Philosophers and Kings

THE DAEDALUS LIBRARY

Philosophers and Kings

Studies in Leadership

Edited by

DANKWART A. RUSTOW

GEORGE BRAZILLER

NEW YORK

Standard Book Number: 0–8076–0540–9, cloth; 0–8076–0539–5, paper

Library of Congress Catalog Card Number: 77–107778

With the exception of "The Marxist Pattern" by Adam B. Ulam, "Sayyid
Jamal ad-Din 'al-Afghani': A Case of Posthumous Charisma?" by Nikki R.
Keddie, and "Uchimura Kanzō: Japanese Prophet" by John F. Howes, the
essays in this book appeared in the Summer 1968 issue of *Daedalus*, the Journal of the American Academy of Arts and Sciences. "The Study of Leadership" and "Atatürk as Founder of a State," both by Dankwart A. Rustow,
and "The Will to Grandeur: de Gaulle as Political Artist," by Stanley and
Inge Hoffmann, which also were published in that issue, appear in the present
volume in revised form.

First Printing

Printed in the United States of America

CONTENTS

vi

Acknowledgments

Gratitude must be expressed to the Carnegie Corporation, which made a grant to the Institute of War and Peace Studies at Columbia University, and to the W. K. Kellogg Foundation for its grant to the School of International Affairs at Columbia. These funds permitted the authors to meet and to consult together at the original planning conference and enabled additional articles to be commissioned. Thanks also go to a number who attended the conference and contributed so much in criticizing the drafts: Conrad M. Arensberg, Lewis J. Edinger, William T. R. Fox, Alexander George, Robert J. Lifton, Lucian W. Pye, Stephen Viederman, Robert G. L. Waite, and James S. Young.

DANKWART A. RUSTOW

The Study of Leadership

I

THE ESSAYS gathered in this volume seek to throw light on the process of leadership in the modern world. Some deal with leadership in politics, others with leadership in ideas. Several trace the links between these spheres of thought and of political action: the views of society that inspire the founding of a state or the formulation of an ideology and the measures of organization that help ensure the victory of a new scientific theory or method.

Most of the men whom the reader will encounter in these pages were innovators. They did not just rule; they founded a new nation-state or recast its institutions. They did not just arrange or spread the teachings of others; they created new systems of thought. Whatever the particular feat of innovation, it was closely bound up with the most intimate hopes, memories, and fears of the statesman or thinker. The major themes of this volume, then, are leadership as a process of innovation and leadership as the recurrent interplay between private personality and public performance.

The portraits included do not form a statistical sample. When taken together, however, they illustrate the scope of statesmanship and of intellectual pioneering in the modern world—from Isaac Newton to Charles Merriam, from James Mill to William James, from Bismarck, Lenin, and Gandhi to Nkrumah and de Gaulle. The intellectual and political forces these men set in motion range from the theory of gravitation in physics to the behavioral method in social studies, from utilitarianism and pragmatism to communism and postcolonial nationalism.

By the very rules of their art, biographers are sometimes seduced into telling the story of a leader's career as the self-contained life of a single hero. Yet it is plain that no one can be a leader in isolation. It is never enough to ask: Who is this leader? A

1

more meaningful question is fourfold: Who is leading whom from where to where? The leader's character, the expectations of his contemporaries, the play of historic circumstance, and the success or failure of a movement in reaching its goals are equally important parts of the over-all process. The authors of this volume pursue very different disciplines—from history to political science, from economics to psychoanalysis. They have assumed that a fuller exploration of the phenomenon of leadership calls for all their various skills—that of the psychologist in relating the leader's outward personality to the intimate experiences of his childhood and his later years, that of the social scientist in tracing the logic of social action that animated the followers, and that of the historian in assessing the influence of leader and followers on a broader stream of events.

Each of these disciplines faces a different sort of challenge in the study of leadership. For the social scientist, there is the excitement of rediscovery; for the psychologist, the exploration of newly charted territory; for the historian, the chance of reuniting seemingly divergent trends within his art.

II

Leadership (by whatever name) was a familiar theme to the distant forerunners of social science in classical antiquity and in the Middle Ages. Historiography, mixing fact with legend, recounted the deeds of heroes of the past; theology explored the truths revealed to prophets, mystagogues, and messiahs. It was taken for granted that such a city as Rome must have been founded by such a man as Romulus, that the discovery of fire must have been made by a Prometheus. Political writers sought to catalogue in their "mirrors for princes" the virtues of the ideal ruler and the principles that must guide his conduct. For all his radicalism, Machiavelli was merely examining a traditional subject from a novel point of view.

A major transformation began in the seventeenth and eighteenth centuries. The consolidation of absolute monarchy and the beginning of the industrial system acted as terrible equalizers, banished the heroic and hierarchical view of the Middle Ages, and left the anonymous individual face to face with a collective society. Modern social thought both reflected and accelerated this trend. Hobbes and Locke, in their theories of social contract, emphasized less the duties of rulers than the rights of individuals. Rousseau pictured political and social institutions as corrupting or liberating the innocent individual; Bentham proclaimed the greatest happiness of the greatest number as the universal moral standard; and Adam Smith traced economic harmony to the workings of an invisible hand whose sinews were the self-interest of innumerable buyers and sellers. In the nineteenth century, German historians saw in the human past the ever-changing manifestations of timeless national genius, whereas their emigrant countryman Marx discovered the mainspring of history in the recurrent tensions between the forces and the relations of economic production. In a world about to be revolutionized by collectivist thought and democratic organization, Carlyle's hero-worship sounded a shrill note of lonely protest. Where the natural-law philosophers had erected their systems on an anonymous individual, the social thinkers of the nineteenth century based theirs on the equally anonymous masses.

In the growing body of systematic social science, there remained less and less room for explicit attention to leadership. Since the days of Smith and Malthus, economists had assumed that political leadership or other deliberate action should not or could not affect the workings of impersonal laws. This impersonal element became even more pronounced as economists of the nineteenth and twentieth centuries proceeded to their calculations of marginal utility, fluctuations in the business cycle, and national input and output ratios. Modern sociology originated largely in the intellectual debate over Marxian thought that was carried on by such figures as Vilfredo Pareto, Emile Durkheim, Max Weber, and Ferdinand Toennies. Whereas these earlier sociologists were still concerned with broad theories of class and social evolution, their successors tended to multiply the detailed statistical correlations of a Durkheim or to refine the abstract definitions of a Weber and a Parsons.

Political scientists continued for a time to people the pages of their treatises with living beings, such as presidents, members of parliament, party leaders, judges, and civil servants. But as the older institutional-legal approach to the study of government came to be considered less and less adequate, they began to adopt a new vocabulary of structure and function from cultural anthropology and a new technique of survey research from social psychology. Amid the verbal abstractions of the one and the quantitative correlations of the other, the political animal—be he citizen or ruler—

3

was in danger of disappearing from the political scientist's view.

Among historians, especially in Britain and in the United States, biography remained a respected genre. Yet historians, too, had to come to terms with the Marxian challenge. The best and most influential work—by men like Henri Pirenne and Marc Bloch—placed political institutions and intellectual movements into a firm framework of economic and social history. Even Lewis Namier, who used biographical material extensively, based his reassessment of eighteenth-century parliamentary politics on the quantitative analysis of vast masses of data. The historian, too, by whatever method or hypothesis, had apparently succeeded in banishing the individual leader from the center of the stage, allowing him to reappear only in the wings as the spokesman for some social or economic interest or as the representative of some statistical trend.

III

Nor did the advent of dynamic Freudian psychology make any immediate contribution to the subject. The psychoanalytic technique had been developed in the constricted cultural milieu of Europe at the turn of the century as a treatment for the neuroses of middle-class patients. Certain of Freud's most suggestive writings dealt with great individuals such as Oedipus, Moses, and Leonardo. Yet, he presented these figures not as statesmen or teachers in close interaction with their followers, but as figures of myth, of religion, or of art who related to their fellow men mostly as symbols—as prophet or genius—to be distantly admired.[1]

Freud's teachings, moreover, left many with the impression that an individual's personality is fully shaped in the first few years of his life, both in its strengths and in its pathology. The temptation was to equate psychic health with social adjustment to middle-class norms and to see in the careers of statesmen or thinkers so many instances of pathological deviation, a blind reliving of the traumatic experiences of infancy. Thus, Harold Lasswell, in a first attempt to introduce Freudian concepts into the study of politics, presented the politician as a man who "displaces private affects upon public objects."[2] In the hands of lesser scholars than Lasswell, the new Freudian terms could easily turn into tools of sensationalism and debunking.

A similar danger of vulgarization lurked in the application of the new psychology to the data of cultural anthropology. Abraham

4

Kardiner and Ralph Linton had carefully explored the connections between the two disciplines. Yet some of the rasher attempts to explain complex social institutions or national character in terms of the prevailing habits of swaddling or breast feeding tended to confirm the skepticism with which the more cautious social scientists continued to regard the Freudian theories. The potentially fruitful effort of Harry Stack Sullivan and his school to link dynamic psychology with the social studies remained encumbered by a vocabulary of "interpersonal relations" as awkward and self-conscious as that of "structure and function" in sociology.[3]

By the 1950's, however, both the more secluded setting of the scholar's study and the more turbulent environment outside became increasingly favorable to a new intellectual attack on a long neglected problem. A half-century of revolution, economic crisis, and war had undermined traditional institutions, challenged accepted ideas, and dramatized the role of individual leaders—such as Hitler, Roosevelt, Stalin, Churchill, Nehru, and de Gaulle. Political scientists proceeded far beyond Lasswell's generalizations and typologies in exploring the psychological dimensions of their subject. A number of biographies combined political and psychological analysis with careful attention to the canons of historical evidence; other studies traced the psychological roots of political attitudes in both children and adults.[4] Above all, political scientists in the United States who had long been imprisoned in a somewhat parochial discipline saw a new worldwide horizon opening up before them.[5] Research on the new states of Asia and Africa and a more systematic examination of Communist dictatorships led to a revived interest in Weber's notion of charisma. Whereas Weber had developed charisma as a somewhat disembodied "ideal type," the newer studies were concerned to apply the concept to concrete historical figures.[6] More generally, the new theorizing about political development and political modernization led to a rediscovery of broad historical questions of change in the social world and broad philosophic questions about the range and limitation of deliberate human control over such change.[7] From either kind of question, it was only a small step to the systematic rediscovery of leadership as a central political process.

Nor did the new interest in leadership remain confined to political science. Over the years, a group of social psychologists had tried to ascertain by experimental methods the individual traits of character associated with leadership.[8] As economists turned to questions of development, they became aware of the political and psychological dimensions of that process; thus, Albert Hirschman's concept of the "reform-monger" explicitly introduced the leadership factor into the development equation.[9] And historians such as William Langer, Stuart Hughes, and Bruce Mazlish have called for closer cooperation between history and psychoanalysis.[10]

The publication of Erik H. Erikson's study *Young Man Luther* in 1958 was the most important landmark in this new trend. Unlike many earlier followers of Freud, Erikson recognized that personality continues its evolution in successive crises from childhood through adolescence and into maturity. His formulations thus became particularly meaningful to historians and social scientists, whose source materials commonly relate to the behavior of adults rather than children. His emphasis on "crises" could serve to highlight the discontinuous, innovative, and creative possibilities in both personal development and a dynamic process of leadership. Above all, Erikson showed a keen awareness that the role of a major innovator in religion or politics must be explained concurrently on two distinct levels: the personal or psychological and the social or historical. Only where personal and social need, each following its distinct logic, broadly coincide does that rare opportunity arise when "an individual is called upon . . . to lift his individual patienthood to the level of a universal one and try to solve for all what he could not solve for himself alone."[11] Lasswell the social scientist had pictured public activity as a screen for the projection of individual pathology. Erikson the psychoanalyst stressed the need for exploring the public arena in its own right. His work also provided an important reminder that the creative as well as the destructive leader—Luther or Gandhi as much as Hitler or Stalin—has a highly individual psychology that sets him apart from the norm. Yet in Erikson's eloquent prose, the psychology of a Luther appeared as a set of common human traits selected, transposed, and magnified, but for all that the more intensely human. In these and other ways, Erikson's work opened up new perspectives of fruitful cooperation between the psychoanalyst, the historian, and the social scientist.

IV

Many of the recent authors on the subject of leadership have had the sensation, now elating and now disheartening, of breaking new ground at the outer frontiers of scholarship. "American political scientists have been inclined to avoid the study of individual leadership."[12] "Few historians have chosen to run the gauntlet of their fraternity's scorn . . . by attempting interdisciplinary work along lines so unsympathetically regarded."[13] "We have few if any studies of the dictator as a personality type . . . a need of political science is going unfulfilled."[14] His eyes firmly fixed ahead, not every scholar has recognized how many others are engaged in similar feats of pioneering.

Instead of multiplying the laments, it is time to explore more concretely the common goal toward which the various effects seem to be converging and to consolidate the gains that the new approach promises in individual disciplines and in the multidisciplinary study of leadership itself.

In a field like political science, a focus on leadership may help resolve some current methodological dilemmas. The generation that participated in the "successful revolt" waged against the older institutional-legal approach in favor of behaviorism[15] has been engaged ever since in a wide search for a new basic unit of analysis. Some have sought it in a "functional" vocabulary too abstruse to be applied in empirical research, some in the making of "decisions" that have proved difficult to isolate from the stream of reality, some in an elusive quantitative measure of power, and some in messages of communication so numerous as to defy inventory. The leader as a figure omnipresent in any political process, as the maker of decisions, originator and recipient of messages, performer of functions, wielder of power, and creator or operator of institutions can bring these disparate elements into a single, visible focus. The study of leadership, moreover, can readily be supplemented with an examination of the social and political organization that he founds and transforms, with an analysis of the psychological appeals and political sanctions that give leader and organization a hold on their mass following. In short, there may be the elements for a new theoretical view, both comprehensive and dynamic, of the political process as a whole.

What Erikson has called the "psycho-historical" approach may similarly serve to reconcile the historian's older emphasis on great men with the newer preoccupation with social and economic forces. In economics, the study of "reform-mongering" may fruitfully link the quantitative abstractions of classical theory with the policy orientation of economic planning and development. For psychologists, finally, an examination of major innovators in thought or organization may firmly place the study of recurrent personality traits and personality conflicts into a wider context of historical and cultural change.

To accomplish any of these advances in various fields of scholarship, there is need for a concerted attack by all of them on the unresolved questions concerning the process of leadership. Such questions may be conveniently grouped under four headings—first, leadership as reflecting the leader's personality; second, leadership as reflecting the character and the situation of the (potential) followers; third, leadership as a craft or technique; and fourth, the study of leadership as a personal relationship between the student and his subject.

V

Lasswell seeks out the personal dimension of leadership: the political man "displaces private affects upon public objects." Leadership makes demands upon the entire person, both on his intellect and on his emotions, and the higher the level of leadership the more exacting those demands. The charismatic leader, as we shall see, makes a direct personal appeal to large numbers of followers. The non-charismatic leader shifts part of his burden to his lieutenants and associates, and these in turn rely on others down each step of the hierarchy. But no matter how many links intervene between leader and rank-and-file, the last set of links connects with the leader himself. In dealing with the inner circle, he is on his own. His personality, therefore, becomes his ultimate resource, the only one under his full control, and the only one for which there can be no substitute. This truth is embodied, positively, in the adage that to rule others you must first learn to rule yourself and, negatively, in Neustadt's dictum about the American president that "no one saves him from himself."[16]

The affects of Lasswell's politician have been displaced by the many deprivations suffered in childhood. Since Lasswell first published his *Psychopathology and Politics* in 1930, both he and his students have restated and refined that hypothesis. Barber, for example, adds "extension" as a second alternative to "compensation," but still stresses the psychological deviation from the norm. "Intense political activity may represent either compensation for low self-esteem, usually resulting from severe deprivations in early life, or a specialized extension of high self-esteem, but seldom does it represent an ordinary or normal adaptation to one's culture."[17]

In this broader form the statement becomes applicable not only to political leaders, but also to scientific discoverers, ideological innovators, and creative artists—all of them pursuing activities that are equally remote from any "ordinary adaptation" to the prevailing culture. No one becomes a leading figure in any of these fields without some intense emotional drive, and compensation and extension between them account for the major possible forms of that impulse. The sources of the drive are likely to lie in the private world of childhood, particularly in the subject's relations to mother and father.

The psychological biographer, having traced the drive to its childhood origins and assessed its strength, also must determine the particular direction it took both in childhood and in adult life. Among politicians, Lasswell has identified three typical syndromes: the dramatizing personality of the agitator, the compulsiveness of the bureaucrat, and the psychological detachment of the judge or mediator.[18] And Nikki Keddie's essay on Afghani shows that such a scheme may be applied to political leaders in cultural contexts quite remote from the early twentieth-century American scene in which it was conceived.

There is need for similar distinctions not only between types of politicians, but between leaders in politics and in other fields of human endeavor. Among the men considered in the following chapters, for example, it seems obvious that a "sick soul" given to the painstaking introspection of a William James would scarcely have been suited for political leadership, nor would a man with the almost fanatical urge to honesty of an Uchimura Kanzō who would rather disavow the "no-church" movement of his followers than have it misrepresent his ideas. A lifelong recluse such as Newton or a cautious, reflective person such as Charles Merriam would be able to give free rein to his power urges, not in politics proper but only in such narrower arenas of attenuated struggle as the Royal Society or the Social Science Research Council. The personal reticence of any of these, as well as of James Mill, contrasts sharply with the histrionic talents of young de Gaulle, the "showboy" qualities of Nkrumah, and the youthful boisterousness of Otto von Bismarck. (The mere listing of these last three also suggests that the

9

"dramatizing character" described by Lasswell recurs among many public political leaders who may or may not be "agitators" in any narrow or derogatory sense of that term.) A more systematic pursuit of the genre of psychological biography might thus alert us to the differential personality traits and childhood experiences of future statesmen, artists, or intellectuals, in general, and of various types of statesmen, artists, or intellectuals, in particular.

Systematic study requires not only many individual biographies, but also explicit comparisons among them. Four types of comparison readily suggest themselves, each holding constant a different element. First, and most broadly, creative statesmen may be compared with the innovators in science, art, literature, or religion, Here the constant element is the mental and psychological process of innovation. Second, on a more restricted scale, statesmen may be compared with other statesmen. Here the common element is political leadership regardless of time and place.

A third type of comparison narrows the focus further still and compares a major political leader (or artist or scientist) in a given setting with other political leaders (or artists or scientists) in the same setting. Here the constant is the situation, and the isolated variable is the personality of various leaders. Edinger's portrayal of Kurt Schumacher as "central actor" in relation to his "counter-players" comes under this heading.[19] The many instances of independent and simultaneous scientific discovery investigated by Robert Merton lend themselves to the same type of comparative treatment.[20] A specific variant of this third type of comparison is that of a given statesman with his nearest rivals for the same leadership position. Generally, if we wish to distinguish the personal factor from the situation, it will prove fruitful to look closely at the period of accession, when personality and situation are first combined in a dynamic leadership process. Such a concern is reflected in Erikson's studies of Luther up to the time of the posting of the Ninety-Five theses and of Gandhi at the time of his first campaign of nonviolent resistance.[21] The essays by the Hoffmanns, Rustow, Ulam, and others in this volume pay special attention to that same phase of preparation or accession. And Tucker advises explicitly "that when we study a case—or possible case—of charismatic leadership, we should always go back to the beginnings of the given leader-personality's emergence as a leader, rather than start with the status achieved at the zenith of his career."[22]

All three types of comparison listed so far trace a leader's public performance to his personal characteristics, his adult style to the experiences of his childhood. What gifts of the imagination enabled Newton to draw together into a coherent whole the theories of Copernicus, Kepler, Galileo, and Descartes? Or Bismarck to propose a scheme of German unification that would appeal to liberals and conservatives? Or William James to formulate a peculiarly American philosophy of pragmatism? What do Bismarck, Lenin, Atatürk, and de Gaulle have in common as political leaders that distinguishes them from intellectual figures such as Newton or James? What resources of personality, and what responses to the Russian revolutionary situation enabled Lenin rather than Martov, Plekhanov, or Trotsky to capture its leadership? Note that the comparative method is just as essential to bring out the unique as it is to establish what is similar. It is a fallacious though widespread view that contrasts the specialist in, say, comparative politics who supposedly searches for general laws with the historian who supposedly is concerned with "mere description" of unique phenomena.

There is also need for a fourth type of comparison, one that traces the personal traits that form in childhood forward into adult performance, whether of leadership caliber or not. This fourth type is concerned with consequences rather than antecedents, and it is essential as a check on any hypotheses developed under the first three headings. A great innovator is, almost by definition, a misfit in his environment; but not every misfit becomes an innovator. "When a superior intellect and a psychopathic temperament coalesce," William James wrote, ". . . we have the best possible conditions for . . . effective genius."[23] The statement sounds entirely plausible, but it should be carefully considered. The "best possible conditions" may not be good enough. A slight shift in the balance between intellect and pathology, a slight change in social environment or early career, and the budding genius may end up as just an ordinary madman. Another subtle shift in personality or environment and a quite normal adjustment may, after all, result.

Any psychological characteristic adduced to explain leadership must be tested on a control group including nonleaders as well. If Wolfenstein, for example, surmises that the early loss of their fathers helped make Lenin and Gandhi into revolutionaries,[24] this raises two kinds of question. Within the total class of revolu-

11

tionaries, or any fair sample of it, what proportion lost their fathers early? Conversely, among early orphans, what proportion becomes revolutionaries and what happens to the rest? In answering the first question, we must start from an acceptable definition of "revolutionary" that avoids any *petitio principii* (in this case, is not skewed toward orphans); in answering the second we must keep in mind the rate of life expectancy in societies such as Russia or India in the late nineteenth century.

The psychological interpretation of great men becomes most dramatic and compelling when it reveals a hidden inner conflict, for example a manifest drive toward extraordinary achievement linked with a latent self-destructive urge. Andrew Johnson's career, as sketched by Barber in this volume, and that of Woodrow Wilson, as examined more fully in the classic study by Alexander and Juliette George,[25] include many episodes when these leaders acted much like any other American politician, only more successfully. They championed the underdog and they made deals with those in power. They thundered against abuses and they promised reforms. They rose by steps up the political ladder. At all these points "straight explanations" from the context of American history or comparative party politics will do just fine. But when Johnson drunkenly rants at the guests of honor attending his inauguration, or when Wilson stubbornly refuses the kind of concession to Lodge that he had often made to others in the past—it is then that we feel compelled (much as do people faced with similar shocks in private life) to call in the psychiatrist. And when we proceed to uncover some clues, usually tenuous, of traumatic experiences in the subject's childhood we feel the thrill of playing both Sigmund Freud and Sherlock Holmes.

There is some justification for this sudden shift in our method of inquiry, but there also are implicit risks. The successful adult, we may argue, lives in the present, the neurotic in the past. At the successful moments of their careers Johnson and Wilson responded to the political needs of the current situation, at the time of their debacles they responded to psychic needs that they carried over from childhood. But by allowing the politician to acquire a psyche only at times of his failure, are we not cheapening politician and psyche alike? Perhaps adult success had also brought its childish gratifications. By shifting from a political to a psychological critique, we risk slipping into an invidious *ad hominem* argument.

By depicting genius as a form of madness, we may fall into a cheap appeal to the reader's complacent mediocrity. Instead of explaining a man's greatness, we merely cut him down to size. It is such rash and selective application of Freudian concepts which, as noted earlier, delayed their acceptance by social scientists.

The remedy, of course, is the one suggested by Erikson's hyphenated phrase "psycho-historical": we must blend psychological with historical (or political, social, literary, etc.) analysis throughout the biographical enterprise, as the Georges have done for Wilson and as Erikson himself has done for Luther and for Gandhi. In embarking on this course, we do not call on psychological explanations only when other types of explanations seem to fail: we no longer introduce psychology as a residual category into a nonpsychological scheme of explanation. In private life, of course, it is our privilege to delay calling the psychotherapist until we are in trouble. In biographical research, the skills of the psycho-diagnostician are equally relevant at every point. The politician who operates the rules of the game successfully is just as much of a psychological being as the one who runs afoul of them. The same maladjusted, or even psychopathic, drive that destroys old forms of culture or of social intercourse to create new ones may turn not only against the environment but at length against the author himself. James' career, as recounted by Cushing Strout, was one long record of self-torture. The Georges found that the same psychic drive that spurred Wilson to ever greater successes in Princeton, in Trenton, in Washington, and on arrival at the Paris peace conference also drove him into ultimate failure: having since childhood been dissatisfied with half-successes he later proved even more acutely dissatisfied with full and over-full success. And of Andrew Johnson, Barber has written that "no amount of success could fully compensate for the needs left from his traumatic childhood."[26]

Comparative study will place such findings in a more meaningful context. To help us understand the "psychopathic temperament" as a "condition for effective genius" we may wish to draw a fourfold distinction between various forms of adjustment to society and to the self. First, there is the vast majority of men who are tolerably "well adjusted" to their society and culture. Second, there is the minority who are, in some sense, "maladjusted." Third, there is an even smaller minority within this group who find a creative outlet for their discontent, who, in refusing to conform to their environment induce the environment in some measure to conform to them. Lastly, there is a subgroup within this creative minority who are first spurred to great achievement and then to the partial or total destruction of that very work of theirs.

Each of these groups is equally amenable to psychological interpretation, but that interpretation includes, at least implicitly, a strong social component. For the social context not only defines such concepts as normalcy, adjustment, and deviation, but also determines, in large part, whether a given psychic endowment will find constructive, destructive, or harmlessly irrelevant outlets. Conscientious study of the first aspect of leadership—the personal, psychological makeup of the leader—thus leads us logically to a study of the social setting, and in particular of the social situation of those whom he comes to lead.

VI

In turning to this second, social aspect—to leadership as reflecting the needs of the followers—we may usefully concentrate on a form of leadership which Max Weber called "charismatic authority." For the concept of charisma has in recent years gained wide currency among students of postcolonial and totalitarian regimes, and it is a central theme in the chapters by Tucker, Apter, and Rustow in this volume.

Erikson's study of Luther traces a particularly close link from the psychic to the social sphere. Young Martin "settled a personal account by provoking a public accounting"; his "individual patienthood" was such that it could be cured only on "the level of a universal one."[27] Weber's notion of charisma implies the reverse linkage. The gist of his theory is that political legitimacy is based in varying proportions on three, and only three, elements: tradition, rational legality, and charisma. Men obey willingly from some mixture of habit, interest, and personal devotion.[28] This does not mean that men always obey: Weber was concerned with authority rather than anarchy. Nor does it mean that those who obey always do so willingly: Weber was concerned with legitimacy, not with coercion. But it does mean that where tradition and rational legality both give way, e.g., in revolutionary situations, charisma alone can restore legitimate authority.

If we learn from Erikson that there are personal problems that can be solved only by transforming the wider social setting, so we learn from Weber that there are social problems the solutions to which require the agency of some single individual. Erikson starts out by reconstructing Luther's early personal experience; he then proceeds to sketch in the social and economic forces of the Renaissance and of early capitalism that challenged the medieval order and thereby helped transform young Martin's lonely protest into a mass movement of Protestantism. Similarly, Weber's sociological analysis of charismatic situations might profitably be supplemented with a psychological study of the person or persons who stand ready to satisfy the "charismatic hunger" of their contemporaries.[29]

One may question whether Weber was well advised to introduce charisma as a technical term into sociological and political analysis.[30] Our understanding of his theory, moreover, is hampered by the fact (overlooked by many critics) that Weber died before completing the final portion of his *magnum opus* on *Wirtschaft und Gesellschaft* that was to have dealt with political sociology.[31] Since the word, however, has found general currency, it seems best to sort out the ambiguities, whether apparent or real, in Weber's extant writings and to incorporate his charismatic model as a special case into a more general theory of leadership. This, at any rate, is the course adopted by Tucker and other contributors to this volume.

Is charisma a personal attribute in the leader? Is it a perception in the minds of the followers? Or is it an aspect of the relationship, of the interaction between them? This is the central ambiguity, and it is one implicit in Weber's choice of word and several divergent passages in his writings. Etymology suggests that charisma is a trait, for the word originally referred to the gift of "speaking with tongues," as described in the epistles of Saint Paul, that is, to a palpable and striking trait of behavior.[32] Weber suggests the same answer, for example, when he defines charisma as "a certain quality of an individual personality by virtue of which he is set apart from ordinary men," or when he cites, as one of his favorite instances of the charismatic, the "Nordic 'berserk,' who like a rabid dog bites into his shield and all around himself until he darts forth in bloodthirsty frenzy. . . ."[33]

Yet, we must remember that Weber's was a sociological, not a

psychological theory. He adduces the frenzied berserk, not to illustrate the psychology or physiology of the charismatic leader; rather
he confronts us with his wild snapping so as to impress on us the
"value-free" character of the concept: having derived it from the
New Testament and applied it to a highly revered figure such as
Christ, he deliberately shocks the reader by extending it to as
irksome and repulsive an example as he can readily think of. When
Weber's concern is with definition he lays stress, instead, on the
attitude of the followers: "The term 'charisma,'" he writes, in his
most detailed passage on the subject, "shall be understood to refer
to an *extraordinary* quality of a person, regardless of whether this
quality is actual, alleged, or presumed. . . . The legitimacy of
charismatic rule . . . rests upon the belief [of the governed] in
magical powers, revelations, and hero worship. The source of those
beliefs is the 'proving' of the charismatic quality through miracles,
through victories, and through other successes, that is, through the
welfare of the governed. Such beliefs and the claimed authority
resting on them, therefore, disappear, as soon as proof is lacking
and as soon as the charismatically qualified person appears to be
devoid of his magical power or forsaken by his god."[34]

Here Weber forthrightly seems to opt for the second position
—that charisma is not a trait but a perception. Not the berserk's
frenzy but the awe of his audience makes the mad biting an
instance of charisma. As beauty is said to be in the eye of the
beholder, so a leader's charisma is in the minds of the followers.
Weber, in this passage, clearly distinguishes between his verbal
analysis and his empirical findings. So long as the followers impute
to the leader such superhuman traits as prophecy, magic, or heroism, he is a charismatic figure—by definition. Empirically the
followers' attitude is influenced by the magnitude and improbability
of the results achieved. No results, no belief; no belief, no charisma.

But if definition and empirical statement are taken together,
Weber is seen to take his stand on the third position: that charisma
is a relationship, a process of interaction. For, the results that are
likely to induce the followers' belief in the leader's charisma are
results achieved on their behalf and in their interest. In the interaction between them, the leader offers miracles for the "welfare
of the governed" and the followers offer faith in the leader's legitimacy. The results of the leader's action induce the followers' belief,
and the followers' belief becomes the criterion of charismatic
authority.

16

Several other ambiguities readily disappear with a careful reading of the same passage. First, charisma is not a fixed datum. Since beliefs can be more or less intense, it follows that there can be degrees of charisma. Second, charisma is not a permanent estate, rather it can grow and wane, appear and disappear. Both of these variations are implicit in Weber's conception of charisma as an ideal type, a phenomenon that in the real world is likely to occur in mixture with other ideal types of authority. As true Weberians we should therefore not ask whether a given system of authority is charismatic; rather we must ask to what extent is it charismatic at a given time. (Apter is on solid Weberian ground when he suggests that Nkrumah's authority was—predominantly?—charismatic during a certain period, namely from 1949 to 1954.)[35]

Third, a ruler's authority may be, at one and the same time, charismatic or chiefly charismatic to some of his followers, and rational-legal or traditional to others, whereas others still may reject his rule as illegitimate. For example, John F. Kennedy had some followers who considered him endowed with unusual, superhuman qualities; there were others who accepted his authority as the elected President of the United States; there were other citizens who simply carried out his orders, as transmitted through an elaborate bureaucracy, from a life-long habit of compliance; and there were some, for instance certain executives of the steel industry, who considered certain of his actions entirely nefarious and illegitimate. If all these different possible reactions are kept in mind, the question becomes not whether a given leader is charismatic, but, charismatic to whom, when, and how much.

Fourth, since beliefs can arise in a variety of ways, it will be useful for some purposes to distinguish between a belief in charisma that stems (a) from direct personal contact between the leader and his immediate followers and (b) from indirect processes of mass communication. This suggests a further distinction between leaders whose first charismatic followers were a small circle of personal associates, such as Lenin in his Genevan exile,[36] and others, such as Stalin, who acquired some reputation of being superhuman or extraordinary only after rising to power by non-charismatic means. But I cannot agree with Tucker that "on the basis of Weber's various formulations . . . it is not easy to distinguish between leaders who are really charismatic and leaders who are not."[37] And, specifically, I am inclined to reject the distinction drawn by other authors between "genuine" charisma induced by direct contact and "spurious" charisma as engendered by the mass media. Weber explicitly states that it is immaterial whether the leader's supernatural powers are "actual, alleged, or presumed." The housewife who is seized by raptures as she listens to her Führer on the radio is just as genuine a believer as the old *parteigenosse* who has experienced his magnetism at first hand.

Weber discusses at length one temporal variation, the disappearance of charisma. Repeated miracles will cease to seem miraculous, and even the most gifted miracle worker may run out of ever-new types of miracles. This is the very reason why charismatic authority is inherently unstable. It is not the rule of any given leader that is necessarily unstable, but he can stabilize it in the long run only by "routinizing" his charisma, that is, by combining charismatic with rational-legal, or over time perhaps, also with traditional, authority. Routinized charisma is thus a prime example in Weber's own scheme of a less intensive form of charisma. The daily miracle of the Mass is not as miraculous as the deeds of Christ in his time; on the other hand it is sanctioned by the tradition and "rational-legal" rules of a far-flung church bureaucracy.

The reverse temporal variation is the sudden appearance of charisma. If legitimacy is the sum total of tradition, legality, and charisma, the balance may shift through an increase in charisma or a decrease in the other two terms. Weber himself suggests the former. "Charisma," he writes, "is the one great revolutionary force in epochs bound to tradition."[38] Recent theories of revolution have instead emphasized the latter, for example Chalmers Johnson's concept of the "power deflation" that precedes revolutions and Tucker's emphasis on charismatic leadership as a response to situations of distress and crisis.[39]

Tradition revolutionized by charisma, charisma routinized within a bureaucracy: this is the part of Weber's scheme that has made it particularly suggestive as a model for the formation of new states in the era of decolonization. There are tensions in that process of transition that seem to cry out for personal, highly concentrated leadership. First, there is the tension of time perspectives. The secession from empire must be accomplished quickly, fateful tactical decisions must be taken from day to day, and yet, the results must prove durable—for to set out to found a state for only a decade or two plainly is not worth anyone's while. The state founder,

Rousseau said, must "toil in one century and reap in another."[40] Second, the negative, destructive attitudes formed during the struggle or the agitation against the colonial power must make way on the morrow of independence for new, constructive attitudes. For only by unity and self-restraint can the economy be developed and a new sense of national identity fostered within the given boundaries. A heroic leader can better than anyone provide the necessary continuity in such an abrupt reversal. Third, the sudden withdrawal of the colonial power, at times without physical contest, may itself provide the initial "miracle" that establishes a claim to charisma. This has been true in many of the countries of Tropical Africa. According to Rustow, it was a similar vacuum or lapse of authority in Turkey after 1918 that made possible the charismatic rise of Atatürk.

Weber's concept, however, is not restricted to heroic figures such as state founders or leaders in successful revolutions, anymore than it is a euphemism for modern dictatorship or the magic powers of primitive medicine men.[41] We saw that Weber stressed the "value-free" rather than normative nature of his concept. Charisma, of course, is unstable and thus a phenomenon of transition. In postcolonial situations the transition is generally assumed to be from tradition to rationality, but for all we know there might also be relapses into tradition. The distress that makes men yearn for charisma is as likely to occur when rational-legal authority crumbles under its own weight of over-organization as when tradition is rudely challenged by modernity. In the eyes of thousands of Sorbonne students in the spring of 1968, Daniel Cohn-Bendit was every bit as charismatic as any contemporary African politician in the eyes of his nationalist followers. The subtlest and most detailed account of an instance of charismatic authority of which I know is contained in Joyce Cary's posthumous novel *The Captive and the Free*. Its hero is a faith healer in post-World War II Britain; needless to say, Cary does not mention the term charisma.[42]

Even in postcolonial situations, charisma is not ubiquitous or automatic in its effects. In Algeria, no charismatic leader emerged from the independence struggle. In many other countries, modernization, economic development, and "nation-building" remained themes of the official rhetoric—and a pious hope of sympathetic American scholars. Even where charisma for a time galvanized the urban masses, disenchantment could easily set in before any of

those tasks were accomplished. The careers of Nkrumah and Sukarno starkly illustrate all that Weber said about the fragility of
charismatic authority.

There is no guarantee, in other words, that charisma will
emerge nor that it will do its job. Weber's threefold distinction is
meant to cover all pure forms of legitimate authority; it does not
claim to account for all possible outcomes. Within the limits of
legitimate authority, of course, any one of the three categories may
be taken as residual in relation to the two others. But for Weber's
scheme as a whole the true residual categories lie beyond those
limits. They are illegitimate authority and nonauthority, that is,
coercion and anarchy.

That charisma is not a personal trait accords with the findings
of a long series of studies by social psychologists that were designed
to isolate the personal traits of leadership—but failed to do so.[43]
But as Robert C. Tucker has stressed, "We do not face a choice
between explaining history by reference to leader-personalities or
assigning them no importance at all."[44] The solution is to view
leadership as a mutual relationship of interaction connecting leader
and followers—and this indeed was the answer formulated by the
social psychologists just mentioned.

We are back then to our initial question—not Who leads? but
Who leads whom? or better Who leads whom from where to
where? Leadership is a process of complex mediation between
the leader's personality, the followers' expectations, the circumstances, and a set of goals. The need for leadership is proportionate
to the distance between circumstances and goals—and a yearning
for charisma represents that need in its most intense form. The
word charisma lays stress on the first part of the fourfold question.
Yet, generally the other three are easier to answer, at least for the
political or social scientist, and the three of them together shed
more light on the fourth than would an examination of the leader's
personality out of its social context.

Different circumstances, different goals, and different followers
put a premium on different personal characteristics in the leader—
although there are other characteristics, related to the technique of
leadership, that all leaders have more or less in common. Of the
figures considered in this volume, for example, de Gaulle, Atatürk,
Uchimura, and others profoundly reflected their various cultures.[45]
They also were attuned to the new forces of technology or of

Westernization that challenged the tradition. Karl Deutsch has proposed that leadership in movements of political integration is typically supplied by a coalition of the "most outside of the insiders" with the "most inside of the outsiders."[46] The most appropriate single leader of such a coalition, obviously, is one who, as it were, represents a one-man combination of outer inside and inner outside. This hypothesis of the founder of a new state or new ideology as a "marginal man"[47] has many applications. Nationalist movements often are founded by border nationals or by men who spent some of their formative years abroad. They were men who through a *Fremdheitserlebnis* had to make a conscious and often painful decision about their national allegiance. Movements of radical social reform or revolution often are led by *déclassé* members of the upper class, or else by self-made men rising from the lower strata.

Yet, neither a social nor even a psychological analysis will account completely for the qualities that make possible the leader's performance. For those qualities tend to become sharply transformed upon his assumption of the leadership role, as he rises or fails to rise to the challenge. Here is another consideration that justifies the emphasis by Erikson, Tucker, and others on the accession phase of the leader's career.

This focus on the process of accession can guard against two related fallacies. The first is the view that the leader was indispensable to the results obtained—leading to the inference, for example, that if Mustafa Kemal had been killed by a bullet at Gallipoli, there would have been no Turkish nation-state. The second is the opposite view, that the result was inevitable, that any other leader would have had to adopt the very same course. The first view pushes beyond the limits of our capacity for causal explanations in history. The second can be shown to be erroneous in its assumptions. Both are forms of overschematization. Both reflect the danger of explaining nothing by attempting to explain too much.

The need for leadership, we found, is proportional to the distress of the followers. Hence, the leader who in fact emerges will be considered indispensable by his followers in proportion to the magnitude of the task at hand. Both the leader and the associates who have thrown their lot with him share an interest in encouraging such a belief in his indispensability by all available means of publicity. Since leader and associates may well be themselves imbued with this belief, no conscious distortion needs to be involved. Foreign journalists and later historians are likely to perpetuate the same myth, for they are notorious for their tendency to endorse the winning faction, applaud power, and adulate success. Still, the notion is the result of a simple optical illusion. In difficult situations of change it is leadership as such, rather than leadership by this or that specific individual, that is indispensable for success.

Most leadership is the result of keen competition among several aspirants—although in a structured movement the crucial rounds of competition may have been fought long before the movement attracted attention. (The leadership fight in the Russian Social Democratic movement, as the chapters by Tucker and Ulam remind us, was raging two decades before the 1917 revolution.) Who is to say that the competitor who narrowly lost out was overwhelmingly less qualified? Or that, if given the chance, he would not have mustered the additional personal resources required for effective leadership? Our method of analysis, in the nonexperimental situations of political history, are too imprecise to allow us to answer such questions with assurance. Accident thus plays its role. But for the rest, the indispensable leader is much like the well-adapted species. In politics as in biology, any appearance of teleology must be accounted for by the Darwinian principle of selection.

Just as there usually is active competition for leadership, so there is always a variety of formulas by which the solution of a given political problem may be attempted. If the situation had only one plausible solution, only one possible outcome, it would create technical or administrative, not political problems. Nor would it require leadership. It is the very multiplicity of solutions that makes the situation cry out for the talents of a leader. Leadership is not the product of inevitability but an instrument of choice.

Here then is a vivid reminder to the social scientist of what is his true function, whatever his specific field of study. "The astronomer tracing the orbit of a star, the biologist raising a culture of bacteria, the chemist testing the composition of a molecule—indeed any outside observer—may meaningfully search for laws of inevitability. But the social scientist is an observer from inside society, and within those confines his task becomes more modest and more difficult. In presuming to predict mankind's inevitable bliss or doom, he is forsaking his vocation. The social scientist's proper function is to ascertain the margin of choice offered by man's social condition and to clarify the choices in that margin."[48]

VII

Successful leadership, we have seen, rests on a latent congruence between the psychic needs of the leader and the social needs of the followers. Hence, many of the characteristics of the political or intellectual leader will be conditioned by the surrounding situation. A comparison of the state founders considered in this volume illustrates the point. Atatürk and de Gaulle made use of their soldierly experience to rescue their countries from imminent or actual military occupation. German unification in the nineteenth century required diplomatic skills such as those of Bismarck. The liberation of an African country from colonial rule was most appropriately achieved by an agitator with the rhetorical gifts of an Nkrumah.

But, the hard work of the leadership process itself is to make the latent congruence manifest, and a large part of this work is done by the leader himself. It is a process of discovery, of adjustment, of consolidation. Insofar as there are traits common to all leaders, they are likely to be traits that help in the performance of these several tasks.

The ideal state founder, according to Rousseau, would be "a superior intelligence acquainted with all of men's passions but liable to none of them; wholly detached from our nature yet knowing to the full; its happiness independent from us yet willing to be concerned with us."[49] The peculiar combination of detachment and involvement that Rousseau describes is one of the most striking features of the leadership process, whether in politics or in intellectual history. During their most active period, political leaders may be detached and involved all at once—seeming remote from their family or personal friends and yet involved with a large number of people in limited ways and through this involvement eliciting intense responses of enthusiasm or loyalty. In the total career of a major leader, on the other hand, there is often a sequence of detachment first and involvement afterward, the first period corresponding to what has been called a psychological moratorium.

The detachment phase is well illustrated in the subsequent essays on Bismarck and on Atatürk.[50] Bismarck for a quarter-century before his appointment as Prussian ambassador to the German Confederation had sampled the life of a bourgeois university student, of a parliamentary orator, of a Junker landowner, and even of a pietist. He thus had come into contact with the major social and intellectual trends, both traditional and emergent, of a Germany groping for a transition from agrarianism to industrialism and from fragmentation to unity. He was forty-seven when he at last found the springboard that propelled him to the traditional position of Prussian prime minister and to the new post of Chancellor of a German Empire. Mustafa Kemal did not change careers as a young man, but he became increasingly detached from the state under whose colors he was serving. He grew up in a border province, and as a young military officer on the Balkans, in Libya, and elsewhere he was in a position to see clearly the weaknesses of the Ottoman Empire. Both in 1908 and in 1909 he participated in political actions that deprived a sultan first of his power and then of his throne, yet, he soon quarreled with the political faction he had joined, and on two occasions gave up his military commands. In the years after 1916, and more intensively in the winter months of 1918–19, he was in contact with military plotters, with parliamentary groups, with court circles, and with the press, until he at last committed himself to his Anatolian-nationalist strategy.

The function of this period of detachment, brooding, or experimentation may readily be seen as one of sizing up the problem by scanning[51] its various aspects and of sizing up one's own inner resources by toying with a number of different roles. There follows a moment of commitment, when one aspect is selected as critical and one role as the suitable one. An inward psychological attitude of detachment is likely to continue, but outwardly there is full engagement.

In this second phase, communication becomes the leader's chief resource. Since leadership usually is competitive, the most effective leaders are likely to be those who first master some new technique. Luther recognized the potential of two new media in combination: the vernacular language as spread by the printing press. Atatürk won his war "with the telegraph wires."[52] The Sultan first had strung them to consolidate his autocracy; the Young Turks later had used them to announce their mutiny and ensure the Sultan's fall; Mustafa Kemal was the first to use them in both directions, for consultation and information as well as for coordination and command. Others who benefited from new techniques included James Mill who fashioned the periodical press into a political and intellectual weapon, Gandhi who was among the first Indians to travel extensively by railroad, and Uchimura who used both magazine and railway to build up a circle of followers throughout Japan. All these examples illustrate two classic generalizations, the first, Charles Horton Cooley's statement that "All leadership takes place through the communication of ideas to the minds of others," and the second, Erikson's warning that "It would be fatal to underestimate the degree to which the future always belongs to those who combine a universal enough new meaning with the mastery of a new technology"—meaning, of course, a technology of communication.[53]

The greatest of thinkers or prophets may be able to express a truly universal meaning fairly unambiguously. Political leaders are more likely to achieve their broad appeal by being "many things to many men." This explains the effectiveness of de Gaulle's technique of statecraft as stagecraft (to use the Hoffmanns' striking phrase). For the stage actor elevates communication to a visible, audible art, an expression susceptible of many interpretations, each of them valid in its way. Among the important services that a memorable stage presence in the theater of history can render is the illusion of movement at times of stagnation or reconsideration and the illusion of consistency at times of hesitancy or reversal of direction.

To help the leader mediate between circumstances and goals, he requires versatility even more than foresight—that is, the ability to make use of unforeseen minor events to pursue major goals that are kept clearly in view. "*Le hasard,*" said Pasteur, "*ne favorise que les esprits préparés.*" Part of the political leader's preparation is to open up clogged channels of communication, to select or find a reconciliation among conflicting goals, and to establish a feasible order of priorities among goals that can be made consistent with one another.[54] All these tasks are accomplished through talents that are often somewhat vaguely known as a "sense of timing."

If the leader is to be a major innovator, a further item in his preparation is likely to be a particular attitude toward the recent and the more distant past of his society. The incentive to invent new political forms—or to push through to victory those already suggested by others—requires profound disaffection from the received forms, and this in turn may be the result of an attachment to even older, seemingly outdated forms. Thus, de Gaulle formed a highly critical view of the secularist republic under which he grew up as a result of his family's religious and monarchist tradition. Atatürk revived the combination of victorious soldier, state founder, and educator that had been nearly forgotten in centuries of Ottoman decay. (Both, significantly, entered the army—the one career which a patriot disaffected from the current regime can pursue with a clear conscience.) The remote past thus may become a powerful ally against the immediate past in the fight for a better future. Finally, as Hirschman reminds us, the successful leader will need the ability not only to promote change but also to become aware of changes that have gone unrecognized.

Detachment, involvement, communication, innovation, and perception of ongoing change—all these are attitudes and techniques that help a leader coordinate the efforts of others. At its most general level, the leadership situation is the one that Rousseau described by his symbol of transition from the state of nature via the social contract to the state of society. Let us imagine that men have arrived at a pass where they cannot singly resist the obstacles to their continued survival. "Now since men can by no means engender new powers, but can only unite and control those of which they are already possessed, there is no way in which they can maintain themselves save by coming together and pooling their strength in a way that will enable them to withstand any resistance exerted upon them from without. They must develop some sort of central direction and learn to act in concert."[55] Here Rousseau points to the close relation between leadership and the learning process, a relation that Hirschman examined in his study of economic policy in Latin America as a process that meanders by trial and error between antagonistic and nonantagonistic solutions, between solutions that would break down a problem into its component parts or enlarge it to be resolved within a wider context—a process, in sum, conditioned by the changing perceptions of all the participants.[56] The reform-monger or the charismatic leader is likely to emerge as the teacher in such a process, but to teach others he must first learn himself. Here once again it is essential to conceive of the leader's personality not as fixed, but as changing; to consider, in turn, the character traits that he may display in long years of waiting for his opportunity, the new resources of personality that he brings to bear as he assumes his role as leader, and the decline which his personality may undergo as his historic task is accomplished.

Both for the leader himself and for his followers or antagonists, leadership is a process of change, often drastic and discontinuous change. Thus, the methods by which a political leader attains power are in most situations strikingly different from those by which he exercises the power so won, and these in turn are different from those by which he transmits it to his successors. One difference between leaders—say, Andrew Johnson, Woodrow Wilson, and Adolf Hitler, whose careers ended in disaster, and others like Franklin Roosevelt, Gandhi, and de Gaulle—may well be that the responses of the former became set at an early age, whereas the latter were able to summon up new resources and adapt to new situations until a far more advanced age.

Having discussed leadership as the reflection of the leader's psychology, as the followers' aspiration, and as the technique of communication between the two, it remains to fit the results into some meaningful framework of historic explanation. The controversy between those who view leadership as a personal trait and those who view it as determined by the situation can be laid to rest by emphasizing the need for congruence between personality and situation. Whether we begin our exploration of this rough mutual fit with an examination of the leader or of the surrounding circumstances becomes partly a matter of taste or of personal interest. But beyond this, it may be useful to think in terms of a twofold spectrum—one dimension being the originality and responsiveness of the leader, the other the compelling or plastic nature of the setting. Both dimensions are implicit in Montesquieu's statement that "At the birth of societies, it is the leaders of the commonwealth who create the institutions; afterward it is the institutions that shape the leaders."[57]

Yet, we must remember that the study of whole societies and their intellectual or political leaders can be comparative, but never experimental. Hence the further we pursue questions of historic causality, the more surely they will elude us. Would Newton's theory of gravitation have been accepted as quickly if its author had not presided over the Royal Society in such autocratic manner? Would the quantitative-behavioral approach to social studies in the United States have prevailed as quickly, or at all, if Merriam and others had not organized the Social Science Research Council? No more than broad estimates are possible. A more accurate appraisal of the personalities of presidential candidates, such as that proposed by James Barber,[58] is surely both desirable and possible— yet no amount of information on the personality development of a Roosevelt or a Kennedy can lead us to anticipate the bombs on Pearl Harbor or the bullet in Dallas.

Even as we turn from comparative generalization or predictions to the evaluation of particular historic cases, ambiguities remain. A leader's achievement must at some point be judged in terms of success or failure, but such judgments will vary with the time perspective. Stanley Hoffmann once observed that "Metternich had succeeded by 1825 and failed by 1848; and writers disagree whether he had succeeded or failed by 1914."[59] Future appraisals of de Gaulle are sure to be conditioned by the manner of his final exit from the political stage, and it is in the hands of future generations of Turks to preserve, modify, or destroy the work of Atatürk. Kissinger reminds us that a leader like Bismarck, by fitting his work to his own personality too closely, endangered its survival— and indeed some Germans have come to view the partition of 1945 as the self-destructive climax of Bismarck's work.

Future refinements in our theoretical understanding of leadership may come from psychology, sociology, or philosophy of history. To stand up to scrutiny, however, they must be accompanied by a corresponding broadening of the empirical foundations. Indeed, nowhere in historical or social study are problems of evidence posed so sharply as in the biographies of famous men. The materials available differ vastly in quantity and quality from one statesman or thinker to the next. The Hoffmanns complain that de Gaulle's "biographers do not give much detail" on his family or childhood;[60] yet the materials that they did find must seem enviable in their richness to any student of James Mill or of Atatürk. Commonly, moreover, the materials are composed or become available only after both the subject and his contemporaries have become conscious of his greatness. Thus, de Gaulle and Atatürk intended their autobiographical accounts to be political manifestoes for the present as well as contributions to the historical record, while Gandhi's *Autobiography* was itself one of the series of "experiments with truth" that it recounts. The testimony of other participants in the events, and the reconstructions of biographers raise further questions of accuracy of information and reliability of judgment.

As the latest of the biographers, the student of leadership must learn to be as critical of his own reactions as he is of his sources. A bad biography, so the saying goes, reveals more about the author than about the subject—and this is nowhere so true as in psychological biography. A good psychological biography provides a more balanced revelation. The more convincingly it portrays the personality of the subject, the more frankly it reveals the range of the writer's empathy and the sharpness of his critical faculties. The scholar who explores the psycho-historical or psycho-political aspects of leadership must remember that his conclusions can be no stronger than the weakest link in his chain of evidence and inference, and that his own sensitivities and judgment are indispensable links in that chain.

REFERENCES

1. Freud's own part in the psychological essay on Woodrow Wilson, later published by Ambassador Bullitt is, as Erikson points out, of dubious authenticity and the interpretation as a whole of even more questionable value. See below, pp. 48f. and note 10.

2. Harold D. Lasswell, *Psychopathology and Politics* (1930), pp. 75–76.

3. Abraham Kardiner and Ralph Linton, *The Individual and His Society* (New York, 1939), and Harry Stack Sullivan, *Conceptions of Modern Psychiatry* (Washington, 1947).

4. See, for example, Alexander L. George and Juliette L. George, *Woodrow Wilson and Colonel House: A Personality Study* (New York, 1956); Lewis J. Edinger, *Kurt Schumacher: A Study in Personality and Political Behavior* (Stanford, 1965); Robert E. Lane, *Political Ideology* (New York, 1962); James David Barber, *The Lawmakers: Recruitment and Adaptation to Legislative Life* (New Haven, 1965); Fred I. Greenstein, *Children and Politics* (New Haven, 1965) and Ann Ruth Willner, *Charismatic Political Leadership: A Theory* (Princeton, 1968). For a more strictly political approach to the theme, see Richard E. Neustadt, *Presidential Power: The Politics of Leadership* (New York, 1960).

5. Compare Dankwart A. Rustow, "New Horizons for Comparative Politics," *World Politics*, Vol. 9, No. 4 (July, 1959), pp. 530–49.

6. For critical appraisals of the recent literature see, for example, Dankwart A. Rustow, *A World of Nations* (Washington, D.C., 1967), ch. 5; and Robert C. Tucker, "The Dictator and Totalitarianism," *World Politics*, Vol. 17, No. 4 (July, 1965), pp. 555–83 and *Personality and Politics: Problems of Evidence, Inference, and Conceptualization* (Chicago, 1969).

7. See, for example, David E. Apter, *The Politics of Modernization* (Chicago, 1965); S. N. Eisenstadt, *Modernization: Protest and Change* (Englewood

Cliffs, 1966); and the seven-volume series of *Studies in Political Development* (Princeton, 1963–1969), sponsored by the Committee on Comparative Politics of the Social Science Research Council.

8. For critical summaries of this literature, see David B. Truman, *The Governmental Process* (New York, 1951), pp. 188–93; Cecil A. Gibb, "Leadership," in Gardner Lindzey (ed.), *Handbook of Social Psychology*, Vol. 2 (Reading, Mass., 1954), pp. 877–920; Sidney Verba, *Small Groups and Political Behavior* (Princeton, 1961), Chapters 3 and 4.

9. Albert O. Hirschman, *Journeys Toward Progress: Studies of Economic Policy Making in Latin America* (New York, 1963).

10. William L. Langer, "The Next Assignment," *The American Historical Review*, Vol. 53, No. 2 (January, 1958), pp. 283–304. H. Stuart Hughes, "History and Psychoanalysis: The Explanation of Motive" in his *History as Art and as Science* (New York, 1964); Bruce Mazlish (ed.), *Psychoanalysis and History* (Englewood Cliffs, 1963).

11. Erik H. Erikson, *Young Man Luther: A Study in Psychoanalysis and History* (New York, 1958), p. 67.

12. Lewis J. Edinger, "Political Science and Political Biography: Reflections on the Study of Leadership," *Journal of Politics*, Vol. 26 (1964), p. 423.

13. George and George, *Woodrow Wilson and Colonel House*, preface to paperback edn. (New York, 1964), p. xiii.

14. Tucker, "The Dictator and Totalitarianism," p. 555.

15. Robert A. Dahl, "The Behavioral Approach in Political Science: Epitaph for a Monument to a Successful Protest," *The American Political Science Review*, Vol. 55, No. 4 (December, 1961), pp. 763–72.

16. Neustadt, *Presidential Power*, Signet edition (New York, 1964), p. 83.

17. Below, p. 380.

18. Harold D. Lasswell, *Power and Personality* (New York, 1948), pp. 88–93.

19. Edinger, *Kurt Schumacher*, p. 272.

20. Robert K. Merton, "Priorities in Scientific Discovery," *American Sociological Review* (December, 1957), Vol. 22, No. 6, pp. 635–659.

21. Erikson, *Young Man Luther* and *Gandhi's Truth* (New York, 1969).

22. Below, p. 77.

23. Quoted by Strout, below, p. 505.

24. E. Victor Wolfenstein, *The Revolutionary Personality: Lenin, Trotsky, Gandhi* (Princeton, 1967), p. 306.

25. Cited, note 4.

26. Below, p. 392.

27. Erikson, *Young Man Luther*, pp. 250–67.

28. The remainder of this section borrows heavily from my book *A World of Nations*, pp. 149–169.

29. The phrase is Erikson's (*Young Man Luther*, p. 16).

30. For critiques see the summary by Tucker (below, p. 69ff.), and the articles cited in notes 3 and 4 to his essay; see also Arthur Schlesinger, Jr., "Democracy and Hero Worship in the Twentieth Century," *Encounter* (December, 1960), Vol. 15, pp. 3–11.

31. The valiant attempt by the editor of the posthumous fourth edition to supply the deficiency with excerpts from Weber's other writings (*Wirtschaft und Gesellschaft*, 4th edition by Johannes Winckelmann [Tübingen, 1956], pp. 551–558 and 823–876) only reminds us how much we are missing.

32. For the Pauline antecedents see, for example, Daniel Bell, "Sociodicy: A Guide to Modern Usage," *The American Scholar* (Autumn, 1966), Vol. 34, No. 4 pp. 696–714, especially p. 702ff.

33. Weber, *Wirtschaft und Gesellschaft*, p. 662; the berserk reappears on pp. 140, 556, and 690. For a slightly different rendering of the passage, see H. H. Gerth and C. Wright Mills, *From Max Weber: Essays in Sociology* (London, 1947), p. 245; their adjective "Arabic" instead of "Nordic" is based on a misprint, corrected only in the 1956 edition.

34. Gerth and Mills, *From Max Weber*, pp. 295f. For other definitions, see the indices of *Wirtschaft und Gesellschaft* and other German and English editions *s.v.*, charisma, and the convenient collection, Max Weber, *On Charisma and Institution Building: Selected Papers*, ed. by S. N. Eisenstadt (Chicago, 1968).

35. Below, p. 115.

36. Below, p. 77.

37. Below, p. 70.

38. Weber, *Wirtschaft und Gesellschaft*, p. 142.

39. Chalmers Johnson, *Revolutionary Change* (Boston, 1966), p. 91; and Tucker, below, p. 80.

40. *Social Contract*, (1762), II, 7.

41. Cf., W. G. Runeiman, "Charismatic Authority and One-Party Rule in Ghana," Archives Européenes de Sociologie, Vol. 4, No. 1 (1963), pp. 148–165.

42. Joyce Cary, *The Captive and the Free* (London, 1959).

43. See above, note 8.

44. Tucker, "The Dictator and Totalitarianism," p. 574.

45. See the essays below on each of these.

46. Karl W. Deutsch *et al.*, *Political Community and the North Atlantic Area* (Princeton, 1957), p. 88.

47. See for that concept, Sigmund Neumann, *Permanent Revolution* (New York, 1942), p. 62.

48. Rustow, *A World of Nations*, p. 17.

49. *Social Contract*, II, 7.

50. Below, especially pp. 208–247 and 317–353.

51. Howes, in similar terms, speaks of Uchimura's "radar-like intuition."

52. Quoted below, p. 219.

53. C. H. Cooley, *Human Nature and the Social Order*, revised edition (New York, 1922), p. 328.

54. Cf., below, p. 218.

55. *Social Contract*, Barker Edition (Oxford University Press, 1948), I, 6, p. 179.

56. Hirschman, *Journeys Toward Progress*.

57. *Considérations sur les causes de la grandeur des romains et de leur décadence* (1734), ch. I.

58. Below, p. 367.

59. Stanley Hoffman (ed.), *Contemporary Theory in International Relations* (Englewood Cliffs, 1960), p. 36.

60. Below, p. 308, note 1.

ERIK H. ERIKSON

On the Nature of Psycho-Historical Evidence:
In Search of Gandhi

I

ABOUT A decade ago, when I first participated in a *Dædalus* discussion, I represented one wing of the clinical arts and sciences in a symposium on Evidence and Inference.[1] I offered some observations of a "markedly personal nature," and this not only from predilection but because the only methodological certainty that I could claim for my specialty, the psychotherapeutic encounter, was "disciplined subjectivity." Of all the other fields represented in that symposium, I felt closest (so I cautiously suggested) to the historian: for he, like the clinician, must serve the curious process by which selected portions of the past impose themselves on our renewed awareness and claim continued actuality in our contemporary commitments. We clinicians, of course, work under a Hippocratic contract with our clients; and the way they submit their past to our interpretation is a special form of historicizing, dominated by their sense of fragmentation and isolation and by our method of restoring to them, through the encounter with us, a semblance of wholeness, immediacy, and mutuality. But as we, in our jargon, "take a history" with the promise of correcting it, we enter another's life, we "make history." Thus, both clinician and patient (and in psychoanalysis, at any rate, every clinician undergoes voluntary patienthood for didactic purposes) acquire more than an inkling of what Collingwood claims history is—namely, "the life of mind" which "both lives in historical process and knows itself as so living."

Since that symposium, the former caution in the approach to each other of clinician and historian has given way to quite active efforts to find common ground. These have been confined for the most part to the joint study of the traditional affinity of case history

33

and life history. But here the clinician is inexorably drawn into super-personal history "itself," since he, too, must learn to conceive of, say, a "great" man's crises and achievements as communal events characteristic of a given historical period. On the other hand, some historians probably begin to suspect that they, too, are practitioners of a restorative art which transforms the fragmentation of the past and the peculiarities of those who make history into such wholeness of meaning as mankind seeks. This, in fact, may become only too clear in our time when the historian finds himself involved in on-going history by an accelerated interplay of communication between the interpreters and the makers of history: Here, a new kind of Hippocratic Oath may become necessary. And as for him who would cure mankind from history itself—he certainly takes on the therapeutic job of jobs.

It is not my purpose, however, to blur the division between therapist and historian. Rather, I would like to try to delineate an in-between field which some of us have come to call the psycho-historical approach. Such a hyphenated name usually designates an area in which nobody as yet is methodologically quite at home, but which someday will be settled and incorporated without a trace of border disputes and double names. The necessity to delineate it, however, becomes urgent when forward workers rush in with claims which endanger systematic exploration. Thus, today, psychoanalytic theory is sometimes applied to historical events with little clarification of the criteria for such a transfer. Such bravado can lead to brilliant insights, but also to renewed doubt in the specific fittedness and general applicability of psychological interpretation. I will, therefore, attempt to discuss here, in a manner both "markedly personal" and didactic, what parallels I have found between my clinical experience and the study of a circumscribed historical event.

Since the symposium on Evidence and Inference, my study *Young Man Luther* has also appeared[2]; and nothing could have better symbolized the methodological embarrassment on the part even of friendly critics than the stereotyped way in which editors, both in this country and in England, captioned the reviews of my book with the phrase, "Luther on the Couch." Now clinicians are, in fact, rather sparing in the use of the couch except in a systematic psychoanalysis; yet, "on the couch" has assumed some such popular connotation as "on the carpet." And it so happens that Luther all his life was a flamboyant free associator and in his youth certainly often talked as if he *were* "on the couch." His urbane superior von

Staupitz, could we inform him of the new uses of this adaptable furniture, would gladly testify to that. He recognized in the young monk's raving insistence that his repentance had not yet convinced God a "confession compulsion" altogether out of proportion to what the father confessor was ready to receive or to absolve; wherefore he told young Luther that *he* was resisting *God,* not God him. And with the recognition of an unfunctional resistance operative within the very act of "free" self-revelation, the confessor of old was on good clinical grounds.

The recognition of an inner resistance to some memories is, in fact, the technical basis for the whole theory of defense in psychoanalysis. As such, it is one of the five conceptions which Freud in one little-known dogmatic sentence calls "the principal constituents of . . . psychoanalysis."[3] To begin on didactic home ground, I will briefly discuss these fundamental assumptions, which have remained fundamental to all modifications of psychoanalysis and to its application in other fields. A "resisting" patient, then, may find something in himself obstructing him in his very determination to communicate what "comes to his mind": Too much may come too fast, or too little too tortuously, if at all. For such *resistance,* Freud blamed the mechanism of *repression* and the fact of an *unconscious,* for what once has been repressed can reassert its right to awareness and resolution only in indirect ways: in the symbolic disguise of dreams and fantasies, or in symptoms of commission (meaning acts alien to the actor himself), or in symptoms of omission (inhibitions, avoidances).

On the basis of his Victorian data, Freud found "behind" repression and resistance primarily what he called the *aetiological significance of sexual life*—that is, the pathogenic power of repressed sexual impulses. But, of course, he included a wide assortment of impulses and affects in the definition of "sexual"; and he considered systematic attention to the *importance of infantile experiences* an intrinsic part of his method and his theory. The last two conceptions led to what has been called the Freudian revolution, although Freud has no more reason than have the fathers of other kinds of revolutions to acknowledge the "liberation" named after him.

But there is one more term, mentioned by Freud in the same study and called "neither more nor less than the mainspring of the joint work of psychoanalysis": *transference*—and for a good historical example of father transference, we again need look no further than Luther's relation to Herrn von Staupitz and the Pope. How he made this, too, historical in a grand manner is, for the moment, another matter. Transference is a universal tendency active wherever human beings enter a relationship to others in such a way that the other *also* "stands for" persons as perceived in the pre-adult past. He thus serves the re-enactment of infantile and juvenile wishes and fears, hopes and apprehensions; and this always with a bewildering *ambivalence*—that is, a ratio of loving and hateful tendencies which under certain conditions change radically. This plays a singularly important role in the clinical encounter and not only in the dependent patient's behavior toward the clinician. It is also part of what the clinician must observe in himself: He, too, can transfer on different patients a variety of unconscious strivings which come from *his* infantile past. This we call *counter-transference.*

All these seeming difficulties, however, are the very tools of the psychoanalyst. To a determined believer in free will, they may all sound like weaknesses, if not dishonesties, while together they are really an intrinsic "property" of the clinical situation. Relived and resolved in each case, they are a necessary part of the evidence; and their elucidation is the only way to a cure. But are they also applicable to some aspects of historical research? Here the difficulties of a hyphenated approach become only too obvious, for in the absence of historical training I can only describe the way in which my clinical tools either hindered or proved handy in an attempt to reconstruct a historical event. Yet, it would seem that even the best trained historical mind could not "live in the historical process" without underscoring and erasing, professing and denying, even loving and hating and without trying to know himself as so living and so knowing. I may hope, then, that the predicaments to be described will remind the reader of his own experiences or of those recorded in the other contributions to this symposium. As for historical data proper, I can only try to introduce a psychological dimension into what would seem to be well-established rules of evidence.

II

Three times in the early-sixties I visited the city of Ahmedabad in the Indian State of Gujarat. The first time I went on the invitation of some enlightened citizens in order to give a seminar on the human life cycle and to compare our modern conception of the stages of life with those of the Hindu tradition. My wife and I occupied a small house on the estate of an industrialist—the city being one of the oldest textile centers of the world. Nearby was the mill owner's marble mansion, always open for rest and work to men of the mind; in its very shadow was the simple house of his sister, a saintly woman called the Mother of Labor, in whose living room hung a portrait of Tolstoy inscribed for Gandhi. It came back to me only gradually (for I had known it when I was young) that this was the city in which Gandhi had lived for more than a decade and a half and that it was this mill owner and his sister (both now in their seventies) to whom Gandhi pays high and repeated tribute in his autobiography. They had been Gandhi's opponent and ally, respectively, in the dramatic event by which labor unionism was founded in India: the Ahmedabad textile strike of 1918.

At the age of forty-five Gandhi had returned to India "for good" in 1914, after having spent his student years in England and the years of his early manhood in South Africa. He had founded a settlement near Ahmedabad, the principal city of the province in which he had been born and had found a liberal benefactor in the man whom we shall simply refer to as "the mill owner" (as, in general, I will endeavor not to name in this paper individuals merely used for "demonstration"). Once settled, Gandhi had immediately begun to travel extensively to become familiar with the life of the masses and to find circumscribed grievances suited to his approach: the nonviolent technique which he had developed in South Africa and had called *Satyagraha*—that is, a method of recognizing and mobilizing the forces of truth and peace in the oppressor as well as in the oppressed. In 1917 he had found an opportunity to move in on the system of indigo growing in faraway Bihar in defense of the rights of the peasants there. And now, in 1918, he accepted at the mill owner's request the mediatorship in a wage dispute in the principal industry at home, in Ahmedabad. He had studied the situation carefully and had decided to accept the leadership of ten thousand workers, a decision which brought him into public, as well as personal, conflict with the mill owner and aligned him on the side of the mill owner's sister, who had been deeply involved in "social work" in the widest sense. In the weeks of this strike Gandhi developed, in deed and in words, his full technique, including even a brief fast. The whole matter

37

ended in a compromise which nevertheless secured to the workers, in the long run, what they had asked for.

This story, then, seemed to harbor fascinating private, as well as public, issues. And it seemed significant that Gandhi would have chosen in the cataclysmic years 1917 and 1918 opportunities to demonstrate his kind of revolution in grievances involving first peasants and then workers and that he would do so on a local and even personal scale—visualize, in contrast, the global activities of other charismatic leaders in the concluding years of World War I. At the time, in fact, the mill strike was hardly noted: "We cannot see what Mr. M. K. Gandhi can win, but we can well see that he might lose everything," wrote the leading newspaper in the area. And in his autobiography, written a decade later, the Mahatma makes relatively light of the whole event—a diffidence which he transmitted to his biographers. Yet, the very next year he would lead the first nationwide civil disobedience and become forever India's Mahatma.

Enter the psycho-historian: Having learned to esteem the mill owner and his family and having become convinced of the historical and biographic significance of the strike as well as of the "resistance" against it, I determined to study both.

First, then, a word on the record of the event as written by Gandhi himself about a decade after the strike. In a previous publication,[4] I have pointed to the general difficulties encountered in using Gandhi's autobiography for either historical or psychoanalytic purposes—not to speak of a combination of both. Maybe more so in translation than in Gandhi's native Gujarati in which it was written, the autobiography often impresses the reader as monotonous and moralistic to the point of priggishness, or, at any rate, as devoid of any indication of Gandhi's presence described by witnesses as energetic and energizing, challenging and teasing. And, indeed, the autobiography originally was not a book at all. It was written over a number of years in the form of "columns" for a biweekly primarily addressed to youth: Each column, like our traditional homilies, had to have a moral. Furthermore, these columns were written when the Mahatmaship of India, gained in the years after the strike, seemed already forfeited both by political fortune and by approaching old age: Gandhi had been jailed and set free only to face again a politically divided India. Temporarily as we now know, but at the time often with depressing finality, he had turned from rebel to reformer. A Hindu reformer approaching sixty must face fully what the autobiography's fore-word clearly states: "What I want to achieve . . . is self-realization, to see God face to face, to attain *Moksha*." And *Moksha* in the Hindu life cycle means final renunciation and withdrawal. The autobiography is a testament, then, even though we now know that Gandhi's leadership had just begun.

One is almost embarrassed to point out what seems so obvious—namely, that in perusing a man's memoirs for the purpose of recon-structing past moments and reinterpreting pervasive motivational trends, one must first ask oneself at what age and under what general circumstances the memoirs were written, what their in-tended purpose was, and what form they assumed. Surely all this would have to be known before one can proceed to judge the less conscious motivations, which may have led the autobiographer to emphasize selectively some experiences and omit other equally decisive ones; to profess and reveal flamboyantly some deed or mis-deed and to disguise or deny equally obvious commitments; to argue and to try to prove what seems to purify or confirm his historical role and to correct what might spoil the kind of immortality he has chosen for himself. Confession-like remembrances often seem to be the most naïvely revealing and yet are also the most complex form of autobiography, for they attempt to prove the author's purity by the very advertisement of his impurities and, therefore, confound his honesty both as a sinner and a braggart.

As pointed out, past events make their often abrupt and sur-prising appearance in the psychoanalytic hour only as part of an observational situation which includes systematic attention to the reasons why they may come to mind just then: Factuality aside, what is their actuality in the developing relation of professional observer and self-observing client? It is, therefore, hard to under-stand how observers trained in clinical observation can accept an event reported in an autobiography—such as, say, Gandhi's account of his father's death—both as a factual event and as a naïve con-fession without asking why the item came to mind in *its* autono-mous setting, the autobiography; and why, indeed, a particular form of autobiography was being practiced or newly created at that moment in history. Gandhi himself states that he knew an autobiography to be a rather un-Indian phenomenon, which makes his own an all the more elemental creation comparable to the confessions of St. Augustine and Abelard or to Rousseau's and Kierkegaard's autobiographic works.

ERIK H. ERIKSON

To put this diagrammatically and didactically, a psycho-historical reviewer would have to fathom—in one intuitive configuration of thought if he can and with the help of a diagram if he must—the *complementarity* of at least four conditions under which a record emerges.

A. *Functions of the Record*

	I Moment	II Sequence
1. INDIVIDUAL	in the recorder's stage of life and general condition	in the recorder's life history
2. COMMUNITY	in the state of the recorder's community	in the history of the recorder's community

Under I-1, then, we would focus as if with a magnifying glass on one segment of the recorder's life as a period with a circumscribed quality. Gandhi's autobiography served the acute function of demonstrating an aging reformer's capacity to apply what he called truth to the balance sheet of his own failures and successes, in order to gain the wisdom of renunciation for himself and to promote a new level of political and spiritual awareness in his nation. But we would also have to consider the special inner conflicts and overt mood swings which aggravated these, his often withdrawn and "silent" years. Under I-2, we would consider all the acute circumstances in Indian history which would make Gandhi feel that he would find an echo for his message in those segments of India's awakening youth who could read—or be read to. Under II-1, we would remember that confession seems to have been a passion for him throughout life and that his marked concern over *Moksha* began in a precocious conscience development in childhood (which, in fact, he shared with other *homines religiosi*). In II-2, however, we would have to account for the fact that Gandhi's record, both in content and style, went far beyond the traditional forms of self-revelation in India and bridged such confessionalism as St. Augustine's or Tolstoy's awareness as Christians, as well as Rousseau's passionate and Freud's systematized insight into the power of infantile and juvenile experience. From the psycho-historical viewpoint, then, the question is not, or not only, whether a man like Gandhi inadvertently proves some of Freud's points

40

(such as the power of the emotions subsumed under the term Oedipus Complex), but why such items which we now recognize as universal were re-enacted in different media of representation (*including* Freud's dream analyses) by particular types of men in given periods of history—and why, indeed, their time was ready for them and their medium: for only such complementarity makes a confession momentous and its historical analysis meaningful.

Our diagrammatic boxes, then, suggest the *relativity* governing any historical item—that is, the "concomitant variability" of passing moment and long-range trend, of individual life cycle and communal development.

III

Let me now turn to the autobiography's rendition of the strike of 1918—the Event as I will call it from here on. There is besides Gandhi's retrospective reflections only one full account of it, a pamphlet of less than a hundred pages by the man who was then Gandhi's secretary.[5] Gandhi's own approach to the matter is even more casual and episodic and is, in fact, broken up by the insertion of a seemingly quite unrelated story.[6] This is the sequence: In a chapter (or installment) called "In Touch with Labor," Gandhi reports on the "delicate situation" in Ahmedabad where a sister "had to battle against her own brother." His friendly relations with both "made fighting with them the more difficult." But he considered the case of the mill hands strong, and he therefore "had to advise the laborers to go on strike." There follows a summary, less than one page long, of nearly twenty days of a strike during which he set in motion all the principles and techniques of his militant and nonviolent *Satyagraha*—on a local scale, to be sure, but with lasting consequences for Ahmedabad, India, and beyond. Then the story of the strike is interrupted by a chapter called "A Peep into the Ashram." Here the reader is entertained with a description of the multitude of snakes which infested the land by the river to which Gandhi, at the time of the strike, had just moved his settlement. Gandhi recounts how he and his Ashramites in South Africa, as well as in India, had always avoided killing snakes and that in twenty-five years of such practice "no loss of life [had been] occasioned by snake bite."[7] Only then, in a further chapter, does Gandhi conclude the strike story by reporting its climax—namely, his first fast in a public issue, in spite of which (or, as we shall see, because of which) the whole strike ended with what looked like a kind of hasty compromise. What was at stake then, and what was still at stake at the writing of the autobiography, was the purity of the nonviolent method: The mill owner could (and did) consider Gandhi's fast an unfairly coercive way of making the employers give in, whereas Gandhi did (and always would) consider a fast only justified as a means of persuading weakening supporters to hold out.

The technical question that arises here is whether the chapter which interrupts the account of the strike could be shown to signify an inner resistance against the whole story, comparable to what we observe and utilize in clinical work. Again and again, one finds, for example, that a child undergoing psychotherapy will suffer what I have called "play disruption"—that is, he will interrupt his play in some anxious manner, sometimes without being able to resume it. And often the very manner of disruption or the way in which play is resumed will suggest to the experienced observer what dangerous thought had occurred to the child and had ruined his playfulness. Or an adult in psychoanalysis will embark on a seemingly easy progression of free associations only to find suddenly that he has forgotten what he was about to say next or to interrupt his own trend of thought with what appears to be a senseless image or sentence "from nowhere." A little scrutiny can soon reveal that what had thus been lost or had intruded was, in fact, an important key to the underlying meaning of the whole sequence of thoughts—a key which more often than not reveals a repressed or suppressed sense of hate against a beloved person. I will later report on Gandhi's sudden awareness of such a disruption in another part of the autobiography.

What, then, could the nonkilling of snakes have to do with the Ahmedabad strike and with Gandhi's relation to the mill owner? Mere thematic play would suggest Gandhiites bent on nonviolence in the first column meet mill owners; in the second, poisonous snakes; and in the third, mill owners again. Do snakes, then, "stand for" mill owners? This could suggest to a clinician a breakthrough of Gandhi's anger against the mill owners—an anger which he had expressly forbidden himself, as well as the striking and starving workmen. If one can win over poisonous snakes by love and nonviolence, the hidden thought might be, then maybe one can reach the hearts of industrialists too. Or the suggestion might be more damaging—namely, that it would be more profitable to be kind to poisonous snakes than to industrialists—and here we remember that another Man of Peace, also using an analogy from the bestiary, once mused that big lazy camels might squeeze through where a rich man could not or would not. Was Gandhi's suppressed rage apt to be "displaced" in such a flagrant way? This would have to be seen.

There is, however, an explanation closer to historical fact and to the propagandistic purpose of the autobiography. He and the mill owner had been involved in a public scandal. Briefly, the mill owner had noted hordes of ferocious looking dogs around his factory on the outskirts of the city and had ascertained that the municipal police, knowing how Hindus feel about killing animals, were in the habit of releasing captured stray dogs outside the city limits. Since hydrophobia had reached major proportions in the area, the mill owner had requested the police to kill these dogs, and some obliging officer, for reasons of his own, had arranged for the carcasses to be carted away through the crowded city streets. Such is the stuff that riots are made of in India. But Gandhi did not hesitate to speak up for the mill owner, saying he himself would kill a deranged man if he found him massacring other people. He wrote in *Young India:*

The lower animals are our brethren. I include among them the lion and the tiger. We do not know how to live with these carnivorous beasts and poisonous reptiles because of our ignorance. When man learns better, he will learn to befriend even these. Today he does not even know how to befriend a man of a different religion or from a different country.[8]

In this prophetic statement we see the reptiles "associated" with carnivorous beasts; and from here it is only one step to the interpretation that Gandhi, before telling the story of how he had made concessions to the mill owner at the end of the strike, had to tell himself and his readers that his basic principles had not suffered on that other and better known occasion when he took the mill owner's side.

Was Gandhi "conscious" of such pleading with the reader? Probably, for the whole trend of thought fits well into the professed aim of his self-revelations: to sketch his "experiments with truth." But factual explanation (and here is the psycho-historical point) should not do away with the underlying and pervasive emotional actuality. For my story, the assumption of an ambivalence toward the mill owner is inescapable. In historical fact it is an example of a mutual and manly acceptance of the Hindu *dharma*—that is, of the assignment to each man of a place within the world order which he must fulfill in order to have a higher chance in another life. If, as Gandhi would put it, "fasting is my business," then making money was that of the mill owner; and Gandhi could not have fulfilled his role of saintly politician (or, as he put it, "a politician who tried to be a saint") had he not had the financial support of wealthy men. This, the Marxists might say, corrupted him, while the Hindu point of view would merely call for a clean division of roles within a common search for a higher truth. The Freudian point of view, however, would suggest that such a situation might cause an unconscious "transference" of unresolved conflicts of childhood to the present.

Young Gandhi had, in varying ways, forsaken his caste and his father when he left to become an English barrister; and he had forsaken his older brother who had wanted him to join him in legal work when he had become a reformer. Such deviations from one's ancestral *dharma* are a grave problem in the lives of many creative Indians. At any rate, when he returned and settled down in Ahmedabad—the city in which both his native language and the mercantile spirit of his ancestors had reached a high level of cultivation—and when he again deviated grievously by taking a family of Untouchables into his *Ashram*, the mill owner alone had continued to support him. The mill owner, thus, had become a true brother; and anyone familiar with Gandhi's life will know how desperate at times was the "Great Soul's" never requited and never fully admitted search for somebody who would sanction, guide, and, yes, mother *him*. This is a complex matter, and it will be enough to indicate here that without the assumption of such a transference of the prime actor in my story to the principal witnesses, a brother and sister, I could not have made sense of the meaning of the Event in Gandhi's life—and of his wish to "play it down."

IV

Nobody likes to be found out, not even one who has made ruthless confession a part of his profession. Any autobiographer, therefore, at least between the lines, spars with his reader and potential judge. Does the autobiographic recorder then develop a kind of transference on the potential reviewer of his record? Gandhi did, as we shall see.

But before reporting this, let me ask another question: Does not the professional reader and reviewer, who makes it his business to reveal what others do or may *not* know about themselves, also feel some uncomfortable tension in relation to them? Yes, I think that he does and that he should know that he does. There are, of course, some who would claim that, after all, they are voyeurs merely in *majorem gloriam* of history or humanity and are not otherwise "involved" with their subjects. But such denial often results only in an interpretive brashness or a superior attitude toward the self-recorder who seems to reveal himself so inadvertently or to hide his "real" motivation so clumsily. A patient offers his motivation for full inspection only under the protection of a contract and a method; and the method is not complete unless the "doctor" knows how to gauge his own hidden feelings. If it can be assumed that the reviewer of self-revelations or of self-revealing acts and statements offered in nonclinical contexts also develops some form of irrational counter-transference, that, too, must be turned to methodological advantage not only for the sake of his work, but also for that of his friends and his family.

I hope to have aroused just enough discomfort in the professional reader to make him share the sting I felt when in the course of my study I came once again across the following passage midway through Gandhi's autobiography: "If some busybody were to cross-examine me on the chapters which I have now written, he could probably shed more light on them, and if it were a hostile critic's cross-examination, he might even flatter himself for having shown up the hollowness of many of my pretensions."[9] Here, then, we seem to have a real analogue to what I described above as "play disruption"; and, indeed, Gandhi continues with a momentary negative reaction to his whole undertaking: "I therefore wonder for a moment whether it might not be proper to stop writing these chapters altogether." After which he recovers, luckily, with a typically Gandhian form of self-sanction: "But so long as there is no prohibition from the voice within, I must continue the writing." There seems to be an awareness, however, of having given in to something akin to free association, though dictated by a higher power: "I write just as the spirit moves me at the time of writing. I do not claim to know definitely that all conscious thought and action on my part is directed by the spirit." Again, he recovers, however, and sanctions his own doings: "But on an examination of the greatest steps that I have taken in my life, as also of those that may be regarded as the least, I think it will not be improper to say that all of them were directed by the spirit." Now he can dismiss his "hostile" reader: "I am not writing the autobiography to please critics. Writing it itself is one of the experiments with truth." And he can distribute the blame for writing at all: "Indeed, I started writing [the autobiography] in compliance with their [his co-workers'] wishes. If, therefore, I am wrong in writing the autobiography, they must share the blame." This concluding remark is, I think, typical of the Gandhian half-humor so easily lost in translation; and humor means recovery.

To say more about this sudden disruption, I would have to know (according to my own specifications) exactly in what period of his life Gandhi wrote this particular installment of the autobiography. Was there a real snooper and critic in his life at the time? Or was the imaginary one an externalization of a second inner voice, one temporarily at odds with the one that inspired his every effort? Much speaks for the latter assumption, for the disruption follows a chapter called "A Sacred Recollection and Penance" in which Gandhi describes an especially cruel outbreak against his wife under circumstances (there were many in his life) both sublime and ridiculous. Once, in South Africa, while cleaning her house which had become a hostel, she had refused to empty a Christian Untouchable's chamber pot (*that* combination was too *much*), and Gandhi had literally shown her the gate. After such extreme and extremely petty moments something could cry out in him: What if all his professions of universal love, all his sacrifices of those closest to him by family ties for the sake of those furthest away (the masses, the poor, the Untouchables) were a "pretense"? So here, the reader and reviewer become an externalization of the writer's self-doubt; and I felt so directly appealed to that I began to think of how I might have explained these matters to him in the light of our clinical knowledge. Not without the sudden awareness of being older than he had been when he wrote that passage, I addressed him in an ensuing chapter explaining that, as a student of another lover of truth, a contemporary of his on the other side of the world, I had a more charitable term than "pretense" for the psychological aspects of his dilemma: namely, "ambivalence." I confronted him with another instance of petty and righteous cruelty and attempted to formulate a pervasive ambivalence: that his marriage at the age of thirteen to a girl of the same age and fatherhood in his teens had prevented him from making a conscious decision at an informed age for or against married life; that this "fate" had been foisted on him in the traditional manner by his father, whom he never forgave. Thus, a lifelong ambivalence toward his wife and children, not to speak of sexuality in general, had perpetuated a predicament in his life as well as in that of many of his followers: Are *Satyagraha* and chastity inseparable? That such conflicts in the lives of saintly men are more than a matter of mental hygiene, I need not emphasize here. Gandhi, I think, would have listened to me, but probably would have asked me teasingly why I had taken his outburst so personally. And, indeed, my impulsive need to answer him "in person" before I could go on with my book revealed again that all manner of counter-transference can accompany our attempts to analyze others, great or ordinary.

And what, we must ask (and he might have asked), legitimizes such undertaking in clinical work? It is, of course, the mandate to help—*paired with self-analysis.* And even as we demand that he who makes a profession of "psychoanalyzing" others must have learned a certain capacity for self-analysis, so must we presuppose that the psycho-historian will have developed or acquired a certain self-analytical capacity which would give to his dealings with others, great or small, both the charity of identification and a reasonably good conscience. Ours, too, are "experiments with truth."

I can offer, for such an ambitious aim, only another schema which lists the minimum requirements for what a reviewer of a record and of an event should be reasonably clear about:

B. *Function of the Review*

	I Moment	II Sequence
1. INDIVIDUAL	in the stage and the conditions of the reviewer's life	in the reviewer's life history
2. COMMUNITY	in the state of the reviewer's communities	in the history of the reviewer's communities

Under communities I here subsume a whole series of collective processes from which the reviewer derives identity and sanction and within which his act of reviewing has a function: there, above all, he must know himself as living in the historical process. Each community, of course, may call for a separate chart: the reviewer's nation or race, his caste or class, his religion or ideological party—and, of course, his professional field.

V

Did Freud live up to our methodological standards? His introduction to what we now know to have been the first psycho-historical essay—namely, the book on Wilson allegedly coauthored by him and William Bullitt[10]—does give an admirable approximation of what I have in mind. But not in the bulk of the book: for here he unwisely relied on Bullitt to review the record for him and to provide him with the data necessary for an application of the laws found in case histories to the life history of a public figure. In my review of this book,[11] I felt it necessary to explain the strange collaboration in this way: As a young man and before he became a doctor, so Freud himself tells us, he had wanted to be a statesman. His deep identification with Moses can be clearly read in his work. Did Bullitt awaken in the old and ailing man (who, in fact, was dying in exile when he signed the final manuscript) the fading hope that his life work, psychoanalysis, might yet be destined to become applicable to statesmanship? The task at hand, however, was obviously overshadowed by Freud's passionate feelings in regard to the joint subject, President Wilson. About this, Freud is explicit in his introduction, the only part of the book clearly written by him, all other handwritten contributions having been "lost" by Bullitt in one way or another. Freud declares that the figure of the American President, "as it rose above the horizons of Europeans, was from the beginning unsympathetic" to him and that this feeling increased "the more severely we suffered from the consequences of his intrusion into our destiny." Wilson's Fourteen Points had promised that a semblance of Christian charity, combined with political shrewdness, might yet survive the first mechanized slaughter in history. Could it be that the destruction or the dehumanization of mankind by the unrestricted use of superweaponry might be checked by the creation of a world-democracy? What followed Versailles played into a pervasive trend in Freud's whole being: a Moses-like indignation at all false Christian (or other) prophecy. A proud man brought up in Judaism, I concluded, even if surrounded by the folklore and display of Catholicism, persists in the historical conviction that the Messiah has not yet appeared and persists with more grimness the more he has been inclined temporarily to give credence to the Christian hope for salvation. Such over-all prejudice, however, even where clearly expressed, is methodologically meaningful only insofar as the slant thus given to the whole work is thereby clarified *and* insofar as it is vigorously counteracted by an adherence to the other criteria for evidence and inference—and for literary form. On the other hand, where a sovereign acknowledgment like Freud's introduction enters an alliance with a vindictive and tendentious case study clearly written by a chronically disappointed public servant such as Bullitt, then the whole work itself becomes a case study of a fascinating, but in its final form abortive, psycho-historical essay. The Wilson book can serve to illustrate, then, if somewhat by way of a caricature, the decisive influence on a bit of history which results from basic differences in *Weltanschauung* among actor, recorder, and reviewer —that is, a world view, a sense of existential space-time which (as a venerable physicist acknowledged in my seminar in Ahmedabad) is "in a man's bones," no matter what else he has learned.

Freud's example leads me back to the days when I first heard of Gandhi and of Ahmedabad and maybe even of the mill owner— all of which remained latent until, at the time of my visit, it "came back to me" almost sensually in the occasional splendor and the pervasive squalor of India. In my youth I belonged to the class of wandering artists who—as some alienated and neurotic youths can and must in all ages—blithely keep some vision alive in the realities of political and economic chaos, even though, by a minute slip in the scales of fate, they may find themselves among the uniformed to whom killing and being killed becomes a sacred duty, or they may perish ingloriously in some mass furor.

As Wilson's image had set in the cruel night of post-Versailles, it was Gandhi's which then "rose above the horizon"—on the other side of the world. As described to us by Romain Rolland, he seemed to have that pervasive presence, always dear to youth, which comes from the total commitment (for that very reason) to the actuality of love and reason in every fleeting moment. The Event had been contemporaneous with Wilson's Fourteen Points; and if these Points were (and with variations still are) "Western democracy's answer to Bolshevism," so was Gandhi's *Satyagraha* (begun so locally) the East's answer to Wilson *and* to Lenin.

As for myself, I was to spend a lifetime finding an orientation in, and making a living from, the field created by Sigmund Freud. But when I decided in advanced years to study the Event—and all

49

I can say is that at a certain time I became aware of having made that decision—I do not think that I set out merely to "apply" to Gandhi what I had learned from Freud. Great contemporaries, in all their grandiose one-sidedness, converge as much as they diverge; and it is not enough to characterize one with the methods of the other. As Freud once fancied he might become a political leader, so Gandhi thought of going into medicine. All his life Gandhi ran a kind of health institute, and Freud founded an international organization with the ideological and economic power of a movement. But both men came to revolutionize man's awareness of his wayward instinctuality and to meet it with a combination of militant intelligence—and nonviolence. Gandhi pointed a way to the "conquest of violence" in its external and manifest aspects and, in the meantime, chose to pluck out the sexuality that offended him. Freud, in studying man's repressed sexuality, also revealed the internalized violence of self-condemnation, but thought externalized violent strife to be inevitable. And both men, being good post-Darwinians, blamed man's instinctuality on his animal ancestry— Gandhi calling man a sexual "brute" and Freud comparing his viciousness (to his own kind!) to that of wolves. Since then ethology has fully described the intrinsic discipline of animal behavior and most impressively (in this context) the pacific rituals by which some social animals—yes, even wolves—"instinctively" prevent senseless murder.[12]

When I came to Ahmedabad, it had become clear to me (for I had just come from the disarmament conference of the American Academy) that man as a species cannot afford any more to cultivate illusions either about his own "nature" or about that of other species, or about those "pseudo-species" he calls enemies—not while inventing and manufacturing arsenals capable of global destruction and relying for inner and outer peace solely on the superbrakes built into the superweaponry. And Gandhi seems to have been the only man who has visualized *and* demonstrated an over-all alternative.

Less nobly, I should admit that I must have been looking for a historical figure to write about. What could be more fitting than (as my students put it) letting "Young Man Luther" be followed by "Middle-Aged Mahatma"? And here I had witnesses: the survivors of a generation of then young men and women who had joined or met Gandhi in 1918, and whose life (as the saying goes) had not been the same since, as if one knew what it might have been. They included, besides the mill owner and his sister, individuals now retired or still in the forefront of national activity in industry, in the Cabinet, or in Parliament. These I set out to meet and to interview on my subsequent visits to India.

If all this sounds self-indulgently personal, it is spelled out here only far enough to remind the psycho-historian that his choice of subject often originates in early ideals or identifications and that it may be important for him to accept as well as he can some deeper bias than can be argued out on the level of verifiable fact or faultless methodology. I believe, in fact, that any man projects or comes to project on the men and the times he studies some unlived portions and often the unrealized selves of his own life, not to speak of what William James calls "the murdered self." The psycho-historian may owe it to history, as well as to himself, to be more conscious of what seems to be a *re-transference* on former selves probably inescapable in any remembering, recording, or reviewing and to learn to live and to work in the light of such consciousness. This, incidentally, also calls for new forms of collaboration such as the father of psychoanalysis may have had in mind when he met the brilliant American diplomat.

To confound things a little further, there are also *cross-transferences* from one reviewer of the same subject to another. For example, in a book on Gandhi's main rivals for national leadership, *Tilak and Gokhale* (both of whom died before his ascendance), S. A. Wolpert[13] calls Gandhi a disciple of Gokhale, and, worse, calls Gokhale Gandhi's "guru." Now, Gandhi, while comparing Tilak with the forbidding ocean and Gokhale (his elder by three years only) with the maternal Ganges and while sometimes calling Gokhale his "political guru," certainly kept *the* guruship in his life free for his own inner voice: an important step in Indian self-conception. But why should Wolpert want to call *his* Gokhale *my* Gandhi's guru with such monotonous frequency—and why should this annoy me? The italics indicate the answer which (as I would judge from my perusal of the literature on Luther) points to a pervasive aspect of a reviewer's "genealogical" identification with his subject as seen through his method, which may make history more entertaining, but rarely more enlightening unless seasoned with insight.

VI

In India, intellectual as well as political travelers could always count on being lodged with friends of means or with friends of friends, and the mill owner related the sayings of many interesting house guests—among them, Gandhi. He had offered me a terrace as a study, saying quietly, "Tagore has worked here." But to be a guest in a man's house is one thing; to be a reviewer of his place in history is another. When I returned to Ahmedabad to interview the mill owner regarding the mill strike, he became strangely distant and asked me to meet him at his office in the mill. This, he made clear, was business: What did I want?

I should say in general that the clinician turned historian must adapt himself to and utilize a new array of "resistances" before he can be sure to be encountering those he is accustomed to. There is, first of all, the often incredible or implausible loss or absence of data in the post-mortem of a charismatic figure which can be variably attributed to simple carelessness or lack of awareness or of candor on the part of witnesses. Deeper difficulties, however, range from an almost cognitively a-historical orientation—ascribed by some to Indians in general—to a highly idiosyncratic reluctance to "give up" the past. Here the myth-affirming and myth-destroying propensities of a post-charismatic period must be seen as the very stuff of which history is made. Where myth-making predominates, every item of the great man's life becomes or is reported like a parable; those who cannot commit themselves to this trend must disavow it with destructive fervor. I, for one, have almost never met anybody of whatever level of erudition or information, in India or elsewhere, who was not willing and eager to convey to me the whole measure of the Mahatma as based on one sublime or scandalous bit of hearsay. Then there are those whose lives have become part of a leader's and who have had to incorporate him in their self-image. Here it becomes especially clear that, unless a man wants to divest himself of his past in order to cure, purify, or sell himself—and there are always professions which receive and sanction such divestment —he must consider it an invested possession to be shared only according to custom and religion, personal style and stage of life. The interviewee, not being a client, does not break a contract with either himself or the interviewer in not telling the whole truth as he knows or feels it. He has, in fact, every right to be preoccupied with the intactness of his historical role rather than with fragmented details as patients and psychotherapists are—often to a fault. After all, this man had been Gandhi's counterplayer in the Event, and he had (as Gandhi knew and took for granted) used all the means at his disposal to break the strike. About this he was, in fact, rather frank, while he seemed "shy" about those episodes which had proven him to be a gallant opponent and faithful supporter. What kind of "resistance" was *that*?

Let me be diagrammatic: The old man's insistence on anonymity turned out to be a lifelong one. In old newspapers I found more than one reference to his charitable deeds which in feudal manner he had always considered his own choice and his own affair. "This is business, not charity," a union official quoted him as saying when he handed him a contribution; and it will be remembered that he did not identify himself when, as a young industrialist, he left money at the *Ashram* gate. Here was a lifelong trend, then, possibly aggravated by some sense of *Moksha,* which supervenes both good deeds and misdeeds. It is not so easy to judge, then, what a man (and a foreigner) does not want to remember or does not want to say or cannot remember or cannot say.

By the same token, the old man's businesslike attitude was later clarified in its most defensive aspects as resulting from an experience with an inquisitive visitor, while in general it seemed to reflect a sense of propriety as though he wanted to delineate what in this matter was "my business" and what his. I have already indicated that this same attitude pervaded even Gandhi's sainthood. When Gandhi said to his friends, who wanted to starve themselves with him, "Fasting is my business," he added, "You do yours." But, then, both he and the mill owner belonged to a cultural and national group referred to in India (admiringly as well as mockingly) as *banias*—that is, traders. And while the whole strike and its outcome are often considered a *bania* deal by Gandhi's many critics (Marxists, or Maharashtrians, or Bengalis), there is little doubt that Gandhi chose to unfold his whole *Satyagraha* technique first in a locality and with people who spoke his language and shared his brand of mercantile shrewdness. And behind such life-styles there is always India and that larger framework of cosmic propriety, which is called *dharma*—that is, a man's preordained place in the cyclic order of things and their eventual transcendence. *Dharma* can excuse much wickedness and laziness, as can Fate or God's Will. But it will help determine, from childhood on, what a man considers proper and what out of line; above all, it provides the framework within which the individual can knowingly take hold of the law of *Karma,* the ethical accounting in his round of lives.

I felt, then, literally "put in my place" by the old man's "resistance." In fact, when he asked me after our first interview what, if anything, I had learned, I could only say truthfully that I had gotten an idea of what Gandhi had been up against with him and he with Gandhi. Only afterwards did I realize how right I was and that the cause of my initial annoyance had been due to a certain parallel between Gandhi's and my relationship to the mill owner. Had I not gladly accepted the wealthy man's hospitality when I was a newcomer to India so that I could venture out into the dangers and horrors of that land from an initial position of friendship and sanitary safety? And had not Gandhi gladly accepted his financial support when he came back from South Africa, in many ways a newcomer to India after twenty-five years of absence? And had not both of us, Gandhi and I, developed a certain ambivalence to our benefactor? Here, a Marxist could find an opening for legitimate questions; and while he is at it, he might well consider the relationship of the social scientist to the foundations which support him. The common factor which interests us here, however, is the unconscious transference on any host—that is, the attribution of a father or older-brother role to anyone in whose home one seeks safety or in whose influence one seeks security. I should add that in my case this theme seems to be anchored in the infantile experience—and, strictly speaking, this alone makes a real transference out of a mere thematic transfer—of having found a loving stepfather in an adoptive country. Every worker must decide for himself, of course, how much or how little he should make of such a connection, and how little or how much of it he should impose on his readers. But first, we must become aware of it.

Now an equally brief word on the other side of the coin—namely, the often sudden and unsolicited revelation of such highly personal material as dreams, memories, and fantasies in the course of interviews. In my case, these were offered by a number of informants in the more informal settings of social get-togethers. Accepting them with gratitude, I was always determined to make use of them only as an auxiliary source of insights, not to be attributed to individuals. I do not know, of course, whether revelations of this kind are common in such work or appeared in mine because my interviewees knew me to be a psychoanalyst. If this most personal data eventually proved to have some striking themes in common, I cannot say whether these themes are typically Indian or typical for men who had followed Gandhi. Here are the themes: a *deep hurt* which the informant had inflicted on one of his parents or guardians and could never forget, and an intense wish *to take*

care of abandoned creatures, people or animals, who have strayed
too far from home. I had secured from each interviewee the story
of how he first met Gandhi only to learn with increasing clinical
admiration how determinedly and yet cautiously Gandhi had induced his alienated young followers to cut an already frayed bond
with their elders. Tentatively, then, I saw these revelations as an
indirect admission of the obvious fact that followers can develop
a more or less conscious sense of having vastly outdistanced their
original life plan by serving a man who had the power to impose
his superior *dharma* on his contemporaries, making a modernized
use of the traditional need for a second, a spiritual, father. A resulting powerful ambivalence toward him is often overcompensated by
the submissive antics of followership. And followership divides
too: Gandhi's disciples had to accept what was his own family's
plight—namely, that he belonged to all and to no one, like the
mother in a joint family. Gandhi's was a unique maternalism, happily wedded in his case with a high degree of paternal voluntarism,
but not always easily shared or tolerated by others.

Followers, too, deserve a diagram. Whatever motivation or conflict they may have in common as they join a leader and are joined
together by him has to be studied in the full complementarity of:

C.

	I Moment	II Sequence
1. INDIVIDUAL	the stage of life when they met the leader	lifelong themes transferred to the leader
2. COMMUNITY	their generation's search for leader-ship	traditional and evolving patterns of followership

As to the last point, Gandhi was a master not only in the selection
and acquisition of co-workers, but also in assigning them to or using
them in different tasks and ways of life—from the position of
elected sons and daughters in his ascetic settlement to that of revolutionary organizers all over India and of aspirants for highest political
power, including the prime ministership, for which he "needed a
boy from Harrow."

The monumental compilation of Gandhi's works[14] undertaken by
the government of India (and now under the charge of Professor

Swaminathan) permits us to follow Gandhi's acts, thoughts, and affects literally from day to day in speeches and letters, notes and even dreams (as reported in letters), and to recognize his own conflicts over being invested with that charismatic cloak, the Mahatmaship. That publication will permit us for once to see a leader in a life-crisis fighting on two fronts at once: the individual past that marks every man as a defined link in the generational chain, and historical actuality. One thing is clear: On the verge of becoming the father of his nation, he did not (as he has been accused of having done) forget his sons, although the manner in which he did remember them was not without tragic overtones and consequences.

VII

The psychoanalyst, it seems, makes a family affair out of any historical event. Does anybody, we may ask, ever escape his internalized folk and learn to deal with the cast of his adult life on its own terms? The answer is yes and no. Certainly, where radical innovation depends on very special motivations and is paired with strong affect, there its impetus can be shown to draw on lifelong aspirations and involvements. It is true that the psychoanalytic method rarely contributes much to the explanation of the excellence of a man's performance—which may be just as well, for it permits the factor of grace to escape classification and prescription—but it may indicate what freed him for his own excellence or what may have inhibited or spoiled it. It so happens that the Ahmedabad Event *was* something of a family affair not only in that Gandhi's counter-players were a brother and a sister, but also because Gandhi here tried to do what is proverbially the most difficult thing for a leader—to be a prophet in his own country. The proverb, too, may gain a new meaning if we can locate the difficulty in the prophet's conflicts as well as in his "country's" diffidence. The very intimacy of my story may seem inapplicable to large events; yet the way Gandhi used his local successes to establish himself firmly as his whole nation's leader—a year later he would command nationwide civil disobedience against the British government—would seem to go to the core of his style as a leader. A man's leadership is prominently characterized by his choice of the proper place, the exact moment, and the specific issue that help him to make his point momentously. Here I would like to quote from a political scientist's work which has aroused interest and on which I have been asked to comment because it uses some "classical" psychoanalytic assumptions rather determinedly.

Victor Wolfenstein, in discussing Gandhi's famous Salt-*Satyagraha* of 1930, asks bluntly: "But why did Gandhi choose the salt tax from among his list of grievances as the first object of *Satyagraha?*"[15] This refers to the occasion when Gandhi, after his long period of political silence, chose (of all possible actions) to lead an at first small but gradually swelling line of marchers on a "sacred pilgrimage" from Ahmedabad to the Arabian Sea in order to break the law against the tax-free use of salt. Wolfenstein's answer is threefold: First, Gandhi "believed that of all British oppressions the salt tax was the most offensive because it struck the poorest people hardest. . . . By undertaking to serve or lead the lowliest self-esteem is raised." This refers to the assumption that Gandhi and other revolutionary leaders overcome a sense of guilt by acting not for themselves, but for the exploited. Wolfenstein's second point is that "the tax on salt constituted an oral deprivation, a restriction on eating." And it is true, Gandhi was preoccupied all his life with dietary prohibitions and dietary choices. But then, Wolfenstein introduces psychoanalytic symbolism in a way which must be quoted more fully:

Another line of interpretation, which is consonant with the view I have been developing of Gandhi's personality, is suggested by Ernest Jones' contention that one of the two basic symbolic significances of salt is human semen. If it had this unconscious meaning for Gandhi, then we may understand his depriving himself of condiments, including salt, as a form of sexual abstinence, involving a regression to an issue of the oral phase. In the context of the Salt March, Gandhi's taking of salt from the British can thus be seen as reclaiming for the Indian people the manhood and potency which was properly theirs.

The choice of issues worthy of a *Satyagraha* campaign must interest us in past as well as in ongoing history, and Gandhi's choice of the salt tax has always impressed me as a model of practical and symbolic action. It pointed to a foreign power's interdiction of a vast population's right to lift from the long shorelines surrounding their tropical subcontinent a cheap and nature-given substance necessary for maintaining work-capacity as well as for making bland food palatable and digestible. Here, Gandhi's shrewdness seemed to join his capacity to focus on the infinite meaning in finite things—a trait which is often associated with the attribution of sainthood. Wolfenstein's suggestion—that the power of this appeal

57

is attributable to an unconscious sexual meaning of salt—while seeming somewhat ludicrous as an isolated statement, appears to have a certain probability if viewed in cultural context. Anybody acquainted with the ancient Indian preoccupation with semen as a substance which pervades the whole body and which, therefore, is released only at the expense of vitality, acuity, and spiritual power will have to admit that if there is an equation between salt and semen in the primitive mind, the Indian people more than any other could be assumed to make the most of it. I suggest, however, that we take a brief look at what E. Jones really said and what the place of his conclusions is in the history of psychoanalytic symbolism.

Jones' classical paper, "The Symbolic Significance of Salt in Folklore and Superstition," was written in 1928.[16] It really starts with the question of the meaning of superstitions that the spilling of salt at a table may bring ill luck and discord to those assembled for a meal. Jones brings together an overwhelming amount of data from folklore and folkcustom which indicate that salt is used in some magic connection with or as an equivalent of semen. A peasant bridegroom may put salt in his left pocket to insure potency; tribesmen and workmen may abstain from both salt and sex during important undertakings; Christian sects may be accused of "salting" the Eucharistic bread with semen—and so on. Jones' conclusion is that to spill salt "means" to lose or spill semen as Onan did: suggesting, then, the sexual model of an antisocial act.

But before we ask how salt may come to mean semen, it is only fair to state that through the ages it has had a powerful significance as itself. When other preservatives were not known, the capacity of salt not only to give pungent taste to the blandest diet, but also to keep perishable food fresh, to cleanse and cure wounds, and even to help embalm dead bodies gave it magic as well as practical value: The very word "salary" apparently comes from the fact that this clean, indestructible, and easily transportable substance could be used instead of money. That it comes from the great Sea, the mythical giver of life, makes salt also a "natural" symbol of procreation as well as of longevity and immortality, wit and wisdom, and thus of such incorruptability as one fervently hopes will preserve the uncertain phenomena of friendship, loyalty, and hospitality. The use of salt on its own terms, then, for the ceremonial affirmation of mutual bonds would do nicely to explain the superstition concerning the unceremonious spilling.

Jones' conclusion is really rather cautious: "The significance naturally appertaining to such an important and remarkable article of diet as salt has thus been strengthened by an accession of psychical significance derived from deeper sources. The conclusion reached, therefore, is that salt is a typical symbol for semen. There is every reason to think that the primitive mind equates the idea of salt not only with that of semen, but also with the essential constituent of urine. The idea of salt in folklore and superstition characteristically represents the male, active, fertilizing principle."

In psychoanalysis, "deeper" always seems to mean both "sexual" and "repressed," an emphasis which made sense within Freud's libido theory—that is, his search for an "energy of dignity" in human life that would explain the fantastic vagaries of man's instinctuality and yet be comparable to the indestructible and commutable energy isolated and measured in natural science. In civilization and especially in his day, he would find pervasive evidence of the systematic repression in children of any knowledge of the uses and purposes of the sexual organs and this most particularly in any parental context —a repression which no doubt used the pathways of universal symbolization in order to disguise sexual and, above all, incestual thoughts and yet find expression for them. Among these, early psychoanalysis emphasized paternal and phallic symbolism more than maternal; yet, if sexual symbolism did play a role in helping Gandhi, as he put it, "to arouse the religious imagination of an angry people," then the Indian masses, with all their stubborn worship of mother-goddesses, surely would have been swayed as much by the idea of free access to the fecundity of the maternal sea as by the claim to male potency.

At any rate, the one-way symbolization suggested in psychoanalysis, by which the nonsexual always symbolizes the sexual, is grounded in the assumption that the erotic is more central to infantile and primitive experience than are the cognitive and the nutritional. But one wonders: Where survival is at stake, where sexuality is not so obsessive as it becomes in the midst of affluence, where sexual repression is not so marked as it became in the civilized and rational mind—could it not be that the symbolic equation of salt and semen is reciprocal? Could not the ceremonial linking of the two have the purpose of conferring on life-creating semen, a substance so easily squandered, the life-sustaining indestructibility of salt? This is, at the end, a question of determining the place of sexuality in man's whole ecology. But in the immediate context of the chronic semistarvation that has undermined the vitality of the Indian masses and considering the periodic threat of widespread death by famine, it would seem appropriate to assume, first of all, that salt means salt. In fact, the further development of psychoanalysis will have to help us understand the symbolic representation not only of repressed sexuality, but also of the ever-present and yet so blatantly denied fact of death in us and around us.[17] If reason will not suffice, then new forms of irrational violence will force us to consider the consequences of man's seeming ability to ignore not only the certainty of his own death, but also the super-weaponry poised all around him to destroy the world he knows—literally at a moment's notice.

Sexual symbolism may help, I would agree, to understand superstitions and symptoms such as, say, the often self-destructive food-fads Gandhi indulged in: At one time, he excluded natural salt from his diet, while at another his friends had reason to tease him over his addiction to Epsom salt. In such matters, however, he was only the all-too-willing victim of a tremendous preoccupation with diet rampant during his student days in vegetarian circles in England as well as in the tradition of his native country, although he adorned this with his own concerns over the impact of diet on sexual desire. In deciding on the Salt March, however, he was obviously in command of his political and economic as well as his psychological wits. And in any context except that of irrationality clearly attributable to sexual repression, one should take any interpretation that explains a human act by recourse to sexual symbolism with a grain of salt.

VIII

A historical moment, we have been trying to suggest, is determined by the complementarity of what witnesses, for all manner of motivation, have considered momentous enough to remember and to record and what later reviewers have considered momentous enough to review and re-record in such a way that the factuality of the event is confirmed or corrected and actuality is perceived and transmitted to posterity. For recorders and reviewers alike, however, events assume a momentous character when they seem both unprecedented and yet also mysteriously familiar—that is, if *analogous events* come to mind that combine to suggest a direction to historical recurrences, be it divine intention someday to be revealed, or an inexorable fate to which man may at least learn to adapt, or regularities which it may be man's task to regulate more engineeringly, or a repetitive delusion from which thoughtful man must "wake up." Psychoanalysis is inclined to recognize in all events not only an analogy to, but also a regression to the onto-genetic and phylogenetic past. This has proven fruitful in the clinical task of treating patients who suffered from "repressed reminiscences"; but out of its habitual and dogmatic application has come what I have called the *originological fallacy* which, in contrast to the teleological one, deals with the present as almost pre-empted by its own origins—a stance not conducive to the demonstration of developmental or historical probability.

The diagrammatic formula for a *historical analogy* would be that another event is considered equivalent to the one at hand because it happened.

D.

	I Moment	II Sequence
1. INDIVIDUAL	to a comparable individual at the corresponding stage of his development	to comparable individuals throughout their lives
2. COMMUNITY	in a corresponding stage of a comparable community	at comparable moments throughout history

Let me use as a first set of examples a thematic similarity between Gandhi's autobiography and that of the most influential Chinese writer of roughly the same period, Lu Hsün (1881-1937).

The memory from Gandhi's youth most often quoted to anchor his spiritual and political style in his oedipal relation to his father is that of his father's death. This passage is often referred to as a "childhood memory," although Mohandas at the time was sixteen years old and was about to become a father himself. One night his father, whom the youth had nursed with religious passion, was fast sinking; but since a trusted uncle had just arrived, the son left the nursing care to him and went to his marital bedroom in order to satisfy his "carnal desire," and this despite his wife's being

61

pregnant. After a while, however, somebody came to fetch him: The father had died in the uncle's arms—"a blot," Gandhi writes, "which I have never been able to efface or to forget." A few weeks later his wife aborted. This experience represents in Gandhi's life what, following Kierkegaard, I have come to call "the curse" in the lives of comparable innovators with a similarly precocious and relentless conscience. As such, it is no doubt what in clinical work we call a "cover memory"—that is, a roughly factual event that has come to symbolize in condensed form a complex of ideas, affects, and memories transmitted to adulthood, and to the next generation, as an "account to be settled."

This curse, it has been automatically concluded, must be heir to the Oedipus conflict. In Gandhi's case, the "feminine" service to the father would have served to deny the boyish wish of replacing the (aging) father in the possession of the (young) mother and the youthful intention to outdo him as a leader in later life. Thus, the pattern would be set for a style of leadership which can defeat a superior adversary only nonviolently and with the express intent of saving him as well as those whom he oppressed. Some of this interpretation corresponds to what Gandhi would have unhesitatingly acknowledged as his conscious intention.

Here is my second example: The writer Lu Hsün, often quoted with veneration by Mao, is the founding father of modern China's revolutionary literature. His famous short story "Diary of a Madman" (1918), the first literary work written in vernacular Chinese, is a masterpiece not only (we are told) in the power of its style, but (as we can see) as a very modern combination of a precise psychiatric description of paranoia (Lu Hsün had studied medicine in Japan) and a nightmarish allegory of the fiercer aspects of traditional and revolutionary China. Later in an essay entitled "Father's Illness," Lu Hsün again mixes a historical theme—namely, the discrepancy of Western and Confucian concepts concerning a man's last moments—with the ambivalent emotions of a son. He had spent much of his adolescent years searching for herbs that might cure his father. But now death was near.

Sometimes an idea would flash like lightning into my mind: Better to end the gasping faster. . . . And immediately I knew that the idea was improper; it was like committing a crime. But at the same time I thought this idea rather proper, for I loved my father. Even now, I still think so.[18]

This is the Western doctor speaking; but at the time a Mrs. Yen, a kind of midwife for the departing soul, had suggested a number of magic transactions and had urged the son to scream into his father's ear, so he would not stop breathing.

"Father! Father!"

His face, which had quieted down, suddenly became tense. He opened his eyes slightly as if he felt something bitter and painful.

"Yell! Yell! Quick!"

"Father!"

"What? . . . Don't shout . . . don't . . ." he said in a low tone. Then he gasped frantically for breath. After a while, he returned to normal and calmed down.

"Father!" I kept calling him until he stopped breathing. Now I can still hear my own voice at that time. Whenever I hear it, I feel that this is the gravest wrong I have done to my father.

Lu Hsün was fifteen at the time (to Gandhi's sixteen). He, like Gandhi, had come from a line of high officials, whose fortunes were on the decline during the son's adolescence. At any rate, his story clearly suggests that in the lives of both men a desperate clinging to the dying father and a mistake made at the very last moment represented a curse overshadowing both past and future.

It is not enough, however, to reduce such a curse to the "Oedipus Complex" as reconstructed in thousands of case histories as the primal complex of them all. The oedipal crisis, too, must be evaluated as part of man's over-all development. It appears to be a constellation of dark preoccupations in a species which must live through a period of infantile dependence and steplike learning unequaled in the animal world, which develops a sensitive self-awareness in the years of immaturity, and which becomes aware of sexuality and procreation at a stage of childhood beset with irrational guilt. For the boy, to better the father (even if it is his father's most fervent wish that he do so) unconsciously means to replace him, to survive him means to kill him, to usurp his domain means to appropriate the mother, the "house," the "throne." No wonder that mankind's Maker is often experienced in the infantile image of every man's maker. But the oedipal crisis as commonly formulated is only the infantile or neurotic version of a *generational conflict* which derives from the fact that man experiences life and death—and past and future—in terms of the turnover of generations.

It is, in fact, rather probable that a highly uncommon man experiences filial conflicts with such inescapable intensity because he senses in himself already early in childhood some kind of originality that seems to point beyond the competition with the personal father. His is also an early conscience development which makes him feel (and appear) old while still young and maybe older in single-mindedness than his conformist parents, who, in turn, may treat him somehow as their potential redeemer. Thus he grows up almost with an obligation (beset with guilt) to surpass and to originate at all cost. In adolescence this may prolong his identity confusion because he must find the one way in which he (and he alone!) can re-enact the past and create a new future in the right medium at the right moment on a sufficiently large scale. His prolonged identity crisis, in turn, may invoke a premature generativity crisis that makes him accept as his concern a whole communal body, or mankind itself, and embrace as his dependents those weak in power, poor in possessions, and seemingly simple in heart. Such a deflection in life-plan, however, can crowd out his chances for the enjoyment of intimacy, sexual and otherwise, wherefore the "great" are often mateless, friendless, and childless in the midst of veneration and by their example further confound the human dilemma of counterpointing the responsibility of procreation and individual existence.

But not all highly uncommon men are chosen; and the psychohistorical question is not only how such men come to experience the inescapability of an existential curse, but how it comes about that they have the pertinacity and the giftedness to re-enact it in a medium communicable to their fellow men and meaningful in their stage of history. The emphasis here is on the word *re-enactment*, which in such cases goes far beyond the dictates of a mere "repetition-compulsion," such as characterizes the unfreedom of symptoms and irrational acts. For the mark of a creative re-enactment of a curse is that the joint experience of it all becomes a liberating event for each member of an awe-stricken audience. Some dim awareness of this must be the reason why the wielders of power in different periods of history appreciate and support the efforts of creative men to re-enact the universal conflicts of mankind in the garb of the historical day, as the great dramatists have done and as the great autobiographers do. A political leader like Mao, then, may recognize a writer like Hsün not for any ideological oratory, but for his precise and ruthless presentation of the inner conflicts that must accompany the emergence of a revolutionary mind in a society as bound to filial piety as China. In a man like Gandhi the autobiographer and the leader are united in one person, but remain distinct in the differentiation of re-enactments in writing and in action. In all re-enactment, however, it is the transformation of an infantile curse into an adult deed that makes the man.

Common men, of course, gladly accept as saviors *pro tem* uncommon men who seem so eager to take upon themselves an accounting thus spared to others, and who by finding words for the nameless make it possible for the majority of men to live in the concreteness and safety of realities tuned to procreation, production, and periodic destruction.

All the greater, therefore, can be the chaos that "great" men leave behind and often experience in themselves in the years following their ascendance. For the new momentum, which they gave to their time, may now roll over them, or their power to provide further momentum may wane from fatigue and age. Uncommon men, too, ultimately can become common (and worse) by the extent to which their solution of a universal curse remains tied to its ontogenetic version. The author of "Diary of a Madman" at the end of a career as revolutionary writer himself died in paranoid isolation as, in hindsight, one would expect of a man who, all his life, could hear his own voice yelling into his dying father's ear. And Gandhi, who could not forgive himself for having sought the warmth of his marital bed while his father was dying, in old age indulged in behavior that cost him many friends. In Lear-like fashion, he would wander through the tempest of communal riots, making local peace where nobody else could and yet knowing that he was losing the power to keep India united. It was then that the widower wanted his "daughters" close (he had never had a daughter of his own) and asked some of his women followers to warm his shivering body at night. This "weakness" the septuagenarian explained as a test of his strength of abstinence, opening himself wide to cheap gossip. This story, too, will have to be retold in terms of life cycle and history.

What was once united by the power of charisma cannot fall apart without exploding into destructive furor in the leader or in the masses or in both. Here life history ends, and history begins in its sociological and political aspects. How a leader survives himself and how an idea survives a man, how the community absorbs him and his idea, and how the sense of wider identity created by his presence survives the limitations of his person and of the historical moment—these are matters that the psycho-historian cannot approach without the help of the sociologist of tradition-building and institution-forming. He, in turn, may want to consider the "metabolism" of generations and the influence of a leader's or an elite's image on the life stages of the led: Kennedy's rise and sudden death certainly would provide a modern model for such a study.

To return once more to my original interest in Gandhi: I have indicated what I have learned since about his personal idiosyncracies as well as about his power of compromise. If some say that his ascendance was unfortunate for an India in desperate need of modernization, I cannot see who else in his time could have brought the vast, backward mass of Indians closer to the tasks of this century. As for his lasting influence, I will endeavor to describe in a book his strategy (as enfolded in the Event) of challenging man's latent capacity for militant and disciplined nonviolence: In this, he will survive. In the meantime, I, for one, see no reason to decide whether he was a saint or a politician—a differentiation meaningless in the Hindu tradition of combining works and renunciation—for his life is characterized by an ability to derive existential strength, as well as political power, from the very evasion of all job specifications. In interviewing his old friends, however, I found ample affirmation of his agile and humorous presence, probably the most inclusive sign of his (or anybody's) simultaneous mastery of inner and outer events. And it is in his humor that Gandhi has been compared to Saint Francis. Luther understood such things even if he could not live them; and at least his sermons formulate unforgettably the centrality in space, the immediacy in time, and the wholeness in feeling that lead to such singular "events" as survive in parables—a form of enactment most memorable through the ages, although, or maybe just because, most effortless and least "goal-directed." Now a man has to be dead for quite a while before one can know what parables might survive him: In Gandhi's case, one can only say that the "stuff" for parables is there. Let me, in conclusion, compare two well-known scenes from the lives of Gandhi and Saint Francis.

Teasing was a gift and a habit with Gandhi throughout his life, and elsewhere I have pointed out the affinity of teasing to non-violence.[19] It was after the great Salt March (he had been arrested again, and while he was in jail, his *Satyagrahis* had been brutally attacked by the police) that Gandhi was invited to talks with the Viceroy. Churchill scoffed at the "seditious fakir, striding half-naked up the steps of the Viceroy's palace, to negotiate with the representative of the King-Emperor." But the Viceroy, Lord Irwin, himself described the meeting as "the most dramatic personal encounter between a Viceroy and an Indian leader." When Gandhi was handed a cup of tea, he asked to be given a cup of hot water instead, into which he poured a bit of salt (tax-free) out of a small paper bag hidden in his shawl and remarked smilingly: "To remind us of the famous Boston Tea Party."

If we choose to insist on the symbolic meaning of salt and would see in this gesture a disguised act of masculine defiance—so be it. But such meaning would be totally absorbed in the over-all artfulness with which personal quirk (Gandhi would not touch tea) is used for the abstention from and yet ceremonial participation in the important act of sharing tea at the palace, and yet also for the re-enactment of a historical defiance, pointedly reminding his host of the time when the British taxed another invigorating substance and lost some colonies which, in independence, did rather well.

Whatever combination of overt and hidden meanings were enacted here in unison, the analogy that comes to mind is a scene from St. Francis' life, when he was asked for dinner to his bishop's palace. A place on the bishop's right was reserved for the ethereal rebel, and the guests were seated along well-decked tables. But Brother Francesco was late. Finally, he appeared with a small sack, out of which he took little pieces of dry dark bread and with his usual dancing gestures put one beside each guest's plate. To the bishop, who protested that there was plenty of food in the house, he explained that for *this* bread he had *begged* and that, therefore, it was consecrated food. Could there be a more delicate and yet finite lesson in Christianity?

The two scenes bespeak an obvious similarity in tone, and artfulness; but in order to make them true analogies, comparison is not enough. Other lifelong similarities in the two men could be enumerated and their respective tasks in their respective empires compared. Gandhi was no troubadour saint, but a tough activist as well as an enactor of poetic moments; and he was a strategist as well as a prayerful man. All this only points to the psycho-historian's job of specifying in all their complementarity the inner dynamics as well as the social conditions which make history seem to repeat, to renew, or to surpass itself.[20]

REFERENCES

1. Erik H. Erikson, "The Nature of Clinical Evidence," *Evidence and Inference* (Boston, 1958); revised and enlarged in *Insight and Responsibility* (New York, 1964).

2. Erik H. Erikson, *Young Man Luther* (New York, 1958).

3. Sigmund Freud, "An Autobiographical Study," *The Complete Works of Sigmund Freud*, Vol. 20 (London, 1959), p. 40.

4. Erik H. Erikson, "Gandhi's Autobiography: The Leader as a Child," *The American Scholar* (Autumn, 1966).

5. Mahadav Desai, *A Righteous Struggle* (Ahmedabad).

6. M. K. Gandhi, *An Autobiography* (Ahmedabad, 1927), Part 5, Chapters 20-22.

7. An old Indian friend recounted to me an event taken almost for granted in those early days—namely, how young Vinoba Bhave (the man who in all these years has come and remained closest to Gandhi in spirit, style, and stature) sat by the *Ashram* grounds and a big and poisonous snake crawled under his shawl. He kept lovingly still, and another Ashramite quietly folded up the garment and took it to the riverbank.

8. L. Fischer, *The Life of Mahatma Gandhi* (New York, 1950), p. 238.

9. Gandhi, *An Autobiography*, Part 4, Chapter 11.

10. Sigmund Freud and William C. Bullitt, *Thomas Woodrow Wilson: Twenty-Eighth President of the United States—A Psychological Study* (Boston, 1967).

11. Erik H. Erikson, *The New York Review of Books*, Vol. 7, No. 2 (1967); also *The International Journal of Psychoanalysis*, Vol. 47, No. 3 (1967).

12. "Psychoanalysis and Ongoing History: Problems of Identity, Hatred, and Non-Violence," *Journal of the American Psychiatric Association* (1965).

13. S. A. Wolpert, *Tilak and Gokhale* (Los Angeles, 1962).

14. *Collected Works of Mahatma Gandhi* (Ahmedabad).

15. Victor Wolfenstein, *The Revolutionary Personality* (Princeton, 1967).

16. Ernest Jones, *Essays in Applied Psychoanalysis* (London, 1951), Vol. 2.

17. Robert Lifton, *Death in Life: Survivors of Hiroshima* (New York, 1967).

18. Translated by Leo O. Lee for my seminar at Harvard from *Lu Hsün ch'üan-chi* (Complete Works of Lu Hsün; Peking, 1956), Vol. 2, pp. 261-62.

19. Erikson, "Gandhi's Autobiography: The Leader as a Child."

20. This paper was presented in outline to the American Academy's Group for the Study of Psycho-Historical Processes at Wellfleet, Massachusetts, in 1966.

ROBERT C. TUCKER

The Theory of Charismatic Leadership

I

IN A recent survey of Max Weber's political ideas, Karl Loewenstein observes that the concepts of "charisma" and the "charismatic leader" have had the greatest impact upon the thinking of our time. Unquestionably, many Western social scientists have been influenced by the Weberian idea of the leader who enjoys his authority not through enacted position or traditional dignity, but owing to gifts of grace (charisma) "by virtue of which he is set apart from other men and treated as endowed with supernatural, superhuman, or at least specifically exceptional powers or qualities."[1] Few aspects of Weber's political sociology have been so much discussed in the recent literature of political science, and interest in the subject is still growing. Yet no scholarly consensus seems to have formed, or even to be in process of formation, on the scientific worth and precise application of the concept of charismatic leadership.

Some writers are impressed with its power or potentiality as a tool for analyzing certain leadership situations of the historical past and present; others are skeptical and doubt whether the idea of charismatic leadership has much place in political science. Loewenstein himself belongs to the latter group. Noting that the idea comes from the religious realm and that Weber undertook to transfer it to politics, he contends that the world of religion re-

While working on the subject of this essay, I greatly benefited from the opportunity to discuss a number of the problems involved with Dr. Ann Ruth Willner, a fellow associate at the Center for International Studies of Princeton University, and to consult her own writings on charisma referred to below.

mains the fundamental locus of charisma. Hence the category applies chiefly to the pre-Cartesian West and, in our time, to those parts of Asia and Africa that have not yet broken away from the "magico-religious ambiance"; and it ceases to have relevance in our age of technological mass democracy.[2] Carl Friedrich, another critic, argues for a restrictive interpretation of charisma. He points out that in Rudolph Sohm's *Kirchenrecht* (1892), from which Weber derived the term and idea of charisma, charismatic leadership was understood as leadership based upon a transcendent call by a divine being in which both the person called and his followers believe; and Friedrich feels that such leadership should properly be conceived as grounded in a faith in God or gods. He objects to Weber's broadening of the category to include secular and non-transcendent types of callings, inspirational leadership of the demagogic type, and so forth. "Hitlers," he asserts, "represent a very different kind of leadership than the founders or even the inspired supporters of a religion." Even psychologically speaking, they fall in different categories, since the totalitarian leaders are typically preoccupied with power, especially organizational power, while the founders of religions are not.[3] Among other, less sweeping criticisms, two closely related ones are especially noteworthy. First, it is pointed out that on the basis of Weber's various formulations—some of which are rather nebulous —it is not easy to distinguish between leaders who really are charismatic and leaders who are not. And secondly, critics have observed that Weber provided no clear statement or catalogue of the personal qualities in charismatic leaders which give rise to the special emotional bond with their followers that charisma implies. In short, the theory of charismatic leadership, as Weber himself expounded it, leaves us in some doubt as to which leaders are charismatic and what makes them so.[4]

Let me begin by placing myself squarely upon Weber's side in the issue regarding the usefulness of the concept of charismatic leadership. I believe that this concept meets a vital theoretical need. Indeed, it is virtually indispensable, particularly for the student of revolutionary movements of various kinds, Communist ones included. Moreover, it was not, in my view, an error on Weber's part but a very great merit to take this category out of the historical world of religion and apply it to political life. For the realms of politics and religion interpenetrate in many ways. Nor does the concept of charisma, despite its mystical component, cease to have relevance to political life in an age of technological mass democracy. The secularization of society does not so much mean the disappearance of religion as it does the weakening of the hold of religion *in its traditional forms,* along with the displacement of religious emotion into other areas, particularly the political. Millenarian political movements have dotted the Western social landscape from the eighteenth century and so far show little sign of disappearing in the highly secularized industrial society of the present century. Societies far removed from what Loewenstein calls the "magico-religious ambiance" may still experience the pervasive influence of a modern political religion. Moreover, modern communications media make possible the *projection* of a charismatic leader of such a movement to a far greater number of people than ever before. And to insist, as Friedrich does, that charisma can properly appear only in the setting of a belief in a divine being ("God or gods") is arbitrarily to equate the realm of religion with a particular set of theologies. The psychological argument with which he supports this thesis is also a shaky one. On the one hand, founders of religions have not invariably been indifferent to considerations of power. On the other hand, it is difficult to generalize concerning the motivations of "totalitarian leaders." While a preoccupation with organizational power is characteristic, there is little evidence that these men seek power simply for power's sake; they appear, on the basis of our still inadequate knowledge of them, to be persons of great psychological complexity in all cases.

But after we have rejected the extreme positions of those critics who would severely restrict the applicability of the concept of charisma or deny its continued relevance in the modern age, we still have to reckon with the arguments about the concept's unclarity and the difficulty of applying it in practice. Here the critics are on stronger ground. Weber's principal statements on charisma appear in the context of his tripartite division of the forms of legitimate authority into traditional, rational-legal, and charismatic. Although a typology of the grounds of legitimate authority is a perfectly valid scholarly objective, it is not necessarily the best framework for developing a theory of charismatic leadership. For this reason, among others, Weber's pertinent writings, though strewn with invaluable insights, present no adequate treatment of charisma as a phenomenon in the realm of political leadership. Above all, they do not make the concept of charismatic leadership sufficiently operational to serve as a guide for further research. The aim of the present essay is to help remedy this deficiency.

Since my approach to the problem differs from the one most characteristic of contemporary writings in the social sciences concerning charisma, it may be useful to preface the essay with a short comment on its origin and relation to the scholarly literature. As shown by the work of writers like Edward Shils, David Apter, and Dorothy and Ann Ruth Willner, Western social scientists have tended in the recent past to approach the phenomenon of charisma in the context of a study of modernization and political development in ex-colonial "new states." The result is a functional theory of charisma according to which charismatic leadership is essentially a fulcrum of the transition from colonial-ruled traditional society to politically independent modern society; and the Weberian typology is, in effect, historicized into a sequence that runs from traditional through charismatic to rational-legal forms of authority.[5] In contrast, I approached the phenomenon of charisma through a study of revolutionary movements, Russia's in particular.

In connection with a work in progress on Stalin and Russian Communism, it became necessary to re-examine the role of Lenin as founder and supreme leader of the Bolshevik revolutionary movement. In the course of this effort, Weber's notion of charisma proved a highly useful tool of analysis of the remarkable personal authority that Lenin exercised over the Bolsheviks from the inception of the movement at the turn of the century to his death. Also, however, the application of the general concept to a concrete historical case, one on which we happen to have quite detailed factual knowledge, suggested some adaptations of Weber's formulation, some ways in which the idea of the charismatic leader might be restated for theoretical purposes. Afterwards, it seemed worthwhile to generalize these results and take preliminary soundings on the applicability of the modified concept to some other historical cases. The outcome is a reformulation of the theory of charismatic leadership from a perspective other than that of political development and modernization, although there is nothing in the reformulated theory that would keep it from being applied to charismatic leadership of "new states." The perspective also differs somewhat from that of Weber himself, but preserves his underlying view that charisma is a phenomenon of universalistic significance whose *political* manifestations, however important from the standpoint of political scientists, are only one of its manifold dimensions.

II

An exposition of the concept of charisma can proceed in either of two ways. One is to bring together all that Weber himself wrote on the subject and systematize this material. Here the aim would be to present a general interpretation of Weber's thinking; and fidelity to his meaning and position would be the chief test of success. The alternative procedure—which is the one to be followed here—is to take Weber's principal pertinent thoughts as a point of departure for an independent reformulation of the concept of charismatic leadership. In doing this, one's aim is not essentially to be exegetic, but rather to develop the theory of charisma into a more workable tool of understanding and research. Accordingly, the outcome may not be a faithful reflection in all ways of Weber's thinking. Certain of his thoughts may be neglected, others may be much more heavily emphasized than they were in his writings, and still others, which were not present in Weber, may be added. Here the result should be evaluated as a contribution not to the history of ideas, but to the needs of scholarship in the field of leadership.

Weber uses "charisma" in a value-neutral manner: To be a charismatic leader is not necessarily to be an admirable individual. In Weber's own expression, the manic seizure and rage of the nordic beserker or the demagogic talents of a Cleon are just as much "charisma" as the qualities of a Napoleon, Jesus, Pericles.[6] Among the examples cited are founders of religions, prophets, warrior heroes, shamans, and great demagogues, such as the leader of the Bavarian leftist rising in 1918, Kurt Eisner. Owing to their extraordinary qualities, or what are perceived to be such, these leaders inspire followings among which their superior authority is freely accepted. Oftentimes, the relationship of the followers to the charismatic leader is that of disciples to a master, and in any event he is revered by them. They do not follow him out of fear or monetary inducement, but out of love, passionate devotion, enthusiasm. They are not as a rule concerned with career, promotion, salary, or benefice. The charismatic following is a nonbureaucratic group. In Weber's words, the disciples or followers tend to live primarily in a communistic relationship with their leader on means which have been provided by voluntary gift.[7]

73

In describing the charismatic authority-relation, Weber stresses at times the obedience that the followers render to the leader, and some commentators have highlighted this theme. We are thus invited, or at least permitted, to infer that in a genuine case of charismatic leadership, it would be virtually inconceivable for a follower to contradict or disagree with the leader or to question his infallibility in any way. It is necessary, however, to enter a caveat here. Weber's thinking on charisma was much influenced by the examples with which he was familiar from the settings of traditional religion, where absolute obedience would of course be characteristic of the charismatic as well as other types of authority-relation. But if charisma is, in principle, a universalistic phenomenon, as we are assuming along with Weber, then we should be more prepared than he was to recognize that codes of conduct in the relations between charismatic leaders and their followers will in certain respects vary according to the political culture. What is specific to the charismatic response is not absolute obedience toward the leader, but simply the fact that by virtue of extraordinary qualities he exercises a kind of "domination" (as Weber puts it) over the followers. Followers can be under the spell of a leader and can accept him as supremely authoritative without necessarily agreeing with him on all occasions or refraining from argument with him. In the highly argumentative atmosphere of a modern radical party, for example, a leader can be both charismatic and contested on specific points, as Lenin often was by his close followers. Indeed, he can even manifest some of his charisma in the inspired way in which he conquers dissent by the sheer power of his political discourse. Immense persuasiveness in argument may, in other words, be one of the extraordinary qualities by virtue of which a leader acquires charisma in his followers' eyes. We should not, therefore, envisage the charismatic authority-relation as one that necessarily involves automatic acquiescence of the followers in the leader's views or excludes the possibility of their disagreeing with him on occasion and up to a point. All the more so since as an innovator the charismatic leader tends at times to break with established ways of thinking and acting, and thus to take positions which diverge from his followers' expectations and consequently raise disturbed questions in their minds. Needless to add, there will always be some among the followers who would never dream of taking issue with him, even on the most trivial points.

It is presumably necessary to possess extraordinary qualities in order to be widely perceived over a period of time as the bearer of them. Yet Weber stresses the response of the followers as the crucial test of charisma. To *be* a charismatic leader is essentially to be *perceived* as such: "It is recognition on the part of those subject to authority which is decisive for the validity of charisma."[8] Furthermore, such recognition of charisma on the part of the followers must be reinforced from time to time by the leader's demonstration of charismatic powers. He must furnish "signs" or "proof" of the exceptional abilities or qualities for the sake of which his followers render him their personal devotion; if he fails to do so over a long period, his charismatic authority may disappear. As Weber puts it:

By its very nature, the existence of charismatic authority is specifically unstable. The holder may forego his charisma; he may feel "forsaken by his God," as Jesus did on the cross; he may prove to his followers that "virtue is gone out of him." It is then that his mission is extinguished, and hope waits and searches for a new holder of charisma.[9]

One other theme that Weber stresses in his treatment of charisma is its innovative and even revolutionary character. Charisma, he says, is alien to the world of everyday routine; it calls for new ways of life and thought. Whatever the particular social setting (religion, politics, and so forth), charismatic leadership rejects old rules and issues a demand for change. It preaches or creates *new* obligations. It addresses itself to followers or potential followers in the spirit of the saying: "It is written . . . , but I say unto you . . . ." In contrast and opposition to bureaucratic authority, which respects rational rules, and to traditional authority, which is bound to precedents handed down from the past, charismatic authority, within the sphere of its claims, "repudiates the past, and is in this sense a specifically revolutionary force."[10]

From this summary it is evident that charismatic leadership, in Weber's view, typically appears in the setting of a social *movement* of some kind or creates such a movement. The charismatic leader is not simply any leader who is idolized and freely followed for his extraordinary leadership qualities, but one who demonstrates such qualities in the process of summoning people to join in a movement for change and in leading such a movement. This is, I believe, a point of central importance for any endeavor to systematize the theory of charisma. And it is one to which Weber himself, although he uses the phrase "charismatic movement" on occasion, does not give due emphasis. To remedy this, let us postulate that charismatic leadership inherently tends to become the center of a charismatic movement—that is, a charismatically led movement for change. To speak of charismatic leaders, then, is to speak of charismatic movements; the two phenomena are inseparable.

Although not all movements for change are charismatic, those that are cover a broad spectrum, ranging from small coterie-movements to genuine mass movements and from those with little organization to those with elaborate organization. They appear in diverse forms of society—democratic and authoritarian, Western and non-Western, highly developed and under-developed economically. And they cross ideological lines. As Robert Michels showed in *Political Parties*, marked charismatic tendencies appeared in various West European socialist movements of the later nineteenth century, the leaders of which became objects of a "cult of veneration among the masses." Ferdinand Lassalle, for example, was received "like a god" when he toured the Rhineland in 1864.[11] In the twentieth century, some Communist movements, starting with Russian Communism under Lenin, have been charismatic. We also find charismatic leadership in many of the fascist movements and in nationalist movements of such widely varying character and locale as the Indian independence movement and the Black Muslims of America.

It would appear that charismatic movements arise in different ways. On the one hand, the movement can be charismatic from the outset—that is, inspired and brought into being by the charismatic leader-personality who heads it. The July 26 Cuban revolutionary movement created by Castro and German National Socialism under Hitler may be cases in point. Alternatively, the movement simply as a movement for change may be in existence *before* the rise of the charismatic leadership and then undergo transformation into a charismatic one. A non-charismatic Russian Marxist revolutionary movement was in existence, for example, before the appearance in its leadership of Lenin, a charismatic leader-personality. As this instance shows, however, when a movement for change exists before the appearance of charismatic leadership, a schism may result. Instead of homogeneously undergoing metamorphosis into a charismatic movement, it divides into those who reject and those who accept the charismatic leader. Thus, Bolshevism arose as Lenin's charismatic following *within* the Russian Marxist revolutionary movement. In time, it split off from the Mensheviks and took shape as an independent movement claiming to be the sole authentic voice of Russian Marxism.

A charismatic movement's growth may be represented in a series of concentric circles. The initial phase is the formation of a charismatic following—a group of persons who cluster around the charismatic personality and accept his authority. The little Bolshevik colony in Geneva at the beginning of the century, which formed the historical core of Lenin's charismatic following, is a good example. The relation of the Geneva Bolsheviks to Lenin was that of disciples to the master, his authority in all things revolutionary was acknowledged, and his mission to lead the revolutionary movement was taken for granted.[12] As a charismatic following grows, attracting new members in larger and larger numbers, it achieves the status of a movement. It also develops an organization, which in the case of a modern-day revolutionary movement is likely to be a party organization. The growth curve of the movement may fluctuate, periods of growth being followed by periods of decline. Under propitious conditions, the movement may turn into a mass movement with tens of thousands of followers. And if it is a political movement, a further critical growth-point is reached at the time when it acquires (if it does acquire) political power. Once in power, the movement becomes a movement-regime with enormous resources of influence. The entire citizenry of the country concerned as well as others abroad now enter into a vastly enlarged potential charismatic following. Finally, a charismatic movement, particularly one that comes to power in a major nation, may become international in scope, radiating across national boundaries and enlisting new followers everywhere. For example, the world Communist movement that came into existence under Russian Communist auspices after 1917 was, in one of its several aspects, an international charismatic movement of followers of Lenin.

Emphasis upon the charismatic movement as the typical habitat or creation of charismatic leaders has important methodological implications for the study of such leadership. It means that when we study a case—or possible case—of charismatic leadership, we should always go back to the beginnings of the given leader-personality's emergence as a leader, rather than start with the status achieved at the zenith of his career. We should look for indications of a charismatic following or movement (which may,

77

as in Lenin's case, be a movement within a movement) very early in the career and in any event before power is achieved. The test of whether or not a charismatic movement takes shape before the leader's advent to power is not, of course, infallible, for there presumably are certain instances in which circumstances (for example, military status) have militated against the growth of a charismatic movement in the early period. Thus, a career officer like Nasser of Egypt might have been a potential charismatic leader without, at an earlier time, having been able to become the center of a movement. But even in such instances, one would expect to find signs of the early formation of at least a small charismatic following with the given figure's milieu.

All this has a bearing upon the problem of identifying charisma. Since scholars usually show a special interest in leaders' careers in power, there has been a certain tendency both to search for examples of charismatic leadership among leaders in power and to study the charismatic leader-follower relation primarily as manifested then. When we concentrate attention upon that stage, however, we run greater risk of error in identifying a given leader as charismatic; for power is a source of phenomena that resemble the effects of charisma without actually being such. It brings prestige and, especially in modern technological conditions, possibilities of artificial inducement or simulation of mass adulation of a leader. Examples that immediately come to mind are the personality cults of Stalin in Russia and Nkrumah in Ghana, neither of whom—as later became clear—were hero-worshiped by their citizens in the way that some foreign visitors believed on the basis of what they saw and heard in the two countries when the two leaders were in power.

To sum up the foregoing, a leader need not achieve power—national or other—in order to qualify as charismatic. What is decisive is whether or not he attracts a charismatic following and shows a marked tendency to become the center of a charismatic movement as defined above. To minimize the risk of error in classifying a given leader as charismatic, it is of great importance, therefore, to study his impact upon those around him *before* he achieves office. We may lay it down as a general rule that when a leader-personality is genuinely charismatic, his charisma will begin to manifest itself before he becomes politically powerful. For the student of charisma, then, the pre-power stage of a leader's career is of critical significance. Unless there is evidence of the spontaneous formation of at least a small charismatic following on a purely voluntary basis, the likelihood of a given figure being a charismatic leader-personality is quite small. Needless to add, none of this is meant to imply that the charismatic leader-follower relation ought not to be studied in later stages of political careers. It merely argues for a genetic approach to the phenomenon in concrete cases.

In what forms does the evidence of early charisma appear? In the cases of contemporary figures—Castro, for example—it may be possible to investigate the responses of others to them at the formative stages of their careers by interviewing erstwhile associates who speak from personal experience and observation. But in most cases of interest to us, we are likely to be dependent to a great extent upon written materials as sources of evidence. The value of the biographical and general historical literature on major figures is limited because biographers and historians, with few exceptions, have not approached the study of these figures with the concept of charismatic leadership in mind, and so have not always been attuned to evidence of it in their researches. On the other hand, for this very reason what evidence we do find of charisma in such general secondary sources is often of considerable value. Memoir literature and letters of those who were closely associated with the given figure early in his career are likely, however, to be of greatest importance in many instances. Certain problems of the critical use of such sources naturally arise, in part from the tendency of some memoirs to project, consciously or unconsciously, upon the past a charismatic response that either was not experienced at the earlier time or was not experienced to such a degree. To minimize the chance of being misled by retrospective exaggeration of charismatic response, it is important to search out any available historical witnesses whose bias, if any, would be against such exaggeration, and who set down their memories under conditions of complete freedom of self-expression. Consider, for example, the following memoir of Lenin by a Russian Marxist who worked closely with him on the newspaper *Iskra* at the turn of the century when Lenin, at thirty, was emerging as one of the leaders of the movement:

No one could so fire others with their plans, no one could so impose his will and conquer by force of his personality as this seemingly so ordinary and somewhat coarse man who lacked any obvious sources of charm. . . . Neither Plekhanov nor Martov nor anyone else possessed the secret radiating from Lenin of positively hypnotic effect upon people—I would even say, domination of them. Plekhanov was treated with deference, Martov was loved, but Lenin alone was followed unhesitatingly as the only indisputable leader. For only Lenin represented that rare phenomenon, especially rare in Russia, of a man of iron will and indomitable energy who combines fanatical faith in the movement, the cause, with no less faith in himself. If the French king, Louis XIV, could say, *L'Etat c'est moi*, Lenin, without putting it into words, always had the feeling, *Le Partie c'est moi;* he had the feeling that in him the will of the movement was concentrated in one man. And he acted accordingly. I recall that Lenin's sense of mission to be the leader at one time made an impression upon me also.[13]

The value of this statement as evidence that Lenin was a charismatic political personality is obviously enhanced because it comes from A. N. Potresov, who long before writing it had become one of the leaders of Russian Menshevism and a political enemy of Lenin. Also noteworthy is the place of writing and original publication of the memoir: Germany, 1927.

III

Why does charismatic leadership emerge in the setting of movements for change, and what is the explanation of the passionate devotion that the charismatic leader of such a movement typically receives from his followers? In answering these two closely related questions, we must focus attention first upon the followers and their needs. Here again we find that Weber himself has made the crucial point although without giving it adequate emphasis and elaboration. He tells us that charismatic leaders have been the natural leaders "in time of psychic, physical, economic, ethical, religious, political distress," and, elsewhere, that charisma inspires its followers with "a devotion born of distress and enthusiasm."[14] In short, the key to the charismatic response of the followers to the leader lies in the *distress* that the followers experience.

Why movements for change arise and spread at times of widespread distress in society is obvious. The further connection between distress in its many forms and responsiveness to charisma in leaders of movements for change is only slightly less manifest. Briefly, the charismatic leader is one in whom, by virtue of unusual personal qualities, the promise or hope of salvation—deliverance from distress—appears to be embodied. He is a leader who convincingly offers himself to a group of people in distress as one peculiarly qualified to lead them out of their predicament. He is in essence a savior, or one who is so perceived by his followers. *Charismatic leadership is specifically salvationist or messianic in nature.* Herein lies its distinctiveness in relation to such broader and more nebulous categories as "inspired leadership" or "heroic leadership." Furthermore, this fundamental characteristic of charismatic leadership helps to explain the special emotional intensity of the charismatic response, and also why the sustaining of charisma requires the leader to furnish periodical "proof" of the powers that he claims. The followers respond to the charismatic leader with passionate loyalty because the salvation, or promise of it, that he appears to embody represents the fulfillment of urgently felt needs; their faith in his extraordinary capacities is kept alive (or not, as the case may be) by the periodical demonstration that he gives (if he does) of powers of efficacious leadership on the road to the salvationist goal. These may be, for example, miracle-working powers if the movement is religiously salvationist, or revolution-making powers if it is a charismatically led revolutionary movement, or war-making powers if it is a movement seeking to effect change by military means.

Of course, not all movements for change arising in society are charismatic or become so. In many societies at many times, there are non-charismatic movements of reform dedicated to the improvement of conditions underlying the dissatisfactions normally experienced by many people. Charismatic movements are likely to appear alongside these others when prevailing widespread dissatisfaction deepens to the point of becoming genuine "distress" (suffering or acute malaise that conceivably could be alleviated); and when extraordinary leader-personalities come forward with appeals of salvationist character, persuasively proclaiming the possibility of overcoming the situation of distress, pointing to ways of doing so, and offering their own leadership along this path to those who are willing to follow. At such a time, numbers of those in distress will usually rally to the salvationist appeal, and charismatic movements for change are born.

The first determinant of charismatic response is situational; the state of acute distress predisposes people to perceive as extraordinarily qualified and to follow with enthusiastic loyalty a leadership offering salvation from distress. This being so, we must reckon with the possibility of at least a low level of charismatic response to leaders who, for one or another reason, would not fulfill, or would fulfill only imperfectly, the second of the two conditions just laid

81

down. Examples are not far to seek. Thus, in the state of threatened national existence experienced by the people of Britain in 1940, when their island lay open to German invasion, there was no doubt some charismatic response to the war leadership of Sir Winston Churchill, who personified the will never to surrender and the determination to fight on to victory; and yet Sir Winston, as both prewar and postwar history shows, was not a notable example of the charismatic leader-personality. Again, when Franklin D. Roosevelt became President in a crisis-stricken U.S.A. in 1933, exuding confidence and proclaiming that there was nothing to fear but fear itself, he evoked from many Americans a charismatic response that for the most part subsided when the acute national emergency was overcome. We might use the term "situational charisma" to refer to instances where a leader-personality of non-messianic tendency evokes a charismatic response simply because he offers, in a time of acute distress, leadership that is perceived as a source and means of salvation from distress.[15]

The foregoing considerations suggest strongly that when the situational determinant of charismatic response is present, the presence or absence of a genuinely charismatic leader-personality may be a critical historical variable. If we ask, for example, why the distress of German society in 1933 should have led to the triumph of National Socialism whereas the distress of British society in 1931 led simply to a rather emotional general election, the presence of Adolf Hitler on the German scene and the absence of a correspondingly charismatic leader-figure on the British scene may go a considerable distance toward providing the answer, although it would have to be added that the German distress was deeper and broader, and the general state of emergency more acute, than in the British case. Again, so great was the importance of the personal charismatic leadership of Lenin in leading the Bolsheviks to power in the Russian Revolution that even Trotsky, who was not given to exaggerating the role of personality in history, observed in later years that without Lenin there probably would have been no October Revolution in Russia.[16]

Distress occurs in such a wide variety of forms that it seems hardly feasible for a theorist of charismatic leadership to catalogue them. They range from the physical and material distress caused by persecution, catastrophes (for example, famine, drought), and extreme economic hardship to such diverse forms of psychic or emotional distress as the feelings of oppression in peoples ruled by foreigners, the radical alienation from the existing order experienced by revolutionaries, or the intolerable anxieties that have motivated many followers of religious millenarian movements in the past and political millenarian movements in the modern age. Although distress in one form or another is more or less endemic in social history, it is at times of crisis, of extremely serious and widespread distress, that charismatic movements for change develop in profusion as would-be messiahs attract followers *en masse*. For example, pretenders to the role of messiah arose among European Jewry during the massacres from the eleventh to the fourteenth centuries, and each time there resulted a wave of millenarian enthusiasm, often expressing itself in a mass migration towards Palestine.[17] It seems likely, moreover, that charismatic movements attain their greatest force at times of confluence of multiple forms of distress in society. Thus, German National Socialism, as a charismatic movement led by Hitler, acquired a mass following at a time when several forms of distress were rampant in German society: wholesale unemployment and poverty in the great depression, economic troubles and status anxiety in the lower-middle class, and injured national feelings resulting from defeat in World War I and the terms of the Versailles treaty.

Deeper and more systematic analysis of the phenomenon of distress—in particular, its psychological varieties—is an obvious requisite for further development of the theory of charismatic leadership. Erik H. Erikson has suggested[18] that there are certain historical conditions, such as the waning of religion, in which people in large numbers become "charisma-hungry." Pursuing the point further, he distinguished three forms of distress to which a charismatic leader may minister: "fear," as in the fear of the medieval European Jews for their lives or the obscure, subliminal fear of nuclear destruction in contemporary Western man; "anxiety," especially as experienced by persons in an "identity-vacuum" or the condition of not knowing just who or what they are; and "existential dread," or the distress that people experience under conditions in which rituals of their existence have broken down. Correspondingly, a charismatic leader is one who offers people salvation in the form of safety, or identity, or rituals, or some combination of these, saying to them in effect: "I will make you safe," or "I will give you an identity," or "I will give you rituals." In the case of Gandhi, for example, the people of India were given a new collective identity.

ROBERT C. TUCKER

Erikson's observations are highly relevant to the "functional" theory of charisma mentioned earlier, for they help illuminate the charismatic role of some leaders of "new states" in the process of transition to independent nationhood and modernity. Anxiety and existential dread, in the senses just defined, are two forms of psychic distress that may, for obvious reasons, be both widespread and acute in societies at this stage of historical development. On the one hand, people for whom the fundamental ambiance of life has always been the village community may be plunged into the anxiety of an identity-vacuum as life becomes urban- and nation-oriented in the transition period. And on the other, the process of modernization may create a great deal of existential dread by upsetting the habits and customs that have regulated life in the society since time immemorial. The leader who at such a juncture can make national identity meaningful and thereby give the people of his country a sense of belonging to a new and greater community, and who at the same time can help them find their way to a new life-style, a new ritualization of existence, will certainly acquire great charisma in the eyes of very many. By the same token, however, he is likely to arouse fanatical hatred on the part of those who remain devotees of the old order of things in the society. Here, by the way, we touch upon what is probably a universal feature of the charismatic leader: his capacity to inspire hatred as well as loyalty and love. Precisely as an exponent of change, the leader who evokes a positive charismatic response from some is likely to evoke a negative one (we might speak of this as "counter-charisma") from others. The same leader who is charismatic in the eyes of people in distress, for whom salvation lies in change, will be counter-charismatic in the eyes of those who see in change not salvation but ruination. Lenin, for example, became a shining hero for many Russian peasants during the revolutionary period, and a veritable antichrist in the eyes of others for whom the old Russian ways remained dear.

A charismatic movement does not necessarily turn into a mass movement. If, for example, a particular social group experiences extreme distress at a time when the general distress level in the society is relatively low, a charismatic movement of great vigor but small size may emerge. Such might be the pattern in a society with an oppressed racial or ethnic minority. Alternatively, and depending upon the character of the charismatic movement in question, events may transform the situation by creating mass misery and thereby greatly augmenting the movement's following. A

84

case in point is the career of Russian Communism before and during World War I. Before 1914, Lenin's charismatic following was quite small and limited almost exclusively to members of the radical intelligentsia. By 1917, however, the war had produced such misery among masses of Russians—particularly workers, soldiers, and peasants—that substantial numbers of them became responsive to Lenin's revolutionary charisma. After the October Revolution, the charismatic following of Lenin, while it included many individuals in the population at large, remained concentrated in the Communist Party. And because he had, through his personal leadership of the Revolution, given stunning "proof" of revolution-making powers, he was quite literally idolized by many of the followers. Characteristic testimony on this score comes from Walter Duranty, who reported at the time of Lenin's death:

I have seen Lenin speak to his followers. A small, busy, thick-set man under blinding lights, greeted by applause like thunder. I turned around and their faces were shining, like men who looked on God. Lenin was like that, whether you think he was a damnable Antichrist or a once-in-a-thousand-years' prophet. That is a matter of opinion, but when five thousand faces can light up and shine at the sight of him, as they did, and I saw it, then I say he was no ordinary individual.[19]

To sum up, charismatic movements for change arise and spread at times when painful forms of distress are prevalent in a society or in some particular stratum of a society. The unique personal authority of the leader and the rapturous response of many of the followers grow out of their feeling that he, by virtue of his special powers as a leader, embodies the movement's salvational promise, hence that which may be of supreme significance to them. Since he ministers to their most pressing need—the need to believe in the real possibility of escape from an oppressive life-predicament—they not only follow him voluntarily and without thought of material recompense, but tend to revere him and surround him with that spontaneous cult of personality which appears to be one of the symptomatic marks of the charismatic leader-follower relationship.

This explains why we cannot rightly view the phenomenon of charisma as belonging primarily to the historical past. Wherever and whenever human beings in serious numbers live in desperation or despair or similar states, charismatic leaders and movements are likely to appear. Depending upon such factors as the quality of the leadership and the depth and breadth of the existential disquiet to which it appeals, these movements will sometimes prove of little consequence and sometimes of great. Finally, there is no evident basis for believing that humanity is about to enter a new age of general content in which charismatic movements will grow more and more anachronistic. On the contrary, at a time when chronic famines may be approaching in various countries in which population burgeons while food supply does not, and when man in the more affluent industrialized parts of the world lives not only with the terrors and anxieties of the nuclear era but also, increasingly, with the deep ennui and distress of unrelatedness that life can breed in mass technological society, the outlook is rather for new messiahs and movements led by them.

IV

We have so far considered the charismatic response from the followers' standpoint, seeing it as the readiness of persons in distress to accept with enthusiasm the authority of a leader in whom the hope of salvation appears to be embodied. Now the question arises as to the nature of the extraordinary qualities that cause a leader to be regarded as a potential savior. This question has not received systematic treatment in the existing literature on charisma and can only be resolved on the basis of numerous future case studies in depth of actual charismatic movements and their leaders.[20] Such studies should make the requisite generalizations possible. Meanwhile, a few preliminary general observations may be hazarded.

Charismatic qualification may, on the one hand, consist in extraordinary powers of vision and the communication of vision, especially when this vision relates to the possibility and ways of overcoming distressful conditions. Alternatively, it may consist in unusual powers of practical leadership of people along the way to such a goal. In the one case, the charismatic leader appears as prophet; in the other, as activist. But there is no hard-and-fast separation between these two basic charismatic leader-roles. In practice, the difference is one of prevailing tendency. If, for example, one were to take Marx and Lenin as illustrations of the prophetic and activist types respectively, it would have to be added by way of qualification that Marx was an organizer of revolutionary movements as well as Communism's great prophet, and that Lenin, whose charismatic powers showed themselves chiefly in the field of practical leadership, was likewise an ideologue of Communist revolution and something of a visionary. Gandhi, too, was a social visionary although he demonstrated his extraordinary leadership powers primarily in the teaching and practice of nonviolence as a practical method of changing men and conditions. Finally, there appear to be some leaders who defy classification according to this dichotomy because they not only combine both kinds of charismatic qualifications, but fulfill both roles in their respective movements. Hitler, who was at once the principal ideologue and inspirer of National Socialism and its *Fuehrer* to the end, might be mentioned as an example.

Although charismatic leaders may vary in type, there appear to be certain qualities common to them as a class. Notable among these is a peculiar sense of mission, comprising a belief both in the movement and in themselves as the chosen instrument to lead the movement to its destination. The charismatic leader typically radiates a buoyant confidence in the rightness and goodness of the aims that he proclaims for the movement, in the practical possibility of attaining these aims, and in his own special calling and capacity to provide the requisite leadership. Needless to say, in the lives of most of these leaders—even those who do achieve success—there are moments of discouragement and despair when they and their cause seem fated to fail. But it is not characteristic of them to display such feelings in public. Rather, they show a stubborn self-confidence and faith in the movement's prospects of victory and success. This, indeed, may be the quality that most of all underlies their charisma and explains the extreme devotion and loyalty that they inspire in their followers; for people in need of deliverance from one or another form of distress, being in very many instances anxiety-ridden, easily respond with great emotional fervor to a leader who can kindle or strengthen in them a faith in the possibility of deliverance.

This belief in the movement and sense of personal mission to lead it is a common element, for example, in the varied biographies of three of the most strikingly successful charismatic leaders of the first half of the twentieth century—Lenin, Hitler, and Mussolini. Potresov's above-cited memoir illustrates much direct testimony to the compelling quality of Lenin's revolutionary faith—his *tseleustremlennost'* or "goal-fixation" as some have called it—and his self-assured belief in his own mission to lead the revolutionary cause. When he put out his powerful tract *What Is to Be Done?* shortly after the turn of the century, there was a widespread mood of discouragement in the Russian Marxist milieu. His actual and literary personality injected into this milieu new confidence in Russian revolution as a historically imminent prospect, something that a small group of determined revolutionaries could seriously hope to spark and lead by their collective efforts under Lenin's guidance. Numbers of Russian Marxists gravitated into his orbit, and Bolshevism emerged as a Lenin-centered charismatic movement within Russian Marxism.

Whereas Lenin's charismatic appeal was concentrated for a long while within the Bolshevik Party, both Hitler and Mussolini comparatively early in their careers found mass followings in their distress-filled nations. In both these cases, moreover, the man's boundless faith in himself, or appearance of it, seems to have been a key to the charismatic response by large numbers of people. Describing the reactions of many Germans to Hitler at the beginning of the 1930's, Hadley Cantril, for example, concludes:

The message of Hitler, his own obvious belief in the righteousness of his program, his sincerity, and his faith in himself made an indelible impression on those who heard him. In a period of doubt and uncertainty, here was a speaker who did not argue the pros and cons of policies but who was fanatically self-confident.[21]

And in an appraisal of Mussolini's impact upon people in the Italy of 1922, Laura Fermi emphasizes his "ability to impersonate, at the most timely moment, the superman and the savior to whom as he had said himself, 'nothing is impossible.'" She explains:

In 1922, to a population that had lost sight of its aims and will, that lacked faith in itself and was affected by a mass inferiority complex, that suffered from both real and imaginary ills, the idea of a savior capable of bringing well-being to all by the sheer force of his will was not only appealing, it was a last hope. And Mussolini, savior and superman, promised law and order, a full appreciation of victory and its worth, an Italy cured of poverty, restored to its dignity, resuming its place among the great nations of Europe, and governed by youth and youthful energy.[22]

I do not mean to suggest that a charismatic leader acquires charisma exclusively because of his inspirational sense of mission and belief in the movement, or even that his personality *per se*, independently of the content of his message, is sufficient explanation for his impact upon his followers. We cannot properly say of charismatic leaders that "the medium is the message," although it is a large part of it. They offer to followers and potential followers not simply and solely their extraordinary selves as instruments of leadership, but also a formula or set of formulas for salvation. They address themselves in one way or another to the predicaments that render masses of people potentially responsive to the appeal of a movement for change and offer some diagnosis of these predicaments. Indeed, they characteristically strive to *accentuate* the sense of being in a desperate predicament, as if following the motto of the young Marx who wrote: "The Germans must not be given a minute for self-deception and resignation. The real oppression must be made still more oppressive by adding to it the consciousness of oppression; the shame still more shameful by publicizing it."[23] And they propound certain ideas, ranging from the most nebulous to the most definite and concrete, as a way out of the predicament.

Thus, Marx, having diagnosed the sufferings of the working class as a necessary outcome of the capitalist mode of production, advocated the class struggle leading to proletarian revolution and Communism as the formula for man's salvation—for the transcending of human alienation in all its forms. Lenin, addressing himself at the turn of the century to the predicament of Russian Marxism *as a revolutionary movement,* provided a complex formula for what was to be done both to cure this movement of its ills (such as the "economist" heresy) and to make Russian revolution a certainty: create a militant organization of revolutionaries as a proselytizing nucleus of a future nationwide resistance movement of the discontented and disaffected of Russia against the Tsarist order. The charismatic response of numbers of Russian radicals to the Lenin of *What Is to Be Done?* was partly a consequence of the cogency of this revolutionary formula to their minds. The infinite fertility of his tactical imagination, his astonishing capacity to devise formulas for the movement's policy at every turn and in every predicament, was undoubtedly one of the sources of the spell that he exerted upon the Bolsheviks. But the impact of a charismatic leader's formulas for salvation (in this instance, salvation by Communist revolution) cannot, in the final analysis, be divorced from that of his personality. Lenin's formulas derived much of their cogency from the immense assurance with which he usually propounded and defended them in party councils, and from his great personal powers of persuasion. Thus, a Bolshevik known for his reserve and self-control reminisced as follows about the effect that Lenin's speeches had upon him when he first heard him speak, at the Bolshevik conference in Tammerfors in 1906:

I was captivated by that irresistible force of logic in them which, although somewhat terse, gained a firm hold on his audience, gradually electrified it, and then, as one might say, completely overpowered it. I remember that many of the delegates said: "The logic of Lenin's speeches is like a mighty tentacle which twines all round you and holds you as in a vice and from whose grip you are powerless to tear yourself away: You must either surrender or resign yourself to utter defeat."[24]

Special mention should be made of one sort of salvational formula that has played an exceedingly important part in social movements of past and present, charismatic ones included. This formula traces the ills plaguing a people, or race, or mankind as a whole to a great and deadly conspiracy the destruction of which, it is held, will solve everything. Franz Neumann distinguished five main variants of such a "conspiracy theory of history" in the postmedieval West: the Jesuit conspiracy, the Freemason conspiracy, the Communist conspiracy, the Capitalist conspiracy, and the Jewish conspiracy. And he found anti-conspiracy gospels associated with "affective leader-identifications," or what we have here been calling the charismatic response of followers to a leader:

Just as the masses hope for their deliverance from distress through absolute oneness with a person, so they ascribe their distress to certain persons who brought this distress into the world through a conspiracy. . . . Hatred, resentment, dread, created by great upheavals, are concentrated on certain persons who are denounced as devilish conspirators.[25]

We may restate the point in terms of the theory of charismatic leadership by saying that some leaders of the charismatic type have attracted followers with formulas that derive from conspiracy doctrines. Offering both a diagnosis of the distress that people are experiencing in times of anxiety and a gospel of salvation through struggle against and ultimate elimination of the purported conspiracy and its bearers, these conspiracy doctrines encourage the followers of a movement to restructure their thinking and their lives in apparently more meaningful and satisfying ways and thereby give the would-be messiah charismatic authority in their eyes. And here again we find that formula and personality are mutually reinforcing. The leader's personality becomes more salient and magnetic for many because of its identification with the conspiracy doctrine, and the latter, however fantastic it may be, becomes more believable because of the leader's paranoid earnestness, the obsessive conviction with which he portrays the conspiracy and inveighs against it. To a generation that remembers Hitler and *Mein Kampf*, lengthy illustrations of the point are unnecessary. Examples closer to home are to be found in the recent history of movements on the radical right in America.

V

In conclusion, a few comments on the problem of what happens to charismatic movements when their founding leaders pass on. Weber treated this problem under the heading of "routinization" and "depersonalization" of charisma. He elaborated these themes in complex ways that I shall not attempt to summarize here in any detail. Suffice it to say that charisma, according to Weber, characteristically undergoes transformation from an extraordinary and purely personal relationship into an established authority structure that is no longer necessarily dependent upon personal charismatic qualification in the incumbent leader. Thus, it is transmitted from leader to leader according to established rules of succession, such as designation by the charismatic leader of his own successor or, alternatively, designation of a successor by the charismatic followers of the leader (as in the selection of a new Pope). In the process of depersonalization, charisma evolves into hereditary or "familial" charisma with its locus in a royal family, for example, or into institutional charisma attached to an office like the priesthood.[26]

Although it is useful and suggestive at many points, Weber's discussion of "routinization" and "depersonalization" of charisma is also, unfortunately, rather confusing and open to serious objections. How can something that has been defined as antiroutine and personal in its essence be routinized and depersonalized? As Carl Friedrich has pointed out, it makes little sense for Weber to speak of "routinized" charisma, since "routine and charisma are contradictory terms, if the initial specification of the term 'charisma' is taken at all seriously."[27] Hence Weber might have stood on firmer ground if he had couched this part of his theory of charismatic leadership—as, indeed, he tended to do in places—not in terms of the routinizing of charisma, but rather in terms of its transformation into other forms of authority.

On the other hand, it is not my intention to argue that charisma, by its very nature, ceases to exist with the death or departure of the original leader in whom it inheres as a personal quality. On the contrary, it appears to be a phenomenon that can and often does live on after the charismatic individual is gone. But the form in which it characteristically lives on is the cult of the departed leader —something to which Weber gives little consideration in his theory of routinization. Thus, the charisma of the founder of a religious movement survives, insofar as it survives at all, primarily in the cult of the founder, the revering of his memory by the followers who live after. It is the same with the founders of charismatic political and ideological movements. Thus, Marx and Engels underwent, as Robert Michels expressed it, a "socialist canonization" in movements that carried on in their names. And Lenin, who had strongly disapproved of the manifestations of Lenin-worship that appeared in the Russian Communist movement in his later lifetime and had more or less succeeded in suppressing them, became on the morrow of his death the object of a great public Lenin cult that expressed not only certain pragmatic needs of the Communist movement, but also, and first of all, the feelings of very many of its members.

But insofar as the charisma of a successful charismatic leader survives in the form of a cult of the dead leader, it does not cease to be personal in quality; it remains his even in death. The cult, in other words, may be a special form of "routinization" of his charisma, but is not a "depersonalization" of it. This conclusion, however, has an immediate and obvious bearing upon the Weberian idea that charisma is transmitted to the original leader's successors according to established rules of succession. Not only does the cult tend to conserve the original leader's charisma and keep it in his own name; it may, as a result, actually *militate against* the transmission of his charisma to a successor, and it may do this even though the practical interests of the movement make transmission desirable. It is not at all evident, therefore, that the successors of a charismatic leader at the head of a movement that outlives him will themselves be leaders of charismatic quality. And insofar as they are, it is not by virtue of succeeding to the dead leader's charisma, but by virtue of what they themselves are and how the followers perceive them.

REFERENCES

1. Max Weber, *Theory of Social and Economic Organization* (New York, 1947), p. 358.

2. Karl Loewenstein, *Max Weber's Political Ideas in the Perspective of Our Time* (Amherst, 1966), pp. 79, 90. For Loewenstein's remarks on the influence of Weber's theory of charisma, see *ibid.*, p. 74.

3. Carl J. Friedrich, "Political Leadership and Charismatic Power," *The Journal of Politics*, Vol. 23, No. 2 (February, 1961), pp. 14-16. On the etymological and theological background, see E. San Juan, Jr., "Orientations of Max Weber's Concept of Charisma," *The Centennial Review*, Vol. 11, No. 2 (Spring, 1967), pp. 270-85.

4. For examples of these two criticisms, see in particular K. J. Ratnam, "Charisma and Political Leadership," *Political Studies*, Vol. 12, No. 3 (1964), pp. 344, 354.

5. See, in particular, David Apter, *Ghana in Transition* (New York, 1963), esp. pp. 320-30, and Ann Ruth Willner and Dorothy Willner, "The Rise and Role of Charismatic Leaders," *The Annals of the American Academy of Political and Social Science*, Vol. 358 (March, 1965), pp. 77-88. The Willners write: "Charismatic leadership seems to flourish today particularly in the newer states that were formerly under colonial rule" (p. 80). The article does not *define* charisma in the setting of the "newer" states, however, but follows Weber in giving the concept a universalitic definition.

6. Max Weber, "The Three Types of Legitimate Rule," *Berkeley Publications in Society and Institutions*, Vol. 4, No. 1 (Summer, 1958), p. 7.

7. Weber, *Theory of Social and Economic Organization*, pp. 359-61.

8. *Ibid.*, p. 359.

9. *From Max Weber: Essays in Sociology*, trans. H. H. Gerth and C. Mills (New York, 1946), p. 248.

10. Weber, *The Theory of Social and Economic Organization*, p. 362. As Reinhard Bendix puts it: "The charismatic leader is always a radical who challenges established practice by going to 'the root of the matter.'" (*Max Weber: An Intellectual Portrait*, p. 300.)

11. Robert Michels, *Political Parties* (New York, 1959), pp. 64-67.

12. N. Valentinov, *Vstrechi s Leninym* (New York, 1953), pp. 71-75.

13. A. N. Potresov, *Posmerty sbornik proizvedenii* (Paris, 1937), p. 301.

14. *From Max Weber*, pp. 245, 249. In their introductory essay in this volume, Gerth and Mills speak of charismatic leaders as "self-appointed leaders who are followed by those who are in distress and who need to follow the leader because they believe him to be extraordinarily qualified" (*ibid.*, p. 52).

15. I am indebted to Ann Ruth Willner for the phrase "situational charisma," as well as for data on American charismatic response to Roosevelt at the outset of his Presidency. On these and other points, see her important

forthcoming study *The Theory and Strategies of Charismatic Leadership*, which views the phenomenon of charisma in the universalistic terms of reference set by Weber.

16. Leon Trotsky, *Trotsky's Diary in Exile: 1935* (New York, 1963), p. 46.

17. Norman Cohn, "Medieval Millenarism: Its Bearing on the Comparative Study of Millenarian Movements," ed. Sylvia Thrupp, *Millenial Dreams in Action, Essays in Comparative Study. Comparative Studies in Society and History*, Supplement 2 (The Hague, 1962), p. 32.

18. Oral remarks at the Tuxedo conference on Leadership (October, 1967), in discussion of the present paper.

19. Walter Duranty, *Duranty Reports Russia* (New York, 1934), p. 170.

20. For a first attempt at a systematic catalogue of qualities characteristic of a large number of charismatic leaders, see the aforementioned forthcoming study by Ann Ruth Willner.

21. Hadley Cantril, *The Psychology of Social Movements* (New York, 1963), p. 235.

22. Laura Fermi, *Mussolini* (Chicago, 1966), pp. 214-15.

23. Karl Marx, "Zur Kritik der Hegelschen Rechtsphilosofie: Einleitung," Karl Marx-Friedrich Engels, *Werke*, Vol. 1 (Berlin, 1957), p. 381.

24. J. V. Stalin, "Lenin," in *Works* (Moscow, 1953), p. 57.

25. Franz Neumann, "Anxiety and Politics," in *The Democratic and the Authoritarian State: Essays in Political and Legal Theory* (Glencoe, 1957), p. 279.

26. For Weber's extended discussions of routinization, see particularly *Theory of Social and Economic Organization*, pp. 364-71, and "The Three Types of Legitimate Rule," pp. 8-10. See also Bendix, *Max Weber*, pp. 308-28.

27. Carl J. Friedrich, *Man and His Government: An Empirical Theory of Politics* (New York, 1964), p. 172.

ADAM B. ULAM

The Marxist Pattern

THERE WAS a bit of the cult of personality from the very beginning. Marx was, after all, in the tradition of the great socialist system-makers who conceived their role not merely as politicians and theorists, but as discoverers of new worlds. St. Simon was creating a new religion. Fourier thought of himself as the Newton of moral sciences. And over Marx's grave Engels could say: "As Darwin discovered the law of evolution in organic nature, so Marx discovered the law of evolution in human history." Carried away by emotion, Engels was to claim for his departed master and colleague significant discoveries in mathematics. This was already the seed of presumption which was to make Lenin "condemn" non-Euclidean geometry, Stalin to formulate linguistic theories, and Comrade Mao's thought to leave its imprint on as varied fields of endeavor as nuclear energy and Ping-Pong. There is, after all, an element of both childishness and grandiose conceit in the claim of having discovered something which has eluded countless philosophers and historians, of having laid bare that which the whole course of history and civilization has tended to conceal and suppress. Khrushchev was right insofar as the logic of the doctrine is concerned when in the beginning of his indictment of Stalin he was to assert that "it is impermissible and foreign to the spirit of Marxism-Leninism to elevate one person, to transform him into a superman possessing supernatural characteristics akin to God. Such a man supposedly knows everything, sees everything, thinks for everyone, can do anything, is infallible in his behavior."[1] But the history of the movement is full of instances of what he finds "impermissible and foreign to the spirit of Marxism-Leninism."

During the last quarter of the nineteenth century, beginning as a matter of fact some years before Marx's death, this demi-urgelike concept of the leader became somewhat attenuated. Marx himself tended to speak in unprophetlike tones. "Perhaps" appears

95

increasingly in his judgments and analyses. The spirit of the age became uncongenial to leaders cut in a superhuman mold. Engels, after Marx's death, is reminiscent not so much of a prophet thundering out anathemas and evoking the visions of cataclysms as of a kindly retired professor encouraging or reproving his pupils, sighing nostalgically over the enthusiasms and impatience of his youth.

Marxism in the hands of the German Social Democracy became indeed weighed down with academic respectability. Kautsky and Bernstein could but with difficulty be differentiated in their personality traits and the style of work from the Schmollers and Sombarts. On the political side, the picture was almost as depressing. The political leaders, not to speak of the trade-union officials, of the German Social Democracy accepted Marxism as a convenient ideology rather than as a bracing revolutionary imperative. In retrospect it is easy to see that prosperity and legality tended to dampen the revolutionary spirit. And, without a sense of struggle and an exhilarating feeling of danger there was no place for *the* leader, the man combining the insight into the future and a sense of mission. There are no Napoleons in peacetime armies. Even a person with as much revolutionary *élan* as Rosa Luxemburg was essentially a theorist. She was endowed with a degree of intellectual toleration and introspection, again qualities which were to prove destructive to or would disqualify the would-be leaders of Communism.

When we turn to the Russian scene, we find, on the contrary, revolutionary leadership in abundance. Soviet historiography is, for a change, not far wrong or tendentious when it depicts the story of nineteenth-century revolutionary movement as consisting of men seeking for—and failing in their endeavors because they could not find—*the* theory. The pages of the nineteenth-century history are full of Lenins and Plekhanovs *manqués*, seeking a key to the understanding of the social reality and to the vast task of transforming it into a better world. From the Decembrist Pestel who got as close as one could at that early time to laying down a blueprint for a totalitarian state to Tkachev who in his ideas on revolutionary organization and mechanics and his notions on propaganda was to anticipate Lenin, many of the revolutionaries longed instinctively for a comprehensive theory of political action, for an ideology which would show why and how the existing regime must be brought down. What aroused their despair was the very intractability of the material they had to work with, the apathy and ignorance of the peasant masses. This, in turn, spurred revolutionary thought into channels of conspiracy. But conspiracy itself unguided by a systematic theory is ineffectual as a guide to revolution, at least under modern political conditions. Thus, what was the purpose of all the heroics and sacrifices of the *People's Will?* The only aim on which its members could agree was convocation of a universally elected Constituent Assembly. But, as the more perceptive of the members of the *People's Will* saw, to the great majority of electors to the assembly such concepts as "democracy," "socialism," and so forth would have been completely incomprehensible. Thus the Russian revolutionary of the seventies and eighties found himself in a predicament somewhat similar to that of a member of the New Left in the America of the 1960's, and in both cases the impasse arrived at by the conflict between revolutionary principles and revolutionary temperament was to lead to wild visions of violence and cataclysms.

It becomes understandable why Marxism did not exert an earlier and greater impact on revolutionary thought in Russia. Marxism teaches patience; the Russian revolutionaries were impatient. Furthermore, especially in the last quarter of the century, Marxism already began to be bedecked with professional and bourgeois respectability which infuriated men brought up to Chernyshevsky's *What Is to Be Done* and its triumphant exaltation of all forms of nonconformity. Just as to the modern Western radical the orthodox Soviet style Communist party with its ritual and organization is somewhat "square" and old-fashioned, so to a rebellious Russian youth of the era, Marx's vision of the industrialized and centralized state was prosaic and repellent. Most of all, the Promised Land of revolution was to be postponed for what appeared eons of time, while the idiocy of rural Russia was being transformed into bustling towns and scientifically run farms, while those corrupt bureaucrats and landlords, so much hated that they almost inspired perverse affection, were being replaced by coldly efficient and calculating industrialists and bankers. This prospect was so repellent that it inspired a *cri de coeur* by Tkachev when admonished by Engels for his impatience: "It is Russia's backwardness which is her great fortune, at least from the revolutionary point of view."[2] Long before Mao Tse-tung, some Russian radicals clearly perceived that true revolutionary spirit cannot cohabit with a highly developed economy.

What then secured the eventual triumph of Marxism in Russia? Mainly the efforts of a small group of devoted and remarkable men. The Bolshevik Revolution, wrote Maxim Gorky in a moment of frankness, was the work of a "numerically tiny group of the intelligentsia leading a few thousand workers who have been indoctrinated by it."[3] Or even more precisely, a few men who by the force of their personality managed to push Marxism to the fore in the revolutionary movement. When the revolution happened Marxism was in the wings. As the other contenders for power, liberals and the Socialist Revolutionaries, dropped out, militant Marxists boldly embarked upon their venture. That individual leadership was of crucial importance has been admitted by all the main parties to the drama. The Bolshevik Revolution would not have taken place without Lenin and himself, Trotsky was to write. Had only Gershuni lived, the Socialist Revolutionaries were to sigh, Lenin would not have been able to mesmerize his opponents and followers alike, their own party would not have disintegrated into innumerable factions. If only the Russian liberals, as represented by the Kadets, possessed a real leader rather than those ineffectual professors and lawyers. . . . Why did the early hope of democratic revolution, Kerensky, turn out in the end to be a conniving windbag? And even on the right the same questions and regrets have been voiced over the last fifty years: Why was there no Witte or Stolypin among the Tsar's wartime ministers? And the one general who attempted to stem the tide of the revolution, Kornilov, revealed himself in the words of his colleague as a man "with the heart of a lion and the brains of a sheep."

But, even before its supreme triumph and tragedy, the rise and development of Russian Marxism was extraordinarily influenced by the qualities and characteristics of a few men. Among them we shall look at three—Plekhanov, Lenin, and Martov. It is not too much to say that without any one of them the events of 1917 would have taken a different turn. Of Lenin's contribution it is superfluous to speak. But, that Russian Marxism arrived at this turning point of history in the condition to play a decisive role was largely the achievement of Plekhanov. That it was not to develop more vigorous antibodies to Bolshevism was largely the fault of Martov.

Plekhanov's intellectual heritage (as against his actual person which counted for little in the events of 1917) and Martov's scruples explain the events of 1917 almost as much as Lenin's determination.

The careers of the three men intersected at several points. Much of the history of the Russian Social Democracy between 1898–1914 is comprised in fact of the collaboration, quarrels, and reconciliations of these three men.

Plekhanov was the Master. Indeed, paradoxical though it may sound, it can be claimed that his was the most important contribution to the future triumph of Marxism in Russia. Almost single-handedly between 1883 and 1900 he created Marxian literature in Russian. Equally important, he established a niche for Russian Marxism, then consisting literally of just himself and his two faithful co-adjutors, Vera Zasulich and Axelrod, in the international socialist movement, and built the foundation for those international contacts and sympathies which were to enable Russian Marxism to survive and thrive in exile. When in the 1890's the Russian revolutionary movement began to revive after its virtual destruction in the preceding decade, it would have been almost inconceivable that young intelligentsia radicals should have been tempted to imbibe Marxism and to forsake the much more romantic and activist gospel of renascent Populism without this distant and already renowned figure, without his cogent and sarcastic criticism of other radical ideologies, and, not least of all, without the example of his personality. Plekhanov, from a distance, was ideally suited for that hero worship which is the cementing ingredient of revolutionary movements. Not merely a writer and theorist, he was one who had as a young man and member of the *Land of Freedom* group "walked in the shadow of the gallows," as he would often remind his disciples. He then had the supreme courage of denouncing the terrorist tactics of the People's Will, but this defiance instead of being, as in the case of the renegade Tikhomirov, a prelude to abandoning the struggle, was for Plekhanov the beginning of a yet more glorious and harrowing revolutionary career. For more than a decade, he had carried the fight both against the Tsarist government and the main currents of the Russian radical thought, and all the while struggling against poverty and a debilitating illness. For a Russian intellectual with his keen sense of inferiority about the "civilized West," it was an impressive achievement of Plekhanov's that he was recognized as an equal by the leading German luminaries of Marxian thought. When the scandalous heresy of revisionism erupted within the bosom of the social-democracy, Karl Kautsky, fearful of offending his old comrade, entrusted the Russian with the task of refuting Bernstein's noxious views. To Lenin and Martov, then in Siberian exile, Plekhanov must have appeared almost superhuman. Imagine Karl Kautsky, the ruling deity of Marxian scholarship, asking a Russian for help in a dispute about theory.

But it was in this moment of crisis and triumph that Plekhanov was to show himself, both, very Russian and his defense of orthodoxy prophetic of future ferocious intellectual intolerance of the Bolsheviks. Bernstein was not only a dissenter, he was a virtual traitor to the cause. The dogmatic structure of Marxism was for Plekhanov not merely a theoretical framework for a political movement, but an all-embracing faith, the canons of which no one had the right to tamper with because of his own private doubts or the weight of statistical evidence. A socialist party could not degenerate into a debating society; it had to be a fellowship of the faithful. Thus, in a burst of intellectual intolerance Plekhanov really destroyed his own position as *the* leader of Russian Marxism, at the moment when it was being transformed from a miniscule sect into a political movement. If all there is to an ideology is really the definition of orthodoxy and suppression of heresies, then the main qualification for leadership becomes not intellectual but organizational ability. There is a deeply ironic quality to the apostolic succession in Russian Marxism: Plekhanov virtually enthroning Lenin as his successor, just as Lenin was to install Stalin as his own, and both men coming to regret bitterly their actions, and yet being unable to undo them. Both sought fitting instruments of repression: Plekhanov of theroetical dissent within the fledgling movement, Lenin of political opposition within the ruling Bolshevik party. Both were to assume that their chosen lieutenant would remain an obedient and deferential pupil, and both were to recoil at discovering that the new man meant not only to snatch the party out of their hands, but to transform it in his own image.

With the Second Congress of the Russian Social Democratic Party in 1903, the Plekhanov phase of Russian Marxism was ended. It was he who helped create Bolshevism by taking Lenin's side and ensuring that on this issue of Lilliputian proportions, as it then appeared, about whether the editorial board of *Iskra* should have three or six members, Lenin's followers should prevail over Martov's. Plekhanov was to remain a figure of great intellectual prestige, whose support was sought both by the Mensheviks and Bolsheviks in their interminable squabbles, whose word was still the law on an intricate problem of Marxian theory, and whose help was called upon when it came to enlisting the services of rich and influential sympathizers. But it was mainly as a monument of the past that he was sought by Russian visitors to Geneva. With advancing years and economic security, he reverted, as people do, to the manners of his class, the Russian gentry. Formal and reserved in his behavior, he would at times scintillate with wit and erudition. A deferential visitor would be dragged through art collections and museums and treated to a lecture by the man who laid down the canons of Marxian art criticism. But, irreverent or disputatious visitors were told to brush up on their Marxism or their argument would be cut short by a withering glance and those now famous words: "You were not even born when I already . . . ."

Like that other veteran revolutionary Prince Kropotkin, 1914 reawakened in Plekhanov the Russian patriot. His bondage to the Germanic ideas and mannerisms disappeared, and to a shocked fellow-socialist who inquired "how about our German comrades," he replied that it would be a great pleasure to him to bayonet some of them.[4] October found him a complete stranger to his country and to the movement which he had created. Shortly before his death he barely escaped being lynched by a band of anarchist sailors. It was a vivid demonstration of his own rueful prophecy: the Russian working class would only disgrace itself by a premature seizure of power.

Plekhanov set a great store by the question of personal style. His first doubts about Lenin were aroused by the latter's admittedly laborious and awkward prose. Trotsky, with his brashness and flamboyance, he disliked from the first. Such scruples in a revolutionary may appear both comical and pedantic. Yet a Russian Marxist before 1917 was bound to feel that the essence of his creed required, strange as it sounds to our ears, a *civilized revolution*. The disgrace of Tsarist Russia lay precisely in the uncivilized character of its social and political relations. An anarchist or a Populist could think of revolution as consisting in unleashing a mob's fury. Some members of the People's Will looked not unfavorably at the

101

anti-semitic pogroms which followed the assassination of Alexander II. They represented a welcome sign of the breakdown of law and order, a necessary prelude to a popular uprising. But, to a Marxist such sentiments were impermissible. Yet, the triumph of the Bolsheviks in 1917 was predicated precisely upon their abandoning this "civilized" concept of the revolution, of giving in to and abetting the anarchist feelings of the masses, of conquering power under essentially anarchist slogans.

It is not too much to see the dispute between Martov and Lenin as being one about revolutionary manners and morals, rather than ideology properly speaking.

In Lenin the disciple of Plekhanov clashed with the one of Chernyshevsky. After the revolution he was to sigh repeatedly over its various "uncultured" aspects, urge that Russia must learn from "the civilized West," scoff at bohemianism and contrived bad manners. But he also used to repeat that "one does not enter the realm of revolution in white gloves." There was a strange quirk in his character which made him delight in the trampling on legal norms and customs, hanker after violence, and elevate terror to a principle of administration.

To Martov, on the other hand, the most vivid memory of his childhood remained the scene of the Jewish pogrom in 1881 in Odessa, when his own family was in jeopardy. From then on he could never, in the famous revolutionary phrase of the 1860's attributed to Chernyshevsky, call upon Russia to "raise the axe." Though as a convinced Marxist, and under the Russian circumstances he could never unconditionally repudiate violence, Martov found it repugnant. World War I was for him a tragedy and an absolute evil.[5] For Lenin it was a unique opportunity to breathe the militant spirit once more into Marxism and to embark upon a world revolution.

The relationship of the two men who embodied the two opposing currents of Russian Marxism is of great psychological interest. Their friendship turned after 1903 into bitter personal hostility, and yet each man retained a strange attraction for the other. Lenin was to struggle hard against his love for Martov, as Krupskaya wrote in her sentimental way. But more than this "love" was at stake. Martov came to epitomize for Lenin the whole humanistic and hence futile side of the Russian revolutionary tradition: a man in principle an uncompromising Marxist, yet in every concrete revolutionary situation filled with doubts and qualifications. The language used by Lenin about his old friend after the Revolution—"cretin," "Miliukov's lackey," and so forth—gives the impression of Lenin trying to exorcise Martov and Martovism from his own nature, not giving in to the temptations of thinking that the Revolution and the socialist state could be won and preserved in a more humane way. Martov for his part could never overcome a certain juvenile admiration for his old friend's daring and defiance of rules. In the memoirs of his youth, he was to write nostalgically of the young Lenin of the 1890's, still willing to learn rather than to be an oracle, still devoid of that morbid intolerance and suspicion toward people which was to characterize him later on. Pathetically and revealingly Martov was to add "I was *never* to notice any element of personal vanity in Lenin's character."[6]

This last remark contains a clue to the tragedy of Martov's life and that of Russian Marxism. Countless times before, he had excoriated Lenin for his presumption and intrigues. In 1903 Lenin was out to steal the Party journal. In the revolution of 1905–06 he authorized "expropriations," armed robberies supposedly for the party treasury but in fact joined in by criminal elements. After 1910 he was, in Martov's words, not a political leader, but the head of a sort of Mafia bent upon seizing the Russian Social Democracy. In 1917 he abandoned Marxism for adventurism and anarchism. Yet, at each point Martov drew back from drawing consequences from his indictments and from pressing to take countermeasures. Had he thrown his already considerable prestige behind such a move, Martov could have been instrumental in expelling Lenin from the party in 1907, when the majority at the London Congress was drawn into furious indignation by the revelation of scandals and crimes perpetrated by the Bolsheviks. In July 1917, when the troops were being moved to Petrograd to quell what had been clearly an attempted coup by the Bolsheviks, Martov accused Kerensky of following in the footsteps of Thiers and setting out to massacre the revolutionaries. And in October, while condemning the this time successful Bolshevik seizure of power, Martov still could not bring himself to advocate countersteps. Revolutionary events on the scale of October could not be traced, after all, to the will of one man or a conspiracy of a power-hungry group. They had to be traced to the aspirations, however misguided they were, of the "masses." A true revolutionary and Marxist could not forcibly oppose the "masses." The Mensheviks then had to educate the people or, as he used to phrase it before October, work to "isolate the Bolsheviks morally." After the Revolution even Martov could not maintain that it was the "masses" which instituted systematic terror, shot or imprisoned veteran political leaders, and finally sent him and other Mensheviks into exile. But in 1922 he still could not discern any element of "personal vanity" in Lenin's makeup!

It would be a gross oversimplification to trace Martov's predicament solely to his personal weakness for Lenin. It was, in part, the product of the intellectual's eternal feeling of inferiority toward the activist. To be sure, Martov was not an armchair philosopher; he had been a revolutionary propagandist and organizer. But in October it was the Bolsheviks who were making the revolution. Most of all the fears and scruples which disarmed Martov and emasculated the non-Bolshevik left at the crucial point are traceable to their concept of their own ideology. It would have been a repudiation of everything that he and his comrades believed in to assume that in the Russia of 1917, the "freest country in the world," one man or a party could effectively change the course of history, that the Marxian laws governing the development of society could be suspended or rendered invalid through a conspiracy. Hence, the real answer to Communism, comical as it sounds to us, was to fit it into the categories of Marxian historical orthodoxy. Wrote Martov in 1921:

We grant to the Bolsheviks that they represent, in essence, the final stage of the destruction of feudal Russia, but we fight them because they are fulfilling this "Jacobinical" role badly and because . . . they corrupt the proletariat and render it impotent. . . . We view the further development [of Russia] as going on *from* Bolshevism rather than returning to a phase before it.[7]

This judgment is truly pathetic from the perspective of nearly fifty years later—the dwindling band of Mensheviks in Paris, Berlin, and finally New York waited for the forces of history to assert themselves and for the blinders to fall off the eyes of the Russian working class. But interestingly enough a variant of the same opinion was expressed by Lenin during his last illness. Appalled by the already evident bureaucratization of the Soviet regime and by the squabbles among his would-be successors, he expressed deep doubts about his life work. Not that he could ever repudiate the Great October; but the Revolution was seen by him as a violation of the Marxian canon, allowable and legitimate only if its subsequent course were to endow it with a socialist and humanistic content. The sick man's inner dialogue, the conglomerate of his doubts and hopes, is expressed in a language which at times borders on the incoherent. October represented a unique chance. The complete hopelessness of the situation, had by the same token increased the strength of the workers and peasants tenfold, and opened "for us the possibility of laying the foundations of a civilization in a different way from all other Western European countries."[8] It was not wrong to conquer power and then "already on the basis of worker-peasant power and the Soviet system to start catching up with other nations." By *catching up* Lenin clearly meant not only industrialization and modernization; he meant also "culture," the word standing in his lexicon principally for humane treatment of the ruled by the rulers. This "culture" was notably missing in old Russia, and much as he had authorized and approved terror during the Revolution and the Civil War, Lenin incongruously looked forward to a period when socialism would be combined, would come to mean in effect, this humane, "feeling" attitude toward people. He himself would not see this promised land, but his followers would.

Plekhanov, Martov, and Lenin epitomize three different temperaments of Russian Marxism, three different styles of leadership. The father of Russian Marxism from his Populist activism turned to the vocation of *intellectual* leadership. The leader's function was to diagnose the forces of history, to certify the given historical moment as suitable or inappropriate for a revolutionary breakthrough. It was not his role to improvise, to stir up human emotions, to struggle for the sake of struggle. The long exile, the virtual isolation of his last years and finally his tragic end—dying neglected and scorned by the very movement which he had done so much to build and preserve—were thus a price paid for the excessive premium put upon theory as against life. It is incorrect to speak of Plekhanov's moderation or democratic scruples as being responsible for his political failure. It was, on the contrary, his own brand of extremism: his extreme devotion to the doctrine. This devotion made him tolerate, at times support, Lenin and the Bolsheviks before 1914 because, for all their undemocratic temperament and behavior, he saw in them a legitimate offshoot of Marxism. His condemnation of Bolshevism at the moment of its triumph in October again proceeded not so much from his revulsion at the tactics employed or even from his Russian patriotism, but from ideological scruples. How could one have socialism or a socialist revolution if the working class did not constitute the majority of the population?

Another dimension of Plekhanov's tragedy was that he lacked that keen appetite for political power which is an almost inevitable component of political success. He was abundantly endowed with pride or, if one prefers, vanity. But he could not endure the strain of continuous polemic, the tedium of constant watchfulness for the opponent's moves and intrigues. Charismatic leadership was not part of Plekhanov's equipment. How could it be? He hewed to the notion of the political leader being the intellectual guide. It had been the revulsion at the romanticized notion of political leadership which had been partly responsible for driving him away from Populism. Some months before his death, in a conversation with Vera Zasulich, he wondered whether and where the two of them, by now completely isolated relics of the earliest era of Russian Marxism, had gone wrong. He could find no answer nor grounds for self-reproach: "Did we fulfill our vow? I think we fulfilled it honestly. Isn't that true, Vera Ivanovna, honestly?"[9]

If Plekhanov viewed politics from a severely intellectual angle which forbade him to depart from his doctrine even when the realities of the political situation cried for flexibility, then for Martov the message of Marxism became essentially moral. He savored in Marxism mostly its quality of dissent, its challenge to all established forms of authority, to force and routine as factors in social relations. The intellectual content of his ideology saved Martov from being an anarchist pure and simple. But when it came to a conflict between orthodoxy and the "people" or the "masses," Martov would always find himself in a quandary. In a way, and much more than Plekhanov, he was curiously apolitical. That politics requires a notion of authority, that the business of government consists largely in the pedestrian tasks of collecting taxes, legislating, and administering—those commonplaces never found a wholehearted acceptance in Martov's philosophy. A man of such a makeup could have never entered a government without a feeling of guilt, without a feeling that to govern is to betray. And this syndrome was strong enough within the non-Bolshevik left to contribute signally to its defeat in 1917.

I have pointed out elsewhere that scruples and attitudes of a similar kind were not absent even among the Bolsheviks.[10] It took all of Lenin's determination to strip the party of its remaining democratic "superstitions," to compel and cajole its top ranks to accept the idea first of one party rule and then of strict intra-party discipline and prohibition of factions. Just as he had taken over the most anarchic of revolutions and turned it into the foundation upon which was to be built the most centralized and despotic state of modern times, so he had to transform a movement in its inception as democratic as it was socialist into a prototype of a totalitarian party. That Lenin had a dictatorial *temperament* was discerned by Trotsky as early as 1903. But the evolution of the Bolsheviks into a party strictly controlled from the top proceeded by fits and bounds, by accident as well as by design. It would not have been possible without first the authoritarian character of Imperial Russia and then World War I. In the post-October period, every abrogation of democratic rights within the party was justified as temporary and due to a special emergency: first the Civil War, then the Kronstadt revolt, then the need of rebuilding the country's economy.

One aspect of Lenin's role, then, was that of a great improviser. However close emotionally and even ideologically he may have been to Martov, *politically* he stood at the opposite pole. An astute observer hit the nail on the head when he wrote that for Lenin an ideological problem never existed in a vacuum. It was always considered in connection with its organizational consequences. Or, to paraphrase it, considerations of political power colored every ideological problem. To be fair, this association was, for the most part, unconscious and uncynical. Yet, the end result was the atrophy of what had remained of democracy and freedom of expression within the Communist Party. The two men once linked by Marxian orthodoxy as well as by intimate personal bonds thus traveled in opposite directions. One arrived at the point where dissent became almost the sole measure of his political position; the other at a position where the problem of power *almost* crowded out every other political consideration. For all of Lenin's hopes, for all his grief at the news that the companion of his early struggles was also ill and dying, he could never have admitted that Martov had been proved right.

Each of the three men had his own brand of intolerance, and this factor contributed in no small measure to the poignant tragedy of their lives. An essentially kind and warmhearted man, Plekhanov could not tolerate intellectual disagreement. He greeted Revisionism with the famous aphorism: "Either Bernstein will bury social democracy or socialism will bury him." Who knows, maybe the memory of this phrase in a textbook of Party history stuck enough in Khrushchev's mind to prompt him to his memorable "we shall bury capitalism." This intellectual prickliness of Plekhanov prevented him also from throwing his weight decisively against Lenin on many occasions before 1914 when such a stance could have definitely isolated the Bolsheviks and changed the whole course of Russian Marxism. He loathed Lenin's adventurist tactics, but the Bolsheviks recognized his *theoretical* authority and stuck to the fundamentalist interpretation of Marxism, while among the Mensheviks there were some who leaned toward the "parliamentary fallacy" or even—terrible to say—revisionism. When the Bolsheviks' "tactics" were shown to be not merely aberrations, but a breach with the whole ideological tradition, and Plekhanov finally thundered against them, it was too late. History could not be reversed by a few quotations from the *Capital*.

In Martov, intolerance extended to the whole problem of governing. No government was wholly justified or could have pure hands. Every act of repression, every hint of use of physical force, was illegitimate. Thus, this devout Marxist could have taken as his motto the aphorism of Leo Tolstoy: "Nobody who has not been in jail knows what the state is"—a sentiment logical for a Christian anarchist, but not for a believer in centralized political and economic power.[11] This notion of political power as being somehow impure prevented Menshevism of Martov's variety from being a positive force during the Revolution. And it weakened fatally the position of his more realistic comrades who tried to shore up the Provisional Government. If Martov, who was the conscience of the Party, was against repression, how could Tseretelli or Dan work wholeheartedly for the suppression of the Bolsheviks, for tightening up military discipline, or for setting limits to the anarchy which was engulfing the country? During the Civil War, Martov and his group preserved exemplary loyalty toward the Bolshevik regime which was already persecuting them, banning their newspapers, dissolving soviets and trade unions dominated by them, and so forth. Martov was unsparing in his criticism of those Mensheviks who were participating in anti-Bolshevik regimes. In return for this support at the end of the Civil War, Martov's partisans were in effect banned from political life. He himself, the man "whom Ilich never ceased to love," according to the testimony of Krupskaya, had to become once again an exile.

Martov's tragedy epitomizes the drama of what might be called "pure social democracy." Standing between revisionism on the one hand and communism on the other, it emasculated Russian democratic socialism of any political influence it could have had without in turn restraining the growing totalitarian tendencies of Bolshevism. The failure of Menshevism in Russia was to have consequences transcending the boundaries of the country; it was the forerunner of the tragedy of the non-Communist left in the world at large. For all the electoral successes of socialism in Great Britain, in the Scandinavian countries, it was but the pale ghost of the movement which in the first decade of the twentieth century promised to inherit the earth, or at least the West. And in due time, democratic socialism was to stand equally abashed before the phenomenon of the New Left. One could not approve of its methods, of its militantly anarchist spirit, but how could one take one's stand on the side of authority, of the state?

As against the intellectual intolerance of Plekhanov and what might be called libertarian one of Martov, Lenin displayed a more involved complex. Of his emotional dislike of parliamentarism and of the entire legal and administrative paraphernalia of the bourgeois state, one does not have to speak at length.[12] Until 1914 he chafed under the democratic and parliamentary phraseology of the European social democracy, sighed at the strange spectacle of the meetings of the 2nd International, where revisionists and, worse, members of the British Labour Party and of Poale Zion rubbed shoulders with militant Marxists. World War I was for him a liberating experience: the militant Marxists could now shed the debilitating post-1870 parliamentary and democratic tradition, toss aside the very name "social democracy" like a "soiled child's shirt," and revert to the earlier and revolutionary traditions of the movement. The supreme quality of political leadership, the realization that *the* moment had come, was thus his in 1914 as it was again to be in 1917.

The post-November leadership of Lenin stamped him as one of the few great historical figures capable both of carrying out a revolution and of mastering it. He set himself resolutely to reverse the trend toward anarchy which had made the triumph of Bolshevism possible. The deepening tragedy of his last years consisted, as pointed out above, in the increasing concern that the Soviet state might have been conceived in sin against the precepts of Marxism, and that this fact would weigh heavily and fatally upon its future development. But this worry could not make him turn to the remedies he abhorred: anything smacking of Western constitutionalism or free political life. And so in his last illness, confronted by the already all too visible phenomena of bureaucratism and passionate struggle for power among the ruling oligarchy, Lenin still sought to cure the Soviet political system through homeopathic prescriptions: an administrative reform, the addition to the Central Party organs of fifty or more "rank and file proletarians," and so forth. It thus fell to this believer in historical necessity, to this thoroughgoing Marxist, to discuss the future of the movement and the state he had built in terms of personalities: not the majestic forces of history, but the personal characteristics of Trotsky, Bukharin, or Stalin were going to determine the future of Russia and Communism. Stalin's "rudeness," as Lenin put it in his testament, loomed as important for the country's future as the rate of Russia's industrial growth, and who now can say that it was not to prove even more important?

Thus, paradoxically, the movement which by its very creed rejects the notion of charismatic leadership, which extolls the forces of history as against whim or random striving of individuals, has been most dependent and most affected by a series of leaders who whether against their wishes (as Lenin) or with their ready concurrence (Stalin) assumed semi-divine status and adulation. Even the dissident and democratically inclined branches of Russian Marxism stressed, to be sure not so drastically as the Communists, the role of the teacher-leader, as we have seen in the cases of Plekhanov and Martov. And going into our own days, it is characteristic how various offshoots of militant Marxism become known by the name of and indeed cannot be separated from the leader: Castroism, Titoism, Maoism. In the case of the last, the cult of the leader has reached proportions which have never been surpassed by a *political* movement. Even at the height of the adulation of Stalin, his discipleship and ideological descent from Lenin were acknowledged; the names of Marx, Engels, and Plekhanov were allowed to appear in the most slavish works devoted to the "genius leader of the world proletariat." But the cult of Mao is *sui generis*: the more recent outpourings about the Great Helmsman mention no predecessors, admit no teachers. From nuclear physics to table tennis, the thought of Mao is to be the inspiration of the Chinese and, indeed, the whole world. One has to go back to the most extravagant of the Roman emperors to find a parallel to this deification of a political leader.

What, then, is responsible for this exaltation of the role of the leader in Marxism and especially in its Communist offshoot? First of all, the importance of the doctrine for the political movement, the need for the ultimate authority in its interpretation and application to the shifting political and social circumstances. Then, as Marxism became implanted in Russian soil, it entered a society where radical thought looked at politics not merely as one of many departments of life, but as *the* supreme discipline encompassing those spheres which in the West had long been relegated to religion, aesthetics, or the individual's personal philosophy. In that sense, Russian radical thought of the sixties and seventies of the nineteenth century bore a striking resemblance to the New Left of today. Marxism in competing with and overcoming Populism had absorbed its universalist pretensions, its view of politics as the way of life. The leader had to become not merely statesman and teacher, but hero and prophet as well. And when the whole premise of the rationality of the political process was challenged by World War I, Lenin was bound to triumph over Plekhanov and Martov.

REFERENCES

1. Quoted in Bertram Wolfe, *Khrushchev and Stalin's Ghost* (New York, 1957), p. 88.

2. P. Tkachev, *Collected Works* (Moscow, 1933), Vol. II, p. 22.

3. Maxim Gorky, *The Russian Peasant* (in Russian; Berlin, 1922), p. 45.

4. Samuel H. Baron, *Plekhanov* (Stanford, 1963), p. 324.

5. Israel Getzler, *Martov* (Cambridge, 1967), p. 139.

6. Martov, *Notes of a Social Democrat* (Berlin, 1922), p. 268.

7. *Martov and His Circle* (in Russian; New York, 1959), p. 58.

8. Lenin, *Sochinenia*, 4th ed. (Moscow, 1954), Vol. 23, p. 438.

9. Baron, *Plekhanov*, p. 352.

10. *The Bolsheviks* (New York, 1965), pp. 382–86.

11. One cannot help wondering how the great writer could have been so sure, after all *he* was never in jail.

12. Those personal characteristics are discussed in my *Bolsheviks* (New York, 1965), pp. 208–16.

DAVID E. APTER

Nkrumah, Charisma, and the Coup

GHANA WAS the first African territory to achieve independence from colonial rule.[1] It is difficult now to recall the excitement and general good will which attended that event. Overtones of race were, perhaps, in the background; but misgivings were mainly confined to the old colonial hands, a few African intellectuals, and the chiefs, the traditional rulers. Their reservations were lost in the shower of congratulations from all sides. Ghana, it was agreed to the point of cliché, was a symbol: to the British, of their liberalism; to the Americans, of anticolonialism; to Negro Americans, of a change in attitude toward their historical and cultural past. For the left, independence represented potentiality, the possibility of an African revolution; for the right, a maneuver to forestall revolution. In Africa, it meant at least a freedom from tiresome expatriate judgments, a time of uncertainty perhaps, but an exciting one. For all, it remained a period of innocence, a rebirth, kindling in some degree vague hopes for a new deal for Africans.

The novelty was, of course, not so great as it appeared. Constitutional patterns and precedents were observed. Indeed, although few realized it, a set piece was now being extended to Africa. Ghana achieved independence in 1957, but through an old procedure—one which had evolved out of earlier struggles for independence. Even in Ghana itself the devolution of authority had begun long before the war; the cases of Burma and India were immediately relevant examples, and Ceylon served as the model. Independence was achieved by staged constitutional steps. Beginning with local government reform aimed at financial and judicial development at the local level, each step fostered increasing popular participation and greater responsibility in central government, and, by means of general elections to legislative and executive bodies, ever larger proportions of elected Africans. The constitutional turning point was the emergence of elected majorities which would lead to cabinet government, party competition, and independence. Although Ghana, like all the African territories, pursued its own path, an institutionalized body of precedents and practices had been followed.

These constitutional punctuation marks may sound quaint to-day, but not if one recalls the events of the general election of 1951, the first in an African territory. A new leadership had emerged, although badly organized and lacking in experience. The authorities felt that there was still time to shape this leadership—a tutelary period of good will in which the spirit of British parliamentary institutions could somehow be breathed into constitutional channels and with which nationalism could be blended. To knowledgeable observers, the pattern of devolution of authority by measured steps seemed to be the best method for combining the forces of "rising nationalism" with the establishment of "age-old institutions" in a new setting. Constitutionalism was to provide the legal framework of a state in which nationalism would create a sense of loyalty and a national identity.[2] This was the immediate political context of Nkrumah's rise to power.

Many private doubts remained: Could parliamentary institutions serve when there were so many difficult and unresolved questions, pressures for development, conflicts over local issues, and struggles for power? All of these could easily lead to corruption or subversion. More important were the reservations expressed about the commitment of the new leaders to democratic institutions, not least by these leaders themselves. On the other hand, if they were forced into opposition or kept out of responsible office, parliamentary government would fail at the start, since overwhelming popular support had rallied to Kwame Nkrumah and his Convention People's Party. If support was strongest from the least responsible members of the community, it remained the government's task to make them responsible. The violence of the 1948 riots in what had been considered a model colony had not been lost on the authorities. The more liberal colonial officials were willing to accept widened African participation, even if the leaders of the C.P.P. were made of ambiguous stuff. It was the best one had to work with, and Nkrumah himself was intelligent. His associations and some of his more declamatory gestures were revolutionary, but that was in public; privately he was capable of talking good sense. To the British, the risks were worth taking.

When Ghana came into being in 1957, the experiment seemed to be working. There was good will on all sides (except in Kumasi). Garden parties marked the festivities; seventy-two countries sent delegations, and over a hundred guests of Nkrumah attended, including Richard Nixon. The Duchess of Kent danced the fox trot with Nkrumah in the State House in celebration of independence.

Today Nkrumah is in exile in Guinea—"learning French," it is said (but, according to his former Attorney-General Geoffrey Bing, "tending his roses"). There is little sentiment for his return. Most of his friends seem relieved he is gone. As one of his former cabinet ministers remarked: "It was as if we were in a bus. The driver was Nkrumah. He drove us around one sharp curve after another. We all swayed, some more, some less, but we all swayed."[3] The present government has been reviewing how much they swayed, and the *Report of the Commission to Enquire into the Kwame Nkrumah Properties,* which gives some indication of how funds were misused, is not very savory reading. Certainly there were large-scale misappropriations of funds by senior C.P.P. and government officials—and at a time when the price of cocoa was going down and the public was called upon to make sacrifices for Pan-Africanism in the name of African socialism.[4] The gap between theory and practice was nowhere wider than in the villages. Rural decline was one side of the coin; showpiece projects, like the massive public buildings in Accra, represented the other.

It is not surprising, therefore, that the current tendency is to view Nkrumah's Ghana as a house of cards, a government inflated out of proportion by contemporary liberal observers anxious only to see good in everything African. True, the Convention People's Party was always a tatterdemalion collection of miscellaneous people, but did it exist only in the rhetoric of its leaders? Was parliamentary government at best a temporary device the British used to divest themselves of a small and potentially annoying colony? Clearly the Ghana government did not build a militant one-party socialist state. Was it merely a weakly organized affair in which the personal dictatorship of Nkrumah kept up appearances of governing by threats and violence when, in fact, everything was a shambles? Today's observers are divided in their views. Nkrumah's government was either too radical or not radical enough.[5]

A few argue that even those most intimately connected with the process were simply taken in.[6] Moreover, observers employed misleading language when analyzing the situation, scholars being among the worst offenders. To describe Nkrumah as a "charismatic" leader was to confuse temporary popularity for something more profound, thus changing a momentary attribute into a "credential" Nkrumah could use to sustain personal power.

The shadow of Nkrumah and what he symbolized remains. Dubious and discredited though he may be today, how he will be seen by future generations depends, in part, on how they interpret his role in the context of his day. Was he an exceptional leader in an exceptional moment of history; or was he simply puffed up, an adder without a sting? In the perspective of today, I hold to my original view of him. For a time he had exceptional normative significance. He had hoped to change the basis of public behavior. He failed, but the effort was genuine and the causes of failure complex. He tried to reach his goals by relying on a small, but crucial band of followers for whom and for a short while he played the role of a charismatic leader.[7] "Charisma" was more than an illusion created by Nkrumah for the benefit of a few foreign friends. (If it was not, the same illusion can be said to have surrounded Sukarno, Ben Bella, Sekou Touré, Nasser, and Nyerere.) There is a wide difference between a Touré and a Houphouet,[8] a Nkrumah and an Azikiwe, a Nyerere and a Mboya; just as there is between a Fidel Castro and an Eduardo Frei. This is not simply a matter of ideology nor degree of personal popularity. Rather, the difference arises from the normative authority the leader seeks to impose. The true charismatic leader accepts his own mystique, his consciousness of his role in history, so that the public or a significant subgroup allows him to relate his personal political goals with a wider moral vision and thereby affect public action. Perhaps the relevance of charisma today is not its fleeting nature nor even its extent or degree, but what happens in its aftermath.

To become the first independent African state was an important political event. The same is true of the development of the one-party state and the search for a revolutionary role. These, as well as the reaction by the military and the current effort to restore liberal democratic institutions, continue in Ghana a tradition which began earlier when it was cast in the role of Africa's political bellwether. In Ghana itself there is considerable sensitivity to the wider significance of the efforts being made by constitutionalists and the army to re-establish a parliamentary framework. The note of reason was struck from the start when General J. A. Ankrah, chairman of the National Liberation Council (which was formed after Nkrumah's downfall on February 24, 1966), indicated in a radio address to the country a month later:

I wish to reiterate that the National Liberation Council expects all Ghanaians to welcome back into the fold of our nation those lost and misguided sheep—whatever might have been their previous political persuasion—who unfortunately strayed away from the path of righteousness through the evil indoctrination of the ex-president. Our traditional Ghanaian hospitality, sweet reasonableness, and fellow feeling must be extended to those who will be released from protective custody so that, in the fresh air now blowing through this great Nation of ours, they might put their regrettable past firmly behind them and contribute to the great task of raising the new Ghana from the ashes of the old.[9]

How long such reasonableness can be maintained after the assassination of one of the most popular leaders of the coup against Nkrumah, General Kotoka (and in the face of pressure from ambitious young officers whose aims for the country may be noble, but whose commitment to military rule is likely to overcome their faith in the people), remains to be seen. Certainly the "heroic" leader tendency—best represented by Brigadier Afrifa—has by no means disappeared. Moreover, we can expect the constitutional issues to become more complicated. Just as Argentina has had to face the problem of Peronism without Perón, so a parliamentary government in Ghana will have to deal with the problem of Nkrumaism without Nkrumah. This concern helps account for the almost cookbook-recipe approach of the present efforts at finding a suitable constitutional framework—and for the tendency to borrow specific political devices employed in different constitutions. Too much preoccupation with the prevention of tyranny and not enough attention to the special problems posed by a developing country have led to deep differences of opinion as well as generational conflicts. Even some of the military leaders have expressed growing concern that the old-style politicians—like the Chief Justice E. A. Akufo Addo, or Professor K. A. Busia, or even younger political leaders who had been jailed by Nkrumah, like R. R. Amponsah and M. K. Apaloo—are not capable of organizing the country politically.[10]

Indeed, the public seems to be divided between those who fear any strong central government in the aftermath of Nkrumah and those who feel that a powerful central government is essential for stabilization. Some—like the Inspector-General of Police, J. W. R. Harlley, one of the three who made the revolution—are sympathetic to "ex-C.P.P." Others, after years of exile or jail, are understandably less charitable. (Dr. Busia, now chairman of the advisory council of the National Liberation Committee, for example, is certainly concerned over their future role.) Other political figures, some of whom are former C.P.P. officials who quarreled with Nkrumah and were forced into exile (such as Gbedemah), have now returned with renewed political ambitions. For the moment they are being bypassed, but no one knows for how long. The chiefs, many of whom were punished for their anti-C.P.P. stand, now expect to see the luster of traditional authorities restored in some manner and have advocated a "non-party state." Meanwhile, a whole new generation is emerging. No one knows what the name of Nkrumah will mean to it. There is little doubt that the youth feel the country has become provincial and quiet. Will they also feel let down by the new leaders? Will they perceive the problems now being confronted as local but real, where before they were grandiose and unreal? Will they prefer the realities of the practical and the mundane, or the drama and opportunity presented by radical politics?[11] These are some of the perplexing questions that remain to be answered.

The Concept of Charisma

In the past few years, the term "charisma" has been applied indiscriminately to most of the "heroic" leaders of nationalist movements who have been instrumental in the founding of new states. Many of the names are well known: Senghor, Touré, Houphouet, Nkrumah, Azikiwe, and Awolowo, in West Africa; Kenyatta, Nyerere, Mboya, Lumumba, and Kaunda, in East and Central Africa. The charismatic leader can be distinguished from more ordinary political leaders less by popularity and role than by the effectiveness with which he combines the potentialities of planning with a moral ideology (particularly in the form of a latter-day "Leninism"). It is unfortunate that the appellation has also come to refer to charm and popularity. Such a conception of charisma mistakes temporary enthusiasm for personalized leaders for something more substantial. There may be historic moments when remedial solutions are phrased as simple rhetorical statements, but when the strategic moment passes, so does support. Certainly the casual ease with which populist loyalists shift from once revered leaders would indicate that charisma when defined as popularity is no less superficial than the solutions offered by the leaders themselves. At best, such leaders have an appropriate moment of glory which quickly fades away.[12]

The term charisma either means more than that or is so flexible that it applies to virtually all leadership situations and cannot be taken seriously. I will attempt to show that the term is meaningful; that it applied to Nkrumah, particularly during the years 1949 to 1954 (reaching its peak in 1951-52); that it began to decline rapidly after that; and that its decline had important structural consequences, most particularly in the establishment of a single-party "mobilization system."

Max Weber, of course, used the word flexibly to describe a normative residual category sandwiched between two stable types of authority, the traditional and the rational-legal. More explicitly, he defined charisma as "resting on devotion to the specific and exceptional sanctity, heroism, or exemplary character of an individual person, and of the normative patterns or order revealed or ordained by him (charismatic authority)."[13] He explained: "The term 'charisma' will be applied to a certain quality of an individual personality by virtue of which he is set apart from ordinary men and treated as endowed with supernatural, superhuman, or at least specifically exceptional powers or qualities."[14] These include divine powers in healing, the hunt, and so forth, exemplified by a Shaman or religious leader, like Joseph Smith (about whom Weber had some doubts) and, more interesting for our purposes, Kurt Eisner, the Bavarian Communist leader who, in Weber's words, was "carried away with his own demagogic success." The criteria established by Weber were exemplary devotion, which the leader demands; the communality of his followers; and the significance of the leader's will and its orientation to the future, which, although rejecting personal gain, nevertheless allows booty and corruption (bribery, "gifts"), rather than rationalized economic activity.

Edward Shils, employing "charisma" in the context of new nations, follows Weber's usage. He sees modern politics as a result of the change from traditional to rational-legal authority. Charismatic leaders facilitate this transition by their ability to attract a populistic following and by means of personalistic rule rallying support for highly generalized goals, such as independence and self-government. For Shils, the charismatic element is based on the leader's capacity to sustain a shift from traditionalistic norms. These are temporarily displaced onto the leader himself, and by a sort of alchemy ("grace"), he transforms them into a more generalized set of modern norms, thus producing a new standard for and type of behavior.

The countries with underdeveloped economies are primarily peasant countries and their national unity is quite new and fragmentary. The uneducated classes are rooted mainly in local territorial and kinship groups; sometimes they are dependents of feudal magnates to whom are directed whatever wider loyalties they have. They do not have the strong sense of nationality which drives the leaders of their country, who are often the creators of the nation and not merely of the new state. These leaders are strong and creative persons who have broken away from the bonds of the old order—the bonds of kin and family and local territory. Even when they claim to speak in behalf of the deeper traditions of those whom they would lead, they have departed from the actual traditions of the culture in which they originated. They are "nationalized" and "politicized" and therein lies their chief novelty. The majority in the state, by contrast, lives in sometimes unthinking, sometimes obstinate, attachment to its traditional symbols. Most of its life is "pre-national" and "pre-political."[15]

Shils also points out that most leaders of this kind are socialist in outlook, and their problem is to develop new motivational patterns likely to produce greater efficiency and better motivation to work.[16]

Both Weber and Shils stress the short-lived quality of charismatic leadership, and both are concerned with the degree to which charisma can affect behavior before such leaders begin to lose ground. Weber discusses the various forms that the transformation of charisma can take, while Shils focuses on the situation that arises when populism becomes less than supportive, disguising hostility and opposition. Charismatic leaders seeking to remain in office under these conditions take steps to protect themselves: They become aloof, where they had been open and accessible to the public; they surround themselves with the trappings and finery of political authority; and they rely heavily on military and police protection and recruit leaders more for their loyalty than for other and better qualities. When charisma declines, the leader characteristically becomes a despotic, uneasy, and certainly undemocratic strong man. The Weber-Shils formulation can be applied to certain new nations where the conflict between traditional and modern values creates a moral vacuum, manifested in structural conflict and behavioral ambiguity. A heroic leader can step in and, if not bestow "instant political grace" by forming new normative standards associated with his own pronouncements, at least give the appearance of doing so.

119

In Ghana, a vague ideological mixture of nationalism and socialism emanating from Nkrumah appeared to define new social norms against which more parochial ones had to give way. Such a combination of appeals was also designed to give the common man a stake in society. If charisma in the Weber-Shils formulation is one side of the coin, populism is the other.

Although I accept this formulation in general, I do not believe that it obtains in such simplistic fashion. The Ghana case (and others as well) indicates that the Weber-Shils usage is too vague. Rarely does the conflict between tradition and modernity occur in such a manner as to produce normative or behavioral schizophrenia, on the one hand, or a normative vacuum, on the other—although behavioral ambiguities may at times have pressed individuals. A sharp normative breach never occurred in Ghana. As David Brokensha suggests in his study of the Ghanaian town of Larteh:

There is clear evidence, from many sources, of the nature and extent of social change in Larteh, that is of changes in specific social institutions. This evidence does not support some of the more commonly held stereotypes, which hold that (a) change necessarily means social and psychological conflicts; (b) contemporary Africans are "men of two worlds"; (c) economic progress leads to individualism and the "breakdown of traditional culture."[17]

Whatever the many merits of the Weber-Shils formulation, neither Weber nor Shils goes far enough in specifying the conditions that give rise to charisma; nor do they articulate with sufficient precision its *modus operandi.*

Indeed, charisma can arise in part when the increase in modernity is not met by a proportioned decline in "traditionalism." Then a charismatic leader is part traditional and part modern.[18] This happened in Ghana. Despite important changes in the structure of authority and rule, traditionalism flourished to a surprising degree and continued to provide the normative basis of propriety. Operating through customary beliefs and practices, traditionalism affected the substance and style of Nkrumah during his charismatic period. If it pitted Nkrumah against the chiefs,[19] a kind of charismatic dialectic resulted which combined the two opposing tendencies. Nevertheless, the Ghana illustration also points up the value of the Weber-Shils formulation. Charisma must be regarded as a normative phenomenon on the basis of which political legitimacy is established. Its role, according to Shils, is to establish authority in new nations which previously were not national units. Shils emphasizes the need to breathe life into what would otherwise remain artificial creations lacking solidarity. For him, the ultimate test of such normative power is whether or not it can affect public behavior, but this "behavioral" impact cannot easily be shown. The Weber-Shils theory of charisma—from norms to behavior—is inadequate here because it lacks a structural variable.

Of course, this normative emphasis does not mean that charismatic leaders will be more successful than the more ordinary popular ones in carrying out basic programmatic goals. For example, the actual opportunities open to most African leaders are narrow. Political leaders there all find themselves with much the same set of options. The major difference lies in the effort made by charismatic leaders to change norms and thus alter the structure of public motivation so that those opportunities will be widened. The failure these efforts usually meet can in some part be attributed to the early stage of development of most African countries. Charismatic leaders are not likely to realize their wider claims under such circumstances. Charisma as a normative phenomenon can only affect behavior when it consolidates itself in a new structural system. When development is small, this is difficult to accomplish. Certainly the attempt to do it in Ghana failed.[20]

We can, therefore, limit the application of the term "charisma." It is likely to arise where there exists an attenuated normative situation which, although it may not challenge pre-existing norms directly, allows new combinations; where behavioral situations show a more random basis for the selection of normative alternatives than is presupposed by an institutionalized acceptance of any one particular set, traditional or modern.

A charismatic leader does not require a large number of devoted followers so much as a relatively small band of disciples who can create a movement and gather support. These disciples need a strong set of beliefs and commitments that enable them to validate their actions and to sanction otherwise unsanctioned acts. Charisma is one method of providing them with these. Nkrumah succeeded with a small group of party associates, but he and his disciples failed completely on the structural side because they were not able to create a new system. They could not mobilize effectively, nor restructure roles and social relationships, nor change the pattern of normative life and public behavior. Instead, life in the villages became poorer. The economy was ground down to pay for the regime —the fate of all charisma in countries with low rates of development. Leaders in these countries can symbolize unity and freedom, but lack the means to create the society they promise. The political kingdom remains elusive; and what it gains temporarily in power, it loses in innocence. Charismatic leaders are rarely prepared for the results.

As the new National Liberation Council works to create a democratic constitution in Ghana today, it is attempting to avoid some of the dilemmas of power in a poor country. Nkrumah has been repudiated. On the day after the revolution, women chalked their faces and wore white in the villages—traditional symbols of rejoicing. Nkrumah's former associates have turned against him. The C.P.P. seems to have vanished, yet Nkrumah's ghost continues to hover. Like Napoleon at Elba or Perón in Madrid, he waits to be recalled. His most important achievement was to confront colonialism, racism, and revolution in an African context. If this gift of grace was small, it was hardly insignificant.

The Populist Origins of Charisma in Ghana

As already suggested, charisma is not merely a matter of personal popularity. Overt signs of popularity, however, may indicate spontaneous affection and devotion leading to an acceptance of hitherto unsanctioned action. During his charismatic period, Nkrumah could always attract crowds, was frequently hoisted on the shoulders of party supporters, and in general was the object of much public festivity. He was extolled in "hi-life" songs, and the market women wore his picture on their clothes. These actions demonstrated affection and some attachment to his person as a symbol (or advertisement, perhaps). Such public predisposition in his favor created a certain "space," so that his immediate followers were able to act in ways that would normally have brought public disapproval. Still, Nkrumah's charisma really applied only to a small band of followers who accepted his hortatory language. This language substituted nationalist and socialist symbols for Christian ecclesiastical ones (and with about the same precision). Emphasis on political unity provided this group with a vague, but useful political charter composed of an organizational dash of Leninism (democratic centralism) and a claim to represent the public as embodied in direct demands to participate in power.[21] Nkrumah would touch upon a wide range of grievances in order to obtain from the wider public a certain "normative exemption,"

122

which extended even to traditional issues. For example, he appealed to groups who were forced against their wills into the Ashanti Confederacy when it was restored in 1935 (which occurred in several of the Brong areas of Ashanti). The dissident chiefs or former chiefs, young men restive under chieftaincy control, and others who had reason to be discontented could be brought together through the amalgamation of grievances, new and old. Although charisma was directly relevant only to a core group, such tactics created a wider supportive public that extended the "normative exemption" and included, most significantly, the urban lower-middle class (rather than the urban lower class, the latter being composed merely of northern migrants who performed the most menial jobs in the towns and were regarded as *declassé* in both ethnic and class terms). The result during the charismatic period was a "movement," rather than an effectively organized party. A loose and diverse following joined with a charismatic nucleus composed primarily of journalists, pharmacists, teachers, ex-servicemen, and small-scale businessmen—or those possessing a variety of entrepreneurial talents that could be employed for organizational purposes. If one appeal was to dissidents on the basis of ethnic life and tradition, another was to dissidents on the basis of class mobility. The first was traditional; the second, modern. The reconciliation of both was the normative indicator of charismatic power. The charismatic appeal, thus, was most effective for the nucleus of disciples and for those groups of "strategic marginals" who sought a new mode of political participation, even though for them the normative element was quite shallow.[22]

Ghana was, of course, by no means unique. The need for better social integration was visible in almost all colonial territories after the war. Many African countries went through similar political crises: urban unrest, trouble with the chiefs, rural backwardness, inadequate educational and occupational opportunities—all leading to bitter anticolonial feeling. Such a politically charged atmosphere resulted in rioting in Ghana in 1948, in Uganda in 1949, in the Ivory Coast in 1950, as well as elsewhere.[23] A change in outlook between generations was also occurring which—in a context of bad housing, outmoded colonial patterns of paternalism, and repression—was aggravated by rising demands from political leaders and ex-servicemen who had spent their readjustment allowances during a period of high prices and postwar shortages. Why, then, did charisma arise in Ghana first?

In Ghana, the United Gold Coast Convention (the particularly nationalistic organization which preceded the C.P.P.) had made strenuous efforts to transform unrest into a major political force. Although it was not successful, it helped prepare the ground for Nkrumah and his charismatic appeal. Indeed, the failure of the U.G.C.C. is as significant as the success of Nkrumah. The organization included most of the best political brains in Ghana, but lacked the normative appeal of Nkrumah and offered none of the new structural solutions to Ghana's problems that could apply to the "strategic marginals." In contrast, Nkrumah not only created an organizational nucleus and secondary leadership, but by means of a coalition of strategic marginals built up political momentum in both rural and urban areas. This required good local organizational work, effective leadership, and a combination of normative appeals and structural programs capable of winning the support of the youth (particularly in the southern part of the country and to an important extent in the non-Ashanti divisions of the Confederacy and even among the younger elements of the Confederacy itself, including the Ashanti Youth Association). Once realized, the combination of dissident marginals with the youth formed the basis for the charismatic following. This combination was critical since both groups—strategic marginals and youth—are likely to be the most dissident in the society and, because their roles are the least institutionalized, to have the least coherent and most vulnerable values. After the war, their acceptance of traditional discipline had declined, and their antagonism was directed against the control exercised by colonial officials, missionaries, or mission-trained teachers.

When the C.P.P. began to gain ground as a populist movement among the groups most likely to challenge authority, a larger and more passive part of the population became vulnerable to Nkrumah's appeal less on positive grounds than on negative ones. They sought to prevent him from driving too deep a wedge between generations, family, and clan. Since the C.P.P., which promised such large benefits, also had the capacity for exceptional mischief when opposed, it seemed easier to "go along" with Nkrumah. When the older nationalists realized what was happening, they made common cause with the chiefs. The chiefs, however, were already under attack from the strategic marginals and the youth. Thus, the most responsible groups in the community—the chiefs and the older, more established political leaders—had underestimated the threat of Nkrumah for too long and were isolated. They did not comprehend their situation until after the general election in 1951, and by then it was too late. They formed an opposition that tried to exorcise Nkrumah as a figure of wickedness, but the results they achieved were quite the opposite of those intended. By accepting the issue as normative, they increased Nkrumah's charismatic significance; by transforming conflicts of interest into conflicts of value, they helped validate his claims; by polarizing the issues, they forced the general public to separate itself from the seemingly isolated and petulant group of chiefs and senior politicians and to opt instead for populist power. Under the circumstances, despite the narrowness of the group for whom Nkrumah's charisma had normative and behavioral consequences, a wider group provided him with the shelter of a "populist umbrella"—what I have called "normative exemption."

During the charismatic period, Nkrumah did not have to bear direct responsibility for ill-conceived actions or for the failure of his policies. The chiefs did; they were agents of administration. Moreover, since Ghana was not yet independent, the British could also be blamed for Nkrumah's mistakes; indeed, the British maintained effective administration until well after their official departure, although representation was increasingly democratic. Nkrumah had not yet declared war on the opposition. Several key C.P.P. leaders thoroughly enjoyed the parliamentary game and were good at debate. Thus, although there were fears that a strong central government would not give sufficient protection to local and individual needs after independence, few worried that Ghana would turn into a police state. (Outright totalitarianism was in bad odor all around.) The parliamentary system favored populism, and democracy helped the party organize constituency parties. In even the smallest villages, the pennant of the C.P.P. symbolized political participation of one sort or another.[24]

Nor should one ignore the attractiveness of the C.P.P. It provided novelty and local color in contrast to the drabness of the old-style politicians and the officials of the British administration. The C.P.P. offered a new panoply of ritual and dance that had previously been the precinct of traditional politics. Another factor, in a more practical vein and at the local level, was the British government agent. Although he may have agreed with the chiefs in private that the C.P.P. middle leadership was a bad lot, he cooperated with Nkrumah all the same. If a C.P.P. leader overstepped his bounds too drastically, however, it was still possible to take him to court or to apply pressure, at least, to the C.P.P. itself. Legal processes were, if anything, being improved.

At the same time, the C.P.P. favored Africanization of the civil service, expansion of education, and other measures aimed at winning support of African intellectuals. (In these early days of partial power, Nkrumah was surprisingly successful with the intellectuals too.) It was a period of general prosperity and stability. The mood was hopeful and marred by few incidents (such as the Anlo tax riots) in which people were killed. Individuals could become significant in their communities simply by becoming members of the C.P.P. The majority of the recruits to the party, as well as its sympathizers, were participating in national politics for the first time. It was not a matter of winning over adherents from some other group.

The movement consisted of a small group of effective leaders around Nkrumah, including Gbedemah, Botsio, and Baako; staff on a militant newspaper, the *Accra Evening News;* a semiliterate, but willing group of up-country hands; and rural and urban groups of strategic marginals who addressed their efforts primarily to organizing constituency parties and using the support of the British to make themselves more credible. The organizational jobs themselves were simple. The accounts did not need to be kept very well. The offices were often little more than hangouts for occupational "dropouts," and the benefits were quite often handouts. It was possible to capitalize on the apparent powerlessness of the authorities: chiefs, British, and "betters." In rendering the "true" authorities powerless, Nkrumah created power for himself. Such power needed not so much substance or effective organization, as control over parliament. Charisma occurred in the context of a parliamentary democratic framework—the need to organize for elections, the manipulation and distribution of posts and favors, and the monopoly of power these provided. The democratic framework established in 1950 and enlarged in 1954 was the structural basis of charisma and the expression of the power and organization of the C.P.P. When it became widely realized that the goal of self-government was close at hand, that the British would depart, the parliamentary framework became vulnerable, and charisma began to wane. When it did, the opposition—in the form of the National Liberation Movement—put forward counternorms in the latter part of 1954, and a serious struggle between norms of authority ensued. By 1955, the situation had reached the proportions of civil war—a state that lasted well into the first year of independence. By then, it was no longer a matter of charisma, but a classic struggle for power.

These points have been discussed elsewhere, and the outlines are clear enough. During the charismatic period, Nkrumah came out strongly against tribalism, but not against chiefs; against religious conflicts (especially in the case of Muslim and Christian), but not against religion; against "divide and rule"—that is, colonialism—but not against the Commonwealth. During the peak of the charismatic period, there was comparatively little dissension on key issues of over-all policy. As was inevitable in such a poorly organized party, there were internal party problems, particularly in Ashanti. Despite these difficulties, the C.P.P. won the 1954 general election handily, a plague of candidates standing as C.P.P. "independents"—candidates not officially approved. As Dennis Austin puts it:

In June and July 1954 there was hardly a sign of the conflict that was soon to break out. At the national level, all was quiet and events took their expected course. Nkrumah submitted his list of names of the first all-African cabinet to the Governor. The new parliament met for the first time under the 1954 constitution, and Sir Emmanuel Quist was reappointed Speaker. The government then announced a detailed program to prepare the country for the grant of self-government, now confidently expected.[25]

Two events portended a break in the charismatic period. The 1954 phenomenon of C.P.P. independents (candidates standing as C.P.P. without party backing and quite often in opposition to the regular C.P.P. candidate) showed the weakness of party organization. Also crucial was the public reaction to the government's attempt to fix the price of cocoa below the market level. This was not simply a matter of price. For the first time, the cocoa farmers were made to realize their vulnerability to government—a vulnerability without the usual possibilities of appeal. In the midst of well-founded rumors of misappropriation of cocoa funds by the C.P.P., an Ashanti-sponsored popular nationalism emerged. The local populists in the C.P.P. were now regarded not as political saviors, but as hoodlums. Moreover, the traditional senior village authorities sought to re-establish themselves at this time. They professed amity and friendship in the villages, but were also willing to use C.P.P. techniques (such as "Action Groupers," against C.P.P. "Action troopers").[26]

By 1955, it became apparent that a combined opposition using all forms of counternorms—religious (the Muslim Association Party) and ethnic (the National Liberation Movement)—was likely to capture two of the country's four regional territories: the Northern Territories, which had remained largely aloof from C.P.P. politics, and Ashanti. A third, Transvolta-Togoland, also had a strong anti-C.P.P. movement, as did the largest state in the coastal region, Akim Abukawa. In addition, the Ga were increasingly opposed in Accra. By now, charisma was dead. The question was whether or not the C.P.P. as an organization was finished. It was not; despite all these forms of opposition, the C.P.P. managed to win the general election in 1956 just prior to independence. It had showed considerable organizational resilience. It was not merely a paper organization, although to what extent the parliamentary system and the British civil service sustained it is difficult to say. The C.P.P. survived under great pressure in 1955-56, but for a year after independence it remained dangerous for a C.P.P. minister to go to Ashanti.

Nkrumah as a Charismatic Leader

Handsome, small, Nkrumah had a natural grace and elegance, a finely shaped head, and a certain delicacy of manner. He was direct rather than devious. His voice, both deep and melodious, had a practiced resonance that audiences found attractive. He radiated warmth and attentiveness. In conversation he appeared to give undivided attention, listening carefully as if seeking advice and maintaining a solicitous manner. He lacked ordinary vanity, but had rather more than his share of delusions of grandeur. He regarded himself in the tradition of great "thinker-politicians," a sort of cross between Ghandi and Lenin (depending upon which ideological mood he favored and whom he wanted to impress). Yet he was not really intellectual. He could give the appearance of sweet reason, and he radiated common sense, which seemed to render his more radical or ideological statements harmless, as if they were so much political window dressing. He could imply sincere devotion to radical ideas; but by shifting his emphasis, he was a radical to the radicals, a liberal to the conservatives, an Afro-American to the Americans, a British-African to the British, an *African* socialist to the nationalists, and an African *socialist* to the Marxists.

He was an inadequate parliamentarian and could be made to look foolish by skillful debaters like William Ofori Atta. His temper was short; when angered, he could be quite irascible, make sudden judgments, and treat his associates like pawns. When he wanted something, he used personal reassurance and charm, directness and patience. When "crossed," he was unpredictable. He enjoyed the company of intellectuals, but primarily when they acted as his attendants. He was a master at quick interviews. Although he could give personal consideration to others, he used everyone. When speaking at village meetings, he was careful to touch on some important local issue and to give the appearance of attempting to solve the problem. He played the role of a new kind of chief, one who wanted to be a socialist theoretician as well as a leader. He was conscious of his youth, resentful of age. Although he enjoyed politics—especially when the C.P.P. won a difficult by-election or defeated an opponent—he was not very brave nor decisive, except in situations where the decisions were clear. He always made sure that there were a few wise heads around him to assist in making decisions and to serve as scapegoats if something went wrong. During the charismatic period, these were mainly British. Later, the task was taken on by George Padmore for Pan-Africanist purposes, by Americans for the Volta Development Scheme, and by a miscellaneous combination of refugees for a variety of other purposes. His most loyal follower was Kofi Baako (originally the head of the League of Ghana Patriots and subsequently Minister of Defense), a tough, energetic, and intelligent man who helped promote Nkrumaism as an ideology.

Nkrumah was well educated by Ghanaian standards (Achimota, Lincoln University, the London School of Economics) and well connected (Azikiwe, the Congress of Peoples Against Imperialism, participation as a co-chairman at the 1945 Pan-Africanist Congress). Influential with the intellectual wing of the Negro community in the United States, he also had a sentimental attachment to the Garvey movement. He came originally from a small ethnic group along the coast (Nzima) and from a "good family."[27] He remembered his friends and cared little for money. He had intimate relationships with Caucasians, particularly Marxist English girls, who continued to write to him after his return to Ghana and to whom he gave repeated assurances that he would never "sell-out"— no matter what appearance his tactics presented. He had become skilled at oratory and public speaking, and had a good sense of the symbolic power of language. Frequently he used evocative expressions that could be interpreted in various ways. "Positive action," for example, was the C.P.P.'s "revolutionary" program, which covered any activity that seemed useful. Nevertheless, his rhetoric gave the appearance of a deep, moral involvement, which on closer inspection was lacking. "Tactical action," which might have otherwise been called opportunism, became a form of cleverness at outsmarting enemies—above all, the British.

Yet for all his charm, Nkrumah remained a deeply suspicious man. He trusted only a few intimates; even these, he knew, could betray him; disloyalty or psychological betrayal offended him most. He could be ruthless, but he could also play the magnanimous chief—provided sufficient begging for grace (in the traditional Ghanaian manner) had been undertaken beforehand. He could accept the idea of having enemies, but he could not accept opponents. A Ghanaian was either with him or against him. An outsider or expatriate could keep his own opinions, as long as he did a job. Nkrumah was not a racist.

About his private life, there is considerable conjecture. He was said to have married early, and had a son, who studied medicine in England, and several children by various mistresses. His marriage to an Egyptian Christian was entirely unannounced and took even his close friends by surprise. He continued to have a variety of mistresses—English, South African, and West Indian.

In the arts, he was quite uneducated and had little appreciation of African art, except when it expressed something unique in African culture. He was interested in African symbolism, but awkward with it, trying always to find something unique, but not "feudalistic." On such matters, his rather "vulgar Marxist" orientation confused him, but he was always willing to listen to creative people, such as Effua Sutherland, poetess and playwright and a founder of the Ghana National Theater. He saw in African art the opportunity to remedy a historical record that classified African culture as primitive; he viewed this art as a political symbol, not an aesthetic one. On the whole, he had bad taste.

The appellation "showboy," which the Ghanaians gave him during his earlier period, remains a good one. He had a good sense of personal drama and role. He observed himself and his own performance with pleasure. In this respect there was something of the small child in him. He lacked maturity and wanted to share his achievement with others, to make them pleased at his success. Within the limits of his suspiciousness, he was also very gracious and quick to forgive.[28]

He would shift from one type of personality to another without apparent inconsistency. Before independence, he could meet in the cabinet room of Christiansborg Castle, where a British cabinet secretary provided the working papers and careful staff work, to discuss parliamentary business. Government business was resolved according to approved canons of rationality. Arguments turned on fiscal necessity, efficiency, need, and development. Cabinet minutes during the charismatic period show issues to have been well considered and decisions carefully worked out. The Governor, Sir Charles Noble Arden-Clarke, helped by pointing out possible difficulties and problems, and Nkrumah was usually open to such advice.[29]

Nkrumah was well briefed by his civil servants. He discussed matters with the permanent secretaries, who provided him with the findings of commissions of enquiry, facts, technical advice, and so forth. The administrative class was sustained by civil servants trained in a system of higher education that was elitist in structure. Overseas study, special courses, and degrees were common. African civil servants moving into the administrative class adopted the same style of life as British civil servants. Church, school, cultural association, and charity constituted the focus of the civil servant's life. The civil service, which almost tripled during this period, remained more hostile to Nkrumah than any other group, except possibly the university staff.

Rather weak politicians like Nathaniel Welbeck or key party people with or without parliamentary posts could call meetings suddenly on their own initiative if a crisis occurred. Cabinet ministers would respond to an urgent telephone call, pile into cars, and rush to Botsio's house or elsewhere, while action-troopers hung about on guard. Big decisions could be made at a moment's notice on the basis of very little knowledge or planning. The party side of things was a little like the Mafia, with elements of favoritism, fraternalism, graft, petty corruption, local tyranny, and petty harassment.

These two faces of Nkrumah's Ghana became blurred as time went on. Public statements expressed sentiments for parliamentary institutions as well as appeals to party unity. The one led to the party secretariat; the other to the Cabinet secretariat and the administrative class of the civil service. Between party officials and administration officials there was real antagonism. In general, civil servants had little use for Nkrumah and remained oblivious to his "grace-bestowing" powers, while the party officials formed the charismatic "nucleus" for whom charisma meant everything.

In the process of the struggle over power between traditionals and non-traditionals, a conflict gradually transformed into an attack on British rule, Nkrumah tried to redefine modernity—to make it African, not British—and at the same time to make tradition corporate and socialist. Socialism became traditionalism; nationalism, modernity. Subsequently he opened an attack on the bureaucracy, waged as a conflict over two principles of rule: populism versus functionalism. Mass support channeled through the party was the basis of the first; the civil service represented the second. The personal factor always remained important, but conditions during the charismatic period favored him. In his show, voice, style, awareness of local problems, ability to pick out individuals in a village and give them power as a form of grace, Nkrumah presumed to the powers of a chief—the super-chief who would protect the people against the mischief of lesser chiefs. He used every device and institution, even the Asafo companies and other tribal groups. Indeed, in the rural areas, the party became a sort of tribal organization. Just as a man from one village could get help in Accra from an association formed of immigrant kinsmen, so the more impecunious and adventuresome young villages could seek similar aid from the local C.P.P. official.

This personalistic and traditionalistic role extended to the secondary leadership as well. When the C.P.P. headquarters was located over the Narrows Drugstore, party chiefs were always accessible. In the back courtyard, the C.P.P. Peugeot 203 vans—painted in party colors with loudspeakers on top—were parked or repaired. This area was usually crowded with young boys and minor C.P.P. hangers-on, who slept on the balcony, ate in the courtyard, relieved themselves along the walls, ran errands, and served as messengers, while the senior officers—like Boi-Doku, Propaganda Secretary, and Madame Hannah Cudjoe, a Women's Organizer and later Chairman of the National Day Nursery Movement—held organizational sessions, checked finances and party lists, planned party meetings and conferences, and so forth. Nkrumah's presence always hung in the air. He would come to headquarters, frequently very early in the morning, and, sitting in front of his portrait, discuss party business and listen to petitions and grievances. Loose papers and old manifestoes were piled on the floor. Party cards and copies of the constitution were scattered on the dusty tables; old

British left-wing books and pamphlets, mostly written after the war, mildewed in the lopsided bookcases. It was ramshackle and familiar, accessible and friendly, with a hint of violence and menace, which, nevertheless, rarely materialized. It was part of the slum.

Indeed, during the charismatic period some of the party leaders, like Kofi Baako, still lived in the slums of Jamestown. When Baako was forming NASSO, the National Association of Socialist Youth Organizations, I visited him in his single-room porch dwelling on the second floor of a ramshackle Accra house. Most of his belongings were piled on the iron bars of his mosquito netting; his bed was unmade. There was one electric light bulb hanging from the ceiling. The floor was very shaky. He was not often there. (His permanent residence was in Cape Coast, his home.) Later he lived in comparative luxury. Later, too, the party was to build large office blocks in an empty field.

A few young party ideologues retained an austere style. For example, Joseph Sigismondi, then a young clerk in the Aglionby Library and a member of the League of Ghana Patriots, lived in a small, clean, cement cell belonging to a Syrian garage owner and filling-station operator. The sound of the mechanics doing their work and the smell of grease and oil contrasted with the spareness and cleanliness of the walls. On the floors were neatly piled copies of the (then) *New Statesman* and *Nation,* publications of the left in general, as well as copybooks and textbooks. Sigismondi was trying to pass the Cambridge School Certificate through correspondence courses. He was a revolutionary with a "shining morning countenance." For him Nkrumah was the reincarnation of Lenin—although he had doubts about Nkrumah's revolutionary perseverance.

Such feelings were shared by others. Even at the height of the charismatic period, everyone doubted Nkrumah; that was part of the paradox. His populist followers worried that he would betray "the cause" to the British, although Nkrumah always succeeded in persuading them that tactical action was designed for the best.[30] The revolutionaries were disturbed by his opportunism and worried about his lack of ideological sophistication. But the "Marxists" were a tiny band. Their main talents consisted of an ability to talk and, much more occasionally, to write. They were used by Nkrumah as his token of comradely and fraternal links to the anticolonial world. Later they would be used more strenuously.

For each group, Nkrumah could make things "all right." Here was the value of charisma. The British found him reasonable when he could have been troublesome. The party followers, the poor, and the young gained comfort. He made them feel that their private ambitions were desirable and freed them of the inhibitions of their elders. The opposition saw him a possible super-chief, as an enemy against whom they could not unite. Hangers-on were his spies; local schoolmasters, his agents; the lorry drivers, his communications network. The British were his administrators. His system did not create power so much as unite existing forms. If it was ramshackle, it worked. His charisma became a vessel into which all authority flowed. One did not need to believe that Nkrumah was a "man of destiny" in some ultimate sense. Rather, one had to feel that "destiny" was in his hands.

The Turning Point

Charisma in Ghana was a function of a parliamentary framework. As already suggested, before independence the parliamentary system protected Nkrumah from the consequences of his own decisions while maximizing the power he could deploy. It provided an organizational rationale, enabling the entire complex of groups to work together. A predicament arose when the same system began to provide a venue for effective opposition. Nkrumah never underestimated that opposition. He knew very well how fragile was his support, and he tried to direct charismatic appeals precisely to those who were only partially "socialized" in the system and needed to rely on a personalized "authority" for sanction. As long as party politics, bargaining and compromise, seizing advantage, balancing party with cabinet decision-making worked to C.P.P. advantage, Nkrumah supported parliamentary government. Below the center, however, paradoxes remained that the parliamentary system could not easily resolve. For example, conflicts of interest were translated into conflicts of value at the local level. In disputes in local government bodies between traditional and secular authorities, each issue became defined as being for or against Nkrumah, for or against independence, for or against "revolution" (in a vague and undefined sense), for or against "the people." At the same time, the opposite was occurring on the national level. The parliamentary pattern forced Nkrumah to convert issues of value into issues of interest, to bargain over grants-in-aid, the siting of bore holes and new schools, and the support of particular candidates in return for favors and "booty" (in the sense Weber suggested that the charismatic leader rewards followers by the allocation of "spoils"). Real opposition thus emerged at the local level—to be "bought off" at the central level (producing real corruption). As a result, anger, frustration, and bitterness increased among the opposition at the local level. Particularly was this so in Ashanti, where cocoa revenue, still the largest single source of wealth for the country, was the basis for governmental financing. It is not surprising that the actual conflict between opposition and government erupted there suddenly in the autumn of 1954 in arguments over the price of cocoa set by the marketing boards. Nor is it surprising that a traditional figure, the senior linguist of the Asantehene, would head the conflict. By challenging Nkrumah, he gained the support not only of the cocoa farmers, but—most significant of all—the Asante Youth Association (which had been an integral part of the C.P.P.). Thus, the Asantehene was able to organize an effective opposition force. Traditional norms and structures were thrown against a fading charisma with such success that it looked as if the C.P.P. would become undone just as quickly as it had become established.[31]

In the beginning, the C.P.P. had championed the parliamentary cause as a method of gaining power, and its support began to wane at this point. In the end, the main support for parliament came from opposition groups. They recognized in it the kind of structure which they needed in order to survive. Despite this, Nkrumah was able to manipulate parliamentary institutions, thereby preventing the opposition from winning power. The parliamentary framework sustained power in the face of waning charismatic authority with parliament a device to establish a single-party system. Parliamentary power controlled by the C.P.P. replaced charismatic authority.

A good example of the predicament of the opposition was the issue of what constitution would come into force when the British handed over power. This was not simply a problem of a unitary versus a federal form of constitutionalism, although the parties phrased the matter thusly. Rather, it was a question of the safeguards that could be created to preserve the parliamentary system after the protective arm of residual British authority was gone. The opposition groups wanted "entrenched" clauses in the constitution that would guarantee regional houses of assembly and houses of chiefs. But the C.P.P. was so much in control that opposition groups refused to participate in hearings and inquiries conducted by the British. Instead, they attempted to petition the Crown for support, a tactic which only weakened their cause. As long as Nkrumah controlled a "legitimate" government, such end-run efforts were bound to fail. Despite an intense political campaign waged by the combined opposition (and they lacked money and experience), the C.P.P. won the general election of 1956. Independence was granted without major concessions.

Thus, during the period of 1954-56 Nkrumah could rely on parliamentary, not charismatic, authority. He concentrated his campaign on groups most likely to be susceptible to party support: taxi drivers, young clerks in commercial houses, some of the market women, and generally those who lived in slum areas and were semi-educated. (These became his urban "toughs," whom he depended on to carry out any activity, including, if necessary, frightening or disciplining other groups.) Nkrumah also supported the traditional anti-Ashantis by employing the power of central disputes, as in certain of the Brong areas long hostile to Ashanti. In such areas, pro-C.P.P. chiefs were established. (Eventually a Brong-Ahafo Region was split off from Ashanti.) To the north, which was not particularly involved politically, but where the chiefs were mainly anti-C.P.P., Nkrumah offered even greater opportunities for rural development.

On the whole, this strategy worked. Entrenched clauses of the new constitution were never put into practice. The National Liberation Movement and the broad coalition of which it became a part, the United Party, remained vulnerable to internal dissension. After independence, however, Nkrumah began to alter the political structure of the country. Through a series of maneuvers (and not without the assistance of a number of expatriate lawyers and intellectuals), he attempted to convert conflicts of value at the local level into conflicts of interest, and conflicts at the central level into conflicts of value rather than interest. The wheel turned full circle, but now the parliamentary system had to go. He used every possible device to threaten, wheedle, cajole, and divide the N.L.M. and its supporters. Such efforts met with success. Nkrumah began to reorganize marketing associations and cooperatives to force the farmers to support the government or suffer the consequences. The trade-union movement, previously independent, became part of the C.P.P. and was identified as a "vanguard" auxiliary of the party. The Young Pioneers was established to organize the youth and establish discipline. In other words, party power replaced parliamentary power, but the shape of society was corporate. The press was controlled; the university, attacked. A compliant national assembly passed a series of ordinances which abrogated most legal safeguards of individuals. These included the notorious Preventive Detention Ordinance, which allowed the government to jail people for up to five years without trial. Certain "rights" in the constitution were interpreted to be without legal force.[32] Opposition went "underground." From a fraternal, open, populist society, Ghana began to change into something else. Fear and a conspiratorial undercurrent became noticeably common. Intrigue and manipulation, factionalism and internal conflict increased until the party was so riddled with opportunism that instead of becoming a nucleus for a new society, it was a bundle of competitive interests—hardly an effective organization.

The Coup

Charisma was virtually dead by 1955; parliament was run by the C.P.P. The result was a lacuna in national political values, a weak national structure, and corrupt behavior on all sides. Nkrumah tried to rectify this situation in several ways. To revive his normative appeal, he repeatedly emphasized his role as "founder" and leader of the party. He attempted a new "scientific socialism" —under the title of Nkrumaism first and then "consciencism"— which was to lead to the mobilization of the society through its own moral momentum. This was never accomplished. Instead, Nkrumah came to treat Pan-Africanism and the African revolution as the key issue, with Ghana residual to that object. Nkrumah had no real blueprint for Ghana after independence; his was rather the art of the grand design—a fatal weakness.

The first populist stage of party organization led to the formation of a movement loosely organized and capable of winning elections, but also of provoking considerable mischief when not provided with a legitimate outlet. The problem was to make that organization responsible. As it became responsible, charisma virtually disappeared. A locally-based opposition developed which challenged the leadership of Nkrumah. While the major emphasis was on the establishment of a popular democratic and participant system, the local C.P.P. organizations were nourished and C.P.P. membership was enlarged by the party's efforts to fight and win

137

elections. As long as the parliamentary system was safe, the constituency parties were the nucleus of this movement. Power at the center depended, therefore, upon the effectiveness of the constituency parties.

When Nkrumah turned against parliamentary government, however, he also turned against the constituency parties of the C.P.P. Once it became clear to him that the parliamentary framework threatened his regime, he not only eliminated the opposition, but rendered the constituency parties impotent. With each case his tactics were different, but the end product was the same. He put opposition leaders in jail or forced them to flee the country. (In the case of traditional leaders, he was able to enforce discipline by a series of ordinances which reduced their powers.) He let the constituency parties of the C.P.P. wither on the vine. A new and corporate party structure was devised for a "great leap forward" which required tightening the party organization in favor of its more militant socialist group. The enemy became the "African bourgeoisie," and the African bourgeoisie were in large measure the constituency parties. Once the United Party had been eliminated, the constituency parties took on many characteristics of the opposition, bringing it inside the C.P.P. Where populism had been the basis of support, it now became the basis of opposition. One response by Nkrumah was to appoint to positions of local control district commissioners, as well as representatives of the auxiliaries: farmers, youth, women's organizations, cooperatives, and other organizations. These auxiliaries of the party were to replace local government and the constituency parties. Each of these groups soon became so involved in intrigue and self-enrichment, however, that they only furthered general discontent. Efforts made to stamp out corruption were largely unsuccessful, especially after 1960. The socialist appeal on the normative level had to rely on attempts to build up Nkrumah as a great Pan-African figure. The results were "petty Stalinism." A "new party structure," organized in 1959 to further the revolutionary aims of the country, remained largely a paper reform. Nkrumaism became the ideology of the revolution, but no one could make out what it meant. Thus, the structural reform failed.

Confronted with public rebuff and organizational failure, Nkrumah accelerated the pace of political change. Hoping to establish his "second coming"—his new and socialist charismatic period on a Pan-African scale—Nkrumah became president by republican referendum in 1960. Emphasis was now on discipline, and the principles of a militant one-party state were applied. But Ghanaians refused to be disciplined; they merely became more hostile to Nkrumah. By 1963, when a referendum was held to make Ghana a one-party state, everyone knew that the election was meaningless (2,773,920 affirmative and 2,454 negative votes). Nkrumah had vanquished all his enemies, but he clearly had very few friends. He now lived under conditions of extreme security. The police, military, and spy networks were expanded. He made every effort to accomplish his purposes through a mixture of threats, calls for revolutionary sacrifice, cajolery, and bribery. But a second coming did not occur.

Perhaps the most important new consequence of these efforts to transform the party into a "vanguard instrument" was the establishment of a "dual" government in which domestic politics were increasingly sacrificed for the Pan-African. On the one hand, there was the formal framework of government. Opposition was allowed to play a miniscule (but important) role for some time before it was entirely eliminated.[33] Parliament thus continued to function in some small degree, insofar as it served as a forum for grievances. Parliamentary questions continued to be asked—sometimes with remarkable frankness—by backbenchers. The government also used parliament as a sounding board and patronage device. But the government could pass any legislation it liked. Just in case of difficulty, the constitution enacted on June 29, 1960, established special powers for the first president of Ghana, including the explicit authority to "give directions by legislative instrument."[34] Parliament had passed a Preventive Detention Act in 1958 as a temporary measure to protect the government following troubles in Ashanti and alleged plots against the government. In 1964, the act was amended to give the president power to detain any citizen for "acting in a manner prejudicial to the defense of Ghana, the relations of Ghana with other countries, or the security of the state."[35] Other ordinances were passed giving exceptional powers to the government vis-à-vis the courts, foreign affairs, and punitive activities.

The Pan-African emphasis gave rise to a second government based in the President's Office and run by the National Security Service. A Special Intelligence Unit reported directly to the President's Office and to the Deputy Chief of Staff of the Armed Forces. A Central Bureau, directly below the President's Office, coordinated military affairs and technical assistance. Directly under the Central Bureau was the Bureau of African Affairs. The National Security Service ran military affairs, and the Bureau of African Affairs administered the African Affairs Center and Secret Training Camps for Ghanaian and other African Freedom Fighters. It also maintained links with "fraternal" parties, trade-union organizations, and similar groups in other African countries. The Special Intelligence Unit of the President's Office maintained its own military force, consisting of two "Guards" Regiments which became the Presidents' personal bodyguards and undertook training in four secret camps.[36] The Bureau of Technical Assistance, actually a special African service, coordinated Pan-African activities. The Bureau had five departments and various information-analysis and technical facilities.[37] The Bureau of African Affairs was the main center for coordinating these activities for the President's Office. It became more and more militant in tone and revolutionary in outlook. It held conferences, such as the Freedom Fighters' Conference of 1962, and ran the Ideological Institute at Winneba. Its Press Branch was particularly important in laying out a "correct revolutionary line," spreading Nkrumaism, and establishing a Marxist center in Africa.[38] In addition, Nkrumah had a book, *Strategy and Tactics of Revolutionary Warfare, with Particular Reference to the African Revolution,* prepared, in which excerpts from *The Selected Military Writings of Mao Tse Tung* appeared as his own. The Kwame Nkrumah Ideological Institute, with a sixty-foot statue of Nkrumah in front, became the center of Nkrumaism (its Marx-Engels' Institute) and taught a vague mixture of Marxism and nationalism. The Ghana Youth Pioneers were to be the instrument of political indoctrination. Each school in the country was to have its Young Pioneer branch. Within the G.Y.P., there were four groupings: from age four to six, it was called African Personality; from eight to sixteen, the Young Pioneers; from seventeen to twenty, the Kwame Nkrumah Youth; and from twenty-one to twenty-five, the Young Party League.

This second political structure, operated from the President's Office, was the new design for African politics. Leaders of various party auxiliaries were given titles, such as Minister Plenipotentiary and Ambassador Extraordinary, to allow them to establish counterpoint organizations elsewhere in Africa. When the party was revamped in 1962 (under the general *Program of Work and Happiness*), it was given a directly instrumental role in ordinary political and social life.[39] Instead of a realistic plan for the development of Ghana, the object was to organize for revolution. The needs of the revolution would determine the shape of Ghana's political institutions. When this became more widely understood, the forces at work to undermine Nkrumah became more determined. There were attempts on his life, and the atmosphere grew increasingly conspiratorial.

What specifically were the causes of the coup? For one thing, the cost of these activities was astronomical. The training camps, show-piece projects, organizational activities, publishing, travel, and conferences voraciously consumed available income. Financial burdens fell mainly on the rural cocoa farmers just at the point when they had been deprived of all political participation both inside and outside the framework of the C.P.P. In addition, the price of cocoa, the main source of income, dropped before the Volta Development Scheme and other industrial projects intended to diversify the future economy of Ghana could become productive. With capital already scarce, private investment opportunities were further restricted by the new revolutionary objectives. Although the new party program allowed both public and private enterprise, continuous debate over the degree of private enterprise to be allowed frightened off potential investors.

On the political side, the decline of the constituency parties only intensified factionalism in the C.P.P. Local opposition continued to rise. This was either ignored in the higher reaches of the party or identified as subversion with punitive results. Hardly a family did not have friends or relatives in Preventive Detention. In such a small country, with its extraordinarily high degree of intimacy and family solidarity, this factor could not be considered negligible.[40] Factionalism became so great that the various groupings of the party, the functional auxiliaries, and the Bureau of African Affairs were in constant competition for Nkrumah's direct sanction. Increasingly he played one off against the other. To maintain control, he allowed them to become corrupt; then he obtained the details of their corruption and, in effect, blackmailed them. Nkrumah thus used countervailing groups to maintain his power, a system which worked fairly well until he sought to control the army in the same manner. The army had maintained its old British structure intact. Increasingly bypassed by the Russian-trained Guards Regiments, it moved while Nkrumah was in Peking and enroute to Hanoi. On February 24, Major A. A. Afrifa, Colonel E. K. Kotoka, and Mr.

J. W. Harlley, Inspector-General of Police, proclaimed the end of Nkrumah's government after a brief struggle with the Regimental Guards.[41] The first radio report reminded the public:

We lived our lives perpetually afraid of prison, poverty, and un-aware of our future. Glorious dreams were continuously unfolded be-fore our eyes. And this beloved country of ours was plunged into a dark night of misery and suffering. Nkrumah and his henchmen became rich, confident, and lorded it over us with all the ruthless instruments at their disposal—security forces, prisons, and torture.[42]

Few tears were shed over Nkrumah's downfall. There was re-joicing in the streets. The life-size statue of Nkrumah in front of Parliament House was pulled down and smashed. The National Liberation Council, which took over the government, pronounced this epitaph:

Ghana's independence and freedom meant to Kwame Nkrumah . . . per-sonal freedom to act as his whims and fancies dictated. He resurrected the colonial District Commissioner (but this time he was almost invari-ably a near-illiterate) and killed democratic local government in the process. His security agents were everywhere making his oppressive presence felt in every nook and corner of this country. His District Commissioners and Party hirelings were party despots scattered all over the country to keep the people in subjection.

He pressed religion into his service and came to believe he was a God. He deliberately encouraged the cult of his personality and appropriated such titles as "Katamento," "Osuodumgya," "Oyeadieyie," "Kasapreko." He was omnipotent. He was a god.[43]

An Evaluation

It is, of course, as easy to exaggerate the apparent success of Nkrumah as it is to dismiss his ambitions and efforts as being entirely fatuous. Nevertheless, what he built was not a house of cards. The party existed, but was inadequate to the many tasks attempted. The ambitions and practices of politicians as well as the acts of the government were more than empty gestures. The party and its leaders kept changing, both in role and structure—changes which had immense consequences for the people. Nkrumah failed to transform Ghana into anything like the militant party state which some people desired, but he did not stop trying. At the highest levels, integrity and a genuine regard for the people were lacking. There was never much middle leadership. Despite all this, there were ideals and honest efforts.

Perhaps the most important failure was Nkrumah. He understood neither charisma nor his normative obligations. He did not realize that charisma in a voluntaristic environment is based on populism, and that when it declined, that same populism was likely to turn the leader and his government into enemies of the people. He never confronted this problem. He tried to deflect his confrontation with the people first by appearing to sustain a parliamentary system with high political participation and then by dismantling democratic government and substituting for it a revolutionary ideal. Nkrumah lacked the imagination and skill to develop a country. He was a revolutionary without a plan—a visionary, but not a builder. The combination was a disaster—not only politically, but economically as well. The charismatic appeal of Nkrumah helped to create a populist movement which expanded the effectiveness of the parliamentary system, but also terminated the charismatic period itself. The alternative was a more authoritarian and revolutionary approach, which became increasingly oppressive at home and aggressive abroad. Could it have ended otherwise? We are left with a fascinating problem.

The events described here are paralleled in many other developing countries. Each must continue to search for the optimal political forms which are better able to provide a moral spirit, a respect for people, a means of progressive development, and some reasonable stability.

REFERENCES

1. This paper was prepared under the general auspices of the West African Comparative Analysis Project. I am indebted for many of the ideas contained herein to the members of the project: James S. Coleman, Robert A. Lystad, and L. Gray Cowan. These materials are based on research supported by the Carnegie Corporation, which I acknowledge hereby with gratitude.

2. In my book, *The Gold Coast in Transition* (Princeton, 1955), I was concerned with this merger under the general rubric of "political institutional transfer."

3. Interview with B. A. Bentum, March 31, 1967.

4. Reports of Nkrumah's personal misuse of funds seem to have been exaggerated in the press. Nevertheless, it is quite clear that he lacked a clear sense of what constituted his personal monies and those of the party

DAVID E. APTER

and, at times, the state. See the *Report of the Commission* and the *White Paper* (Accra-Tema, 1967).

5. For opposing views, see Henry Bretton, *The Rise and Fall of Kwame Nkrumah* (New York, 1966); and B. Fitch and M. Oppenheimer, "Ghana: End of an Illusion," *Monthly Review*, Vol. 18, No. 3 (July-August, 1966).

6. I recall, however, an interview with the contemporary Governor, Sir Charles Noble Arden-Clarke in 1953, when, in response to a question about the future of Ghana, he said: "It will be one cut above a banana republic."

7. This period, from 1949 to 1954, we will call the "charismatic period."

8. I would dissent from the view put forward by Aristide Zolberg in his excellent study *One-Party Government in the Ivory Coast* (Princeton, 1964), p. 323, that Houphouet-Boigny was a charismatic leader.

9. Lt. General J. A. Ankrah, *The Aspirations of Our New Nation* (Accra-Tema, 1966), p. 7.

10. In an interview shortly before his death, General Kotoko told me that the politicians and the university people were given to too much talk, and that the people needed a strong guide and central direction. He said that during the Nkrumah period people simply voted in the elections which were held in the way they were expected in order to oblige the most powerful leaders. He was increasingly doubtful that democracy could work in Ghana, but was willing to give it a try. Among the political names referred to, Akufo Addo was a former leader of the United Gold Coast Convention and one of the "original six" detained by the British in March, 1948—one of whom had been Nkrumah; Busia had been leader of the opposition; Amponsah, a general secretary of the N.L.M.; and Apaloo, a leading opposition journalist. All but Akufo Addo had either been detained by Nkrumah or exiled.

11. The students at the University of Ghana—who, by and large, consistently maintained an antigovernment attitude during the years of Nkrumah's rule—are now becoming much more restive and radicalized than ever before. To some extent, this is no doubt a part of a more general pattern of student unrest and political involvement. To some extent, however, it is dissatisfaction with the present N.L.C. government and military rule, benevolent though it might be. But the mood is radical in general, not pro-Nkrumah in particular.

12. The attempt by Runciman to reformulate the definition does not seem to help very much. Indeed rather than restricting the term, he makes it looser. See W. G. Runciman, *Arch. Europ. Sociol.*, Vol. 4 (1963), pp. 148-65.

13. Max Weber, *The Theory of Social and Economic Organization* (London, 1947), p. 301.

14. *Ibid.*, p. 329.

15. Edward Shils, "The Concentration and Dispersion of Charisma," *World Politics,* Vol. 11, No. 1 (October, 1958).

16. In my own work, I have tried to suggest that the ideological result is a mixture of nationalism and socialism, a movement between the two which combines the "primordial" attachments of the first with the more instrumentalistic qualities of the second, a new form of national-socialism. See D. E. Apter, *The Politics of Modernization* (Chicago, 1965), pp. 327-40. See also Clifford Geertz, "Ideology as a Cultural System," *Ideology and Discontent,* ed. D. E. Apter (New York, 1964). On "primordial" attachments, see also Geertz, "The Integrative Revolution; Primordial Sentiments and Civil Politics in the New States," *Old Societies and New States* (New York, 1963).

17. See David W. Brokensha, *Social Change at Larteh, Ghana* (Oxford, 1966), p. 269. Indeed, Brokensha goes on to make the point that in Larteh at least the people have "accepted, with few violent reactions, many intrusive elements in their culture; and far from being in constant conflict, socially or psychologically, they have displayed a resilience and tolerance in keeping with their values of calmness, decorum and propriety; their saying *Bekoe toko,* 'It does not matter,' reflects their feeling that one should not oppose or offer violence but accept, a feeling which has helped them to accommodate to the many changes without losing their identity or abandoning their institutions. *In this respect Larteh is typical of many other West African communities.*"

18. For example, in the important central area of Ghana, Ashanti, what was surprising was how strong the force of traditional loyalties remained even after the traditional king had been exiled for years and then limited to rule in a single division, Kumasi. When the Ashanti Confederacy was restored, the old patterns re-established themselves to a surprising degree (including the old disputes); but this also improved the quality of local government and administration along more modern lines. There were changes of course. According to William Tordoff: "The fact was that the office which Prempeh (the Asantehene, or King of Ashanti, who was restored to power in 1935 after the arrest and exile of the previous Asantehene in 1896) filled was a very old one; but the situation and the functions which he now had to fulfill were new." See William Tordoff, *Ashanti Under the Prempehs* (London, 1965), p. 361.

19. Indeed, the traditional sector of Ashanti was an important source of continuous opposition against Nkrumah and the C.P.P. See Dennis Austin, *Politics in Ghana 1946-1960* (London, 1964), *passim.*

20. Here I agree with the point made by Henry Bretton that most observers exaggerated the organizational capacities of the C.P.P. to work structural change in the society. See Bretton, *The Rise and Fall of Kwame Nkrumah,* pp. 74-76.

21. In more technical terms, I call these three functions: goal specification, institutional coherence, and central control. See my article, "Notes on a Theory of Non-Democratic Representation," *Nomos,* Vol. 10 (New York, forthcoming).

22. For many earlier followers, the appeal disappeared quickly, and they became open opponents of Nkrumah right away: for example, Joe Appiah, Kwesi Lamptey, Dzenkle Dzeu, and many others.

23. For a good discussion of the Ivory Coast riots, see Ruth Schachter Morgenthau, *Political Parties in French-Speaking West Africa* (Oxford, 1964), pp. 194-96.

24. Nor should one minimize the sheer fun and pleasure this engendered. Central and Southern Ghana is, after all, composed of villages which have a certain homogeneity and intimacy as well as traditions of local participation. In the first stages of Nkrumah's rule, the presence of the C.P.P. organizations simply enlivened the dispute—the pre-existing pattern of conflict and argumentation which had been going on for generations among the men who continuously ate together in the compounds. The blaring loudspeakers of the traveling politicians were like road shows. Old and new issues clashed—involving, in particular, the young men of whom neither the chiefs nor older politicians of the professional class were particularly fond, but who had been traditionally disrespectful of chiefs. All this formed the basis of a new vitality in the village and linked it to the center, the metropole.

25. See Austin, *Politics in Ghana,* p. 251.

26. They also "captured" control of the Asante Youth Association from the C.P.P.

27. See K. Nkrumah's autobiography, *Ghana* (London, 1957).

28. This description is based on personal knowledge of Nkrumah: observations made by his former secretary, Miss Joyce Gittens; former party officials who knew him well, such as James Markham; as well as notes, letters, and other materials filed by Nkrumah from the time he was in the United States until his second year in office and to which I was given access in 1957.

29. This information is based on interviews with senior government officials in 1953 and 1957 as well as confidential access to cabinet minutes.

30. And it seemed to work. After all, the Jagen affair in 1952 (when the liberal constitution was suspended) did not go unnoticed by the C.P.P. stalwarts, who in the last analysis doubted that the British really would go all the way to independence.

31. See Austin, *Politics in Ghana,* pp. 250-315.

32. For a description of these and other types of disciplinary measures taken by the C.P.P. government, see my article on Ghana in J. S. Coleman and

C. G. Rosberg, Jr. (eds.), *Political Parties and National Integration in Tropical Africa* (Berkeley and Los Angeles, 1964). See also my *Ghana in Transition* (New York, 1963); and more recently: Bretton, *The Rise and Fall of Kwame Nkrumah.*

33. At the same time, the number of members of parliament was increased, and certain reserved seats were made available for women.

34. See Part I of the Constitution of 1960, Special Powers for the First President. For a good discussion of the Constitution, see Leslie Rubin and Pauli Murray, *The Constitution and Government of Ghana* (London, 1961). A more up-to-date and thoughtful analysis is contained in William B. Harvey, *Law and Social Change in Ghana* (Princeton, 1966).

35. The Preventive Detention Act, 1964, Article I.

36. These camps were at Afienys, Akosombo, Elmina, and Okponglo. Russian instructors were employed first, but proved unsatisfactory. Chinese instructors were regarded as superior.

37. The departments included: OCAM states, Freedom Movements in Dependent Countries, Former British and American Territories (Liberia being considered former American), South African and Southwest African, and other African states.

38. The Press Branch published *The Spark* (weekly), *L'Etincelle* (the French language edition of *The Spark*), *Voice of America* (monthly), *Freedom Fighter* (weekly), *Pan-Africanist Review* (quarterly), *African Chronicler* (weekly), and the *Bulletin on African Affairs.*

39. Even local government areas were dismantled in 1962; the more viable among them were broken up in order to decrease their autonomous power, and more district commissioners were appointed.

40. See the account provided in Col. A. A. Afrifa, *The Ghana Coup: 24th February 1966* (London, 1967).

41. *Ibid.*

42. Radio Broadcasting Company, *Our Destiny in Our Hands* (Accra, 1966).

43. *Ibid.,* pp. 24-25.

NIKKI R. KEDDIE

Sayyid Jamal ad-Din "al-Afghani": A Case of Posthumous Charisma?

I

THE PEOPLES of the Middle East came under the West's imperial sway later than most other non-Westerners, and they have resented the experience more keenly than most. During Sayyid Jamal ad-Din al-Afghani's lifetime (1838/9–1897), the Western onslaught gained its full momentum. The British established the first European colony at Aden at the time of his birth and were suppressing the Sepoy rebellion (1857), led mainly by Muslim units in their army, when Jamal ad-Din traveled to India as a young man. At the height of his political career, he was involved in activities aimed at ending the British occupation of Egypt.

Jamal ad-Din's lifetime was a period not only of Western intrusion and Muslim resistance, but also of intense intellectual ferment among Middle Easterners. Generally the most determined resistance was offered by traditional groups in remote areas—the tribesmen under Abd al-Qadir in Algeria, the Mahdist sect in the Sudan, the Muslim recruits in the British-Indian army. In the capitals and other large cities, leading political and intellectual figures were championing the acceptance of Western patterns of administration and thought. Jamal ad-Din, however, offered a blend of traditional and modern ideas with a sharp political edge turned against the West. He was the first Muslim with an international reputation to reinterpret the Koran and the early Islamic traditions in order to emphasize the virtues of science, technology, military strength, and political unity. By deriving these virtues from Muslim rather than Western sources, he exerted an influence on believing Muslims unmatched by those who simply imitated the unbelieving West. Jamal ad-Din embodied in his teachings, his writings, and his political activities characteristic Muslim attitudes that formed in the period of struggle and came to prevail among Arabs, Persians, and other Middle Easterners.

Jamal ad-Din admired the technical and scientific achievements of the West, yet passionately struggled to break the grip that technology and military power allowed the West to establish over the Middle East. He despised the conventional forms of Islamic devotion that, in his view, condemned the masses to ignorance, apathy, and subjugation. He attempted to instill a vision of Islam that would reflect the glories of the classical period of Muhammad and the early caliphs and yet prove fully compatible with modern science, technology, and military power. In a combination of religious identification and national pride, he sought a principle of solidarity that would enable Middle Easterners to shake off the foreigner's rule.

Jamal ad-Din's activities were far-flung. He was at times orator, preacher, theologian, pamphleteer, teacher, journalist, ideologue, political organizer, adviser to rulers, secret agent, and conspirator in assassination. His activities were wider in scope than those of any prominent post-medieval Muslim, and he left a permanent imprint on many areas. In Egypt his disciples founded the school of Islamic modernism and worked to revitalize Al-Azhar as the leading theological school of Islam. In Iran he is credited with inspiring the first effective nationalist mass protest—the tobacco boycott of 1891–92 that, a quarter-century before Gandhi's first *satyagraha*, forced the cancellation of a foreign monopoly. In Istanbul he worked with Sultan Abdülhamid in promoting pan-Islam, a doctrine of which he is generally considered the foremost exponent. In Paris he gained a hearing among European intellectuals for his spirited defense of Muslims against fashionable charges of obscurantism and backwardness. His hatred of imperialism was focused on the British. Like others three-quarters of a century later he sought to enlist the help of Russia against the West. Echoes of his rhetoric may be heard in the speeches of modern nationalists like Muhammad Musaddiq and Gamal Abd al-Nasir, and also Islamic revivalists like the founders of the Muslim Brotherhood in Egypt. His political weapons were primarily those of the weak—oratory, conspiracy, assassination; but his teachings demonstrated throughout the Middle East the strength of ideology as a political and spiritual force. Few of Jamal ad-Din's innumerable schemes and combinations had any immediate success in the world of politics, and the ideas expressed in his writings do not achieve the intellectual level found among many of his successors. Yet he had a personal magnetism that proved irresistible to many who encountered him in the palaces, study rooms, or market squares of the Middle East or in the salons of Paris. His posthumous reputation is steadily growing. He is generally considered, both by Muslims and Western scholars, the single most influential Middle Eastern ideologist of his period.

To small circles of his contemporaries and to a much wider posthumous audience, Jamal ad-Din had many of the characteristics of the charismatic leader—personal magnetism, ideological innovation, and new and determined patterns of political action. Like many other charismatic figures, he lived in a period of crisis and was, in several senses of that suggestive phrase, a marginal man. Whether born in Afghanistan, as he claimed, or in Iran, as recent research has conclusively established, he came from a border area somewhat peripheral to the Muslim world within which he was active and through which his influence spread. As an Iranian, moreover, he was brought up in the heterodox minority, or Shi'i, branch of Islam.[1]

Like at least two other major leaders of nationalist movements based on a religious identity, Muhammad Ali Jinnah and Theodore Herzl, Afghani in his early life evinced little religious orthodoxy or exclusiveness. Much as the Westernized young Jinnah cooperated with the predominantly Hindu Indian National Congress, and the secularized young Herzl was an assimilationist who believed at one point in solving the Jewish question through a mass conversion of Jews to Christianity,[2] so the young Afghani believed in the unification of Islam, Judaism, and Christianity and voiced ideas that brought down upon him the wrath and persecution of the defenders of orthodoxy. Such assimilationist ideas elicited little mass response. Only when these three men turned to an essentially nationalist restatement of a widely followed religious and cultural tradition did they achieve greater success and a large following. Living before Herzl, Jinnah, Tilak, or Gandhi, Afghani was a precursor of their type of mass nationalism which, through its reshaping of religious traditions toward political activism, awakened new powers in the East.

The successful charismatic leader has often been a borderline man both spatially and spiritually—born and brought up on the margins of his own area of operation, with one foot in the old world and one in the new. Afghani was such a borderline man, who had the components needed for successful charismatic leadership. The question remains as to why his political efforts ended in failure despite his genius and partially favorable circumstances.

II

There is little information about Jamal ad-Din before the age of thirty, but in the account that Jamal ad-Din gave to his disciples in his mature years, he claimed that he was born and brought up in Afghanistan. The title "sayyid" indicates a family claim to descent from the Prophet Muhammad. Afghanistan, of course, is a country where the upper class and those who live in western regions speak Persian, but where, in contrast to neighboring Iran, most of the population belongs to the orthodox majority, or Sunni Islam. The account based on Jamal ad-Din's word continues as follows: As a youth, Jamal ad-Din showed great proficiency in the traditional Muslim fields of learning. At the age of about eighteen he traveled to India where he took up the study of Western science; later he went on the traditional pilgrimage to Mecca. The standard biography then recounts his involvement in the Afghan civil disorders of the 1860's. It says that he helped lead the army of the Amir Dust Muhammad in the siege and capture of Herat in 1863; and that after that ruler's death, he supported one of the pretenders, A'zam Khan, whom he later counseled on political reforms. The British supported another pretender, Shir Ali, and helped him displace A'zam. Because of Jamal ad-Din's great popularity, the British, it is said, did not dare expel him. Only when the new ruler, Shir Ali, began to spread lies and calumnies about him did Jamal ad-Din think it best to leave the country.

Jamal ad-Din next went to India, where, we are told, he was received with great respect and veneration, but where the British kept him closely confined and eventually insisted that he leave. When he then stayed in Egypt for forty days, he attracted great attention and admiration. Afterwards he went to Istanbul where he was received respectfully by the reformist Grand Vizier Ali Paşa and other high dignitaries, but also aroused the jealousy of the Şeyhülislam, head of the Ottoman religious establishment.

151

When Jamal ad-Din gave a lecture on crafts and industries before a distinguished Istanbul audience, it is said that Şeyhülislam distorted his words, giving them a heretical meaning, and had him expelled.

Jamal ad-Din returned to Egypt for a longer stay, from 1871 to 1879. He attracted a circle of young students to whom he expounded his modernist and rationalist interpretation of Islam. Once again his opponents are accused of distorting his ideas, making them sound heretical. Once again he rapidly acquired political influence through newspapers launched by his disciples, through his own public speeches, and through his influence on the heir-apparent, Taufiq. Upon the latter's accession, the British and various local detractors are accused of turning the new ruler against Jamal ad-Din and having him expelled.

Afterwards he went for a third time to India (1879–1882), where he is said to have been harassed by the British authorities, but did find time to write his major treatise, *Refutation of the Materialists*. Jamal ad-Din spent the next several years in Paris and London. In Paris he published his "Answer to Renan" and (with his Egyptian disciple Muhammad Abduh) an Arabic pan-Islamic newspaper *al-Urwa al-Wuthqa* (*The Strongest Link*—meaning the Koran as the bond of Muslim unity). The British Arabophile Wilfrid Scawen Blunt introduced him to leading political personages in London where Jamal ad-Din, as the self-proclaimed chief European representative of the Sudanese Mahdi, is said to have sought a resolution of the British-Sudanese conflict.

From London, Jamal ad-Din proceeded to Iran where he met the Shah, and is said to have influenced powerful men. When the Shah requested that he leave, he went to Russia for two years. Next Jamal ad-Din had an "accidental" meeting with the Shah in Munich at which the Shah is said to have begged him to return to Iran, offered him the prime ministership or the ministry of war, and asked him to reform and codify the laws of Iran. When Jamal ad-Din arrived in Iran, however, the intrigues of the incumbent prime minister forced him to take sanctuary in a Shi'i shrine, and five hundred soldiers were said to be required, at the Shah's and the prime minister's orders, to escort him out of the country.

Jamal ad-Din next went to Iraq from where he sent the chief Shi'i a religious letter that is cited as the force persuading this leader to call for a boycott of tobacco by all Iranians, forcing the cancellation of the British-owned monopoly concession. In England Jamal ad-Din received a pressing invitation from Sultan Abdül-hamid, whom he is said to have greatly influenced in the formulation of his pan-Islamic policies. Although he is said to have received numerous offers of high government posts or other political responsibilities from various Middle Eastern rulers, Jamal ad-Din spent the remaining years of his life in Istanbul where he died of cancer in 1897 at the age of fifty-eight.[3]

The mythological nature of Afghani's account of his own life can be seen in the many biographies in several languages that derive from Afghani's own word. The neat and repetitious pattern of this account alone should awaken suspicion about its accuracy. Essentially the same thing happens to Jamal ad-Din in nearly every country to which he travels—from his entry into the highest government circles in Afghanistan in the 1860's to his death in Istanbul in 1897. He is first received with the highest marks of welcome by the notables and educated persons of the country, and its rulers almost always seek his advice on important matters and usually offer him a high office, which he rejects. Then, suddenly, he is expelled or otherwise forced to leave because unfounded suspicions are aroused in the ruler by evil men or because of the machinations of the British, who are seen as following Jamal ad-Din around the world with single-minded devotion.

A rather different account of Jamal ad-Din's adult career emerges from the documents and archival sources that scholars in Iran, in Europe, and the United States have recently brought to light. There is confirmation of each of his major sojourns, but also evidence of early stops he never mentioned. There is ample proof also of Afghani's unusual ability to make a strong impression on Muslim rulers and statesmen on his first encounter with them and also of his equally remarkable propensity quickly to lose their confidence. Yet the reality is far more complex and a good deal less glamorous than the legend.

Jamal ad-Din, in fact, first appeared on the Afghan political scene in 1866, three years after the capture of Herat in which he claimed to have taken a prominent part. His advice to A'zam Khan does not seem to have concerned domestic reforms; rather it was in favor of an offensive alliance with Russia against the British. Shir Ali did not (as the legendary biography has it) owe his throne to the British, and he expelled Jamal ad-Din not on their advice, but rather because he considered him a Russian agent. There is no record of Jamal ad-Din's reception by Ali Paşa and other dignitaries in Istanbul, and it seems unlikely that the Şeyhül-islam should have been seized with jealousy of a young and unknown foreign visitor. The speech that Jamal ad-Din gave was not an important public event until it was attacked because Jamal ad-Din did, as his opponents said, call prophecy a craft. This notion was bound to seem heretical or even blasphemous to orthodox Sunnis, and his expulsion on the request of the Seyhülislam thus seems amply accounted for.[4]

Once again Jamal ad-Din's importance in Egypt in the 1870's was not so great as the official biography would have us believe; and it is doubtful that he had so much influence on Taufiq, either before or after his accession as Khedive, as he claimed. But Taufiq did owe his throne to British (as well as French) intervention. Since Jamal ad-Din just before his August, 1879, expulsion was occupied with delivering fiery speeches and organizing other political activities against these foreign powers, it was only natural that the Khedive should seize an early opportunity to rid himself of the embarrassing foreigner.

The 1880's were the period of Jamal ad-Din's most intensive literary and journalistic activity. The nature of that activity, however, comes through in rather distorted fashion in the standard biographies. It is remarkable, for example, that Jamal ad-Din should have attacked with such venom Sayyid Ahmad Khan whose ideas on acceptance of modern Western elements of technology and organization by Muslims were rather akin to his own. Afghani's book becomes explicable when it is remembered that Sayyid Ahmad Khan was the chief advocate of Muslim collaboration with British rule in India, a policy that Afghani bitterly opposed and wanted to discredit by stressing the heretical and nefarious nature of its author. *The Refutation of the Materialists* was also the beginning of a campaign by Jamal ad-Din to stress his own identification with Islam and orthodoxy at a time when a defensive pro-Islamic mood was growing in the Muslim world, partly as a result of increasing Western encroachments.

The same desire to appear as a defender of orthodoxy also explains why Jamal ad-Din and his followers took pains to avoid having his "Answer to Renan" translated into Arabic, for the article was a document of skepticism addressed specifically to a French audience. It was a response to Renan's lecture on "Islam and

Science," in which Renan had spoken of Islam in general and the Arabs in particular as being hostile to science and philosophy. In his answer Jamal ad-Din was at least as strong as Renan regarding the hostility of Islam to science and reason, but stated that all religions were equally hostile to philosophy and science, whose truths could only be understood by a small intellectual elite. Significantly, Renan in a rejoinder, agreed with most of Jamal ad-Din's points.

The standard account of Jamal ad-Din's political activities in the 1880's again is remarkable for the familiar omissions and distortions. *Al-Urwa al-Wuthqa*, for example, was widely circulated free of charge, apparently thanks to money received in part from his friend Blunt, in part from his former enemy, the ex-Khedive Isma'il, and in part from a General Husain at-Tunisi. Despite his money from Isma'il, Jamal ad-Din was openly championing in his newspaper the cause of Sultan Abdülhamid, hardly a friend of Isma'il's; he also struck a far more stridently anti-British tone than could have been to the liking of Blunt or the ex-Khedive. *Al-Urwa al-Wuthqa* folded when its financial support was withdrawn. There is no evidence whatever that Jamal ad-Din had any contact with the Sudanese Mahdi, whose European representative he claimed to be. Although Jamal ad-Din evidently was trying to attract the attention of Sultan Abdülhamid II, the many contradictory intrigues and claims of this period led the Sultan to suspect that Jamal ad-Din was an agent in a British plot to support an Arab claim to the caliphate against the Sultan's own.[5]

During the first trip to Iran in his adult life, Jamal ad-Din was indeed received by the Shah. But according to a courtier's account, Jamal ad-Din frightened Nasir ad-Din Shah by offering himself to be used as a sharp sword against the ruler's foreign enemies—the same suggestive phrase that Jamal ad-Din was later to use in speaking to Sultan Abdülhamid—and the Shah soon asked Jamal ad-Din's host in Tehran to take him from Iran. There is no evidence that the Shah sent him on any secret diplomatic mission to Russia, although Jamal ad-Din may have conceived that notion while introducing himself into the Shah's suite in Europe. Jamal ad-Din's second stay in Iran and its sequel once again were rather less dramatic than the standard biography would have us believe. There is not the slightest indication that he was offered the prime ministership or any other cabinet position. It did not take five hundred soldiers to remove him from his sanctuary and escort him across the frontier. And it was an ulama-led mass movement, more than a single letter from Jamal ad-Din, that produced the successful tobacco boycott. It is true that Jamal ad-Din's expulsion from sanctuary filled him with lasting hatred of Nasir ad-Din, and from this period onward he occasionally spoke of the need to kill the Shah. But the Shah's actual misrule was flagrant enough to be perceived by Iranians and foreigners without any need for Jamal ad-Din's propaganda and the tobacco boycott was possible only within this atmosphere of general discontent. Jamal ad-Din's one solidly successful plan was for the assassination of Nasir ad-Din Shah, carried out in 1896 by one of his disciples who had just visited the master in Istanbul.

Afghani did go to Istanbul at the invitation of Sultan Abdül-hamid, but documents now indicate that the invitation was suggested as early as 1885, years before it was accepted, and that the Sultan mainly wanted to keep his guest under close surveillance in order to stop his supposed intrigues with the British for an Arabian caliphate.[6] Jamal ad-Din in the end yielded to a combination of promises and thinly veiled threats. He played no such important role in the Sultan's pan-Islamic program as the biographies suggest, but was increasingly a prisoner in a gilded cage, permitted to publish nothing and to give no public speeches. This forced confinement and idleness, after a life in which he had always been allowed or even forced to flee from uncomfortable situations, seems to have further affected Jamal ad-Din's sense of reality. It is from his last years in Istanbul that disciples have recorded a whole series of fantastic stories about offers of high government positions and responsibilities from various oriental rulers, many of which have entered the biographical literature.[7]

What emerges from this examination of Jamal ad-Din's adult career is a legend dear to Jamal ad-Din and perpetuated by his devoted followers—one that included elements of the dramatic, the grandiose, and the paranoid. If one now turns from his adult years to his childhood and youth, the distortions are even more striking and hence their analysis becomes more revealing.

III

The most crucial circumstance established by recent research is that Sayyid Jamal ad-Din "al-Afghani" was not at all, as his chosen name indicates, an Afghan but rather an Iranian; consequently he was not brought up as a Sunni, but as a Shi'i. He arrived in Afghanistan for the first time in 1866 at the age of twenty-seven or twenty-eight and was known to everyone as a foreigner, spoke Persian in the Iranian manner, and claimed to be a Turk from Istanbul.

The most reliable account of Jamal ad-Din's youth, done by his nephew and the nephew's son, says that he was born into a family of sayyids (descendants of Muhammad) in Asadabad, a large village in Northwest Iran. As a result of a quarrel between Jamal ad-Din's father and other sayyids, the father quit the village when Jamal ad-Din was ten and went to the city of Qazvin, leaving the rest of the family behind. The two later went to Tehran and finally to the centers of Shi'i religious education in Ottoman Iraq, where the son was left in the hands of teachers. Jamal ad-Din's nephew writes that Jamal ad-Din left these cities for India because some of the local ulama (religious scholars) were plotting against him, while his grandnephew has said that this hostility to the adolescent Jamal ad-Din was due to his neglect of mandatory religious duties, like the fast of the month of Ramadan. Jamal ad-Din's grandnephew adds that his choice of India as his next destination was due to its relative religious freedom.[8] Jamal ad-Din spent over a year in India, right before and probably during the Indian Mutiny in which Muslim leaders played a prominent role. His lifelong hatred of the British probably stemmed initially from his late adolescent experiences in India, the first country in which he had contact with the disruptive effects of British rule in Muslim lands. Between 1858 and 1865, Jamal ad-Din apparently spent much time in traveling and seems to have visited Mecca, Baghdad, the Shi'i holy cities in Iraq, and possibly Istanbul—all then parts of the Ottoman Empire.

What appears, from internal and external evidence, to be the earliest remaining document in Jamal ad-Din's handwriting is suggestive of a whole series of possibilities about his character and beliefs that have scarcely been raised before. This is a "Treatise on the Crafts" by the late founder of the innovating Shaiki school of Shi'ism, Shaikh Ahmad Ahsa'i, whom some of the orthodox had condemned as an unbeliever, and is copied in Jamal ad-Din's hand-writing. At the end of this treatise, Jamal ad-Din wrote: "I wrote this in the Abode of Peace, Baghdad, and I am a stranger in the lands and banished from the homelands, Jamal ad-Din al-Husaini al-Istanbuli." After his 1866–68 trip to Afghanistan, Jamal ad-Din

wrote "Kabuli" over "Istanbuli" in red ink and also tried to obliterate "Baghdad" in red ink by writing a different word over it.[9] This
stop in Baghdad must have occurred before Jamal ad-Din's well-
documented trip to Afghanistan via Iran in 1865–66; what is intriguing is his attempt to cover his tracks. Both here and on his
trip to Afghanistan, Jamal ad-Din calls himself "al-Istanbuli" and
claims to be from Istanbul, evincing concern here, as in his subsequent use of the name "al-Afghani," to hide his Iranian origins. It
seems likely that Jamal ad-Din indeed traveled to Istanbul between
1858 and 1865, since he apparently never claimed to be from a
city or country that he had not at least visited, and such a claim
might be dangerous if he confronted someone who actually knew
Istanbul. Subsequent to his 1868 expulsion from Afghanistan, however, Jamal ad-Din is never recorded as referring to a prior visit
to Istanbul, nor is such a visit suggested in any biography—another
indication of a need to hide something about his early years. Even
more intriguing is his effort to obliterate the reference to his being
in Baghdad, a stay which he never refers to in his later accounts
of his own life. Whether this visit and the attempt to obliterate
reference to it are connected with the presence in Baghdad at this
time of the leaders of the Babi religion, a heretical offshoot of
Shaikhism, is a matter for speculation. Finally, in this same document there is the reference, repeated in later texts, to himself as
"a stranger in the lands and banished from the homelands." This
reference may confirm an expulsion from the Shi'i shrine cities or
from Iran. Thus, by his twenties, Jamal ad-Din is already denying
his Iranian origins, attaching himself elsewhere, probably showing
religious heterodoxy, and seeing himself as a wandering exile.

Jamal ad-Din's connections with the Shaikhi movement and
possibly with the Babi heresy that grew out of Shaikhism are new
discoveries that may help explain some of his ideas. Shaikh Ahmad
Ahsa'i (1753–1826), whose treatise Jamal ad-Din copied, founded
a religious movement that included many ideas taken from philosophy and from mysticism. The Shaikhis interpreted allegorically
many of the supernatural features of orthodox Islam and also stated
that, following the disappearance of the Twelfth (Hidden) Imam,
there must always be in the world a "perfect Shi'i" who was the
intermediary between mankind and the infallible Hidden Imam.
In his "heretical" talk in Istanbul in 1870, Jamal ad-Din stressed
a parallel concept—the need of every generation of mankind for a

158

philosopher who will guide them in the world. At least two and probably all three of the earliest treatises that Jamal ad-Din copied in the 1860's and carried around with him until 1891 are by Shaikhi leaders—the one by Ahmad Ahsa'i, already noted, and another one, copied in 1866 in Qandahar, by Hajji Muhammad Karim Khan Qajar, the head of all the Shaikhis in the mid-nineteenth century.[10] The Babis were a heterodox messianic offshoot of the Shaikhis whose leader in the 1840's declared himself to be the *Bab*, or gate, to the Hidden Imam, and later said that he had brought a new dispensation that superseded the Koran. Jamal ad-Din was always well informed on Babi thought, and it seems likely that the active militance, reformism, and messianism of the early Babis may have influenced his later ideas and activities. The quarrels with shrine ulama noted by Afghani's grandnephew might be connected with Shaikhism or Babism, as also might be Afghani's messianic self-image as well as his hiding of his beliefs and background.

In 1865 Jamal ad-Din entered Iran from the West (that is, the Ottoman Empire) and spent several months there, another stay to which he never referred in speaking to his non-Iranian biographers and disciples. He now reportedly made the last visit of his life to his home village, which he ignored on his two later trips to Iran, and stayed for three days with his parents, two sisters, and nephews. A family report says that Jamal ad-Din's father and others pleaded with him to end his constant traveling, but that Jamal ad-Din replied: "I am like a royal falcon for whom the wide arena of the world, for all its breadth, is too narrow for flight. I am amazed that you wish to confine me in this small and narrow cage."[11] This report of his words may be given some credence, as the comparison of himself to a bird, the need to keep moving, and the horror of being caged were often repeated in his later words and actions. After several months in Tehran, Jamal ad-Din traveled east to Afghanistan. In Eastern Iran he wrote a poem saying he had been terribly oppressed by the demons and beasts of Iran, and was quitting Iran for Turan, where he would lay his troubles before the Sultan. Another poem refers several times to Bokhara as his destination.[12] Again there is evidence of strong feeling against oppression experienced in Iran, although no source tells us what this oppression was.

In Afghanistan, Jamal ad-Din wrote in his diaries a series of personal reflections and reminiscences noting his experiments and disillusionment with various religious schools and reflecting a mystical outlook. He again speaks of himself as "the stranger in the lands, exiled from the homelands." In one piece of rhymed prose he shows that his beliefs were then, as later, the subject of controversy:

> ... The English people believe me a Russian (*Rus*)
> The Muslims think me a Zoroastrian (*Majus*)
> The Sunnis think me a Shi'i (*Rafidi*)
> And the Shi'i's think me an enemy of Ali (*Nasibi*)
> Some of the friends of the four companions have believed me a Wahhabi
> Some of the virtuous Imamites have imagined me a Babi
> The theists have imagined me a materialist
> And the pious a sinner bereft of piety
> The learned have considered me an unknowing ignoramus
> And the believers have thought me an unbelieving sinner
> Neither does the unbeliever call me to him
> Nor the Muslim recognize me as his own
> Banished from the mosque and rejected by the temple
> I am perplexed as to whom I should depend on and whom I should fight ...
> Seated in Bala Hisar in Kabul, my hands tied and my legs broken,
> I wait to see what the Curtain of the Unknown will deign to reveal to me and what fate the turning of this malevolent firmament has in store for me.[13]

New documentation enables us for the first time to form an accurate, though sketchy, picture of some of the key events of Jamal ad-Din's life before his expulsion from Afghanistan in 1868 when he was twenty-nine or thirty. This picture illustrates some of the dominant themes of his later and better-known periods. From the time of his first private writings, Jamal ad-Din denies his Iranian origin, calling himself an Istanbuli when in Baghdad and Afghanistan, and then switching to an equally fictitious Afghan origin for the rest of his life. He also refers to himself frequently as one expelled from his homeland. This self-image, combined with his reference in a poem to oppression by Iranian demons and beasts of prey who have burnt his soul, implies strong hostility to some powerful Iranians, whom he sees as having expelled him either from Iran or from Shi'i Iraq. Afghani's denial of his Iranian origins is usually attributed to his desire to present himself as a follower of the majority (Sunni) branch of Islam, rather than its minority (Shi'i) branch. Yet, when one finds this denial extending even to his most private diaries and papers, including a treatise by Shaikh Ahmad Ahsa'i, whose ideas most Sunnis would have found more heretical than those of the average Shi'i, one is led to conclude that something more than a calculus of religious acceptability is involved. As the frequent references to enemies and expulsion from the homeland indicate, events must have occurred to make Jamal ad-Din regard himself from an early age as a mistreated exile.

Also significant is Jamal ad-Din's attitude to his own family; he apparently had no contact with them between 1856 (possibly earlier) and 1865. He returned to his village for only three days in 1865, apparently rejected pleas that he stay longer, and then broke contact with them completely. Only in 1884 did he think to send copies of his widely distributed Arabic newspaper *al-Urwa al-Wuthqa* from Paris to his family in Asadabad. This elicited correspondence from two of his nephews, who wrote that they had been trying for years unsuccessfully to locate him. One nephew, Lutfallah, wished to join him in Paris, but Jamal ad-Din strongly discouraged it.[14] When Jamal ad-Din later spoke of his father, he made him a member of a noble family of Afghanistan, but there is no record of his talking about other relatives. Jamal ad-Din may have felt his family had abandoned him in childhood. In any case, he felt himself to be a deracinated exile, and his invention of a fantasy young manhood in which he helped a great Afghan Amir lead successful military battles may be a compensation for an unsatisfactory and hostile youth.

In putting forth the preceding and subsequent hypotheses about Jamal ad-Din's behavior, I recognize that psychological biographies of historical figures can never have anything like the documented certitude that attaches to some of their external actions. In addition, psychological analyses of heroes are often resented, and doubly so when a non-Muslim Westerner writes about a Muslim Easterner. Numerous studies indicate, however, that effective mass leaders, whether Eastern or Western, who devote their whole lives to a deeply held cause, tend to have a somewhat special psychological makeup and experience, as compared to their more average and colorless compatriots. In addition, striking psychological similarities often appear among heroes and popular leaders, even when they come from very different cultures. To analyze the special psychological features of a great man like Jamal ad-Din does not imply any negative judgment regarding the political and human value of the cause to which he devoted himself, nor does it indicate that he should no longer be regarded as a hero. Despite the objective and subjective problems of a psycho-historical analysis of Jamal ad-Din, it appears worth undertaking, with a recognition that its results are somewhat speculative, in order to find what light such analysis might shed both on Jamal ad-Din's activities and on other political movements in the modern Middle East.

IV

Jamal ad-Din's fantasies about his family and homeland bear striking resemblance to the widespread hero myths analyzed by Otto Rank in *The Myth of the Birth of the Hero*. In innumerable myths, the hero is raised by humble persons who are not his true, illustrious parents. After years of exile or wandering from his parental homeland, he returns and establishes his dominance through brilliance or military exploits, sometimes killing the reigning king. Rank ties the mythical substitution of parents to widespread adoption fantasies, based on the ambivalence of children toward their parents (particularly of boys toward their fathers). Such ambivalence sometimes results in a fantasized splitting of the father into a heroic good father, seen as the perfect Ruler, and a fallible or bad father. Rank's discussion refers to several Iranian examples; indeed, stories about the founders of many Iranian dynasties include themes of a humble childhood spent away from the true parents and a return accompanied by heroic military exploits.[15] The close parallel of Jamal ad-Din's fantasies to myths prevalent both within and beyond Iran suggest, as do other features of Jamal ad-Din's life, a psychological background similar to that analyzed by Rank.

Rank indicates that the child who sees himself as more talented than his parents and as having been slighted by them is especially prone to fantasize a good, illustrious father. Jamal ad-Din must early have recognized his own intellectual and leadership potential, and he may have felt slighted by a family that left him on his own from an early age. Jamal ad-Din's whole life was characterized by a search for an ideal authority figure who would treat him with respect and follow his suggestions—a search that was repeatedly followed by bitter disillusionment. His profound ambivalence toward male authority figures is shown in his initial excessive expectations of rulers, which then changes into excessive hostility. Jamal ad-Din's creation of a mythical noble Afghan father and family suggests a splitting of father images, as does the strongly ambivalent pattern of his relations with rulers. Jamal ad-Din's inability to integrate mixed feelings toward authority and his perception of himself as a mistreated exile may thus be exaggerated versions of fantasies and anxieties common in talented, sensitive, and imaginative children.

Another theme of Afghani's political life and of his repeated political failures appears already in the Afghan period—his propensity for grandiose and ultimately unrealistic schemes. In his Afghan period, Jamal ad-Din was advising the Amir to seek an alliance with Russia and to fight the British, even though the political realities of the 1860's were such that this action would be doomed, as even the anti-British Amir A'zam knew. Jamal ad-Din even hoped to draw the new pro-British Amir Shir Ali into his plans, but he succeeded only in bringing about his own expulsion. The fantasy of a successful holy war against the British recurs in Jamal ad-Din's life. Although useful as a means of arousing mass sentiment for Muslim unity, it was hardly viable on the practical level that Jamal ad-Din seems to have intended to use it.

Also typical of Jamal ad-Din's later life is his relationship with the Amir A'zam Khan. The documents show that Jamal ad-Din quickly became the Amir's most intimate adviser, demonstrating the magnetic attraction of personality and intellect that was later to be evinced repeatedly. The documents also report, however, that after a few months Afghani broke with the Amir and requested permission to leave the country. He did not (as he claimed) try to accompany A'zam on his successful attempts to regain power, but rather stayed in Kabul and tried to gain favor with the new Amir. A pattern of personal influence on holders of power followed by a break with them occurs again and again in Afghani's life. Although Jamal ad-Din seems scarcely to have had personal friends that he regarded as equals, his intellect and magnetism often gained him rapid entrée into politically powerful circles, where he usually suggested violent and unrealistic anti-British plans. Partly because of the fantastic and possibly dangerous nature of his proposals, partly because of his refusal to grant the usual deference to the powerful, and partly because he was a man who needed to control a situation and wanted to impose a total policy rather than bargain for small concessions, Jamal ad-Din almost always broke with the powerful men whom he had so quickly attracted. The rulers from whom he first hoped for so much he then attacked as being evil or misled; the good authority figure was transformed into an evil one.

Although there is not enough information to say whether Jamal ad-Din had a band of disciples before his arrival in Egypt in the 1870's, from then on one of his greatest achievements was educating his circles of disciples in Egypt, Iran, and Istanbul. Here again the relationship was not only unequal, but rather absolute. The reports of Jamal ad-Din's discussion circles indicate that he was always given the last word, while the letters his disciples wrote him are full of almost religious devotion. When disciples entered on political paths that Jamal ad-Din did not approve, he was quick to denounce them in untempered language. In many cases disciple-ship was either absolute or nothing. Muhammad Abduh, a major reformer and thinker in his own right, was an adoring disciple of Jamal ad-Din for years and wrote both to and about him in terms of the most mystical worship. For example, in a letter that Abduh wrote to Jamal ad-Din in 1883, Jamal ad-Din is referred to in terms more usually reserved for the Deity:

You have made us with your hands, invested our matter with its perfect form and created us in the best shape. Through you have we known ourselves, through you have we known you, through you have we known the whole universe . . . from you have we issued and to you, to you do we return.

I have been endowed by you with a wisdom which enables me to change inclinations, impart rationality to reason, overcome great obstacles, and control the innermost thoughts of men. I have been given by you a will so powerful as to move the immovable, deal blows to the greatest of obstacles, and remain firm in the right until truth is satisfied.[16]

After two years of close political work with Jamal ad-Din in Paris in 1884–85, however, Abduh broke with his former master, entered a reformist rather than revolutionary course of action, and rela-tions between the two cooled considerably.

In his relationships both with the politically powerful and with

164

his disciples, Jamal ad-Din needed to control the situation and to impose his own line of thought and action. This need, whatever its psychological springs, together with the grandiose and unrealistic nature of most of his schemes, helps explain his ultimate political failure. While a man of strong will, such as Lenin, who imposes on his colleagues views consonant with realities, may become a successful charismatic political leader, one who seeks to impose unrealistic views must end a political failure.

Jamal ad-Din's personal reflections and poems before age thirty also show features that were to remain characteristic of his life. First, in his long poem from Eastern Iran, he sees himself as having been persecuted by unnamed Iranians, and in several inscriptions he refers to himself as an exile, a stranger in the lands. The image of persecution and unjust treatment recurs in letters to Amir Shir Ali.[17] As noted above, in 1870 Jamal ad-Din was exiled from Istanbul because of a talk in which he allegedly referred to prophecy as a craft, not unlike other crafts. This exile Jamal ad-Din wrongly attributed to jealousy of his influence on the part of the chief Ottoman religious leader. In 1879 Afghani was expelled from Egypt by the new Khedive Taufiq, with whom he had earlier had good relations; this exile Jamal ad-Din wrongly attributed to the British or to scheming political enemies. Jamal ad-Din rightly attributed his forcible expulsion from Iran in 1891 to the Shah, for whom he thereafter expressed a burning hatred, and on whom he frequently vowed a revenge that was to be fulfilled when one of Jamal ad-Din's disciples assassinated the Shah in 1896. In addition to resentment over his various unjust exiles, Jamal ad-Din frequently voiced his conviction that he was being followed and persecuted by the British. He also told stories of personal betrayal by those in whom he had had confidence. British documents show that the Foreign Office and the Government of India did not try to keep any systematic tabs on Jamal ad-Din except in 1887, when he was writing anti-British articles from Russia. Whatever mistreatment he had received from the British was the routine treatment handed out by lower officials to anti-British figures in India and not part of a large plan or conspiracy directed specifically against him.

The two main objects of Jamal ad-Din's hostility were the British and the Shah of Iran. Interestingly, these two remained, until recently, the main objects of hostility for many Iranians, especially intellectuals. In the case of the British, the main mechanism at work in building this hostility seems to have been the same for Jamal ad-Din as it has been for more recent Iranians. Jamal ad-Din observed the disruption of Muslim culture and economic life and the oppression of Muslims on his various visits to British India, and from this he derived a picture of the British as diabolical schemers out to destroy Islam. More recently Iranians have observed the negative results of British power in their own country and from this have built up a picture of the clever British as having masterminded the major events of Iranian history for decades, if not centuries. Hostility to the Shah, both for Jamal ad-Din and for more recent young Iranians, seems to go beyond the bounds of what can reasonably be attributed to the royal power alone. One wonders if the authoritarian patriarchal character of Iranian family and social life may be related to the Iranian attribution of unlimited power and cleverness to the patriarchal Shah (and perhaps also to the British) while the individual Iranian perceives himself as being too weak to do anything but indulge in verbal or disorganized aggression.[18]

The Iranian Shah had for Jamal ad-Din an importance not shared by any other political figure, and this importance may have been tied to the Shah's position as ruler of Iran, Jamal ad-Din's renounced fatherland. Jamal ad-Din's passionate hatred for the Shah after the latter had expelled him from Iran in 1891 was quite special. Although the Khedive Taufiq and the Ottoman leaders had also expelled Jamal ad-Din, there is no record of his calling for personal vengeance on them, or even on the British, whom he disliked so passionately. Only the Shah of Iran called forth his frequently stated vows of vengeance, vows that were fulfilled when one of Jamal ad-Din's disciples returned from Istanbul to Iran in 1896 to assassinate the Shah.[19]

The documents emanating from Jamal ad-Din before his expulsion from Afghanistan also show his propensity for role-playing as well as his allied confusion about his own identity. His manufactured identity in Afghanistan is only one of a long series of roles that he was to adopt. In Istanbul immediately after his Afghan trip, he claimed to be an Afghan, and his recorded speeches show that he adapted almost immediately to the Westernizing environment of official circles in the *Tanzimat* period of government-sponsored reform. In one speech he praised highly the Westernizing and civilizing efforts of the Ottoman rulers, and he quickly got an appointment to the official and reformist Ottoman Council of Education. In Egypt, after his expulsion from Istanbul, Jamal ad-Din adapted to the role of teacher in the years before any active political life was possible. But with the beginning of the growth in political awareness in 1878–79, he took advantage of new possibilities by becoming a pioneer in oppositional journalism, political use of a freemasonic lodge, and public speech-making. The only consistent themes of his talks and writings are anti-imperialist and anti-British aims, tied to a desire to revivify the military strength and dynamism of the Islamic world. These central goals he adapted to the most varying political schemes and personal roles. In Afghanistan it was alliance with Russia against Great Britain; in Istanbul, Westernizing reform; and in Egypt and elsewhere, the attempted use of the most diverse allies to lessen British domination.

Jamal ad-Din's religious and ideological identity also changed frequently. In Afghanistan, Istanbul, and Egypt, he did not try to adopt a particularly religious posture and was suspected of heresy; but in India, he chose to write a treatise defending Islam against the attacks of all sectarians and free thinkers, the so-called *Refutation of the Materialists*. From 1883 on, he put himself forth as a leading ideologist of pan-Islam, an idea whose popularity in the Muslim world was already growing when Jamal ad-Din picked it up and became its most eloquent defender. Even in pan-Islam he was not consistent, as he varied his public support for Sultan Abdülhamid with suggestions for alternative leaders in the Muslim world. In 1884–85, Jamal ad-Din referred to himself as the European agent of the Sudanese Mahdi, whose claim to be the Muslim world's awaited messiah was opposed and denied by the Sultan. There is not a shred of documentary evidence that Jamal ad-Din had the slightest contact with the Mahdi. Jamal ad-Din's Arabophile friend Wilfrid Blunt, however, was able to use this claim to put Jamal ad-Din in contact with the governmental figures Randolph Churchill and Sir Henry Drummond Wolff, and to start him planning to work with Wolff for the British evacuation of Egypt. On returning to Iran in 1886 and again in 1889, Jamal ad-Din revealed to certain Iranian leaders that he was, in fact, an Iranian; and in his dealings with the Shi'i religious leaders during a movement against a British tobacco monopoly in Iran, Jamal ad-Din wrote and spoke as a Shi'i. In the same years that he was playing a religious role to Muslim audiences, Jamal ad-Din displayed quite a different face to Westerners, both in his religiously skeptical "Answer to Renan" and in various public and private talks to British audiences and representatives, where he stressed his political liberalism and affinity for British ideals. Near the end of his life, he spoke to his disciples of his lifelong commitment to constitutional ideals, but in fact none of his writing stresses constitutional or parliamentary rule. Indeed, one of his 1883 articles strongly criticizes an Ottoman liberal exile for demanding political reform in the Ottoman Empire, when first priority should be given to strengthening the Muslim world against the West.[20]

To a large degree, Jamal ad-Din's role-playing was responsible for what success he had, particularly for his ability to rise rapidly in the most varied environments. Certainly his claim to be a Sunni from the main capital in the Muslim world must have helped him in Afghanistan, just as his Shi'i claims aided him in Iran and his liberal claims found a sympathetic hearing among Westerners. Nor is it surprising that these contradictory claims were made by someone who was, in fact, a Persian Shi'i by background, a background closely reflected in a number of facets of Jamal ad-Din's character and in his legendary biography. Shi'ism, particularly in its Persian form known as the Twelver Shi'ah, includes many elements of martyrology. Among the highest holidays of the year are those celebrating the battlefield deaths of the Prophet's son-in-law Ali and especially his sons in their attempts to assert their legitimate claims to the Caliphate, or temporal succession of Muhammad. Shi'i attitudes toward political authority are colored by the doctrine of the Hidden Imam, which asserts that the rightful ruler of the world of true believers went into hiding, and that full political legitimacy will be restored only at the time of the future reappearance of that Hidden Imam. Moreover, there is the Shi'i doctrine of dissimulation—the claim that the true believers have not only the right, but the duty to disguise their beliefs in order to save true religion from continual persecution by wicked illegitimate authority. No one without a certain versatility at role-playing could have appealed effectively to practical politicians and to intellectual followers throughout the Muslim world of the nineteenth century. No one without the gift of adaptation could have experienced so strongly and intimately the profound appeal of the Islamic tradition to the masses of common Middle Easterners and the compelling claims of intrusive Western patterns of technology and organization. And to no one but a Shi'i—and better yet a Shi'i in exile—

would the required feats of versatility, adaptation, and dissimulation have come so naturally. Jamal ad-Din's true national-religious background and his efforts to disguise it would seem to have been useful qualifications for his chosen role as political and ideological unifier of the peoples of Islam against the onslaught of the West.

While role-playing may have been essential to Jamal ad-Din's task, it plainly was not enough. That task implied challenging the entire economic and military resources of the West—the power of its technology and its organization—at the peak of its imperialist period. In throwing down the challenge, Jamal ad-Din repeatedly offered himself to rulers as a "sharp sword" and eloquently wrote of the "strongest bond." But the only sharp sword in his cause was the words that poured from his lips and his pen; the strongest bond of the movement he envisaged was his own abiding faith in the spiritual and political unity of Muslims. Even for someone of Jamal ad-Din's outstanding talents and qualifications, the task he had set himself proved impossible to accomplish in his own lifetime. His failure must be attributed, therefore, more to circumstances than to the limitations of his own character. His reputation has risen steadily as his ideal of Muslim liberation from Western imperial rule has come closer and closer to fulfillment.

Operating within the circumstances in which he found himself, Jamal ad-Din was bound to discover that the parts even the most talented leader can play without finally outsmarting himself are limited. Indeed Jamal ad-Din often seems to have gone beyond this limit. For example, he appears not to have decided whether he should influence policy as an adviser to Muslim rulers or as an educator and agitator among those opposed to these rulers. He tended, in fact, to do both at the same time. In Egypt, he expected to influence the young Khedive Taufiq, who was a client of the British, while he was at the same time carrying on mass agitation against the British. In Iran, he tried to influence the Shah and his prime minister, but also dealt with opponents of the government. While protesting his loyalty to Sultan Abdülhamid, he also treated with his enemies and with rival claimants to a revived caliphate. Such behavior helped bring about his expulsion from Egypt and Iran and also the Sultan's more clever policy of confining him as a prisoner in a gilded cage. Near the end of his life, he recognized his own error in having appealed to rulers more than to their oppressed subjects.[21]

Related to the exaggerated role-playing that characterized

Afghani's life is his propensity to picture himself largely through the roles that he believed or fancied others assigned to him. This tendency is already indicated in the rhymed reflections from Afghanistan, quoted above, in which he emphasized the varied and contradictory views that others have of him. Another aspect of it is seen in his constant exaggeration of the role or position that important people have offered or given him. Afghani's exaggerated claims may have been made mainly to impress his listeners, but at times his exaggerations are so careless and foolhardy that they lead one to suspect that he did not always distinguish fact and fiction. Specifically, Jamal ad-Din always stresses interviews with rulers, official missions, and offers of high office, such as a fictitious offer of the prime ministership by the Shah of Iran or an official mission from the Mahdi. A weak sense of identity is often combined with compensatory boasting about recognition by the great and powerful. Jamal ad-Din seems to have had a genuine confusion about his real identity, a confusion that helped him adapt to the most varying needs and situations, but that also involved him in grandiose exaggerations of what he might accomplish through such cleverness at adaptation.

V

Related to his role-playing, but going beyond its more mundane aspects, is Jamal ad-Din's tendency to see himself as a kind of prophet or messiah, destined to reform, reawaken, and reunite the Muslim world and free it from its infidel conquerors. This role is suggested in Afghani's frequent comparison of himself to Luther, in the conviction of some of his followers that he was the *mahdi*, and in his letters in the 1890's in which Afghani says that the exact events of the martyrdom of the great Shi'i Imam Husain have been repeated in his own persecutions. In one of these letters, he compares the Iranian prime minister who expelled him from Iran in 1891 and falsely claimed to have sent him provisions for his journey to the governor of Kufa who ordered the killing of the Imam Husain, Ibn Ziyad:

When did Ibn Ziyad show mercy to the family of the Prophet? . . . He who accusses the descendant of Ali of being Armenian and uncircumcised, would he provide a journey's provision for him? May the curse of God be on the liars!

Yes, the events of the past and the present must parallel each other in every respect. Because the evil ones, although they may enter the world of existence in different epochs are all from the same malevolent tree. Their deeds and their words have always been alike and the same. And the way of God in the world of creation has always been and shall remain the same. Now one must await the wonders of the Divine Power.

I verily performed the duty advised by religion. In traveling the path of Truth I did not allow fear and trembling, which are the behavior of a majority of people, to take hold of me. I did not remain silent in offering warnings because of vain superstitions. And the evildoers did whatever they could. Now it remains to be seen what God will do. Of course, whoever is weak of character and infirm in faith can imagine whatever he wishes, and can say whatever he wants, and can make any kind of accusation—just as was done and said in the distant past.[22]

The most complete document of Afghani's messianic self-view is a petition he addressed to a high Ottoman statesman, unfortunately undated, in which he asks to be used as a wandering pan-Islamic emissary. He hopes to travel among the divided and conquered peoples of Muslim Asia and reawaken them to unity and holy war against the unbelievers. He will tell them to "expect the time and the hour and the arrival of the end of the period"—the exact words traditionally utilized to herald the advent of the *mahdi*.[23] Scattered throughout Afghani's writings and talks are numerous other hints of this messianic role.

Afghani's messianism was a factor in both his successes and his failures. In a time of profound internal crisis and external defeat for the Muslim world, an inspiring messianic leader who could reawaken confidence in the ability of an aroused and reunited Islamic world to fight off oppressors and unbelievers helped to reawaken Muslim pride and stimulate his hearers to efforts in behalf of their own people. On the other hand, the unreality of Jamal ad-Din's actual schemes for instant liberation and revival nullified the effectiveness of almost all his political plans.

Related to his messianic self-image was Jamal ad-Din's view of himself as a persecuted martyr. Not only are the two roles often found in close juxtaposition both psychologically and historically, but in Shi'i tradition all the imams are believed to have been martyrs (particularly, the two most important imams: Muhammad's cousin and son-in-law, Ali, and Ali's son Husain). In his petition to Sultan Abdülhamid requesting permission to leave Istanbul, Jamal ad-Din confuses his roles so far as to compare his oppressors to Yazid and Shimr, the men most responsible for killing Husain—

this in a petition to the Sunni caliph whom he was trying to convince of his own Sunni orthodoxy. The petition's tone of unjust persecution and injured innocence characterizes many of Jamal ad-Din's letters and recorded conversations. It reads, in part:

I had offered my soul to be a cutting sword . . . in Your Caliphal hands, to be used against internal and external enemies. But it was not accepted. When I received the Caliphal edict ordering me to submit and expound my humble opinion concerning the possibilities of a unification of Islam, I felt as happy as if the eight gates of Paradise had been opened to me, and I wrote a summary of my humble opinion on this subject, in accord with Your High Imperial Order, and submitted it to the Caliphal threshold. Since not a word concerning this matter has been uttered until now, I have unfortunately concluded that the project has been thrown into the corner of oblivion, or that it has been burned by the fire of malice of partial and malicious persons, or its contents were misinterpreted by latter-day sages so as to diverge from its sublime intent, and it was consequently lodged among subversive literature. . . .

. . . What can I do against those intriguers and slanderers who have access to every heart and mind? God give me patience! I have not the slightest doubt that these cruel Yazids and these tyrannical Shimrs like the robbers of Kufa and Damascus will continue to weave their hundreds of intrigues against me. Of course, with the help of God it is the easiest thing for me to hang the ruses of these intrigues on their own necks like necklaces of damnation. As God the Almighty has made my heart free from aspirations of rank and glory and from love of glitter and pomp, and as God the Almighty has created me as I am, devoted only to serve the world of Islam, it is clearly forbidden for me to waste my time with the hallucinations and futilities of base individuals. Every intelligent person will admit that His Sacred Caliphal Highness will not suffer that I lose my time and vital energy for the undignified and trifling occupation with the calumniations of these people here, and that, consequently, they will accelerate their gracious permission for my departure, seeing that my leaving is preferable. . . . It is impossible to live among people who do not know the fear of God and who do not refrain from intrigues, like fabrication, lies, and incitement, in order to render fruitless the services and acts of loyalty of those who are really and unselfishly devoted to Your Caliphal Highness.[24]

This petition was as unsuccessful as his other attempts to escape Istanbul, and Jamal ad-Din was forced to remain in involuntary captivity. It seems likely that the forced inactivity and captivity of his last years contributed to his projection of grandiose fantasies onto his past; these fantasies were in the clearest contrast to the frustrations of life in Istanbul, where the Sultan no longer paid attention to his advice or desires. Lacking any significant influence or activity in these years, Jamal ad-Din told repeated stories of how the Shah, the Tsar, and even the hated British had offered him major posts and turned to him for advice.

Although many men, and particularly younger men, were his adoring disciples, there is evidence of only one woman with whom he had personal relations. Only adoring letters from this young German woman to Jamal ad-Din remain, and we do not know to what degree her feelings were reciprocated, although two of her four letters were found unopened and unread, which is suggestive. That this relationship was a sexual one seems definite not only from the content of the letters, but also from a report of the French police noting that Jamal ad-Din had to leave his lodgings when he brought this woman to sleep with him because his landlord considered her a German spy.[25] To his male followers, Jamal ad-Din recurrently voiced hostility to maintaining sexual or marital ties with women. Although believing in reform in most spheres, he defended the inferior position, isolation, and veiling of women. Jamal ad-Din reportedly stated that if the Sultan insisted on his plan of marrying him to one of the women of the court, he would cut off his own "organ of procreation."[26] In general, Jamal ad-Din's emotional affects seem to have been tied primarily to his larger goal of uniting and liberating the Muslim world from conquest and oppression and secondarily to his relations with his male disciples. It is difficult to imagine that his disciples were misled in their view that Jamal ad-Din avoided relationships with women.

Despite the differences in cultural background, one is struck by the many similarities in personality between Afghani and the political agitators analyzed by Harold Lasswell in *Psychopathology and Politics*. Lasswell's own analysis of several agitators shows them to be characterized in different degrees by hyperactivity; high verbal ability; a desire to control others and sway crowds; impostorship and role-playing; a capacity to make friendships quickly, but soon to feel betrayed by important friends; a sharp division of the world between friends and enemies; and delusions of grandeur and persecution. Lasswell relates the paranoid features of their personalities to strong evidence of latent homosexuality and fears of impotence.[27] Freud linked all cases of clinical paranoia he had seen to latent homosexuality, and some relationship be-

tween paranoia and latent homosexuality seems to be borne out
by more recent clinical and statistical studies.[28] How far statements regarding clinical cases of paranoia severe enough to require
medical treatment can be applied to the mild paranoiac tendencies
found not only in Afghani, but in numerous other ordinary and
extraordinary persons is problematical. Lasswell's analysis of influential political agitators suggests, however, that for them latent
homosexuality and subclinical paranoia remain associated features.
It is important to stress that paranoia is predominantly associated
with homosexual feelings that are *only latent*, as revealed in close
personal ties with men—ties often broken when they threaten to
become too close—and in other emotional attitudes. It is apparently
rare for a paranoid to be an active homosexual and common for
him to be either heterosexual or totally or largely celibate. Although
Afghani's ties to his disciples were of a type common in Islam, his
hostility to ties to women and to marriage seemed noteworthy
even to his own followers.

A most interesting paper by R. P. Knight suggests that the
latent homosexuality of paranoids is often based on a combination
of love for and murderous rage against the father. This observation
helps to account for the common psychiatric phenomenon that
clinical paranoids are not cured by being brought to recognize
their own latent homosexuality, since it includes a strong unacceptable component of murderous and destructive rage.[29] A strong repressed hatred toward the father was also noted in many of the
agitators analyzed by Lasswell. The hatred was often displaced
onto political authority figures, while the agitator stressed the need
for the unity, love, and brotherhood that he had missed in his
own family life. A murderous rage toward authority figures cannot
be denied in Jamal ad-Din—especially toward his earliest political
authority figure, Nasir ad-Din Shah of Iran. The pattern of close
friendships followed by breaks and accusations of betrayal, noted
by Lasswell, is also found again and again in Jamal ad-Din. If one
looks both at Lasswell's cases and at Jamal ad-Din, one may conclude that relatively mild, non-clinical paranoid tendencies may
contribute both to the partial success of political agitators and to
their failures. Such men tend to have a single-minded devotion to
a public cause, a dynamic activism, a verbal facility, and a dramatic presence before crowds that help win them a devoted follow-

174

ing. In addition, the conviction that they are being unjustly persecuted by evil forces gives them the drive to devote tremendous
efforts to overcoming those forces and to bringing themselves and
their just cause to power. There seems little doubt that many of
the most successful charismatic political leaders, particularly those
who started as leaders of mass movements, belong in this agitator
category. But when, as in the case of Afghani, paranoid tendencies
involve a serious distortion of the world and political realities, this
personality type may destroy many of his own successes before they
come to meaningful fruition.[30]

This analysis is not intended to negate the objective significance of the causes to which Jamal ad-Din and other important
agitators devoted their lives. Indeed, the great and continuous success in the Muslim world of Jamal ad-Din's writings and of the
myth of his life stems, in part, from increasing relevance of what
he said to that world. Although his own overconfidence in the
possibility of quickly achieving his goals helped thwart the direct
political efficacy of his actions, Jamal ad-Din's life and words
touched on numerous themes that were to become increasingly
important to Muslims. His approach of seeking within a reinter-
preted Muslim tradition the sources of revival and political strength
and independence found a growing number of practitioners and
followers after his death. These ranged from Islamic modernists
and reformers through various Middle Eastern nationalists to the
Islamic revivalists in movements like the Muslim Brethren. Not
only did Jamal ad-Din indicate sources of pride and strength to an
Islamic public at a low point in its collective strength and self-
confidence, but he pioneered among Muslims in the use of tools
and media that were to become increasingly influential. His understanding of the modern political use of secret societies, political
speeches, the telegraph, and above all political journals was highly
developed, and such tools were to become increasingly important
in the Muslim world after he employed them.

One may say that Jamal ad-Din's failure in his directly political
efforts, which contrasts so sharply with the great influence of his
legacy and legend, was due in part to his being ahead of his time.
Although the psychological components of Jamal ad-Din's political
failures have been stressed here, it is also true that the anti-imperialist goals he was pursuing were not so much fantastic as vision-

ary—visions that could be largely realized in the future, but not with the immediacy that Jamal ad-Din, like so many messianic reformers, imagined possible.

Analysis of Jamal ad-Din's personality would matter little if so many of his personality features and modes of expression and behavior did not recur with frequency and political impact in the Middle East. The modern Middle East has provided increasing examples of the traits found in Jamal ad-Din: violence of speech and temperament, overconfidence about the unity and military potential of Muslims, personalization of the evils brought by the British and other Westerners, and exaggerated sense of the power of words and rhetoric. The more positive features of political concern are also evident: self-sacrifice and activism; a striving for political strength, independence, and reform; and a belief in the power of people to change their own destinies. To a surprising degree, the successes and failures of Jamal ad-Din have been re-echoed in the successes and failures of modern Middle Eastern nationalism. A study of the causes of Jamal ad-Din's failures and successes may, therefore, suggest an avenue for further inquiry into the political and intellectual transformation of the modern Middle East.[31]

REFERENCES

1. Evidence for this point is summarized in my "Sayyid Jamal ad-Din al-Afghani's First Twenty-seven Years: The Darkest Period," *Middle East Journal*, Vol. 20, No. 4 (Autumn, 1966), pp. 517–33, and in my forthcoming full biography of Jamal ad-Din. On the border and crisis origin of charismatic leadership, see especially Dankwart A. Rustow, "Atatürk as Founder of a State," in this volume.

2. On Herzl, see especially Alex Bein, *Theodore Herzl* (Meridian Books, 1962) and the forthcoming biographical article in *History and Psychoanalysis* (Basic Books) by Peter Loewenberg. There is as yet no scholarly biography of Jinnah, and some have guessed that the reason his papers have not been opened to scholars is the religious unorthodoxy of his early years. To a degree Gandhi's early experiments with Western ways fit him in this pattern.

3. For English language versions of the standard biography, based on the words of Afghani and his disciples, see the section on Afghani in E. G. Browne, *The Persian Revolution*, 1905–1909 (Cambridge, 1910), or the article "Djamal ad-Din al-Afghani," in the *Encyclopedia of Islam* (second edition).

4. Full documentation of these points appears in my forthcoming *Sayyid Jamal ad-Din al-Afghani: A Political Biography* (University of California Press: Berkeley and Los Angeles, 1970); the Istanbul stay has been de-mythologized in Niyazi Berkes, *The Development of Secularism in Turkey* (Montreal, 1964), pp. 180–88.

5. Documentation on these points appears in my forthcoming biography and in Homa Pakdaman's important new biography, with substantial appended documentation, *Djamal-ed-Din Assad abadi dit Afghani* (Paris, 1969).

6. The correspondence proving this point has been unearthed and printed in the chapter on Jamal ad-Din in a Persian book, Khan Malik Sasani, *Siyasatgaran-i daureh-yi Qajor* (Tehran, 1334/1959–60).

7. The two main eyewitness records of Jamal ad-Din's conversations in Istanbul are in Arabic: Muhammad al-Makhzumi, *Khatirat Jamal ad-Din al-Afghani* (Beirut, 1931), and Abd al-Qadir al-Maghribi, *Jamal ad-Din al-Afghani* (Cairo, 1948).

8. Interview with Aga Jamali (Tehran, 1966). Mirza Lutfallah Asada-badi, *Sharh-i hal va asar-i Sayyid Jamal ad-Din Asadabadi ma'ruf bi "Afghani"* (Tabriz, 1326/1947–48). These men's accounts are considered to be the most reliable, not only because they originate in genuine family recollections, but also because much of what they relate, including the Shi'i education in Iraq and the trip to Afghanistan, has been confirmed by documents in the *Documents inédits*.

9. *Documents inédits*, p. 15, doc. 9 (4); plate 7, photo 19. I have seen the original at the Majlis Library in Tehran.

10. *Documents inédits*, p. 15, doc. 9 (2); I have a microfilm of the treatise. Thanks must be given to Abdul Husain Zarrinkub for identifying it as *Mir'at al Arifin* by Hajji Muhammad Karim Khan. Homa Pakdaman first suggested Shaikhi influence on Afghani's thought.

11. Preface by Sifatallah Jamali to *Maqalat-i jamaliyyeh* (Tehran, 1312/1933–34).

12. *Documents inédits*, plate 2, photo 3; pp. 81–82.

13. *Documents inédits*, plate 3, photo 9. Thanks to Homa Pakdaman and my colleague, Amin Banani, for help with this translation.

14. See the letters from Lutfallah and his brother Mirza Sharif catalogued in *Documents inédits*, pp. 28–29. These are discussed in my forthcoming biography.

15. Otto Rank, *The Myth of the Birth of the Hero and Other Writings*, ed. Philip Freund (New York, 1959), pp. 3–96; Richard N. Frye, *The Heritage of Persia* (New York, 1963), p. 104.

16. Translated from the *Documents inédits* in Elie Kedourie, *Afghani and Abduh* (London, 1966), Appendix I, pp. 66–69.

177

17. Cf. the letters reprinted in Nikki R. Keddie, "Afghani in Afghanistan," *Middle Eastern Studies*, Vol. 1, No. 4 (July, 1965), pp. 334–36.

18. Such a relationship between the authoritarian patriarchal Iranian family and the ineffectual, though often violent, oppositionist is suggested in F. M. Esfandiary's interesting novel, *The Day of Sacrifice* (New York, 1959). The attribution of diabolical cleverness to an omnipotent Shah is a related obverse to the traditional picture of the ruler as a source of unlimited beneficence. Like the exaggerated adoration or abomination of leaders in all countries, both have their origin partly in strong ambivalent emotions to the father, whom the child, especially in strongly patriarchal cultures, perceives as omnipotent.

19. See my forthcoming biography and chap. 3 of E. G. Browne, *The Persian Revolution*, 1905–1909 (Cambridge, 1910).

20. See my forthcoming biography and Nikki R. Keddie, *An Islamic Response to Imperialism: Political and Religious Writings of Sayyid Jamal ad-Din "al-Afghani"* (Berkeley and Los Angeles, 1968), p. 52, n. 19.

21. See the letter to a Persian friend translated in Browne, *The Persian Revolution*, pp. 28–29, which reads in part: "Would that I had sown all the seed of my ideas in the receptive ground of the people's thoughts! Well would it have been had I not wasted this fruitful and beneficent seed of mine in the salt and sterile soil of that effete Sovereignty! For what I sowed in that soil never grew, and what I planted in that brackish earth perished away. During all that time none of my well-intentioned counsels sank into the ears of the rulers of the East, whose selfishness and ignorance prevented them from accepting my words. . . . The stream of renovation flows quickly towards the East. The edifice of despotic government totters to its fall. Strive so far as you can to destroy the foundations of this despotism, not to pluck up and cast out its individual agents. Strive so far as in you lies to abolish those practices which stand between the Persians and their happiness, not to annihilate those who employ these practices. . . ."

22. *Documents inédits*, photos 192–93. Thanks must be given to Amin Banani for help in the translation.

23. The petition is translated and analyzed in Nikki R. Keddie, "The Pan-Islamic Appeal: Afghani and Abdülhamid II," *Middle Eastern Studies*, Vol. 3, No. 1 (October, 1966), pp. 46–47. I would no longer date it 1885, but more likely around 1879, for reasons discussed in the forthcoming biography.

24. Ottoman Archives, Yildiz Kiosk register, item no. 11030. Thanks are due to Andreas Tietze for the translation.

25. The police documents were discovered by Homa Pakdaman. I have read the originals at the archives of the Paris Prefecture of Police, file labelled "Cheik Djemal Eddin el Afghan." The letters from this woman are in the Jamal ad-Din collection at the Majlis Library in Tehran, and one of them is reproduced in *Documents inédits*, plates 66–67.

Afghani: A Case of Posthumous Charisma?

26. Makhzumi, *Khatirat Jamal ad-Din al-Afghani* (Damascus, 1965 ed.), pp. 66–67. Although this recollection was published years after the event, it seems unlikely that this admirer invented it.

27. Harold D. Lasswell, *Psychopathology and Politics* (New York, 1960), especially chaps. 6–7.

28. Sigmund Freud, "Psychoanalytic Notes Upon an Autobiographical Account of a Case of Paranoia," *Collected Papers*, Vol. 3 (London, 1950); S. Ferenczi, "On the Part Played by Homosexuality in the Pathogenesis of Paranoia," *Sex in Psychoanalysis*, ed. Ernest Jones (New York, 1950); Philip M. Kitay, *et al.*, "Symposium on 'Reinterpretation of the Schreber Case: Freud's Theory of Paranoia,'" *The International Journal of Psycho-Analysis*, Vol. 44, No. 2 (1963), pp. 191–223; H. M. Wolowitz, "Attraction and Aversion to Power: A Psychoanalytic Conflict Theory of Homosexuality in Male Paranoids," *Journal of Abnormal Psychology*, Vol. 70, No. 5 (1965), pp. 360–370, and the sources cited therein.

29. R. P. Knight, "The Relationship of Latent Homosexuality to the Mechanism of Paranoid Delusions," *Bulletin of the Menninger Clinic*, Vol. 4 (1940), pp. 149–59.

30. I must confess some trepidation that this attempt at psycho-historical analysis of a Muslim hero will be regarded by Middle Easterners only as the latest of a long series of attacks on the Muslim East by Western Orientalists. Without entering into a long discussion of this real problem, I can only state that I do not find Jamal ad-Din any more aberrant than numerous great Western political leaders and agitators, nor is an analysis of his character intended to deny or denigrate the genuine and positive achievements of his life, example, and writings.

31. Thanks are due to the John Simon Guggenheim Foundation, the Social Science Research Council, the American Philosophical Society, and the U.C.L.A. Near Eastern Center and Humanities Foundation for fellowships and grants that contributed to my work on Jamal ad-Din. Thanks go also to the friends who have helped my research, named in the preface to my *An Islamic Response to Imperialism: Political and Religious Writings of Sayyid Jamal ad-Din "al-Afghani"* (Berkeley and Los Angeles, 1968); to Dankwart A. Rustow for his editing and suggestions; and in addition to my colleague Peter Loewenberg, who commented on this paper and introduced me to the Los Angeles Interdisciplinary Psychoanalytic Study Group, which kindly devoted an instructive evening to a discussion of Afghani.

JOHN F. HOWES

Uchimura Kanzō: Japanese Prophet

I. *The Society*

IN THE century since the Japanese Imperial Restoration of 1868, society's perception of the individual has changed. The Tokugawa government viewed him as a tool of society. Now society increasingly exists to serve him. In the course of this development, the Japanese have adopted much of the Western tradition of individualism. Many persons have contributed to this change. Among them, Uchimura Kanzō occupies a special position. He lived as a heroic individual who at the same time venerated Japanese traditional group ethics and challenged the right of society to exact conformity from its members. His voluminous and popular writings described the pain which resulted and the solution he found in a Christianity free of institutional ties with Christendom. He is considered a cultural giant in Japan today; his works are constantly republished and his contribution to history re-evaluated. A study of his life and how he used it in his writings illustrates the kinds of strain introduced when the Japanese attempted to become nineteenth-century Western individuals in a group-oriented society.

Uchimura was born into a low-ranking samurai family. The samurai, who made up the top 5 per cent of the population, served in the beginning of the Tokugawa Period as a military police force, but with the passage of time became scholars and bureaucrats in a land which for over two centuries needed no soldiers. By the nineteenth century, samurai boys aspired to high government office. Very few realized their ambition, for the qualified candidates far outnumbered the positions. To utilize available talent and to insure maximum consideration for any decision, individual government posts were often assigned to groups of men, each of whom took responsibility in turn, working closely with colleagues in the same post. This government by committee reflected a general policy of checks and balances which minimized individual initiative. Though conscious of his elite status, the samurai recognized that it gave him little opportunity for self-expression.

A state-supported rational orthodoxy provided the ethical basis for the society in which these samurai moved. The Tokugawa family had unified Japan in the early seventeenth century over the determined opposition of the Buddhist establishment and feudal houses deeply influenced by the Christianity which Portuguese and Spanish missionaries had introduced to Japan. Shortly after they had unified Japan, the Tokugawa proscribed Christianity and crippled Buddhism by making its priests and temples party to their system of population control. While they remained in power, Japan's two other religious traditions showed the greatest vitality. The first was the belief in *kami*, semi-divine and largely benevolent local gods who had been seen throughout Japanese history to exist in a hierarchy which led up to the Imperial household. This religious system, known as Shinto, or "the way of the Gods," linked the individual Japanese to the rest of his people, past and present. Existing parallel to Shinto, but serving the more rational side of man's nature, was the official faith of neo-Confucianism. The Tokugawa government had adapted this highly sophisticated rational humanism to promote its own ends of social harmony. Both systems of belief located the individual in the group, and neither provided him with a basis for action apart from its other members. Even membership in the elite samurai class did not entitle the individual to question communal beliefs.

The intrusion of the United States and other Western nations into Japanese affairs which began in 1853 led to many changes in this system. These affected every person in Japan. Because the source of domestic change could easily be identified as foreign, attitudes toward new domestic policies were transferred to the foreigners that appeared to have caused them. Japanese felt both attracted to Western culture and threatened by its strength. This ambivalence was to condition their whole history for the next century. They admired Western achievements and hoped to equal them. At the same time, they feared loss of national identity. If they did not Westernize, they might follow India into colonial status. If they did Westernize, their very success would cut them off from their own past. As they increased in strength and maintained their independence and distinctive identity, the rational basis for their fear of the West declined; but, like most fears, this one did not respond in proportion to the removal of the original threat. The West remained a unit, opposed to things Japanese, the object at once of emulation and irrational hostility.

The actual innovations legislated by the leaders of the Restoration affected the samurai in particular. The new government saw their continued support as unjustified, in particular since the success of a conscript army had invalidated their original claim to preferential treatment. Accordingly, it abolished the stipends and the other distinctions which had set the samurai apart. Deprived of their perquisites, some found positions in the new bureaucracy or in business, but a sizable number never discovered other satisfactory employment. Uchimura came from a family that during his childhood lost everything because of the Restoration.

Though the West had ultimately brought about the dissolution of the samurai class, the need to achieve equality with the West provided a socially acceptable means by which ex-samurai from displaced families could gain a position in the new dispensation. They started out to gain the tools, particularly Western languages, through which Japan could achieve equality with the West. In the course of their study, they imbibed the whole corpus of the Christian culture which seemed responsible for Western strength. This conflicted with their strong Japanese identity. Gradually the love-hate relationship to the West, which characterized society as a whole, became a part of each individual to the extent that he knew the West and in particular its languages. He lived as a man divided against himself and considered the rational Western superstructure of his being in constant tension with his innate Japanese nature.

This tension was reflected even in the different way a man said his name when he addressed a Westerner. Throughout East Asia the patronymic precedes given names. The Chinese in their contacts with the West have in general retained this order. Thus, Mao Tse-tung is the son named Tse-tung of the Mao family. The Chinese adherence to tradition has caused Westerners some difficulty. We are told that the ebullient Texan Patrick Hurley, whom President Roosevelt sent as ambassador to China in World War II, first greeted the head of the Nationalist government with the words, "Glad to meet you, Mr. Shek!" If this story is true, it must have given Chinese officials cause for some condescending reflections about American competence. Japanese would have been deeply disturbed. From the beginning of their nineteenth-century contacts with the West, the Japanese as a nation decided to continue their native order at home and use the Western order in contacts with the Westerners. This convention continues to the present. Uchimura Kanzō had two parts to his being which he contrasted, and when he wrote in English or moved among Westerners, he knew himself as Kanzō Uchimura. One of his great problems as a young man was that he considered Kanzō Uchimura superior to Uchimura Kanzō. Since World War II Western scholars of Japanese studies have tried to reduce the confusion which this simultaneous use of two systems has introduced into catalogues and bibliographies by writing the patronymic first at all times. I have followed that convention here.

The adoption of the Western order in giving one's name was accompanied by the rapid integration of Western material culture into Japanese society. By World War I the Japanese dressed and increasingly ate like Westerners. This widespread change to Western material life was not matched by a parallel development in ethics. Beginning in the last years of the nineteenth century, there was a concerted effort to halt the acceptance of Western values. This resulted in the Imperial Rescript on Education which the Emperor bequeathed to his people in 1890. It reflected the concern felt by the Emperor's advisers over the rapid increase in Christian influence and proposed a return to Confucian and Shinto values:

Ye, Our Subjects, be filial to your parents, affectionate to your brothers and sisters; as husbands and wives be harmonious, as friends, true; bear yourselves in modesty and moderation; extend your benevolence to all; pursue learning and cultivate arts, and thereby develop intellectual faculties and perfect moral powers; furthermore, advance public good and promote common interests; always respect the Constitution and observe the laws; should emergency arise, offer yourselves courageously to the State; and thus guard and maintain the prosperity of Our Imperial Throne coeval with heaven and earth. . . .

The way here set forth is indeed the teaching bequeathed by Our Imperial Ancestors, to be observed alike by Their Descendants and the subjects, infallible for all ages and true in all places.[1]

The original Japanese resounds with phrases that link these words to the core of the samurai ethic, and through this document the attitudes that had nurtured the samurai class became the norm for the whole of the Japanese people. No one could object to them because they expressed the best in the moral sensibilities of the Japanese tradition. In fact, it was not the wording of the Rescript but the attitude with which it was treated that was to give it its great symbolic significance. It came to occupy a position in the Japanese educational system somewhat analogous to that accorded the Pledge of Allegiance to the American Flag in the United States except that a highly centralized educational system in Japan could insure much more effective acceptance of it. Veneration accorded the Rescript in early youth resulted in internalized ethical attitudes that could not be questioned. Any other ethical standards the Japanese might gain in later life had to be engrafted onto these attitudes acquired in primary-school classrooms. If later he adopted a transcendent ethic like Marxism or Christianity, he either qualified his new faith to accord with the official interpretation of the Japanese nature or he lived in a state of spiritual inequilibrium.

As part of the sweeping reforms after World War II, the Education Rescript was abandoned along with the whole fabric of State Shinto which had maintained it. Since that time, Japan has had no official definition of what constitutes the essence of the Japanese national character. On several occasions conservatives have suggested that something similar be devised to counteract that widespread increase in moral laxity which Japan has experienced along with other advanced nations. The most recent attempt was set forth by a committee of moralists brought together by the Ministry of Education. They published a draft report which evoked a storm of opposition, largely from those who feared any attempt to define the nature of a good Japanese as the first step in the reintroduction of prewar ethical rigidity. The contents of the draft made it impossible for responsible critics to dismiss it so lightly. It included little reference to Japanese tradition, and appeared to depend more on the imperatives of Christendom than those of China. One of its most perceptive critics dealt less with its contents than with its overly rational tone and recommended the use of the Bible instead. The influential *Asahi* newspaper said in its critique: "a sermon coming from the brain will not convince young people. . . . The New Testament is so persuasive because it begins with familiar and concrete examples."[2] The public opinion which the *Asahi* editorial writer reflects appears to consider the great book of Christianity more pertinent than the Confucian tradition to the formation of contemporary ethical standards.

It is at this point that the story of Uchimura Kanzō becomes relevant. During his lifetime, from 1861 to 1930, he labored to make the Bible the national classic of Japan, and in his last years he felt at times that he had succeeded. Yet, before he could reach that conclusion in the calm retrospection of old age, he had become a symbol of how conversion to Christianity deprived the Japanese of his spiritual birthright. A refusal to bow before the Education Rescript followed by intense autobiographical and pacifist writings reflected his alienation from Japanese society. Subsequent exegesis of the Bible led him back to gradual acceptance of society and himself. Both his alienation and reconciliation grew out of the relation between the events of his youth and the society in which he grew.

II. *The Man*
Render unto Caesar ...

Kanzō entered the world as the first of five children born to the personal secretary of a daimyo. He was about seven when two of the opposing armies in the War of the Restoration passed within a short distance of his Takasaki home west of Tokyo. Although we do not know, it is possible that he observed the armies as they passed by. Whether he actually saw them or not, he considered the Restoration that followed shortly thereafter as one of the most important events in his life. For the next few years the family's fortunes rose as his father received a number of new appointments; each gave him additional scope and responsibility. Then, as suddenly, he found himself without employment, as the daimyo to whom he had been so loyal lost his fief and most of his income. The father continued to observe the pitiful forms of irrelevant loyalty even though his master had in fact neither work which required doing nor payment to reward it. Kanzō's occasional condescension mingled with filial admiration for his father seems to have resulted from his own sense of emergency and the inability of his father to adapt to the changes brought on by the Restoration.

Kanzō concluded that his family's straitened circumstances resulted from the incursion of the West into Japan, and so he followed a route of professional training which would equip him to meet the West's threat. He started to study English at age eleven. When at sixteen he arrived in the new Sapporo Agricultural College in the capital of Japan's northernmost island, he could use English well. The government had established the school to aid in the development of the virgin territory and to that end had imitated the new land-grant college at Amherst, Massachusetts, which would later become the University of Massachusetts. The man whose name is most closely connected with the early days of that institution, W. S. Clark, came to Japan to help found its similar school. In addition to designing the physical plant and the curriculum, Clark converted all the students in the first class to his own type of pietistic evangelical Calvinism. Though Clark had returned home before Kanzō arrived with the other members of the second class, Clark's spirit lived on in the members of the first class who immediately converted the newcomers. Living habits like those of Western students accompanied the Western faith. As they donned the Western military-style uniforms in the morning, they warmed themselves by Franklin stoves. In their class-rooms they perfected their English. After they had worked with their hands and received token payments for what they grew in the school garden, they feasted off venison, salmon, and thick slices of bread served with butter and sugar. By the time of his graduation four years later, Kanzō had become a new man of the sort his generation emulated. And he gloried in the distinction, for to him it meant he had escaped the confines of narrow Japanese identity and become an international man. Only some years later would he doubt the value of this development.

Immediately upon graduation, Uchimura set about with his schoolmates to develop the small church they had started while students. His closest friends were Nitobe Inazō, who would go on to found the field of colonial administration in Japan and serve as one of its leading internationalists, and Miyabe Kingo, who would become a world-renowned botanist. The three were the best students in the class, but try as they might neither of the other two could best Kanzō in any academic enterprise. Though unequal competitors in the classroom, the three became the closest of friends and spiritual confidants. The church which they had founded flourished, as they decided to align themselves with neither of the denominations which had sent missionaries into Hokkaido. Their decision led one missionary to demand the return of four hundred dollars which he had made available to them to erect a church building. The sum represented a large part of the total income of the church's members, but by dint of great effort they managed to repay it within a year. In the meantime, Kanzō's official responsibility for the development of the fisheries industry in Hokkaido had ceased to interest him. He resigned and took the four hundred dollars with him to Tokyo where he returned it to the mission-board representatives. His later dogged determination to remain independent from foreign funds dates from this experience, where he saw the threat of foreign domination lend a vitality to his church which those that remained more closely connected with missionaries lacked.

In the capital, Kanzō found Christianity flourishing. He was one of five hundred young converts to attend a general conference of Christians where some of the delegates who occupied responsible positions in society freely predicted the Christianization of Japan. Their optimism did not strike their colleagues as farfetched. Christianity with the unofficial encouragement of numerous government officials had increased its numbers tenfold in the preceding few years. Its modern and Westernized adherents included many who, like Kanzō, could anticipate important careers in the new Japan.

Yet among them, Kanzō found neither a church nor a job which satisfied him. The Christians seemed cold and insincere, and none of the positions he accepted, each of which could have led to a successful career, held his interest. Psychosomatic symptoms ("severe throbbing of my heart")[3] drove him to spas for rest cures. From their inns he wrote letters to Miyabe in Sapporo which reflect a soul in turmoil over the unavoidable choices of late adolescence. Kanzō longs for his friends in Sapporo, he says, and then turns to involved analyses of the career opportunities open to him. For each he finds himself disqualified. His final letter from an inn ends with an offhand reference to girls, and the next letters to Miyabe deal with his suit for the hand of a Christian girl he has met near his home in Takasaki. Everyone—his parents, his friends in Sapporo, to say nothing of the biographer—could tell from his attitude that marriage would mean trouble. Yet, he went ahead with it and had the ceremony performed by the missionary who had baptized him, only to discover within a few months that the girl had been a "wolf in sheep's skin"[4] and returned her, pregnant, to her family. Mortgaging his future, Kanzō purchased passage to the United States and obtained addresses of contacts there from acquaintances in Tokyo. His marriage over the objections of his parents left him with feelings of guilt for his offense against the canons of filial piety, and his refusal to heed his wife's pleas for reconciliation cost him the respect of his Christian friends in Tokyo.

During his three and one-half years in the United States he continued his search for a suitable career. His first job found him caring for feeble-minded boys in one of the early institutions which provided such service. At the suggestion of the understanding superintendent, he vacationed for two weeks during the summer at Gloucester, Massachusetts, where his letters reflect continued turmoil over the future. Even in that state, however, he commanded sufficient strength to write in English a magazine article about traditional Japanese ethics and pay his hotel bill with the royalties he received for it. From Gloucester he went to Amherst College, there to settle down for two years of fruitful study where he came under the influence of Amherst's president, Julius Seelye, who viewed the shy and pious Japanese young man as an object of special concern. Seelye became the most important among a number of surrogate parents that Kanzō adopted. Under Seelye, Kanzō read widely in biography and history, studied Greek and Hebrew, and earned a second undergraduate degree. Then he moved on to train for the ministry in Andover Theological Seminary. There it became obvious that he could not stand the prospect of life as a professional man of religion, and, after a number of further distressing psychosomatic symptoms, he returned to Japan without definite prospects for the future.

In Japan he continued unable to discover a job which would let him work according to the dictates of his demanding conscience. He accepted the principalship of a Christian school, but resigned within a few months when missionaries, who had been employed to teach under him by the Board of Trustees, objected to his invitation to a Buddhist priest to lecture. Back in Tokyo, Kanzō was invited to teach English at the high school which prepared students for entry into the Imperial University of Tokyo. It was here that his hesitation to bow before the Imperial Rescript on Education made his name a household word.

At this point with Kanzō on the verge of his most famous act, he demonstrated many characteristics common to the prophetic personality. He had grown up a shy, sincere, God-fearing, and prudish boy. He could not recognize his intense ambition, but in fact tried to control his entire environment, out of fretful apprehension. He saw himself as the pawn of capricious fate. Having been brought up in a tradition that considered ambition selfish, he had drunk deep at the font of nineteenth-century hero worship and the heady Christian tradition which taught responsibility to God alone. His attempt to live by these ideals had led to his offense against his parents and flight abroad.

And in America, rudest shock of all, he had discovered that his intensive training in things Western had not made him an international man. He had staked his future on his ability, once trained, to escape parochial Japanese society. Instead, in America he had to conclude that he could be nothing but a Japanese, and that was second best; one of his tasks for many years would be to plead the cause of his people against the West. Yet, while in the United States, he had also discovered that he could be nothing but a Christian; as a result, he must on return to Japan attempt the conversion of his fellow Japanese, so that they could merit the respect they coveted from the West as equals. Kanzō could accept no subordinate life role. He had to bring together within himself the Christian and the Japanese. It was all or nothing.

This jumble of conscious and unconscious motives and fears struggled within Kanzō as he anticipated the approaching ceremony at which his school would officially receive its beautiful copy of the Education Rescript. The chief source for what happened that day is a letter Kanzō wrote to an American friend, David C. Bell, some two months after the event. It says that he had been surprised by the request. "I was not at all prepared to meet such a strange ceremony. . . . I had scarcely time to think upon the matter. So, hesitating in doubt, I took a safer course for my Christian conscience . . . and did *not* bow!"[5] Painstaking research[6] indicates that Kanzō had been neither so surprised nor so decisive as he indicated to Bell. A letter to Miyabe in Sapporo the night before requested that his name be erased from the rolls of the church lest Kanzō do something which might embarrass his friends. The few other schools which had held similar ceremonies had set no consistent precedent in the regard they accorded the Rescript. Other reports from eyewitnesses of Kanzō's act indicate that he bowed slightly with a nod of the head rather than a deep obeisance. He could neither obey the request nor refuse it. Students who resented Kanzō's prudish reaction to manly talk of sexual prowess on a student outing may have blown up the event to revenge their own earlier grievances.

Though he may not have remembered exactly what happened, it is clear that Kanzō's time for indecision had passed. Fledgling news services spread the story throughout the nation. On the same day, the new constitutionally elected Diet which included numerous Christian members had begun to show its opposition to government policy. Because of his hesitation, deep obeisances while listening to the contents of the Education Rescript became a required part of the public-school curriculum until 1945. He had become a symbol for both those who feared individualism and those who idealized independence.

". . . to write *about . . . convictions I came to in my experience*"

When Uchimura provoked the storm over his loyalty to the symbols of the state, he had finally ended his long period of personal indecision. Many years would pass before he could relax in an assured professional role, but at least from this time on he knew the complete dimensions of the task that his life to date, ambitions, capabilities, and fears had cut out for him. He knew who he was and what he had to do. It remained to find out by what means he could do it.

After months of despair, Uchimura began to teach at a number of small Christian schools, and to write, at first in response to the critics of his action before the Education Rescript. As he gained greater confidence in his ability as an author, he gradually ceased classroom teaching. Then in 1893 he moved with his bride, who would bear him a daughter and a son and outlive him, to settle in the ancient capital of Kyoto. There in the space of three years he completed the works for which he is still best known. They include: eight books and five major articles which deal with history (including a biography of Christopher Columbus and a teleological geography of the world), Biblical exegesis (of the books of Ruth and Amos), career choice (on how to select a career which at the same time meets the requirements of personal ambition and societal needs), contemporary events (a defense of the Sino-Japanese War followed by a stinging rebuke of the government for its actions against China), confessional writings (the difficulties which attend the Christian life in Japan), and works in English intended to introduce Japan abroad. At last Uchimura had found a medium in which he could work and support himself.

Some of the books have become modern classics. They include

the confessional writings and the works intended to introduce Japan to foreigners, which have been translated into Japanese at home. A compelling style refuses to leave the reader uninvolved. Either he lays the book aside because he cannot stand the intensity of the author, or he continues and becomes a partner in Uchimura's concerns.

The confessional writings deal with two kinds of alienation. *Search After Peace* (*Kyūanroku*) describes the pain occasioned by the sin which separates man from God; and *Consolations of a Christian* (*Kirisuto shinto no nagusame*) describes how the Japanese, true to his convictions as a Christian, finds himself cut off from all contact with his fellows. His last remaining consolation is that in this progressive removal from elements of society he discovers how to stand alone, the precondition for free communion with God. Thirty years after he had written this, Uchimura recorded in the introduction to a new edition that he had taken "my pen simply impelled by the thoughts which burned up within my soul."[7]

This passage describes how opposition from his fellow Christians makes Uchimura doubt his own faith and consider apostasy:

Oh! am I not an evil man? I have been called a heretic by a theologian recognized both by others and me myself for his great knowledge; *am I not a heretic?* A certain man of great virtue who has believed in Christianity for ten-some years longer than I have, who commands the confidence of the greats in Europe and America and who is revered as a pillar of the whole church has called me an atheist; *am I not really an atheist?* A certain senior missionary whose name reverberates throughout religious society, who has spent several decades preaching the gospel in India, China and Japan and who has two or three doctor's degrees has called me a Unitarian; *am I not really a Unitarian who believes not in the atonement of the savior but depends only upon his own good works?* A certain famous missionary physician has diagnosed me as insane; *have I really lost my senses?* All the churches have kept their distance from me as a dangerous object; *have I really been born into the world as an envoy of the devil in order that clad in sheep's clothing I might lay waste the church of God?* Everyone considers me an evil man; I alone defend myself. Which has more weight, the evidence of everyone or the assurance of one? *Yes, I was not a Christian.* I had been deceiving myself and was in fact a demon. Why did I not today throw off the name of "Christian" and return to the life of a normal man of the world? Why should I stop there? Why not use the sincerity and enthusiasm which I have up to now used for Christianity to attack the Christian Church which considers me its enemy? How can I pray to the God of

191

my enemies? How can I respect and study the Bible of my enemies? I am a Unitarian, an atheist, a hypocrite, a person who should not belong to God's church; a wolf, a madman. *All right! From now what if I were to learn from the colleagues of Hume, Bolingbroke, Gibbon and Ingersoll; what if I were to hang a sword above Christianity?*[8]

Here Uchimura, cut off from his fellow Christians and full of aggression against them, remains pitifully dependent on external authorities whose opinions seem to gain in credibility as they exist apart from his own time and place. Finally after the descriptions of numerous catastrophes which have befallen him, Uchimura presents his one real consolation in a few simple phrases:

If I have not the power to distinguish good from bad, to select this and reject that, I will become the slave of others. The soul is valuable because of its ability to stand alone. Even though I am the smallest among men, I can to some extent converse directly with the Almighty. *God teaches me directly without working through the hands of the Pope, bishops, ministers, theologians.*[8]

Though these closing lines describe in eloquent terms the ultimate security of towering faith, the bulk of the work rather describes the terrible pain of increasing isolation. A reader receptive to Uchimura's evangelical message could agree with the last paragraph; others who shared his symptoms of alienation could identify with the bulk of the work and ignore its conclusion. But, in either case Uchimura appealed powerfully to the intellectual who felt society had no place for him.

If these works set forth the problems the new intellectual felt at home, the English-language books expressed the concerns he felt when he faced the Western world. They may be called works of justification, for they plead the righteousness of the whole Japanese people before the West. Their assumption that somehow the Japanese require justification reflects the great lack of confidence Japanese felt in this encounter. Uchimura's barbed comments against Western provincialism also provided in translation expression for some of the vexations which Japanese felt against the West, but could not otherwise express. *Japan and Japanese* (later republished in abridged form as *Representative Men of Japan*) consists of six biographies of important figures in Japanese history, each of whom represents a type. They have stood the test of time well, and in some cases remain the only mention of the men concerned in a language other than Japanese. *How I Became a Christian*, which is subtitled "Out of My Diary," describes Uchimura's life up to his return from the United States. It is his best known work and has enjoyed considerable popularity in a German translation, though the American edition sold very poorly. Because of Uchimura's de Tocqueville-like treatment of Calvinist New England and its religious institutions in the latter-nineteenth century, it would probably enjoy a larger audience today than when originally issued.

One of the most striking passages in *How I Became a Christian* describes Kanzō's introduction to President Seelye of Amherst College:

Miserably clad in an old nasty suit, with no more than seven silver dollars in my pocket, and five volumes of Gibbon's Rome in my valise, I entered the college town, and soon appeared in the president's gate. A friend of mine had previously introduced my name to him; so he knew that a young savage was coming to him. I was introduced to his parlor, and there waited for my doom to be stunned by his intellectuality and Platonic majesty. Hush! he is coming! Prepare thy soul to stand before his sinless presence. He may look through thy heart at once, and take thee for what thou really art, and refuse to own thee as his pupil. The door opened, and behold the Meekness! A large well-built figure, the leonine eyes suffused with tears, the warm grasp of hands unusually tight, orderly words of welcome and sympathy,—why, this was not the form, the mind, the man I had pictured to myself before I saw him. I at once felt a peculiar ease in myself. I confided myself to his help which he most gladly promised. I returned, and from that time on my Christianity has taken an entirely new direction.[10]

Through passages like these, Uchimura could speak to the doubts felt by all Japanese when they stood before the great representatives of the West. Uchimura made of his personal experience an expression of community concern.

Though on first reading the autobiographical works seem to reveal their subject completely, extended contact with them shows that Uchimura has selected what he will reveal to emphasize his helplessness. He pictures himself as without a will. Numerous situations which excite our sympathy happen to him through no fault of his. These lead to his anomie and alienation. Uchimura had to use a format which ignored his volition because he could not admit the part his ambition had played in his decision to become a Christian and his later divorce. Rather than publicize the impurity of the original motive which brought him to his pitiable state, he preferred to see his whole history from his conversion until he arrived in the United States in terms of a vacuum which sucked him along. It is the sense of helplessness that he uses to deal with this period that gives his works their great poignancy.[11]

This poignancy enabled readers who felt themselves alienated from society for whatever reason to identify with Uchimura's plight. The biographer who has to use autobiographical works as an important source seeks a complete revelation beyond the ability of the author, the requirements of his art, or the needs of his readers. The Japanese young men who found in Uchimura's autobiographical works echoes of their own experience did not concern themselves over the motives which led Uchimura to write. Instead they thrilled to the greatness of lonely individuality he described even as they shared with him the pain such individuality invites.

Shortly after he had completed these works based largely on his experience, the satire Uchimura had written against the Japanese treatment of China in the Sino-Japanese War drew the attention of a capable and aggressive publisher in Tokyo. He persuaded Uchimura to join him as a columnist. Here, in the company of a number of other gifted newspapermen, Uchimura helped shape the most influential newspaper of the day. Uchimura contributed articles both in English and Japanese. The former presented Japan to Westerners in a way that would counteract the condescension and criticism of the treaty-port foreign language press, while the latter criticized the Japanese establishment in an attempt to elevate it to Western standards. For a brief period, Uchimura enjoyed the high salary, prestige, and interesting colleagues that accompanied the job, but he resigned when, in 1903, the editor of the newspaper announced his support for those who desired war with Russia. Uchimura retired from the limelight to support himself with a magazine devoted to the study of the Bible.

During the months before and after his resignation from the newspaper, Uchimura wrote what continues today as the most detailed Japanese treatment of pacifism. He started with astringent attacks on the warmongers in the government, but as it became clear that the war could not be avoided and he would have to live through it in Japan, he turned to a series of articles which outlined the Christian attitude toward war. They emphasized retreat from society and fidelity to one's Christian ideals in preparation for the day when the return of peace would once again enable the Christian to pursue his calling. In response to the argument of the just war in the name of freedom, he replied: "Freedom is not obtained by felling the foe of freedom. Freedom is taken captive by its enemies, suffers their insults, is finally killed by them and then is reborn. This is a basic doctrine of Christianity."[12] The Christian answer to force is meek submission in the faith that God will make final amends. This attitude toward the question of war represented Uchimura's new conviction about the role of the Christian in the non-Christian society. The Christian's objection to war was just one specific in his more general opposition to the ways of this world. He could only respond by defense of the faith on the fringes of society, in the hope that later he could once again return to its center.

Uchimura's resignation along with those of a number of other columnists on the newspaper marks the end of Japan's first experiment with loyal opposition, for after that date the socialists and the other Christians who had joined him in criticism also stopped. Most of them later agreed, either through their words or silence, with the government. The government quieted the few who persisted in outright disagreement. Uchimura turned to a new way of life which allowed him to nourish his potential for outspoken criticism even as he also refrained from it.

In these early works Uchimura had expressed the hopeless anomie into which the acceptance of Western tradition had forced him. Whether or not his readers shared his faith, they understood his lack of security in the presence of his countrymen and Westerners. They experienced through his pathos their own lack of confidence and desire for faith. In this common experience they also gained confidence in their own weak and unvoiced aspirations toward individuality.

The Bargain with God

Uchimura had by 1903 already lived through the events which would gain him recognition in every high-school history text. His achievement of psychic and fiscal stability as he entered his fifth decade enabled him to live much like other middle-class intellectuals. In part, the shift can be seen as a normal career development for one who has lived in such dire psychic contingency for so long.

Some who, as young men, endure a severe identity confusion burn themselves out and soon die. Others who, like Uchimura, manage to find an equilibrium move on to positions of responsibility in relaxed middle age. When Uchimura opted for his quiet life, no one would have predicted that he would once again step into the limelight some fifteen years later.

In the suburbs of Tokyo, Uchimura settled down to edit the magazine whose title he translated into English as *The Biblical Studies* and to work with a small number of carefully selected students. He became a *sensei*, or teacher in the Confucian sense. The *sensei* accepted only those students who by their persistence and loyalty demonstrated their sincere desire to learn. Everything he taught them had ethical implications, and they as the *deshi*, or followers, took with them the responsibility to remain loyal to his dictates. In Uchimura's use of this traditional system he introduced a new classic; whereas the *sensei* in earlier days had based his ethical maxims on Confucian teachings, Uchimura used the Bible. His magazine and the new railroad network enabled him to enlarge his circle of *deshi*. The traditional *sensei* worked with twenty or thirty *deshi* at most, but Uchimura's readers grew, at their greatest, to an estimated ten thousand. Extended correspondence and traveling enabled him to offer many of his readers who were distant from Tokyo the fruits of personal contact, enjoyed by the few who came to his home for instruction each Sunday. He formed ties of mutual dependence with all of them, and in time of emergency he was prepared to spend the night on a train en route to a personal conference in a lonely provincial village. They reciprocated with support when he needed it.

The particular kind of Christian teaching that Uchimura offered came to be known by a word that he coined, *mukyōkai*. The word *kyōkai* is the Japanese equivalent for the English "church," either as a common or proper noun. The *mu* is best translated "absence of," though it is very easy to impart into this affectively neutral word a strong sense of negation, particularly when it is attached to a word with such strong affect as "church." For Uchimura the whole of the accretions of Western history to the Christian tradition had no relevance to Japan. Christianity justified its claim among men only to the extent that it could be understood through careful reading of the Bible and reference to the actions of Christians. Anything beyond that resulted from man's work and

might either hinder or help true understanding, but was not necessary to it. Uchimura did not develop the sense in which he meant
the word beyond a few short epigrammatic passages early in the
twentieth century.[13] They demonstrate how, even this early in the
negative sense of the character *mu* had aroused the concern of
church members. Uchimura soon ignored their concern, preferring
to give content to his idea through the careful exposition of the
Bible which he presented through his Sunday meetings and through
his magazine.

That Uchimura could support himself with this work surprised
even him, for time had not borne out the sanguine expectations of
Christian growth entertained by some at the 1883 conference of
Christians in Tokyo. Very shortly after that conference the conservative reaction that culminated in the Education Rescript had set
in. It then became clear that the interest in Christianity shown in
the mid-eighties had resulted, in part, from political considerations.
Many Japanese had hoped that if they became Christian, the West
would immediately recognize them as equals. When they realized
that this consequence would not follow upon conversion, they lost
much of their interest. Growth continued, but at a slower rate.
After the events leading up to the Sino-Japanese War, when
Uchimura declared his pacifism, the Christian movement split into
three groups. Those interested primarily in social reform went into
what would become the Socialist and Communist movements. The
vast majority of Christians continued on in their church. Since these
did not speak out against government policy, they gradually became accepted as a part of the Japanese scene. But, split into a
multitude of denominations, each of which claimed universality and
harked back to a different European or American tradition, they
seemed "foreign." Uchimura's *mukyōkai* lacked Western ties and
depended upon the traditional *sensei-deshi* organization, hence it
was "Japanese" and enjoyed wide potential appeal. It did not
grow quickly, but produced followers of intense piety and dedica-
tion.

During the years between 1903 and 1918 Uchimura developed
his *mukyōkai* ideas and learned the skills necessary to insure a
regular diet of incisive and inspiring commentary for the magazine.
He also lived through the problems connected with entry into the
responsible generation, that period between the death of those in
the preceding generation, who, while they live, insulate the indi-

vidual from direct confrontation with eternity, and one's own death. Once a man's forebears have all died, the individual finds that the whole past of his family now lives or dies with him, and he has the responsibility to transmit what will continue to live in future generations. During these years Uchimura came to grips with death and the problems of direct responsibility. His parents died early in the twentieth century; the Meiji Emperor and Uchimura's daughter Ruth followed them in 1912, and he witnessed the ritual suicide of Western Europe which began in 1914.

The effect on Uchimura of this confrontation is not as yet clearly understood. It is a fact, however, that as he passed through these experiences, the idea of Christ's return to earth as the end of history began to interest him. His good American friend David C. Bell had urged the faith on him for years. Finally, during the summer of 1917, Uchimura became convinced of its truth. On October 31 of that year he planned a lecture in the large central YMCA auditorium to commemorate the four-hundredth anniversary of Luther's Ninety-Five Theses. Fearful of failure on this his first attempt at so large a meeting, Uchimura later remembered that he paused on a street corner en route to the lecture hall. There he promised God that if the meeting succeeded, he would take that success as evidence that God had caused him to *leave the study and mount the lecture platform in the center*" of Tokyo.[14] The meeting succeeded beyond all expectations.

The following January, Uchimura announced a series of lectures in the same auditorium. He had enlisted as co-sponsors the Japanese representatives of the world millenarian movement which spread through Europe and the United States at the end of World War I. Two thousand people came to hear him talk on "The Second Coming of Christ as Viewed by a Scholar of the Bible." For the next few months he traveled widely to expound his new conviction in all the major cities.

Uchimura's cooperation in this millenarian movement vexes the biographer intent on the discovery of an inner logic in his subject. It is difficult to understand why Uchimura moved as he did at this time. His own writings do not provide sufficient information though they make it clear that he recognized a deep-seated connection between this action and his most profound emotions. It seems that it loomed so important to him because it enabled him, finally, to unite his religious commitment to the Christian God and his loyalty to Japanese society. American entry into World War

I proved that it had lost moral superiority over Japan. Japan's national tutor in the Christian faith had thus died, as Uchimura's personal father surrogates had passed on. Uchimura had the responsibility to convert his countrymen before Christ returned to judge the whole world. This seems to represent the subliminal logic behind his actions.

He reacted with a sense of his own historical importance. As he started his large meetings downtown, he began to print his daily diary in *The Biblical Studies*, and he identified himself increasingly with the problems of Japan's national moral health. Thus, he became a national priest, a political figure in the broadest sense who felt responsible for the health of his nation and reserved the right to radical criticism.

As he worked with his colleagues in the Second Coming movement, he recognized in the American Scopes Trial and the unbalanced mental state of many who came to his lectures the dangers inherent in the doctrine. He rejoiced that his son Yūshi had entered psychiatry, "a partial fulfillment of his father's youthful dreams,"[15] and discussed with Yūshi the psychiatric problems which belief in the Second Coming might complicate.

Satisfaction with Japan's basic ethical integrity accompanied this understanding of the relation between psychology and faith. After the end of World War I, Japan entered a period when it appeared to those like Uchimura that the forces of liberal democracy would at last win out. At the same time, word of the social dislocation caused by the war made the Japanese recognize the advantages provided by their nation's stability. Here at last the tensions which had goaded Kanzō on to prominence fell into quiet repose. Neither the individual Uchimura nor his nation required special justification or intervention before God. He could now return to the center of his society as a respected man of faith and letters.

By Faith Alone

During the last twelve years of his life, Uchimura completed a systematic study of the main parts of the Bible, achieved a sense of relaxed equality with Westerners, and effected his last great act of independence by freeing himself from the unanticipated ill effects of his own charisma.

With the passage of time the lectures of the Second Coming

movement developed into regular Sunday afternoon expositions on the Bible. Many of the *deshi* had now grown into positions of responsible adulthood. They organized a lecture series and hired Uchimura to address their members. For a decade, audiences of more than five hundred persons regularly paid lecture fees to hear him speak. Freed of managerial details he could concentrate on what he wanted to say, and he developed long coordinated series of talks based on sections of the Bible. His most famous series dealt with the Ten Commandments, Daniel, Job, Romans, the Life of Christ, and Galatians. Of these the *Romans* and the *Life of Christ* best represent his mature thought.

In the *Romans* Uchimura dealt with the problem of tradition, the connection between the old and new dispensations, and the significance of Christ in history. Before Uchimura started the series early in January, 1921, he made preparations which reflected his gravity of purpose and sense of importance. He had the Bible society bind special copies of the *Romans* with blank sheets inserted so that members of the audience could make notes. He entered into his work with such vigor that when after twenty months he finished his sixtieth lecture he felt a sense of loneliness. The texts appeared in print shortly thereafter and were reprinted six times before Uchimura's death. They can still be bought in paperback form.

Though Uchimura considered the *Romans* to be his most important work, it may well be that his *Life of Christ* better summarizes his method and message. Begun the week after he ended the *Romans,* it consisted of seventy-four lectures in two large series between December, 1922 and July, 1926. His introduction to the printed form describes his method:

No one can write the biography of Christ. Only Christ can write it well. And he sent down the holy spirit to write it for us. Matthew, Mark, Luke, John: these are what resulted. No later lives of Christ can improve on those first biographies. In our desire to weave anew the life of Christ, we simply add commentaries to these earliest attempts.[16]

He used Matthew as the major text with some reference to Mark and Luke, ignoring the problems raised by both higher and lower criticism. Instead he presented only the relevant facts without reference to the difficulties in interpretation which the conflicting views presented by the various authors of the Gospels bring on.

Within Matthew, he omitted reference to Christ's geneology, birth, youth, and visit to the temple; he also did not deal with numerous teachings and parables. Yet he spent 20 per cent of the total on the Sermon on the Mount, preferring to "make clear through Christ's teaching and actions that he was the savior, both as the son of God and of man."[17]

The *Life of Christ* exemplifies a number of points with regard to Uchimura's mature method. He did not write systematic theology, though he knew its leading exponents and frequently referred to them. His verse-by-verse approach approximated the way that the traditional Japanese studied his Confucian texts, and Uchimura went far beyond the Western literalists to an interpretation for which he sought justification in the experience of the individual believer.

In this way we may term his approach "existential" with a small initial "e." For him Christianity was the simple total of the sincere attempts by individuals to live in accordance with Christian imperatives. An individual could best study Christianity in the lives of those who called themselves "Christian." For Japanese the lives of Japanese Christians provided the best model. Here Uchimura transmuted the pains and satisfactions of his own experience into a paradigm of Christian life for his countrymen. These works of Biblical exegesis thus formed the final stage in his scholarly and yet intuitive method. His Biblical commentaries still provide the best sources in the Japanese language.

The writings and reminiscences of many among his auditors attest to his impressive lecture style. He worked on effects, avoiding contact with others for hours before each appearance in the apparent conviction that small talk might short-circuit some of the charisma building up within him. His care produced results which made it difficult for members of the audience to escape the emotions he projected.

Detailed analysis of Uchimura's Biblical works awaits the attention of future scholars. Casual contact makes it appear that Uchimura's main contribution resides in his interpretation of the particular power that the Bible can exercise over the hearts of men not nurtured in Christian society when they approach it with an open heart. The weakness of this method is that it ignores the centuries of Christian tradition which separate twentieth-century men from the authors and compilers of the Bible.

He again wrote Miyabe to disassociate himself from the church of his youth with which he had renewed his relationship early in the twentieth century:

No matter how long I consider the matter, I still feel that the church system is not in the spirit of Christ and that to continue it hinders the progress of the Gospel. . . . On the basis of our long friendship I have . . . consciously continued a contradiction with regard to you and the Independent Church. . . . Now as I mark "finis" to my life's work, I must reject all human ties and retain a clear confidence in the next world. Therefore, I hereby cut all relationships with anything which calls itself a church, and I want to end my life as a pure *mukyokai* believer.[18]

As he cut his ties with his old church, so Uchimura cast off the two *deshi* who had worked for him on his lectures and helped him edit his magazine for years. Perhaps "cast off" is too strong a word; Uchimura used the verb "to make independent," but in the context of the traditional *sensei-deshi* relationship his act reflected what would be considered a ruthlessness better expressed by a stronger verb. In the traditional system, the *deshi* served his master well to the extent that he loyally transmitted his *sensei's* ideas. Great *sensei* lived on through the careful preservation accorded them by those whom they had nurtured to maturity. Although Uchimura taught man's independence from his fellows through complete dependence on God and this lesson properly learned could in theory have been transmitted through traditional channels, in fact it could not be. The *deshi* shared the personality characteristics which had goaded Uchimura into his creativity. They were ambitious, sharp, sensitive, and fearfully in need of a leader. Uchimura was flattered by their loyalty and awed by their ability. Tsukamoto Toraji was his special favorite, and his attempt to deal with Tsukamoto provided the final tragedy and triumph in Uchimura's life.

Uchimura praised Tsukamoto. He was "a great linguist, a Dante scholar, and a good evangelical Christian. He lost his wife by the earthquake of the year before last, and since then, evangelical zeal came suddenly upon him. He is what we may call, an 'earthquake-made preacher,'[19] . . . a very learned man, great Bible-scholar, and in every way, superior to myself."[20] There is no doubt that Uchimura had considered Tsukamoto as his successor on several occasions and even told Tsukamoto that he had been chosen, but Uchimura's concern over Tsukamoto's interpretation of *mukyōkai* made him change his mind. Uchimura's own tortured road to religious understanding had finally led him to a relaxed view of direct communion with God, but for his *deshi* he had become an intermediary between them and God. They considered *mukyōkai* the core of Uchimura's genius, and Tsukamoto, just because it appeared that he might succeed Uchimura, had to clarify for himself the essence of *mukyōkai* in preparation for his own role. In this attempt Tsukamoto fell into the trap posed by the *mu*; he emphasized the negative aspects of the concept and seemed about to define a new form of church based upon negation of other churches.[21] Uchimura refused to print one of his articles without revisions and also refused him permission to use the word *mukyōkai* as the title of a new periodical which he planned to start because the term was too "negative." Tsukamoto finally gave in, but with very little grace, before Uchimura's intransigence.

Uchimura then told Tsukamoto to set up his own meeting where he could hold any views he desired, but they would not be attributed to Uchimura. Uchimura's diary entries reflect the pain it caused him. "Today I finally broke with Tsukamoto. Although it could be called cordial, it was not happy."[22] "As youths we declare our independence from elders and as elders we declare our independence from youth."[23] Tsukamoto, stunned by Uchimura's action, found himself unable to return to Uchimura for the ceremonial admission of error custom required in such circumstances. He felt apology would be insincere since it seemed to him that Uchimura had wronged him. When Tsukamoto finally determined to make amends, in spite of this conviction of innocence, he arrived at Uchimura's home to find that his *sensei* had died fifteen minutes earlier after weeks of wondering why Tsukamoto had not come to receive his pardon.

Tsukamoto first felt a strange sense of liberation, but guilt rather than liberation came with the passage of time to dominate his recollections. He felt he had "crucified"[24] Uchimura. Seven years later he recalled, "even now, . . . his little smile and fearsome gaze always float before my eyes. And the little smile, along with the fearsome gaze, consoles me, encourages me, warns, and also admonishes."[25] The vexed relationship with the aged Uchimura had become the curse in Tsukamoto's life.

Before he had felt it necessary to break with Tsukamoto, Uchimura had made up his mind about *mukyōkai*. He told his youngest *deshi* that a very important statement would be found among his papers at the time of his death. It said in part:

My *mukyokai* principle was not principle for principle's sake but principle for the sake of faith. . . . It was not an idea with which to attack the Church. It was a concept with which to further faith. . . . I speak to make my position clear. I am not a mukyokai *believer in the sense of the word's popular use today.* . . . I believe in *mukyokai* to the extent that I have no interest in the Church. . . ."[26]

Uchimura's act of final independence in death thus renounced the religious concept for which he had become most famous. The apparent renunciation of himself that this implied imposed a severe identity crisis upon the *deshi* who have struggled with it ever since. They considered themselves *mukyōkai* believers now faced with the painful necessity of working out the concept anew for themselves. Uchimura's expression of independence had been so strong and persuasive that it had bound his followers to him as he had earlier been bound to his American mentors. He had been able to leave them and return to Japan. The *deshi* had enjoyed no such alternative and so had forced him, as the price for his own integrity, to disown them. Only then could he move on freely to the next world.

Uchimura's death one year before the Manchurian Incident has left us no way to predict how he would have responded when the liberal political optimism of the twenties suddenly proved groundless. Could he have once again spoken out against government warmongering? The only answer comes from the act of another of his *deshi*, Yanaihara Tadao. Yanaihara held the post of colonial administration at the Imperial University of Tokyo. Appalled by army excesses in China during 1937, he spoke out against them and was forced to resign his post. Through the war he supported himself on his savings and his meager income from lectures on the Bible and his own magazine. His exegesis of Isaiah left no doubt that he continued to disagree with the government which finally censored his magazine by refusing him a ration of newsprint with which to publish. He continued to send out the essence of his ideas on postcards. Katō Shūichi, who rose to prominence in postwar Japan as a social critic, recalls that for him and his fellow students at Tokyo University Yanaihara's continued intransigence served as the one source of encouragement through the remainder of the war. "The whole world was mad, but we knew that as long as Yanaihara lived there was still hope for the future."²⁷ Thus, though in death Uchimura repudiated *mukyōkai*, his principal lesson of God-fearing individualism continued to find eloquent expression.

III. *Conclusion*

Uchimura appears as one of those rare leaders in the spiritual history of the world for whom analogues can be found only across great stretches of time and distance. He can be compared with Gandhi and Luther in his rejection of foreign influences in the name of native culture; with Kierkegaard and Luther in his development of his language as a tool to handle the problems posed by new situations; with Luther in his insistence upon the priesthood of each believer; and with the Japanese Nichiren (1222–1282) in his stubborn conviction of his rightness and his challenge to the government.

Although, in general one must seek outside Japan for parallels to him, Uchimura attracts attention because of his contribution to his native land. To the men of his own time and nation he exemplified the independent individual. Since he had to support himself by his opinions, he knew that to deviate too far from what people could and would believe would cost him both his influence and his livelihood. Yet his radarlike intuition continued to help him discover and develop audiences where others recognized no potential. Timid as a person, he projected an image of uncompromising strength. To a nation which had not known great heroes for over two centuries he reintroduced the concept and provided an example. When Yanaihara resigned and continued to criticize the government, increasing numbers of Japanese came to regard both him and his *sensei* as prophets. And as such they may be regarded, for they stood out against their contemporaries and staked their all in the faith that He who led them could not be disregarded.

REFERENCES

1. W. T. deBary, Ryusaku Tsunoda, *et al.*, *Sources of Japanese Tradition* (New York, 1958), pp. 646–47.

2. "Thoughts on the Discussion of 'The Ideal Japanese' ('*Ningenzō rongi e no kitai*')," morning edition (January 12, 1965), p. 2.

3. Letter to Miyabe (original in English), Christmas 1883, in *Complete Works of Uchimura Kanzō* (*Uchimura Kanzō zenshū;* hereafter *"Zenshū"*), Vol. 20, p. 96.

4. Letter to Miyabe (original in English, October 27, 1884; *Zenshū*, Vol. 20, p. 126.

5. March 6, 1891; *Zenshū*, Vol. 20, p. 207. W. T. deBary, Ryusaku Tsunoda, *et al.*, *Sources of Japanese Tradition*, pp. 852–54, includes most of this letter.

6. Ozawa Saburō, *Uchimura Kanzō: the Case of Lese Majesty* (*Uchimura Kanzō: fukei jiken;* Tokyo, 1961).

7. "Retrospection After Thirty Years (*Kaiko sanjūnen*)," Zenshu, Vol. 1, p. 8.

8. *Zenshū*, Vol. 1, pp. 31–32.

9. *Zenshū*, Vol. 1, p. 35.

10. Tokyo, 1895, p. 131; *Zenshū*, Vol. 15, p. 113. This work is now available only in Japanese translation, though W. T. deBary, Ryusaku Tsunoda, *et al.*, *Sources of Japanese Tradition*, pp. 848–52, contains several extended passages from it.

11. For an extended treatment of this subject, see my "Western Words and Japanese Pre-occupations: The English-Language Works of Uchimura Kanzō," *Pacific Affairs*, Vol. 38, Nos. 3–4 (Fall-Winter, 1965–66), pp. 307–25.

12. "The Gospel of Peace (*Heiwa no fukuin*)," *The Biblical Studies* (*Seisho no kenkyū*), No. 44 (September 17, 1903), pp. 563–4; *Zenshū*, Vol. 14, p. 291.

13. One of these translated in W. T. deBary, Ryusaku Tsunoda, *et al.*, *Sources of Japanese Tradition*, pp. 854–55.

14. "Personal Experience in the Second-Coming Faith (*Sairin shinkō no jikken*)," *Seisho no kenkyū*, No. 222 (January 10, 1919), p. 32; *Zenshū*, Vol. 9, p. 865.

15. Letter to David C. Bell, November 11, 1922; *zenshū*, Vol. 20, p. 1074.

16. *The Galilean Way* (*Gariraya no michi*), *zenshū*, Vol. 5, p. 407.

17. Yamamoto Taijirō, ed., *The Complete Exegetical Works of Uchimura Kanzō* (*Uchimura Kanzō Seisho chūkai Zenshū;* Tokyo, 1961), Vol. 15, p. 303. My analysis of *Romans* and the *Life of Christ* owes much to Yamamoto's careful annotations.

18. October 14, 1929; *Zenshū*, Vol. 20, p. 1334.

19. Letter to David C. Bell, February 2, 1925; *Zenshū*, Vol. 20, p. 1160–61.

20. Letter to David C. Bell, November 3, 1926; *Zenshū*, Vol. 20, p. 1224.

21. *My Mukyōkai* (*Watakushi no mukyōkai shugi*; Tokyo, 1962) contains Tsukamoto's articles on the subject published between 1925 and 1929.

22. December 22, 1929; *Seisho no kenkyū*, No. 354 (January 10, 1930), p. 31; *Zenshū*, Vol. 18, p. 903.

23. December 1, 1929; *Seisho no kenkyū*, No. 354 (January 10, 1930), p. 27; *Zenshū*, Vol. 18, p. 896.

24. "Uchimura Sensei's Death and I (*Uchimura Sensei no shi to watakushi*)," *Uchimura Kanzō Sensei and I* (Uchimura Kanzō Sensei to watakushi; Tokyo, 1961), p. 17.

25. "On the Seventh Anniversary of Sensei's Death (*Sensei yuite shichi nen*)," *Uchimura Kanzō Sensei and I* (*Uchimura Kanzō Sensei to watakushi*; Tokyo, 1961), p. 118.

26. *Articles in Memory of Uchimura Kanzō* (*Uchimura Kanzō tsuioku bunshū*; Tokyo, 1931); *Zenshū*, Vol. 9, pp. 204–41.

27. Statement to the author, January 8, 1969.

Atatürk as Founder of a State

"KEMAL ATATÜRK was born in Salonica in 1881." This opening statement of the conventional Turkish biography sounds as innocuous as it is anachronistic and misleading. In fact, the boy born in Salonica in 1881 was named Mustafa. Twelve years later a teacher, whose own name was Mustafa, gave him the second name Kemal ("perfection"). Only in 1934, a decade after his founding of the Turkish Republic and four years before his death, did the Turkish legislature bestow on him the honorific surname Atatürk, or "Father Turk." The statement, therefore, begs the biographer's central questions: How the boy Mustafa grew into the man Kemal, and how Kemal came to be Atatürk.

The political scientist may well wish to consider role before actor and raise three questions in turn: First, how did vast numbers of Turks come to feel so orphaned that they accepted a new father figure? Second, why was it Mustafa Kemal who became leader of the nationalist movement of 1919 and, in due course, founder of the Republic and *pater patriae*? And third, in what ways might another man's performance in these roles have differed from his? In the investigation of this third question, political and biographical analyses converge. (How did Mustafa's childish endowment and Kemal's mature character influence the destiny of Turkey as ruled by Atatürk?) Yet by their own nature, and also that of the available sources, the first two of these questions can be answered with greater assurance than the third.

Charisma and Organization

The role that Kemal played in the transition from Ottoman Empire to Turkish Republic is one that, with a Weberian term, has often been called charismatic. All legitimate authority, Max Weber asserts, is in varying proportions traditional, rational-legal, or char-ismatic. Men obey willingly—from habit, from interest, or from devotion to a person. A charismatic leader, according to Weber, is one who in the eyes of his followers is out of the ordinary human range and is capable of working miracles for their benefit. Weber does not suggest that all authority is legitimate—he leaves aside coercion—and he is, of course, aware that legitimacy can dissolve or be forfeited. But wherever political tradition and rational legality fail, his hypothesis implies that if legitimacy is in some degree to be maintained, then charisma must to that extent fill the void. Weber does not explain in detail how a claim to charisma arises or is substantiated. It would seem that the ability to produce powerful results in the absence of apparent power is the true political miracle, the most common warrant for charismatic legitimacy. However it may arise, such legitimacy in Weber's view remains shaky because it must be forever reasserted by new mir-acles—and miracles tend to become less miraculous as they multi-ply. This defect can be remedied only by "routinizing" charisma, notably by supplementing it with bureaucracy. Charismatic au-thority can become secure by shifting toward other forms of legitimacy.[1]

Charisma is based only in part on personal qualities—such as a combination of wide sensitivity, active energy, and aloofness of manner. It is, above all, a relationship, a link of expectation, that ties leader and followers. As beauty is said to be in the eye of the beholder, so charisma may be said to reside in the perceptions of those under its spell. The political analysis of charisma, therefore, must begin not with the leader's personality, but with the vacuum that he fills. Just as in physics a vacuum requires a vessel to contain it, so a political vacuum is not the mere absence of leadership, institutions, or legitimate authority, but rather the default of these at a time when they are intensely felt to be needed. Hence, typical charismatic situations are those of a sudden collapse of established authority or a profound but vague threat to the welfare of a human group. Charismatic leadership is a form of crisis leadership.

The defeat of the Ottoman Empire in World War I created such a crisis situation. The six-hundred-year-old state, after four cen-turies of victory and two of intermittent defeat, had suffered a crushing military blow. Its decimated troops remained in control of barely half the prewar territory. The major non-Turkish na-tionalities—Arabs, Armenians, Greeks—had seceded before the war or were turning openly hostile. British and French forces controlled the capital and major ports and rail junctions; in the south, the Allies were on one pretext or another advancing gradually. The landing of Greek troops in Anatolia in pursuit of the "great idea" of resurrecting a Byzantine Empire raised the specter of total dismemberment of what remained of the Ottoman state.

The Empires of the Romanovs and the Habsburgs had just collapsed in slightly worse and that of the Hohenzollerns in slightly better circumstances of defeat. It was a wonder that Sultan Mehmed Vahideddin managed to cling to his throne for four more years. Of the breakdown of his government's authority, there could be little doubt. Nor did the Allied powers try to build up any alternative structure of legitimacy. Their leaders at Paris were too divided on Germany, on Austria-Hungary, on Russia, and on the League to sort out their disagreements over Turkey. (When they began to do so, at San Remo in the spring of 1920, Turkish resistance already had a head start of more than a year.) In Istanbul and Anatolia, the Allied forces proceeded too much by coercion and piecemeal interference to allow any sense of a new order to grow up.

In this confused situation, a single act of defiance against Sultan or Allies by some prominent individual might easily establish a claim to charismatic authority. Kemal, as one of the few victorious generals in the demobilized army, was such a prominent individual, and in the spring of 1919 he publicly launched his political career by disobeying the Sultan and defying the British. For two months after his arrival as army inspector in Anatolia, he had toured the country on horseback or by automobile, had tested the political temper, made contacts, and laid plans. At British insistence, the Sultan's War Ministry tried to secure his return to Istanbul, but Kemal procrastinated and at length resigned from the army some hours before a peremptory order of dismissal could reach him. The military officer whom Istanbul had designated as Kemal's replacement continued to take his orders, and the governor who was to have arrested him resigned his post. Kemal himself redoubled his political activities in Eastern Anatolia and eluded two ambushes— one laid by a British intelligence officer and the second by one of the Sultan's governors. The impotence of Kemal's antagonists was plain.

Two nationalist congresses, at Erzurum and Sivas, appointed a "Representative Committee," headed by Kemal, which acted as a provisional government in all but name. Under such pressure from the provinces, the Sultan selected a moderately nationalist cabinet which called for general elections. The new House of Representatives unanimously endorsed the Kemalist program of independence within the armistice line of 1918. When the British tried in March 1920 to retrieve the situation by establishing full control in Istanbul and encouraging the Sultan to send troops against the Anatolian "rebels," Kemal was ready. He called a National Assembly to Ankara, defeated the ragtag army that the Sultan sent against him, and quelled a series of loyalist risings throughout Central Anatolia. Diplomatic recognition followed upon internal success. By 1921, only the Greeks were left in the field. In September of that year, Kemal turned back their military advance a few miles west of Ankara. A year later, his government was undisputed master of Istanbul as well as Anatolia.

Throughout the three years of their War of Independence, the nationalists benefited greatly from the lack of purpose and coordination among their antagonists. If Sultan's condemnation, Anatolian risings, Greek invasion, and British support had all come at once, their cause would have been hopeless. Even if the three main Anatolian risings had been simultaneous, they might have changed the outcome.[2] As it was, the nationalists attained their full aims of independence and territorial integrity. Turkey, which during World War I had been far weaker than Germany or Austria, became the only one of the Central Powers to obtain a negotiated peace. Three months after its signature, Kemal proclaimed his Republic.

This much of Kemal's story well fits the charismatic hypothesis: the personal initiative, the narrow escapes, the mounting successes, the widening popular support—all leading to the chance to rebuild the institutions and to remold the attitudes of an entire people. "Charisma," says Weber, "is the one great revolutionary force in epochs bound to tradition."[3]

But Kemal himself remained notably diffident about the personal, charismatic basis of his power. Before his landing in Anatolia, he had spent six months in consultations in Istanbul, all designed to avoid a course likely to lead to rebellion, civil war, and charisma. In Anatolia, he delayed flagrant disobedience as long as possible and, having disobeyed the Sultan, kept open the possibility of reconciliation and made several positive overtures in that direction. At most, therefore, Kemal proved a reluctant revolutionary and a very cautious charismatic.

The charismatic leader, according to Weber, scoffs at fixed rules, sneers at steady income, and generally scorns predictable regularity. On any of these counts, too, Kemal was the very opposite of a charismatic figure. All his adult life he drew a regular (if modest) government salary. His instinct, moreover, was to solve any and all problems by organization. One organization, the War Ministry at Istanbul, had sent him to Anatolia, and Kemal had taken a personal hand in the staff work that prepared his mission. On arrival, he established contact with another set of organizations—groupings of local notables and members of the defunct Union and Progress Party who were rallying to the slogans of "Defense of Rights" and "Rejection of Annexation." What distinguished Kemal most clearly from other public figures of the period was his most uncharismatic trait: He envisaged a larger and more intensive effort at organization. One is tempted to call him an organization man thrown into a charismatic situation.

These details suggest distinction among charismatic founders of new states in the twentieth century—between leaders like Sukarno and Nkrumah, who had little organization to back them up and felt constrained by what little they had, and others like Atatürk and Nehru, who inherited or were able to reconstruct a far-flung political network. The greater stability of the second variant is obvious. Nowhere in this model, however, is there the neat sequence, envisaged by Weber, of charisma first and routinization afterwards. Even while their reputations were at their most charismatic, Nehru and Atatürk were fully absorbed in perfecting their organizations. Routinization proceeded as or even before charisma became manifest.

Why does one person rather than another come to still the "charismatic hunger" of his contemporaries?[4] In Turkey in 1919, circumstances, default of some persons, and the positive ambition of others provide three concurrent lines of explanation. The circumstances were defeat and occupation, widespread desire for national resistance, and hence a need for a combination of military and political leadership. The Sultan—morbidly shy, irascible, suspicious, and lacking in political experience—defaulted by collaborating with the enemy. The three most prestigious generals, including Enver Pasha, defaulted by leading the country into defeat and then fleeing abroad. Other leading generals were Ottomans of Albanian, Kurdish, or Arab descent, and they hesitated to take the lead in what was likely to become a specifically Turkish movement of national resistance. Kemal was one of the three highest-ranking generals of Turkish nationality to stay behind. Only thirty-seven years of age (in 1918), he was the youngest holding such rank. At any rate, he was the first to seek the task of nationalist leadership.[5] In the soldierly politics of the preceding decade, he had been on the periphery of the ruling Union-and-Progress circle; his career thus illustrates Karl Deutsch's hypothesis that leadership in a new movement of political integration is likely to come from the outermost of the insiders or the innermost of the outsiders.[6] He also had developed marked political ambitions.

There probably is no simple prescription for training someone as a leader for a future time of crisis, let alone as prospective founder of a new state. Deeper personal qualities are as little amenable to deliberate social planning as they are to precise analysis by the methods of social science. The next best thing to such a prescription would appear to be a plan for educating an elite responsive to the tasks of the future—a plan that allows for natural selection to provide the leader, while the rest of the elite furnishes the necessary organized support. Such a regeneration of the political elite had been one of the prime concerns of Ottoman policy for several generations before 1919. The contrast between this late Ottoman elite and the English Puritans is instructive. The Puritans were men outside the established order trained in a new ideology; they became radical revolutionaries.[7] Kemal and his associates had been trained in a new, Western-style curriculum, but they had been trained at state expense in preparation for the highest offices in army and state. Thrown into a revolutionary situation, they became conservative revolutionaries. The same process of elite recruitment accounts in large measure for the greater political stability of Turkey in contrast to the Ottoman successor states in the Balkans and in the Middle East, for the Turkish Republic inherited roughly nine tenths of the political elite trained for an Empire far larger in area and population.[8]

Force, Right, and Foreign Policy

Throughout the period of national resistance and the War of Independence, Kemal's actions rested on a few basic convictions that he applied to shifting circumstances with great flexibility. Justice, he believed, is absolute, but Force is required to make Right prevail in this world. A Turkish state had a right to independent

213

existence; but to assert that right, the Turks had to muster the necessary energy, determination, and leadership. In the world of the early-twentieth century, moreover, the only claims to independence likely to be honored were those on behalf of a nation.

By temperament and training Kemal was a man of action, not an abstract thinker. But he reflected on his actions and had a superb gift of articulation, so that these tenets can be readily documented from his speeches and other statements. "There certainly is a Right, and Right is above Force. Except that the world must be persuaded that the nation knows its rights and is prepared to defend and retain them." A people which has exercised dominion for more than six centuries, so he never tired of telling the defeated Ottoman subjects, will not willingly become a colony. He also warned his listeners that "today the nations of the whole world recognize only one sovereignty: national sovereignty." Hence his "basic goal" was "that the Turkish nation should live in dignity and honor. This goal could be achieved only by the possession of complete independence."

Several principles derive from Kemal's central tenet. Rights can be effectively asserted only through one's own force, not vicariously through someone else's. World War I had made Britain the preponderant power in the Middle East, and leaders of almost every nationality set their hopes on winning British support: Sharif Husayn and the Arab nationalists, Weizmann and other Zionists, Venizelos with his Panhellenic plans, the signers of the Anglo-Persian treaty of 1919, and several Kurdish and Caucasian factions. In Istanbul many of the Sultan's ministers adopted a similar Anglophile course in hopes of winning more lenient peace terms at Paris. Kemal, on the contrary, saw in the British the most dangerous antagonists and assumed that only British war-weariness and Turkish resistance could soften or deflect their enmity. In his *Six-Day Speech* he reserves some of his most scathing language for a group in Istanbul in 1919 that styled itself the Society of Friends of the English. He similarly rejected the plan of an American mandate favored by the "Society of Wilsonian Principles." But since this pro-American faction included some of his closest supporters, Kemal's language about Wilson was a shade more charitable.

Kemal was well aware of the use of treaties in defining rights. To claim rights in the abstract, however, without regard to legal precedent or present force, may make you a good humanitarian—a word that from Kemal's lips carries a distinct tone of contempt. In

214

the real world, such abstract claims are idle and foolish, and Kemal saw in Wilson an example of just such sentimental folly. "I confess that I, too, tried to define the national border somewhat according to the humanitarian purposes of Wilson's principles," Kemal later stated. But he explained himself at once: "On the basis of these humanitarian principles, I defended boundaries which Turkish bayonets had already defended and laid down. Poor Wilson, he did not understand that lines which cannot be defended by the bayonet, by force, by honor and dignity, cannot be defended on any other principle." On another occasion, he expressed his realistic appraisal of force even more bluntly: "Before reorganizing Anatolia, I had to conquer its people"—leaving it open whether he was referring to his suppression of the Anatolian risings in 1920 or to his expulsion of the Greek armies.

Kemal's central tenet, moreover, works both ways. Force must back Right, but no rights must be claimed beyond what force can hold; and it was this type of realistic, even pessimistic, appraisal of the situation that had repeatedly put him at odds with his superiors during World War I. Realistic self-limitation, a readiness to fit ends to means, remains one of his lasting contributions to Turkish statecraft. In his own mind, it no doubt provided the most compelling justification for the transition from imperial to national government.

Kemal's belief about right as the end, force as the means, and the necessary proportion between them led him to insist on a neat separation between political and military affairs. As a young officer, to be sure, he had (like most of his contemporaries) taken an active part in the conspiracies that prepared the Young Turk revolution of 1908 and in the factionalism that followed. As early as 1909, however, he had proposed that officers should be prohibited from partisan activity, and for the next nine years he had fully concentrated on his military assignments. He reasserted the same principle even more emphatically when he himself had taken over the political direction of the War of Independence: "Commanders, while thinking of and carrying out the duties and requirements of the army, must take care not to let political considerations influence their judgment. They must not forget that there are other officials whose duty it is to think of the political aspect. A soldier's duty cannot be performed with talk and politicking."[9]

Kemal's convictions reflected (as we shall see more closely) national, social, as well as personal character: the legalism and militarism of Ottoman culture, the training and experience of the

215

Ottoman military-political elite of his generation, and the concern about authority and the streak of violence in his personal makeup. But he differed sharply from Enver and other contemporaries. Enver confounded political rhetoric with strategic calculation and responded to defeat with compensatory dreams of glory, whereas Kemal coordinated strategy and politics in preparing for retrenchment. A Turkish journalist who knew both leaders closely has surmised that Enver, after a battle such as Kemal had won on the Sakarya, would have thrown away victory and independence itself by marching off to the conquest of Syria or Macedonia.

A final implication of Kemal's political thinking was his unquestioning commitment to the primacy of foreign over domestic policy. This represented a tenet so obvious to him that it can be better documented from his deeds than his words. During the War of Independence, he postponed all internal differences for the sake of defending the country. In the face of the Greek attack, he protested his loyalty to the Sultan who had declared him a rebel and an outlaw. Later the immediate motive for declaring the Sultanate abolished was his concern to prevent the Western powers from inviting a rival Istanbul delegation to the Peace Conference at Lausanne. Only after the peace was signed did he proclaim a Republic, frame a new constitution, and abolish the Caliphate. Characteristically, his most explicit justification of the nation-state (in a passage already quoted) refers to the concept of sovereignty accepted in the international community and to its customs of recognition.

Communication, Dictatorship, and Democracy

Kemal's domestic policies were more variable, partly because they remained subordinate to foreign affairs, and partly because international problems tend to recur whereas domestic ones have a better chance of staying solved while policy moves on to new tasks. Three periods can be distinguished. The War of Independence, when Kemal broadly rallied all available forces; a second period (1923-27), when he forcibly consolidated his dictatorship; and a third, when he leniently exercised it. To call the Kemalist regime a "democracy," as Lord Kinross does at times in his biography, is slightly misleading even for the first period.[10] Kemal's political moves after the armistice give a better indication of his own attitudes: He first attempts to enter the cabinet through contacts in the palace and audiences with the Sultan; he then uses parliamentary lobbying in a vain attempt to bring down a collaborationist ministry; next, he wages a press campaign publicizing his role in the defense of Gallipoli in 1915 among the literate audience of the capital; he entertains passing thoughts of a *coup d'état*; and finally he decides to bring together military and civilian resistance in the provinces. The priorities are clear. The soldier turned politician starts from the traditional, autocratic center of power and moves in a widening spiral outward toward the people.

In Anatolia, Kemal was to find uses for popular support that were in part opportunistic and in part genuine. To convince his antagonists in Istanbul and London that the nationalist movement could not be quelled, he set out "to make the world hear the nation's voice in robust tones." A secret circular from Ankara, for example, unloosed a "hurricane of telegrams" to forestall an unfavorable cabinet change in Istanbul. In only three days, as many as 217 of these were received by the House of Representatives alone, which duly reprinted them in its minutes. How many more the British Embassy may have received over the months we do not know, since its chief political officer, the Dragoman, stuffed them uncounted, and perhaps unread, into what he aptly called the "*vox populi* sack."[11] At one time, when the Istanbul war minister inquired about the origin of such floods of messages, Kemal replied with an air of great innocence that these were "entirely an expression of the grief and concern emanating from the bosom of the nation."

Aside from the megaphone effects of the *vox populi*, Kemal naturally enough used in his more public statements the idiom of popular government long customary in the West and, for a decade or so, familiar to the Turkish elite as well. In Anatolia he published a newspaper first called *National Will* and then *National Sovereignty* (*Irade-i Milliye, Hakimiyet-i Milliye*), and he signed his circulars on behalf of a "Representative Committee." Yet no formal meetings of that group were held, no one quite knew who its members were supposed to be, and Kemal acted as its sole spokesman—so that, in fact, the committee represented Kemal himself and his conception of the country's good.

At other times the search for wider support was in earnest. During a period of supreme danger to the country, Kemal did his best to rally monarchists and populists, Unionists who had survived their party's debacle and anti-Unionists returning from exile, Westernizers and Muslim clerics, Bolshevik sympathizers and social conservatives. Meanwhile, to sharpen his own tactical judgment, he kept a steady exchange of telegrams with military commanders, administrative officials, and chairmen of Defense of Rights Societies in all parts of his zone of control—informing them of over-all political developments, asking for news from their areas, and at times explicitly inviting suggestions about his next moves. "I was faced with the necessity," Kemal explained later, "of piecing together with the greatest care and sensitivity all the private and public opinions and sentiments, to gauge the real trend and to arrive at a feasible decision. . . . So as to secure the application of a decision it also was very important to ascertain the point of view of the army." The cables received at Ankara from colonels and district officers throughout Anatolia embodied the true representative process of the early Kemalist movement.

Kemal's tactical secret was not, as his *Six-Day Speech* seems to imply, infallible foresight, but a sheer inexhaustible resourcefulness.[12] No sooner had one plan run into difficulty than he came up with another that bypassed the obstacle. When unexpected opportunities offered, he stood ready to seize them. The long-range goal of independence was fixed, but to reach it Kemal was tacking with every changing wind.

When it came to setting up a new institution, Kemal deliberately used vague terms that would veil its novelty and preserve his freedom of action: not a provisional government, but a "Representative Committee" that was to be "the nation's agency for communication"; not a "constituent assembly" (this, his correspondents in the provinces warned, would rouse the twin specters of dictatorship and revolution—that is, of Jacobinism and Bolshevism), but an "assembly with extraordinary powers." Although this body soon became known as the Grand National Assembly, no one for the next several months officially specified whether it was an Ottoman or a Turkish nation in whose name it was assembled. The very term *millet* was conveniently ambiguous since to the educated townsman it already meant "nation" in the Western sense, whereas to the illiterate peasant it still suggested "religious community"—that is, Islam.

"Agency for communication" was a fitting term. An American journalist visiting the Sivas Congress exclaimed: "I have never heard of more efficient communications. . . . Within half an hour,

Erzurum, Erzinjan, . . . Diyarbekir, Samsun, Trebizond, Angora, Malatya, Kharput, Konya, and Brusa were all in communication."[13] On important occasions, Kemal would be directly at the side of the telegraph operator, spending several hours in telegraphic dialogue with a single respondent. "How did you win this war?" a journalist asked in 1922; "with the telegraph wires," Kemal replied with a smile. Kemal's leadership in these early years was based on receiving and imparting information, on consulting with associates who formed a network over the country, on harmonizing and concerting the actions of the most diverse regions, social groups, and individuals. It was a virtuoso performance of leadership by conciliation, by connection, by communication.

But communication can indicate a two-way or one-way flow of power. The wires that Kemal kept humming had been strung decades before by Abdülhamid the better to control his governors and his competing networks of informers. Kemal's second period of domestic politics brought many changes, some of them quite abrupt. He still responded to events and was still ready to shift plans. But he kept his own counsel much more than before, and even his oldest friends found him evasive. Instead of taking time for detailed consultations, he would now egg the Assembly on into some procedural impasse and then announce his own plan—with all the trappings of surprise—as the magic solution.

By his choice of personnel for given tasks, Kemal still was eager to disarm possible opposition. In 1920-21, he had included in his cabinet in Ankara a maximum of high civil servants and anti-Unionists so as to compensate for the Unionist antecedents and the military backing of his movement. (Conversely, the Sultan appointed to his cabinets in Istanbul a large proportion of military officers.) One of the key speakers in the Assembly's debate on adopting a Republic was Abdurrahman Şeref, one-time imperial historiographer. Among the many deputies who jointly sponsored the bills to abolish the Caliphate and the religious or şeriat ministry, the Muslim clerics were listed first.[14] And a former Young Turk conspirator from Macedonia presided over the trial of ex-Unionists in 1926. Clearly, Kemal preferred to have the *ancien régime* provide its own undertakers and pronounce its own obituaries.

Even aside from this macabre touch, what had once been genuine solicitude on one side or accommodation on the other now smacked of Machiavellianism and sycophancy. The era of postponed issues and of veiled intentions was followed by a new era of the showdown, the *fait accompli*, and the dropped mask.[15]

The reasons for these abrupt changes are not difficult to uncover. With victory in sight, Kemal's followers felt relieved of the pressure of national emergency and proved unwilling to postpone their differences. Some took the occasion to vent long-smoldering grudges against Kemal and his current group of ministers. Kemal himself, victorious in his struggle and vindicated in his predictions and his crucial gambles, felt less dependent on support, less inclined to compromise. And just when old friends might be most conscious of past debts of gratitude, Kemal proved eager to assert his long-fettered freedom of action.

In dealing with obstreperous followers, Kemal now was not above using threats or force. A lengthy committee debate on the abolition of the Sultanate he cut short by jumping on a table. Sultanate meant dominion, he shouted, and it was not attained by pettyfogging niceties, but by power. Whatever the committee might report, the outcome would be the same—except that some "heads might be cut off." He did not have to carry out his threat just then. Yet over the next few years, a few conspicuous prosecutions subdued the noisy and restless Istanbul press. An emergency decree in 1925 closed the Progressive Republican Party, which some old associates of 1919-20 had formed in opposition to Kemal's own Republican People's Party. A score of ex-Progressives and ex-Unionists were executed in 1926, following a plot against Kemal's life, though only a few of them had had any prior knowledge of the plot. The charges that the Progressive Party had abetted the Kurdish rising of 1925 were even flimsier.

Ali Fuat Cebesoy, Kemal's friend since their childhood and later a founder of the Progressive Party, was to write in 1957 that he believed then as in the 1920's that "the Gazi would have administered the revolutionary program better by remaining an impartial head of state. But perhaps," he generously adds, "I may be mistaken." Many others believed from the start, with equal sincerity, that Turkey in Kemal's days was not ready for democracy, that any organized opposition was sooner or later bound to endanger secularism and the Republic itself. Kemal, in any case, was unwilling to tolerate the experiment. Rather, he was prepared to wield personal power through a party dictatorship and, if necessary, to make his more headstrong or ambitious opponents pay with their lives.

Readers of a generation inured to the mass murders of a Hitler and of a Stalin—and to those following Sukarno's overthrow in Indonesia—should at once be reminded that in an average day those regimes killed off more victims than the Kemalist regime did in all its two decades. Although the exact arithmetic is hard to establish, it is clear that those who lost their lives for political reasons in Turkey in the twenties and thirties numbered several dozen, at most a few hundred (or, if we include the risings in Anatolia in 1920 and in Kurdistan in 1925, a few thousand). Nor did the regime create any sizable number of exiles—again the number hardly exceeded a few hundred. Proportions are of the essence in politics, and in judging Kemal's performance, it must be borne in mind that in modern times few political transformations of such magnitude have been accomplished at such modest cost in lives.

Not only was Kemal restrained in his use of violence, but the violent interlude ended after a few years. His one-party regime was tempered after about 1927 by full respect for parliamentary and legal procedures. Having suppressed the opposition and executed a few of his more serious rivals, he could afford to be more lenient and broad-minded. No longer could a deputy with impunity shoot his colleague dead in the very lobby of the Assembly, as happened in 1923. No longer could a score of Assembly members, regardless of their parliamentary immunity, be summarily tried and sentenced as in 1926. In the internal deliberations of the People's Party parliamentary group, major issues could be debated freely, and even on the Assembly floor dissident members could cast occasional nay votes without fear of reprisal. Flagrant cases of corruption were prosecuted—including impeachment proceedings against a cabinet minister. A number of potential malcontents were sent into honorable exile as ambassadors to Warsaw, Tirana, or other minor capitals. The few determined opponents which the regime still had in the 1930's—Communists, extreme clericalists, and Kurdish tribal leaders—were likely to draw prison sentences or terms of forced residence away from their homes. Elections were held on a regular four-year schedule, and Kemal himself was re-elected President by each new Assembly. Most importantly, perhaps, Kemal after the days of the War of Independence enforced a clear separation between military and civilian affairs—as only a victorious general turned politician can.[16]

In launching his political career, it was noted, Kemal had begun from the top with his connections with the Sultan, and then, as successive plans failed, worked his way down to the small-town level. But his populism was not all by default. Having for years commanded troops raised by a comprehensive system of conscription and embarking now on a mission of national self-defense, he knew that the success of his enterprise would depend on a combination of resolute leadership from the top and broad support from the common masses. This was to remain Kemal's political position throughout his career—that of an elitist out to awaken a popular response. These two poles of his thinking already appear clearly in the speech he gave to the notables of Ankara when first setting eyes on that city late in 1919. It was one of his most significant speeches, and several passages, including his justification of national sovereignty, have already been quoted. A longer excerpt at this point will illustrate not only Kemal's manner of thought, but also (so far as a translation can) his spoken style.

If a nation does not become concerned about its existence and its rights with its entire strength, with all its spiritual and material powers, if a nation does not rely on its own strength to secure its existence and independence, then it cannot be rescued from becoming this person's or that person's puppet. Our national life, our history, and our system of administration in the last epoch are a perfect demonstration of this. Therefore, within our organization the principle has been adopted that the national forces are supreme and that the national will is paramount. Today the nations of the whole world recognize only one sovereignty: national sovereignty. If we now look at the other details of the organization—we begin our work from the village and the neighborhood and from the people of the neighborhood, that is, from the individual. If the individuals do not do their own thinking, the masses can be led in an arbitrary direction, can be led by anyone in good directions or in bad directions. To be able to save himself, every individual must become personally concerned with his destiny. A structure that in this way rises from below to the top, from the foundation to the roof, will surely be sturdy. Nonetheless, there is need at the beginning of any undertaking to go not from below upward, but from above downward.

If the former could be done, all mankind could achieve their hearts' desire. But since no practical and concrete way of doing this has yet been found, certain initiators are providing guidance in giving to nations the directions that they need to be given. In this way, organization can be built from above downward. In my travels in the interior of our country, I have been extremely gratified to observe that our national organization, which naturally began in this same way, has reached down to its true point of origin, to the individual, and that from there the real structuring upward has also begun. Nevertheless, we cannot assert that any degree of perfection has been attained. Therefore, it must be considered a national and patriotic duty that we should make great efforts especially to attain the goal of a structuring from below upward.[17]

Authority and Ambivalence

Kemal's adult personality revealed several distinct facets, one during his army career until 1918 and three others during the successive phases of his political leadership that were distinguished earlier. The first of these phases was that of the War of Independence (1918-23), a time when Kemal succeeded in coming to terms with his ambivalence about authority. The second phase (1923-27) was that of consolidation of his dictatorship, when Kemal was able to relate the personal experience of his youth to the cultural situation of Turkey as a whole. The third phase (1927-38) included the last decade of his life, when he was the country's unchallenged ruler, but when the resources of his personality, so sharply focused earlier, began to blur and decline.

To many of his classmates in military school and to his fellow officers, Kemal appeared morose and taciturn. In the years of World War I, he often seemed a querulous malcontent who increasingly disapproved of the entire drift of military and political events and who therefore refused to participate and withdrew into himself. The measure of this withdrawal is provided by the spectacle of one of the ablest and most energetic Ottoman generals refusing at the height of the war (1917-18) to accept any command and instead, at the age of thirty-six, taking several months to accompany the Crown Prince to Germany and to undergo a medical cure at Karlsbad.

But from his arrival in Anatolia and for the next eight years (that is, during the first and second periods of his political career), Kemal developed a gift of persuasive speech that was to become the principal tool of his new trade—addressing small groups of notables, congresses, assemblies, and popular crowds. Not surprisingly, his major published works were all spoken, rather than written: the memoirs of the period from 1914 to 1919, composed in the form of lengthy interviews with two journalists in his entourage; the *Six-Day Speech,* delivered before the 1927 Congress of the People's Party; and his *Speeches and Addresses,* delivered over the years both inside and outside the National Assembly (mainly be-

223

tween 1919 and 1925), and collected posthumously by the Institute of the History of the Turkish Revolution.

In searching for the man behind the politician, one may well take one's clue from three episodes that are featured more prominently in those three oral works than any comparable events. Not surprisingly, each episode relates closely to one of the periods just outlined. His reaction to the armistice of 1918, described at length in the 1926 memoirs, constituted the beginning of the first phase, and his response to the reinforced occupation of Istanbul, as described in great detail in the *Six-Day Speech*, constituted its climax. The emancipation of women was a recurrent theme during his speaking tours in Anatolia in 1923-25, during the second period. And the delivery of the *Six-Day Speech* itself marks the turning point to the third or final phase.

At the time of the armistice, Kemal was in command of the Syrian front, and his memoirs justify in detail and with full documentation the tenacious opposition he put up against the orders received from Istanbul for evacuation of the strategic port of Alexandretta. It was his inability to impose his interpretation of the armistice—of the rights and duties of defeated Turkey—on the political leadership in Istanbul that prompted him again to resign his military command, this time not to go off to Karlsbad or Berlin, but to move in on Istanbul and to tackle the political situation head on. The months that followed (November 1918 to April 1919) were not a mere withdrawal, but rather a constructive "moratorium" in which he pondered and explored the basic strategies of his newly chosen career—including the Anatolian strategy that he eventually adopted, with its risks to himself, the dynasty, and those who might be caught in the struggle between the two. His gradualism was designed to reduce these risks. It took him months to make his decision public (with his resignation from the army in July 1919) and four more years for that decision to be fully and dramatically confirmed (through his election as President of the Republic).

Kemal's transition from soldiering to politics and from silence to speech brought into the open his central ambivalence toward authority. The statement about Force and Right quoted earlier implies this ambivalence. To trace it back into Kemal's childhood is an undertaking that a political scientist's limited competence renders difficult and the scanty sources on his early life make impossible.[18] But before returning to the significance of the armistice of 1918 for Kemal's life and thought, it is appropriate to document that ambivalence from his mature years.

That Force should have been a major theme in Kemal's thinking, particularly about foreign affairs, is not surprising. He was a military man and later a political leader in wartime. Throughout his formative and most active years—indeed until he himself established the Republic—foreign dangers loomed large for the Turkish state, which was at war from the time Kemal was thirty until he was forty-two.

Against this background, his deep feeling about Right and Law becomes all the more meaningful. "There certainly is a Right, and Right is above Force." Throughout his career, Kemal respected outward forms of legality. This was, of course, a national as well as a personal characteristic. As rulers over a far-flung Empire, the Ottomans had for centuries been called upon to formulate and uphold the law that Serbs, Greeks, Arabs, and many others might cheerfully defy. Hence it is difficult to know to what extent Kemal upheld legality because it could rally fellow Turks to him or because of his own conscience, because he could not bring himself to apply force other than in a righteous cause.

Whatever these dual origins of his attitude (which Kemal had little need to distinguish), there is a clear difference in its application to others and to himself—and it is here that his ambivalence about law, power, and authority becomes manifest. In dealing with subordinates, he lets them feel the full rigor of the law. In shaping his own actions and his relations to superiors, he is inclined to stretch the law without actually breaking it.[19]

Several of these elements are blended in his account of the abortive plot of 1916 led by Captain Yakub Cemil, designed (if we may believe Kemal's later account) to bring Kemal, the victor of Gallipoli and the youngest general in the Ottoman army, to power. Kemal sneers at the Unionist rulers of the day for their cowardice and hesitancy in proceeding to the execution of the culprit. Had the plot succeeded, Kemal explains, he would have accepted the gift of power—though not from such sullied hands; one of his first acts of state would have been to have had Cemil hanged for treason.

In considering his own actions, he is at once more lenient and more inventive. His mission to Anatolia, in fact, may be more political than military, but he has taken care to insert in his instructions a number of elastic clauses that can be stretched to legalize the situation. Nor, so long as he takes off his uniform just a few hours before the dismissal notice can reach him from Istanbul, does he feel that he is guilty of insubordination. The Defense of Rights Society may, in fact, be supplanting the Sultan's authority, but first it duly registers with the local emissaries of Imperial authority.

Kemal's assertion of the armistice line of 1918 as the national frontier brings together the personal and the national experience and intertwines the strands of Kemal's political thinking that were earlier considered separately—right, force, and law; nationhood, diplomacy, and politics. Kemal did not define the boundary as an ethnic or linguistic line. In his early statements, he was careful to speak of areas with an "Ottoman Muslim majority" so as to include Kurds as well as Turks. For the nation within that line, he claimed no common primordial history, no Rousseauian general will, no Wilsonian plebiscite, and no Hegelian *Volksgeist*—only six hundred years of a common tradition of rule. Self-determination and other "humanitarian" arguments might serve as convenient talking points. In its essence, however, it was a military line, a line that Ottoman Turks had defended even in the extremity of defeat and, in the crucial Syrian sector, under Kemal's personal command. It was a legal line recognized by the armistice of Moudros, and all Allied encroachments beyond it were so many breaches of international law. It was a political line, because the nationalist movement under Kemal's leadership, measuring ends to means, had based its political program on that line, had staked its honor on that claim, and had redeemed that claim with the bayonet.

To found a new state on military frontiers was a task that gave full scope to Kemal's soldierly virtues, even in his later role as a politician. The same constructive blend is evident in his execution of the over-all plan. His resourcefulness, his careful exploration of alternatives, his keen sense of timing, and his reliance on surprise may be seen as so many political applications of the precepts that he had learned from his Prussian and Ottoman instructors at the military staff college.[20]

Whereas the armistice bore directly on the themes of Force and Right, it may seem curious that Kemal, the antisentimental realist, should dwell in his *Six-Day Speech* at such length on the reinforced occupation of Istanbul on March 16, 1920. Materially, in terms of bayonets, that move affected the situation very little. Allied troops had been stationed in Istanbul since the end of 1918 and had continually interfered in the conduct of the Sultan's government. In

Anatolia, Kemal remained in control: It was not the British in Istanbul nor the Sultan—with his hastily assembled "Disciplinary Forces" and "Muhammadan Forces"—who later in the year challenged Kemal's hold on the hinterland, but rather the Greeks moving inland from Izmir.

Still the emphasis in the *Six-Day Speech* is quite accurate, for the British by their move drastically changed the relations between the Sultan and Kemal. By arresting nationalist deputies in the very building of the Ottoman parliament and by occupying telegraph offices throughout the capital, the British cut Kemal off from any further means of pressuring the Sultan and his government. By getting the Sultan to outlaw Kemal and raise troops against him, they forestalled, for the time being, any reconciliation between Istanbul and Anatolia—which Kemal had repeatedly sought on his own terms over the months. The Sultan, of course, might have come around: After Kemal's victory over the Greeks in 1920-21, the Istanbul government was only too ready to negotiate with Ankara the re-establishment of monarchical normalcy. After 1908, Sultans Abdülhamid and Reşad had conceded political control to the Young Turks; why should their brother Vahideddin or, if he proved unwilling, the next prince in the line of succession have done less for Kemal after 1922?

But in the meantime the British had given Kemal the trump card that would allow him to challenge the Sultan to a showdown— although the full extent of the challenge did not become apparent until later. In response to the Şeyhulislam's *fetva*, which declared him an outlaw and a rebel, Kemal secured a *fetva* from leading clerics in Anatolia pronouncing the Sultan a captive of the infidel enemy, hence releasing Muslims from their duty of obedience.

The British (in the view espoused by Kemal) had cut the legal bond between himself and the Sultan, absolving the one of the crime of tyranny and the other of the crime of rebellion. They had put power in his reach—under circumstances more dangerous, but also more honorable and promising than the Yakub Cemil plot of 1916. In 1916 and 1919, Kemal's ambition had gone no further than the ministry of war or perhaps the prime ministership. Now all of a sudden there appeared a far more thrilling vision: He would be able to supplant the Sultan himself, exercise full sovereignty, and yet suffer no torments of guilt for having destroyed the existing legal order. Throughout the spring and summer of 1920, to be sure, Kemal protested his devotion to the Sultan and his determination to liberate him from captivity. But by 1922 that notion had been quietly abandoned. Still, the abolition of the Sultanate retroactive to 1920 was no mere legal sophistry; for Kemal, it became the final act relieving his old ambivalence about authority, accommodating his overweaning desire for power to his deep-seated respect for law, and reconciling Force and Right.

Culture and Personality

Following this reconciliation, Kemal's program of Westernization by decree proceeded during the second period even as he consolidated his dictatorship: Republic for Monarchy (1922-23), abolition of Caliphate and religious schools (1924), the Hat Law outlawing the wearing of turban and fez (1925), the shift from the Muslim to the Christian era (1925) and from Arabic to Latin letters (1928), the adoption of the Swiss civil and Italian penal codes (1926), and the abrogation of the constitutional clause making Islam the state religion (1928).

Throughout these eventful years, Kemal's tactical instinct continued to be unerring. By announcing his reforms piecemeal and forcing each of them through within a few weeks, he forestalled any crystallization of opposition and instilled a sense of momentum in his followers. As earlier in his shaping of political institutions, he carefully chose the labels. His aim this time was not to disguise novelty—there was no need for this now that he was in unchallenged control—but to spare national sensibilities. He spoke of the international, not the Christian, calendar; of the Turkish, not the Swiss, civil code; of the Turkish, not the Latin, alphabet; of civilized, not European, dress.

Few of the reforms were original with Kemal. Most of them had been advocated in the decade of political change and debate after 1908—with the significant exception of the republican form of government and the abolition of the Caliphate; a few had solid antecedents in the earlier, nineteenth-century era of Ottoman reform. Much of Kemal's program was sketched in a utopia (entitled, *A Very Wakeful Sleep*) that Abdullah Cevdet, most consistent Westernizer among Young Turk writers, had published in 1912.[21] But Cevdet's voice had been only one in a confusing babble of Ottomanism, Westernism, Turkism, and Pan-Islam, whereas Kemal picked out only this single clear theme. Among the several types of successful political leader, the state founder, by definition, creates new political forms. The need for a new political circuitry typically arises from an overloading of the old channels of communication. When it comes to substantive measures, his task is less one of innovation than of clarification, less one of composing new messages than of sorting out the old ones; it is one of selection, of rerouting, and of establishing priorities.

The criticism sometimes leveled at Kemal's reforms—that they dealt with surface trivia such as headgear, letters, and family names—does not stand up under closer examination. Kemal, it is true, cared far more deeply about cultural matters than about social and economic problems as these are commonly defined in a post-Marxian world. But culture consists of a set of symbols, and in the context of his time and place these externals had profound symbolic meaning. Throughout the millennia, Middle Eastern society had been a mosaic of language groups, religious communities, and social classes. The distinctions among these had always been clearly visible in contrasting forms of dress; thus, social behavior could be adjusted on first encounter and at a glance. To prescribe a different set of clothes, therefore, did imply profound social changes. The Hat Law meant an ostentatious break with Islam, which required the faithful to touch his covered head to the ground in his daily prayers.[22] The alphabet change produced its intended effect by cutting off later generations from most of their pre-1928 literary heritage. The abolition of the fez (adapted a century earlier from a current Venetian fashion as a brimless compromise between Muslim turban and Christian hat) implied a death sentence on the bastard Levantine culture that pervaded Istanbul (and Kemal's Salonica) in the nineteenth century and cities like Cairo and Damascus well into the twentieth. Kemal evidently agreed with Abdullah Cevdet that "there is no second civilization: civilization means European civilization, and it must be imported with both its roses and its thorns."[23]

The issue of Westernization had bedeviled Ottoman politics since 1774 and 1839. It had begun as a problem of military defense, but it had grown in due course into an issue of cultural transformation and at length posed sharply the question of national identity. Having solved the military and the national questions in the War of Independence, it was natural that Kemal should turn next to a solution of the cultural problem. And Kemal's background equipped him peculiarly well to apply intimate personal experience to the resolution of these broader public issues.

Like most of the leading figures of the Young Turk generation,

Kemal was a native of the European part of the Empire, with its mixed Slav, Greek, Albanian, and Turkish, Christian, Muslim, and Jewish population. Among those leaders, he belonged to the minority that had risen from humble origins. His father had at one time been in the lowest rank of the customs service and later made a modest living in the lumber trade. His mother was an uneducated woman of peasant stock and, after the father's death, married a Turkish-Macedonian farmer.

Yet in his attitudes he differed markedly from his contemporaries. Enver, for example, was the son of a small official in Istanbul and later showed evident relish for the life of high Ottoman society which his political successes opened up for him; his marriage to one of the Sultan's nieces marks the pinnacle of his career as a parvenu. The political associates whom Kemal rallied around him in Anatolia in 1919, on the other hand, mostly came from good families: Ali Fuat Cebesoy was the son and grandson of a *pasha*; Rauf Orbay's father had been an admiral and senator; and Kâzim Karabekir's, a gendarmerie officer. All of them tended to be far more cautious in their political tactics and more conservative in their aims. Kemal's attitude contrasted with both Enver's and that of his own upper-class companions. He found it hard to conceal his impatience with court etiquette or his contempt for social climbers. He often deliberately shocked his associates with his passion for intellectual debate instead of polite conversation, with his abrupt shifts from conciliation to blunt threats, with his love for Western dress, music, and dance, and with his somewhat vulgar tastes in drinking and wenching.

Kemal's predilections become understandable when his social and geographic background are considered together. In Salonica in his youth, there were two distinct upper classes: the Ottoman government officials, who spent their days in the office and their evenings in the all-male company of the coffeehouse, and the Greek merchant class, among whom both men and women led a freer, noisier, and more visible social life. Like Enver and others of modest origins, Kemal may have been impressed with a style of high social life to which he had not been born; but the social forms he admired were European, not Ottoman. It is no coincidence, then, that the issues of Westernization and nationalism were resolved by a Turkish leader who came from a region of mixed nationality where Ottoman and European culture were in close contact—or that the social question for that leader was primarily one of cultural transformation rather than of economic reallocation. Kemal's humble Macedonian origins served him as a sort of Archimedean point from which to unhinge the Ottoman cultural as well as political tradition.

Several hypotheses in the literature on leadership are clearly relevant here. It has often been noted that the originators of nationalist ideologies typically come from border areas or spend some of their formative years abroad. Because of this *Fremdheitserlebnis*,[24] national identity for them becomes something not to be taken quietly for granted, but rather to be consciously (and sometimes painfully) chosen and vocally asserted. European examples abound, and Kemal and his Macedonian-Turkish contemporaries, as well as the more ideologically oriented Turkish nationalists from the Tsarist Empire, fit the pattern closely.

On a psychological plane, Harold Lasswell long ago suggested that the politician "displaces private affects upon public objects."[25] And Erik Erikson more recently has said of Luther that he set out "to solve for all what he could not solve for himself alone."[26] There is a significant difference of emphasis: Lasswell suggests an unwarranted intrusion of psychopathology into politics, Erikson a creative blending of the personal and the political. The difference may well coincide with that between leaders like Hitler or Wilson who, after spectacular successes, destroy themselves and their work, and those like Luther or Gandhi whose works endure.

Of all of Kemal's Westernizing reforms, the emancipation of women carries a double distinction: It was not formally embodied in any law,[27] and yet some of Kemal's most eloquent speeches of this period deal with this theme: To keep women secluded is to waste one half of Turkey's most precious resource. Even to do properly their jobs as wives and mothers of future citizens, women must be educated. Only as a nation of modern men and women can Turkey take its rightful place in the modern world.

Accustomed all his life to giving orders to men, and later to laying down the law for them, Kemal preferred, in dealing with the problem of women, to rely on the persuasive power of speech. The mid-twenties, of course, were the time when Kemal, having gained power, had to show for what purposes he meant to use it, and perhaps thereby reveal the deeper motives from which he had originally craved power. Since his speeches on female emancipation are so prominent among those on Westernization, it seems likely that his feelings about women and their relation to men

231

point to the most intimate link between Kemal the man and Kemal the political leader.

Lord Kinross's account of Kemal's personal life may not be accurate in every detail, but it does represent the most careful sifting fo date of the evidence readily available. On the subject of women, it is to be commended especially for avoiding the twin temptations of prudery and salaciousness.[28]

After his father's death, Kemal grew up for some years as the only male in a house that he shared with his mother and younger sister. The relations between mother and son remained stormy till the end. Zübeyde wished Kemal to become a man of religion, but he insisted on a military career. When the mother remarried, young "Mustafa was jealous as a lover of another man in his mother's life." Years later, Zübeyde reciprocated with hearty disapproval of Fikriye, an attractive cousin who had come to share Kemal's house in Ankara. To the end, Zübeyde scolded "little Mustafa" as if he were a schoolboy.

As an adolescent, Kemal felt attracted to the Christian women in Salonica; as a young military attaché in Sofia, he eagerly took ballroom lessons in the waltz and the tango. Both he and his friend the ambassador fell in love with Bulgarian girls; yet to their discreet inquiries, the father of one replied: "I would rather cut off my head than have my daughter marry a Turk." Most of Kemal's relations with Western or Westernized women remained casual—although from Sofia and during World War I he carried on an intimate correspondence in Turkish occasionally interspersed with French with the Christian widow of a Muslim officer. Kinross judges that "Kemal was a man without love in his nature" to whom women "meant little save as a source of distraction, an outlet for his appetites, and a stimulus to his masculine vanity. Asked once what qualities he admired most in a woman, he replied, 'Availability.'" Kemal "throughout his life chose women who took the initiative in showing their feelings. But he could not bear to be loved too much."

Zübeyde died early in 1923 in Izmir, reconquered three months earlier by her son's armies. Three days later, he married Lâtife, an intelligent, Westernized, strong-willed woman of good Turkish family. Zübeyde, before her death, had for once approved of her son's choice. Kemal now took pride in showing off his young wife without a veil, hearing her take part in debates at the dinner table, and having her ride with him on horseback at parades. But Lâtife tried to control his drinking, grew fiercely jealous when he flirted with others, on occasion made him feel her social superiority, and took to scolding him in public, much as his mother had.

In his attitude toward women, it is fair to conclude, Kemal was caught in an ambivalence as deep as that toward male authority. At one pole stood his mother—domineering, uneducated, traditionally secluded. Around the other revolved a quick procession of Westernized women—intelligent, educated, and "available." Yet Lasswell's hypothesis of private feelings displaced upon public objects fits none too closely. Kemal's task was of such magnitude that he could ill afford the luxury of displaced affects, of being at odds with himself. He drank and indulged his appetite for mistresses only as war and politics left him the time—indeed he required these distractions precisely whenever his nervous energies were not employed on what to him were more serious tasks. On those occasions, he caused much gossip, since the banquet table and the ballroom were his favorite settings for letting women "take the initiative in showing their feelings." Otherwise, most of his affects remained under firm control, both in public and in private.

His marriage, by contrast, was rather a displacement in the opposite direction. "He had married as much for sociological as for personal reasons"[29]—that is, to set an example of a Westernized, emancipated relationship between the sexes. Yet the marriage, Kinross concludes, was marked by "the failure of two headstrong Oriental natures to come to terms with the give-and-take problems of a Western relationship." After two years, Kemal divorced Lâtife unilaterally in the traditional fashion.

Even though Kemal transcended the Lasswellian model of political psychopathology, he fell short of the Eriksonian ideal, for he clearly did not resolve his ambivalence about traditional and Westernized women for himself. Still, the official policy of female emancipation that he instituted soon after his divorce proved a more promising way of resolving (or forestalling) similar feelings of ambivalence for future generations of Turkish men. In his later years, Kemal combined private feelings of affection with public principles of female equality by adopting as his daughters several intelligent young women and sponsoring their education in Turkey and abroad. One became an aviatrix, and another served as his assistant in the formulation of his historical speculations.

233

Among all of Kemal's public statements, the most personal one on record is the brief speech that he pronounced at his mother's grave in Izmir on January 27, 1923. It is couched in Kemal's simplest, most direct language and bears all the marks of spontaneity; on careful reading of both content and context it gives us perhaps the most important single clue to his attitudes toward authority, toward women, and toward his own political career.

Kemal did not come to the graveside until a full twelve days after his mother's death. On the day before Zübeyde died, he had set out on his first post-war speech-making tour. Although he was informed of her death, he stuck to his full schedule, reaching Izmir after six or seven stops and as many political addresses. Needless to say, both his absence from the mother's funeral and his conduct of political business as usual at a time when there was no pressing emergency were grave departures from Muslim and Turkish conventions of piety. An even more striking departure from the rituals of mourning was his marriage only three days after his visit to the grave. Kemal evidently could not bring himself to rush to his mother's side in death any more than he had been able to live harmoniously with her since his childhood. Nor could he bear to remain without a new, formal attachment to another woman of strong character with whom he would soon engage in similarly intimate battles of will.

"My mother, who lies here," Kemal told the assembled friends and dignitaries, "has been a victim of oppression, of violence, of an arbitrary administration which has brought the entire nation to the precipice of disaster. If you allow me to explain this, I should like to submit a few prominent points of her life of suffering. It was in the era of Abdülhamid. . . ." The first two episodes recalled relate to his earliest political activity as a young staff officer, when he was jailed for a month and then posted to a distant assignment in Damascus (to which Kemal refers obliquely as his "place of banishment"). "Only three to five days were vouchsafed to us to see each other, because again the secret agents, the spies, the hangmen of tyranny . . . carried me away. . . . My mother was forbidden to see me and she was abandoned . . . in her sorrows and her grief." The third episode is the time in 1919 when the government of Vahideddin, Abdülhamid's brother, had sentenced him to **death** *in absentia*. When Kemal sent a manservant of his back to

Istanbul alone, "my mother . . . suspected that the death sentence which had been pronounced on me by the Caliph and Sultan had been carried out and this suspicion caused her to be paralyzed. After that . . . she always was under the pressure and the torture of the Sultan and of his government and of all the enemy powers. . . . For three and a half years my mother spent all her nights and all her days in tears. These tears made her lose her eyesight. Finally, very recently, I was able to rescue her from Istanbul. I could rejoin her but she had already died in body and was only living on in spirit."

The speech is equally remarkable for what it omits as for what it says. It begins as an expression of the son's grief for the mother, but it quickly turns to a political theme. There is no mention of the other members of their family, the father and the stepfather from whom Zübeyde was widowed, the sister Makbule who survived her mother and who was to survive Kemal as well, or the other children of Zübeyde's who died earlier. The main characters in the melodrama at the graveside are the mother, Kemal himself, and two of the sultans—Abdülhamid and, in a lesser role, Vahideddin. The former, of course, had been the ruler throughout Kemal's childhood and youth—in fact, until his deposition in 1909, in which Kemal, as staff officer of the "Action Army" that marched on the capital, took a prominent if indirect part. Zübeyde, we know, had taken little if any interest in public affairs; yet it is to political vicissitudes, to the "torture of the Sultan," that Kemal attributes her lifelong suffering and her death. Zübeyde, we know, had wanted young Kemal to become a man of religion, and it was the son himself who had insisted on preparing for the army and, once in the officer corps, had joined in the political conspiracies then rife among the military. Yet at no point does Kemal acknowledge his own choice in these matters. He evidently felt *compelled* to join the army and later to launch into politics—compelled by the Sultan's despotism which let the country's defenses decay, which made first Kemal's native Macedonia and then all of Turkey a prey to foreign intrigue, to sedition, and to invasion. It is the Sultan, therefore, first Abdülhamid and then Vahideddin, who is explicitly blamed for the mother's suffering and sorrow, for her paralysis, for the loss of her eyesight, for her death in body and at last in spirit.

But for a death that he blames on political tyranny, at a

graveside from which political preoccupations had detained him, there is a political consolation in Kemal's own recent triumph. The final passage of the speech moves easily from mother Zübeyde to mother country:

"There is no question that I am much grieved by the loss of my mother. But there is one circumstance that removes this grief of mine and that consoles me: to see that the administration, which brought our mother the country to destruction and ruin, has itself been brought to the graveyard of oblivion, never again to return. Let my mother be underneath this soil, but let national sovereignty stand on its feet forever. That is, the greatest force that consoles me is that. Yes, national sovereignty will continue forever. To the spirit of my mother and to the spirit of all ancestors let me repeat the oath that I have given in my conscience. Before the grave of my mother and in the presence of God I vow and swear: to preserve and defend that sovereignty which the nation has obtained and established by shedding so much blood, I will, if necessary, not hesitate in the least to go to the side of my mother. To sacrifice my life in the cause of national sovereignty shall be for me a duty of conscience and honor."[30]

Kemal did not consider authority self-justifying or inherently beneficent. The claims of authority, while it remained legitimate, to him were stern and inexorable. But to retain legitimacy, the holder of authority must prove himself, the commander on the battlefield, the ruler by warding off invasion and suppressing rebellion. In short, authority must accomplish its proper tasks.

It was noted that Kemal—like many a successful rebel—felt deeply ambivalent toward authority. While recognizing its claims in principle, he found it hard to take orders from those in authority above him. From childhood on, his favorite solution to the dilemma was to perfect his own understanding of the authority-legitimating tasks. In school, the teacher recognized him as Mustafa "Kemal" (Mustafa "the Excellent") and put him in charge of a group of younger and duller pupils. From his days as a young officer, Kemal toward the end of his life recalled with pride the time when, over the objections of his superiors, he worked out an independent plan for a military exercise—only to be rewarded by the praises of the German military inspector, the great Field Marshal Baron Colmar von der Goltz.[31] Later on, Kemal was to perfect the same technique. By waiting for events to demonstrate the failure, and hence the illegitimacy, of his superiors, he could at last assume legitimate authority for himself, and thus reconcile his ambivalence. But unlike the Sultan, he did not claim personal or arbitrary power: it was his oath to the service of national sovereignty that he invoked to justify his commands.

In the graveside speech the authority figure is the Sultan, first Abdülhamid and then Vahideddin, in the deposition of both of whom Kemal was instrumental. The relationship between the three *dramatis personae*—mother, son, and Sultan—thus is intimate. The Sultan, one readily infers, represents the evil father figure: his emissaries are hangmen, and he is guilty of the bodily destruction of mother Zübeyde and mother country. Kemal himself appears as the loyal son, who avenges mother and country by exposing the hollowness of the Sultan's—any Sultan's—authority, by consigning him to "the graveyard of oblivion," and by replacing the Sultanate with a more legitimate regime of his own creation and with himself in command.

In his speech to the National Assembly that declared the Sultanate lapsed, Kemal had revealed the depth of his feeling— while at the same time disclaiming any guilt for Vahideddin's demise, which he characterizes as a political suicide:

Finally, during the reign of Vahideddin, the 36th and last Sultan of the house of Osman, the Turkish nation was brought to the deepest ditch of slavery. There was a desire to push the Turkish nation, which for thousands of years had been the noble symbol of the concept of independence, into that ditch with a single kick. But to deliver this kick there was need for a traitor, a senseless, uncomprehending traitor . . .

Who would be capable of rising to his feet and of accepting with his whole being the death sentence on Turkey, that would put an end to the independence of the Turkish state, that would destroy the life, the good name, the honor of Turkey's population? Unfortunately, none other than the man this nation had allowed to be at its head as its sovereign, its Sultan, its Sovereign, its Caliph: Vahideddin. By this vile act of his, Vahideddin only accepted a transaction of which he amply deserved.

Vahideddin through this act of his killed himself and rendered inevitable the obliteration of the form of government that he represented.[32]

Now, four months later, Kemal at his mother's grave found comfort, as do other bereft mortals, in the certain hope of immortality. But it is not Zübeyde herself, but rather the mother country under Kemal's new dispensation of national sovereignty, of whom he says that she will live forever. And only in this public cause of national sovereignty does Kemal vow to "go to the side

DANKWART A. RUSTOW

of his mother"—something he could not bring himself to do in his private grief for Zübeyde. Only to the country at large could Kemal unstintingly give that love that he so often withheld from his mother and the many other women in his life. But on this grand, countrywide scale, that love would be more fully returned than Zübeyde had ever been capable of returning it. The avenging son's crowning reward was that he would be acknowledged by his countrymen, and indeed by history itself, as the Father Turk.

Testament and Decline

The delivery of the *Six-Day Speech* itself marks the last personal turning point revealed in Kemal's oral works. It was a grand account of his political performance since his arrival in Anatolia in 1919, with the main emphasis on the early years when he laid the basis for the new state. It was supported by numerous verbatim documents that interlard the narrative and fill a bulky appendix. In perusing the *Six-Day Speech,* the reader should not forget that it was an account rendered by a statesman in office. Kemal is silent on a number of topics that would have been embarrassing, notably his relations with the Young Turks in exile (several leading Young Turks had been executed in 1926) and with the Bolsheviks (Communism had been outlawed in 1923). He avoids the entire topic of his attempts to come to power in Istanbul under the Sultan by beginning his account with May 1919 and goes into little detail on later moves toward reconciliation with the Ottoman dynasty. He understates the degree to which he compromised with the plan of an American mandate. Throughout the work, moreover, Kemal tends to project his later quarrels with old associates (for example, Rauf Orbay) back into an earlier period. For all these minor faults, the *Six-Day Speech* is likely to remain the single major source on his leadership, and it has set a high standard of factual detail for later Turkish memoir writers. The impression of a political testament is reinforced by the peroration which is addressed to the future youth of Turkey. Significantly, it is a repetition of the calamities of 1918 and 1919 of which he warns future generations: defeat, occupation, a government collaborating with the enemy, and a desperate need for national resistance.

As a performance, the *Six-Day Speech* was a unique tour-de-force. For three months Kemal had exhausted relays of secretaries in assembling his materials and polishing passage after passage.

238

When he delivered it (to a captive audience of delegates to the Second National Congress of his People's Party), he remained at the rostrum with little respite for an average of six hours a day. It was not exactly his speech to end all speeches; yet during his remaining eleven years he rarely spoke in public for so long as an hour at a time. And soon after his marathon feat of oratory, he proceeded to abolish the alphabet in which the *Six-Day Speech* had been composed and to initiate drastic changes in the very language that he had used so superbly throughout his political leadership.

Drinking, mistresses, the so-called National History Thesis, and the invention of a somewhat arbitrary language known as Pure Turkish—these were to occupy much of his time until, by about 1937, his health began to decline. (At Gallipoli in 1915 and on the Sakarya in 1921, he had refused to attend to such ailments as malaria or a broken rib; the only previous time when he allowed his health to preoccupy him was in 1917-18, when he saw the imminent collapse of the Turkish state and no chance for him to save it.[33])

The National History Thesis—on the basis of a mixture of truth, half-truth, and fiction—asserted that Sumerians, Hittites, Indo-Europeans (almost all civilized peoples, in fact, except the Arabs and other Semites) were descended from Central Asian Turks, who had originated human speech and writing. It was the kind of tendentious rewriting of history, the kind of search for remote and glorious antecedents, characteristic of many early nationalisms. It also followed the standard rule for that search: Find the historic peoples or persons who in the world at large today command the widest respect and to whom you can claim a closer connection than your political antagonists or national rivals. For Kemal, that excluded the Arabs as associated with Islam, the Ottomans as ancestors of Sultan Vahideddin, and the Byzantines as precursors of Venizelos' "great idea." The Sumerians and Hittites, on the other hand, had the advantage of focusing such historic dreams not on Russian Central Asia, but on solid Anatolian homeground.[34]

This type of historical romanticism, however, serves its purpose in arousing a national consciousness among intellectuals which politicians can then convert into the institutions of a territorial nation-state: It is appropriate to the generation of Fichte and Mazzini, not of Bismarck and Cavour. Among Turkish poets, such patriotic and nationalist themes can be traced from Namik Kemal in the

1870's to Ziya Gökalp at the time of the Balkan Wars. But when Mustafa Kemal some years later rallied his countrymen to a desperate defense, when he battled the Greeks, proclaimed the Republic, and Westernized its cultural and legal life, nothing had been further from his mind than Central Asian inscriptions or Sumerian artifacts. It is this reverse timing that marks Atatürk's historical speculations as an aimless pastime.

Kemal's language reform was directed against those Arabic and Persian elements of vocabulary and grammar that sharply separated the ornate rhetoric of educated Ottomans from the peasant's plain speech. Yet the words culled from medieval Central Asian texts or even more freely invented were often less comprehensible to peasant or townsman than those long naturalized from Arabic. By their arbitrary, assembly-line methods, Kemal's coterie of philological autodidacts rather retarded the continuing process of linguistic purification. Once again, the timing was out of phase.[35] Just as he had in the adoption of Latin letters, Atatürk set a personal example of mastering the new idiom. It gives a pang of sadness to think of Turkey's most eloquent orator delivering an entire speech in this self-imposed non-language and causing the newspapers to publish detailed glossaries so that the public might learn its content.[36]

The Alexandretta crisis of 1937-38 brought out a strong flicker of Kemal's old self. Once again he could launch into his favorite sphere of foreign policy. Once again he could review troops poised for action. Once again he could apply his mind to the locale of the major turning point in his career, of his rebirth from soldier into politician in the days after the armistice. By naming the border district Hatay, or Hittite-land, he even managed to connect it with his latest hobby. But Kemal had saved Turkey's independence more than fifteen years before, and the incorporation of Alexandretta removed but a minor blemish on his life's work. Even before the annexation was completed, on November 11, 1938, Kemal died of cirrhosis at the age of fifty-seven.

Innovation, Tradition, and Achievement

In chemistry there is a distinction between the energy that brings about and that which maintains a compound; similarly, in politics the talents of the founder of a state are different from those of the ruler of an established one. Kemal's greatness lies in his triple accomplishment as defender of his country, creator of the Republic, and radical Westernizer. Having acquitted himself superbly of these three tasks, he became (as Hegel has said of "world-historical individuals" who have attained their goal) a mere husk.[37]

Yet in the two middle periods from 1919 to 1927, his personality was fully focused on the task he had set for himself. He had staked his ambition of personal power on the preservation of independence for his country. The course of the War of Independence vindicated his political pessimism of the previous decade, renewed his faith in his own powers, resolved his ambivalence toward authority, and rekindled his pride in being a Turk. But power for Kemal and independence for Turkey were not isolated ends in themselves. After a century and a half of double-dealing at the hands of Europe, the Turks had for once used Force to assert Right and thus swept away a long accumulated legacy of ill will and resentment on both sides. By deposing the Sultan (or better yet, declaring him deposed by European action in the last scene of the old nefarious interplay), Kemal had also liberated the Turks from the weight of Ottoman and Muslim tradition. Future Turkish generations would now be able to Westernize without a sense of shame or duress. And as Turkey became a Westernized, forward-moving nation, future Turkish adolescents would no longer be despised as Muslim and backward while their womenfolk sat veiled behind latticed windows. After a century or more of half-hearted Westernization, Kemal found that by assuming full personal power he could attempt the job in its entirety, could try to solve for all Turks what young Kemal in Salonica could not have solved for himself alone.

Still, his national and cultural revolution preserved important links to the past. Indeed, the speed and scope of the transformation were facilitated through continuity in leadership and in political method.[38] Kemal and his collaborators were members in good standing of the Ottoman elite, and his performance was an answer to the nagging question that a stream of memorials to the Sultans had asked since the late-eighteenth century: How can this state be saved? His particular solution employed methods and symbols that harked back to the most glorious Ottoman period. Like the early Sultans, he combined the three roles of victorious battlefield commander, founder of a state, and sponsor of a large-scale educational establishment.[39] His policy thus provides a striking

instance of what Robert Ward has called "reinforcing dualism"—
the use of traditional techniques and symbols to speed up modernization itself.[40]

Although this continuity was an incalculable source of strength
for Kemal's immediate tasks of state-founding and Westernization,
it also implied a weakness in the longer run—a weakness apparent
in the relative slowness of Turkey's economic development and
in the wide gulf that still separates her educated rulers from the
peasant masses. Kemal indeed displayed little interest in social or
economic change as these terms have come to be understood since
the Mexican, Russian, and anticolonial Revolutions. For him,
economic improvement and a bridging of class differences were
practical requirements of national solidarity and international
stature, rather than deeply felt needs of human justice and dignity.
There is no reference in his speeches to inequalities of property.
To the Kemalists as to the Ottomans, education remained the
chief tool of social change, and even in this field the achievements
of his reign remained modest.

Yet there are statements and implications in Kemal's nationalist and secularist thought that transcend the purely political and
cultural scope of his reforms. He proclaimed the ideals of popular
sovereignty and of civic participation by the masses and fashioned
the parliamentary and party institutions that would in the decade
after his death begin to make such aspirations more meaningful.
In a culture that for centuries had been deeply steeped in religion,
one of his most widely quoted sayings proclaimed: "Science, the
truest guide in life." His party, though led by officers, government
officials, and provincial notables, was called the Republican *People's*
Party, with the key word *halk* denoting "common people." And
its slogan *inkilâpçilik*, which may be translated with equal inac-
curacy as "reformism" or "revolutionism," implied the desire for
constant forward momentum, for radical change whether by
peaceful or violent means.

It was entirely consistent with Kemal's thought that this
momentum should carry Turkey beyond his own accomplishments.
Kemal himself, as we saw, acknowledged that his efforts at political
organization from the top would fully succeed only as they reached
deep into the social structure and evoked a responsive echo there.
As organization has been pushed downward to the village and the
individual level as a result of the transition to competitive party
politics since the late-forties, it is the long neglected social and

economic items that have come to the top of the agenda.

Inevitably some of the directions earlier formulated have become subject to re-examination, and some of the previous achievements have been endangered. In the politically supercharged atmosphere of the 1960's, such Kemalist goals as the secularization of education, the withdrawal of the military from politics, and an independent foreign policy combined with a firm cultural orientation to the West must be vigorously reasserted. They must also be boldly supplemented with new policies for social justice and rapid economic development. Above all, on a political stage crowded and noisy as never before, new techniques must be devised to accommodate demands and to conciliate conflict. The difficulties of the fifties and sixties and those yet to come thus represent part of the deferred cost of Kemal's gradualist revolution.

Nevertheless, the broadening of the elite movement to embrace the entire citizenry is now well under way, and it will be an indispensable part of the total process of modernization. The final heirs of the ideology of modernization that in two centuries filtered down from Sultans and vezirs to schoolteachers and lieutenants will be a socially and politically conscious lower class. Only at that point will the "structuring upward" that Kemal anticipated be ready to start.

Rousseau said of the founder of a commonwealth that he must be able "to toil in one century and to reap in another."[41] Atatürk's accomplishment in rebuilding the Turkish state in a national and modern image will be secure in proportion as the Turkish masses of the future will claim as their own his full inheritance.[42]

REFERENCES

1. I have elaborated this interpretation of Weber's concept of charisma in my book, *A World of Nations* (Washington, 1967), pp. 148-69, where full references are given.

2. Cf. [Patrick Balfour] Lord Kinross, *Atatürk: The Rebirth of a Nation* (London, 1964), p. 238.

3. Max Weber, *Wirtschaft und Gesellschaft* (4th ed.; Tübingen, 1956), p. 214; cf. his *Theory of Social and Economic Organization*, tr. Henderson and Parsons (New York, 1947), p. 363.

4. Erik H. Erikson, *Young Man Luther* (New York, 1958), p. 16.

5. For details on the Sultan and the Ottoman generals of 1914-19, see my articles, "The Army and the Founding of the Turkish Republic," *World Politics*, Vol. 11, No. 4 (July, 1959), pp. 513-53; "'Djemal Pasha" and "Enwer Pasha," *Encyclopaedia of Islam* (rev. ed.).

6. Karl W. Deutsch *et al.*, *Political Community and the North Atlantic Area* (Princeton, 1957), p. 88.

7. On the Puritans, see Michael Walzer, *The Revolution of the Saints: A Study in the Origins of Radical Politics* (Cambridge, 1965); on educational policy in the late Ottoman Empire, Bernard Lewis, *The Emergence of Modern Turkey* (London, 1961), pp. 175 f.

8. Cf. R. E. Ward and D. A. Rustow (eds.), *Political Modernization in Japan and Turkey* (Princeton, 1964), p. 388.

9. During the decisive phase of the War of Independence, in 1921-22, Kemal personally assumed the supreme military command. By that time, however, the task of political organization on which he had concentrated for nearly three years had proceeded far enough so that he could largely leave the management of political affairs to others. After the war, he returned to his political tasks, and in 1924 forced his associates to choose between political or military careers.

10. Kinross, *Atatürk: The Rebirth of a Nation*, p. 221. Elsewhere, Kinross gives a more balanced judgment on Atatürk's politics: "His was a dictatorship based on democratic forms, within a legal and constitutional framework which he scrupulously observed" (p. 438)—scrupulously, that is, from about 1927.

11. Sir Andrew Ryan, *The Last of the Dragomans* (London, 1951), p. 226.

12. In the *Six-Day Speech*, Kemal suggests that his performance should be viewed "as a chain of logical propositions." Atatürk, *Nutuk*, Vol. 1 (Ankara, 1934), p. 11.

13. Louis Browne, of the *Chicago Daily News*, quoted in Kinross, *Atatürk: The Rebirth of a Nation*, p. 193. The inclusion of Mosul, for which I have put an ellipsis, gives Kemal a little too much credit; it had been under British occupation since November, 1918.

14. Cf. my article, "Politics and Islam in Turkey, 1920-1955," *Islam and the West*, ed. Richard N. Frye (The Hague, 1957), p. 73.

15. Cf. Kinross, *Atatürk: The Rebirth of a Nation*, pp. 237, 240.

16. Kemal's brief experiment in controlled opposition in 1930 illustrates all at once his inability to operate a democratic system, the mildness of his dictatorship, and the contribution it made to the future establishment of democracy. See Walter F. Weiker, "The Free Party of 1930 in Turkey," Ph. D. Dissertation, Dept. of Politics, Princeton University (1962).

17. The speech is reprinted in *Nutuk*, Vol. 3, pp. 258 f., and *Atatürk'ün Söylev ve Demeçleri*, Vol. 2 (Ankara, 1945-54), pp. 11 f., where the date is erroneously given as 28 December 1920, instead of 1919.

18. For example, of the four leading biographies, the least reliable states flatly that his father died when Mustafa was seven, the most authoritative gives a seven-year range (ages five to twelve), and the other two give no specific date. What little is known about the relationship between father and son goes back to one or two passing reminiscences by Kemal years later. Considering his profound ambivalence to authority, one is tempted to speculate about that relationship; but causes inferred from effects are, of course, no addition to our knowledge.

19. Similarly, his *Six-Day Speech* often omits or blurs certain inconvenient parts of the truth without actually telling a falsehood. See below.

20. I am indebted for this observation to Halil Inalcik.

21. Cevdet's utopia is summarized in Lewis, *The Emergence of Modern Turkey*, p. 231.

22. Pious Turks, of course, have continued to pray, and ways have been found of obeying both God and Caesar. The Anatolian peasant prefers, among all the authorized Western forms of headdress, the visored cap which at prayer time can easily be turned back to front.

23. Cevdet in *Ictihad*, No. 89 (Istanbul, 1913), as quoted by Lewis, *The Emergence of Modern Turkey*, p. 231.

24. Cf. Karl W. Deutsch, *Nationalism and Social Communication* (New York, 1953), p. 85; Hans Kohn, *The Idea of Nationalism* (New York, 1948), pp. 5-6.

25. Harold D. Lasswell, *Psychopathology and Politics* (Chicago, 1930), pp. 75-76.

26. Erik H. Erikson, *Young Man Luther*, p. 67.

27. Whereas the turban and fez were outlawed by the Hat Law, only local ordinances were directed against the veil. The Swiss civil code presupposed rather than prescribed legal equality between the sexes.

28. On Kemal and women, see Kinross, *Atatürk: The Rebirth of a Nation*, pp. 10, 295 (Zübeyde); p. 12 (Salonica); p. 64 (Sofia); pp. 60 f., 97 ff. (correspondence with widow); p. 164 ("Without love in his nature"); p. 259 (Fikriye, "availability"); p. 391 ("chose women who took the initiative"); pp. 367 f., 390 f. (Lâtife); p. 423 ("two headstrong natures," divorce); p. 421 ("sociological reasons"); pp. 471 f. (adopted daughters).

29. One wonders whether political motives also may have played their part, and whether the marriage failed in this respect as well. Few readers have credited General Karabekir's assertion that Kemal in 1923 had plans of making himself Sultan and Caliph. (Kâzim Karabekir, *Istiklâl Harbimiz* [Istanbul, 1960], pp. 978, 1058, 1065, 1067, 1137.) If monarchy was on his mind at all, a secular monarchy would seem to have been more in character. But whether religious or secular, monarchy would have required an heir, and it may thus be no coincidence that Kemal was married during the interval between abolition of the Sultanate (November

1922) and proclamation of the Republic (October 1923). Again, there are no more than hints in the literature of Kemal's sterility (see, for example, Şevket Süreyya Aydemir, *Tek Adam: Mustafa Kemal*, Vol. 3 [2d ed.; Istanbul, 1966], pp. 485 f.), presumably the consequence of an ill-cured case of gonorrhea (see note 33). If indeed he was sterile, the early months of his marriage may well have been the time when he himself found out about his condition. The question obviously cannot be resolved unless more reliable sources become available.

30. *Söylev ve Demeç*, II, 74–75.

31. *Belleten*, vol. 14, no. 56, pp. 502–514 (September, 1950). Kemal told the story in 1947 to his adopted daughter Âfet Inan.

32. *Nutuk*, III, 317; *Söylev ve Demeç*, I, 269 (November 1, 1922).

33. Kemal had suffered from malaria at Gallipoli (Kinross, *Atatürk: The Rebirth of a Nation*, pp. 87, 91, 94), and a broken rib at the Sakarya (p. 274). A case of gonorrhea in his early years had been inadequately treated and caused later complications (p. 113), including a recurrent kidney ailment (pp. 113, 166). He also suffered from chronic constipation (p. 261), and once had a bout with ear trouble (p. 144). In 1923 he had a heart attack, followed several years later by another (pp. 262, 475).

34. Lewis, *The Emergence of Modern Turkey*, p. 315. On historical romanticism of early nationalists generally, cf. Rustow, *World of Nations*, pp. 40–47.

35. For a more favorable view of Kemal's language reform, see Uriel Heyd, *Language Reform in Turkey* (Jerusalem, 1954).

36. See *Oriente Moderno*, Vol. 14, No. 11 (November, 1934), p. 522.

37. "Sie sind, wenn sie ihr Ziel erreicht hatten, nicht zum ruhigen Genuss übergegangen, nicht glücklich geworden. Was sie sind, ist eben ihre Tat gewesen; diese ihre Leidenschaft hat den Umfang ihrer Natur, ihres Charakters ausgemacht. Ist der Zweck erreicht, so gleichen sie leeren Hülsen, die abfallen." *Einleitung in die Philosophie der Weltgeschichte*, II, 2, d. I am indebted for this quotation to Albert O. Hirschman. See also Erikson, *Young Man Luther*, p. 260.

38. It has been characteristic of Turkey's gradualist pattern of political development that its political elite changed more drastically at times when political institutions underwent little change (for example, 1908-18 and since 1950), and that its political institutions were extensively recast (in 1919-25) when the composition of the elite remained essentially unchanged. Cf. Rustow, *Political Culture and Political Development*, eds. Lucian W. Pye and Sidney Verba (Princeton, 1965), pp. 197 f.

39. Two symbolic acts of the Ankara government made manifest this organic link between Kemalism and the earliest Ottoman tradition. After the decisive victory over the Greeks on the Sakarya in 1921, the National As-

sembly conferred upon Kemal the title of Gazi, or Victor—the very appellation that the Turkish-Muslim frontier warriors who founded the Ottoman state in the thirteenth century had earned in their encounter with Greek-Christian enemies on the same Bithynian battlefields. And just as Sultan Mehmed II (reg. 1451-81), after the conquest of Istanbul, proceeded to establish his famous palace school, so the Ankara government in November 1928 adopted a decree concerning the "Organization of a National School." Article 3 of that remarkable and concise document provided that "every Turkish citizen, man and woman, is a member of this organization"; Article 4 appointed that "the headmaster of the National School is the President of the Republic His Excellency Gazi Mustafa Kemal." See Gotthard Jäschke and Erich Pritsch, *Die Türkei seit dem Weltkriege* (Berlin, 1929); also in *Welt des Islams*, Vol. 10, pp. 131 f. (It was the time of the alphabet change, and soon the Gazi could be seen, chalk in hand, instructing his citizen-pupils.)

40. Ward and Rustow, *Political Modernization in Japan and Turkey*, pp. 445ff.

41. Jean-Jacques Rousseau, *Contrat Social*, Book 2, Chapter 7.

42. I am indebted for critical comments on an earlier version of this essay to Talat Helman, Halil Inalcik, Gotthard Jäschke, Bernard Lewis, and Sabra Meservey, and for research assistance to Sabri Sayari. My views of recent Turkish history and of Atatürk have greatly benefitted from frequent discussions with the late Professor Yavuz Abadan, whose rich store of knowledge and subtle and balanced judgment I came to admire over the years. A somewhat expanded version of the present essay appears both in English and in Turkish translation (kindly prepared by his widow, Professor Nermin Abadan) in a memorial volume published in his honor. Fuller references to the Turkish sources will be found in that Turkish language version. See *Prof. Dr. Yavuz Abadan'a Armagan* (Ankara Üniversitesi Siyasal Bilgiler Fakütesi Yayinlari No. 280; Ankara, 1969) pp. 517–71 ("Atatürk As Founder of a State") and 573–634 ("Devlet Kurucusu olarak Atatürk").

STANLEY AND INGE HOFFMANN

The Will to Grandeur: de Gaulle as Political Artist

"S' élever au-dessus de soi, afin de dominer
les autres, et, par là, les évènements."
(—Vers l'armée de métier)

THE LEADER, Charles de Gaulle, twice the savior of France, knight-errant for her grandeur, believer in the cultural values embodied in a national tradition, appears all of one piece. It is as if he had chosen to tailor himself to his role in history from the very beginning of his childhood, as if he had carefully selected from his heritage and from his personality the elements that would allow him to play that role to perfection. When the events did not conform to the demands of his self-imposed role, he has waited for the most effective entrance. Once on the scene, he has "arranged" himself so as to meet these demands, and no one, however critical of the play, can deny the merits and mastery of the performance.

It is therefore tempting simply to study from where he derived his characteristic style, how he has shaped his role, and how he has imposed it on his nation—as if he were not really much more complex. Indeed, we do not know whether there is more to him than the public personage. We suspect that there is, behind it, a face both greater and smaller than the public figure: greater, for the public figure draws its life from the man beneath; smaller, because the man is surely restricted by the personage he has chosen to become.

What the man demonstrates is the triumph of the will over personal and national conflict, over inner doubts and external dramas. It is a will to restore, preserve, promote an abstraction, France, which has always been more important to him than any other commitment. That "certain idea of France," of which he speaks, has to be served by a certain kind of leader. And

248

de Gaulle's will has also, indeed primordially, been to be that leader. His career shows a remarkable blend of thought and action, a rare capacity to fulfill one's vocation by giving to oneself and to one's mission exactly the shape of one's dreams and ambitions; in other words, de Gaulle displays an aesthetic talent worked out in a political arena.

It is not the purpose of this paper to pass judgment on de Gaulle as a political leader. Such a judgment would require an evaluation of the intrinsic merit of those dreams and ambitions, a detailed assessment of the means he has used in order to realize them, and a discussion of the lasting effects of his achievements and failures. Our concern is narrower: It is to study de Gaulle as a political artist not by looking at his techniques, at his craft, but by concentrating on what he has called his gift—that is, his "character" and the way in which he has shaped it to fulfill his self-appointed role. We will examine first the development of his personality, then the definition, psychological requirements, and psychological implications of his vocation, and finally, the charismatic link between the political artist and his public—the people to whom he must communicate his gift in order to fulfill his mission.

I. *Genesis*

We will discuss three factors among all those that may have shaped the General's personality and leadership style: his family, his own reactions to his milieu during his youth and adolescence, and the influences of some contemporaries.

The Milieu

A discussion of his family is essential to an understanding of de Gaulle.[1] We are not suggesting that his milieu "determined" him, but it put him on certain tracks that he has never left and also provided him with a point of departure which he both accepted and left behind.

He was born on November 22, 1890, the third of five children, the second of four boys. His father, Henri de Gaulle, descended from a long line of impoverished nobles—belonging both to the *noblesse d'épée* and to the *noblesse de robe*—who lived, at first, in the provinces (Burgundy and Flanders) and, since the seventeenth century, in Paris. The fascination with history which Charles was going to display was already in his family, on Henri's side.

Henri's father had written a history of Paris, edited one of King St. Louis, and traced the genealogy of the family. One of Henri's brothers, called Charles de Gaulle, was a poet and scholar who, in a book about the Celts in the nineteenth century, anticipated his nephew and namesake, both in celebrating the resilient independence of the Celts (as well as their spread to America), and in writing that "in a camp surprised, at night, by an enemy attack, when each one fights alone, one does not ask his rank of whoever raises the flag and takes the initiative of rallying his men."[2] Henri's mother, a prolific writer of edifying novels, showed sympathy for various revolutionary figures like Proudhon and Jules Vallès, and wrote a book glorifying O'Connell.

Henri de Gaulle was forty-two when Charles was born. He had originally intended to follow a military career, but, according to Charles' biographers, he was stopped by a reversal of his family's fortunes. He was wounded near Paris in the Franco-Prussian War and, later, often took his children to visit the battleground. He became a professor of philosophy, history, and literature and headmaster in a distinguished Jesuit high school in Paris. There is no doubt that his impact on Charles was great; Henri's former students have testified to his mystical love for France, and it is he who supervised his sons' extensive readings in French history and in the classics of French literature.

Charles' mother, Jeanne Maillot, shared her husband's devotion to France and Catholicism; she came from a bourgeois lineage—a line of austere, small businessmen from northern France, in whose families the youngest sons usually pursued military careers. One of her uncles, Charles Maillot, an officer of unusual height, was legendary in the family. Little is known about her.

Charles de Gaulle's milieu was both typical and yet somehow *en marge*, in two essential respects. On the one hand, socially, it is hard to imagine a family more French than one that believes its ancestry goes back to the thirteenth century. Yet de Gaulle was not born in a family typical of nineteenth-century French society: As he pointed out later, his parents' outlook, concerns, and resources were not those of the bourgeoisie, and there must always have been a contrast between the dignified appearances—an apartment in Lille, one in Paris, a summer home in the Dordogne—and the financial realities. De Gaulle's detachment from the class preoccupations of France's social categories thus becomes easier to understand. On the other hand, his family was typical of the

258

values of the French Right: At the end of the nineteenth century, a deep attachment to the monarchy (which the de Gaulle family had served, either as officers or as lawyers), a fervent Catholicism, fierce patriotism, and fear for the decline of France were characteristic of all those families to whom Maurras was pitching his appeal. In one vital respect, however, the de Gaulles did not conform: *"Monarchiste de regret,"* Henri de Gaulle was not, it seems, moved in any way by the passionate anti-republican hatred, the anti-Semitism, and xenophobia so characteristic of the Right; there was no sectarianism here, and Henri de Gaulle did not believe that Dreyfus was guilty.

De Gaulle's family thus transmitted to him three essential messages. First, as the preceding example suggests, it was profoundly inner-directed. Not only were the values it believed in, for all their lack of originality, those of a minority of Frenchmen in an impious republic, a fact that did not prevent the de Gaulles from sticking to their beliefs with dignity and firmness. There was also here a willingness to examine issues *independently*, on their own merits, and to judge them from a viewpoint that left its mark on Charles: what might be called intense moderation—intense, because of the depth of Henri's "feeling" and of Mme de Gaulle's "passion,"[3] yet moderate, because the tone of the family, the manners of the father, above all the lessons of French classicism and history all seem to have pointed to the condemnation of excess. Self-respect, later so crucial to de Gaulle, was undoubtedly a family value and achievement.

Secondly, the values inculcated by the parents were above all public values. This was a family where a child would quickly learn to sublimate his private dreams and drives into public ones: the love of France, Christian faith, honor, the lessons of history, respect for culture, the nation as both the highest temporal good and as a cultural partnership of the living and the dead, the virtues of the soldier as both the defender of the nation and the carrier of the Christian faith. Most striking is the way in which, in this dignified but impoverished home of a family whose beliefs ran against the dogmas of the established regime, history—France's past—and the legacy of French culture seem to have served as a consolation for the present as well as a yardstick. Charles' enthusiasm for Rostand's *Aiglon*, seen at the age of ten, fits in easily.[4]

The sentimental story (played by Sarah Bernhardt) of the ailing, oppressed, innocent son of the great Emperor, protected and inspired by a soldier called Flambeau, who symbolizes the average Frenchman and keeps the memories of Napoleon's epic alive in captivity, could not fail to arouse in Charles the patriotic feelings and sense of service cultivated by his family and to strengthen his military vocation, already indicated by his childhood games, where he always insisted on playing the role of France.

Third, and perhaps most importantly, Charles' milieu must have communicated to him a deep sense of distress about the present. Toward the internal situation of France, the emotions must have ranged from discomfort to disgrace, as the nation moved from the unfinished truce of the *ralliement* years, to the turmoil of the Dreyfus case (where all sides, as de Gaulle's father saw it, behaved lamentably), the separation of church and state, the closing of the Jesuit schools (including Henri's), the rise of socialism, labor unions, and strikes. Externally, the dominant feeling was one of persistent national humiliation; the father and mother had been traumatized by the fall of France in the war of 1870 and remained obsessed by the need for *la revanche* and the fear of further French setbacks like Fachoda—another reason why *l'Aiglon,* with its evocation of past exploits to exorcise both the humiliations of the era after Napoleon the First, of which it talks, and those of the era after Napoleon the Third, in which it was written, would appeal to the boy. But the basic fact remains: The de Gaulles' beloved France, the "princess or madonna" of the religious and nationalistic boy, was seen and felt as troubled, threatened, almost tragic rather than healthy, heroic, and expanding.[5] Her present condition could only be deplored, and as for the future, one could and should of course hope, but it was hard to imagine improvement without drama. His martial spirit and his desire to protect thus strengthened each other.

That he picked up all those "messages" we know from the first three paragraphs of the *Mémoires.* For all its opposition to present trends, for all its nostalgia and misgivings, his family life and holidays teamed with activities, fun, and games, of which learning became a part. In short, the family provided a rich and harmonious (*non-conflicted*) cultural legacy.

Childhood and Adolescence

In this setting, the picture of a little boy emerges: a "perfect little devil," who is "neither docile nor naïve"—"when Charles appears, tranquillity disappears"[6]—full of mischief, practical jokes, and energy (books and papers are sent flying around his room). This double concern which never left him: for *statecraft* and for *stagecraft* began in childhood, in his fondness for reliving in his readings and in his games various episodes (usually martial ones) of French history.

This period of joyful ebullience, of passionate abandon in adventure stories and war plays, gradually receded as he approached adolescence. Someone in the family says he must have fallen into an icebox. This fits with his stiff distant bearing in secondary school, where he was reported to have begun to stand apart. Why a child's sense of uniqueness, which it shares with all other growing children, should have matured into a style of life, is a puzzle that we must now try to elucidate.

The key seems to lie in his relation to his family. We see a tension between his respect for it, his acceptance of its beliefs, and his intense desire to make his own mark, to be his own master— *to be himself* and not merely one more relatively undistinguished member of old, respectable, but uncelebrated families. Independence became his claim, not just a family value. The very lessons he received from his father and from his Catholic teachers must have created dissonance. They taught him the honor and pride of loyalty to unpopular values.[7] They, as well as the books he devoured, celebrated service, submission to causes, discipline. But those same books also revealed that history is a tale full of sound and fury, in which whole bodies of doctrines have been blown away, in which, as he was going to write later, "evangelical perfection does not lead to empire."[8] Moreover, the world around him taught him that pure loyalty to traditional dogmas and the perfect practice of Christian values were no way of saving them. His books and teachers, however, provided him with an answer to the dilemma. The young reader of Corneille and history knew that mastery of self and others brings its own rewards[9]; his whole education, at home and in school, was pervaded by the Greek ideal, so powerful in France's classical age and culture (as indeed throughout continental Europe): that of the self-sufficient, self-controlled, and sovereign personality, who controls events, so to speak, from within through force of character. Thus the solution to his tension was sought in a way that was to become typical of his style: by *transcending* the legacy.[10]

He must have experienced, at home, both opulence and deprivation—the opulence of affection, example, and high ideals, but also a double deprivation; on the one hand, this obviously remarkable boy seems to have been treated, out of fairness to his brothers and sister, with no special privileges; on the other hand, as one perceptive commentator has put it, it was a "frustrated family,"[11] frustrated socially and politically by France's domestic and external political conditions. There was but one way both to put an end to those frustrations *and* to emancipate oneself from them; to serve the values of the family *and* to save them from obsolescence; to remain loyal to that culture and that history so dear to his parents *and* to remove culture and history from the realm of morose meditations, genealogical explorations, and imaginary recreations; to be a son and brother to his parents and their other children *and* to make a name for oneself: by becoming the man who saves the respected past by shaping a future worthy of it. The solution was to put himself at the service of a great cause that would give him the opportunity to be great by doing great things. The cause could have been that of the church, but the boy seems to have been too fond of battle, too much in love with temporal glory and domination; it thus became that of France, to which he transferred the religious devotion that was in him. He would serve France in such a striking way that the past would be *renewed* rather than just enshrined, and the nation might live according to the family's ideals. This meant accepting—as a precondition for success—the political framework that his parents found so distasteful: to be a nostalgic monarchist and Catholic was not going to help.

It meant, above all, leaping above the family's horizons. De Gaulle says he was tempted by "the play" of French politics, whose permanent confrontation of great characters must have appealed to his imagination and love of drama.[12] But this would have hurt his family's feelings, and the play affronted its and his own values. He could, however, resolve his dilemma harmoniously. In a military career, Charles could try to do what his father had been prevented from doing by fate. He would be at the service of France, rather than of the Republic, and repudiate all divisive ideologies as so many traps. That desire to be France's protector without intermediaries, so characteristic of his career and so clearly marked in the very first page of the *Mémoires* (where he talks first of her, and then only of his "milieu"—his word), had been, after all, authorized, indeed encouraged, by his family and education. Thus, military service was both a family tradition and a personal solution. By serving the cause of the *revanche*, he would begin to solve for all Frenchmen the problems that could otherwise not be solved for his family alone, and he would find glory in it.

He may have found the family horizons stifling, but there was no revolt; rather, there was a kind of externalization: a desire to fight and remove what had made those horizons stifling. Similarly, later, his acts of defiance would never amount to mere rebelliousness, nor would he ever be a revolutionary. But serving France only and directly also asserted his independence from everyone else—as if he had originated from her alone: de Gaulle would appear both as self-made and as the product of two thousand years of history.

There is nothing unique in the case of a young man to whom history and making his mark on it appear the only worthy goals in life. But what is unique is the continuity of concern and purpose. The love affair with France and history, the love of battle and *"rêve de gloire au pied d'un étendard,"*[13] the determination to be at current history's rendezvous so as to be in future history's texts have known no interruption. What is unique is the total identification of his personal destiny with that of his nation, and the strength of will to fulfill the purpose beyond childhood, through a long period of trial and waiting.

In order to understand better how he managed to act out his dreams without losing touch with reality, one has to examine more carefully what seems to have happened in his adolescence, between the ages of fourteen and sixteen. As in every important period of his life, external events coincided with internal developments. The events are well known: France's crisis between church and state (which hit not only France but home) and the Tangiers crisis with Germany. Simultaneously, a *sense* of being different, separate, chosen[14] is strengthened, and a *will to be* unique and self-contained arises in him. These are the years when he grows to be taller than his brothers, to tower over his schoolmates, when he must have felt (and been made to feel) awkward; when he must have also felt the need to distinguish himself from that omnipresent father, who taught him constantly in school as well as at home. Precisely, this is the time when his father, worried by the proliferation of Charles' gifts, by a certain tendency to dispersion, a certain lack of discipline in him, challenges him to study harder in order to be able to enter Saint Cyr, France's West Point. Charles' reaction announces his future style: He uses the challenge as an opportunity and makes of the peculiarity not only an asset, but a mark. Tallness becomes the physical symbol of a moral ambition—to be above the others, to be straight and erect. His imagination feeds his will, and his will disciplines his imagination. *Grandeur* becomes his motto, for himself, others, and France: He will join the army because it was then *"une des plus grandes choses du monde."*[15] Aware of how his height and his concerns distinguish him from his schoolmates, he becomes even more aware of his uniqueness and enchanted with it. But if there is narcissism in him, as in every adolescent (and every leader), it is, once more, transcended narcissism, for his reply to the threat of identity diffusion is not totalism, but the mobilization, or, to use two of his favorite words, the *rassemblement* of all his faculties toward the goals of success and service, which will *elevate* him above himself and others.

In this transition from childhood to adolescence, nothing is more interesting than the playlet he wrote at age fourteen and got published the following year: *Une mauvaise rencontre* is the last display of youthful exuberance and the first use of the pen toward the adult goal. It is a frothy skit about an "amiable thief" whose method of robbing is as smooth and painless as Madison Avenue's persuasions, except that there are shiny pistols which underline the persuasion.[16] This theme of coercive persuasion and even the episodes and refrain are taken from an inconsequential *poème à jouer* (poem to perform) by Gustave Nadaud, a popular chansonnier-poet.[17] But Charles transformed its style into sweepy Alexandrines (with a good lacing of Rostand), changed the nameless "amiable thief" of Nadaud into the grand César-Charles Rollet, who declares he was born brigand as others are born kings, officers, . . . or masons (that is, born to their own uniqueness, which they have only to fulfill); a brigand of promise who by great dramatic misfortune lost his superb garb. Unloved and hunted, he "needs" to be comforted by his victim: a ruse indeed, but one which *Charles*, not the original songster, supplied and elaborated. Here are some excerpts of Charles' additions to the original (emphasis added):

> . . . *César-Charles Rollet, qu'on connaît en tout lieu*
> *Voleur de grands chemins par la grâce de Dieu* . . .
> *Certains naquirent rois. . . . Moi je naquis brigand;*
> *On peut le voir d'ailleurs très bien à mon costume.*
> *Sur ma tête, autrefois, s'agitait une plume*
>
> . . . (with melancholy)

. . . Pourquoi me rappeler ce superbe panache
Dont un coup de bâton cruel trancha les jours? . . .
O jour fatal *et sombre! Eh! Oui, Monsieur,* tout passe! (Epique)

(One wonders what happened "one day" to our young Charles, to transform him from the carefree prankster into the straight, stiff-cordial, but distant schoolboy. . . .) *"Eh, oui—tout passe."* (How like the style of the grown man, how prophetic of his fatalism half a century later![18])

Oh! Ce fut un combat *terrible,* horrible, laid
Grand, géant, *furieux, effroyable. C'était*
Le chaos monstrueux, sans grâce, *horrible et morne—*
D'un brigand révolté *contre un homme à bicorne.*
Ma plume *tomba près d'un gendarme à cheval,*
Auquel j'avais ouvert le ventre! . . .
. . . C'est très mal!
Me direz-vous. Ma foi! Je n'en sais rien moi-même.
Personne ne nous voit, personne ne nous aime.

He describes how his featherless hat became sad, and, *"selon la nature,"* gradually lost its *antique* colors.

Il restait sur mon chef droit—les grandes *douleurs*
Sont muettes—fier, grand, défiant *la fortune*
Il rêvait, dans le jour serein, dans la nuit brune
Partout, c'était un corps inerte, *laid, rêveur,*
Et pensant à sa plume

And later:

La vie humaine n'est qu'un tissu de misères . . .

There are two kinds of messages the play appears to convey. One concerns the young de Gaulle's struggle with his own development, the other foreshadows some of the mature de Gaulle's mastery.

As to the first, the adolescent boy who wrote this play in fun added these characteristic themes of his own to Nadaud's ditty: grandeur, struggle, chaos and loss, loneliness, dreams of glory and fatalism. The idea *great* is repeated again and again. Loss is symbolized by the superb feather which leaves him (that is, his hat) "un corps *inerte,* laid, rêveur"[19]; also, in elaborate jest and as a ruse to arouse pity, he refers to his loss of three sisters and three brothers. This may be a fanciful bit of analysis, but since these are de Gaulle's own additions to and transformations of the original, and since they also check (by extrapolation) with the observations reported by his biographers, they warrant being taken seriously, as reflecting the principal preoccupations of young Charles.

Both versions of this boring tale cynically relied on the ultimate persuasive power of force. But Nadaud lacked Charles' subtle blend of flattery and ruse, his lusty and ironic manipulation of gullible pity (de Gaulle's *mépris* for a certain kind of man appeared early), which explained why the use of overt violence was unnecessary. Finally, Charles added the glorification of his hero's pride and egoism; he celebrated his force and his ruse. Compare this with what the mature de Gaulle wrote some twenty years later in his prophetic "credo": *"l'homme d'action ne se conçoit guère sans une forte dose d'égoisme, d'orgueil, de dureté, de ruse."*[20] But the world forgives him because he dares great deeds: "Il séduit *les subordonnés et lors même qu'il* tombe sur la route *garde à leurs yeux* le prestige des sommets *où il voulait les entraîner."* Or: *"Pas d'orateur qui* n'agite *de grandes idées autour de la plus pauvre thèse."*[21] Is it stretching the reader's imagination excessively to ask him to compare these lines with the grand feather which *"s'agitait d'autrefois"* on his hero's head . . . ?

In his childhood play, the seduction is so successful that the victim cries, sincerely, *"enchanté"* at the curtain; later, in his reality play with reluctant opponents (such as General Giraud, or General Salan, or foreign leaders), the victim would often, however, dream of or try for revenge after having been had.

It would seem, then, that at least at the age of fourteen, de Gaulle's fate had been sealed. Obviously, the young man's concern is already for the exercise of power. The play expresses the drive for mastery in a world marked by mediocrity and violence; what is missing from it is what was, so to speak, already *given*—the values and the cause on behalf of which de Gaulle (unlike the brigand) would use the brigand's cynical experience and bouncy dash.

Charles' character now changes and tightens. His sister had described him as "poet and soldier."[22] From now on, his pen will serve first to reflect upon action so as to put action in the lofty perspective that makes it meaningful and, second, as a substitute for action whenever the times are not ripe for it. The sense of fun, so strong in his games and in his playlet, does not disappear, and never will—he will go on performing in plays at Saint Cyr—but a new austerity emerges. Fun will be externalized and transcended, like rebellion: used as a weapon against others and sought in the craft and pleasure of mastery. The sense of drama, so strong in the rambunctious boy, turns into a desire to play a part in a national drama, for which the young man must prepare himself[23]: As he will say later, his gifts must be shaped by skills.[24] The fascination with history continues, but history stops being a playground for childish re-enactments and becomes a judge, a springboard, a reality principle. The need to protect, once turned to the defense of smaller schoolboys mistreated by bullies,[25] is oriented toward France. Already, as throughout his career, the will-to-do or be something feeds on *and* magnifies that something's existence; sensing his difference, he cultivates it. The desire to play a great role leads to double domination—of oneself, as a way of dominating others[26]; the strain increases further the distance from others: Steeped in history, taught to find in its sweep a recourse against the present, he will manifest his ambition by disdaining (once more, *dominer*— that is, both stand above and master) the petty concerns of his contemporaries and all those human entanglements that divert or slow one down. Haughtiness, separateness will be both the condition and the cost of his success.

It is as if, in those years, Charles de Gaulle had experienced a loss that stimulated his creativity and that was reflected or anticipated in his play: the national loss represented by the events recalled above, which made him fear for *his* France, and a more intimate one—the growing awareness of childhood's end, the end of family protection and of mere playacting in a harsh and troubled world, the call of responsibility. Combativeness remains, and indeed grows; but a certain note of bitterness appears—perhaps as a reaction to those events, perhaps also as the by-product of the price the young man felt he had to pay, in his human relations, for his ambition and uniqueness. The years of preparation for action suggest already the double feeling which his whole career inspires: on the one hand, the sense of an extraordinarily effective use of all his resources; on the other, that of a certain repression or compression of ordinary humanity, as if his family and education had provided him with enough human warmth to avoid any real mutilation, yet somehow made him distrustful of his own spontaneity and incapable of dealing with men except on behalf of great abstractions. For such a man, a military career—in which his size and stiffness would be exemplary, where his awkwardness in human relations would be concealed by the hierarchy of ranks, and where his need both to serve and to command would be fulfilled—was an excellent choice. And the selection of infantry is equally significant, for it meant both the certainty of being in the thick of battles and the choice of a branch in which he would be in contact not with men recruited from those elites and middle classes who had been his companions in school and for whom he had little penchant, but with those average Frenchmen—mainly peasants—who must have appeared to him as less corrupted, easier to lead, and easier to keep at a distance.

In his later life, after his admission to Saint Cyr, three events are worth noting. One was a national trend. In the years that preceded World War I, a "nationalist revival" brought back prestige to some of the values that de Gaulle's parents and teachers had cultivated—if not Catholicism, at least a militant and passionate concern for the nation's honor and rank spread from the Right to the Republican establishment.[27] Thus de Gaulle learned that if one sticks to beliefs one deems true and great, whatever the costs of temporary unpopularity, one will be proven right when the circumstances at last consecrate the permanent relevance and the specific aptness of those beliefs.

The two other events were personal tragedies which aggravated, on the contrary, his sense of loss, his intense need for self-respect, and his isolation; both also strengthened in him the sense that realities, however sinister, have to be accepted, that they should not crush one's will, but be faced in order to be overcome. First, there were his two years in German captivity—a crushing blow to the dreams of glory of the young officer and also, probably, to his self-respect. It frustrated him of his share in the final victory; it separated him from his comrades and pushed him even more into himself. Since his repeated attempts to escape were defeated by his very tallness, there was only one thing to do: to use this forced separation in order to reflect on the meaning of the great events to which he could not contribute. Out of those reflections, readings, and lectures came his first book[28]—characteristically enough, a study of civil-military relations in Germany in World War I. It was, first, a plea for moderation, for "the limits traced by human experience, common sense, and the law"[29]; second, a study of the crucial role of morale: collective will, confidence, and unity, and of its collapse in Germany largely because of party divisions and the civilian leaders' lack of stamina when faced with the rabid demands of military leaders. The de Gaulle that came out of a German prisoners' camp immediately went to fight in Poland, against the Russian Revolution; he reflected on the strength of the Polish sense of identity across class barriers—seeing both what there was and what he wanted to see. He returned to France in order to marry Yvonne Vendroux, the twenty-year-old daughter of a biscuit manufacturer from northern France, and to teach military history at St. Cyr. As a student at the Ecole de Guerre in 1922-24, he left on his superiors the same kind of impression he had made on his classmates as an adolescent, only stronger—that of a bright but haughty young man. He was contemptuous of strategic "lessons" that enshrined what the French army had learned from the Great War (but that he, who had missed half of it, obviously felt to be foolish, too mechanical, too rigid, too petty); he was extremely sure of himself and disdainful of criticism.[30]

The second tragedy was more intimate. His third child, born in 1928, was a retarded daughter. De Gaulle and his wife decided to keep her with them, and for twenty years, the General was, it seems, the only person capable of making the little girl laugh. His powers of affection were thus lavished on a poor creature with whom no real intimacy was possible.

Influences

During those formative years, it is interesting to see who, among the countless writers the young man was reading, and who, among the several superiors he had, impressed and influenced him most. He picked up what he needed—that is, what resembled him and encouraged him most to "be himself." As a youngster, he had copied a phrase of Hugo's: "concision in style, precision in thought, decisiveness in life" (qualities far more true of him than of Hugo).[31] He read Nietzsche. The vigor with which he resisted him in his own first book shows the appeal which the call for supermen had had on him (and which *Le fil de l'épée* would dramatically display), for one is always marked by what one fights so hard. Yet it also shows the differences between the philosopher's ethics and de Gaulle's; for he denounces in supermen not only "the taste for excessive undertakings," but also the selfishness of an elite that while "pursuing its own glory believes it pursues the general interest."[32] In de Gaulle's own life, personal glory would loom large, but only as the servant of the general interest (as seen, of course, by de Gaulle . . .).

He read Péguy, whose incandescent mixture of nationalism, love for the soil and people of France, and distaste for parliamentarianism (as opposed to the mystique of the Republic), whose celebration of France as the soldier of Christ, repudiation of the formalistic and systematic "systems of thought" derived from Kant, and raising of Hope—active Hope—as the cardinal virtue, corresponded to his own feelings and left their mark even on his style.[33] He read Barrès, but interestingly enough he chose to see in him only the man who "gave back to the [French] elite a consciousness of national eternity,"[34] not the rather xenophobic, intensely conservative and frightened bourgeois writer, turned far more to the past than to a future that spelled possible decadence. He may have appreciated Maurras' (and undoubtedly Bainville's) views on foreign affairs, but there is no sign of any acceptance of the rigid, doctrinaire, and antiquated "system" of integral nationalism with its divisive and "continuous song of hate."[35]

Above all, he read Bergson, whose philosophy of intuition (as against analytic intelligence), *élan vital* (as against established doctrines), emphasis on time as "the vehicle of spontaneous creation," and stress on how personality transcends all "stable, ready-made categories,"[36] obviously seduced a young man eager to transcend and transmute his own categories, to stop his formidable memory from being a museum and to turn it into a fuel for the future. And he could recognize not yet his own destiny, but his own aspirations in Bergson's question:

By what sign do we ordinarily recognize the man of action, who leaves his mark on the events into which fate throws him? Isn't it because he embraces a more or less long succession in an instantaneous vision? The greater the share of the past that he includes in his present, the heavier the mass he pushes into the future so as to weigh on the events in preparation: his action, like an arrow, moves forward with a strength proportional to that with which its representation was bent backwards.[37]

A final influence was even more profound, because it was more direct—it exerted itself in de Gaulle's own chosen career: Pétain's. De Gaulle, as a cadet, served in Colonel Pétain's regiment; he fought under his orders when the war began; he became his aide and protégé in the 1920's. There were obvious differences between the cautious peasant's son and the ardent young officer, but de

Gaulle recognized in his superior what he wanted to develop in himself: "the gift and the art of leadership."[38] He must have recognized himself in that man who "dominates his task through his mind, and, through his character, leaves his mark on his task"; in that "master who . . . has disdained the fate of servants—thus showing the greatness of independence, which receives orders, seizes advice but closes itself to influences—the prestige of secrecy, preserved by deliberate coldness, vigilant irony, and even by the pride in which his loneliness is wrapped."[39] "Too proud for intrigue, too strong for mediocrity, too ambitious for careerism, [Pétain] nourished in his solitude the passion to dominate, hardened by his awareness of his own merit, by the obstacles he had met, the contempt he had for others."[40] He must also have recognized himself in Pétain's impervious disregard for official doctrine, even at a cost to his own career, for Pétain, on the eve of the war, was holding out against the established dogma of impetuous offensive— and de Gaulle was able to observe how costly that dogma proved to be, to conclude (again) that dogmas mislead instead of guiding, and to learn that Pétain's concern for firepower (artillery) and machine guns) was more justified than official emphasis on manpower in a country with a relatively small population.

This is, then, the capital of influences, experiences, and resources that de Gaulle had accumulated by the mid-1920's. Sure of and eager for the great destiny he had announced since he was seventeen,[41] he now turned to his first great task: the intellectual elaboration, clarification, and anticipation of his future mission.

II. *Vocation*

De Gaulle's leadership will be examined from three viewpoints. How has he conceived the character and role of the *leader?* How has he made *himself* the leader he wanted to be? How has he made *France* conform to his own requirements?

Leadership

Whoever examines the General's career as a leader cannot fail to be struck by three aspects. First, the theme of transcendence is essential: de Gaulle is a man who has, so to speak, stretched himself throughout his life so as to be able to meet the needs created by the circumstances and thus to fulfill himself. This has required, on the one hand, the capacity to put himself in a state of readiness and active waiting until the events occur—he was forty-nine when France fell, and he spent twelve and a half years out of power between his two reigns. It also has required, on the other hand, the capacity to grow so as to meet new challenges not with old formulas but with appropriate inner strength.[42]

Secondly, de Gaulle has always been more concerned with being right than with achieving immediate results: There is, throughout his career, a preference for all-or-nothing in every issue he considers important; his uncompromising presentation of the *armée de métier,* his tactics as leader of the R.P.F., his foreign policy all indicate a determination to be right even at the cost of immediate effectiveness or popularity, and to let either events or his own acts prove that any other course than his own is wrong.

Finally, one cannot fail to be struck by the ideological emptiness of Gaullism. It is a stance, not a doctrine; an attitude, not a coherent set of dogmas; a style without much substance—beyond the service of France and French grandeur, itself never defined in its content, only by its context.[43]

All three features reflect de Gaulle's personality and conception of leadership. What he has started with—after studying in his first book what leadership should not be—is not a doctrine, but a portrait. The mission is absent—both because it is *generally* taken for granted and because it *specifically* depends on events. What he presents is a self-portrait in anticipation: the portrait of the leader, in *Le fil de l'épée*—a "Plutarchian hero created in the imagination by the values that will create in History the destiny of this hero, and thereby resembles him."[44] The values that created him were those de Gaulle had picked up from his family, but also from his classical and romantic readings (especially, one senses, in Corneille, with his emphasis on self-mastery, and in Chateaubriand and Vigny, with their glorification of the lonely hero). He had picked up these values, too, from the current of ideas that marked the pre-1914 nationalist revival and that "Agathon's" famous inquiry[45] ascribed then to French youth—a reaction against the Republican dogmas of positivism, optimism (in its liberal or socialist versions), scientism, continuous progress, and prevalence of great forces over individual men. Here, the emphasis is on struggle, competition, and above all on the great men who tame events. Thus de Gaulle, "the man of the day before yesterday and the day after tomorrow," indeed goes back to earlier notions than those of the Kantian and Comtean Republic, so as to shape the future with them.

In de Gaulle's case, the values that created the great man in his imagination are primarily psychological. Once again, as a true Corneille hero, and exactly as in Erik Erikson's concept of identity, he blends what he knows he is and what he would like to be, so as better to become what he is. The way to tame history and to leave a mark (for this is the name of the game) is to be and to have *un caractère*—the *caractère* of the leader. Without such a character, no set of ideas will help; indeed, they will harm, for they will interpose a screen between reality and the leader (echoes of Sorel and also results of de Gaulle's reflections on World War I). The right *caractère* will, by definition, have the craft and strength to dominate events. The leader is the man who owes his power to no one but himself[46]—who imposes himself, who is propelled by what is in him, not by other people's doctrines. He is literally self-generated and perpetually renewed by challenges, possessor of and possessed by a gift that is unexplainable and somehow compelling, because men are political animals who need order and turn to leaders in periods of trouble. When de Gaulle tries to describe the craft that must shape the gift, again it is not to techniques of action nor to ideas that he turns, but to psychological traits: secrecy, mystery, distance, silence, and protectiveness— all summarized as "the contrast between inner strength and self-mastery,"[47] all enhanced by *"la culture générale,"*[48] his father's preserve.

No conception could be more alien both to the prevalent style of French political leadership of his time or to the style of incremental decision-making of modern bureaucratic systems (including armies); yet none could be more fitting to a young man impatient for action and creation, but reduced—in his mid-thirties —to expectation and anticipation and endowed primarily with his own *caractère,* since he accepted neither the attrition of bureaucracy,[49] nor the ideas and habits of the regime, nor the counter-ideologies that offended his realism or his desire for purposeful national unity. *Le caractère,* as defined by de Gaulle, would necessarily be the man who stretches his resources to meet the challenges by "forcing his own nature"; the man whose "contempt for contingencies" and concern for "elevation" would dictate an all-or-nothing, an *unbending,* attitude; the man whose very condition of success would be to combine a stance of energy, responsibility, and domination with doctrinal indifference and flexibility. "His character would be his destiny."[50]

Indeed, the three features of de Gaulle's leadership are all derived from the essence of his conception: Leadership, that mysterious gift, is itself an essence, revealed in acts, in attitudes, and in its very aptitude to outgrow, repudiate, and free itself from specific policies and past courses—an essence that is preserved by constant, conscious effort and renewed by practice.[51] Yet *Le fil de l'épée* does not provide the whole picture: It neither gives the full sweep of de Gaulle's conception of leadership, nor constitutes the single key to his subsequent career.

There is both a backdrop and another side. The backdrop is provided by de Gaulle's cyclical notion of time, in which there are shades of Nietzsche's "eternal return" and of Péguy's "epochs and periods." It expresses itself in the last page of the *Mémoires*[52]: History is made of peaks and depressions; nations, as well as great men and like nature, must ride out the storms and come back up again. At any given moment, the world provides a stage: The great man is the actor, both in the theatrical and in the political sense. The metaphor of the play, of the stage, of the drama, appears in all his works; the actor's duty is not to follow a preconceived script, but to write his own and to play it as well as the circumstances allow.

When one analyzes de Gaulle's idea of the good actor and the right script, the other side of the picture appears. First, the good actor must be able to play on all the registers of history. On the one hand, he must wait for the circumstances to be ripe, and when they are, seize them decisively, for "events, in great moments, tolerate in positions of leadership only men who know how to chart their own course."[53] On the other hand, he must also know "how to put himself on the side of time,"[54] how to discern and work for the long range—to *rise above* the moment. Second, the good actor is not out only for himself: for "the leaders of men—politicians, prophets, soldiers who obtained most from others—identified themselves with high ideas."[55] The notion of the *cause* is crucial to this conception of leadership. The great leader fulfills himself by becoming the militant missionary of a function, at the service of which he puts all the resources of the word and of action. Charles de Gaulle identifies with France, makes of himself a personage—called General de Gaulle in the *Mémoires*—whose vocation is to be the voice of the nation. History calls him in emergencies, and he calls the French on behalf of France. He has to serve the present needs of France, to protect her legacy, and to guarantee her future. He must maintain her personality, so that she can keep playing on the world stage; he must, in his own moves, follow only what he deems the national interest, apart from all categories, ideologies, and special interests. He is a unifier, by being above and lifting others above their daily selves.

Thus, he fulfills a function that "goes far beyond his person"; he serves "as destiny's instrument."[56] His role is to provide "that inspiration from the summits, that hope of success, that ambition of France which sustain the nation's soul . . . something essential, permanent,"[57] whatever specific or institutional role he may be performing at any moment. Malraux speaks of a *dédoublement* of de Gaulle—the man and the personage. But it is really a *détriplement:* There is *Charles;* there is the public-political *de Gaulle,* the temporal leader, who happens to be the head of the Free French, or provisional Premier, or opposition leader, or President; and there is the public-historic person, the embodiment of France's cause, *General de Gaulle,* who dominates the other two, transcending the first and controlling the second.

France provides Charles de Gaulle not only with the transcendence he needs, but also with the limits he craves. To be "France's champion" means depending on no one, yet being oneself completed; but the need to preserve France's personality, the subordination of the self to her service impose prudence, harmony, moderation, and protect both the nation and the missionary from the excesses of those (like Napoleon or Hitler) who use their nation as tools of personal glory or to work out their ideological or psychological obsessions. The vocation is thus all-consuming, yet a restraint. It is all-consuming not only insofar as it must become the leader's *raison d'être,*[58] but also insofar as the missionary and guide, who takes his cue only from history and the national interest, can—as *leader,* as missionary for the cause—take initiatives that are denied to lesser people. (He can rebel against the disgrace of the armistice, but others cannot rebel against him.) It is a restraint, because of the constant need not to do anything that would, by sullying his own public personage, spoil the chances and soil the honor of the nation. The great leader imposes his will and denies fatalism[59]; but he must also know how to balance ends and means, how to distinguish what is irresistible from what is reversible, so as not to be destroyed by *hubris*.[60] The key is provided by the elusive but essential notion of grandeur.

"De Gaulle's" relation to his mission is the relation of a high priest to his God, executing only His will (as he sees it), and leading his flock with a hand that both points to the summits and hides the petty obstacles so as to inflame his people's energies. Hence the mystical quality, noted by many observers,[61] and the lofty assurance of his language. Just as the religious leader must at times protect his people from sin, at times redeem it from sin, de Gaulle's function is to redeem his nation from the secular equivalent of sin, which he himself calls the fall.[62]

It is also the relation of a monarch to his kingship. One can only admire how he has combined his parents' nostalgia, his own acceptance of the Republic as a necessary framework, and his determination to provide that framework with a completely different type of leader, recalled from the monarchic past, detached from heredity, and reshaped for the dramas of the future.

Last but not least, the link between the public figure and his cause is the relation of the artist to his work of art. Charles himself has been very conscious of this. He has pointed to the aesthetic dimension of military leadership[63] and of statecraft,[64] to the analogy between *"le chef et l'artiste."*[65] He has, in his books and speeches which describe or express the public figure, tried to transform ordinary or chaotic experience into aesthetic form, in a style that has two essential features: its deliberateness, reflected in the complexity of highly structured and patterned sentences, and its oratory, as if it were written to be read aloud, for a stage. The calm which surrounds his work is that of the artist who needs deep quiet to transcend the conflicts in himself and the data provided by his experience. The central themes of his published works have remained unaltered since his adolescence; they have been constantly restated, each new statement being superimposed over the last one; each book, each major address has in it *all* of himself (as leader), as well as something about his mission. And each of his major political acts, however tortuous the means or the details, has been whole, indivisible, and unmistakably his own, like any artistic act. There is in him a quality that rises far above force and ruse, beyond the skillful use of all available tactics. But if in de Gaulle's conception the relation of the *leader*—that is, of "de Gaulle"—to the *mission* of "General de Gaulle" is that of an artist to his creation, so, first of all, has been *Charles'* relation to his *public* self. It is to the creation of "de Gaulle" by Charles that we must turn.

The Leader as a Work of Art

How did Charles de Gaulle apply to himself his notion of leadership, make of himself a work of art, and thus "create in History" his own destiny? The answer can be described chronologically and sought psychologically.

It may well be that his captivity in 1916-18, which deprived him of the opportunity to meet his first major challenge in a way that would have satisfied him, both heightened his fervent desire for a future chance and saved him from the risk of rigidity, of mechanically re-enacting later in life the ways in which one has succeeded in meeting one's first test. This accident of fate thus left him *disponible*—in particular, for first building up in his mind and works the image of the leader and also for moving the scene of the mission from military prowess to statecraft. For his choice of a military career, explained above, was not a full nor satisfying answer to his need to serve by saving. The self-portrait that he paints in his two books of 1932 and 1934 goes much beyond military leadership. It already stretches toward statecraft.[66] Only as a national leader could he solve for all Frenchmen the problems—external and domestic—that had plagued his family and his youth. To be sure, if he groped toward supreme power, he did not expect it. His first moves in London, in June 1940, showed that he was still willing to serve under more prestigious French leaders who would reject Vichy's armistice. But he had made himself ready for supreme power and stepped into the void decisively.[67] Eighteen years later, the man who no longer expected a new call again stepped into the void, with supreme ease and tactical skill, because he had, once more, kept himself ready for the unexpected.

One can therefore distinguish in his career two important thresholds: 1940 and 1958. Before June 1940, he is a military man whose concerns, to be sure, far exceed those of his superiors and colleagues; yet they still remain essentially within the realm of strategy. From June 1940 to the early-1950's, he becomes—first as leader of the Resistance, then as head of Liberated France, lastly as head of the Opposition—the political trustee of his beloved France who judges all events from a single yardstick: French substance and survival. His fear of loss of and for her is so great that, in his actions on the world stage, he acts primarily as a restorer and preserver of her traditional legacy, conceiving her interests in classical terms, as if the future had indeed to be the prolongation (and rectification) of the past. But finally, with the *Mémoires* and the return to power, a third de Gaulle appears, still concerned above all with France, yet more serene, more willing to let go, more universal (in the sense of being more able to take other peoples' aspirations into account, more eager to adapt and renew than to maintain and restore), and also more detached both from Charles and from his temporal political self, to whom he refers in the third person, *sub specie aeternitatis,* or, rather, from the lofty vantage point of the historic figure.

In each case, the crossing of a threshold has been prepared both by the failure of action within the previous framework, which makes him again *disponible* for action when the framework collapses (for example, the failure of his lobbying for a motorized army in the 1930's, the fiasco of the R.P.F. in the early-1950's) and by the kind of catharsis which his indirect form of action—writing —performed for him. Whereas the man of action, even when he takes so long a view or so high a point of view as does de Gaulle, must take into account the necessities of the moment, the writer can judge those necessities from the viewpoint of future history. The man of action aims at the future, but stands in the present; the writer can put himself already in the future and assess the present from that vantage point. Before 1940 and before 1958, writing both raised his horizon and sharpened his lucidity—about himself, as shown by his call for a "master" in *l'Armée de métier*[68] and by his analysis of "General de Gaulle" in the *Mémoires,* and about the world around him, as shown by his assessment of Germany and France in his two books of 1934 and 1950 and by his re-evaluation of the international scene in the *Mémoires.* There, he also re-judges, and usually absolves, the men he had fought or condemned during the war. He wrote, quoting Faust, that in the beginning was action, not the word.[69] But in his case, although the word is always about action, action was always preceded and defined by the word.

Chronology thus sends us back to psychology—to de Gaulle's double determination not to let failure discourage him from his mission, and to prepare himself through the disciplined reflection of writing for the role that events might allow him to play. It is as if *Charles,* the artist, had put all his efforts into shaping *de Gaulle,* the work of art. This has meant, deliberately, an attempt to de-personalize himself, to remove, as Malraux puts it, Charles from the public eye. Yet Charles, the private man, exists. And the public figure, the work of art, is intensely, uniquely personal.

His private self has not been absorbed by his public role: de Gaulle has married a woman whose milieu is very close to that of his mother, he has had three children, has led a normal family life, and is a discreet but devout Catholic. Private affects and public objects have lived side by side. Those who have been able to get through to the man have found him courteous, devoid of arrogance and of awkwardness (indeed the descriptions remind one of those we have of his father).[70]

However, there is a great deal of evidence about the subordina-tion of Charles to de Gaulle: Charles is a rather pale and banal figure, tailored in such a way as to leave all the energies to de Gaulle. His private life is quiet and low key—marked "neither by quarrel nor by laughter."[71] As Malraux has pointed out,[72] other great men have had colorful private personalities. (He mentions Napoleon, but one could add Pétain, who, in addition to episodic liaisons, spent much of life courting a young woman to whom he wrote very intimate letters and whom he finally married.[73]) The private de Gaulle, says Malraux, is merely the one who does not talk of public affairs. His courtesy does not abolish the distance between himself and others; it protects distance—indeed, it is merely, adds Malraux, a feature of his "priesthood." As far as one knows, there is no real intimacy between him and others. His wife is a devoted but reserved figure; his son, physically a carbon copy of himself, has had an unspectacular career as a navy officer; he has had admirers and circles of close acquaintances, but no very close friends, and displays little spontaneity. "He accepts from himself neither impulsiveness nor abandonment."[74] The private self seems always on its guard both against indiscreet questioners who want to get behind the public figure, and against those who, admitted into his restricted privacy, would try to take advantage of it so as to influence the public figure.[75] There is no such thing as happiness, he once "barked out"[76] under this kind of questioning. To such a man, everything that is not public life, service, the personage, and the cause, far from being a haven, a respite, a shelter, means exile and solitude.[77] This does not mean that he is never tempted by it; but when he yields to or chooses that temptation, it is in order to pursue his interior monologue, not in order to find ordinary human warmth. The monologue feeds the public figure and prepares him for the next phase of his role; human warmth and entanglements would only distract him from his task.

This task—the exercise of power—is also solitary, if one chooses to perform at such an altitude. Yet in *that* kind of performance lies "the interest of life." The dominant relation between the two selves, between Charles and General de Gaulle, could be characterized by that Lasswellian phrase, the displacement of private affects on public objects. But displacement, here, is deliberate and elaborate— like artistic creation. The first of those public objects is none other than himself, or rather "de Gaulle," the epic figure that has to be shaped so as to fill the part that history and Charles have prepared for it. Private feelings have to be transmuted into public service; the requirements of the mission rule out the personage's being influenced either by the whims and demands of the private person or by the pressures and results of others.[78] Hence there is that formidable "internal distance" noted by Malraux and Gide,[79] that refusal to let the internal monologue appear in the open; hence, especially in the months after June 1940 (when the man had to act out the public figure he had created in his mind, when this figure had to meet, to fit, and to make its mission, and when his torment must have been extreme) there is that formidable, gloomy, bitter, and closed look in eyes which "reflected nothing from the world outside."[80] The sense one gets is of a deeply passionate and sensitive man—indeed, one who, during the war, was so raw and scorched that he did not yet always control his feelings and public face[81]— but one whose real passions are public, whose moods are determined by the state of public affairs, whose serenity, a self-imposed necessity for the great leader, is the product of an effort, a conquest, and whose real dialogue is not with specific human beings, but with those abstractions that *to him* are human. Gide's Thesée said: *"Je n'aime pas l'homme, j'aime ce qui le dévore."* De Gaulle could say: I don't like men, I like what elevates them.[82]

It is as if there were two parallel de Gaulles: the private person with a father and mother of flesh and blood, to whom he was, so to speak, normally attached—yet no part of that trilogy sufficed him. And then there are the higher, public objects of his affections—General de Gaulle as the "national necessity" for troubled times, because he is "alone and erect"[83]; and the General's mythical (or real?) parents: History, the father to whom he is responsible[84] (just as others must report to him), and which will judge him according to his works; France, his mother—an old cliché which the long tradition of describing France as a person had somehow frayed, yet which finds in de Gaulle, the protector and knight, the new force of authenticity. The feelings that animate de Gaulle are at that level, in that realm. His failures affect him not because they are his own, but because they are France's. The warmth he needs is not the intimacy of equals, but the support and sympathy of the led. The "melancholy" that is the accepted price of domination, that willing sacrifice of ordinary human relations,[85] becomes intolerable and leads to "ill-explained retreats" only when the *leader's* soul becomes engulfed by what Clemenceau (twice quoted by de Gaulle)[86] called its worst pain: cold—the indifference or hostility of the led. The warmth he needs is public. Since his goal is not self-expression, but self-fulfillment through service, and since his mission is to lead men, he cannot perform his task alone; when they abandon him, then, rather than letting his private self take over, he remains his public person, but in waiting.

Between Charles and General de Gaulle, there are undoubtedly no conflicts. The stoicism with which he faced his third child's illness resembles his imperial way of facing the realities of power. Indeed, "de Gaulle" is Charles' accomplishment. If France is "de Gaulle's" *raison d'être*, "de Gaulle" is Charles'. How could that double need for glory and for distance be better served than by stretching oneself into, and merging with, a function of historic significance, yet one that requires that one keep one's distance even from oneself, to make sure that the performance will be great? For a man to be his own creator, what a revenge over solitude and separateness; also what pride, and, once again, what a way both of externalizing and of transcending narcissism—for it is in his historic figure that he takes the pride of the artist who has mastered his craft; it is not vanity.

The values *Charles* had absorbed from his family have been grafted on *General de Gaulle's* "parents." He resembles Vigny's Moses: "*Seigneur, vous m'avez fait puissant et solitaire. Laissez-moi m'endormir du sommeil de la terre.*" What saves the missionary from inhumanity is, first, a very Christian sense of man's frailty— even the great man's (see his astonishing portrait of Hitler: "but, beaten and crushed, perhaps he became a man again, long enough to shed a secret tear, at the moment where everything ends"[87]). Secondly, rather than serving a harsh God, he serves, on the one hand, History—which requires of its most appreciated servants not only that they court glory, but also that they respect moderation (hence his persistent rejection of dictatorship)—and, on the other hand, France, the beacon of light, the threatened princess, the nation that has to be saved from its vices.

It is by shaping his public figure that de Gaulle has resolved that tension analyzed earlier. The mission is a transmission of the parents' legacy (but as rescued and remade by the leader); the missionary is the receptacle of the cynical lessons that history also teaches, and of the ego's will to power (but to be used for a great cause).

It does not matter if we know little directly about Charles, the artist, who created de Gaulle, the work of art. Even if we knew the last intimate detail of the artist's childhood, schooling, and marriage, what we are able to say about the personal life of the artist is, usually, irrelevant to the evaluation of the work of art. It helps us only to understand the man who made it, rather than the work itself; it may provide the key to the content, but not to the intimate relation of form and content which is the essence of every work of art. Conversely, understanding this relation tells us a great deal about the man.

Indeed, the public figure from whom the Memoir writer who says "I" strived to be detached, and who is supposed to be only the protector of France and incarnation of history, in the real cycle of identifications takes on the features of Charles the artist. The more he bends himself to the public figure and to France, the more the "character" and France resemble the artist—but as in every work of art those features are transformed, re-created, mastered, *dominated*. Charles de Gaulle has continued to marshal all his resources. He has displayed all the qualities associated with artistic creation: the mix of detachment and commitment which allows him to watch his personage from afar, yet to shape its destiny; the blend of passion and decorum, so characteristic of a man whose style often appears as its own reward, yet always serves a cause; the willingness to be dominated by the object—in this case, the character and France, which "haunts" him[88]; the combination of deferral and immediacy. What must be resented as obstinacy by all those who hold dissenting views, and what represents a neurotic flaw in the character of Charles? His old need always to be right reflects the artist's sense of the inner appropriateness of a particular decision, of its perfect fit into the whole vision; his "feel" that his conception "works" or must ultimately work. Very often, his skill as a craftsman (politician) *makes* it work, even as his skill as an artist (statesman) helps him to assess correctly the *"pâte"* (reality) he is trying to reshape. It is an instinctive, instinctual activity, one which involves all the gifts of the artist-leader.

It is easy to see why Malraux should have become fascinated by the General, for the public figure is like the embodiment of Malraux's ideal. He is a character in a novel that Malraux never wrote, but that would combine all of Malraux's strivings; he is also the work of art so much admired by Malraux, that which takes off from past masterpieces, expresses a transcendent faith, and conquers time. De Gaulle is that adventurer with a cause that Malraux had looked for in his early years, and the cause is not the excessively abstract ideology that Communism had represented and that the Soviet Union exploited for its purposes, but the preservation of a cultural entity—the nation, whose importance Malraux had discovered in defeat and whose personality (not superiority) de Gaulle wants to assert. De Gaulle's mission is to leave a scar on history, to shape his destiny, and thus to defy death, chance, oblivion by linking creatively the past and the future. To de Gaulle as to Malraux, men are what they do, what they reveal of themselves not in introspective analysis, but in creative action. If creativity is the "working out of conflict and coalition within the set of identities that compose the person,"[89] then de Gaulle's leadership is highly *creative*, even if it is not so *innovative*.

Some witnesses have seen him as all of one piece. In reality, we find a harnessing of all the pieces. Thus, there is a skillful transformation of his psychological peculiarities into unique tools of leadership. This is true of many of his gifts. His memory has become not only the thoroughly reliable servant of his eloquence, but also a source of prestige and awe. His literary talent and his imagination have blended in the *Mémoires*, written at a time when he seems to have thought that his chances of ever coming back to power were slim; these volumes served not only as a catharsis, as noted before, but also as a reliving in the imagination of the exploits of the recent past and as a legacy of examples for the future. His old gift for drama, acting, and performing on a stage has become ritualized in his press conferences and ceremonial appearances: From his early playacting, he has shifted to role-acting. His energy finds outlets in constant journeys, which feed his curiosity, provide him with the "soul's warmth" he needs, allow him to carry his message to all the corners of his widening stage, and preserve his sense of the realities.

We have stated that the army fitted some of the peculiarities of his character—his sense of distance, his shying-away from intimacy, and that incapacity to share decisions that results from his drive for independence. All of those traits have become the trademarks of his political leadership. The "King in exile"[90] has become the Republican monarch. The mold which the army had given to his way of organizing action, its institutionalization of distance, he has elevated and perpetuated in a constitution that makes of the President a kind of commander in chief, aided by a chief of staff, the Premier. His impatience with details that could clutter the mind of the leader has also been institutionalized. His dislike for discussions and debates that dilute the will and confuse the issues,[91] his awkwardness in small groups have led him to replace such negotiations with "consultations" in which he is usually alone with whomever he consults.[92] His preference for infantry, which put him as an officer in direct but dominating contact with average Frenchmen, is relayed by his way of leaning on the people, of short-circuiting the "elites."[93] His preference for a certain protective isolation has driven telephones out of his offices and saved almost all his weekends in France for a return to Colombey. When some feature, left untamed, could have harmed his vocation, he has curbed his own nature. The early reluctance to let himself be interviewed, photographed, or put on display has been disciplined, although not at the expense of the imperatives of mystery and surprise. And even intransigence, his trademark, has gradually been put back into limits—that is, reserved for two kinds of issues, both significant of his leadership: symbolic or protocol issues, involving "nothing but" self-respect, and vital national interests.

Next to the transmutation of personal traits into tools, there is the welding of opposites, or of polarities, in such a way that, far from destroying each other and the man, they complement each other and help him fulfill his mission by becoming ingredients of leadership—externalized and transcended. Some of those polarities can be seen as variations on two permanent themes—picked up from his parents, and later developed in memorable statements: the passionate and the reasonable.[94]

The most obvious are the polarities of rebellion and rallying,[95] or defiance and assertion. The natural *démarche* of de Gaulle is to defy either whatever offends his concept of leadership (such as the instruction he received in military schools, the military policy of the interwar period, or the political styles of the declining Third Republic and of the Fourth Republic), or whatever "insults the future" as he both wants it and deems it possible (such as Vichy's resignation to defeat, or the two postwar "hegemonies, or the French Communists' servility toward Moscow after 1947). This defiance can be brutal and intransigent. But de Gaulle is neither a nihilist nor (adds Malraux)[96] a Trotsky. The rebel in him wants it known, as he once told a delegation of labor-union leaders, that "General de Gaulle has no predecessors"[97]; but he wants to have successors and to represent historic continuity. The defier, or resister, does so in order to "save and put in order."[98] The purpose of his domestic calls to action was to unify the French; of his external acts of negation, to reshape the world in safer fashion, which to him means, characteristically, into equilibrium. His one substantive domestic notion (beyond the constitutional design he announced in 1946 and realized in 1958-62) has been the association of capital and labor. On the other hand, the unifier and servant of order knows he can succeed only through battle—be it against an overpowering ally, or other French regimes or parties, or business and labor unions attached to their ways.

Another set of polarities, close to the previous one, is the General's romanticism and classicism (his admiration for Chateaubriand, who assured the transition, is no surprise). It is the romantic who says "me and history,"[99] asserts his lack of origins, sees the world as a turmoil in which the man of action, occasionally, discreetly, discontinuously "decides and prescribes . . . and then, after action has been launched, seizes again by spurts the system of his means which facts relentlessly put out of shape."[100] It is, however, the classicist who insists on measure and balance, who sees in the leader a kind of grand entrepreneur, the function of whose investments and innovations is to preserve the continuity and flow of history, who rules like a Cornelian Emperor, and knows that in this century "no man can be the people's substitute."[101] Romanticism and classicism blend in de Gaulle's military programs and use of technological innovations; he has put the radio, during the war, and television, since 1958, at the service of *le caractère;* his old hostility to the "system of armed masses," which inspired first his design for a professional army and, later, his reconversion of the French army to the atomic age, reflects both the romantic love for mobility, decisiveness, lightning action that had made him admire

Hoche, Foch, and Clemenceau and the classic concern for maximum efficiency in the use of limited resources, which had made him celebrate Louvois and Turenne, Carnot and Pétain.

Two other sets of features that are kept in balance and blended for the mission are, on the one hand, his inflexibility and brutality; on the other, his tactical skill and patience. The former have been displayed abruptly throughout his career—from his relations with Churchill to his speech in Montreal. A psychological tendency that goes back to his childhood and stems both from his loyalty to transmitted values and from his self-assertion has thus been used to shape, delay, or accelerate history. But, on the other hand, there has been—in this transformed prankster and critical *connaisseur* of dubious means to lofty ends—a deliberate use of ambiguity (*"je vous ai compris!"*), a willingness to wait and ponder until the moment is ripe, especially when there was either no other, better way of affecting events or no vital interest involved. Temporization, it seems, was already a trait in the student and young officer whenever his mind was not fully engaged.[102]

Another tension, also resolved, is that which exists between his taste for flamboyance and his sense of finitude. One drives him toward heroic assertions of will, toward grand attempts at making his policies irreversible; the other toward a certain fatalism, a strange readiness, if not to accept defeat, at least to admit partial failure as the price for being human.[103] Once again, he marries the two, and each heightens the other: The more one is aware of the limits of one's possibilities—one's own and those of "the nation as it is in the world as it is"—the more necessary it becomes to do what can be done with *panache*, flair, and style; but those, in turn, are justified only so long as they serve the cause realistically.

One keyword of de Gaulle's political vocabulary illuminates his acts as a leader, his way of mobilizing and welding his resources: "arbitration." It does not mean mediation, finding a common denominator among pre-existing tendencies (within him) or factions (outside); it means deciding—both after taking into account in one's calculations all the givens provided by one's own nature or by the "nature of things," and with the higher interest as a goal. Once again, we find mastery without mutilation; the "arbiter" is none other than *le caractère*, determined to take charge, respectful of the need for equilibrium, and resolving his inner tensions by the tough "internal discipline and heavy yoke"[104] of subordination to the higher goal.

But arbitration does not take care of all inner tensions. There is one between him and the cause that is supposed to transcend and elevate both his private and his public selves—between the artist and the mission for which he shaped his work of art. There are, inevitably, opposite pulls. There is, in particular, a contradiction between the *private man*'s desire to assert his personality— his egotism, if you like—his sense of personal adventure, a certain drunkenness with his own destiny, a heady enchantment with having made of himself such a precious capital,[105] and the *historic figure*'s desire to be above all the expression of *France*, his concern for *raison d'Etat*. The former injects occasionally into the leader's acts an element of vindictiveness or into his words a paean of self-praise.[106] The latter may demand some self-abnegation, and in any case prudence in the use of the capital, skepticism about the ego's reach. Yet the reconciliation is usually provided in a way that both protects the mission and satisfies the artist—by exalting the public-political figure. The personality that is spread over the map is the *public* personage, not the private self, and since that personage is nothing but the tool of the state, his successes, resentments, assertions, claims, and setbacks become those of the nation. To leave him "in the desert" (as did the Fourth Republic) is to waste France,[107] to slight him is to slight France, to plan his assassination is a crime against the state, to serve him is to ennoble oneself. If *le caractère* wants full power for himself and denies anyone else's capacity to exert power adequately, it is because there is between "de Gaulle" and his mission a mystical link that allows him to claim historical legitimacy. De Gaulle, quoting Roosevelt who had taxed him with egotism,[108] asks whether F.D.R. thought him egotistic for himself or for France; in fact, he has solved the problem by equating his *public* self with the *higher* interest of France.

Yet this solution poses one more problem: It may reconcile the artist with the *final* work of art—the historic personage which the public-political figure must create. But it does so by boosting the *artist*'s work of art: that public figure. And, like every work of art, this one tends, once it gets under way, to take on a life of its own, with its own demands for wholeness. Since its artist is so closely tied to it by his own needs and in his person, the work tends also to take over the artist. If it does so, he has failed—he is no longer master of himself, of the others, or of his creation. This time he needs to use his resources not to *blend*, but to *separate*. He has

279

resorted to three familiar aids, mobilized on behalf of self-distance and perspective: his sense of humor and irony; his habit of describing himself in the third person as an actor on a stage whom he would watch from the audience; and his discipline of detachment by moving away from the all-absorbing present in time (the recourse to history) and space (travels). These three devices have been (as usual) instinctively and deliberately used by Charles to keep himself from fusing entirely with the *éclat* and *grandeur* of his "over-determined" work of art, similar to the over-determination of fantasy and dreams, as of all rich artistic creation. There is a gigantic battle between the artist's attempt to fuse and project his highest aspirations onto *le caractère* who lives for France, and his own narcissistic needs to hold onto that artistic projection by completely identifying with it.

France as de Gaulle

What makes this battle so difficult to win is not only the resemblance of the work of art, "de Gaulle," to the artist, but also the resemblance to the artist of that higher work of art, France, which the public figure has both to serve and to shape as "de Gaulle's" work of art.

Not only have many of Charles' psychological and even physical peculiarities been turned into tools of leadership, they have also been projected by him onto his beloved France. This is especially striking in the case of those traits that are essential to an understanding of the man: his own highest aspirations, blends of the *is* and the *ought* since they reflect both psychological needs and moral values[109] he has assigned to France. A pragmatist in his daily politics, de Gaulle as a political high priest is concerned above all with making France behave according to those values; a Machiavellian in his tactics, he is a moralist in his highest goals. (As an associate has described him, he is "Caesar reshaped by Christianity.") De Gaulle, from adolescence on, has felt the need for a strong internal discipline to guard him against waste and dispersion, to harness his gifts and prevent internal tensions from paralyzing him. The solution, as we know, has been to unify his talents and traits in the service of a great cause, which will provide the harness and heighten the efficiency of his personality. This is exactly what he ascribes to and prescribes for France: France is full of "ferments of dispersion," has often yielded to "chimeras," been threatened by mediocrity and disasters.[110] For France, the harness is to be provided by a unifying and galvanizing "national ambition," a "great undertaking"—by grandeur, by the "choice of a great cause." Once again what he proclaims necessary for her is what he has assigned to himself—*"viser haut et se tenir droit."*[111] Both he and France need a higher *"querelle";* without one, he is convinced that she will not "be herself" for she is truly herself neither in mediocrity nor in misfortune. Similarly, he is at his best only when carried by his mission. When he writes of "Old France, burdened by history, bruised by wars and revolutions, relentlessly going back and forth from grandeur to decline, but straightened, century after century, by the genius of renovation,"[112] or describes France as a "great people, made for example, enterprise, combat, always the star of History,"[113] or says that he always felt that Providence "had created her for perfect success or exemplary misfortune,"[114] he is describing himself as much as her.

The identification goes further. Just as he has proclaimed throughout his life that the hero was both his own law and the servant of France, France is seen by him both as *the* nation par excellence and as the servant of what he called, during the war, *"la querelle de l'homme"*—the cause of freedom, of equilibrium, of generosity in a world threatened by mechanization.[115] Just as he has used all his resources in his mission, but put them at its service, he has always wanted to use all the spiritual and political "families" of France, refused to discard any so long as it was willing to contribute to the cause, but tried to convert them all from their separate concerns to the common goal. Just as, for him, grandeur meant an attitude of the will and soul rather than a specific doctrine, grandeur for France means a state of mind and resolve, a rejection of pettiness, an ambition rather than a concrete program: the ambition, more cultural and moral than political, to preserve certain values that are like a blend of Christianity's and of the Revolution's.

The precondition for grandeur, in both cases, is the same: independence. De Gaulle's foreign policy—his central concern—has aimed persistently at giving France "free hands," at restoring her freedom of decision (the more interdependent the nations of the world, the greater the need for a margin of autonomy); in recent years, he has made of this a universal doctrine. It is impossible not to recognize in his philosophy of international relations, in his dismissal of ideologies, in his assertion of the primacy of national interests, in his stress on the incommunicable uniqueness of each nation,[116] in his view of states on the world stage as separate national essences with accidental existences shaped by the twists of history and the turns of national consciousness,[117] once again a projection of his own conception of leadership—ultimately, of his personal stance, of his own determination to "belong to all and nobody"[118] (a formula that fits his view of France)—and a blend of the *is* and the *ought* (for his mission and France's as defined by him are justified only if he is right). It was Vichy's crime to have renounced French independence, thus losing its legitimacy.[119] And if he was able to restore France's independence, in 1944 and after 1958, it was because he had never alienated his own.

The emphasis on independence for him and her is tied to another essential notion: that of integrity, meaning both wholeness and faithfulness. Independence is the condition for integrity; integrity is the substance of self-respect; and self-respect, or dignity, a central value, can be found only in grandeur. "Not to disappoint oneself"[120] seems to be the motto he gave both to himself and to France. There is no self-respect in humiliation, or in mediocrity, or in *"bassesse"*[121] (there may be some in failure, if it is honorable). For the leader, there is no loss of self-respect in a resort to deception and cunning so long as the higher cause prevails; there is, for France, no loss of self-respect in revising her alliances and reversing her policies so long as her own higher goals are served. The association of capital and labor that de Gaulle keeps trying to establish, so much like the combination of opposites within himself, makes more sense as a promotion of dignity than as an economic reform. De Gaulle offers France's aid to the French Canadians, who have preserved their independence and integrity and are now claiming a modern role of their own, but the French Algerians, who did not know how to adapt and spoiled the image of France, were less well treated by him.

Grandeur, independence, integrity: just as his leadership tends to give France his own profile, France's leadership aims at making of the world a collection of ideal types of Gaullist nations, each one embodying its unique values and virtues, and kept within the limits of moderation by the balancing of power. There is an underlying assumption here that just as man is truly free and responsible only when he can fully develop and master his personality, there can be no true world order outside that which would be a structured harmony of multiple uniquenesses. And just as the leader sets the example for France, France must set it for the world.

France in international relations indeed behaves as de Gaulle writ large. Just as his conception of leadership consists of discerning what he deems right, providing an example, and asking others to follow rather than forcing them to do so, France's stance on the world stage consists of showing the way imperiously and exhorting others to follow; but just as he has always refused entanglements for himself so as to save his freedom to maneuver, his France refuses commitments with obscure purposes and binding procedures. His difficulty in negotiating, his way of never letting a concession be bargained out of him but, instead, of granting (*octroyer*)[122] concessions to which the other will respond freely become France's vetoes, boycotts, and unilateral moves. His personal intransigence becomes France's intractability; the leader's *âpreté* becomes France's toughness; the man's preference for dealing with other great leaders, lonely masters, and artists becomes France's disdain for taking seriously powers incapable of "charting their course." His need for drama becomes France's stealing the show in world affairs, or attempts to steal it.

The same polarities that he combines in himself he projects onto and harnesses in France. A traditionalist, but also an empiricist thirsty for action, he wants France both to preserve her personality and to innovate—for without innovation, modernization, mechanization, industrialization, there is no way to be great anymore. Yet all these changes must not be allowed to turn France into a bastardized America. (Hence the emphasis on saving her language and culture in which he finds, not surprisingly, her essence.) His own mixture of narcissism and discipline becomes the blend of often strident French self-assertion and recognition of the need for "modesty." And just as the awareness of personal finitude increases the desire for flamboyance, the realistic awareness of the limits of France's present power heightens the need for self-pride: France's foreign policy today combines a colossal *repli* from overseas and abandonment of excessive commitments, with a spectacular determination to exploit every possibility of influence.[123]

III. *Charisma*

The artist does not need a responsive public immediately. He may write or paint for the "happy few" and posterity. The political artist needs a public *now*, even if his ambition is to build for the ages; without one, his work of art remains a conception. The political artist succeeds only if public response allows the figure of the leader, privately shaped by the artist for a public role, to become a public figure. Political leadership is a relationship between the leader and his followers; and charisma is not only a gift, it is also a form of authority, a link between a certain type of ruler and the ruled. If charisma is communicated self-confidence,[124] what we must discuss now is why, when, and how de Gaulle has managed to impose his gift to the French, to preserve his authority after coming to power, and at what costs for the nation and for the future of his own work.

Conditions

De Gaulle has always known and said that he could not carry out his mission without public support. From 1940 to 1944, he literally forged it. He resigned in 1946 when he felt it slipping and lacked the institutional means to preserve it *in his style*. He tried in vain to recreate it as leader of the R.P.F. He found it again in 1958. What were the conditions for his success?

He has succeeded in establishing that cycle of identifications— of France to himself, of himself to France, of the people with him, of himself and France to higher causes—whenever the circumstances have been exactly what the script required; whenever he has been able to enact or re-enact on the stage of history the great drama that he had wanted to perform: that of bringing *alone* a decisive and famous service to his nation in distress; whenever history brought his nation to the point where his own need (for drama, leadership, a call, unity, and salvation) became France's, and when France at last had no alternative but to turn to the lonely leader; whenever the missionary who had subordinated his private self to his public function met men whose public drama had become a private crisis.[125] It was the man's great chance that when he projected his formidable will and imagination into the future, events obligingly provided the great dramas that he called for *à la* Chateaubriand (*"levez-vous, orages désirés"*), that World War I foreshadowed in his mind, and that his relative failure in it made even more imperative for his ambition. This was a chance that his political genius has, of course, fully exploited; but it was also part of his genius to have anticipated, announced, and denounced those events clearly.

Here we find the first ingredient of his charisma: the awe-inspiring capacity of *le caractère* to predict the *circonstances*—that is, to be right. Prescience did for him what victory over paralysis had done for F.D.R. in the American people's eyes. (It is no accident if de Gaulle's symbolic domain was public, F.D.R.'s was private.) The somewhat suffocating statement of May 19, 1958: "The Algerians shout: Vive de Gaulle as the French do instinctively when they are deep in anguish or carried by hope,"[126] reflects a reality.

However, what has been required for success has been a perfect adequacy and a perfect prophecy. It is only when the circumstances were those of extreme and irremediable disaster, when the leader could appeal both to the present fears, anxieties, and sufferings of the people and to their hopes, to Péguy's *"espérance"* and Corneille's *"beau désespoir,"* when he could appear as the prophet, the unifier, the remover of the roadblocks to and the guide toward the "summits" of self-respect and greatness that he has succeeded. The counter-example is provided by the long episode of the R.P.F. There, adequacy was missing. The General prophesied titanic turmoil and cataclysmic conflict between East and West: It did not happen. Although his goals were as lofty as ever, he could not appear as a unifier, since his very attempt to "rally" the nation outside and above the parties divided the French—a dilemma that could have been resolved (as in the fight against Vichy) only if they had gradually deserted the parties out of a personal sense of tragedy and need for salvation, the precondition for which would have been the correctness of the prophecy (as shown later, in 1958). Moreover, because "hope had a tragic accent for him," he had to put the spotlight on tragedy in order to justify his call for action; thus, he appealed almost exclusively to people's fears and anxieties, and exploited them stridently, with dismal results. Those who heard him and came were often those who wanted to save not France but their possessions, and of course they deserted him when the fear of loss vanished, but not without having given to the R.P.F. a cramped, regressive, and repressive air, in which Barrès prevailed over Péguy, conservation over innovation.

For de Gaulle to be able to be the voice of hope and effort, the disasters must already have happened. Before, he can denounce their coming, but by the very nature of his personage, to try to be more than a *recours* if they come is likely to be counter-productive. If they fail to occur, his prophetic gift will be tarnished, but if he tries as a political leader to contribute to their coming so as to prove himself right and to awaken the missing "great ambition," he will, by *la force des choses*, be forced to exploit the least grand side of men. Moreover, his methods—intransigence, *politique du pire* yet refusal to go all the way to dictatorship (since dictatorship, to his eyes, means excess *unless* it is prompted by a great national ambition or by a national disaster, both precisely absent)[127]—will simultaneously appear like a wrecking operation and keep him and his followers from power. The attempt of the R.P.F. was explainable only in terms, once again, of the man and the mission: At fifty-six, the man had too much energy for internal exile, and he saw his beloved France under mortal threat. The fiasco of the R.P.F. taught him that before catastrophes his strength was in his very solitude,[128] and the writing of the *Mémoires* cleansed the sullied image of the savior: He erased the re-enactment *manqué* in action by a successful re-enactment in writing.

The reason why de Gaulle's effectiveness begins only in the midst of disaster has to do with the second ingredient of his charisma. It is only in the depths of crisis and despair that the fear of losing one's personality breeds millennial hopes of rescue: otherwise, complacency prevails, and the would-be guide has that unsavory choice between frustration and deliberate contribution to the dreaded yet necessary *secousse*. But when the crisis comes, then de Gaulle's peculiar message—that France must regain her greatness by saving her identity—strikes the deepest chord. For the message, as we have noted, is far more pedagogical than ideological (and thus is related to the messages of religious leaders or of a Gandhi): To de Gaulle (as to the Caesar-Charles of his early play), what matters most is *that* one face the turmoil, and *how* one confronts danger, rather than *what* specific measures one should take (for they depend on circumstances). Here is the strength of Gaullism; its roots lie, again, in the adequacy of a personal case to a national one. For de Gaulle, as we know, the goal in life was not to realize a program, but to be a character, to have a firm identity, shaped by internal balance and control for great but pragmatic action, and faithful to certain values; leadership so defined was its own purpose. For France, a very old nation, identity did not have to be defined in substantive, programmatic terms, necessary perhaps for recent nations still unsure of their national consciousness, but positively harmful in the case of a country where an intense feeling of nationhood coincides with fearful divisions on policies. Thus, in times of acute crisis, the thing for a leader to do is to underemphasize the *substance* of action, but to stress the *essence*—which is self-respect and style. There was no need to define a French identity; there was a need to save and proclaim it, to make the French feel proud of being French and relevant to their times: Nobody could *feel* and *understand* this better than de Gaulle.

It is in emergencies that the threat to national identity makes the citizens willing to give up their established way of life, cherished possessions and institutions, in order to overcome the crisis. De Gaulle's personal message—mystical attachment to an idea of France and detachment from any specific social pattern, fixed policy, overseas position, all of which are merely transient manifestations of the mysterious essence that alone must be preserved —could thus only be heard in extreme moments, when he could play his role of innovating protector. His constant and baffling theme—France must be herself—which may seem like gibberish to many foreigners, is the second source of charisma, for it succeeds whenever, in peril, the French feel the need both to assert their personality in the world and to unify and adapt in order to survive. De Gaulle's charisma thus has an element of poetry in it—the sound and the rhythms are more important than the words' actual meanings; they shape or reshape the meanings. In this way, he can preserve the authenticity, the freshness of the nation's *élan vital,* instead of hardening or freezing it in a program.

A third factor in his charisma is his appeal to a certain style of authority, the style of crisis leadership, represented in French literature by Corneille and in French history both by the *Ancien Régime* and by the Napoleonic Empires. The kind of leadership celebrated in *Le fil de l'épée,* for all its distance from parliamentary leadership, was a French archetype. One of us has analyzed this in detail elsewhere.[129] *Le style du Général*—of political action and of eloquence—fits into a mold perfected and conceptualized by Richelieu. His very sense of distance and restraint, his conception of action by individuals each of whom has his own personality to preserve and is linked not to others on the same level as himself, but to a superior (or, in de Gaulle's own case, a higher calling), fits both the Frenchman's *horreur du face à face*[130] and his fear of arbitrariness.

One understands, then, the nature of de Gaulle's appeal in a crisis. He tries to address himself to some of the highest qualities in men—a sense of sacrifice and responsibility and duty; he calls on them to find in the crisis an opportunity to *grow*, rather than to succumb to the irrational fears, hatreds, and delusions so often flattered by demagogues. (Indeed, his own lack of "the physique, taste, attitudes and features that could flatter"[131] crowds, his indifference to being loved, and his rejection of a personality cult justify Malraux's comment: His strength lies in authority, not in contagion.[132]) Yet there is no doubt that the crisis itself brings out those fears, hatreds, and delusions, produces a kind of mass regression of helplessness, and makes the helpless eager to let the decisive leader "arbitrate" for them. One finds among his followers different kinds of men whose attachment to him varies in motivation and in intensity. There are some who need idols, or who attach themselves to the hero because of an inner need for a father figure—de Gaulle, this time, is each one of *them* completed; there are many such men in his entourage. Others are attracted more by what is compelling in de Gaulle's mission and message than by a personal need of their own—except for one widespread need, so important in crises or in otherwise mediocre periods, yet neglected by political scientists: the need to admire. Some are fascinated less by the work of art, the mission, than by the artist: They are the romantics of adventure, action, and great-men-defying-history.[133] Others, finally, are occasional followers, attracted by a temporary or partial element of de Gaulle's action, led by their own predilections and by his ambiguity to confuse this element for the essence or to misinterpret its meaning; they are grievously disappointed when they discover their error. The closer they had been to him, the more passionate their rejection.[134]

Preservation

But the qualities necessary for a charismatic (or other) leader's coming to power are not those that he needs in order to stay in power or to protect his work. A number of possibilities arise. One, the charismatic leader, having accomplished his task, responded to, and taken care of the distress that made people turn to him, may lose both his charisma and his power, or at least his power: Having saved, his role is over. Two, he may, in order to stay in office and to avoid the "routinization of charisma," perpetually recreate conditions of distress that will allow him to play the savior (Mao, for example). Three, he may decide that his best way of protecting his accomplishments is to institutionalize, so as to leave to his successors more than a memory of glory; but then there is a problem of preserving, while still in power, his own charisma from the disenchantments of routinization.

De Gaulle's career has managed to embrace all those alternatives. His personality and conception of leadership, on their romantic side, are so much in love with being a lonely savior that the prospects of institutionalization are, at first sight, incompatible with the claim to uniqueness, to direct communication with France and history, with the view of the French as somewhat weak and fickle and ungrateful children or prodigal sons of France: Between them and their big brother, the relations have never been easy. In 1945-46, partly by inclination, partly because of the circumstances (which made of him a national symbol, but put institutionalization into the parties' hands), he had to choose between trying to hang onto power at the expense of his *caractère* and charisma, and saving his charisma by "leaving things before they left me"[135]; which he did, following once again the script of *Le fil de l'épée*.

Since his return to power in 1958, he has succeeded in ruling already ten years. He has applied a fascinating mixture of alternatives two and three. Conditions of distress have been, it is true, provided in abundance by events that were not of his creation—especially during the Algerian war; but he has seized them with characteristic glee so as to re-enact his mission and to renew his charisma: when he put on his general's uniform before the TV cameras while Algiers was rioting in January 1960; when he smashed the army rebellion in April 1961; when he used the 1962 assassination attempt against him as the occasion for a Blitzkrieg on his political enemies. Moreover, the style of his foreign policy since the end of the Algerian drama, while it corresponds to his nature, also serves the function of producing, so to speak, minidramas that rejuvenate his appeal, as if he, too, needed to create crises for whose solutions he will be "erect and necessary" (for example, the press conference of January 1963, the Common Market crisis of 1965, the Canadian venture).[136] The mixture of dread and excitement with which he interpreted the Middle East crisis of

1967 as a possible gateway to world war is significant and reminds one of the false prophecies of 1947-50.

But precisely because a world drama, today, would be less a challenge than a calamity; because he remains concerned above all with protecting France's heritage and chances to grow; and because he knows (at a time when the problems of economic development dominate people's minds) that the public mood is no more heroic than the international scene is adequate for grand ventures, alternative two is kept in check by his sense of reality and limits. The problem thus becomes how to realize alternative three in a way compatible with the unique personality of the leader and with the preservation of his charisma. Earlier, the challenge was to grow by stretching; now it is to grow by knowing how to fit his enormous and epic frame into a more complacent and limited framework. He has tried to solve this problem by giving France institutions that correspond both to his own personal ideal and practice of leadership and to what he thinks French unity, stability, and efficiency require. The distance that he needs is assured not only by the constitution and by his interpretation of the President's role as one that dominates all other organs and groupings, but also by the ingenious creation of a Gaullist party that provides him with a lever, gives to his supporters highly interested reasons for loyalty, yet maintains the necessary separation between the President of all Frenchmen and a political party with which he has no direct connection, but without which he would be in the same situation as in 1945.

Yet he obviously doubts that institutionalizing his mission will do the trick after him, since leadership remains in essence a personal attribute; and he himself also tries, while alive, to preserve his charisma from the attrition of even well-oiled institutions. His decision to run for office (facing universal suffrage for the first time in his life) at the end of 1965 is highly symbolic, for while it meant that he wanted to give to his "historic" legitimacy the seal of his institutions, it also meant that he doubted that the latter could survive without the benefit of his own charisma. During the brief election campaign that preceded the disastrous first ballot, he resorted again to the apocalyptic language of fall and salvation. Elected, he continues to try to be both the first President of the Fifth Republic and "General de Gaulle." Of the three ingredients of his charisma— prophecy, stress on "being oneself," embodying the style of crisis authority—neither the first nor the third quite fits the present circumstances, not tragic enough to inspire the former nor to justify the latter. But the second one still has its appeal, as shown by the broad approval given by the French to a provocative foreign policy of independence which preserves France's identity even as the French society and polity lose much of their old distinctiveness.

What buttresses, completes, and inspires that appeal are two other factors, of uneven importance. One is memory—his capacity to remind people of the mess they were in, due to the old parties and to outside humiliations, before he came to clean it up. But the very fact of having cleaned it up attenuates the fears of a relapse; and the memories begin to fade away.

The other factor is precisely that which lies behind all his works, that which is most intensely personal, his artistry: de Gaulle's residual charisma lies almost entirely in his own *caractère,* now that the original appeal, the pristine adequacy between his call and the circumstances, has vanished. What people still follow is the great actor on the stage. A charisma that once moved the French to follow him or to cling to him, in circumstances that gave him tasks commensurate with his needs, now persists despite the narrower range of deeds and makes the French watch him as a spectacle—partly because, on the more modest scale where he operates today, they remember how in the past he stretched his potential to whatever scale was required, partly because they sense that even on that smaller scale he performs more impressively than anybody else could, partly because, as Malraux puts it, he is their alibi, and they bask in the sun of his prestige, whose rays illuminate them.[137] And so they watch him accomplishing those grand rites which mark both the institutionalization of his charisma and the periodic occasions of its reassertion, both the symbolic re-enactment of his mission and the reassuring return of normalcy. And they watch him rebelling for France wherever he still can—against the hegemonies, against the power of the dollar, against American violence in Vietnam and English-Canadian "oppression" in Quebec. The times having changed; in an international system that frustrates achievements and multiplies denials, in a nation both dulled and enervated by what Raymond Aron once called the "querulous satisfaction" of an industrial society devoid of deep cleavages but deprived of enthusiasms, a charisma once fed by accomplishments becomes a charisma based on drama. Statecraft becomes stagecraft and thus remains a protest against and remedy for the banality or "melancholy" of a duller period: "Judging the leader capable of adding to the effectiveness of familiar procedures the full weight of a unique authority [*une vertu singulière*], confidence and hope keep any obscure trust in him."[138] Indeed, the suspense about how his own drama will end nourishes his charisma.

Costs

Yet the problem of what will happen to his work in the future remains. It cannot be answered fully, but elements of an answer can be found if one looks at some of the costs of de Gaulle's leadership. In the first place, his very identification with France, just as it has subordinated "Charles" to "de Gaulle," and both to "General de Gaulle," has left out of France all that is not in de Gaulle's vision of France: Things have been compressed and repressed that will inevitably reassert themselves, since they have not been suppressed. He has, by his style of leadership, raised in acute form a problem of participation that has been amply discussed elsewhere.[139] His personality and conception of leadership, on the one hand, and his repulsion for French parliamentary politics, on the other, have created a system that may well, once the leader is gone, provoke a swing of the pendulum in the direction that he has so often denounced. His very exclusion of all "intermediaries," because of their discordances and confusion, has only increased their desire for revenge, especially in the old parties' case. His way of unifying the French is to rise above their cleavages and to ignore these cleavages' representatives. But even if some of the alignments they champion have lost much of their relevance thanks to his acts and to circumstances, they are still waiting in the wings. Surrounded by docile men whose docility annoys him, but incapable of bearing near him those who resist him and whom he respects,[140] he may have eased the way for opponents he despises. The great man has dwarfed and distorted his own institutions, which remain both fragile and marginal. The necessary synthesis between the two poles of French political authority—heroic crisis leadership and weak routine authority—continues to elude his nation.

His fascination with long-range national goals—those that can be achieved on the world stage, or whatever is required for playing on it—perhaps also his personal conviction, once more projected onto France, that dignity and greatness are worthier goals than mere material happiness have led him to brush aside or neglect values and concerns of crucial importance to many[141]: hence the re-

current divorce between himself and the French. His own style—
the quest for high drama and distant perspectives—has its reverse
side: a certain indifference, or temporization and lassitude, when
confronted with problems that seem to him less essential than those
lofty goals and on which his advisers differ.[142] As for the French,
their willingness to give priority to France's greatness decreases
whenever the requirements of the latter cease being the same as
their own daily necessities. Once order is restored, independence
insured, the threat of great crisis removed, this divorce leads to
mutual disenchantment, as in the winter of 1945-46, when the
Frenchmen's obsession with the daily difficulties and deprivations
conflicted with de Gaulle's ambitions, or in the years 1965-68: that is,
whenever the French do not live up to the imperative of grandeur,
but satisfy themselves with what he deems mediocrity and, so to
speak, give the lie to his claim that France is not herself without
greatness. *He* may not be himself without it, nor France in *his* eyes,
but France can be in *theirs*, and they do not always crave it. He
needs it always; but he can enact it for France only when both the
circumstances and the French allow him. When they cease being,
to use a famous and autobiographical quotation, an "elite people,
sure of itself and dominating" (master of its fate), the memory of
what they had to do or to give up in order to follow him leads to
"scowling, howling, and growling" (*la hargne, la ronge, et la
grogne*).

Not only have other (to him lesser) goals been discarded
within, but—most importantly—higher goals than those that can be
served by the present system of (more or less) cooperating nation-
states have also been ruled out. For the greatness he seeks, for himself and France, is that of the nation-state. A man who sees his
mission as the perpetuation of France and who sees in "being oneself" the highest duty can give to France's higher cause a noble,
humanitarian tone and goals of extensive coordination with others,
but certainly not the "ambition" of disappearing into a higher
grouping: that kind of higher goal would be self-abnegation or
abdication, the opposite of self-assertion; and so every merger of
sovereignties, beyond revocable association, must appear to him
like a fading of the will to live. But whereas, in the domestic realm,
the lack of participation and subordination of "lower" goals may
lead to a reaction that will show the intermediaries and the "lesser"
concerns to be just as destructive as he has always warned (even
more so for having been neglected), outside the mechanism of the

self-fulfilling prophecy may work differently: not through reaction against what he stood for, but through the contagion of nationalism.[143]

Other costs have to do not with things ruled out, but with things created by his leadership. Both his deeds and his style have made enemies—for himself within France, for France in the world. Although he sees international relations as a struggle and puts being right far above being surrounded with friends, the occasional isolation of France in world affairs—when his initiatives or words are not followed by others or when his words and his grand refusal to see things from any perspective but his own antagonize others—is a dangerous price for "grandeur"; for diplomacy does not prosper by, nor morale feed on very distant chances of ultimate success or prospects of final vindication.[144] And the inevitable creation of domestic hostility cannot please the man who wants to unify the French, but who antagonizes many, either because of specific policies they dislike, or because of his haughty style of personal leadership. There can be no greatness without struggle; but the animosities which the struggle provokes impede greatness insofar as, in the temporal world, leadership has to be more than a moral posture: It must bring a payment in cash.

Also, his high image of France and his identification with her have often bred a kind of intoxicating self-delusion in him. A policy followed by other, weaker men can (indeed must) fail. The same policy endorsed by him must succeed—because he can speak for France and because he is "de Gaulle"; he discovered, in dealing with the Algerian F.L.N., that this was not the case. Nor have his pronouncements and visits always been followed by the results he had expected (for instance, in Latin America, or his warning to Israel in May 1967). Thus, hopes have often been dashed, energies wasted, imprudent acts performed, or words expressed because character was not convertible into, or backed by the commitment of, material power, or because he misread events, or because his grand moves were no substitute for those detailed measures of execution with which he does not like to bother.

More serious (because they are more lasting) are the illusions he may have created among the French. His message has bred its own misunderstandings. It is pride that he has wanted to restore in the French; it is vanity that he may have fed. (Their reaction to his Canadian outburst is significant: He wanted to make his people proud of their overseas cousins, both for their past resilience and for their new ambition; French opinion blamed him for having given France a bad name on the world stage.) He has tried to replace a chauvinism of nostalgia, envy, resentment and to displace self-doubt with a national pride in the recovery of independence, harmony, economic progress; yet in its reverberations his own assertiveness has often led to silly manifestations of misplaced gloating or xenophobia. Moreover, in his pedagogic attempt at moving men by making them believe either that they are better than they really are so as to make them better, or that they are doing more than they actually do so as to get them to do more, while knowing the sad truth himself, he has spread myths (such as that of France's almost unanimous role in the Resistance, or share in the victory of 1945, or voluntary decolonization, or atomic prowess). These may in the end detract from the very adjustment to reality that he was also trying to promote and without which the will to greatness would operate in a vacuum.

Ultimately, the reason why the protection of the work remains unsure is quite simple. Some of the deeds are history, irreversibly so: the resistance and liberation of France, and decolonization. Others are fragile—the nuclear force, the stand against supranational integration, the constitution—because they embody a highly personal reading of reality, and above all an attitude rather than a program. Should this attitude be repudiated by the French after him, either by deliberate choice of another course or by incapacity to follow any (through dispersion and discord), then that part of his work would be lost, partly through *their* fault, and—for the reasons just given—partly through his own; but these are so intimately tied to the essence of his personality and leadership that it is hard to see how they could have been avoided. And even if that part of his work disappears, there would always remain the two things which de Gaulle, political master and artist, has most cared about: the trail of glory and the tales of greatness in the history textbooks of the future, and the inspiration and example for action. "Since everything always begins anew, what I have done will sooner or later be a source of new fervor after I have disappeared."[145] For "there is something contagious in greatness."[146]

We have observed that de Gaulle's conception of the leader as missionary of a national cause had religious overtones, and that this missionary figure was itself the creation of a political artist. Indeed, it is the artist, revealed by his work of art, who resembles

295

in many ways the great religious leaders, or the statesmen with a religious dimension, of the past.

A desire to redeem his father and a sense of being chosen; a strong moral conscience and a love for "activity on a large scale"; a long effort of building up in oneself all the resources needed for the task to come; the capacity to make one's childhood crises representative of collective problems, to make of one's personality the answer to a historical crisis, to fill a collective identity vacuum with one's own identity through one's acts or writings; the capacity to wait for the right moment, to engage one's whole personality when it comes, and to prefer settling for nothing rather than compromising one's integrity; a self-fulfilling (and early) sense of omnipotence and omniscience, combined with enormous energy and mental concentration; narcissism absorbed in charisma and lifted into deeds; a sense of being unique and unprecedented—all these traits, assembled by Erik Erikson,[147] apply to de Gaulle. The central values of integrity and fidelity, honor, self-respect developed in adolescence, a kind of telescoping of the adolescent and mature stages of psychosocial identity are also present here, along with the bypassing of intimacy, although there is no apparent bypassing of generativity in the case of a man who has not only had children, but also expressed his concern for the expansion of French youth. At first sight, we do not find one element that characterizes many great leaders: the search for a wider identity than the one that existed before. To him, France remains the highest temporal good; yet the universalist component of French culture, the expansion of de Gaulle's horizons since the mid-1950's, his assertion of the essential equality and dignity of all self-respecting cultural entities, whatever the hierarchy of political power, and, within his country, his effort to transcend traditional class or ideological divisions ought not to be ignored.

If the artist is thus confirmed as a great politico-religious leader, what about the work of art to which he has devoted his life?

For an evaluation of "the work-of-art in history," so much *hubris* is required—even more than that of the artist who created it. In comparison with other art, its ultimate value is dependent on its timeliness, on its permanent "fit" into history, on the lasting appreciation of its audience, as well as on its intrinsic value.

By definition, the intrinsic value of a work of art is to be found not in its timeliness, nor in its social contribution, nor in the applause it gets, but in something hidden entirely within its own complex structure. Whether people like it or not, find it useful, pleasing, or ugly, is irrelevant here—not just because the audience does not matter to its *artistic* evaluation, but because whether it is good or bad is not even the issue. The issue is, rather: Is it or is it not a work of art? If it is, then by definition, "it works, it will last"; it will leave its mark somewhere, sometime.

Just as the artist, at his best, does not care about his immediate impact on his audience, one finds in de Gaulle a certain indifference to it, partly out of faith, partly out of fatalism, partly because he looks to the long-range audience of history, but mainly because he is concerned above all with his artist's work—his public figure and the latter's mission—for its own sake. This concern helps explain the relative ideological poverty of the Gaullist pursuit of grandeur. It also explains de Gaulle's frequent preoccupation[148] with *ending well*. Like Corneille's Augustus, he has the actor's temptation—*"quitter la vie avec éclat."*[149] What shall the rest of the story be?

The *political* artist, the man of action, needs the support of the public. His mission could end dramatically, if he were to be repudiated by the French after some political crisis. He could then no longer claim—as after January 1946—that he still represented French legitimacy, since the institutions in which the drama would unfold are this time his very own, supported massively by the people. Even rejected as a political leader, however, the historic figure—the ultimate work of art—would continue to exist: "General de Gaulle" could, like any masterpiece, be great (and thus contagious) out of office as well as in power. But for the work of art to persist and endure, the style of the exit would have to be grand, like that of January 1946, and unlike the falls of so many French leaders.

In other words, the real danger lies elsewhere than in the mere withdrawal of assent. It lies in that mysterious and delicate relation of the artist with his creation. Will the artist in him, despite his lucid resolve, become incapable of new creativity? There are two threats, within himself. The artist could become the prisoner of the public figure, from which he would have lost his distance, and which would have turned into a rigidified and uncontrolled caricature of itself, like a huge, heavy fish left on an empty shore. Or else the artist could succumb to the self-indulgence of old age, when all the private fears and flaws, once conquered and transcended, take over, making of the public figure the hostage or the victim of the private man's afflictions. In either case he would become the captive of his past, which he could no longer renew nor transcend.

Maybe fate will save him from either disgrace. The man who has so eloquently described old age as a shipwreck, who warned himself against Pétain's "majestic lassitude," who watched Adenauer's decline and Churchill's decay must surely be on his guard against personal exhaustion. Against irrelevance, and the tendency to re-enact incongruously his missionary role, he may be protected by his acute sense of reality—and also, one hopes, by his aesthetic concern. For the man who has tried to make of his public figure, of his career, and of his nation an integrated work of art needs an aesthetic end to the script he has written and the character he has shaped. Maybe he will put an end to the work of art—public figure and mission—in time, becoming again, as in his childhood and adolescence, a human being alone with his dreams. Whatever the rest of his story will be, de Gaulle is and has been the incarnation of Bernanos' fragile ideal—the man who has never lost that "*esprit d'enfance*" that consists of all the early aspirations and ardors; he has never betrayed the vision which he formed in those early years and has put a formidable mix of vitality, determination, and sheer exhilarating sense of fun and play into the realization of his dreams.

"*On a l'histoire qu'on mérite.*"[150] This was de Gaulle's first lesson, which he read to his students when he was a young officer. Perhaps it is also his last lesson as an old man.

Postscriptum (sed non postmortem)

This essay was written a few weeks before the revolutionary events of May–June, 1968 and a year before de Gaulle's second and probably final resignation from political leadership. We have left the previous analysis unaltered, based as it was on our view of de Gaulle at the height of his power. In the following epilogue, we try to examine what accounts for the dramatic change in the relations between the political artist and his public. Do these changes, and his behavior during the crisis, require a different view of his work of art? Was the "style of exit" sufficiently grand to allow that work of art to endure after the end of his political leadership?

Crisis

In the crisis of May–June, 1968, de Gaulle's charisma at first waned so fast that his political demise appeared inevitable to many, but *le caractère* once again turned the tables on his enemies.

The crisis itself resulted from the costs of his kind of charisma, discussed above. Ten years of solitary rule by a leader who needed the people's confidence but shunned their involvement had made many Frenchmen eager to take into their own hands their problems as they saw them. Reforms aimed at modernizing the academic system and at moving toward de Gaulle's old ideal of workers' "participation" in industry had been delayed. The high quest for grandeur had given priority to the financial and military demands of the world role over the demands of the French consumers. Feeling neglected, they rebelled: all that had been denied and repressed exploded in May. Centralization at the top of a heavily bureaucratic system had not only made the state insufficiently responsive to social discontents, it had also prevented the leader and his government from realizing the scope of diffuse dissatisfaction. It insured that even a localized breakdown (such as that of the universities in Paris) would challenge the regime and spread to other sectors. During the crisis, whether out of wounded pride or out of obstinate clinging to long-range national goals de Gaulle maintained his planned visit to Romania and entrusted the handling of the crisis to the government, which left him at the mercy of his ministers' skills.

The crisis also resulted from the inevitable limits of any charisma. De Gaulle had given France his own features. But a nation is not a man. The crisis reflected deep and ancient traits of the French body politic, which no regime had been able to change. The weakness of intermediate bodies between the electorate and the government facilitated spontaneous combustion—the fire could spread without any resistance.[151] De Gaulle's contempt for such bodies, his "institutionalization of distance" had accentuated but not created this weakness, which was already at the root of Tocqueville's gloomy reflections on the French. The national tendency, described by Tocqueville as well as by de Gaulle, to resist reforms unless they grow out of a revolution was reflected in de Gaulle's own style of leadership; but it was also, much of the time, a genuine obstacle to his own reformist inclinations.[152] Also, he was a very old man presiding over a nation with a vast and growing population of youth; the generation gap was colossal and explains his difficulty in understanding a student movement so different from anything even in his own long experience. Finally, and by a supreme paradox, the "great mutation" of France, which he promoted as the precondition for modern greatness, was leading to an increasingly "mechanical" society—one dominated by economic imperatives, organized along bureaucratic lines, and thus deprived of the *élan* of individual prowess, poor in opportunities for romantic creation or leadership, and, to many Frenchmen, dull. This may explain why de Gaulle, contrary to so many of his supporters, showed some sympathy for the wave of *contestation*: The man who had, albeit in his dutifully patriotic way, sought an escape from the boredom of bourgeois society, could understand a revolt against the tedium of technocratic society. But the hierarchical anonymity of this society also explains why the rebellion broke out.

When it did, de Gaulle's charisma was almost destroyed. This time he had not only failed to foresee a crisis; he had repeatedly celebrated the stability of his ten-year-old regime. There was a threat of disaster, but it seemed to spring out of the very inadequacies of his own rule. Moreover, what first appeared at stake was not, as in past emergencies, saving France's identity from a threat of dissolution, but appeasing a bewildering variety of grievances, concrete and vague. Indeed, to many Frenchmen, de Gaulle's own theme—"France must be herself"—now meant that the time had come to be without him. Yet he reacted as in earlier crises, some of which included attacks on his leadership (such as the settlers' revolt in Algiers in January 1960). He waited in order to gain perspective, then appealed to the nation for confidence in him, asked to be confirmed once more as the lone savior resolving France's distress. He called for a referendum that would give him a mandate for reform. But now his appeal fell flat. This time it seemed as if a majority of the public wanted to be saved from *him*. They had revolted, precisely because of his earlier failure to reform, in order to be active, not in order once more to leave "public affairs to the sovereign wisdom of the highest authority."[153] Past rebellions against him had been limited; his strength had consisted in his refusal to change his course. This time he offered to change it—a confession of weakness in the present and error in the past. He did thereby appeal to hope, as he had in 1940 and 1958; but in the minds of many, the hope of change was no longer associated with him, or was associated with his fall. He had reenacted his role at a time when the events no longer fit the conditions in which this self-imposed mission could "work." *Les circonstances* being wrong, *le caractère* appeared like "the specter of a ghost, or the ghost of a specter."[154]

This was on May 24. Six days later, charisma was reborn and chaos tamed. The conditions had changed. His government's policy for negotiating an end to the strikes had failed. Anxiety was beginning to replace exaltation and to displace *Schadenfreude*. His antagonists were no longer a huge, anonymous mass of workers and students—that is, "the people"—but a familiar battery of discarded politicians and labor leaders who at first were just as stunned as he had been, but who now incautiously claimed his succession, which his own fiasco of May 24 had appeared to open. The situation was no longer *insaisissable*. De Gaulle could replay, for the third time, his familiar role. He had always warned that if his own regime were challenged, the result would be anarchy followed by totalitarianism. By May 30, that prophecy seemed convincing again. Now there was a threat of national dissolution, and he seemed to provide the only way out: once more, the heroic stance—"me or chaos"—could rally the "silent majority." An appeal for personal trust, irrelevant on the 24th, worked on the 30th—especially as, in the past couple of days, he had somehow been retransformed from the *Président* of a stumbling regime into a *caractère* alone. Pompidou's soft line had failed, the ministers were in spectacular disarray. Thanks to de Gaulle's grand display of stagecraft: his disappearance, his visit to the French army in Germany, his use, once more, of mobility and mystery, and his formidably apt recourse to the skills of the *Mauvaise Rencontre*—cunning and the threat of force—the crisis was turned into a re-creation of the past, of 1940 and 1958. The leader won, because in circumstances made adequate by his very errors, the historical personage now dictated the script: General de Gaulle would once more play his savior role and be the first French statesman whose regime would not be overthrown either by defeat or by a street revolt. Again, he saved so as to unify. His appeals in June were for both order and change. But this last, spectacular re-creation of charisma contained the seeds of his final failure. This time, the "mess" from which he had saved the French was nevertheless one which had been produced by his own regime; moreover, on May 30 (as in the days of the RPF), he had had to appeal primarily to the fears of the people, to the instincts for "law and order." Finally, at the insistence of his Prime Minister, and in order to wage battle on the most promising grounds, he had substituted new legislative elections for the referendum now postponed; and even though he interpreted the Gaullists' victory as a plebiscite,

301

it reinforced a trend he did not like: a reassertion of the public's desire for a less charismatic, more "representative" regime, one that would listen more to the humble needs of the electorate and be less in need of a permanent savior.[155]

Exit

The months that followed witnessed a growing *malentendu* between the General and his people. He was no longer able to maintain his newly restored charisma in the three old ways, examined above. First, the call to greatness on the world stage had been damaged beyond immediate repair by two major blows. The crisis of the franc exposed the Achilles' heel of his leadership: the tremendous shock of May had bared the fragility of French society, inflation returned both as a result and as a remedy, and atavistic reflexes of suspicious prudence and profitable speculation damaged the currency. This time he was not able to transfuse, speedily, his self-confidence into his compatriots. He could, in November, "save" the franc alone, as he had saved France in May, but he had to save it, again, from the French: His feats were becoming defensive —a lonely dam holding back the flood. The means for a "great national ambition" in the world had been shattered by the crisis. The second blow, the Soviet invasion of Czechoslovakia, shattered the design: the grand ideal of Europe's reunification at the expense of the superpowers was temporarily smashed.

His second strength—the appeal to memory—had been damaged by the fact that people tended to be more aggrieved by the troubles of May than by the mess of ten years before, and Pompidou, dismissed in July but not disinherited, emerged as a reassuring alternative both to de Gaulle and to chaos. The General's third asset— being a great actor on the stage—was now a liability. The new stage was drastically smaller and trickier, and he looked incongruous on it. Moreover, a charisma based on drama was precisely what the nation seemed tired of.

He understood that his people were willing to let him save them from themselves, and were also eager to save themselves from what his leadership had been in the past. De Gaulle was faced with a difficult choice. He could change the style of his leadership: re-enter the disenchanted world of normalcy, let charisma wane, stake his political future on institutionalization by de-emphasizing the presidential monarchy, and patiently re-create the psychological and economic conditions for a new forward march later, either on the world stage or on the road to internal reform. But this would have been no more in character than his resigning under fire in May. He had served as a healer before, but always by rallying the French for action. He had often temporized, but only for a momentary lull in a strategy of movement. To slow down at the age of seventy-eight, in the second half of his last mandate, was to risk letting the French settle into mediocrity and losing the opportunity offered by the great *secousse*. The man who had written that only vast undertakings could overcome France's "ferments of dispersion," and knew that this was also true of himself, could not shirk his precept and shrink his personage. To act as any ordinary president —bargaining with his own supporters, balancing pressure groups— was to betray himself.

Concerned with maintaining his work of art, rather than with maximizing his chances for political success, he had to gamble for the highest stakes and propose a new national undertaking. He would not *"voir petit dans cette grande affaire."*[156] He would attach, once more, his leadership to the reforms he deemed essential. He would help the French save themselves from reliance on him alone, but not by dulling his leadership. He would lead them into a new social order, one that would make mechanized civilization bearable, that would be neither communism nor *laissez-faire* capitalism, and that would be based on "participation," in the universities, in new territorial units (the regions), in industry. France would be, so to speak, "de-Napoleonized," but in his way: by him, and by becoming exemplary once more, for the new post-industrial order. This last "national ambition" corresponded both to the needs of France, as he saw them, and to his own need for rekindling charisma. It was not enough for him to propose reform; he had to stake his political future on its adoption, to ask again for a personal vote of confidence.

But his appeal did not work. There was, for the first time, a double contradiction between the essence of his statecraft and the demands of the new mission. There was a problem of substance. Previously, he had paid attention to domestic reform because it appeared essential for France's greatness on the world stage. This was again the case; but his first concern had been the latter; now, it had to be the former. Here he was on unchartered territory. The great reforms of 1944–1945 had resulted from national unanimity; this time he had to reforge unanimity through reform. Then, daring was logical, and timidity would have been divisive; now, grandeur in design was important, so as to take advantage of *la secousse*, but caution in detail was necessary, in order not to wound the body politic further. De Gaulle had to be both leader and manager. He was a great crisis leader, but he had never been a good manager.[157] He always acted as the lone embodiment of France. On the world stage, acting *for* the French, he could be brutal and bold; on the domestic stage, acting *on* the French, not only did he feel that he could not begin to move until there was sufficient consent (created by shock),[158] but he also had to squeeze his huge frame through the narrow openings of entrenched interests and bureaucratic forts. This showed in the drafting of the complicated, cumbersome, and confused bill that he submitted to the people on April 27, 1969. Although he had defined grandeur in terms of domestic reform, his very concern for balance made the measure look anything but grand.

Moreover, there was a problem of style. There was an inherent contradiction between his imperious (or imperial) style, his demand for a personal bond of trust between the leader and the led, and the very notion of participation, which requires the institutionalized and direct involvement of the citizens in the management of their own affairs. His attempt at reconciliation was to offer participation, just as he had granted independence to Algeria: by fiat. But his insistence on keeping the last word and power of execution to *l'État* emptied university and regional autonomy of much of their substance.

There was also a contradiction between "participation" and the habits and desires of the French. A nation caught for centuries in the vice of authority relations that were fundamentally non-participatory, knowing no middle ground between dictates from above and resistance from below, could learn the compromises of face-to-face relations only through patient institution-building and experimentation. After the shock of May, however, "the convulsions of the serpent of messiness"[159] reduced the chances of early success. The rebels of May were not interested in his balanced schemes. They wanted either apocalyptic change or permanent *contestation*. His supporters of June wanted peace and quiet. "*La secousse*" of May had been strong enough to shake his grip on them in the beginning, yet despite his hopes, and thanks in part to his own mastery, it was not strong enough to "open their eyes."

Thus, instead of a new fusion, there was a falling out between de Gaulle and the French. He disappointed both those who wanted tranquility and those who wanted not merely greatness in conception, but also boldness in execution. The doubts the French had about the substance of the bill he submitted to them—a substance which appeared unsettling to some, minuscule to others, irrelevant to many—were compounded by the style in which de Gaulle acted: somehow, the substance was not familiar enough, or not enough in his character; the style was all too familiar, all too much in character. It was not in this way—on this ground and by repeating the homage of their personal loyalty—that they wanted him to teach them to reform. Many who could still conceivably be mobilized by his appeal were reluctant to follow him there; many who were only too eager to participate refused to do it at the General's command.

If de Gaulle's artistry was not at its best in the shaping of the measure on which he staked his leadership, if, in other words, the political leader had chosen to wage his customary battle on dubious ground, he was however, as usual, more concerned with style than with substance, with the long run than with the issue at hand, and above all, with his image in history. The reform itself, for all its mediocrity, bore his mark. He was reviving the past in order to make it serve the future, by restoring France's provinces as the regions for modern economic development. He was both rallying and defying, by inviting interest groups to become participants in decision-making (instead of bringing pressure to bear on it as outsiders), and thus by challenging hosts of local and professional notables. But he had higher goals. If he won, his charisma would be reaffirmed: He could draw on it to overcome obstacles to further reform; he could bring his association with his people to a quiet end, on his own terms, by 1972. If he lost, he would at least save *le caractère* from attrition, as in 1946, and now also from the possible shipwreck of old age—he would, as before, exit on behalf of a grand cause (once more, institutional change). The coldness or detachment which observers noticed in his last appeals must have reflected his discomfort with the battleground imposed by circumstances, his sense that the outside warmth he needed—the support of his people—was waning, and his greater concern with his artist's work than with winning.

Unless there could be dramatic proof to the contrary, the time had come again to "leave things before they leave me" totally. If de Gaulle could not end in the quiet glory of a savior in harmony with his people, or in the tragedy of assassination in the service of his country, if the choice was between a mediocre, endless last act—wasted on managing a damaged *status quo* or on introducing reforms in the way of ordinary politicians—and the "exemplary misfortune" of public repudiation, he would prefer the latter as far better for the historic personage. For it would, as in the 1930's, as in 1966, as in the days of the RPF, read as a failure of the French, not as a failure of de Gaulle. He would stand in history as the man who, for the last time, had "been himself" in trying to get his people *ad augusta* (albeit *per angusta*) at a moment when they wanted to stay put.[160] The end of his political leadership would come at a time chosen by him, and in his style. It was the French who were flunking their test, for the test he lost was—in his terms—that of France's will to greatness. It was symbolic that they refused to follow him on a march "to the heights" of social cooperation, along a *juste milieu* between extreme solutions. It was also symbolic that the specific issue of his fall was an attempt to loosen the hold of centralized, anonymous bureaucracy. As in 1945, he would rather appear as the only true revolutionary than sink into the marsh of immobilism.

There was a risk that he would thus preserve the integrity of the leader only at the cost of a debacle of some of his main achievements. His figure in history would then have been as badly hurt as if the leader had lost his grip not merely on his people but on himself. This has not happened. He made his mark by leaving in time. His last re-enactment of his old threat—"if you desert me, you'll have chaos"—failed to work its magic, precisely because there was a chance for orderly succession. By resigning with immense dignity, he consolidated the achievement dearest to him—the regime. He provided France with her first smooth transition from charisma to normalcy. He got in defeat what he had failed to gain in triumph, and what might have eluded him had he tried to hang on until the end of his term[161]—a consensus around the Constitution of the Fifth Republic. Winning the elections of 1968 had weakened presidential supremacy; losing the referendum of 1969 consolidated it. Having avoided the "routinization of charisma," but also having made his people tired of the recurrence of conditions of distress-and-salvation, he succeeded both in giving his tarnished charisma that sunset glow of final defeat, so much appreciated by the French ever since Vercingétorix, Louis XIV, and Napoleon, and in leaving behind him institutions that the people promptly entrusted to his own disciples.

End?

The political leader is dead. True, the French killed him when *they* judged that his re-enactment of his missionary role had become "incongruous" or "irrelevant." But the artist had not become "the prisoner of the public figure."[162] He submitted the political leader to Russian roulette, not out of mechanical habit but in order to determine whether his people were still willing to accept from him the only kind of leadership that allowed him to "be himself." Playing any other role would have betrayed the work of art. *Le caractère* was badly fitted for the kind of delicate reshaping that an old and battered society needed. He could undertake it only if it were done in his style, as part of a new *grande querelle*; and he was not at all fitted for the kind of undramatic tinkering to which most Frenchmen now aspired. De Gaulle would not let his rule outlive his charisma. Even if the circumstances were no longer so grand, the exit was in style. In his last act as a leader he preserved his self-respect, by committing himself to his cause, and the self-respect of his people, by submitting himself to their will. Therefore, the work of art endures.

The dialogue between the private person and the historical personage persists. Rejected by the French, de Gaulle, once more, "rather than letting his private self take over ... remains his public person"—not this time "in waiting" for new leadership, but in writing, shaping his statue the way he wants it remembered. Whatever regrets he must feel about losing the opportunity to repair the damage suffered by his internal and external policies in 1968, whatever misgivings he may have about the text of the reform rejected in 1969, he will surely transform the story of the political leader in recent years so as to make it exemplary and magnify the impact of General de Gaulle in years to come. Only thereby can the artist reconcile the demands of an undoubtedly bruised ego and the demands of the historical personage. This last act of self-transcendence still requires what has served him so well in his political career: irony, detachment, perspective.

De Gaulle's final place in French history is not yet clear. In the end, his stature will be measured not simply by what he did to improve that of France or by the way in which he came and left, but by his greatest contribution: the creation of General de Gaulle, the embodiment of a great style of French leadership, the figure who mobilized old cultural values, ancient traits of "national character," France's language, literature, and philosophy to protect France's integrity and renew France's grandeur. The artist, in his own quest for grandeur, will now make history by writing it. The ultimate test of de Gaulle as a political artist thus lies where, as a child, his artistry began: in the realm of the imaginative re-creation of the past, aimed at leaving a mark on the future.

REFERENCES

1. His biographers do not give much detail, they do not indicate their sources, they copy one another often without acknowledging it, and sometimes contradict each other. The most interesting indications are in: Georges Cattaui, *Charles de Gaulle: l'homme et le destin.* (Paris, 1960); Jean-Raymond Tournoux, *Pétain et de Gaulle* (Paris, 1964)

2. Cattaui, *Charles de Gaulle,* p. 16.

3. De Gaulle, *Mémoires,* Vol. 1, p. 1. (All references to the Memoirs are to the original French volumes; the translations are ours.)

4. Cattaui, *Charles de Gaulle,* p. 20.

5. Compare, André Malraux, *Antimémoires* (Paris, 1967), p. 157: "I think that, ever since his decision of June 18 [1940] hope had a tragic character for him." We think that this tragic vision developed much earlier.

6. Tournoux, *Pétain et de Gaulle,* pp. 24-25; Philippe Barrès, *Charles de Gaulle* (Montreal, 1941), p. 30.

7. Compare, Roger Wild, "De Vaugirard au Quartier Latin," *Revue des Deux Mondes* (March 15, 1962), pp. 275 ff.

8. *Le fil de l'épée* (Paris, 1962), p. 87.

9. The impact of *Cinna* on de Gaulle deserves a long (if hypothetical) discussion. When, in Act II, Augustus appears, his first statement refers to *"cette grandeur sans borne et cet illustre rang"* that he has acquired. His discourse on the melancholy of domination, the *"destin des grandeurs souveraines"* that deprives them of friends they can trust, his call for lucidity, his final mastery—*"je suis maître de moi comme de l'univers"*—all are reflected in *Le fil de l'épée.*

10. There is an extraordinary passage in *Vers l'armée de métier* ([Paris, 1944 ed.], p. 217), where he explains that whoever possesses the germ of leadership qualities cannot develop them by exerting them only in "military categories." *"La puissance de l'esprit implique une diversité qu'on ne trouve point dans la pratique exclusive du métier, pour la même raison qu'on ne s'amuse guère en famille."*

11. Emmanuel d'Astier de la Vigerie, *Les Grands* (Paris, 1961), p. 90.

12. *Mémoires*, Vol. 1, p. 2.

13. Speech at St. Cyr in 1957; quoted in Tournoux, *La tragédie du Général* (Paris, 1967), p. 227.

14. Tournoux (in *Pétain and de Gaulle*, p. 39) suggests that Charles was far ahead in his studies, which would have accentuated his sense of being different and superior. But we have not been able to find a confirmation.

15. *Mémoires*, Vol. 1, p. 2.

16. The text is in Tournoux, *Pétain et de Gaulle*, pp. 29-36.

17. Gustave Nadaud, *Chansons à dire* (Paris, 1887), pp. 303-6.

18. Compare his press conference of Nov. 27, 1967: *à propos* of "*l'après gaullisme,*" he said: "*tout a toujours une fin. Chacun se termine*" (*Le Monde*, Nov. 29, 1967, p. 4).

19. That feather seems to owe a great deal to Rostand's *Cyrano de Bergerac*.

20. *Le fil de l'épée*, p. 87. In his *Mémoires*, de Gaulle talks of several leaders (Churchill, F.D.R., Hitler) as "seducers."

21. *Ibid.*, pp. 86, 87.

22. Cattaui, *Charles de Gaulle*, p. 23.

23. Jean Lacouture, in his *de Gaulle* ([Paris, 1964], p. 15) notes that de Gaulle in his *Mémoires* (Vol. 1, p. 2) describes his ambition to "*rendre à la France quelque service signalé*" as "l'interêt *de la vie*," not as duty. In 1958, when faced, in Dakar, with picketers asking for independence, he exclaimed that when de Gaulle is there, "*on ne s'ennuie pas.*" (Passeron, *de Gaulle parle 1958-62* [Paris, 1962], p. 462.)

24. *Le fil de l'épée*, p. 78.

25. Cattaui, *Charles de Gaulle*, p. 23. Tournoux, *Pétain et de Gaulle*, p. 25.

26. Compare, *Vers l'armée de métier* (Paris, 1944), p. 197. "*Le rôle du chef est toujours de concevoir d'après les circonstances, de décider et de prescrire en forçant sa nature et celle des autres.*"

27. See Eugen Weber, *The Nationalist Revival in France 1905-1914* (Berkeley, 1959).

28. *La discorde chez l'ennemi* (Paris, 1944; first published in 1924).

29. *Ibid.*, p. viii. On p. x, he celebrates the "*jardin à la française*" with its "magnificent harmony," despite the "noble melancholy" that sometimes pervades it because "each element, by itself, could have shone out more," but only "at the expense of the whole."

30. See, on his experiences at the Ecole de Guerre, in addition to Tournoux

(*Pétain et de Gaulle*, Part 1, Chs. 5-6, and pp. 380 ff), Jacques Minart, *Charles de Gaulle tel que je l'ai connu* (Paris, 1945).

31. Cattaui, *Charles de Gaulle*, p. 29; Gaston Bonheur, *Charles de Gaulle* (Paris, 1958), p. 32.

32. *Discorde chez l'ennemi*, p. ix.

33. On Péguy's influence, see Edmond Michelet, *Le gaullisme passionnante aventure* (Paris, 1962). The prose poem which ends the third volume of the *Mémoires* closes with the image of the Old Man (de G.) who "never tires of watching, in the shade, for the glimmer of Hope."

34. *La France et son armée* (Paris, 1938), p. 228.

35. Alexander Werth, *de Gaulle* (New York, 1965), p. 60.

36. H. Stuart Hughes, *Consciousness and Society* (New York, 1958), pp. 117-18.

37. Quoted by Lucien Nachin in his preface to de Gaulle's *Trois études* (Paris, 1945), p. xlvi.

38. *Mémoires*, Vol. 1, p. 2.

39. *La France et son armée*, p. 274.

40. *Mémoires*, Vol. 3, p. 60.

41. See Tournoux, *Pétain et de Gaulle*, p. 41.

42. Compare, in *La France et son armée*, p. 191: *"grandir sa force à la mesure de ses desseins, ne pas attendre du hasard, ni des formules, ce qu'on néglige de préparer, proportionner l'enjeu et les moyens: l'action des peuples, comme celle des individus, est soumise à ces froides règles."*

43. See S. Hoffmann, "de Gaulle's memoirs: the hero as history," *World Politics* (Oct., 1960).

44. Malraux, *Antimémoires*, p. 152. *Le fil de l'épée*, published in 1932, was based on lectures and articles written since 1927.

45. *Les jeunes gens d'aujourd'hui* (Paris, 1913).

46. Compare, *Vers l'armée de métier*, p. 221: *"les puissants se forment eux-mêmes. Faits pour imprimer leur marque, plutôt que d'en subir une, ils bâtissent dans le secret de leur vie intérieure l'édifice de leurs sentiments, de leurs concepts, de leur volonté."* This is a constant theme in this book and in *Le fil de l'épée*.

47. *Fil*, p. 83.

48. *Vers*, pp. 217-18.

49. *Fil*, p. 96-97; *Vers*, pp. 224 ff; Lucien Nachin, *Ch. de G.* (Paris, 1944), pp. 88-89.

50. François Mauriac, *de Gaulle* (Paris, 1964), p. 24.

51. *Fil*, p. 77 ff.

52. See also *Vers*, p. 154, about the "perpetual return" of human affairs.

53. *Mémoires*, Vol. 2, p. 67.

54. Malraux, *Antimémoires*, p. 155.

55. *Fil*, pp. 87-88.

56. *Mémoires*, Vol. 2, p. 312.

57. *Ibid.*, Vol. 3, p. 287.

58. André Passeron, *de Gaulle parle 1962-6* (Paris, 1966), p. 132. (TV interview, Dec. 13, 1965.)

59. Compare de Gaulle's lectures at St. Cyr in 1921, in Tournoux, *La tragédie du Général*, pp. 513 ff.

60. Compare his balanced judgment on Napoleon in *La France et son armée*, pp. 149-50.

61. Compare D'Astier, *Sept fois, sept jours* (Paris, Coll. 10/18, 1961): "*comme un grand prélat glacé dont la France est le royaume qu'il ne veut pas partager et qui n'est peut-être pas de ce monde*" (p. 102). See also: Malraux, *Antimémoires*, p. 135; Pierre Bourdan, *Carnets des jours d'attente* (Paris, 1945).

62. *Mémoires*, Vol. 1, Ch. 2.

63. Compare "*le caractère esthétique des choses militaires,*" in *Vers*, p. 142.

64. ". . . *César, qui ne procède que des exigences profondes de son temps, est un homme* sur la scène, c'est à dire forcément un artiste" (emphasis added). Letter to M. de Bourbon-Busset, quoted by Tournoux, *La tragédie*, p. 486. In the *Mémoires*, Vol. 1, p. 47, he called Churchill "*le grand artiste d'une grande Histoire.*"

65. "*De même* que le talent marque l'oeuvre d'art *d'un cachet particulier de compréhension et d'expression, ainsi le* Caractère imprime son dynamisme propre aux éléments de l'action. . . . *Moralement, il l'anime, il lui donne la vie, comme le talent fait de la matière dans le domaine de l'art.*" *Fil*, pp. 54-5.

66. Compare the quotation in fn 9. The final call for a master, in the same book, is a call for a "*ministre, soldat ou politique.*"

67. When General Catroux, a much higher-ranking general, joined de Gaulle in October 1940, there was no doubt any more about de Gaulle's leadership.

68. "*Il faut qu'un maître apparaisse, indépendant en ses jugements, irrécusable dans ses ordres, crédité par l'opinion. Serviteur du seul Etat, dépouillé de préjugés, dédaigneux de clientèles; commis enfermé dans sa tâche, pé-*

nétré de longs desseins, au fait des gens et des choses du ressort . . . assez fort pour s'imposer, assez habile pour séduire, assez grand pour une grande oeuvre . . ." (p. 227); Robert Aron, in *An explanation of de Gaulle* ([New York, 1966], p. 70), quotes this revealing sentence from de Gaulle's *Mémoires*: "In human endeavors, due to a long and slow effort, a sudden, unique spurt may be achieved in different and disparate spheres:" a good account of de Gaulle's own course.

69. *Fil,* p. 15.

70. See, for instance, Col. Passy, *Souvenirs,* Vol. 1. (Monte-Carlo, 1947), p. 122; André Gide, *Journal 1942-45,* (Paris, 1950), p. 185.

71. D'Astier, *Les Grands,* p. 124.

72. Malraux, *Antimémoires,* p. 150.

73. Compare Henri Amouroux, *Pétain avant Vichy* (Paris, 1967).

74. Malraux, *Antimémoires,* p. 151.

75. Passy, *Souvenirs,* p. 123.

76. D'Astier, *Les Grands,* p. 137.

77. Compare, *Mémoires,* Vol. 3, pp. 288-89. He spent very little time as a "private" person after his resignation in January 1946. He made his first public statement in June, and after the fiasco of the R.P.F., he wrote his *Mémoires,* still unfinished when the Fourth Republic collapsed.

78. In his *Mémoires,* Vol. 3, p. 287, he says that he decided, after his resignation to stay in metropolitan France so as to show that the flood of insults *"contre moi"* could not touch him. A few lines further, he speaks of "de Gaulle."

79. Malraux, *Antimémoires,* p. 134. Gide, *Journal 1942-49* (Paris, 1950), p. 185.

80. Bourdan, *Carnets des jours d'atteute,* p. 35.

81. Passy, *Souvenirs, passim;* compare also Major-General Edward Spears, *Two Men Who Saved France* (London, 1966), pp. 148 ff.

82. D'Astier, *Sept fois sept jours,* pp. 60-61, writes: *"Il n'aime pas les hommes. Il aime leur histoire, surtout celle de la France, dont il agit un chapitre qu'il semble écrire au fur et à mesure dans sa tête."*

83. *"C'est pourquoi, dans les heures tragiques où la rafale balaie conventions et habitudes, ils (les chefs) se trouvent seuls debout et, par là, nécessaires."* (*Vers,* p. 221.)

84. Pierre Viansson-Ponté, *Les gaullistes* (Paris, 1963), p. 49: insults leave him cold, but he is concerned about how the press treats "his historical figure."

85. *Fil,* p. 89; *Mémoires,* Vol. 2, p. 322.

86. *Fil,* p. 70; *Mémoires,* Vol. 3, p. 243.

87. *Mémoires,* Vol. 3, p. 175.

88. Malraux, *Antimémoires,* p. 135.

89. Jerome Bruner, *On Knowing* (Cambridge, 1962), p. 29; the characteristics listed in the previous paragraph are borrowed from his stimulating essay.

90. Tournoux, *Pétain et de Gaulle,* p. 389 (evaluation by one of de Gaulle's superiors in 1924).

91. *"Le dialogue traditionnel, dans les affaires de l'Etat, lui était étranger."* Malraux, *Antimémoires,* p. 156.

92. D'Astier, *Les Grands,* p. 108.

93. Compare Mauriac, *de Gaulle,* pp. 22-23.

94. Albert Hall Speech, June 18, 1942, in *Mémoires,* Vol. 1, pp. 672 ff; also, *Mémoires,* Vol. 1, p. 1.

95. Compare Jean Lacouture, *de Gaulle.*

96. *Antimémoires,* p. 135.

97. Tournoux, *Secrets d'Etat* (Paris, 1960), p. 351.

98. Portrait of Mussolini, *Mémoires,* Vol. 3, p. 172.

99. Malraux, *Antimémoires,* p. 156: "nous et le destin du monde."

100. *Vers,* p. 197.

101. *Mémoires,* Vol. 3, p. 232.

102. See Tournoux, *Pétain et de Gaulle,* pp. 383 ff, and d'Astier, *Les Grands,* pp. 119 ff.

103. Compare the portrait of Stalin, *Mémoires,* Vol. 3: He quotes Stalin as saying "after all, only death wins." p. 78.

104. *Mémoires,* Vol. 1, p. 111.

105. Compare *Mémoires,* Vol. 2, p. 294.

106. Compare d'Astier, *Les Grands,* p. 137.

107. Compare his refusal to participate in any public ceremony or go to any public edifice of the Fourth Republic. On his failures, see his press conference of Nov. 1953, in Alexander Werth, *De Gaulle,* pp. 227-28.

108. *Mémoires,* Vol. 2, pp. 240-41.

109. Compare Erik Erikson's concept of *virtue,* in "Human Strength and the Cycle of Generations," *Insight and Responsibility* (New York, 1964).

110. *Mémoires,* Vol. 1, p. 1; see also Vol. 3, p. 21, and Passeron, *De Gaulle parle 1962-66,* pp. 134-37.

111. The epigraph to *Le Fil* is a quote from Hamlet, *"être grand, c'est soutenir une grande querelle"*; see also *Mémoires*, Vol. 1, p. 1.

112. *Mémoires,* Vol. 3, p. 290.

113. *La France et son armée,* p. 277.

114. *Mémoires,* Vol. 1, p. 1.

115. Oxford speech, Nov. 25, 1941: *Mémoires,* Vol. 1, pp. 565 ff.

116. Compare his remarks on Syria and Lebanon, while serving there in 1930: "People here are as foreign to us (and vice versa) as ever." Only two possibilities existed, according to him: coercion or departure (Nachin, *Trois études,* 56-57). He has, later, applied both. At least one possibility was thus ruled out—that which had served as the myth of the French Empire under the name of assimilation and was going to serve as the myth of French Algeria under the name of integration.

117. See the comparison of the French and the Germans in *Vers,* pp. 22-23.

118. See the press conference of May 19, 1958, in Passeron, *de Gaulle parle 1958-62,* p. 5.

119. *Mémoires,* Vol. 2, p. 321.

120. Malraux, *Antimémoires,* p. 130.

121. See the portraits of Hitler and of Laval in *Mem.,* Vol. 3, pp. 173-5.

122. Compare Tournoux, *La tragédie,* p. 278.

123. In *La France et son armée,* writing about the 1890's—the years of his childhood—he said: France "cultivates melancholy while enjoying her wealth." His task today seems to be to make her increase her wealth without melancholy, thanks to an active foreign policy.

124. See Lloyd and Suzanne Rudolph, *The Modernity of Tradition* (Chicago, 1968), pp. 199-200.

125. Compare Louis Terrenoire, *de Gaulle et l'Algérie* (Paris, 1964), p. 58, reporting that de Gaulle in March 1958 told him: "People are worried about France, but this feeling of national concern has not yet become a personal anxiety."

126. Passeron, *de Gaulle parle 1958-62,* p. 7.

127. *Mémoires,* Vol. 3, pp. 238, 650 (Bayeux speech of June 16, 1946).

128. Compare Eugene Mannoni, *Moi Général de Gaulle* (Paris, 1964), p. 106: "The R.P.F. merely taught de Gaulle what he had already known: in History's absence, solitude is preferable to promiscuity."

129. S. Hoffmann, "Heroic Leadership in Modern France," in Lewis Edinger

(ed.), *Political Leadership in Industrialized Societies* (New York, 1967), pp. 108-54.

130. Michel Crozier's expression, in *The Bureaucratic Phenomenon* (Chicago, 1964).

131. *Mémoires*, Vol. 2, p. 311.

132. Malraux, *Antimémoires*, p. 156.

133. Emmanuel d'Astier de la Vigerie is the best example.

134. Soustelle is the best example.

135. *Mémoires*, Vol. 3, p. 271.

136. The photos of his return from Montreal to Orly Airport, in the middle of the night, showed an elated and combative de Gaulle surrounded by sleepy and sullen cabinet ministers.

137. Malraux, *Antimémoires*, p. 140.

138. *Fil*, p. 79.

139. See S. Hoffmann, "Paradoxes of the French Political Community," *In Search of France* (Cambridge, 1963).

140. Compare D'Astier, *Les Grands*, p. 99; Tournoux, *La tragédie*, p. 194.

141. Compare D'Astier: "I am a French ant, that brings . . . a bit of material for his history. . . . I have been in a theater of history, I want to go back to life, to my life." *Sept fois, sept jours*, pp. 60-61. See also Malraux, *Antimémoires*, p. 131.

142. Compare Paul de la Gorce, *de Gaulle entre deux mondes* (Paris, 1964), Ch. 10, on de Gaulle's hesitations over economy and financial policy in 1944-45.

143. For further details on his European policy, which tries to reconcile a desire for a "European Europe" capable of supplementing France's limited power and voice, with a determination to avoid supranational federalism, see S. Hoffmann, "de Gaulle, Europe and the Atlantic Alliance," *International Organization*, Vol. 18, No. 1 (Winter, 1964), pp. 1-28; "Europe's Identity Crisis," *Dædalus* (Fall, 1964), pp. 1244-97; "Obstinate or Obsolete? The Fate of the Nation-State and the Case of Western Europe," *Dædalus* (Summer, 1968), pp. 862-915; *Gulliver's Troubles, or the Setting of American Foreign Policy* (New York, 1968), Ch. 11.

144. This is the main criticism of his Middle East policy of 1967, which condemned Israel's resort to force from a long-term perspective on war that completely neglected the short-term plight of Israel in the tense circumstances of May 1967.

145. *Mémoires*, Vol. 3, p. 289.

146. *Vers,* p. 154.

147. The authors of this paper express their gratitude to him, from whom they have learned so much.

148. Compare Tournoux, *La tragédie,* pp. 502-3.

149. *Cinna,* Act IV, Scene II.

150. Tournoux, *La tragédie,* p. 514.

151. See Reymond Aron, "La Revolution Introuvable" (Fayard: Paris, 1968), pp. 38 ff., 95 ff. See also François Bourricaud, "Une Difficile Reprise en Mains," *Preuves,* No. 218 (May–June, 1969), pp. 38–48.

152. Cf. de Gaulle's television interview, June 7, 1968: "Until now, our structures and our groups . . . have resisted this kind of change."

153. Stanley Hoffmann, "French Psychodrama," *The New Republic* (August 31, 1968), p. 19.

154. Aron, *op. cit.,* p. 43.

155. See Stanley Hoffmann, "De Gaulle's Legacy to Pompidou," *The New Republic* (July 12, 1969), pp. 19–21.

156. Television interview, April 10, 1969.

157. His timidity as a domestic reformer had already shown, in very comparable circumstances, when he refused to follow Pierre Mendès–France's austerity plan in 1945.

158. Television interview, June 7, 1968: "Such a reform, nobody, including me, can undertake it alone. It has to be sufficiently accepted and the circumstances must be right. . . . Now, there has been a shock, a terrible shock, which must have opened the eyes of many."

159. De Gaulle, speech of March 11, 1969.

160. In the television interview of June 7, 1968, he compared himself to the angel in a "primitive painting," who tried to keep a crowd from letting itself be driven to hell by devils, and pointed in the opposite direction— only to become the target of the crowd's anger.

161. It is not at all clear that, had de Gaulle remained in power until 1972, his successor (after fourteen years of Gaullist rule) would have been a Gaullist.

162. These quotes are from our earlier conclusion. For another assessment, see Emmanuel Berl, "Le crépuscule du magicien," *Preuves,* Nos. 219–220 (July–September, 1969), pp. 82–5.

HENRY A. KISSINGER

The White Revolutionary: Reflections on Bismarck

FEW STATESMEN have altered the history of their society so profoundly as Otto von Bismarck. Before he came to power, Prussia—and the rest of Germany—seemed to be undergoing the "normal" evolution toward parliamentary, constitutional rule. Indeed, the crisis that brought him to office in 1862 was the familiar issue of parliamentary control over the budget, which in every other West European country had been resolved in favor of parliament. Five years afterwards, Bismarck had changed the domestic orientation of Germany and the pattern of international relations by solving the issue of German unification which had baffled two generations. His solution had not occurred previously to any significant group or to any major political leader. Too democratic for conservatives, too authoritarian for liberals, too power-oriented for legitimists, the new order was tailored to a genius who proposed to restrain the contending forces, both domestic and foreign, by manipulating their antagonisms.

"People are born as revolutionaries," the German liberal Bamberger wrote during his Parisian exile in 1862, as he attempted to explain the enigma of Bismarck's personality. "The accident of life decides whether one becomes a Red or a White revolutionary."[1] Many years later Bismarck said that Bamberger was one of the few authors who had understood him.

What is a revolutionary? If the answer to this question were not ambiguous, few revolutionaries could succeed; the aims of revolutionaries seem self-evident only to posterity. This is sometimes due to deliberate deception. More frequently, it reflects a psychological failure: the inability of the "establishment" to come to grips with a fundamental challenge. The refusal to believe in irreconcilable antagonism is the reverse side of a state of mind to which basic

317

transformations have become inconceivable. Hence, revolutionaries are often given the benefit of every doubt. Even when they lay down a fundamental theoretical challenge, they are thought to be overstating their case for bargaining purposes; they are believed to remain subject to the "normal" preferences for compromise. A long period of stability creates the illusion that change must necessarily take the form of a modification of the existing framework and cannot involve its overthrow. Revolutionaries always start from a position of inferior physical strength; their victories are primarily triumphs of conception or of will.

This is especially true when the challenge occurs not in the name of change, but by exposing institutions to strains for which they were not designed. Even the most avowedly conservative position can erode the political or social framework if it smashes its restraints; for institutions are designed for an average standard of performance—a high average in fortunate societies, but still a standard reducible to approximate norms. They are rarely able to accommodate genius or demoniac power. A society that must produce a great man in each generation to maintain its domestic or international position will doom itself; for the appearance and, even more, the recognition of a great man are to a large extent fortuitous.

The impact of genius on institutions is bound to be unsettling, of course. The bureaucrat will consider originality as unsafe, and genius will resent the constrictions of routine. In fortunate societies, a compromise occurs. Extraordinary performance may not be understood, but it is at least believed in (consider, for example, the British respect for eccentricity). Genius in turn will not seek fulfillment in rebellion. Stable societies have, therefore, managed to clothe greatness in the forms of mediocrity; revolutionary structures have attempted to institutionalize an attitude of exaltation. To force genius to respect norms may be chafing, but to encourage mediocrity to imitate greatness may produce institutionalized hysteria or complete irresponsibility.

This was the legacy of Bismarck. His was a strange revolution. It appeared in the guise of conservatism, yet the scale of its conception proved incompatible with the prevailing international order. It triumphed domestically through the vastness of its successes abroad. With a few brusque strokes Bismarck swept away the dilemmas that had baffled the German quest for unity. In the process, he recast the map of Europe and the pattern of international relations. Like the mythological figures Solon or Lycurgus, he created a society in his image and a community of nations animated by his maxims in their dealings with one another.

Everything about Bismarck was out of scale: his bulk and his appetite; his loves and even more his hatreds. The paradox of his accomplishments seemed embodied in his personality. The man of "blood and iron" wrote prose of extraordinary simplicity, plasticity, and power. The apostle of the claims of power was subject to fits of weeping in a crisis. The "Iron Chancellor" loved Shakespeare and copied pages of Byron in his notebook. The statesman who never ceased extolling reason of state possessed an agility of conception and a sense of proportion which, while he lived, turned power into an instrument of self-restraint.

But the gods sometimes punish pride by fulfilling man's wishes too completely. Statesmen who build lastingly transform the personal act of creation into institutions that can be maintained by an average standard of performance. This Bismarck proved incapable of doing. His very success committed Germany to a permanent tour de force. It created conditions that could be dealt with only by extraordinary leaders. Their emergence in turn was thwarted by the colossus who dominated his country for nearly a generation. Bismarck's tragedy was that he left a heritage of unassimilated greatness.

The Making of a Revolutionary

On May 17, 1847 a tall, powerfully built man mounted the speakers' rostrum of the Prussian Parliament, which had been assembled in fulfillment of a promise made by the Prussian king during the Napoleonic Wars a generation before. A reddish-blond beard lined a face marked by many duels of student days. Proud in bearing, self-confident in expression, the speaker represented the *beau-ideal* of the Junkers, the large landholders who had built up Prussia.

The occasion was trivial. In the course of a debate about agricultural relief, one of the speakers had pointed out that the national enthusiasm of what in Prussia was called the War of Liberation had been due to the bonds forged in 1807 between the Prussian people and its government by a series of reforms. As soon as Bismarck began his maiden speech, an incongruity became apparent. Despite his size, Bismarck's voice was weak and somewhat high-pitched. His

319

sentences emerged hesitantly as if each phrase had to tear itself loose from his large hulk. The prosaic words therefore conveyed an impression of immense, barely controlled passion:

I must contradict the proposition that the uprising of the people in 1813 required other motives than the shame of having outsiders command in our country. Our national honor is ill-served by the implication that the degradation suffered at the hands of a foreign autocrat was not enough to subsume all other sentiments in the common hatred of the foreigner.[2]

Faced with a wave of liberal indignation, Bismarck had great difficulty finishing this passage. (The stenographic report lists loud murmurs after almost every sentence.) One of the most moderate rejoinders denied Bismarck the right to judge a period which he had not experienced. Quickly Bismarck returned to the rostrum. While the enraged liberals hooted and the president vainly called for order, Bismarck turned his back on his colleagues and began to read a newspaper. When order had been somewhat restored, he began again in his irritating, rasping, and yet compelling voice:

I cannot deny of course that I did not live then, and I have always deeply regretted that it was not given to me to participate in this movement. That sentiment is ameliorated, however, by the information which I have just received. I had always assumed that the slavery against which we fought came from abroad. I have just learned that it was domestic and I am not very obliged for being enlightened.

Nobody then in the room in Berlin would have believed it possible that this man, standing so nearly alone, would solve the problem of German unity which had eluded the efforts of two generations. Nor could any have imagined that his ideas—seemingly so incongruous in a century of liberalism and nationalism—would eventually shape the destiny of their country. But not every revolution begins with a march on the Bastille.

A revolutionary must possess at least two qualities: a conception incompatible with the existing order and a will to impose his vision. Bismarck's colleagues in the Parliament could not have been aware of his ideas. Had they understood the road which he had traversed, however, they would have known that they were dealing with an elemental, perhaps even a demoniac, personality.

Otto von Bismarck was born on April 2, 1815, the year of Napoleon's banishment to St. Helena. His parents represented the two pillars of the Prussian state: the aristocracy and the bureaucracy. His family, Bismarck remarked once, were already Junkers when the Hohenzollerns (Prussia's kings) were still an insignificant

South German dynasty. Bismarck's father had served briefly in the army, but neither the disaster of Jena nor the War of Liberation could induce him to leave his ancestral estate again. He had preferred independence to service even when the king took away his commission and he lost favor at the court.

Independence had not proved sufficient for his bride. The daughter of a Privy Councillor, risen from the bourgeoisie, she insisted that her sons live according to the maxims of the Enlightenment and justify themselves by intellectual attainment. "I had always thought," she wrote, "that my greatest happiness would be to have a grown-up son . . . whose calling would permit him to penetrate much deeper into the realm of the spirit than was possible for a woman."[3]

To penetrate the realm of the spirit meant leaving the ancestral estate in Pomerania and the discipline of the Max Plaman Institute in Berlin. Bismarck never lost his nostalgia for nature or the illusion that his real happiness lay in a bucolic existence. He always spoke of his stay at the Gymnasium with distaste and of the relations with his mother with bitterness.

"I left the Gymnasium," wrote Bismarck sarcastically in his memoirs, "the normal product of our educational system, as a Pantheist and if not a Republican at least with the conviction that a republic was the most reasonable form of government."[4] Republican or not, all roads were open to the aristocrat. Bismarck planned to enter the bureaucracy because he thought that it would demand a less stringent discipline than the army. Thus the first Bismarck who proposed to serve his king with the pen enrolled at the University of Goettingen. But formal study proved unbearably confining. In rebellion, Bismarck turned himself into the "mad Junker," extravagantly dressed, proud of the ability to drink anyone under the table, always ready to duel, distinguished by linguistic ability and sarcastic wit. Heavily in debt, physically run down, Bismarck left Goettingen after one year, at the insistence of his parents, for the University of Berlin.

Berlin wrought no fundamental change, however: "I live here like a gentleman," he wrote to a friend in Goettingen, "and gradually adopt an affected behavior. I speak a good deal of French, spend much time getting dressed, the remainder making visits and with my old friend the bottle. In the evening I sit in the first tier of the opera and behave as rowdily as possible."[5]

Only once was his nihilism interrupted by three aphorisms tracing Bismarck's future: "Constitution inevitable; in this manner to outward glory; but is it necessary to be inwardly pious besides?"[6] The first two thoughts were reasonable predictions. The third outlines a dilemma that Bismarck never solved. He always understood the requirements of success, but was less clear about whether to approach his task with a certain sense of reverence for the finiteness of the human scale. A statesman who leaves no room for the unforeseeable in history may, however, mortgage the future of his country.

Advised to leave the University of Berlin, Bismarck prepared for the state examinations with the aid of a private tutor. At last he was ready for his first governmental post with the President of the Province of Aachen (Aix-la-Chapelle). Appropriately enough, this official was a friend of Bismarck's mother.

But the routine of a civil servant proved intolerable. So Aachen grew to know the "mad Junker" who preferred foreigners to his stodgy compatriots, a splendid conversationalist whose love affairs and gambling debts soon became notorious. One year later he left Aachen without leave. Nothing is known of the sudden decision except Bismarck's cryptic account:

I had every prospect for what is called a brilliant career . . . had not an extraordinarily beautiful Briton induced me to change course and sail in her wake for six months without the slightest leave. I forced her to come aside; she lowered the flag, but after possession of two months I lost the booty to a one-armed colonel fifty years of age with four horses and 15000 dollar revenue.[7]

The deeper reason for giving up his governmental career was not to be found in Bismarck's love affair, however. Bismarck gave the best explanation in a letter to a friend who had questioned his decision by appealing to his patriotism:

That my ambition is directed more towards not having to obey than towards giving orders is a fact for which I can give no reason save my taste. . . . The Prussian official is like an individual in an orchestra. Whether he plays the first violin or the triangle he must play his part as it is set down whether he thinks well of it or ill. *I however want to make music as I consider proper or none at all* [emphasis added].

Besides patriotism was probably the motive force of but a few of the famous statesmen particularly in absolutist states; much more frequently [it was] ambition, the desire to command, to be admired and to become famous. I must confess that I am not free of this passion and many distinctions . . . of statesmen with free constitutions, such as Peel, O'Connell, Mirabeau (etc.), won as a participant in energetic political

movements, would exert on me an attraction beyond any abstract consideration. . . . I am less allured however by the successes to be attained
on the well-worn path through examinations, connections, or seniority
and the good will of my superiors.[8]

This self-portrait was only deepened by a lifetime of public
service. It was extraordinary for a member of the aristocracy of a
state built on the notion of duty and service to assert that the
chance to command was a more compelling motive than patriotism.
The insistence on identifying his will with the meaning of events
would forever mark Bismarck's revolutionary quality. Neither the
sense of reverence for traditional forms of the conservative nor the
respect for intellectual doctrines of the liberals was part of Bismarck's nature. He could appeal to either if necessary, but aloofly,
appraisingly, and with a cool eye for their limits. It was no accident
that the three statesmen whom the letter described as worthy of
emulation represented either rebellion or a break with the past:
O'Connell, the Irish revolutionary using the rules of the House of
Commons to paralyze it; Peel pushing through the Corn Law
against his own party and splitting it in the process; Mirabeau
presiding over an attempt at legal revolution.

Bismarck was back on the ancestral estate now. Restless, he
read voraciously: Shakespeare and Byron, Louis Blanc and Voltaire, and always Spinoza. His escapades multiplied. After another
broken engagement, Bismarck left on a journey through England,
France, and Switzerland. He even made tentative plans to serve
with the British army in India. But "my father wrote me a letter
moist with tears which spoke of lonely old age (seventy-three years,
widower, deaf), of death and meeting again. He ordered me to
return. I obeyed. He did not die."[9]

At this point in his life, Bismarck received a provisional answer
to the question about the need for piety. Though the solution was
more in the nature of a diplomatic pact with God than the mastering of a spiritual dilemma, it sufficed to bring about the measure of
balance that enabled Bismarck to give direction to his elemental
energies.

In a personality that reduces everything to a manifestation of
the will, the spiritual and the sensual are never far apart. Thus
Bismarck came to a degree of belief through two women.

Marie von Thadden came from a family of "Pietists," a fundamentalist sect believing in the most literal interpretation of the
Bible. This group was significant because it contained many of the

most influential members of the aristocracy, including Leopold von Gerlach, later the adjutant of the king and Bismarck's principal sponsor at court. They combined rigid orthodoxy in religion with inflexible conservatism in politics. No group less likely to appeal to Bismarck could be imagined. "Of Cromwell's famous phrase 'Pray and keep your powder dry,'" he mocked, "they forget the second and most important half."[10]

Marie von Thadden was beautiful and passionate. When in 1843 she became engaged to his friend Moritz von Blankenburg, Bismarck stopped at her estate to make her acquaintance. Marie von Thadden was attracted to Bismarck who seemed to her "a great and interesting man of the world with a brilliant appearance." She decided to save the soul of this "Pommeranian Phoenix known as the epitome of wildness and arrogance."[11]

Two days later Bismarck returned to Marie von Thadden's estate. Once more they discussed religion. After he left, Marie von Thadden invoked her fiancé's assistance. But three letters from Moritz von Blankenburg full of maudlin exhortation remained unanswered. A direct confrontation proved equally unsuccessful.

Married now, Marie von Thadden continued her efforts. She introduced Bismarck to her closest friend and fellow Pietist Johanna von Puttkammer, who also attempted to convert him. But pressure was not the way to reconcile Bismarck with his Maker. It took an event of elemental power to teach Bismarck the meaning of finality, if not a sense of limits. For on November 10, 1846, Marie von Thadden died.

Marie von Thadden was the victim of an influenza epidemic that had already claimed her younger brother and her mother. From the deathbed of her mother, Marie had written to Bismarck asking him to come to see her as quickly as possible. When he arrived, she had fallen ill herself. Even now she was still concerned with the salvation of his soul and sent him a message pleading "with the utmost earnestness" that now was the moment for conversion. This caused Bismarck to pray for the first time since his sixteenth year not *to* a God, much less to a theology, but *for* a person. For once he confronted a situation, however, which was beyond his power: "This is the first time," he wrote to his sister, "that I have lost someone . . . close to me and whose parting created a profound and unexpected void." To his widowed friend, he said: "This is the first heart that I lose of which I truly knew that it beat for me. . . . Now I believe in eternity—or God has not created the world." Otto von Bismarck came to God on the basis of strict diplomatic reciprocity whereby God in return for faith guaranteed the permanence of a profound passion.

Marie von Thadden's death had another and more immediate consequence: Bismarck's engagement with Johanna von Puttkammer. Two months before he had written to Moritz von Blankenburg that he did not yet trust his feelings. But four weeks after Marie's death, Bismarck spoke to Johanna von Puttkammer about marriage. She encouraged him to ask her father's permission. To convince the forbidding, dour, intensely religious, old Heinrich von Puttkammer that the "mad Junker" was a fit husband for his daughter would have discouraged a man less bold.

The result was Bismarck's first major diplomatic document, a letter asking for permission to visit the Puttkammer estate to put his case in person. As he was to do so often, Bismarck confounded his opposite number by complete frankness and with a sweep unknown in the unimaginative circle of Bible Readers. Bismarck's letter began:

It may appear presumptuous that I whom you have met but recently . . . ask of you the strongest proof of confidence which it is in your power to grant. I also know that I . . . will never be able to give you in my own person those guarantees for the future which would justify the pledge of so dear a collateral on your part, unless you make up through confidence in God what cannot be supplied by confidence in man.

Here was the case against Bismarck stated more powerfully than Heinrich von Puttkammer would ever have been able to, only to be transformed into an appeal to the Pietist's deepest conviction. Bismarck did not ask for Johanna's hand because he was worthy of God—this would have seemed presumptuous to a Pietist in someone far more religious—but because only God could make him worthy. To reject him would have indicated not lack of faith in the suitor, but an absence of trust in God. On this plane, the subsequent account of Bismarck's fall from grace accentuated the merit of his redemption:

At the time of my sixteenth birthday I had no other faith than a naked deism which did not remain long without Pantheist overtones. About this time, I stopped praying, not out of indifference but as the consequence of ripe reflection. . . . I told myself that either God produced everything, including my own thoughts—in which case He was praying to Himself; or that my will was independent of God's—in which case it would be presumptuous and indicate a doubt . . . in the perfection of the

HENRY A. KISSINGER

Divine decrees, to believe that one could influence Him by human entreaties.

To the pious von Puttkammer, this could have seemed as nothing short of the voice of the devil, but it only served to heighten the power of the moment of conversion:

About four years ago . . . I came into closer contact with Moritz von Blankenburg and I found in him what I had never had in life: a friend. . . . Through Moritz I also became acquainted with the [Thaddens] and their circle. . . . That hope and peace were with them did not surprise me, for I had never doubted that they accompanied faith. But faith cannot be given nor taken away and I was of the opinion that I would have to wait resignedly until it was vouchsafed to me. . . . What had stirred within me became real when at the news of the fatal illness of our deceased friend . . . the first fervent prayer tore itself from my heart, without any concern about its reasonableness, together with a stinging sense of my unworthiness to pray and with tears as had been unknown to me since childhood. God did not grant my prayer then, but he also did not reject it, for I did not lose again the capacity to appeal to Him and I feel if not peace, at least a confidence I never knew before. . . . Daily I entreat God to be merciful to me . . . and to awaken and to strengthen my faith.[12]

What could a pious man reply? Bismarck was demanding of Heinrich von Puttkammer no more than what by his own description he was daily asking from God. And because this was the letter of a man who had made his peace with his Maker, there was in it nothing of an apology to mortals, so that even Bismarck's catalogue of sin became a manifestation of his defiant pride.

Having won the moral terrain, Bismarck followed the letter with one of the lightning moves which were always to accompany his careful preparation. He reported to his brother:

Around Christmas I wrote to the father who was extraordinarily horrified because the idea that his daughter might marry frightened him in any case, but in particular in connection with a man of whom he had heard a great deal of ill and little good. Upon my return home I received a letter from him which contained in essence nothing but a few quotations from the Bible with which he had consoled himself in his sorrow and a dubiously phrased invitation to Rheinfeld [the Puttkammer estate]. There I found . . . a disposition for prolonged negotiations, of doubtful issue, had I not moved the whole affair to a different plane by a decisive embrace of my bride, immediately upon first seeing her, to the greatest astonishment of the parents.[13]

To the moral conquest was thus added a *fait accompli;* many a later opponent of Bismarck might have been less astonished by his tactics had he known of his courtship.

The episode achieves an additional dimension through the conclusion of Bismarck's letter to his brother:

I have had a great and no longer expected stroke of fortune because I am marrying, speaking quite cold-bloodedly, a woman of rare spirit and nobility. . . . In matters of faith we differ, somewhat more to her sorrow than to mine, if not as much as you may think . . . for events . . . have produced certain transformations in me. . . . Moreover I love Pietism in women.

Ever since these letters became public, German historians have debated the degree of Bismarck's sincerity. But if Bismarck was insincere, it did not necessarily have to be in the letter to his future father-in-law. In any event, sincerity has meaning only in reference to a standard of truth of conduct. The root fact of Bismarck's personality, however, was his incapacity to comprehend any such standard outside his will. For this reason, he could never accept the good faith of any opponent; it accounts, too, for his mastery in adapting to the requirements of the moment. It was not that Bismarck lied—this is much too self-conscious an act—but that he was finely attuned to the subtlest currents of any environment and produced measures precisely adjusted to the need to prevail. The key to Bismarck's success was that he was always sincere.

Bismarck's new-found relationship to God played the crucial role in the formation of his public personality. Until his introduction into the Thadden circle, Bismarck's naturalism had led to virulent skepticism. In a world characterized by struggle, death was the most recurrent phenomenon and nihilism the most adequate reaction. This had produced the restless wandering of Bismarck's early years, the seeming indolence, and caustic sarcasm.

God provided the mechanism to transcend the transitoriness of the human scale: "I am a soldier of God," he wrote now, "and I must go where He sends me. I believe He will mould my life as He needs it."[14] "God has put me at the place where I must be serious and pay my debt to the country," he wrote to his wife upon receiving his first diplomatic appointment in 1852. "I am firmly decided to do His will and if I lack wisdom I shall ask it of Him; He gives plentifully and never presents accounts."[15]

Bismarck's faith thus represented a means to achieve a theological justification of the struggle for power; its distinguishing characteristic was not acceptance, but activity—Darwinism sanctified

327

by God. God became an ally by being subjected to Bismarck's dialectic; for would He permit what had not found favor in His eyes? Bismarck's fatalism, erstwhile so hopeless, now found a sense of direction. "With confidence in God," he wrote to his bride, "put on the spurs and let the wild horse of life fly with you over stones and hedges, prepared to break your neck but above all without fear because one day you will in any case have to part from everything dear to you on earth, though not for eternity."[16]

After his introduction to the Thadden circle, there was about Bismarck a new sense of purpose and a calculation of the main chance. Following his father's death in 1845, he even left the Kniephof and moved to the other ancestral estate, Schoenhausen on the Lower Elbe. The reason was eminently practical: There existed a good prospect of a vacancy in the position of Deichhauptmann, the officer in charge of building and repairing the dikes. When the incumbent failed to resign as expected, Bismarck saw to it that he was relieved by bringing charges of unauthorized absences. Deichhauptmann was a position of great prestige since the welfare of the predominantly agricultural region depended on it. It was not surprising, therefore, that the Estates nominated Bismarck as an alternate to the Parliament in Berlin. It only increased his sense of mission that the regular deputy fell ill and he was elected as his replacement.

This, then, was the man who stepped to the rostrum on May 17, 1847. He had sown his wild oats. He had spent nine years in the solitude of his ancestral estates and had emerged hardened, extremely well read, and infinitely more imaginative than his fellow Junkers. Once embarked on a public career, he lived for little else. Though he appeared as the defender of traditional Prussia, he needed only the opportunity to demonstrate that he gave this conviction an application which would revolutionize the map and politics of Europe.

The Nature of the Challenged International Order

The stability of any international system depends on at least two factors: the degree to which its components feel secure and the extent to which they agree on the "justice" or "fairness" of existing arrangements. Security presupposes a balance of power that makes it difficult for any state or group of states to impose its will on the remainder. Too great a disproportion of strength undermines self-restraint in the powerful and induces irresponsibility in the weak. Considerations of power are not enough, however, since they turn every disagreement into a test of strength. Equilibrium is needed for stability; moral consensus is essential for spontaneity. In the absence of agreement as to what constitutes a "just" or "reasonable" claim, no basis for negotiation exists. Emphasis will be on the subversion of loyalties rather than on the settlement of disputes. Peaceful change is possible only if the members of the international order value it beyond any dispute that may arise.

The statesmen who met at Vienna in 1815 to end the Napoleonic Wars had been taught this lesson through twenty-five years of nearly uninterrupted struggle. They had learned that the peace of Europe depended on a balance of power that removed the temptation of easy conquest, especially by France. They tried to create "great masses," to use Pitt's phrase, in Central Europe to remedy a state of affairs which had enabled four generations of French rulers to exploit Germany's dissensions for purposes of conquest. Russia, in turn, had used each conflict to advance farther into Europe.

Conditions in Germany, therefore, were the key to European equilibrium. If Germany was too centralized or too powerful, it would bring about a combination of expansionist France and Russia to counterbalance it. If Germany was too divided, it would tempt constant pressure. The peace of Europe depended on three factors: (a) an over-all balance of power in which the states of Central Europe—primarily in Germany—would be sufficiently strong to resist pressures from East and West; (b) a special equilibrium *within* Germany that would create among the German states a structure strong enough to resist attacks from both East and West, but not so powerful as to disquiet Germany's neighbors, sufficiently unified to be able to mobilize for defense, but not so centralized as to become an offensive threat; (c) a moral consensus which caused most disputes to be settled by recourse to a superior principle rather than to force. The balance of power was to be a last recourse, not the sole arbiter. This is what came to be known as the "Metternich system" after the Austrian Foreign Minister who was instrumental in devising it and who was its principal manipulator until he was overthrown in 1848.

No element of the Metternich system was more intricate than the arrangements for Germany. The constitution of the German Confederation was as subtle as the membership was complex: Austria belonged to the Confederation only with its German third, and the Confederation did not include the Polish provinces of Prussia. On the other hand, the Netherlands was represented because of its possession of Luxembourg, and Denmark was included because its king was also ruler of Schleswig-Holstein. Prussia, the largest purely German state, had only one vote out of seventeen. It was theoretically possible that a grouping of states comprising less than a quarter of the population or resources of Germany could outvote the major powers, Austria and Prussia.

Usually, however, the interests of Austria ran parallel with those of the minor states. Austria and the minor states were interested in maintaining the *status quo*: They were concerned with preventing Prussian hegemony, but wanted to achieve this goal without open conflict. The Assembly of the Confederation meeting in Frankfurt was therefore designed to inhibit decisive action except in case of overwhelming foreign danger. The very complexity of its procedures was well suited to delay, to ameliorate, to evade. Moreover, Austria controlled its proceedings to a considerable extent. The Austrian representative was *ex officio* president of the Assembly of the Confederation. The Assembly met in the Austrian Legation at Frankfurt; its secretariat was under Austrian control; and until 1848, the seal of the Confederation was the Austrian seal. In these circumstances, it was not too difficult to transform the Assembly of the Confederation into a diplomatic congress bound by the instructions of its member governments.

Nevertheless, the Confederation was not simply a diplomatic congress. To begin with, it owned directly five fortresses facing France. It could receive as well as accredit ambassadors. It had the power to declare war. It was possible, therefore, for a German state to pursue two contradictory policies at the same time: one as an independent power, the other in its capacity as a member of the Confederation. As happened during the Crimean War and again during the Schleswig-Holstein crisis, it was even possible for three different foreign policies to be pursued concurrently in Germany: that of Austria, that of Prussia, and that of the minor states. Such a structure could act in union only when confronted by an overwhelming common danger—a threat sufficient to menace the European equilibrium. It was not likely to be able to generate consensus on positive aims; it would not itself be able to threaten the European balance.

Had the Metternich system been maintained only by considerations of power, it would not have lasted fifty years. Prussia accepted a subordinate role—far smaller than its power would have justified—because its rulers became convinced that they had more to fear from liberalism domestically than they could gain by relying on Prussia's strength abroad. They therefore placed an alliance with Austria above their political and strategic opportunities within Germany. Similarly, Russia was restrained from expanding into the Balkans at least in part by the doctrine of the unity of conservative interests. For a generation, the Holy Alliance of Russia, Austria, and Prussia acted as a brake on domestic upheaval. It also restrained two expansionist powers—Prussia and Russia—by appealing to their moral inhibitions.

The unity of conservative monarchs survived even the Revolution of 1848. The Prussian king refused the crown of a united Germany when it was offered by the National Assembly in Frankfurt, because he believed that only Austria had a historical claim to it. Russian troops assisted Austria in suppressing a rebellion in Hungary, and Russian threats helped Austria to re-establish her dominance in Germany. When another Napoleon came to power in France, the revolutionary threat of the previous generation seemed to reappear, and the three Eastern courts drew closer still. In the early 1850's, the Metternich system appeared destined to dominate European politics for the indefinite future.

The Challenge: The Postulate of Prussian Uniqueness and Invulnerability

At this precise moment, a theoretical challenge developed that unexpectedly came not from the liberals, but from a man who owed his public career to the Prussian conservatives' conviction that he epitomized their values. Appointed Prussian Ambassador to the German Confederation in 1852, Otto von Bismarck almost immediately attacked the Metternich system. Bismarck did not accept the fundamental axiom that Prussia's domestic structure was so vulnerable that it could be protected only by rigid adherence to the unity of conservative monarchs. On the contrary, Bismarck insisted intransigently on the postulate of Prussia's uniqueness and invulnerability.

This conviction was not without foundation, for Prussia was not simply another German state. Its rigid domestic policy could not eradicate the consciousness of nationalism brought to Germany by the French occupation nor eliminate the prestige acquired by Prussia through its tremendous efforts during the Napoleonic Wars. To be sure, for a generation after the Vienna settlement, Prussia's policy of repression was even more effective than that of Austria because it was not leavened by Austrian inefficiency. The very shape of Prussia—athwart Germany from the partly Polish East to the Catholic and somewhat Latinized Rhineland—made it the symbol of the quest for German unity. Even liberals looked to it for the attainment of their objectives. Prussia, which in the seventeenth century was an idea before it became a reality, accomplished the even more extraordinary tour de force in the nineteenth century of becoming an idea *contrary* to its reality.

For over a generation after the Congress of Vienna, however, Prussia seemed paralyzed by the vastness of its challenge. As long as nationalism was identified with liberalism, Prussia was able to realize its German mission only by giving up its historic essence. It remained for Bismarck to challenge this identification. He insisted that nationalism and liberalism need not be parallel phenomena. They could be separated, and traditional Prussia could play a national role:

> If someone, in the name of German unity, presses for a parliamentary union I should like to warn him not to confuse two concepts: German unity and the right to deliver parliamentary speeches from a German rostrum. For me the two concepts are far apart.[17] . . . There exists nothing more German than the development of rightly conceived Prussian interests.[18]

If this was true, Prussia could perform its German mission only if it preserved its historic essence. Far from adapting to the liberal trend, Prussia had to overcome it—all the more so as parliamentary institutions were not required to guarantee Prussian liberties:

> Prussia has become great not through liberalism and free-thinking but through a succession of powerful, decisive and wise regents who carefully husbanded the military and financial resources of the state and kept them together in their own hands in order to throw them with ruthless courage into the scale of European politics as soon as a favorable opportunity presented itself. . . . It is undoubtedly just that every Prussian should enjoy that degree of liberty which is consistent with the public welfare and with Prussia's career in European politics but no more. This degree of liberty is possible even without parliaments and at the present stage of Prussia's intellectual development, the abuse of royal power belongs to the most improbable contingencies.[19]

Bismarck saw no point in political constructions that destroyed Prussia's identity. In 1848, he resisted the attempt of the liberals to achieve German unity through a democratic constitution. "[Our] people has no desire to see its kingship dissolved in a ferment of South German indiscipline. Its loyalty is not to the paper head of an Empire . . . but to a living and free king of Prussia. . . . I hope to God that we shall long remain Prussians when this piece of paper [the German constitution] will be forgotten like a dried-up autumn leaf."[20] Bismarck wanted to preserve the existing order in Prussia so that Prussia could overthrow the Metternich system within Germany. Thus, he opposed even the liberals' offer of the Imperial Crown to the king of Prussia:

I would prefer that Prussia remain Prussia. As such it will always be in a position to prescribe its laws to Germany and not to receive them from others. I therefore feel duty-bound to oppose a motion designed to undermine the edifice cemented by the blood of our fathers. The crown of Frankfort may seem very brilliant but its luster is to be obtained by smelting it with that of Prussia and I do not think that this will succeed.[21]

Theories of popular sovereignty could only weaken Prussia's international role: "The Prussian army will always be the army of the king and seek its honor in obedience. . . . Prussia's honor does not consist of playing the Don Quixote for vexed parliamentary celebrities all over Germany. I seek Prussia's honor in that Prussia never admit that anything occur in Germany without its permission."[22]

German unity, in short, was to be justified by the facts of Prussian power. It was made necessary not by doctrines of liberalism, but by the security requirements of a state whose very shape inhibited equilibrium. Prussia, spread across the North German plain in a series of enclaves with frontiers following no natural boundaries, needed the resources of Germany for its own defense. Prussia should absorb Germany, rather than the opposite. This conception seemed so incredible to both liberals and nationalists that the stenographic report notes "hilarity" at the end of this passage. It was not the first time that revolutionaries succeeded because their opponents could not believe in the reality of their objectives.

Had the Prussian conservatives who admired Bismarck listened closely, they would have realized that he was separated from them by a gulf scarcely less wide. Bismarck's aphoristic phrases, like the statements of French President Charles de Gaulle—the leader who most resembles him in our century—had meanings not understood by his supporters. Bismarck was defending not a principle, but a fact; not a doctrine, but a reality. "I do not consider the Prussian constitution the best of which history informs us," he said on one occasion; "its chief advantage is that it exists."[23] Bismarck attacked liberalism not because it violated *universal* history, but because it ran counter to *Prussian* traditions. He sought to rescue Prussia's uniqueness from dissolution; the conservatives were interested in defending general principles. Bismarck fought domestic upheaval because he wanted Prussia to focus on foreign policy; his allies wanted to defend legitimate rule as such.

As a result, the postulate of Prussia's domestic invulnerability proved the prelude to a proposition unimaginable to the conservatives: that Prussia could afford to adapt its domestic institutions to the requirements of foreign policy. Once the royal authority had survived the Revolution of 1848, Prussia not only had nothing to fear from liberalism, but could even use it as an instrument of foreign policy. Bismarck reported during the Crimean War:

Towards my colleagues I use privately the following language: Prussia has adopted a policy of peace on behalf of Germany in the process risking the enmity of half of Europe. . . . Should the other German states desert Prussia, however, it must think of its own security. . . . No choice will be left to us but to join the enemies of Russia. But such a shift toward the West can win the confidence of Britain and France only if implemented by a more liberal government which, carried by the Westwind of public opinion, would soon outdistance Austria.[24]

Once in office, Bismarck carried out these prescriptions. During the Austro-Prussian War of 1866, he attempted to foment a revolution in Hungary; only the rapid victory kept his plans from being carried out. Under his stewardship, Germany was the first continental country with universal suffrage, albeit with a constitution that sharply limited the powers of Parliament.

For four decades Prussian policy had been stymied by the paradox that it could achieve hegemony in Germany only by allying itself with forces believed to be contrary to its domestic structure. Bismarck showed that the paradox was only apparent. Prussia's sense of cohesion was sufficiently strong for it to combine a repressive policy at home with revolutionary activity abroad. Even liberal institutions could be used to strengthen the king's authority:

The sense of security that the King remains master in his country even if the whole army is abroad is not shared with Prussia by any other continental state and above all by no other German power. It provides the opportunity to accept a development of public affairs much more in conformity with present requirements. . . . The royal authority in Prussia is so firmly based that the government can without risk encourage a much more lively parliamentary activity and thereby exert pressure on conditions in Germany.[25]

Just as de Gaulle's brutal cynicism has depended on an almost lyrical conception of France's historic mission, so Bismarck's matter-of-fact Machiavellianism assumed that Prussia's unique sense of cohesion enabled it to impose its dominance on Germany. Like de Gaulle, Bismarck believed that the road to political integration was not through concentrating on legal formulae, but emphasizing the pride and integrity of the historic states.

There is one important difference, however. In the contemporary world, France is only one of several medium-sized states of roughly equal strength. Within nineteenth-century Germany, Prussia was by far the strongest purely German state. Bismarck did not, therefore, depend entirely on the persuasiveness of his arguments and would have been doomed to failure had he done so. Unlike de Gaulle, he could impose his convictions on the other contenders by force—provided international conditions were favorable. Thus, a great deal depended on Bismarck's conception of international affairs.

The Art of the Possible

It is fortunate for posterity that Bismarck was in the relatively subordinate position of ambassador for ten years. Appointed Ambassador to the Assembly of the Confederation in 1852 and to St. Petersburg in 1858, Bismarck's principal means of influencing public policy was through reports to his superiors. The result was a flood of memoranda passionate, brilliantly written, remarkably consistent—the outline of Bismarck's later policy. Increasingly Bismarck urged that foreign policy had to be based not on sentiment but on an assessment of strength. Prussia had to abandon the self-restraint that had characterized its policy since 1815:

We live in a wondrous time in which the strong is weak because of his moral scruples and the weak grows strong because of his audacity.[26] . . . A sentimental policy knows no reciprocity. It is an exclusively Prussian peculiarity. Every other government seeks the criteria for its actions solely in its interests, however it may cloak them with legal deductions.[27] . . . For heaven's sake no sentimental alliances in which the consciousness of having performed a good deed furnishes the sole reward

335

for our sacrifice.[28] . . . The only healthy basis of policy for a great power . . . is egotism and not romanticism.[29] . . . Gratitude and confidence will not bring a single man into the field on our side; only fear will do that, if we use it cautiously and skillfully.[30] . . . Policy is the art of the possible, the science of the relative.[31]

Policy depended on calculation, not emotion. The interests of states provided objective imperatives transcending individual preferences. "Not even the King has the right to subordinate the interests of the state to his personal sympathies or antipathies."[32] When, early in Bismarck's career, his Austrian colleague in Frankfurt made a personal appeal to stop his harassing tactics in the Assembly of the Confederation, he replied:

It is my task to conduct Prussian policy just as it is yours to vindicate that of Austria. That these do not aim for the same results is a necessity produced by history and it cannot be eliminated either by ourselves or our Cabinets. If you constantly keep this in mind I am inclined to believe that our relationship can be freed of the painful impressions you describe even in the face of more substantial divergencies.[33]

The Metternich system had insisted on the closest ties between Prussia and Austria in order to defeat the revolution in Germany and, if necessary, in the rest of Europe. Bismarck, however, not only argued that Austria was not needed to control the domestic situation within Prussia, but contended that it was an obstacle to Prussia's real vocation. It was not a fraternal but a foreign country: "Our policy has no other parade ground than Germany and this is precisely the one which Austria believes it badly requires for itself. . . . We deprive each other of the air we need to breathe. . . . This is a fact which cannot be ignored however unwelcome it may be."[34]

The idea that Prussia should separate itself from Austria gave way in short order to the proposition that a wise Prussian policy would seek to evict Austria from Germany—a proposition which would have been inconceivable even five years previously when the Prussian king believed that only the Austrian emperor was "entitled" to the crown of a united Germany. Moreover, the German Confederation, far from being a natural forum for Prussian policy, was an obstacle to it:

The secondary states . . . find in the Assembly of the Confederation a pedestal from which they can discourse about the affairs of Germany and Prussia, indeed even about European policy, more loudly than would be permissible were they in immediate contact with world affairs. . . . It is not surprising that they are interested in developing an institution in which with a minimum of effort they obtain not only security but an accretion of influence. Thus in case of war, Hesse-Darmstadt has the right to claim the assistance of the Prussian army and in return assists Prussia with 6,200 men.[35]

If Prussia wished to remain a great power, it could not submit to an illusory consensus of the German states. It should seek instead to utilize the resources of the secondary German states for its own ends. The justification for German unity was not nationalism, but Prussia's requirements as a great power: "A great power desirous of conducting its own foreign policy based on its intrinsic strength can agree to a greater centralization of the Confederation only if it assumes its leadership and insists on the adoption of its own program."[36]

Since Austria would never accept Prussian hegemony in Germany, Bismarck argued, Prussia had to seize every opportunity to weaken her. Within three years of being sent to Frankfurt as the best guardian of the unity of conservative interests, Bismarck counseled that Prussia use Austria's embarrassments during the Crimean War to attack her: "Could we succeed in getting Vienna to the point where it does not consider an attack by Prussia on Austria as something outside of all possibility we would soon hear more sensible things from there. . . . We should march into Austria, quickly and unexpectedly, while Bohemia is still without troops."[37] During Austria's war with France and Sardinia, Bismarck wrote: "The present situation once more presents us with the great prize if we let the war between Austria and France become well established and then move south with our army taking the border posts in our field packs not to impale them again until we reach Lake Constance or at least the limits where the Protestant confession ceases to predominate."[38]

Nothing illustrates Bismarck's revolutionary quality more dramatically than his advocacy of a Prussian attack on Austria for no other reason than the auspicious moment. Even in the heyday of the Metternich system, it was not unusual for a state to seek to improve its position; but every effort was made to endow change with the legitimacy of a European consensus. Pressures for change without even lip service to existing treaty relationships or to the Concert of Europe involved a revolution in prevailing diplomatic method. Heretofore the major outlines of the Vienna settlement had been treated as inviolate; its legitimacy was a key aspect of its stability.

Bismarck proposed to base the Concert of Europe on precise calculations of power; when they conflicted with the existing order, the latter had to give way or be forcibly overthrown.

To be sure, the difference was one of degree. The Metternich system did not ignore considerations of power even while seeking adjustments through European congresses. Bismarck, in turn, would have been the last person to reject the efficacy of moral consensus: He would have treated it as an important attribute of power, as one factor among the many to be considered. But the stability of the international order depended on this precise nuance.

The Metternich system had been inspired by the eighteenth-century notion of the universe as a great clockwork: Its parts were intricately intermeshed, and a disturbance of one upset the equilibrium of the others. Bismarck represented a new age. Equilibrium was seen not as harmony and mechanical balance, but as a statistical balance of forces in flux. Its appropriate philosophy was Darwin's concept of the survival of the fittest. Bismarck marked the change from the rationalist to the empiricist conception of politics.

The Empiricist Assessment of the International Order

In 1854, during the Crimean War, Bismarck wrote:

We have three threats available: (1) An alliance with Russia; and it is nonsense always to swear at once that we will never go with Russia. Even if it were true we should retain the option to use it as a threat. (2) A policy in which we throw ourselves into Austria's arms and compensate ourselves at the expense of perfidious confederates. (3) A change of cabinets to the left whereby we would soon become so "Western" as to outmaneuver Austria completely.[39]

Here was the distillation of the new diplomacy. The same report listed as equally possible an alliance with Russia against France, an arrangement with Austria directed against the secondary German states and presumably against Russia, and an understanding with France (the purpose of the "Western" course domestically) directed against Austria and Russia. The ultimate choice depended strictly on considerations of utility. Hence the apparent Russophile was discussing an arrangement with France, then at war with Russia. The seeming reactionary found it possible to envisage a shift to the left. Domestic policy was manipulated for the purposes of foreign policy.

This cynicism as to method has given rise to the argument that

Bismarck was above all an opportunist. The charge of opportunism, however, begs the key issue of statesmanship. Anyone wishing to affect events must be opportunist to some extent. The real distinction is between those who adapt their purposes to reality and those who seek to mold reality in the light of their purposes.

Bismarck—as all revolutionaries—belonged to the latter group. To be sure, his policy had a streak of opportunism. Yet pure opportunism tends to be sterile; it absorbs more energy in an analysis of where one is than of where one is going. A policy that awaits events is likely to become their prisoner. The flexibility of Bismarck's tactics was the result of a well-developed conceptual framework. It grew out of the conviction that the "Metternich system" stifled Prussia's natural role; it was animated by a clear picture of the new international order that Bismarck wanted to bring about. Bismarck sought his opportunities in the present; he drew his inspiration from a vision of the future.

Obviously, Bismarck's conception could not be put to the test so long as the key pillar of the Metternich system—the unity of the conservative courts of Prussia, Austria, and Russia—remained unshaken. Unexpectedly, the Holy Alliance disintegrated, because Austria, unable to comprehend its peril, lost the masterly touch with which Metternich had conducted its affairs until 1848. Except for Schwarzenberg, who died prematurely in 1852, Austrian policy was in the hands of mediocrities. Like many men of limited vision, Metternich's successors confused maneuver with conception and sought to hide their timidity by restless activity. As a result, Austria abandoned the anonymity that was one of the tactics which enabled Metternich to deflect major crises from his rickety state. Henceforth, Austria found itself increasingly at the center of European disputes. Its vacillations made the Crimean War inevitable. Its confusion caused Russia to see it as a principal obstacle to St. Petersburg's designs in the Balkans. During the Crimean War and after, Austrian policy suffered from the inability to define priorities. Its measures took so long to conceive that they were irrelevant by the time they were executed; the Imperial Cabinet was so afraid of recklessness that it left itself no room for maneuver, save in sudden fits of panic which had the same effect as recklessness. As its position grew more desperate, its measures became more fitful. The Austrian government sought to compensate for each lost opportunity by redoubling its energies when it finally brought itself to act— which was usually at the wrong moment. "Austria wants to garner all the fruits across which it stumbles on the road which fear forces it to take," Bismarck wrote sarcastically. "I doubt that Buol [Austrian Foreign Minister] has a clear goal unless it is that Austria pocket everything it can obtain by sleight of hand."[40]

The Prussian calculator in Frankfurt understood that the significance of the Crimean War resided not in the terms by which it was settled, but in the diplomatic revolution it brought about: "The day of reckoning is sure to come even if a few years pass. . . . Austria has put itself as a barrier in Russia's way. The latter's policy will henceforth be directed against this barrier. . . . Through this transformation of the constellation of the powers we can only gain in freedom of action."[41]

Thus the most important document of the Crimean War was a report that found its way into the file of the Foreign Ministry of Berlin with marginalia indicating that its author had not succeeded in convincing his superior. Shortly after the conclusion of the Crimean War, Bismarck set down his analysis of the new situation in a memorandum that assumed the perfect flexibility of international relationships limited only by the requirements of national interest. German historiography has justly called it the "Prachtbericht"—the master report—for here in one memorandum was assembled the essence of the new diplomacy, although its novelty robbed it of immediate impact.

The report began with an exposition of the brilliant position of France upon the conclusion of the Crimean War. All the states of Europe were seeking Napoleon's friendship, but none with greater prospect of success than Russia. "An alliance between France and Russia is too natural that it should not come to pass. . . . Up to now the firmness of the Holy Alliance . . . has kept the two states apart; but with Tsar Nicholas dead and the Holy Alliance dissolved by Austria, nothing remains to arrest the natural reapproachment of two states with nary a conflicting interest."[42] Nor could Austria escape its dilemma by anticipating Russia in establishing closer relations with France. In order to maintain the support of his army, Napoleon required an issue capable of supplying at any time "a not too arbitrary and unjust pretext for intervention. Italy is ideally suited for this role. The ambitions of Sardinia, the memories of Bonaparte and Murat, furnish sufficient excuses and the hatred of Austria will smooth its way."

This acute prognosis of the immediate future was preliminary to a discussion of Prussia's position. If a Franco-Russian alliance was inevitable and a Franco-Austria conflict probable, where lay Prussia's safety? According to the Metternich system, Prussia should have tightened its alliance with Austria, relied on the German Confederation, and established the closest relationships with Great Britain.

Bismarck demolished each of these elements in turn. Britain would have difficulty maintaining control of the seas against a resurgent French navy aided, perhaps, by the United States. In any event, Britain's land forces were so negligible that the central powers would have to bear the brunt of the conflict. The German Confederation would add no real strength:

Aided by Russia, Prussia, and Austria, the German Confederation would probably hold together, because it would believe in victory even without its support; but in the case of a two-front war toward East and West, those princes who are not under the control of our bayonets would attempt to save themselves through declarations of neutrality, if they did not appear in the field against us. . . . With a million troops of the Holy Alliance behind it, the German Confederation may seem durable; in the present situation it is unable to resist a foreign danger.

What about the alliance with Austria, for over a generation the cardinal postulate of Prussian policy? Not only was Austria a weak ally, Bismarck replied, but an incongruous one. "If we remained victorious against a Franco-Russian alliance for what would we have fought? For the continuation of Austria's predominance in Germany and the miserable constitution of the Confederation . . . for that we cannot possibly risk our existence or bleed to death victoriously." On the contrary, Austria was the chief obstacle to Prussia's growth:

Germany is too small for the two of us . . . , as long as we plough the same furrow, Austria is the only state against which we can make a permanent gain and to which we can suffer a permanent loss. . . . For the past thousand years the German dualism has regulated its internal relationships through a war every 100 years and in this century too, no other means will be able to make the clock of history tell the proper time.

Thus Bismarck resolved whatever contingency he considered into an argument that Prussia break its confederate bond to Austria.

How then could a power survive in the center of the Continent? After 1815, Prussia's answer had been adherence to the Holy Alliance almost at any price. Bismarck's solution was aloofness. He proposed to manipulate the commitments of the other powers so that Prussia would always be closer to any of the contending parties than they were to each other. If Prussia managed to create a maximum of options for itself, it would be able to utilize its artificial isolation to sell its cooperation to the highest bidder:

> The present situation forces us not to commit ourselves in advance of the other powers. We are not able to shape the relations of the great powers to each other as we wish, but we can maintain the freedom to utilize to our advantage those relationships which do come about. . . . Our relations to Austria, Britain and Russia do not furnish an obstacle to a rapprochement with any of these powers. Only our relations with France require careful attention so that we keep open the option of going with France as easily as with the other powers. . . . I believe that our position loses weight to the degree that the chance of an alliance with France is eliminated from the range of possible options for Prussia. . . . This may be regrettable, but facts cannot be changed, they can only be used.

Facts can only be used—this was the motto of the new diplomacy which sought to keep the situation fluid through the dexterity of its manipulations until a constellation emerged reflecting the realities of power rather than the canons of legitimacy. Such a policy required cool nerves because it sought its objectives by the calm acceptance of great risks, of isolation, or of a sudden settlement at Prussia's expense. Its rewards were equally great—the emergence of a united Germany led by Prussia.

A call to greatness, however, is often not understood by contemporaries. Prussian hegemony in Germany meant little to the Prussian legitimists if it was obtained through an alliance with Napoleon. A unified Germany was unacceptable to the liberals if it occurred in the name of Prussia's greatness. It was inevitable, therefore, that Bismarck should stand alone and that his most bitter battle should be fought against his former allies, the conservatives, who reacted with incredulous horror at the policy he unfolded. They may have had a premonition that Prussia would lose its essence even while it increased its power. Whether their motive was a limited horizon or instinctive wisdom, the conservatives were met with ever-increasing sharpness by Bismarck's eloquent denial that any state had the right to sacrifice its opportunities to its principles.

The Relativity of Legitimacy

Nobody in the states which had experienced French occupation could see in the emergence of a new Napoleon anything but a threat. The nationalists feared foreign bondage, and the conservatives, as always, dreaded domestic upheaval.

Yet the basic postulate of Bismarck's policy was that the fear of a possible Franco-Prussian alliance would be a far better tool for increasing Prussia's influence than reliance on Austrian good will. It took considerable daring to suggest that the state which in 1860 had nearly shared the fate of Poland should use its erstwhile conqueror to bring pressure on its closest allies. Thus the conflict between Bismarck and the conservatives turned on ultimate principles. Bismarck asserted that power supplied its own legitimacy; the conservatives argued that legitimacy represented a value transcending the claims of power. Bismarck believed that a correct evaluation of power would yield a doctrine of self-limitation; the conservatives insisted that force could be restrained only by superior principle.

This conflict found expression in a poignant exchange of letters between Bismarck and his old mentor, Leopold von Gerlach, the military adjutant of the Prussian king. Leopold von Gerlach had grown up during the wars of the French Revolution and had experienced Napoleon's occupation of Prussia. Bismarck was born in the year of Napoleon's banishment to St. Helena; to him Napoleon and the French Revolution were personally distasteful, but not beyond sober calculation. Throughout their exchange, Gerlach appears stodgy and at a distinct disadvantage intellectually. Yet his very unimaginativeness lends pathos to their correspondence, for Bismarck owed everything to Gerlach: his first appointment and his access to the court. The extent of Gerlach's misunderstanding is also the measure of Bismarck's revolutionary quality.

It was only natural that the exchange between Gerlach and Bismarck should have its origin in the "master report" with its recommendation that Prussia develop an option toward France. Bismarck sent this report to Gerlach with a covering letter which placed the principle of utility above that of legitimacy: "I cannot escape the mathematical logic of the fact that present-day Austria cannot be our friend. As long as Austria does not agree to a delimitation of spheres of influence in Germany, we must anticipate a contest with it, by means of diplomacy and lies in peace time, with the utilization of every opportunity to give a coup de grace."[43] Gerlach, however, would not accept the proposition that Prussia's future justified its seeking support across the Rhine. On the contrary, he argued that Prussia should bring Austria and Russia closer together and restore the Holy Alliance which had enforced France's isolation.[44]

343

The spring of 1855 found Bismarck in Paris. He had gone there to divine the character of the statesman who most fascinated him among his contemporaries, Napoleon III. The French Emperor was a symbol of the revolt against the treaties of 1815, the cardinal principle of Bismarck's policy. Since Bismarck wanted to use Napoleon to demonstrate Prussia's superior maneuverability, he proposed to Gerlach that Napoleon be invited to attend the maneuvers of a Prussian army corps: "This proof of good relations with France . . . would increase our influence in all diplomatic relations."[45]

The suggestion that a Napoleon participate in Prussian maneuvers produced an outburst by Gerlach: "How can a man of your intelligence sacrifice his principles to such an individual as Napoleon—Napoleon is our natural enemy."[46] Had Gerlach seen Bismarck's cynical marginalia—"What of it?"—he might have saved himself another letter in which he repeated the principles that had animated the Holy Alliance for over a generation:

My political principle is and remains the war against revolution. Bonaparte is a revolutionary because his absolutism, just as that of the first Napoleon, is based on popular sovereignty and he understands this as well as his predecessor. Prussia's policy must be anti-revolutionary not only in principle but in practice so that at the proper time the vacillating powers such as perhaps Austria and Britain will know what to expect of it. For only he is reliable who acts according to principle and not according to changing concepts of national interest.[47]

It is difficult to escape the pathos of Gerlach, being forced, at the end of his life, into a theoretical defense of his values by the protégé whom he sponsored as the best defender of the very principles now at issue. Gerlach's frustration was compounded because Bismarck, with his marvelous diplomatic skill, immediately transferred the dispute to a plane on which Gerlach was at a distinct disadvantage both intellectually and morally.

Bismarck began by denying that his proposal was motivated by a personal weakness for Napoleon: "The man does not impress me at all. The ability to admire men is in any case only moderately developed in me and it is a fault of my eye that it is more receptive to the weakness of others than to their strengths." On the other hand, Gerlach's insistence on the unity of conservative interests was incompatible with Prussian patriotism. The interests of states transcended abstract principles of legitimacy:

As for the principle I am alleged to have sacrificed, if you mean a principle applicable to France and *its* legitimacy, I admit that I subordinate this completely to Prussian patriotism. France interests me only insofar as it affects the situation of my country and we can make policy only with the France which exists. . . . As a romantic I can shed a tear for the fate of Henry V (the Bourbon pretender); as a diplomat I would be his servant if I were French, but as things stand, France, irrespective of the accident who leads it, is for me an unavoidable pawn on the chess-board of diplomacy, where I have no other duty than to serve *my* king and *my* country [Bismarck's emphasis]. I cannot reconcile personal sympathies and antipathies toward foreign powers with my sense of duty in foreign affairs; indeed I see in them the embryo of disloyalty toward the Sovereign and the country I serve.[48]

What could a traditional Prussian reply to the charge that the principle of legitimacy was inconsistent with Prussian patriotism, that upholding traditional rule involved the possibility of disloyalty toward the legitimate king of Prussia? Lest Gerlach should seek refuge in asserting the identity of the claims of legitimacy and of national interest, Bismarck anticipated his argument:

Or perhaps you find the principle I violated in the fact that Prussia must always be an enemy of France. . . . I could deny this—but even if you were right I would not consider it politically wise to let other states know of our fears in peace time. Until the break you predict occurs I would think it useful to encourage the belief that a war between us and France is *not* imminent . . . that the tension with France is not an organic fault of our nature on which everyone can count with certainty. . . . Alliances are the expression of common interests and goals. . . . But we have indicated our willingness for an alliance precisely to those whose interests are most contrary to ours: Austria and the other German states. . . . If we consider this the last word of our foreign policy . . . we must get used to the idea that in case of war we shall stand alone in the palace of the Assembly of the Confederation holding in one hand the German Constitution. . . . I want nothing else than to take away the belief of others that *they* can ally themselves with whomever they please while *we* would rather lose our skin piecemeal than to defend it with the aid of France. When I advocate this . . . I expect that I am shown that these advantages are illusory or else that I am given a better plan into the combinations of which the semblance of good relations with France does not fit.

Gerlach had no better plan. What was at issue between him and Bismarck was not a policy, but a philosophy. To Gerlach an alliance with Napoleon was contrary to the maxims of morality and the lessons of Prussian history; to Bismarck it depended entirely on political utility unencumbered by moral scruples. Gerlach tested policy by an absolute moral standard; Bismarck considered success the only acceptable criterion. Gerlach sought fulfillment in

345

commitment; Bismarck sought it in dexterity. Because he was of a generation which had known disaster, Gerlach was obsessed by the risks of a power in the center of a continent. Because disaster indicated to Bismarck only a false assessment of forces, he saw primarily the opportunities of the central position.

Thus the exchange between Bismarck and Gerlach had reached an impasse, even though Gerlach was reluctant to admit it. Gerlach invoked Bismarck's great days as the spokesman of the conservatives and repeated his maxim that Prussia would be the weaker partner in a Franco-Prussian alliance. Prussia would lose the confidence of the other German states and therefore Bismarck's policy lacked principle and objective.[49]

Bismarck understood that their disagreement reflected not "misunderstanding," but incompatible values. He therefore proceeded to demonstrate that the maxims of legitimacy, so self-evident to Gerlach, were themselves only relative.

How many governments exist in the contemporary world which do not grow on revolutionary soil? Take Spain, Portugal, Brazil . . . Sweden or England which still prides itself on the Glorious Revolution of 1688. . . . Before the French Revolution not even the most Christian and conscientious statesman ever conceived the idea to subordinate all his political efforts . . . to the fight against the Revolution . . . and this despite the fact that the American as well as the British Revolution represented the same principles which brought about an interruption of legal continuity in France. I cannot believe that there should not have existed before 1789 a few statesmen equally Christian and similarly conservative as we and just as capable of recognizing evil.[50]

This cynical paragraph demonstrates both Bismarck's strengths and weaknesses. To be sure, foreign policy in the eighteenth century had been cold-blooded and seemingly indifferent to domestic upheaval. But neither the British nor the American Revolution had claimed universal applicability. As long as European governments felt secure at home, they were able to ignore internal upheavals abroad. When these conditions no longer existed, Europe learned the "truth" of the postulate which Bismarck derided—that opposing systems of legitimacy are likely to clash if one of them claims general validity.

The debate was resumed two years later by Gerlach. By then he was in retirement and Bismarck had become Ambassador to St. Petersburg. Gerlach's letter has been lost and a page is missing in Bismarck's reply which heightens its abruptness. Impatiently emphasizing the gulf between them, Bismarck proclaimed that the inhibitions of the generation of 1815 had become irrelevant:

Who rules in France or Sardinia is a matter of indifference to me once the government is recognized and only a question of fact, not of right. I stand or fall with my own Sovereign, even if in my opinion he ruins himself stupidly, but for me France will remain France, whether it is governed by Napoleon or by St. Louis and Austria is for me a foreign country. . . . I know that you will reply that fact and right cannot be separated, that a properly conceived Prussian policy requires chastity in foreign affairs even from the point of view of utility. I am prepared to discuss the point of utility with you; but if you pose antinomies between right and revolution; Christianity and infidelity; God and the devil; I can argue no longer and can merely say "I am not of your opinion and you judge in me what is not yours to judge."

Even this bitter declaration of faith paled before a wounding reminder of Gerlach's role in Bismarck's career couched in the religious categories of Gerlach's Pietism:

I did not seek the service of the King. . . . The God who unexpectedly placed me into it will probably rather show me the way out than let my soul perish. I would overestimate the value of this life strangely . . . should I not be convinced that after thirty years it will be irrelevant to me what political successes I or my country have achieved in Europe. I can even think out the idea that someday "unbelieving Jesuits" will rule over the Mark Brandenburg together with a Bonapartist absolutism. . . . I am a child of different times than you, but as honest a one of mine as you of yours.[51]

This was the last letter exchanged between Bismarck and Gerlach.

The Revolutionary Tragedy

With the exchange with Gerlach, the main lines of Bismarck's thought were established. One by one, he had attacked the assumptions on which the "Metternich system" was based. He had declared the German Confederation a fetter to the development of Prussia's power. He had seen in the Holy Alliance a means to perpetuate an unjustified subordination of Prussia to Austria. Austria, the traditional ally, had been asserted to be Prussia's antagonist and France, the "hereditary" enemy, was considered a potential ally. The unity of conservative interests, the truism of policy for over a generation, had been described as subordinate to the requirement of national interest. The state transcended its fleeting embodiments in various forms of government.

347

The significance of Bismarck's criticism did not, of course, reside in the fact that it was made—the tenuousness of the Metternich system was a shibboleth of the mid-nineteenth century—but in the manner by which it was justified. Heretofore the attacks on the principle of legitimacy had occurred in the name of other principles of presumably greater validity, such as nationalism or liberalism. Bismarck declared the relativity of *all* beliefs; he translated them into forces to be evaluated in terms of the power they could generate.

However hard-boiled Bismarck's philosophy appeared, it was also built on an article of faith no more demonstrable than the principle of legitimacy—the belief that decisions based on power would be constant, that a proper analysis of a given set of circumstances would necessarily yield the same conclusions for everybody. It was inconceivable to Gerlach that the principle of legitimacy was capable of various interpretations. It was beyond the comprehension of Bismarck that statesmen might differ in understanding the requirements of national interest. Because of his magnificent grasp of the nuances of power relationships, Bismarck saw in his philosophy a doctrine of self-limitation. Because these nuances were not apparent to his successors and imitators, the application of Bismarck's lessons led to an armament race and a world war.

The bane of stable societies or of stable international systems is the inability to conceive of a mortal challenge. The blind spot of revolutionaries is the belief that the world for which they are striving will combine all the benefits of the new conception with the good points of the overthrown structure. But any upheaval involves costs. The forces unleashed by revolution have their own logic which is not to be deduced from the intentions of their advocates.

So it was with Bismarck. Within five years of coming to power in 1862, he had solved the problem of German unity along the lines of the memoranda he had written during the previous decade. He first induced Austria to separate herself from the secondary German states and to undertake a joint expedition with Prussia against Denmark over the status of Schleswig-Holstein. With Austria isolated from its traditional supporters, Bismarck brought ever increasing pressure on her until in exasperation she declared war. A rapid Prussian victory led to the expulsion of Austria from Germany. Prussia was now free to organize North Germany on a hegemonic basis.

Shortly after taking office, Bismarck had obtained Russian good will by adopting a benevolent attitude during the Polish rebellion of 1862. Napoleon was kept quiet by the lure of gains now in the Rhineland, now in Belgium, now in Luxembourg—prospects that always proved elusive when Napoleon sought to implement them. When Napoleon sought compensation for his miscalculation that Austria would win the Austro-Prussian war, he found himself out-maneuvered. When his mounting frustrations led to the Franco-Prussian war, German unification became a reality at last in 1871.

This united Germany was far from the ideals of those who had urged it for nearly two generations. It was a federation of the historical states and came into being not through the expression of popular will, but through a diplomatic compact among sovereigns.

The very magnitude of Bismarck's achievement mortgaged the future. To be sure, he was as moderate in concluding his wars as he had been ruthless in preparing them. The chief advocate of reason of state had the wisdom to turn his philosophy into a doctrine of self-limitation once Germany had achieved the magnitude and power he considered compatible with the requirements of security. For nearly a generation, Bismarck helped to preserve the peace of Europe by manipulating the commitments and interests of other powers in a masterly fashion.

But the spirits once called forth refused to be banished by a tour de force, however great. The manner in which Germany was unified deprived the international system of flexibility even though it was based on maxims that presupposed the infinite adaptability of the principal actors. For one thing, there were now fewer participants in the international system. The subtle combinations of the secondary German states in the old Confederation had made possible marginal adjustments which were precluded among the weightier components of the modern era.

Moreover, once the resources of Germany became subject to central direction, pressures toward rigid coalitions increased. In trying to deal with its worst nightmare—an alliance between France and Russia—Germany made this alliance inevitable. As German defense policy was geared to coping with a two-front war, it presented an increasing threat to all its neighbors. A Germany strong enough to deal with its two great neighbors jointly would surely be able to defeat them singly. Thus Germany tended to bring on what it feared most. During the period of the German Confederation, joint action was only possible in the face of overwhelming danger.

The uncertainty of these arrangements was one of the reasons why Bismarck had insisted on German unification under Prussian leadership. But he paid a price. What had been a remote contingency became at first a nightmare and then a reality.

These tendencies were reinforced because, with the annexation of Alsace-Lorraine by Germany, France disappeared from the list of potential German allies. The irreconcilable hostility of France meant the elimination of the French option, which in the 1850's Bismarck had considered essential. Henceforth French enmity was the "organic fault of our nature" against which Bismarck had warned in the 1850's. This precluded the policy outlined in the "master report"—of remaining aloof until the other powers were committed. With France available as a potential ally to an opponent of Germany, Bismarck had to attempt to forestall isolation by superior adaptability. But only four great powers remained available for Bismarck's subtle combinations, of which one—Great Britain—was tending toward isolation. Obviously the fewer the factors to be manipulated, the greater is the tendency toward rigidity.

To be sure, while Bismarck governed, these dilemmas were obscured by a diplomatic tour de force based on a complicated system of pacts with Germany at their center. But the very complexity of these arrangements doomed them. A system which requires a great man in each generation sets itself an almost insurmountable challenge, if only because a great man tends to stunt the emergence of strong personalities. When the novelty of Bismarck's tactics had worn off and the originality of his conception came to be taken for granted, lesser men strove to operate his system while lacking his sure touch and almost artistic sensitivity. As a result, what had been the manipulation of factors in a fluid situation eventually led to the petrification of the international system which produced World War I.

Bismarck's less imaginative successors failed even when they strove for "calculability" or "reliability." These qualities seemed more easily attainable by rigid commitments than by the delicate, constantly shifting balancing of Bismarck's policy. Thus Germany wound up with the unconditional commitment to the "worm eaten hulk" of Austria which it had been the whole thrust of Bismarck's policy to avoid.

In this manner it became apparent that the requirements of the national interest were highly ambiguous after all. Bismarck could base self-restraint on a philosophy of self-interest. In the hands of others lacking his subtle touch, his methods led to the collapse of the nineteenth-century state system. The nemesis of power is that, except in the hands of a master, reliance on it is more likely to produce a contest at arms than self-restraint.

Domestically, too, the very qualities that had made Bismarck a solitary figure in his lifetime caused his compatriots to misunderstand him when he had become a myth. They remembered the three wars that had achieved their unity. They forgot the patient preparation that had made them possible and the moderation that had secured their fruits. The constitution designed by Bismarck magnified this trend: The Parliament was based on universal suffrage, but had no control over the government; the government was appointed by the Emperor and was removable by him. Such a system encouraged the emergence of courtiers and lobbyists, but not statesmen. Nationalism unleavened by liberalism turned chauvinistic, and liberalism without responsibility grew sterile.

Thus Germany's greatest modern figure may well have sown the seeds of its twentieth-century tragedies. "No one eats with impunity from the tree of immortality,"[52] wrote Bismarck's friend von Roon, the reorganizer of the Prussian army, about him. The meaning of his life was perhaps best expressed by Bismarck himself in a letter to his wife: "That which is imposing here on earth . . . has always something of the quality of the fallen angel who is beautiful but without peace, great in his conceptions and exertions but without success, proud and lonely."[53]

REFERENCES

1. Quoted in Erich Eyck, *Bismarck: Leben und Werk,* Vol. 2 (Erlenbach-Zurich, 1943), pp. 316-17.

2. Horst Kohl (ed.), *Die politischen Reden des Fursten Bismarck, Historische-kritische Gesamtausgabe,* Vol. 1 (Stuttgart, 1892), p. 9. Hereafter referred to as "Kohl." Refers also to subsequent quotation.

3. Eyck, *Bismarck: Leben und Werk,* Vol. 1, p. 14.

4. *Gedanken und Erinnerungen,* Vol. 1, p. 1.

5. Otto von Bismarck, *Die gesammelten Werke,* Vol. 14, No. 1 (3d ed.; Berlin, 1924), November 14, 1833, p. 3. Hereafter referred to as *G. W.*

6. Eyck, *Bismarck: Leben und Werk,* Vol. 1, p. 26.

7. *G. W.*, Vol. 14, No. 1 (January 30, 1845), p. 30.

8. *Ibid.*, Vol. 14, No. 1 (September 29, 1838), pp. 14-15.

9. *Ibid.*, Vol. 14, No. 1 (January 9, 1845), p. 31.

10. Eyck, *Bismarck: Leben und Werk*, Vol. 1, p. 40.

11. Emil Ludwig, *Bismarck: Geschichte eines Kämpfers* (Berlin, 1926), p. 67.

12. *G. W.*, Vol. 14, No. 1, p. 46.

13. *G. W.*, Vol. 14, No. 1 (January 31, 1847), p. 50.

14. *Ibid.*, Vol. 14, No. 1 (May 3, 1851), p. 208.

15. *Ibid.* (May 12, 1851), p. 210.

16. *Ibid.* (March 7, 1847), p. 76.

17. "Kohl," Vol. 1, p. 273.

18. *G. W.*, Vol. 2 (the "little book"; March 1858), p. 302,

19. *Ibid.*, Vol. 1 (September 1853), p. 375.

20. "Kohl," Vol. 1 (June 9, 1849), p. 113.

21. *Ibid.* (April 4, 1849), pp. 93-94.

22. *Ibid.* (December 12, 1850), pp. 267-68.

23. *Ibid.* (April 21, 1849), p. 88.

24. *G. W.*, Vol. 1 (October 20, 1854), p. 505.

25. *G. W.*, Vol. 2 (March 1858), p. 320.

26. "Kohl," p. 110.

27. *Briefwechsel des Generals Leopold von Gerlach mit dem Bundestags-Gesandten Otto von Bismarck* (Berlin, 1893), p. 334. Hereafter referred to as *Briefwechsel.*

28. *Ibid.* (February 20, 1854), p. 130.

29. "Kohl," p. 264.

30. *G. W.*, Vol. 2 (June 2, 1857), p. 230.

31. *Ibid.*, Vol. 1 (September 29, 1851), p. 62.

32. *Briefwechsel* (May 2, 1857), p. 334.

33. *G. W.*, Vol. 1 (January 19, 1852), p. 128.

34. *Briefwechsel* (December 19, 1853), p. 128.

35. *G. W.*, Vol. 2 (March 1858), p. 310.

36. *Ibid.*, Vol. 2, p. 311.

37. *Briefwechsel* (October 13, 1854), p. 194.

38. *G. W.*, Vol. 14, No. 1, p. 517.

39. *Briefwechsel* (October 19, 1854), p. 199.

40. *G. W.*, Vol. 2 (June 17, 1855), p. 55.

41. *Ibid.* (December 8-9, 1859), p. 516.

42. *Ibid.* (April 26, 1856), p. 139. Subsequent quotations in these pages refer to the same source.

43. *Briefwechsel* (April 28, 1856), p. 315.

44. Otto Kohl (ed.), *Briefe des Generals Leopold von Gerlach an Otto von Bismarck* (Stuttgart and Berlin, 1912), pp. 192-93 (May 5, 1856). Hereafter referred to as "Kohl-Gerlach."

45. *Briefwechsel* (April 28, 1856), p. 315.

46. "Kohl-Gerlach" (April 29, 1857), p. 206.

47. *Ibid.* (May 6, 1857), p. 211.

48. *Briefwechsel* (May 2, 1857), pp. 333-34.

49. "Kohl-Gerlach" (May 21, 1857), pp. 213-16.

50. *Briefwechsel* (May 30, 1857), pp. 337-39.

51. *Ibid.* (May 2-4, 1860), p. 353.

52. Quoted in Ludwig, *Bismarck: Geschichte eines Kämpfers*, p. 494.

53. *G. W.*, Vol. 14, No. 1, p. 61.

ALBERT O. HIRSCHMAN

Underdevelopment, Obstacles to the Perception of Change, and Leadership

DURING A recent visit to a Latin American capital, I wished to resume contact with X, an economic historian who had returned there some time ago after spending several years in Europe. I had been invited for dinner by a sociologist whom I asked whether he knew X; he did indeed, quite well, but did not have X's telephone number; no doubt, however, he could find it by calling a common friend. Unfortunately the friend was not home. I asked whether there might be a chance that X would be listed in the telephone directory; this suggestion was shrugged off with the remark that the directory makes a point of listing only people who have either emigrated or died. After a while, the other dinner guests, an economist and his wife, appeared. They were asked about X's telephone number. The economist said that X must be both much in demand and hard to reach, as several people had inquired about how to get in touch with him within the past few days. The subject was dropped as hopeless, and everybody spent a pleasant evening.

Upon waking up the next morning in my hotel room, I noticed the telephone directory on the night table. I could not resist opening it to look for a listing under X's name. I found it immediately and dialed the number, still sure that it must be the one he owned five years ago before leaving for Europe. But the familiar voice answered my call from the other end of the line.

I. *Special Obstacles to the Perception of Change in Underdeveloped Countries*

It so happens that X is Claudio Véliz, at present the director of a new Institute of International Studies in Santiago and editor of the

354

recent volume *Obstacles to Change in Latin America.*[1] In the course of our conversation, he asked me to give a talk at his Institute. Since the episode I had just lived through confirmed my long-standing suspicion that obstacles to change are intertwined in Latin America and in other less developed areas with considerable obstacles to the *perception* of change, I suggested that an exploration of these obstacles might be an interesting, if somewhat disrespectful, topic. The observations in this section are based on the talk that ensued and also owe much to the lively discussion it provoked.

To a considerable extent, the difficulties of perceiving change are universal. At all stages of development, men are loath to abandon the old clichés and stereotypes that have served them so well, for they make the world around them intelligible, comfortable, and meaningful—or, as in our episode, almost endearingly absurd. Historians and psychologists have documented the difficulties of perceiving what, on the basis of previous experience, is felt to be incongruous as well as the reluctance to absorb new information that conflicts with established beliefs or is otherwise unpleasant.[2] Here, however, I am not so much interested in the general phenomenon as in the possible existence of *special* or additional obstacles to the perception of change in countries where economic and social development has been laggard.

As a preliminary, a not quite terminological point must be briefly discussed. A distinction is often made between "real" and "apparent" or between "fundamental" and "superficial" changes: This device permits one to categorize as superficial a great number of changes that have, in effect, taken place and to assert in consequence that there has not yet been any real change. The decision to assert that *real* change has occurred is made to hinge on one or several tests. For example, it is often affirmed that there has been "no real change" *unless* the absolute distance which separates the per-capita income of the underdeveloped countries from that of the developed has been substantially narrowed or *unless* there has been the kind of radical and sudden redistribution of wealth and power which comes as the result of a socialist revolution. But to set up such demanding tests is in itself an indication of a special difficulty and reluctance to concede change except when it simply can no longer be denied. It is precisely our task to explain this reluctance and this difficulty.

355

PERSISTENCE OF THE "LITTLE TRADITION"

A first, still rather general obstacle to the perception of change derives from the persistence of traits which are related to what Robert Redfield has called the "little tradition." An example: I land at the Bogotá airport after a five-year absence, and the first thing I notice on leaving the plane is the characteristic manner in which several of my fellow passengers are folding handkerchiefs around their noses; having long known this to be a strange custom of the Bogotanos as they emerge from their homes, movie theaters, or bordellos into the dangerous open air, I immediately whisper to myself: "Nothing has changed here!"

Numerous traits of this kind are both harmless and perfectly compatible with the highest levels of economic and political development. Since they were first encountered at a time when the country was backward, however, they have taken on an aroma of backwardness, and the impression is created—by no means only among foreign visitors—that modernization requires a surrender of these traits.

Clearly the observer is in error when he decides that nothing has changed because a number of traits of the "little tradition" are still extant. But the error is not only pardonable, it is almost inevitable. When backwardness is pervasive, it is easy to overestimate the interrelatedness of its components and correspondingly difficult to diagnose correctly which traits will and must be changed in the course of modernization and which ones may be—and perhaps should be—safely kept.[3]

THE BIAS IN THE PERCEPTION OF CUMULATIVE CHANGE

Our next obstacle to the perception of change depends more critically on the division of the world into advanced and less developed countries and is, therefore, central to our argument. It arises because what leads to cumulative change in one country does not necessarily do so in another. In other words, the extent to which a given social event or innovation—industrialization, agrarian reform, the achievement of mass literacy, and so forth—involves a society in further important social and political changes varies considerably from country to country and from period to period. A fundamental transformation of the socio-political structure accompanied the coming of industry to England and France; for Germany, Russia, and Japan, the transformation was less radical or more delayed; and for the "late-late-comers" of Latin America, industrialization has ordinarily brought even less immediate and fundamental socio-political changes. Somehow the existing structures in these countries seem to be better at absorbing and accommodating the new industries and their promoters, technicians, and labor force than was the case in those societies where industry first raised its head.[4]

A similar development may be in the making *within* Latin America with respect to agrarian reform. Whereas the elimination of the *latifundio* in Mexico, Bolivia, and Cuba required nothing less than a revolution, a number of countries (Chile, Venezuela, Colombia, and perhaps even Peru) seem to be able to achieve substantial progress in land-tenure conditions without a concomitant or prior drastic change in the socio-political environment.

Marx said that when history repeats itself, it reproduces in the form of comedy what first appeared as tragedy. The preceding situations suggest a slight variant: It looks as though a given change or innovation appears for the first time with revolutionary, history-making force, but tends to be reported the next time in the "News-in-Brief" column. If we had put our finger on a historical law here, we would then have encountered a reason why fundamental change is less easy to come by in countries which introduce the "revolutionary" innovations of the advanced countries after a substantial time lag.

The matter is not settled so easily, however, for our historical law breaks down as soon as we consider some additional examples. While some innovations cause less cumulative change among the latecomers than they did among the pioneers, the opposite relationship can be shown to hold for others. Take, as a striking example, the transistor radio; its impact is far more revolutionary in countries where a large part of the population had previously been wholly out of touch with national and international events than in countries where, as a result of fairly universal literacy and electrification, the transistor radio is merely one additional medium for the transmission of information.

Another example is the truck (or bus), which has become an important medium of not only geographical, but *social* mobility in some African and Latin American countries. While social mobility had long been a feature of the societies which *invented* the truck, the possibility of achieving truck ownership opened up an important new avenue toward social improvement in more rigidly stratified societies. In a similar vein, I have related recently how the telephone led to the replacement of cash by credit operations in Ethiopia[5]; such a revolutionary role was obviously denied the telephone in North America and Europe, where credit instruments had been perfected for several centuries prior to Bell's invention.

Objectively, therefore, it is hardly possible to assert that cumulative change is more difficult to ignite in underdeveloped countries than in advanced ones. But subjectively the situation looks quite different, for observers in the less developed countries will expect a cumulative change to be connected with those processes which had a revolutionary function in the advanced countries. When these processes fail to perform in this way in their own countries, the observers will disappointedly conclude that "nothing ever changes here." Instances of the opposite relation—namely, that some innovations which were easily accommodated by the existing sociopolitical structure of the advanced countries will cause considerable ferment when transplanted to the less advanced—are not likely to occur to these observers since they always expect changes to take place in accordance with the patterns of the "leading" countries which they emulate and with which they attempt to catch up. This expectation, then, induces a bias in perception—that is, an emphasis on those processes which wrought considerable change in the advanced countries, but are easily domesticated when they are transplanted, while the opposite situations are ignored.

STYLES OF CHANGE IN DEPENDENT AND LEADING COUNTRIES

The less-developed countries are usually *dependent* countries: They have considerably less freedom of movement than the leading or more nearly independent countries.[6] This situation is likely to have important consequences for the manner in which change is typically brought about in each kind of country, and it turns out that such differences in styles of change once again create special difficulties for the perception of change in the dependent countries.

In its extreme form, dependence of a formally independent underdeveloped country is revealed through military intervention of a leading power. But, operating as it does in an open international economic system, the dependent country is also subject to a whole range of intermediate pressures and potential threats: denial of international financing, domestic capital flight, diversion of purchases of goods for export and of tourist services to alternative suppliers, and so forth. Some of these potential threats are likely to become actual not only when the interests of a dominant foreign country are under direct attack, but even when a determined attempt is made to change the domestic social and economic structure. Often there is considerable uncertainty about the international repercussions of internal reform moves. Leading countries are subject neither to such threats nor to such uncertainties.

The consequence for the style of change of the two kinds of countries is obvious: The leading countries can afford to place all their cards on the table and to shout about their achievements in change from the rooftops. When, on the other hand, the desire for change comes to the fore in a dependent country, *and as long as dependent status is accepted as a datum and a constraint,* there will be an instinctive tendency to play it safe by introducing change in small doses so that each individual unit of change will either not be noticed at all or will remain below some "foreign repercussion threshold." The dependent country, thus, will endeavor to dissimulate change by making it as gradual and non-spectacular as possible. Brazil's well-known record of gradual and comparatively nonviolent transitions may be an example of this *stealthy* style of change, and Colombia supplies us once again with an illustrative story. A Polish mission recently visited Colombia and found out all at once about the many basic and not-so-basic economic activities which are at present in the hands of the government, the Central Bank, or other public bodies; not realizing that this state of affairs is the end result of a gradual process which had extended over a period of many years, the Poles are reported to have asked: "Excuse our ignorance, but in which year did you make The Revolution?"

The non-spectacular, stealthy style of change is a defense mechanism used by political leadership in the dependent countries, and in many ways it is admirably clever. Like any human institution, moreover, the style has a tendency to perpetuate itself even when the circumstances which have given rise to it no longer prevail. There is something to be said for turning necessity into virtue and for celebrating the style, as has often been done in Brazil, as a genuine invention and contribution to the art of history-making.

The trouble is that the style is too clever. It may fool the intervention-prone foreigner or the traditional domestic power-holder whose position it slowly erodes. But the general public and, even more, the intellectuals also fail frequently to recognize that change is being achieved. The reason is clear: Because of the over-

ALBERT O. HIRSCHMAN

riding prestige of the dominant countries, change is widely equated with that particular "loud" *style* of change which these countries can so well afford; thus, change is denied to have occurred at all until and unless it takes the particular shape—violent revolution, civil war, and so forth—which is familiar to us from the history of change in the leading countries. A country that is not taking this particular road to change is considered by its own countrymen as too "lazy to make history" or as a country of "ambiguity and half tones."[7] Thus, once again, fascination with the patterns of change characteristic of the leading, dominant countries makes it difficult to perceive processes of change actively at work among latecoming and dependent countries.

THE SPECIAL MISFIT AND DURABILITY OF IMPORTED IDEOLOGIES

In addition to the biases in perception already described, observers in less-developed countries can be affected by a special difficulty in detecting changes in their own societies, regardless of any comparison with what happens or has happened elsewhere. A reason for this difficulty can be found in the image which these observers have of their own societies, in the lenses they use to look at them, or, for short, in their ideologies. It is probably a principal characteristic of less-developed, dependent countries that they *import* their ideologies, both those that are apologetic and those that are subversive of the status quo. There always exists a considerable distance between variegated and ever-changing reality, on the one hand, and the rigid mold of ideology, on the other. The distance and the misfit, however, are likely to be much more extensive when the ideology is imported than when it is homegrown. In the latter case, an important social change which is not accounted for by the prevailing ideology will soon be noted and the ideology will be criticized and either adapted to the new situation or exchanged for a new one. A good example is the Revisionist criticism of orthodox Marxism which appeared even during the lifetime of Engels as a result of certain developments in German society which were hard to fit into Marxist doctrine.

When the ideology is imported, on the other hand, the extent to which it fits the reality of the importing country is usually quite poor from the start. Given this initial disparity, additional changes

360

in the country's social, economic, or political structure that contradict the ideology do not really worsen the fit *substantially* and are therefore ignored or else easily rationalized. The free-trade doctrine imported from England into Latin America in the nineteenth century and so poorly adapted to the needs of that continent was fully routed there only as a result of the two World Wars and the Depression.[8] The long life of the oft-refuted explanation of Latin American societies in terms of the dichotomy between oligarchy and mass may be another case in point. On the North American Left, the notion, imported by Marxist thought, that the white working class is the "natural ally" of the oppressed Negro masses also held sway for an extraordinarily long period, considering the overwhelming and cumulative evidence to the contrary.[9]

Thus, an ideology can draw strength from the very fact that it does so poorly at taking the basic features of socio-economic structure into account. Among ideologies, in other words, it is the least fit that have the greatest chance of survival! And as long as the misfit ideology survives, perception of change—and of reality in general—is held back.

To illustrate the point further, I must tell one last story: A man approaches another exclaiming: "Hello, Paul. It's good to see you after so many years, but you have changed so much! You used to be fat, now you are quite thin; you used to be tall, now you are rather short. What happened, Paul?" 'Paul' rather timidly replies: "But my name is not Paul." Whereupon the other retorts, quite pleased with his interpretation of reality: "You see how much you have changed! Even your name has changed!"

In sum, our search for obstacles to the perception of change specific to underdeveloped countries has been surprisingly successful. This success will give us pause and concern: When there are special difficulties in perceiving ongoing change, many opportunities for accelerating that change and taking advantage of newly arising openings for change will surely be missed. The obstacles to the *perception* of change thus turn into an important obstacle to *change itself.* The matter can also be put in the form of a vicious circle: To the extent that a country is underdeveloped, it will experience special difficulties in perceiving changes within its own society; hence, it will not notice resulting opportunities for even larger and more decisive changes. A country that fails to perceive these opportunities is likely to remain underdeveloped.

II. *Perception of Change and Leadership: Charisma vs. Skill*

Might it not be possible, one could ask, to break out of this vicious circle by the right kind of change-perceiving leadership? To link in this way the problem of perception of change to that of leadership may seem farfetched; yet these problems are so difficult that roundabout approaches are worth trying. One useful indirect approach to the leadership problem would consist in first ascertaining, as I have just done, some *average* beliefs, attitudes, and perceptions that prevail not only in the community at large, but also among its elites. One could then inquire whether and how leaders are liable to deviate from these averages and try to define leadership in terms of such deviations.

The trouble with such a definition (but also its interest) is that deviations from average attitudes and perceptions can take several contrasting forms. In the first place, leadership may be achieved by those who hold to the average perceptions with an uncommon degree of "passionate intensity," who articulate them most forcefully, and who best reflect and express what is in everybody's heart and mind. Average *mis*perceptions, such as those we have reviewed, are of course also reflected and accentuated by this sort of leader, and his ability to empathize with them or his blindness to ongoing change may be an important part of his appeal. Robert Tucker observes elsewhere in this volume that *charismatic* leadership rests to a considerable extent on the leader's ability "to accentuate the sense of being in a desperate predicament,"[10] presumably regardless of whether this sense is justified by actual events.

Yet, accentuation, exaggeration, and forceful articulation of prevailing attitudes and perceptions cannot be the only basis for leadership. Another is surely the ability to overcome and transcend some of these attitudes. In our case, it is precisely the ability to perceive change when most of one's contemporaries are still unable to do so that would enable a leader to take advantage of new opportunities as soon as they arise; in this situation, a leader often appears to *create* such opportunities singlehandedly.

An illustration of this sort of leadership which is based on the perception rather than the denial of opportunity was recently supplied by Carlos Lleras Restrepo, whose masterful "reform-mongering" performance in initiating agrarian-reform legislation and then seeing it through the Colombian Congress I reported on a few years ago.[11] Elected President in 1966, but lacking the two-thirds majority in Parliament that is required for passing all legislation of any importance, he and his Administration seemed condemned to even more immobilism than had plagued earlier governments elected under the "National Front" arrangement in which Conservatives and Liberals shared the responsibilities and privileges of power. But in the first year of his Administration, Lleras had given so many tokens of a determination to push for socio-economic reforms that he was able to attract votes from the opposition which included a left-wing Liberal group that had split from the main Liberal Party in the late-fifties. Eventually, this group decided to rejoin the main party in August 1967, thereby enabling the Administration to muster the needed two-thirds majority. On commenting on these developments in a televised speech, Lleras exclaimed:

[There are those] who took pleasure in predicting difficulties, who were sure that we would never be able to resolve our problems. . . . [They said that] because we did not have the two-thirds majority, the whole life of the country was threatened and that the future was somber. *As though there were not the art of politics! As though all situations were unchangeable! As though there were no possibilities of achieving agreements!* The truth is that all these predictions came to naught—in fact, even *before* the Liberal union was sealed and *before* the two-thirds majority was secure, several important laws had been passed.[12]

Here is a leader who excels at perceiving opportunities, takes great pleasure in his special powers of perception, acts successfully on what he perceives, and strengthens his claims to leadership as a result.

Through our indirect approach—ascertaining first some "average" attitudes and perceptions and then defining leadership in terms of deviations from the norm—we have, in fact, come upon two contrasting components of leadership: skill, on the one hand, and charisma, on the other. Skill requires a stronger-than-average ability to perceive change, while charisma is based in part on a stronger-than-average refusal to do so. The charisma and the skill requirements of leadership, thus, are often at loggerheads, and the most effective leaders are likely to be those who can somehow accommodate both. Lenin with his extraordinary powers to rouse people to action *and* the "infinite fertility of his tactical imagination"[13] is a particularly fascinating example.

But such an even blend of charisma and skill is most uncommon. Usually any one leader is likely to be better either at charisma

363

or at skill, precisely because these two qualities are in part based on opposite deviations from the norm. Once in a while, one encounters a "division of labor" between leaders working in informal concert toward the same goal, as in the remarkable case of the charismatic Garibaldi and the skilled Cavour. Again, however, such an arrangement is not easy to come by.

Finally, the contradiction between the two ingredients of leadership may be attenuated because one ingredient, usually charisma, can be allowed to predominate in the first period of struggle and mobilization, while the skill requirements are more needed in the next stage, when the leader moves closer to or actually into power. That leadership often requires this successive display of contrasting characteristics by the same person is noted by several contributors to this volume.[14] It is indeed a fundamental point about the difficulty of securing continuity in effective leadership. As such, the point was unlikely to escape Machiavelli who made it while discussing the chances that violent seizure of power might change a corrupt republic for the better:

> The project to reform the state presupposes a generous and upright citizen. To become sovereign by force . . . presupposes, on the contrary, an ambitious and evil citizen. Hence it will be difficult to find a person who would wish to use reprehensible means to achieve a just end, or an evil man who will suddenly act like a fine citizen and make virtuous use of an ill-gotten authority.[15]

However the conflict between the skill and charisma requirements may be resolved, a minimum of skill will have to be forthcoming in almost any conceivable situation if leadership is to be at all successful. In recent theorizing on leadership, we probably have had an overemphasis on the charisma component—and in recent practice, we certainly have had an *overdose* of it and a corresponding underdose of skill, particularly in the Third World. Names of highly charismatic leaders who failed because they were short on skill come to mind only too readily.

What has been said applies to both revolutionary leaders and "reform-mongers." Both need a minimum of skill—or, in terms of our preceding analysis, both would do a better job if they trained themselves to overcome the obstacles to the perception of change and to recognize change when it happens. Only in this way can they do better for the communities which they pretend to lead than these communities would be expected to do if one were to predict their future on the basis of their average attitudes, perceptions, and misperceptions. This is the ultimate function and justification of the leader: to improve on the *average* prospects for advance of those whom he leads, to raise the expected value of their future.

REFERENCES

1. Claudio Véliz, *Obstacles to Change in Latin America* (New York, 1965).

2. Some basic references from the psychological literature are Jerome S. Bruner and Leo Postman, "On the Perception of Incongruity: A Paradigm," *Journal of Personality*, Vol. 18 (1949), pp. 206-23; and Leo Festinger, *A Theory of Cognitive Dissonance* (Stanford, 1957). For a remarkable historical case study of blocks to perception in a highly developed country, see Roberta Wohlstetter, *Pearl Harbor: Warning and Decision* (Stanford, 1962).

3. See my article "Obstacles to Development: A Classification and a Quasi-Vanishing Act," *Economic Development and Cultural Change* (July, 1965). It can be argued that keeping some seemingly backward traits is essential if modernization is to be successful since one element of success is the maintenance of a separate identity on the part of the modernizing society.

4. "Latin American politics is something of a 'living museum' in which all the forms of political authority of the Western historic experience continue to exist and operate, interacting one with another in a pageant that seems to violate all the rules of sequence and change involved in our understanding of the growth of Western civilization." Charles W. Anderson, *Politics and Economic Change in Latin America* (Princeton, 1967), p. 104. See also my article, "The Political Economy of Import-Substituting Industrialization in Latin America," *Quarterly Journal of Economics*, Vol. 82 (February, 1968), pp. 1-32.

5. See my *Development Projects Observed* (Brookings, 1967), pp. 151-52.

6. The term "dependent," in lieu of underdeveloped, less-developed, and so forth, is beginning to have currency in Latin America. See, for example, Osvaldo Sunkel, "Politica nacional de desarrollo y dependencia externa," *Estudios Internacionales*, Vol. 1 (Santiago, Chile; April, 1967).

7. The first term is used by Antonio Callado in *Tempo di Arraes* (Rio de Janeiro, 1965), p. 16; the other by Fernando Pedreira in the *Correo da Manhã*, July 16, 1967.

8. See, for example, Nicia Vilela Luz, *A luta pela industrialização do Brasil* (São Paulo, 1961).

9. See Harold Cruse, *The Crisis of the Negro Intellectual* (New York, 1967), pp. 174-75, 262-63, and *passim*.

10. Robert C. Tucker, "The Theory of Charismatic Leadership," p. 751.

11. See my *Journeys Toward Progress* (New York, 1963), Chapter 2.

12. *El Tiempo* (Bogotá), September 14, 1967.

13. Tucker, "The Theory of Charismatic Leadership," p. 751.

14. "The talents of the founder of a state are different from those of the ruler of an established one." (Dankwart A. Rustow, "Ataturk as Founder of a State," p. 821.) "The qualities necessary for a charismatic . . . leader's coming to power are not those that he needs in order to stay in power or to protect his work." (Stanley and Inge Hoffmann, "de Gaulle as Political Artist," p. 869.) I would add that, in many cases, the required switch from one set of qualities to another must take place not after the conquest of power, but at some point prior to it, when agitation and mobilization give place to negotiation with and partial winning over of the existing powerholders.

JAMES D. BARBER

Adult Identity and Presidential Style:
The Rhetorical Emphasis

EVERY CHIEF executive of a great state is required in fact, if not in
law, to make speeches to a national audience, to receive advice and
information, to represent his nation to the world, to bargain, to
exercise authority, and to manage the ordinary business of his
office. These requirements leave much room for choice, which
makes the national leader's behavior politically intriguing, psychologically interpretable, and fateful for the world's welfare. Choices
among these available emphases can amount to a distinctive political style. In this essay, I want to illustrate, by means of a single
example, how we might be able to explain—perhaps even to anticipate—the shape and force of such a distinctive style long before the
man is a leader.

Our American predictions have so often been wrong that some
new system of prescience seems necessary.[1] One thinks of Woodrow
Wilson, the scholar in the White House who would bring reason to
politics; of Herbert Hoover, the Great Engineer who would organize chaos into progress; of Franklin D. Roosevelt, that champion
of a balanced budget; of Harry S. Truman, whom the office would
surely overwhelm; of Dwight D. Eisenhower, a militant crusader;
of John F. Kennedy, who would produce results in place of
moralisms; and of Lyndon B. Johnson, the southern conservative.

We should do better at prediction if we considered the President as a person who tries to cope with an environment by using
techniques he has found effective. For all the complexities of
personality, there are always regularities, habitual ways of handling
similar situations, just as the demands and opportunities of the
Presidency are complex, but patterned. Thus, the President-as-
person interacts with the set of recurrent problems and oppor-

tunities presented by the Presidency; the pattern of this interaction is his political style. He copes, adapts, leads, and responds not as some shapeless organism in a flood of novelties, but as a man with a memory in a system with a history.

The main outlines of presidential style are not hard to discern. One major dimension is activity vs. passivity, the standard way of classifying our chief executives. A second dimension, which does not always coincide with the first, is the emotional flavor or flair he displays—whether he generally appears happy or depressed by what he is called upon to do. These two main clues[2] can help our understanding of many other aspects of the style of political leadership. For example, once we know that Calvin Coolidge husbanded his energies and was usually bored or depressed as President, we are not surprised to discover his emphasis on a rhetoric of high principles and his avoidance of "political" relations with Congress.[3]

Once the main features of a style are grasped, one must find out what holds the pattern together. The best way to discover that is to see how the pattern was put together in the first place—how at a critical juncture the person brought together the motives, resources, and opportunities life handed him and molded them into a distinctive shape, and how the style he adopted then presaged the main ways in which he would shape his energies as President.

I will illustrate with one case (alluding occasionally to others) how a President may select rhetoric as a major outlet for his energy. The President is Andrew Johnson. I shall try to show how his peculiar rhetorical style, which had important political consequences, can be traced directly to that critical period in his life when he made politics a major factor in his adult identity. The facts can be presented only briefly, and the theory only tentatively. My purpose is not to characterize the President Johnson of a century ago, but to suggest that a focus on the formation of adult identity provides an important clue to presidential style.

The Man Close Up: Johnson in the White House

The first President Johnson was habitually restrained in his day-to-day relations with those who worked closely with him. Nicknamed "The Grim Presence," Andrew Johnson impressed his secretary by his "chilling manner" and "sullen fixedness of purpose." "Never once in more than two years did I see him unbend from his grim rigidity, to the flexibility of form and feature which belongs to ordinary humanity." Johnson "cracked no jokes and told no stories"; his rarely seen smile was a "grim cast-iron wrinkle on the nether half of his face at public receptions." His favorite line of poetry was from Gray's *Elegy*—"The dark, unfathomed caves of ocean bare"—a phrase he frequently recited and relished for its grandeur and solemnity. Always dressed "with extreme fastidiousness in sober black," he impressed "ever those who dislike him" with "the great dignity with which he bore himself and the remarkable neat appearance of his apparel." The contrast with Lincoln's appearance may have highlighted these perceptions.

Even in crisis situations, Johnson typically retained his reserve. At the news of Lincoln's assassination, he was "grief stricken like the rest" and "oppressed by the suddenness of the call upon him to become President," but "nevertheless calm and self-possessed." With his back to the wall in the impeachment crisis, he bore himself with "dignity and forebearance"; his "mood fluctuated, from bitterness in the early days of the trial to grim and philosophic amusement as it entered its closing phases."

The Johnson biographers mention a few exceptions to his restrained, humorless, formal behavior in close relations, but their rarity only emphasizes his habitual stern self-control. With children he was sometimes relaxed and easy; he did have one long, rambling conversation with his secretary in two years; he may have been "melted by a woman's tears" when wives of imprisoned Confederates sought his pardon; he may have had "a soft spot in his heart for animals"; and in his last days in the White House, he did hold several gay parties. When Johnson was a Congressman, he and a few companions "got in kind of a bust—not a big drunk," as he wrote to a friend in Tennessee, and went to Baltimore to see "The Danseuses Viennoises," who performed so enticingly "that Job in the midst of his afflictions would have rejoiced at the scenes before him."

No such relief was available to Johnson in the White House. "Devoid of outside interests, an indefatigible worker," following the same grinding schedule from day to day, Johnson plodded through his tasks and endured stoically the attacks of his enemies. Johnson worked standing up; "never free from physical pain," he sometimes endured "excruciating torture" from a kidney ailment and severe pains in his arm that made writing difficult. His wife Eliza "lay a constant invalid in a room across the hall from his library, where through doors ajar, her cough, her sobs and sometimes her moans of anguish summoned him to her bedside." His recourse was work—"work, work, work, with a sullen fixedness of purpose as the sole means of rendering tolerable his existence." With time out for lunch (a cup of tea and a cracker), he "worked incessantly, often making of himself for days and sometimes for weeks a prisoner in the White House."

Johnson in the White House had no close friends to whom he could unburden himself. He "gave his full confidence only to the members of his family, notably to his invalid wife and to the official White House hostess, his daughter Martha Patterson." As Gideon Welles, Secretary of the Navy, observed:

There is a reticence on the part of the President—an apparent want of confidence in his friends—which is unfortunate, and prevents him from having intimate and warm personal friends who would relieve him in a measure. . . . It is a mistake, an infirmity, a habit fixed before he was President, to keep his own counsel.[4]

Eric L. McKitrick captures this aspect of Johnson's orientation in his chapter titled, "Andrew Johnson, Outsider." And Jefferson Davis, in what Johnson's most sympathetic biographer calls a "not unkind and in many ways acute analysis," gave this interpretation:

This pride—for it was the pride of having no pride—his associates long struggled to overcome, but without success. They respected Mr. Johnson's abilities, integrity, and greatly original force of character; but nothing could make him be, or seem to wish to feel, at home in their society. Some casual word dropped in debate, though uttered without a thought of his existence, would seem to wound him to the quick, and again he would shrink back into the self-imposed isolation of his earlier and humbler life, as if to gain strength from touching his mother earth.[5]

Andrew Johnson was rarely aggressive in his close personal relations. If he was a "hard-word, soft-deed man," his hard words seldom came out in conversation. To the importunings of the Radicals Johnson responded, shortly after assuming the Presidency, by "listening to everybody, nodding at everything and staying as far away as possible from controversial issues." Later when Thaddeus Stevens called on the President to criticize his policies and to threaten desertion by the Congressional Republicans, "Johnson gave no indication of yielding but pleaded for harmony." Beset by mobs of pardon-seeking southerners in his office, he remained "mild and subdued, and his manner kindly"—even though in 1861 a mob in Lynchburg, Virginia, had dragged him from a train and beaten him severely, and in 1862 a Confederate mob had thrown his invalid wife and family out of his Tennessee home into the street. Repeatedly his noncommital and somewhat enigmatic responses conciliated Radical Senator Charles Sumner. Johnson tolerated Secretary of War Stanton's presence at his Cabinet meetings for more than two years, although he knew Stanton was plotting against him. "Johnson's failure to do anything about it was a topic of avid speculation." When Stanton was finally asked to resign and replied with insolent refusal, Johnson "was neither surprised nor upset"; he did not call Stanton in for a confrontation. Welles wrote of Johnson's performance with Stanton: "Few men have stronger feeling; still fewer have the power of restraining themselves when evidently excited." He was similarly conciliatory in face-to-face talks with Grant and others who let him down.

Throughout the impeachment trial, Johnson remained impassive in personal conversation, with one significant exception. He expressed considerable impatience with his team of attorneys, who had decided it would be strategically inadvisable for the President to do as he wanted: to "march into the Senate and do a little 'plain speaking.' "[6]

For almost all of his time in the White House, in almost all of his personal relations with those with whom he had to deal as President, Andrew Johnson expressed neither affection nor antagonism, but patient consideration. These observations of others are consistent with Johnson's own self-image. He saw himself as "generally temperate in all things" and judged that "mercy and clemency have been pretty large ingredients in my composition. . . . I have been charged with going too far, being too lenient." He disliked "demagogues," such as Benjamin Butler (although he was courteous to Butler in person), braggarts like Schuyler Colfax, and those who were "all heart and no head," like Horace Greeley. "The elements of my nature," Johnson said, "the pursuits of my life have not made me either in my feelings or in my practice aggressive. My nature, on the contrary, is rather defensive." He felt he might have been a good chemist: "It would have satisfied my desire to analyze things."

The Speaker: Johnson Before Crowds

The contrast between Andrew Johnson's restrained, mild, hesitant style in conversation, and his performance in certain wider rhetorical situations can hardly be overstated. His image as just the

371

kind of aggressive demagogue he denigrated was fixed in the public mind at his inauguration as Vice President on March 4, 1865, just forty-one days before he became President.[7] Shortly before Lincoln's brief speech ("With malice toward none, with charity for all . . ."), Johnson delivered a defiant and muddled diatribe to the crowded assembly. Interrupting the administration of his oath of office, he launched forth in this fashion:

I'm a-goin' for to tell you here today; yea, I'm a-goin' for to tell you all, that I'm a plebeian! I glory in it; I am a plebeian! The people—yes, the people of the United States have made me what I am; and I am a-goin' for to tell you here today—yes, today, in this place that the people are everything.[8]

Speaking without notes, "on and on he went, his voice loud and unclear, his words tumbling over one another and losing themselves in their own echoes." The Supreme Court, the senators, and in particular Mr. Seward and Mr. Stanton, he shouted, "are but the creatures of the American people. . . . I, though a plebeian boy, am authorized by the principles of the government under which I live to feel proudly conscious that I am a man, and grave dignitaries are but men."[9] Each lot of "grave dignitaries" was reminded that they were subordinate to the people Johnson personified—including, according to one account, "you, gentlemen of the Diplomatic Corps, with all your fine feathers and gewgaws." Part way through, the Vice President forgot the name of the Secretary of the Navy and stopped to ask someone sitting close by so that he could include Gideon Welles in the list of those to be put in their place.

Judging from reports of the audience's immediate reaction, Johnson's manner was even more shocking than were his words. "Senators were struck with consternation, and diplomats with difficulty restrained their laughter." Shortly after the speech began, Senator Sumner "put his hands over his face and bent his head to his desk." Lincoln came in during Johnson's speech and, perceiving the situation, sat quietly through it with an expression of "unutterable sorrow," his "head drooping in the deepest humiliation." As he walked out to the Capitol steps to deliver his address, Lincoln told the marshall: "Do not let Johnson speak outside."

A reporter summed up the event in a private letter:

The second official of the Nation—drunk—*drunk*—when about to take his oath of office, bellowing and ranting and shaking his fists at Judges, Cabinet and Diplomats, and making a fool of himself to such a degree that indignation is almost compelled to pity.[10]

In the next few days, "Andy the Sot" was derided throughout Washington and celebrated in song at Grover's Theater on E Street. A few days later, a senatorial caucus "seriously considered the propriety of asking him to resign as their presiding officer"; the Senate voted to exclude liquor from the Senate wing of the Capitol; and two Senators were dropped from all standing committees, "because of their habitual inebriety and incapacity for business." Lincoln quickly passed over Johnson's inaugural performance: "I have known Andy for many years; he made a bad slip the other day, but you need not be scared. Andy ain't a drunkard." The Cabinet, however, discussed the affair at length the following week in an atmosphere of grave concern. Gideon Welles noted that Secretary of State Seward's "tone and opinion were much changed since Saturday. He seems to have given Johnson up now." The Democratic press reviled Johnson editorially, pleased to denounce the supposedly Radical Vice President; the New York *World* called him "an insolent drunken brute, in comparison with whom Caligula's horse was respectable." And the Radical press hit him from the other side: "It is the plain duty of Mr. Johnson either to apologize for his conduct, or to resign his office." Johnson retreated to the Blair family estate in Silver Springs to recuperate. On March 9, 1865, he wrote to the Senate reporter, requesting "an accurate copy of what I said on that occasion."

Johnson's biographies have worked and reworked the explanations for this remarkable speech that brought him national disgrace as he assumed national office. A combination of illness, fatigue, and anxiety affected him that morning, and he took too much brandy. Clearly he was not (as were both his sons) an alcoholic. Nor do we need to rely on the immediate details to explain his behavior; he was displaying a pattern, not an exception. Johnson's speaking style, under certain special conditions, continually subverted his reputation as a steady, stern, and reliable leader.

During the campaign of 1865, Johnson had made a less widely publicized, but equally revealing speech to a large crowd of Negroes in Nashville. On the night of October 24, he faced "a mass of human beings, so closely compacted together that they seemed to compose one vast body, no part of which could move without moving the whole," over which "torches and transparencies . . . cast a ruddy glow."

Johnson began by reviewing Lincoln's Emancipation Proclamation, put into effect the year before. He pointed out that for "certain reasons" the Proclamation's benefits "were not applied to the Negroes of Tennessee."[11] He then proceeded, entirely on his own, to announce: "I, Andrew Johnson, do hereby proclaim freedom, full, broad and unconditional, to every man in Tennessee." This amazing statement stimulated great applause. Thus urged on, Johnson launched into an attack on the local aristocrats and concluded:

Colored men of Tennessee! This, too, shall cease! Your wives and daughters shall no longer be dragged into a concubinage . . . to satisfy the brutal lust of slaveholders and overseers! Henceforth the sanctity of God's holy law of marriage shall be respected in your persons, and the great state of Tennessee shall no more give her sanction to your degradation and your shame![12]

The crowd was ecstatic: " 'Thank God,' 'Thank God' came from the lips of a thousand women." Johnson was carried away by their response. Before "this vast throng of colored people," he said, he was "almost induced to wish that, as in the days of old, a Moses might arise who should lead them safely to their promised land of freedom and happiness." At which point someone shouted, "You are our Moses!"—a cry echoed again and again by the crowd.

On taking the presidential oath of office on April 15, 1865, the day after Lincoln was shot, Johnson delivered a brief, calm address, stressing continuity. But the next day, meeting with the Congressional Committee on the Conduct of the War, he responded to Senator Ben Wade's comment—"Johnson, we have faith in you. By the gods, there will be no trouble now in running the government"—with a sentiment he had earlier expressed in various speeches, one which would completely mislead the Radicals as to Johnson's intentions: "I hold that robbery is a crime, rape is a crime; murder is a crime; treason is a crime and must be punished. Treason must be made infamous, and traitors must be impoverished." He repeated these phrases on April 18 and 21, in nearly the same words, to delegations from Illinois and Indiana—on both occasions as an "impromptu response" to expressions of support. Johnson was misunderstood, as he was at other times, because he made ringing general statements subject to opposing interpretations.

By December 2, 1865, his relations with the Radicals had deteriorated, and his patience with Senator Sumner had given out in an interview marked by Johnson's "caustic" questions.

On December 5, Johnson's son Robert read to the new Congress the President's message, composed by the historian and writer

George Bancroft. Johnson had sent Bancroft only two suggestions: passages from Thomas Jefferson's inaugural and from a speech by Charles James Fox. The result was a "lofty," "cogent," and "restrained" message, generally well received. On December 18, he sent another report, calmly advising a reconstruction policy less stringent than that of Thaddeus Stevens. He discussed dispassionately with the Cabinet his veto of the Freedman's Bill in February 1866, an event which created a national sensation and clearly divided Johnson's supporters from the Radicals.

Three days later, on Washington's Birthday, a crowd of well-wishers who had been celebrating Johnson's veto at a Washington theater came to the White House and called for the President to greet them. Earlier in the day, friends had urged him not to speak, and Johnson had replied: "I have not thought of making a speech, and I shan't make one. If my friends come to see me, I shall thank them, and that's all." But he gave in at last to the crowd's importuning, climbed onto a low wall, and, as the day darkened, delivered a diatribe by the light of a guttering candle. When he referred indefinitely to leaders opposed to the Union, a voice called out— "Give us the names." Johnson responded:

A gentleman calls for their names. Well, suppose I should give them. . . . *I say Thaddeus Stevens of Pennsylvania* (tremendous applause)—*I say Charles Sumner* (great applause)—*I say Wendell Phillips and others of the same stripe are among them.* . . . Some gentleman in the crowd says, "Give it to Forney." I have only just to say: That *I do not waste my ammunition upon dead ducks* (Laughter and applause).[13]

Johnson went on and on, reiterating for an hour and ten minutes the old themes of his personal life history, the false accusations against him, and his similarity to Christ. Johnson asked:

Are those who want to destroy our institutions not satisfied with one martyr? . . . If my blood is to be shed because I vindicate the Union . . . let an altar of the Union be erected, and then if necessary lay me upon it, and the blood that now animates my frame shall be poured out in a last libation as a tribute to the Union; and let the opponents of this government remember that when it is poured out the blood of the martyr will be the seed of the church.[14]

Several weeks later Thaddeus Stevens entertained the Senate by mockingly denying that this speech had ever been made. The affair "gave rise to a wave of wonder and dismay" throughout the country.

The suspicions that the President was a drunkard were revived. The hands of Thaddeus Stevens and the other Radicals in Con-

gress were strengthened. Senator John Sherman, who tried vali-
antly to patch up relations between Johnson and the Congress,
deeply regretted the Washington's Birthday speech: "I think there
is no true friend of Andrew Johnson who would not be willing to
wipe that speech from the pages of history." On April 18, 1866,
Johnson repeated this performance at a soldiers' and sailors' sere-
nade, in a speech that "resembled the other in all particulars, with
the possible exception that this time the personal note, the sense of
persecution, was even less controlled than before."

President Johnson's disastrous rhetoric reached its culmination
in his famous "Swing Around the Circle" in August and September, 1866. Convinced that he could win the people if only he
could address enough of them in person, Johnson was repeatedly
drawn by a crowd's reaction to extreme flights of vituperation.
Apparently unmindful that his speeches were being reported by the
press throughout the nation, the President followed the same
course time and again, first denying he would make a speech,
then delivering a harangue full of blood and religion, and ending
by leaving "the Constitution and the Union of these States in your
hands." At St. Louis on September 8, 1866, he complained that he
had been called a Judas.

Judas Iscariot! Judas! There was a Judas once, one of the twelve apostles.
Oh yes; the twelve apostles had a Christ. . . . The twelve apostles had a
Christ, and he could never have had a Judas unless he had had twelve
apostles. If I have played the Judas, who has been my Christ that I
have played Judas with? Was it Thad Stevens? Was it Wendell Phillips?
Was it Charles Sumner?[15]

In a nineteen-day tour, during which he traveled some two thousand miles and delivered eleven major and twenty-two minor
speeches, Johnson was repeatedly harassed by hecklers and wildly
enthusiastic supporters, both stimulating his angry rhetoric. As an
observer recalled: "Whenever cheers on the route would be proposed for Congress, he would stop and argue the case between himself and Congress. . . . It is mortifying to see a man occupying the
lofty position of President of the United States descend from that
position and join issue with those who are dragging their garments
in the muddy gutters of vituperation."

Again and again, Johnson's friends warned him against extemporaneous speaking. Senator Doolittle of Wisconsin wrote to say:

I hope you will not allow the excitement of the moment to draw from
you any extemporaneous speeches. You are followed by the reporters of

a hundred presses who do nothing but misrepresent. I would say nothing which had not been most carefully prepared, beyond a simple acknowledgment for their cordial reception. Our enemies, your enemies, have never been able to get any advantage from anything you ever wrote. But what you have said extemporaneously in answer to some questions has given them a handle to use against us.[16]

When Gideon Welles advised him similarly, "President Johnson always heard my brief suggestions quietly, but manifestly thought I did not know his power as a speaker." Repeatedly, he tried to resist giving speeches, but then gave in and delivered another highly emotional diatribe. As Johnson himself put it in a speech on the "Swing": "I tell you, my countrymen, that though the power of hell, death, and Stevens . . . combined, there is no power that can control me save you . . . and the God that spoke me into existence. . . . I have been drawn into this long speech, while I intended simply to make acknowledgments for the cordial welcome."

There can be no doubt that Johnson's speaking style had important effects on his presidential power, although it was only one of many elements in that equation. As McKitrick sums up the effect of the "Swing Around the Circle":

It is probably fair to say that few truly confirmed Johnson partisans were likely to have changed their minds as a result of it, dignity or no dignity. Yet the problem for Johnson was not simply that of keeping what following he had, but also of persuading large numbers of not yet fully hardened Unionists to make the decision of deserting to him. Not only did the tour fail in this function for the doubtfuls; but for great numbers of those that remained, it seemed to have provided the perfect excuse to throw away all lingering reservations and to do what they were already on the point of doing—return to the Republican fold for good. It was then that they could insist, while having no more use for Thad Stevens than ever, that they could not support a man who had so debased the dignity of the presidency as had Andrew Johnson.[17]

At his impeachment in early 1868, the first nine articles referred to his supposed violations of the Tenure of Office Act (which severely restricted the power of the President to control his cabinet) and the tenth accused him of making "scandalous harangues." Clearly the man's reputation had undermined the President's authority, and his performances on the stump had contributed heavily to that decline. He left the Presidency to return to Tennessee for another speaking tour, to devote "the remainder of his life to a vindication of his character and that of his State." Despite the disastrous effects of his impromptu speeches, he intended to "indulge in no set speeches, but [to] have a few simple conversations with the people here and there." He toured Tennessee delivering unrehearsed speeches to large crowds. He was defeated for the Senate in 1869, but returned there in 1875. Johnson died on July 31 of that year. He is buried in Greeneville, Tennessee, his body wrapped in an American flag and his head resting on his copy of the Constitution.

The Rhetorical Emphasis

Words can trap thought, and speech can subvert action. Johnson's words—indeed, his way of saying words—came close to doing what the Civil War did not do: altering the fundamental structure of the American Presidency. His rhetoric was clearly patterned, and he exhibited a strong consistency of style which can be discerned in the midst of the many inconsistencies of policy. The examples refer to Johnson and rhetoric, but the applicable analytic distinctions have more general significance to Presidents and their styles.

From the full repertoire of presidential roles, Johnson selected speaking and detailed office work as channels for his immense emotional force. We cannot imagine him operating as his namesake of a century later does, devoting endless hours to negotiation in search of consensus. Johnson spent himself in work and words. Sometimes he could give a calm address; most of his speeches in the Senate, for example, were reasoned arguments, more like a lawyer's brief than a stump harangue. But as his performance on the Swing Around the Circle made clear, he repeatedly—almost uniformly—burst forth in fiery rhetoric whenever he faced a crowd of partisans. Had he learned from the reactions to his inaugural disaster to rely only on written speeches, his reputation probably could have been salvaged. But he never learned that lesson. Again and again, he repeated the same performance, illustrating how a particular strategy can become a permanent feature of presidential style. His friends implored him to restrain himself; his enemies gave him unmistakable evidence that he could only harm himself by continuing. Johnson recognized the problem and repeatedly resolved to change. The impulsive character of his blurted pronouncements testifies to the compulsive element in his rhetoric.

Johnson had an exaggerated faith in the efficacy of his rhetoric. Although he "knew" or saw the destructive effects of his speeches, he believed that he had extraordinary power as a speaker. He felt that he would succeed if only he could speak his heart to those on whom his power depended. In a sense, he was right: Success in terms of audience responsiveness, success in the immediate environment, was often his. He won applause and (perhaps equally important to him) challenge from the crowds. He would not or could not, however, make a balanced assessment of his impact as a speaker. Even as he was being impeached, in part because of his wild speeches, he had to be restrained from addressing the Senate. At the extreme, he shows how a political leader may come to believe that he has a magic strategy, a way of acting that is not subject to the ordinary rules of political evaluation, one that is bound to work if rightly performed.

Johnson was wild on the stump, but subdued in the office; he, like Moses, called for action, but was beset by the vice of procrastination; he was generous and patient with Stanton and Sumner in person, but damned them in his speeches. These contradictions demand explanation. Johnson's obvious feelings of elation in the exercise of rhetoric, his reiteration of personal history and status, and the highly symbolic language he used—all point to the expressive, tension-releasing importance he found in speaking.

If one proposed to explain Andrew Johnson's particular rhetorical style, many other significant elements could be noted even at this descriptive level. The major themes of his speeches, his rhetorical reactions to contemporary political conflicts, and the relations between the symbols and values he expressed and those of the particular historical-cultural environment of the 1860's could be analyzed. But I am concerned here not with the flesh and blood of individual political psychology, but rather with the extent to which a rhetorical specialist like Johnson may share a skeletal structure with other Presidents who emphasize their own strategies. For example, Woodrow Wilson trusted that he could personally persuade the American people to adopt his version of the League of Nations; Herbert Hoover demonstrated a strange disparity between private works and public words; and Calvin Coolidge combined dinner-party acerbity, good-natured banter with reporters, and the preaching of moralistic platitudes over the radio.

The Springs of Political Energy: Motives and the Self

Intense political activity may represent either compensation for low self-esteem, usually resulting from severe deprivations in early

379

life, or a specialized extension of high self-esteem, but seldom does it represent an ordinary or normal adaptation to one's culture.[18] In analyzing the development of a distinctive style that emerges in the adult identity crisis, the style's genesis is of less interest than are its structural and dynamic properties at a particular critical period. In order to understand the background against which the distinctive style emerged and to estimate the degree to which the style was compensatory or extensive, however, one must first trace the deeper and older dimensions of personality.

This is not difficult to do in Johnson's case. He reached late adolescence with a long heritage of deprivations and assaults on the self, and no clear success other than success in survival. His father, a genial handy man at a Raleigh, North Carolina, tavern, died when Andrew Jackson Johnson (named after General Jackson) was three, leaving the family destitute and completely dependent on the mother's drudgery in washing and sewing. The Johnsons were "mudsills," landless poor whites, in constant contact with the privileged guests at the tavern. His mother, an ineffectual woman nicknamed "Aunt Polly," later took up with a ne'er-do-well drifter; Andrew had to care for both of them throughout his late teens. At the age of fourteen, just at the time when noise and movement and a certain graceful clumsiness are natural, he was bound as an apprentice tailor, made to sit quietly and be still, and thrown prematurely into adulthood and enforced concentration. At sixteen, this "exceedingly restless" and "wild, harum-scarum boy" ran away from home and work for about a year to escape prosecution for stoning the house of some local girls. The tailor offered a reward for his arrest and return. Wandering to South Carolina, he fell in love with a Sarah Word, but his suit was rejected. On his return home, the tailor refused to take him back, and Johnson began, at sixteen, a two-year trek, wandering through western North Carolina and eastern Tennessee looking for work, with his mother and impecunious "stepfather" in tow. When Andrew was eighteen, the family finally settled in Greeneville, Tennessee.

Childhood had left him hurt and nearly helpless, but he had a skill—tailoring—which would sustain him while he found himself. Undoubtedly Johnson's lifelong detestation of aristocrats, his championing of the Homestead Bill, his extreme independence, and many other themes in his adult personality can be traced to these early years. But the scant evidence available can be interpreted with fair confidence in a simpler and more general way. The pattern is one of severe deprivation, which roused in Johnson strong needs for enhancing self-esteem. While it is difficult to explain precisely why and how this energizing force was channeled into a distinctively rhetorical style, the force was clearly there to be channeled.

The School of Life: What Johnson Learned

Andrew Johnson had no formal schooling, but from an early age (perhaps ten) he hung around the local tailor shop and listened to what went on there. To palliate the tedium, the tailors hired someone to read aloud to them. They worked in silence, listening to the spoken word. Later Andy was apprenticed: "Many hours a day, shut out from fresh air, crouched down over a needle and thread, deprived of the joys of childhood, the lad bent to his tasks; the inside of a schoolhouse he never saw."

His mother could not read nor write. The foreman in the tailor shop later recalled teaching the boy how to read, but most probably Andy devoted little, if any, time to reading in his early teens, particularly in comparison with the long hours spent listening to the tailor's reader. Thus, for Johnson, words came late and in the spoken form. The newspapers, possibly some novels and poems, but particularly political speeches were read. A special favorite of Andy's was a volume of the orations by British statesmen.[19] In somewhat overdrawn terms, L. P. Stryker recounts the effect of the reading of these speeches:

To Johnson it was like a torch to tinder. It lighted in his soul the fire of high resolve. . . . Painfully and slowly from these classics of the forensic art he learned to spell and to read. A new and undiscovered country lay before him. Cross-legged, he plied with his fingers his busy tailor's needle, while his mind, white hot with a new hope, was far away within the English Parliament. And at night he found and pursued the company of books and stayed with them until, worn down from the long day's toil, he fell asleep.[20]

Or as his contemporary biographer John Savage put it: "This volume [of orations] molded into form and inspired into suitable action the elements of his mental character, and thus laid the foundation of his fame and fortune"; in hearing the speeches, "his own thoughts struggling through took form and color from their influence." Johnson told Savage that his favorite speeches were those of Pitt and Fox, both vehement orators and champions of democracy, whose words—thick with wit and studied insult, and aggressive in tone—were meant to wilt the opposition.

Johnson's running away and subsequent wandering interrupted his rhetorical education, though he kept the book of speeches until his library was destroyed in the Civil War. In Greeneville, his young wife Eliza, whom he married in 1827 when he was nineteen, taught him to write and read to him in the tailor shop, again a learning experience in a context of high emotional involvement. Johnson borrowed books from the few Greeneville collections and began to attend the Polemic Society, a debating group, at Greeneville College. He may also have read a number of books from the college library, a collection of three thousand volumes which "came chiefly from the private libraries of the Mathers, Jonathan Edwards and other New England theologians of the day" and was composed "mainly [of] volumes of sermons and theological discussions."

Every week he walked four miles each way to the college. Memories of his participation, mostly gathered much later, vary from references to his "natural talent for oratory" to his being "a very timid speaker, afraid of his own voice." Sometime in 1829, he was part of a separately organized debating society of Greeneville youth.

Students from the local colleges habitually gathered at his tailor shop during this period, because, as one of them remembered: "One lived here whom we know outside of school, and made us welcome; one who would amuse us by his social good nature, one who took more than ordinary interest in catering to our pleasure." He and Eliza lived in the back room—the only other one—and the students and other casual visitors sat around in the front room while he worked. In 1831 he moved the family, now Eliza and their two boys, into a new house and purchased a separate tailor shop. He hired a schoolboy to read, "not the novels of Jane Austen and Maria Edgeworth, but Eliot's debates, Jefferson's messages, and over and over again the Constitution of the United States."

Johnson's biographers make much of his earliest political ventures, but these were probably little more than extensions of his role as owner and operator of a convenient gathering place for townsmen and students interested in politics. It is not clear that he "organized" the Greeneville debating group, except by providing a place for it to meet, or that he was the leading light in forming a "Worker's Party" in town. He was first elected alderman in 1829.

The ticket of nominees was put together on the Saturday night before the election on Monday. Johnson's name appeared first on the ballot, but despite this favored position he received the lowest vote of the seven elected—eighteen votes, as compared to thirty-one for the front-runner. Johnson was elected alderman again the next year and was mayor for the following three years. In 1832 the county appointed him a trustee of the Rhea Academy.

These early political experiences did not represent a marked deviation from Johnson's regular round of life. The duties of alderman and mayor could not have been onerous in a town of about seven hundred people whose electorate was unable to muster more than thirty-one votes for the leading aldermanic candidate. The idea that he conducted a hard campaign for alderman against the town aristocrats is hardly believable—surely most of them were in church on the intervening Sunday before his first election. The flavor of Johnson's participation is probably best caught by one of the young men of Greeneville, who later recalled that despite the boisterousness of his visitors in the tailor shop:

Andy neither lost his temper nor suspended his twofold employment of reading and sewing. The moment the needle passed through the cloth, his eye would return to the book, and anon to the needle again; and so, enter when you would, it was ever the same determined read and sew, and sew and read. His sober industry and intelligence won the favor of the grave and sedate, and his genial tolerance of the jovial groups which frequented his shop secured him unbounded popularity with the young men of the place.[21]

In other words, Johnson let them use his shop, did not interfere with them, and out of gratitude and affection they put him up for office and elected him. Like his father, Andrew was tolerant; unlike his stepfather, he applied himself with extraordinary diligence to his work. His friends were men of his own class who gathered around him mainly for reasons other than his friendship. There is no clear evidence that Johnson was an active leader of the tailor-shop caucus. Johnson at this point was a localist, a figure well known to the Greeneville working class, a businessman whose occupation naturally brought him into the circle of the town's political actors and talkers. In 1834, probably because he was mayor and a trustee of Rhea Academy, he joined in the call for a new Tennessee constitution, but whether his participation went beyond a signature is uncertain. In the following year, Johnson's horizons underwent a radical expansion.

The Rehearsal: Gathering Resources

Johnson's childhood left him with a need to cure the pain of deprivation and with a way of sustaining himself until he found the right medicine. In many cases, men who become Presidents have gone through what Erik Erikson calls a moratorium, "a span of time after they have ceased being children, but before their deeds and works count toward a future identity." In retrospect, such a period may be seen as a preparation for the full use of an important political strategy, a free rehearsal—free in the sense of not being counted at the time in the calculus of success. The rehearsal is a learning time, but much of the learning is latent, even playful, and its significance may not be evident until much later. Learning in such a rehearsal period may be passive or active; usually it is both. The typical pattern may begin with the passive collection of images or impressions, often at the periphery of attention, and progress slowly through a series of apparently unrelated experiments in action. Some of the features of this process in Johnson's life have wider applications.

In many cases, the *timing* or phasing of learning in relation to a normal set of life stages is important. For example, each of the rhetorically peculiar Presidents previously mentioned was slow to catch on to the written word. Wilson could not read well until he was eleven; Coolidge failed his first set of entrance examinations at Amherst; Hoover was unable to pass his English courses at Stanford. Such retardation may be only one aspect of a more general phenomenon: the special importance of out-of-phase learning for the development of distinctive strategies. Perhaps learning that comes "too early," as well as learning that comes "too late," acquires a particular significance because it offers a way of resolving conflicts before they have become severe or after their severity has accumulated to a disproportionate degree. In any case, learning appropriate to the grammar-school age may take on immense personal importance if postponed until adolescence, when all the emotional conflicts of the earliest years come back again. Most generally, one would want to know whether a period of intensive learning relevant to strategy distinctiveness occurred, in what period of life it took place, and what major conflicts accompanied this learning. Johnson first heard great oratory while passively immobilized on his tailor's table; he first began to read with one of the few kind adults he knew as tutor; he first learned to write from his new bride; and he first began to speak in the need-supplying society of younger friends. At each stage, the *learning* took place *in an atmosphere of emotional intensity*, during which Johnson was working on some fundamental problems of his own.

Similarly, the *sequence* of learning may shape distinctive strategies, particularly in terms of the form of earliest exposure. Johnson began with the spoken word. He heard much oratory *before* he could read; messages came to him in an oral medium *first* and then in writings about speeches. Early lessons in the strategies of action set a context into which subsequent lessons must fit. Sequence is also important in understanding how the learner shapes a cumulative development from a stream of individual lessons.[22] For Johnson, the talent for oratory grew step by step, in large part because of a series of lucky connections.

Johnson received a double introduction to oratory: He heard it, and it was about speeches. The *character* of the material learned obviously influences the development of skills relevant to strategy, although there is rarely a simple correspondence between what is purveyed and what is perceived and retained. The character of the material is a variable in learning many different kinds of skills— from bargaining to dominating—but it has a special significance in rhetoric, because the word form allows so many different types of representations. For Johnson, the curriculum was first the aggressive oratory of the parliamentarians and then the fiery Biblicism of New England divines. In neither case did the material itself have much to do with Tennessee in the mid-nineteenth century, but Johnson later found that he could draw on it for many a speech. In tracing the roots of a rhetorical style, one wants to keep an eye out for the man more interested in speeches than in facts, more imitative of styles than insightful of content.

Johnson as President has frequently been described as a scholar rather than a doer, a theorist rather than a political operator. The *degree of abstraction* of learned material—in the sense of its direct applicability in the immediate environment—may be an important factor here. The historical movement of Johnson's intellective process, insofar as his rhetorical development is concerned, was from far away (England and God) to near at hand (Jackson and Tennessee). Abstract thought, particularly in a context of passive reception and no responsibility for consequences, is freely available for need-fulfilling purposes and for all varieties of vicarious experimentation in fantasy. Strong emotional linkages can develop in such a context precisely because the matter is removed from the restraints of compromise and calculation inherent in practical affairs. Johnson's school was in this sense a totally permissive one: No one would give him a failing mark or an honors grade for what he thought of Pitt and Fox and Jonathan Edwards. Surely a special clue to watch for in tracing the rehearsal for a particular type of political strategy is *the interplay between the abstract and the voluntary in the learning process.*

To the way in which words came to Johnson must be added the way he found to turn them back on the world. In his early teens, his activity was intense, but not in speaking. Slowly the distant and the impersonal had to be linked with the close and the personal in order for what was passively learned to acquire relevance for action. No simple formula can encompass the complexity of those steps, but at least two features are common to this and other cases.

Johnson's active learning of oratory began only after he located in Greeneville, when a particular combination of personal successes and community opportunities made possible his political emergence. Johnson's shop in Greeneville was a place for conversation, for clubhouse talk about the issues of the day. There he heard and began to join in words closely related to the local political situation, to the possibilities and probabilities of organization, action, and achievement by those present. Politics took on a new dimension for him; to Pitt and Fox were added Andrew Jackson and his national enemies (still relatively distant), the local aristocrats and speakers (close but absent), and the leading conversationalists in the room (at hand). He began to see, one supposes, how a person like him might play a part, how the gap between himself-as-auditor and himself-as-orator might be bridged. His early trials in the debating societies, pursued with diligence, gave him a chance to experiment with his voice without committing his future or risking his present. And the nominations, campaigns, and elections in Greeneville, as small steps beyond a secure station, taught him that some form of political life was not impossible for him, that he could perform as acceptably as the others he knew. The linkage here is through persons. The lesson was I *can* learn, *am* learning, *know* how, as well as or better than others do. The mechanisms are *identification with a group in which the strategy is practiced, experimentation without risk,* and *minor gambles in commitment.*

Issues as well as persons provide linkage. Johnson could "remember" when he listened to the tailor-shop conversations about the aristocrats and the other themes of the "Greeneville Democracy" what he had heard before from the young English orators of a previous generation. He could see, or at least feel, the connection between the injustice to his namesake Andrew Jackson in the 1824 election and the thunderings of the New England divines. An ideology of sorts—one that fitted his own history, the myths he had imbibed, and the situation in which he found himself—began to form in his mind. Learning came to encompass a set of ideas in addition to the set of techniques he had started to master. His experience and his anticipations began to take on expressible meanings, made explicit at last in a speech in which he conjured up a path from obscurity and degradation, through effort, to a grand achievement: the joining of Godliness and government. In terms of rhetorical strategy, he had found what to say. In terms of distinctive strategies in general, he exemplified *the significance of rationalization for action and the ways in which available rationalizations can speed or delay cumulative individual development.*[23]

The Man Becomes a Politician

On another Saturday night, in the spring of 1835 when Johnson was twenty-six, he nominated himself for the state legislature. Johnson was there when conversation at Jones's store was interrupted by someone bearing news from a "muster" a few miles away at which Major Matthew Stephenson and Major James Britton had been entered in the race for the Tennessee lower house. Stephenson, from neighboring Washington County, was a Whig who had performed effectively at the constitutional convention the previous year. He was also, by East Tennessee standards at least, an aristocrat, "a wealthy citizen of character and social position." After listening for a while to the discussion of this news, Johnson "sprang from his seat to say: 'I, too, am in the fight.'" Like any other uninvited volunteer, Johnson had only to follow this statement with a formal public announcement to get on the ballot. Several of his friends coached him for his first meeting with Stephenson, to be held in the latter's territory at Boon's Creek in Washington County. Stephenson "was thought to await an easy victory." Johnson's friends researched his political record and otherwise prepared carefully. Stephenson began by expounding various Whig doctrines. Johnson, the "audacious youngster," then "hacked and arraigned" the aristocratic major, challenging his claims for Whiggism in Tennessee. He dealt with several issues and gave a preview of a lifelong theme: "He assured the boys that he was neither a lawyer, a major or a colonel, but a plain man laboring with his hands, for his daily bread, that he knew what they wanted and would carry out their wishes." Johnson was elected by a small margin.

Johnson had thus nominated himself in response to the news that an aristocrat was in the race, had set out to attack his enemy personally, and had found the weapon—spoken words—to succeed. The rehearsal was over; Andrew Johnson had entered a new and much broader arena of action equipped with a strategy for success: in close interpersonal relations (as with the politicos of the tailor shop), restraint; with enemies at a distance (as with the "aristocratic" Major Stephenson), attack. He had found not only the place in which speech could serve his needs for vindication: political oratory; but also the themes which would serve him the rest of his life: self-justification and righteous indignation against the privileged. And he had discovered the language with which to express these themes—that of principles and abstractions and personal allusion. His school had done its work. One can hear in nearly all his speeches the words of the New England divines and Old England parliamentarians, transformed to bear on his cause and reflect his high purposes, particularly in those peculiar diatribes which marred his Presidency.

One other feature of his strategy for success seems to have been critical: his identification with Andrew Jackson. Part of the development of identity is the imitation of models, done with or without awareness. Such models link the person to something beyond himself. Arising from the past, they point the way to the future. The passionless abstract ideal is translated to human form, to an embodiment not so impossible to achieve.

Johnson's very name—Andrew Jackson Johnson—gave him an original connection with a defiant fighter who became President. Jackson's followers felt he had been cheated of the Presidency in 1824, when, despite receiving the largest popular vote, he was defeated after the election was thrown into the House of Representatives. His followers were organizing vigorously in the years leading up to 1828, and Jackson must have been a frequent topic of conversation in Johnson's tailor shop just as he was taking his first political steps. In his maiden speech against Stephenson, Johnson invoked "Old Hickory"; his first speech in Congress was a defense of Andrew Jackson. He helped institute an annual Jackson-Jefferson celebration in Greeneville, ran on a ballot headed with Jackson's picture, and heard again and again almost from the time he began in politics: "You are a second Andrew Jackson"; "You are a man, every inch of you, standing in the shoes of 'Old Hickory' "; or you are "trying to ape Andrew Jackson but cannot make the grade." At least "from 1840 onward, 'Old Hickory' was Andrew Johnson's political pilot, the model of his conduct and the idol of his heart." The roots of the connection with Jackson were personal and local: the name and the particular significance Jackson had for politics in East Tennessee just as Johnson was emerging to the state arena. The idol who was there at one's birth and reappears as one is forging an identity has an immense advantage over competing symbols.

Andrew Jackson was in many ways different from Andrew Johnson. As one sympathetic account says: "Externally, of course, no two men were more unlike, Jackson being a rollicking fellow, fond of horseracing and cockfighting, and more fond of sports than books; Johnson, caring nothing for sports, too serious-minded, and always plugging away at some problem of government." But these were not the features Johnson's early companions and supporters stressed when they constantly reiterated the Jackson-Johnson similarities. Friends would point out: "They came from the same stock; they had both hewed their fortunes from the rough rock of adversity; both were of the people and knew their hopes and fears; both were men of physical as well as intellectual courage; both hated sham and both were passionate lovers of the Union." The identification persisted; as President, Johnson refused to allow Jackson's desk to be moved, despite its inconvenient location. "I love the memory of General Jackson," he said. "Whatever was Old Hickory's I revere."

The Break-out: Confluence of Motives, Resources, and Opportunities

Andrew Johnson's campaign against Major Stephenson seems to mark a turning point in his life. At that time, he brought together the motives from his childhood, the skills from his period of rehearsal, and the political opportunities in the close environment to form a distinctive political strategy that would serve him for the rest of his life. His emergence does not have the same clarity and concentration of development that we find in some other cases.[24] But if one had been able to observe Johnson closely in 1835, had analyzed his life situation in relation to his history with careful attention to the elements of presidential leadership style, at least the following generalizable elements would have emerged.

Perhaps the most important feature of the break-out phase is the marked *infusion of confidence*. Deprivation may so damage self-esteem that success is incapable of rescuing it, or strategies of adaptation developed to meet extreme emergencies of deprivation may be fixed too early to be much affected by later experience. In Johnson's case, however, as in many others, the break-out period was one in which the achievement of success coincided with the culmination of the development of skill and the community's readiness to respond in such a way as to fix a political style.

As is evident from the account of Johnson's success in Greeneville, his fortunes changed rapidly for the better, contrasting markedly with his situation of only a few years before. This picture is efficiently clarified in the following table based on Harold D. Lasswell's well-known formulation of values,[25] noting the degree and character of Johnson's attainment in each of his pre-Greeneville years and at the time of his candidacy for the state legislature.

The *rapid pace* of these changes, their *simultaneous* development, and particularly the *contrast* with his previous fortunes made this period a special time of growth and increasing self-esteem such as Johnson had never known. Aside from some primitive learning (on which he could build) and his skill at his trade (which he could perfect and which taught him that he could develop a skill), he brought to early adulthood very little. Within a few years, he had attained success and adopted a style. The two are closely related: To discover the critical period of commitment to a set of distinctive strategies, one must watch for massive increases in supplies of confidence.

Johnson's breakthrough period shows two other features of particular significance for distinctive political strategies: a special kind of relatedness to a close group and a sudden, radical expansion of the politician's "field of power."[26] Johnson, like others with pronounced emotional conflicts, probably experienced strong tendencies to withdraw from society, to escape into a kinder internal world. Such a person may find communication difficult and communion impossible, because he has meanings a common language cannot express and feelings he can hardly formulate, much less

Changes in Value Attainments in Johnson's Critical Period

Value	Pre-Greeneville (1808-26)	At time of candidacy for state legislature (1835)
Power	None except in family	Public official
Wealth	Extreme poverty	Moderate means
Enlightenment	No formal schooling; heard oratory and learned reading late	Much learning; Academy official
Skill	Dependent on single skill: tailoring	Expert in his trade; developing speaking skill
Respect	Very low; a homeless "mud-sill"	Host to students; nominations and elections
Well-Being	Fatherless; ineffective mother; much discomfort and insecurity	Stable family; own home; relative ease and happiness
Affection	No male or female friends among peers; rejected by home-town adults	Wife, children; surrounded by friendly group
Rectitude	Runaway lawbreaker; no religious life	Decent achievement; developing ideology; attached to religious colleges

share. But thrown, by occupational or other necessity, into continual company, a person cannot avoid talk and may slowly learn, as Johnson did, to be *at once one with and slightly apart from a band of brothers.* This closeness can meet important needs. People learn to rate themselves in part by the ways others react to them, and one such reaction is simply acceptance as a member of the group. Young people, like old people, come together at times not to accomplish anything in particular or even to talk, but simply by their physical togetherness to "say" to one another "we are not alone." When much talk—talk about politics, in particular—is added to this simple juxtaposition, the context is arranged for powerful combinations of affection, experiments in expression, and linkage to broader social arenas. Johnson was surrounded with friends—representing the local working class, intelligentsia, and out-of-office politicians—whose whole entertainment was conversation.

There was in Johnson's case, again as in many others, a *relatively radical expansion of his "field of power"* at the time he adopted a distinctive strategy. His focus of attention shifted from a narrow to a broad arena of action. The home-town politician considering a relatively big-time candidacy thus comes to see his present place in a new perspective. Johnson's candidacy for the state legislature represented to him a significant leap beyond the arena of power he had mastered. Yesterday's inadvertently accumulated resources suddenly appeared in a new and larger context.

The Explanation of Presidential Styles

Johnson's success was incomplete; no amount of success could fully compensate for the needs left from his traumatic childhood. For the rest of his life, he would struggle to make up for what he had suffered. His habit of restraint at work and at close quarters with others continued to serve as a maintenance technique, a way of surviving a chaotic future. But oratory offered him much more: power to control a crowd and, at last, a country; respect, even from the aristocrats; rectitude, as vindication; affection, in the applause; pleasure in the effective use of skill; well-being, in that calm of the soul which follows speaking his mind and heart. And in a more complex and indirect way, oratory gave Andrew Johnson a way of setting the world at odds, of putting the others in their place and thus confirming his own place of defeat and failure.

Johnson's distinctive political style, formed in late adolescence and early adulthood, presaged his style in the Presidency. Much intervened between this early coalescing of disparate elements into a structured identity and the exercise of his presidential style. The backings and fillings of his career on the way to the nation's highest office present a confused picture, in contrast to the clear connections between these two widely separated life stages. Any moderately attentive person could have predicted, in 1865, that Johnson would be an outsider, that he would not be socially lionized by the Washington elite, that he would have difficulty coping with the violent political forces in that age of hate and sentimentality. But how would he react to these challenges? How might his ways of approaching and dealing with them have been foreseen?

I have suggested one analytic system for tracing the roots of presidential style. There are many uncertainties in it; one would especially want to see it applied to more Presidents, including some not yet elected. But in most biographical accounts, the period during which an adult identity was forged can be readily isolated, particularly when one is sensitive to marked infusions of confidence, coming fast, simultaneously, and in contrast to a deprived past; to a special kind of relationship to a close and supportive group life; and to a relatively sudden expansion of the "field of power." Once located, this period can be surveyed in the light of a short list of requirements for a presidential role. Those particularly emphasized can be traced back into the learning process, viewed as a rehearsal for the emergence of the distinctive style. Together with a general assessment of self-evaluation gathered from accounts of early life, these explorations may reveal, in clearer form than they would in later adulthood, the fundamental shape of a potential President's strategies for adapting to the challenges he will confront.

When a man is chosen to lead a great nation, he stands in a uniquely high and lonely place, one not much like the steps he has recently been climbing. But in his memory is another time when he came out of relative smallness into relative greatness. Then he had tried a style, and it worked. What would be more natural than for him to feel that it might work again?[27]

REFERENCES

1. This is not to imply that the record is any better in other political contexts; but we ought to do better in the United States, where the assumption of power is at a definite time and for a definite period *via* a well-defined system, than in situations where the leader himself defines anew—even creates—the office. I am indebted to Dankwart Rustow for this point.

2. I have tried to show a way of using these distinctions in *The Lawmakers: Recruitment and Adaptation to Legislative Life* (New Haven, 1965).

3. See my "Classifying and Predicting Presidential Styles: Two 'Weak' Presidents," *Journal of Social Issues* (forthcoming).

4. Lloyd Paul Stryker, *Andrew Johnson, A Study in Courage* (New York, 1930), pp. 313-14.

5. *Ibid.*, pp. 333-34. For bibliographic essays showing how Johnson fared with successive waves of historians, see Willard Hays, "Andrew Johnson's Reputation." *East Tennessee Historical Society Publications*, Nos. 31-32 (1959); Carmen Anthony Nataro, "History of the Biographic Treatment of Andrew Johnson in the Twentieth Century," *Tennessee Historical Quarterly*, Vol. 24, No. 2 (1965); Albert Castel, "Andrew Johnson: His Historiographical Rise and Fall," *Mid-America*, Vol. 45, No. 3 (1963).

For a sense of the poverty of basic documentation on Johnson's early years, see Leroy P. Graf and Ralph W. Haskins (eds.), *The Papers of Andrew Johnson, Vol. 1, 1822-1851* (Knoxville, Tenn., 1967).

6. It was at this point that Johnson began giving interviews to friendly reporters, defending himself vigorously against the impeachment charges. See Milton Lomask, *Andrew Johnson: President on Trial* (New York, 1960), pp. 307-10.

7. For detailed accounts of this event, see Lomask, *Andrew Johnson: President on Trial*, pp. 28 ff; Stryker, *Andrew Johnson, A Study in Courage*, pp. 166 ff; Eric L. McKitrick, *Andrew Johnson and Reconstruction* (Chicago, 1960), pp. 135-36; George F. Milton, *The Age of Hate, Andrew Johnson and the Radicals* (New York, 1930), Ch. 8; Robert Winston, *Andrew Johnson, Plebeian and Patriot* (New York, 1928), pp. 264-66; Brazilla Carroll Reece, *The Courageous Commoner: A Biography of Andrew Johnson* (Charleston, 1962), pp. 51-52; Benjamin C. Truman, "Anecdotes of Andrew Johnson," *The Century Magazine*, Vol. 85, p. 435.

8. Quoted in McKitrick, *Andrew Johnson and Reconstruction*, p. 136.

9. The day before inauguration, Johnson had written Stanton "to express my highest regard to you personally, and also thank you sincerely for the uniform kindness which you have been pleased to extend to me personally and officially during my service" as Brigadier General and Military Governor of Tennessee (Milton, *The Age of Hate, Andrew Johnson and the Radicals*, p. 144).

10. *Ibid.*, p. 147.

11. Lomask avers: "It was generally assumed that Johnson himself had asked Lincoln to exempt Tennessee from the proclamation as a means of holding in line the state's pro-Union Whigs, many of whom were slaveowners" (*Andrew Johnson: President on Trial*, pp. 24-25).

12. *Ibid.*

13. McKitrick, *Andrew Johnson and Reconstruction*, p. 294, quoting from the strongly pro-Johnson New York *Herald*. Johnson's words carried the drama of these speeches, even when his manner of speaking was calm. See the recollections of one of his guards, William H. Crook, *Through Five Administrations* (New York, 1907), p. 106. On the other hand, he could ignite platitudes through his style of delivery. See Howard K. Beale, *The Critical Year* (New York, 1930), pp. 362-63. Beale assesses Johnson's 1866 speeches as "disastrous," but attributes his tendency to "talk overmuch of himself" to "an inferiority complex" rather than to "egotism." *Ibid.*, pp. 367, 11.

14. Johnson frequently spoke of himself as being, like Christ, Moses, a martyr: "In imitation of Him of old who died for the preservation of men, I exercised that mercy which I believed to be my duty" (Lomask, *Andrew Johnson: President on Trial*, p. 196). "Caesar had his Brutus, Jesus Christ his Judas, and I've had my Ed Cooper. Get thee behind me,

Satan" (Stryker, *Andrew Johnson, A Study in Courage*, p. 784). And themes of blood are frequent: "If I were disposed to play the orator and deal in declamation tonight, I would imitate one of the ancient tragedies and would take William H. Seward and bring him before you and point you to the hacks and scars upon his person. I would exhibit the bloody garments saturated with gore from his gushing wounds" (*ibid.*, p. 356).

15. McKitrick, *Andrew Johnson and Reconstruction*, p. 432.

16. Stryker, *Andrew Johnson, A Study in Courage*, p. 361. For an account stressing Johnson's "political ineptitude," the effects of his speeches in alienating northern moderates (such as James Russell Lowell, who wrote, "What an anti-Johnson lecturer we have in Johnson!"), and his failure to learn "that the President of the United States cannot afford to be a quarreler," see David Donald, "Why They Impeached Andrew Johnson," *American Heritage*, Vol. 8, No. 1 (December, 1956). For a more sympathetic account stressing the content of and the reactions to Johnson's speeches, see Gregg Phifer's series of articles in the *Tennessee Historical Quarterly*, Vol. 11, Nos. 1-4 (1952).

17. McKitrick, *Andrew Johnson and Reconstruction*, pp. 437-38. Of course, factors other than Johnson's speeches were at work. For broader political interpretations, see David Donald, *The Politics of Reconstruction* (Baton Rouge, 1965); LaWanda and John H. Cox, *Politics, Principle, and Prejudice, 1865-1866* (New York, 1963); Kenneth M. Stampp, *Andrew Johnson and the Failure of the Agrarian Dream* (Oxford, 1962), an inaugural lecture delivered before the University of Oxford on May 18, 1962.

18. Barber, *The Lawmakers . . .*, Ch. 6.

19. Variously reported with the titles *American Speaker, United States Speaker, Columbia Speaker*, Enfield's *Speaker, Standard Speaker*, but without disagreement as to its primarily British content. See Winston, *Andrew Johnson, Plebeian and Patriot*, p. 10; Stryker, *Andrew Johnson, A Study in Courage*, p. 3; John Savage, *The Life and Public Services of Andrew Johnson* (New York, 1865), p. 14. The fifth edition, published in 1818 (Philadelphia: Abraham Small) is titled *The American Speaker; A Selection of Popular, Parliamentary and Forensic Eloquence; Particularly Calculated for the Seminaries in the United States*. The name of the compiler is not given. The preface reads, in part: "Without some proficiency in Oratory, there seems to be an insurmountable barrier to the patriotic aspirations of genius—with it, the road to distinction is obvious. The many Legislative bodies in our Federal form of government, and the diversified character of our Courts, present a suitable field for every grade, from the unfledged effort of the callow young, to the mature, eagle-eyed flight in the face of the God of Day.

"It has been our aim, in making this selection, to endeavor to fire the minds of our young men, by placing in their view some of the brightest examples of Genius: to enable them 'With lips of fire to plead their country's cause!' . . . Although a great part of our selection is of an ardent and glowing character, we would not be suspected of denying the superiority of cool deliberate argument and reasoning—but how often have these failed of their effect, by a neglect of appropriate declamation? How often has truth herself been indebted to a happy appeal to the feelings, for all the impression she has made? . . . We are fully convinced of one truth—that to impress, we must feel—it is this that captivates the heart—without feeling, the electricity of Speech is never felt—with the impression which feeling produces, even ungracefulness is overlooked—and the man lost in the Orator." *Ibid.*, pages iii-v.

20. Stryker, *Andrew Johnson, A Study in Courage*, p. 3.

21. Milton, *The Age of Hate, Andrew Johnson and the Radicals*, p. 74.

22. Fred Greenstein's *Children and Politics* (New Haven, 1965) makes clear the significance of sequence in political learning.

23. An early biographical sketch for *The New York Times*, May 21, 1849, shows how these themes were presaged in his experience in Congress: "Whenever a member drops an expression that may be twisted into disrespect to the people, a want of confidence in their integrity or intelligence, or a hint that there are interests in society other than his which should be cared for, Mr. J. fires up; and, springing to his feet, ten to one he will, by well-put questions, extract something from the speaker either equivalent to a retraction of what has just fallen from his lips, or a bold avowal of principles and opinions tending materially to weaken him with his constituents. . . . Mr. J. will never suffer an interruption. In the course of the six years I have known him in the House, I do not recollect ever to have seen him consent to give way for an interruption. He says—'No, sir; my hour is short enough. If my facts or conclusions are not sound, obtain the floor and disprove them.' . . . Owing to the want of early advantages, of which I have written above, Mr. J. at times slashes his mother-tongue—pronouncing words of many syllables, or of recent foreign derivation, with little regard to rules laid down by Walker or Webster. More or less of his fellow-members will titter and sneer at Mr. J.'s many false anglicisms; yet I have rarely seen it done, save by some one smarting under the point of his oratorial bowie-knife. Though expressed in uncouth phraseology, his views are easily understood; for he talks strong thoughts and carefully culled facts in quick succession. He thrusts his opponents through and through, as with a rusty and jagged weapon, tearing a big hole and leaving something behind to fester and be remembered. Woe be unto the luckless wight who offers him a personal indignity—cast a slur upon him, in debate; for if he has to wait two years for the opportunity, when it *does* come, Mr. J. makes the best use of it. He puts no bridle upon his tongue; yet he is never guilty of a personal disrespect to a fellow-member, or even to the opposite party as a whole. Perhaps I may fairly characterize his efforts as being crushingly slashing and slashingly crushing; for he chops to mince-meat and then grinds to powder the men, measures and principles he may be contending against. He takes and maintains positions, at times, which I can hear no *other* man advocate without writing him

down a demagogue. Yet no one can listen to him without feeling morally sure that the man is speaking without the least regard to the effect of his words upon his own prospects as a public man." Graf and Haskins, *The Papers of Andrew Johnson,* pp. 677-78.

24. One thinks, for example, of the critical events concentrated in Coolidge's junior year at Amherst.

25. For the list of values and an illustration of their use, see Lasswell's *Power and Personality* (New York, 1948), p. 17. Many of Lasswell's insights on political agitation apply to Johnson. See his *Psychopathology and Politics* (New York, 1960), Chs. 6-7.

26. The phrase is Alexander George's. See his forthcoming article in the *Journal of Social Issues.*

27. See also Erik Erikson, *Young Man Luther: A Study in Psychoanalysis and History* (New York, 1962); Alexander L. and Juliette L. George, *Woodrow Wilson and Colonel House* (New York, 1956); James Jones, *Life of Andrew Johnson* (Greeneville, Tenn., 1901); Helen Merell Lynd, *On Shame and the Search for Identity* (New York, 1961).

FRANK E. MANUEL

Newton as Autocrat of Science

AMONG THE many stories that sprang up after Isaac Newton's psychic crisis of September 1693 and set tongues wagging in England and abroad was a rumor that he was dead. Had his life actually been cut off when he was in his early-fifties, the consequences for the long-range development of Western science would not have been overwhelming. The *Principia* had been published in 1687; the calculus, at least in its Leibnizian form, had been known since 1684; and his theory of light, though not in the final version of the *Opticks* (1704), had been communicated to the Royal Society in the seventies. His alchemical papers, interpretations of prophecy, and radical revision of world chronology, though they are respectable, rational texts in the spirit of the age, would not, in the long run, have been missed. And other men would have made the corrections for the later editions of the *Principia* without his supervision. Nor would the loss of Newton's "philosophy" recorded in the sibylline "Queries" to the *Opticks* and the "General Scholium" to the second edition of the *Principia* have left a major gap in the annals of thought.

Newton lived on for about thirty-four years after the encapsulated episode and the mild depression that followed. There was an opinion among some eighteenth- and nineteenth-century scientists, echoed in Lord Keynes's impish address on the tercentenary of Newton's birth, that he was never the same after that black year, that he was sort of gaga. In fact, a transformation in his person did take place, though not in this simple, pejorative sense. His genius for solving mathematical problems with incredible speed as if by sudden illumination was by no means impaired, as the continental scientists learned when they dared to test him. What occurred after his crisis was a dramatic rechanneling of his capacities. To say that an aggressiveness which had once turned inward was allowed to manifest itself outwardly during the last thirty years of his life is an oversimplification of his psychological history; but since it is not my intention to present a full-length portrait in this paper, the crude formula will perhaps suffice.

A royal appointment in 1696 made it possible for Newton to leave the university cell in which he had immured himself for decades, alter his whole mode of life and conduct, and give overt expression to a deep need for the exercise of power and to manipulatory skills which had previously been dormant. The tremendous energy with which he was endowed found new materials to mold in the world of men. A juxtaposition of the first portrait of him by Kneller in 1689 with the late ones by Vanderbank tells at a glance the story of the transformation from a sensitive, melancholy, and rather dreamy scholar clad in black to the bloated, pompous, irascible administrator in rich brocade and velvet. Through the influence of Charles Montague (later Lord Halifax), who had been his student at Trinity, Newton was made Warden (and subsequently Master) of the Mint, and to occupy the post he moved to London. For him the office was no sinecure, though it had been the original intention of his patron to provide one, and Newton spent years on the recoinage and on the organization of a campaign against clippers and counterfeiters, venting his rage in the interrogation of prisoners, wielding powers of life and death over them. Though this magistracy continued to the eve of his death and teaches us much about his character, it is less significant for our present purpose than a second office which he assumed in 1703 and held simultaneously—the presidency of the Royal Society.

The political, social, and religious worlds through which Newton moved over the years were subject to mercurial change, and no shift in his mature life was more abrupt than the passage from Cambridge to London. A fixated man and a Puritan in spirit, from the early Restoration on he had led a monastic life under a rule established by his own harsh censor. When he emerged to participate actively in a war against Papism and the Stuarts, he was from the outset an ardent supporter of the House of Orange, and he remained consistently Whig until his death. But the Whiggery of the turn of the century and the reign of Queen Anne, though it might raise popular tumults and burn pope, cardinals, and Dr. Sacheverell in effigy, was hardly consonant with a mid-seventeenth-century Puritan morality, not with Somers and Halifax at the helm.

The looseness of society in the reign of Queen Anne and the first George perceptibly modified the manner of Isaac Newton, if not the demands of his austere censor. Carried about London in a sedan chair, he grew quite corpulent. As a public figure, he met regularly for business with the corrupt and uninhibited Whig politicians and received foreign noblemen, virtually all of whom were accursed Papists. Newton did not participate in Halifax's orgies, nor was he invited to membership in the Kit-Kat Club. He was more likely to be drawn to the millenarian Prophets of London who swallowed up his young friend Fatio de Duillier than to the witty literary society of Pope, Swift, and Gay. Yet he was no longer ignorant of the ways of the world. In the privacy of his chamber, he remained a devout believer, a man of learning, concentrating more and more on history sacred and profane as the final revelation of the divine intent. His absolute, though secret, unitarianism was known only to a few intimates—to William Whiston, to Hopton Haynes, an assistant at the Mint, to John Locke, perhaps to Fatio— not to the bishops and archbishops of the realm who sought out his company and later left testimonials to his piety. But his style had changed. The break between the public and the private man is now sharp; more than ever he leads a double life.

During one of the annual elections of officers of the Royal Society, John Chamberlayne, a Fellow who was a court official under Queen Anne, wrote Newton surrendering to him his vote for members of the Council and voicing a desire to see him made "Perpetual Dictator" of the Society.[1] This sentiment was shared by many others. Disciples dedicated their books to the "divine Newton," and the man who married his niece, John Conduitt, wrote that if Newton had lived in the ancient world, he would have been deified. Fatio de Duillier, Genevan bourgeois that he was, yearned for an extra hundred thousand *écus* to raise statues and a monument to him, and Edmond Halley proclaimed in Latin verse that no mortal could more nearly approach the gods.[2] Such adulation was more than mere baroque extravagance, for Newton did indeed become the "dictator" of the English scientific establishment, and standing on that solid base, he was apotheosized into the symbol of Western science. With more than a soupçon of envy, Laplace later remarked that since there was only one universe, it could be granted to only one man to discover its fundamental law. When one remains attuned to the religious as well as the scientific meaning of a law in a Christian society, one begins to understand how those of his contemporaries, especially the young ones, who could read the hieroglyphic tablets of his law divinized the new Moses. If the hunger of Newton for recognition could ever be appeased, this was the moment.

A multiplicity of factors contributed to the making of the Newton image—it was not only the work of the later eighteenth-century popularizers of his philosophy. In large measure, it was created by Newton himself during the quarter of a century that he ruled the Royal Society. Longevity can be, as we have observed in contemporary politics, an important element in leadership, and Newton lasted long enough to institutionalize himself and his system. Such duration is not, of course, an unambiguous good. When the founder of a scientific movement lives on for decades after the spark in him has been extinguished, he may harden and even fossilize the system. His spiritual sons grow up in the shadow of an ancient oak and their own capacities are often stunted.

The creation of the headship of science may involve acts akin to the processes of winning political, military, or religious leadership. But while primacy in war, politics, and religious movements has been studied critically ever since the Greeks and the Romans, rising to titular hegemony in science—a more recent phenomenon —has in the nature of things been the subject of relatively little scrutiny. Qualities essential for scientific leadership are not the same in all times and places. The historical situation of Isaac Newton was unique, and in some respects his performance was idiosyncratic. But the later Newton, who is usually only of anecdotal interest, emerges from an examination of his doings as the first of a new type in European history—the great administrator of science. An exploration of this phase of Newton's career suggests analogies and may throw light on a historical subject of wide scope—the changing role of the man of science in Western society.

Scientific truth can speak for itself, but requires an agency through which it may be amplified and diffused. As part of a larger study of the social and psychological forces at play in the creation of the "Newtonian world view," it may be worthwhile to observe the actual practices and instruments with which Newton operated in the scientifically less creative part of his life. His triumph was furthered by a complex of circumstances that did not obtain for either Galileo or Descartes in the previous generation nor for Leibniz who was his contemporary. The grandeur and genius of the Newtonian synthesis are here taken for granted, as is its emotional appeal to a monotheistic culture not yet divested of the religious swaddling clothes that had protected it in its early period. It has been noted often enough that the growth of a commercial society in a centralized state like England and its consequent concern with the products of "mathematicall magick," the affinity between the precise, methodical behavior of the experimental scientist and the comportment of the self-disciplined, puritanical Protestant helped fashion a general social environment in which science could flourish. The interaction of Protestantism, nascent capitalism, and the new philosophy can be recognized without the establishment of mechanical historical relations of cause and effect among them. Even the most refractory English scientists had been able to survive the Civil War: No Bruno had been burned, nor had a Galileo recanted and been sequestered. An organized university system had evolved with professorships in mathematics and astronomy, and no major victims among the scientists had been claimed by the purges of the Commonwealth and early Restoration. Moreover, under the Restoration there was a curious royal court which at least played with science and to which its practitioners had access. The very insularity and provincialism of English scientists provided them with a foundation on which to build a scientific structure, an opportunity denied to those wanderers and exiles, Descartes and Leibniz, without roots in any soil. But when all of the auspicious economic, religious, and social factors are weighed—and there are many more that overdetermine English precedence—it still remains to inquire into the methods pursued by Isaac Newton in attaining a position of leadership in his own country and in the European world, after the heroic age of the founding fathers of the Royal Society had passed, as had the peak of his own creativity. If one descends from the realm of grand generalizations about the relationships of English science and religion, or English science and social structure, a description of how the first scientific "establishment" in the modern world was organized under Newton's governance may be of more than parochial interest. There is little likelihood that Newton deliberately set himself the task of devising a strategy to capture the Royal Society and transform it into his creature. Viewed retrospectively, however, his tactics and maneuvers show an underlying purposiveness and reveal the functioning of an organizational will.

To secure the ascendancy of his philosophical principles and to establish his unquestioned pre-eminence, Newton recruited a group of scientific adherents—younger men of varying degrees of talent—joined in absolute loyalty to his person and his doctrine. There were intrigues among the followers and inevitable ostracisms from the group; but his scientific supremacy was accepted by every one of them. It was a relationship of master and disciples, with all the complexity inherent in that bond. To make the Royal Society a worthy institutional vehicle for the propagation of Newtonian science, over the years he perfected administrative methods to bolster the Society through better housekeeping and closer supervision of its operations. Its unique personality was affirmed through a physical structure, a new building all its own. In the hope of insuring continuity in its scientific work, Newton even drafted a scheme for the introduction of an order of paid pensioners. He was also responsible for weaving a sacred and aristocratic aura around science through the development of ceremonials.

Newton's personal ties with the Whig politicians made him the ideal figure to work out a pattern for the role of science in a loose parliamentary regime, a pattern whose traces have not completely disappeared even in recent years. Science and government came to use and promote each other, but, in contrast with some continental models, English science retained a large measure of autonomy.

Finally, since no major creation is achieved without negation, Newton waged fierce battles to consolidate his scientific empire and destroy competitive or insubordinate rivals both within and outside the Royal Society. The bitter quarrels with the English Royal Astronomer Flamsteed and with the cosmopolitan philosopher Leibniz, which punctuated the first decade of his presidency and in which he was spectacularly victorious, forcefully demonstrated his authority within the English establishment and in the international scientific world. In the presentation that follows, the acts described are representative rather than comprehensive; it is of course possible here only to set forth the lines of his policy and to show its wholeness.

The Gathering of the Followers

For the first half century of its existence, the Royal Society had been a rather loose fellowship. Its central figures tended to be the secretaries, who served as a clearinghouse for scientific correspondence. The presidency was largely an honorific office, and though the chair was occasionally occupied by scientists, many of the incumbents were aristocrats and politicians, mere amateurs of science who often failed to attend either the meetings of the Council or the general sessions at which experiments were presented and papers discussed. After the fifteen-year tenure of William, Lord Viscount Brouncker, from 1662 to 1677, there followed a succession of ten presidents, each of whom occupied the office for only a few years. They were intelligent men like Pepys, Montague, and Somers, but with no pretensions to science. No one man dominated the institution until Newton took control. (If any single figure had been outstanding, it was Robert Hooke, who had been a mainstay of the Society for forty years, but by the 1690's he was ailing in body and spirit.)

Though Newton was a member of the Council in 1697-98 and 1699-1700, he did not participate too frequently in the administration of the Society until he had a clear field, and he would not accept the presidency so long as his old enemy Robert Hooke was alive. From his earliest childhood, he feared and shunned competition. He either dominated a situation totally or refused to play. Immediately upon Hooke's death, however, Newton took over, and he reigned for the rest of his life. Isaac Newton had a way of recasting any office he occupied in his own image. During his years as president, he changed the character of the Royal Society, as he did the Mint's, and shed upon it the luster of his own pre-eminence in the world of science. "The very title was justly rever'd, both at home and abroad. . . . Infinite were the encomiums they received from foreign countrys; in a great measure owing to the superior capacity and unbounded merit of so illustrious a president," wrote one of the younger Fellows, Dr. William Stukeley.[3]

When Newton assumed the presidency in 1703, at the age of sixty, his genius was universally recognized though his great work was understood by few men and the continental reception of the *Principia* did not measure up to the admiration of the English. Virtually the whole generation of the Society's founding fathers and the second generation to which Newton belonged had died. Of the original group, only Christopher Wren was still alive (he died in 1723 at the age of ninety-one), and he continued to grace committees with his venerable presence—but he was no longer very active. Of Newton's contemporaries there remained Flamsteed and Francis Aston—the latter a compliant agent of no particular distinction; the former, the stiff-necked Royal Astronomer.

the only major internal threat to Newton's authority. Thus sheer longevity, combined with political favor and towering achievement, made Newton's position almost unassailable.

Since the Royal Society was Newton's base of operations, the composition of its membership has an intimate bearing on his use of men in the furtherance of his ends. For Newton, persons were usually objects, not subjects. The Society's hundred-odd members over whom he presided were divided roughly half and half between men with some professional competence in science and aristocratic or gentlemanly amateurs. The scientists, in turn, were concentrated in two major groups—the medical doctors and physiologists and the mathematical-astronomical contingent. The doctors prominent in the Society—men like Hans Sloane, John Arbuthnot, and Richard Mead—were prosperous and influential court physicians who had easy entry to the palace and the aristocratic houses of the realm. Whenever Newton needed something at Court, the doctors could serve as convenient bedside intermediaries. Sloane, whom Newton had inherited as secretary of the Society, had begun to resuscitate it after the Glorious Revolution, and he had a penchant for keeping matters in his control during the early years of Newton's tenure. Newton chafed at his behind-the-scenes direction, a hangover from the traditional pattern in which the president was a changing figurehead and the secretary was the effective officer, and he could be provoked into denouncing Sloane as unqualified, and further as a villain, a rascal, and a tricking fellow.[4] With the same persistence with which Newton had secured actual, not merely nominal, control of the Royal Mint, he moved into the Royal Society. Though he used Sloane when he needed him, by 1713 Sloane had been persuaded to withdraw to his house in Chelsea and devote himself to his famous collection of natural curiosities and manuscripts. With Sloane's departure, Newton chose as secretaries two men who were of his own creation, Edmond Halley and John Keill. Sloane did not return to the center of activity until Newton's death, when he succeeded him as president. His disappearance was no great loss to science, since he was an old-fashioned gatherer of nostrums and a purveyor of traditional remedies who stuffed the *Transactions* of the Society with his questionable discoveries. Mead was a doctor of more philosophical bent and was Newton's personal physician during his last years. Arbuthnot, one of the numerous Scots who made good in the London scientific world, was close to the Prince of

Denmark, Queen Anne's husband, and a great wit as his satirical writings show. He occupied a pivotal post as physician extraordinary to Queen Anne. When Newton cannily appointed him to committees in both the Flamsteed and the Leibniz contests, he does not seem to have taken his functions too seriously, casually performing in the manner expected of him by the president. The medical men in the Society gave Newton no serious trouble, and one of their number, Dr. Stukeley, a young man from Lincolnshire, became a favorite of his old age and his first biographer—though when Stukeley, against Newton's will, ran for office in the Society after Halley's resignation, he was punished with exile from the presence for several years.[5] As men of independent means, the doctors were not so beholden to Newton as the young mathematicians and astronomers, but so great was the prestige of his person and his system that they obeyed him and aligned themselves with him in any controversy.

The earnest young men upon whom Newton relied for the energetic building of his fame were the astronomers and mathematicians, who had come to the *Principia* as to a new revelation. They eagerly accepted the role of apostles. A few he had known and favored before he assumed office; others he continued to recruit through the decades of his long tenure, and he even outlived some of his earlier protégés. By the time of his death, the academic map of England and Scotland in the mathematical-astronomical sciences had been completely Newtonized. Year by year, as a professorship or a royal office to which a scientist could be appointed became vacant or a new chair was created, he filled it with one of his candidates. They became the king's men in Newton's realm, for there was a secular as well as a spiritual side to his sovereignty. The ties which bound these professors to him were often affective as well as scientific. For the young men, Newton was the father of the clan. The president who had lectured to empty halls during his Lucasian professorship now found himself the head of a scientific family. The old man who had never known woman acquired sons.

David Gregory, who had been one of the first to teach the Newtonian philosophy at Edinburgh in the 1680's, was appointed Savilian Professor of Astronomy at Oxford in 1692, largely through Newton's intervention. Roger Cotes, a mathematician and another of Newton's protégés, became Plumian Professor of Astronomy and Experimental Philosophy at Cambridge in 1706, when he was only twenty-four years old. Newton, who had defined the terms of the new chair himself, as an administrator of science took a very different attitude toward publication than he had in his youth: The Plumian Professor would be required to publish regularly either at Cambridge or in the *Philosophical Transactions of the Royal Society.* The handsome Cotes was a dearly beloved disciple, and Newton lamented his premature death in 1716, saying: "If he had lived we might have known something."[6] William Whiston, who as an undergraduate had heard a few lectures by Newton, first made his acquaintance in 1694. On Newton's nomination, he became Lucasian Professor of Mathematics at Cambridge, after having substituted for him when he went up to London. John Keill, one of David Gregory's students, was named Savilian Professor of Astronomy at Oxford in 1712 and gave courses on the new philosophy there. He also served as "decypherer" to Queen Anne. Keill was a warhorse whose ardor was so intense that Newton sometimes had to pull in the reins.

The one major scientist who remained by Newton's side throughout the whole period of his tenure was the astronomer Edmond Halley, and the nature of their bond may some day be more fully defined if the Halley papers on Newton—which existed at one time—ever turn up. A strange event marks the beginning of their relationship. In 1684, when the twenty-eight-year-old Halley first visited Newton at Cambridge and received from him the fundamental propositions of the *Principia,* his father had been found dead on the banks of a river near Reading. The coroner's verdict was murder, and a wild insinuation was later made by the academic gossip Thomas Hearne that Halley was implicated in the crime. According to the same Hearne, Newton's death was hastened by a violent scene between him and Halley.[7] But for more than forty years Halley behaved toward Newton with great circumspection. He knew how to mollify him when he was in a wrath, and in the great wars with Newton's enemies, he made himself indispensable as chief-of-staff. In the fight with Hooke, he was a reporter and an agent whose primary function was to see the *Principia* through the press and keep Newton from destroying the third part in his anger at Hooke's accusation that the law of gravity had been stolen from him. When Newton needed an astronomer to finish and force publication of Flamsteed's star catalogue, Halley was appointed editor. And when, in 1712, the Royal Society's *Commercium Epistolicum* against Leibniz was to be printed, Halley ran the editorial committee and did much of the paper work. Newton protected him and, though his reputation for religious skepticism was an impediment to his advancement, secured him an appointment as deputy comptroller of the Chester Mint in 1696. After a series of scientific voyages, through Newton's assistance he became Savilian Professor of Astronomy at Oxford in 1703, Secretary of the Royal Society in 1713, and Royal Astronomer in 1721.

Nicolas Fatio de Duillier, an erratic young genius from Switzerland, was another of the elect. Toward him Newton had had a strong emotional attachment back in the early 1690's, the feelings of a man of fifty toward his replica aged twenty-five. By the time Newton had become president of the Royal Society, however, Fatio had fallen into disfavor, though he lingered on the sidelines for a while. Samuel Clarke, who had been converted to the Newtonian philosophy in Cambridge about the same time as William Whiston, had refused a post at the Mint that was in Newton's grant and served as chaplain to the Princess of Wales, a vantage point from which he became the expositor of the philosophical and religious conceptions of the Newtonian philosophy in his famous correspondence with Leibniz—but only after careful consultation with Newton himself. Colin Maclaurin, Henry Pemberton, and John Stirling were of the second generation of disciples in the 1720's, after Fatio de Duillier was swallowed up by the Prophets of London, Whiston was estranged, and Gregory and Cotes had died. Maclaurin became Professor of Mathematics at the University of Edinburgh through Newton's sponsorship, and Henry Pemberton ultimately was made Professor of Physics at Gresham College.

Thus were the young mathematicians and astronomers rewarded with chairs in Oxford, Cambridge, and the Scottish universities. Few academic appointments in this field were made without consulting Newton, and his advice was almost always heeded. Sometimes he gave his protégés munificent gifts as well: Five hundred pounds went to Clarke—one hundred pounds for each of his children—for his translation of the *Opticks* into Latin. When a minor and rather unreliable disciple, George Cheyne, refused his bounty, he was peremptorily dropped.

Newton usually dealt with people on the basis of "commutation," except on those rare occasions when his feelings became involved. He distributed academic posts and royal offices, and the beneficiaries acquitted their debts to him through service and loyalty. There is something feudal as well as paternal about his ties with these younger men. They fought his battles, and he awarded them university professorships as their fiefs. This formidable man sometimes inspired love—surely in Fatio, perhaps in Halley and Conduitt. More often, it was his masterful authority that gave the group of his adherents cohesion.

There was work for the protégés that related directly to Newton's writings. Before his London period Newton had timorously allowed certain of his mathematical papers to be shown only to a few elders, like Isaac Barrow and John Collins, but once he had stopped creating, he granted a number of younger men among his followers freer access to his private mathematical hoard. John Craig, David Gregory, John Raphson, Edmond Halley, Fatio de Duillier, William Jones, John Keill, Henry Pemberton, Abraham de Moivre, and Nicholas Bernoulli were among those who enjoyed the occasional privilege. Corrections and emendations of the *Principia* were begun soon after it was published, primarily by Newton himself, who in characteristic fashion blamed all but one of the errors on his ignorant amanuensis. Fatio de Duillier had thought of himself as the only disciple worthy to prepare the second edition. When he went off into the wilderness of religious enthusiasm, the mantle fell on Roger Cotes, whose long preface became an integral part of the work and in popularizations of Newtonianism was usually cited as proof positive that the structure of the universe as revealed by Newton presupposed an infinitely good and wise architect. The third edition a decade later was the labor of Henry Pemberton. Throughout this period, the disciples also busied themselves with teaching the doctrine in the universities and with popularizations—usually with Newton's blessings, though sometimes accompanied by an underground rumor that the new renderings were endangering the prestige of the original, because they might become more widely diffused than Newton's work, whose grandiose architectural quality and elegant proofs few contemporaries were capable of understanding thoroughly. Whiston, Gregory, Cheyne, Clarke, Maclaurin, Pemberton, Keill, and Desaguliers all wrote books on Newtonianism during the Master's life or immediately after his death. Even the doctors and the divines in the Royal Society exerted themselves to show the application of the Newtonian philosophy in their respective fields of endeavor—the physicians often producing a literature bordering on the absurd, like Cheyne's proposal for a "Principia Medicinae Theoreticae Mathematica." The men in holy orders, who illustrated the religious

409

nature of the Newtonian philosophy, used its principles as a lauda-
tion. The tendency that Dr. Richard Bentley initiated in the Boyle
lectures for 1692 was brought to a climax in William Derham's
lectures for 1711 and 1712, published as *Physico-Theology, or a
Demonstration of the Being and Attributes of God from his works
of creation,* which saw twelve editions by 1754. John Craig's
Theologiae Christianae Principia Mathematica (1699) is perhaps the
most outlandish example of the Newtonian fashion in religion. The
first commentaries of the Newtonian movement were thus written
under the watchful eye of the Master, and he allowed its ramifica-
tions into the strangest areas without dissent.

Although Newton protected his young men and fostered them,
he demanded absolute obedience; the father would brook no criticism, opposition, nor actions that might reflect upon him and
jeopardize his position as a Crown official and luminary of the realm.
He insisted upon social conformity in their public behavior. William
Whiston proved to be an incautious man who could not restrain
his tongue nor mask his views. Differing from Newton over matters
of Biblical interpretation and chronology, in which he believed himself superior to his patron, he could not withhold his criticism,
and such contumely did not sit well with the Master. When
Whiston openly expressed Arian convictions that in reality were
not very dissimilar from Newton's own secret faith, the lack of
prudence was punished. Newton did not lift a finger when Whiston
was ousted from the university for religious heterodoxy. And there
is anecdotage to the effect that he kept him out of the Royal
Society on grounds that he was a heretic, threatening to resign if
Halley and Sloane went through with his nomination.[8] Whiston
suffered deeply from this rejection and, like a lover denied, vented
his spleen against those still in the entourage and against Newton's
intolerance. He settled accounts in his *Memoirs:* "But he then perceiving that I could not do as his other darling friends did, that is,
learn of him, without contradicting him, when I differed in opinion
from him, he could not, in his old age, bear such contradiction."[9]
Fatio de Duillier was excluded when he became involved with the
seances of the wild Prophets of London and served as their secretary. When Fatio, whom Newton had once invited to live close
to him in Cambridge, stood in pillory, Newton went about his
business at the Treasury seemingly unconcerned. Fatio did not
easily free himself of his hero-worship of Newton, and for years
after Newton's death, he considered himself the only true disciple

and interpreter of the system, until in his very old age, stricken with illness, he began to murmur that the Newtonian philosophy without Fatio's explanation was meaningless.

There was one other group in the Royal Society whom Newton befriended by supporting them in more modest positions than university professorships—the Huguenot émigrés. Though he seems to have recovered from the more violent seizures of anti-Catholicism which possessed him and his contemporaries in the eighties and nineties, he retained a deep sympathy for the victims of Louis XIV's laws against Protestants, who took refuge in England in a flight reminiscent of the movement out of Germany in the twentieth century. Most of the exiles sought security and respectability in their new home and were dismayed by the scandal of the Prophets from the Cévennes in which Fatio de Duillier had become enmeshed. Newton helped the reasonable ones—the mathematician Abraham de Moivre, the translator and compiler of scientific letters Pierre Des Maizeaux, and John Theophilus Desaguliers, who had been brought to England as an infant and became an occasionally paid experimenter of the Royal Society.

Newton kept in close touch with his disciples and his favored Huguenots, meeting with them regularly. David Gregory has an account of a session with Fatio, Halley, and himself at which Newton unfolded his publication plans.[10] Ralph Thoresby in his diary describes the agreeable Fellows he encountered at the Royal Society and afterward accompanied to the Grecian Coffee-house— President Isaac Newton, attended by the two Secretaries Halley and Keill, both his protégés and both professors at Oxford.[11] On many evenings, Newton picked up de Moivre at the coffeehouse he frequented, Slaughter's in St. Martin's Lane, and brought him to his own home nearby for philosophical conversation. There was a gentle side to the man that manifested itself in some of these relationships, but their function was primarily to nourish a scientific movement organized around a set doctrine.

Virtually nothing was done in behalf of the Newtonian philosophy without the Master's surveillance and permission. His manuscript legacy shows that in the great controversies in which he engaged, he supervised and usually corrected with his own hand the drafts of whatever the disciples wrote in his defense, but there was a tacit understanding among them that he was never to be exposed. An official portrait was being created of the calm, majestic genius who was above worldly concerns, a paragon of all

411

the virtues of Christianity and the Enlightenment. Keill would send a piece to his friend Edmond Halley, inviting him and Newton to make changes as they saw fit. Cotes asked Newton to write anything he chose as the polemical, anti-Leibniz preface to the second edition of the *Principia* and offered to put his name to it and defend it as his own. The famous "review," or *Recensio*, of the *Commercium Epistolicum*, published in the *Transactions of the Royal Society*, every bit of which Newton himself composed, was passed off as Keill's. In Clarke's philosophical interchange with Leibniz, the manuscripts make it abundantly clear that Newton's is the guiding hand. And in Des Maizeaux's collection of documents, Newton permitted himself the license of final revisions of his disciples' letters, even after they had been sent. The Newtonians in the Royal Society—and the collective name had begun to be used— were really what Leibniz called them, Newton's *enfants perdus*, his reconnaissance patrol.

A Being of Their Own

During his tenure as President of the Royal Society, Newton adopted a series of measures intended to introduce sound administrative procedures and firm discipline among the members. The meticulous, puritanical scientist could not tolerate slipshod ways, and the Society would be a mirror of his personality. While previous presidents had attended irregularly, according to count he was present at 161 out of 175 Council meetings.[12] And in order to participate in the general assemblies, he shifted the weekly session of the Society from Wednesday to Thursday, a day when he was not occupied at the Mint.

The last decades of the seventeenth century were an especially trying period for the Society as an institution: The membership fell off, dues were in arrears, and changes of officers were unusually frequent. The Society had not been able to afford the printing of the *Principia*, having exhausted its treasury on Willoughby's history of fish, and the publication of the *Philosophical Transactions* had been suspended for a time. The Society was on the verge of bankruptcy when Newton took over, and he attempted to make it solvent through a reorganization of its finances. In 1706, the Council ordered that every newly-elected member should pay his admission fee before his official induction and give bond that he would make regular weekly contributions. Nobody could become a member of the Council if his dues were in arrears. In 1723 Newton invested Royal Society funds, along with his own, in the South Sea Company, in order to profit from an enterprise whose stock was rising spectacularly. This was one occasion, however, when his manipulations were less fortunate—though he did not live to see the total debacle.

Newton's psychic owing was boundless, and he could not endure to be obligated or indebted to any man. Whenever he could, he tried to substitute paid for volunteer services. He was uncomfortable with anything but a *do ut des* arrangement. In 1720, he had a stipend fixed for the two chief secretaries of the Society as well as for a foreign secretary. When Desaguliers was appointed a curator of experiments, Newton allocated special funds for his work. But, in return, he insisted that every order of the Council be scrupulously obeyed. When he felt that Desaguliers was not performing a sufficient number of experiments, he had him reprimanded, much to the scientist's dismay.[13] At the last Council session that Newton attended, a few days before his death at the age of eighty-five, he bawled out Halley, then a mere seventy-one, for not transmitting astronomical observations from Greenwich to the Society with the annual regularity stipulated by royal order.

One of Newton's plans of institutional reform was a *Scheme for establishing the Royal Society,* of which six drafts in his hand are extant. Though the plan did not come to fruition, it tells us a good deal about the authoritarian direction in which he was moving. "Establishing" in this context meant giving the Society's projects a sound financial and organizational frame, though one is tempted to read his meaning as re-establishing the society anew under his aegis. Newton envisaged a system of appointed learned pensioners who would be obliged to attend all sessions of the Society and, if they wished to retain their positions, to produce inventions and discoveries on schedule. The plan classified science into five divisions, into each of which a pensioner would be fitted. Newton's early sense of the fluidity of science and the fantasies of the youth who dabbled freely in all forms of knowledge have vanished with age. Science is now organized and structured. In this document, the divine consecration of science is conspicuously absent, as he describes its mission in purely institutional terms. The ultimate goal is secular: to make the Society "famous and lasting"—in one draft he had written "perpetual," the language of the French Academy.[14] The recluse of Trinity turned administrator was moving along the path of the academies that were agencies of the French crown.

Before Newton's incumbency, the Society had fallen to such low estate that Sloane's "unfit entertainment" became the subject of a public satire.[15] Newton devoted himself to the moral as well as the financial renovation of the Society. He made a ceremony of the sessions over which he presided, the first high priest of modern science officiating at its rites. Dr. Stukeley, a hushed witness, has left a description of the performances:

Whilst he presided in the Royal Society, he executed that office with singular prudence, with a grace and dignity—conscious of what was due to so noble an Institution—what was expected from his character. . . . There were no whispering, talking nor loud laughters. If discussions arose in any sort, he said they tended to find out truth, but ought not to arise to any personality. . . . Every thing was transacted with great attention and solemnity and decency; nor were any papers which seemed to border on religion treated without proper respect. Indeed his presence created a natural awe in the assembly; they appear'd truly as a venerable *consessus Naturae Consiliariorum*, without any levity or indecorum.[16]

If the solemnity was fractured, the culprit was ousted. In 1710, a famous fracas occurred between the notoriously choleric geologist and physician John Woodward, Professor of Physic at Gresham College, and Dr. Hans Sloane, who was reading a communication about bezoars, secretions found in the intestines of goats in Persia and India, which he called a kind of gall-stone and used as an antidote against poison. Woodward kept interrupting him with the remark that "no man who understands anatomy would make such an assertion." Upon Sloane's complaint to the Council that he had been insulted, Woodward countered with the charge that Sloane had been making grimaces at him. When Woodward refused to apologize, Newton had him removed from the Council to the accompaniment of reflections that he was a good natural philosopher, but not a good moral one.[17]

Newton's dread of disorder and tendency to ritualize his own behavior, along with a desire to imitate the elaborate manners of the great, led him to assign specific places to the officers who attended him at meetings, like the members of a royal court. The president was to sit at the head of the table, with the secretaries at the lower end, one on each side. The sacred configuration could be altered only to accommodate some "very Honourable Stranger." A liveried servant installed at the door and carrying a staff that bore the arms of the Society set the tone of the weekly meetings. Only when the president occupied the chair could the mace be laid, no lesser dignitary being permitted to enjoy this distinction.

Whenever Newton was identified with an institution, it became an extension of his person, and he sought to protect its position with the same zeal that he would his own. The feeling of identification with Trinity College that he had had during the Francis Alban case, with the Mint in his fight with the Lord of the Tower, he now transferred to the Society. His fierce sense of independence made intolerable the location of the Royal Society—with its museum, meeting room, and library—in the building of Gresham College, where it was subject to the will and desire of the Mercers' Company. Moreover, there were intimations that the Society might be asked to vacate. Newton first tried in vain to obtain a royal grant for a new house, then toyed with a plan for a union of the Queen's Library, the Cotton Library, and the Royal Society—a proposal which Halifax supported in the Lords, but which came to naught. Newton's final solution was to give the Society "a being of their own," as he phrased it, and he proceeded to find another site—a Dr. Brown's house at 2 Crane Court. Once Newton had made the decision to move, he perfunctorily called together a meeting of the Fellows on short notice, arrogantly refused to explain the reasons for the impending change, "which he did not think proper to be given there," and went ahead despite opposition and in the face of general perplexity as to why the members had been assembled.[18] Like many a modern administrator, he sought democratic assent to his decisions and was outraged when it was not forthcoming. In abandoning the old quarters, there was also a desire on Newton's part to break completely with the epoch during which Robert Hooke had controlled the Society. As it happened, in the process of transferring from Gresham College, Hooke's portrait—the only one in existence—and many of his instruments seem to have disappeared forever.[19] Newton wanted the Society to have a being of its own, but he equated that being with *his* being.

Science and the Government

When, in 1705, Queen Anne knighted the yeoman's son Isaac Newton in a formal ceremony at Trinity College, the first scientist to be so honored, the bond between science and the Crown was given symbolic representation. For Newton, this was a great personal triumph, staged in the College where he had once performed menial duties as a subsizar. In issuing a charter to the Royal Society and in founding the Royal Observatory, Charles II had expressed an interest in the advantages that might accrue to the kingdom through the promotion of scientific discoveries. Under Newton, Master of the Mint and dominant figure of British science, a much closer link was forged between science and the government than had ever existed before. Since he was frequently summoned by the Lords of the Treasury in his capacity as Master of the Mint, the leading scientist was looked upon no longer as a closeted Cambridge experimenter, but as a part of the governmental mechanism. Though his fixing of the gold standard in 1717 was a function of his office at the Mint, it was not alien to his long metallurgical experiments and even the alchemical ones which had continued until the eve of his departure for London. Newton always managed to capitalize on his past experience, however remote from current concerns it might appear; nothing seems to have been lost. Once a member of the government, he began to appear at Court. He was consulted by Caroline, the Princess of Wales, about the education of her children, and to her he gave the first copy of his revision of chronology. Scientific events became matters of national interest. Even if his purpose was *méchant*, the intrusion of George I into the Leibniz controversy—in one case reviewing a reply of Newton to Leibniz before it was sent off—is indicative of the new status of science.

The Leibniz controversy brought the Royal Society and its president before the eyes of European aristocrats. Those who could not understand Newton's works were at least able to enjoy the exchange of insults. The very notoriety of the quarrel gave prestige to science, as the King, his mistress, Princess Caroline, and the whole diplomatic corps took part in reviewing the documents in the case, expressing their opinion of the appropriate tactics to be employed in its settlement. When science and the Royal Society became fashionable, foreign ambassadors sought membership to the Society as one might to an exclusive club, and many more were admitted in Newton's day than ever before. The snob in him was not averse to their presence. On occasion the yeoman's son presided at Royal Society meetings surrounded by European ambassadors, like a monarch holding court. The Journal Book describes the occasion when Signor Grimani, the Venetian Ambassador, Signor Gerardini, Envoy from the Grand Duke of Tuscany, and the Duke d'Aumont,

Ambassador Extraordinary of France, were there together, entertained with experiments on "The productiveness of light by friction; The mutual attraction of the parts of matter; . . . preparations . . . of the veins and arteries of a human liver."[20] Newton became a major source of national pride among important segments of the upper classes. In hundreds of eulogies while he was still alive, he was hailed as the glory of the English nation, and his science was saluted as an exemplification of the national genius.

If in the previous generation the religious nature of scientific inquiry had been given fervid expression—and to the very end science remained for Newton a worship of God—the utility of science was now recognized not only in philosophical works like Bacon's and formal apologiae like those of Sprat and Joseph Glanvill, but in practical state measures. As if Marx had been stood on his head, Newton, having devoted the first half of his creative years to the development of a magnificent intellectual superstructure, turned in his latter days to its substructure. In 1709, he accepted offices in the societies of the Mines Royal and the Mineral and Battery Works.[21] Having already given advice on curriculum reform of the Mathematical School at Christ's Hospital in 1694,[22] he turned to plans for reorganizing university education, with greater emphasis on science and upright conduct.[23] The Royal Society became royal not only in name, but in fact. It was represented on any governmental body which might remotely be involved with a scientific question. And its advice was sought on any parliamentary bill that concerned invention. As Stukeley wrote: "The Government, the great Council of the nation, paid a distinguished regard to their judgment in all matters of public utility."[24] The relations between the Society and the state were reciprocal. On February 7, 1713, Bolingbroke informed the Fellows that henceforward Her Majesty's envoys to foreign parts would promote the design for which the Society was founded by gathering information and answering inquiries that might be addressed to them by the scientists. (Among the first fruits of this union of science and the state was the dispatch to the Society of a giant's tooth discovered near Albany on the Hudson.[25]) Honorific appointments to the Society could serve the simple economic interests of the nation and its traders in foreign parts. Prince Alexander Menzicoff, an adviser to Peter the Great, was elected a Fellow on July 29, 1714, at the request of English merchants who sought concessions in Muscovy. And Newton in his own hand carefully prepared three drafts of the letter in response to the Russian nobleman's acceptance, a correspondence that is florid with love for science and humanity.[26]

It is well known that Charles II was moved to found the Royal Observatory because Flamsteed, in criticizing a charlatan's solution to the problem of longitudes, had pointed out how faulty existing star catalogues were. To say that the growing British Empire was anxious over safe navigation and the prevention of losses at sea is to labor the obvious. The Royal Navy, the merchants of London, and the ship's captains themselves were all vitally concerned. In May 1714 a petition was presented to Parliament asking that an award be offered for the discovery of the longitude, and a vast committee was appointed with the power to send for persons, papers, and records. Newton appeared at the hearing, as might a scientific administrator in a present-day inquiry, flanked by his scientists Clarke, Halley, and Cotes. The event presaged hundreds of similar confrontations between parliamentary committees and the new elite of science. The aged Newton was especially honored with a seat near the Committee chairman, and though he would have preferred to limit himself to the meticulous scientific analysis of alternative ways of proceeding with the discovery of the longitude, which he read from a prepared paper, neither the chairman nor the Committee, it seems, would move the bill until the oracle of science would say that one of the methods currently proposed was likely to be useful. William Whiston, among many other longitudinarians—as Arbuthnot satirized the profusion of inventors—had a plan of his own about which Newton was unenthusiastic; and it was only with great reluctance that he permitted a few words to be extracted to the effect that Whiston's method might be useful near the shores. Whereupon a bill passed the Committee and the Parliament offering £20,000, a huge sum, for a practical method of determining longitude within half a degree, and a Board of Longitude was established to sit in judgment on the various proposals and to allocate the awards for a full or partial solution. Newton was, of course, appointed a member of the Board.[27]

Though prominent Fellows of the Society like Arbuthnot had written about the manifold uses of mathematics for military as well as civil affairs and had stressed the need for more widespread mathematical education among officers, Newton himself seems to have been ambivalent about the scientists' participation in the development of military machines. David Gregory reports Newton's proposal to "cure the Bucking and wideness of touch-hole of great Gunns" by means of a new metallurgical mixture, another use of his chemical experiments with alloys,[28] but there is a contrasting story to the effect that Newton was hostile to the application of science to warfare. When the disciple's father, also named David, made an invention to improve artillery, Newton urged his son to destroy it on the ground that it would soon become known to the enemy and that it tended to the annihilation rather than the preservation of mankind.[29]

If scientists aided only sporadically in perfecting military weapons, they gave the government direct assistance in preventing public disorders. The comet of 1680 had generated a wave of terror and superstition. In 1715, Halley published a description and a map of the precise path of the eclipse before it happened on April 22, and public tranquillity was maintained. The utility of science to civil authority thus was dramatically demonstrated.

In the 1670's, John Evelyn dined with Flamsteed and referred to him with veneration as "the learned *Astrologer* & *Mathematician,* whom now his Majestie had established in the new *Observatorie* in *Greenewich* Park, and furnish'd with the choicest Instruments . . . ," as if he were a magus at an Eastern court.[30] By the second decade of the eighteenth century, such individual scientific positions of prestige and influence were virtually eliminated. Newton had systematically consolidated science in one body and under one head and had curtailed the independence of separate scientific agencies. Around him, a corporate scientific establishment with an authority of its own had taken shape. It did not enjoy munificent gifts from the Crown, and its leading members were fairly independent economically, being supported by university posts, lucrative medical practices, or ecclesiastical appointments. Despite its relative autonomy, however, the activities that involved science with the government were being constantly multiplied.

The Wars of Truth

Of the events that established Newton's hegemony, the conflicts with Flamsteed and Leibniz were the most dramatic and the noisiest. The institutionalization of the Newtonian philosophy, like the victory of any great historical doctrine, required the slaughter of enemies both at home and abroad. The quarrels with Flamsteed and Leibniz, though they had earlier origins, flared up in earnest during the period of Newton's presidency. By defeating Flamsteed, Newton established his unquestioned supremacy in the English scientific world, and thereafter no competitor dared raise his head during Newton's lifetime. Before he was through with Flamsteed, Newton had invoked the power of the secular arm of the state to have himself and the Council of the Royal Society appointed overseers of the formerly independent Greenwich Observatory and to publish as he saw fit and over Flamsteed's strenuous objections the Royal Astronomer's observations made at Greenwich during a period of more than three decades. The Leibniz quarrel was the vindication of English science against the "continentals." The enemy from without was routed, and Newtonian science could reign supreme and uncontested, except for the rear-guard actions of the French Cartesians. By the time Voltaire, that great propagator of the new faith, arrived in London, the issue was settled, and he wrote the famous eulogy of Newton in the *Letters Concerning the English Nation*, which perhaps more than any other single document popularized and universalized Newton's image. In *Elements of the Philosophy of Newton,* Voltaire became the Paul to Newton's Christ, though it may well be doubted whether Christ or Newton would have been satisfied with his respective apostle.

In the years after 1704, the president of the Royal Society was in prime shape for personal and scientific infighting, and he engaged simultaneously with Flamsteed on one flank and Leibniz on the other. There was a difference in the nature of the contests. Though the battle with Leibniz struck at his vitals, the combatants never confronted each other in person, nor did they exchange accusations except through intermediaries. Baroque pomp and circumstance presided over the conduct of the war, and grand secular potentates witnessed the fray as amused spectators. Wrangling with Flamsteed—hardly an equal struggle, for the Royal Astronomer was generally regarded as an eccentric—was of a different order. The conflict between the two officers of the English Crown had a corrosive family intimacy, and their vociferous quarrels at the Royal Society, in the Greenwich Observatory, and in Newton's house afforded Newton an opportunity for the direct release of brutal rage upon another human being. After the turn of the century, intoxicated with power and authority in his dual capacity as Master of the Mint and president of the Royal Society, he allowed his angel of destruction, mightily armed, free rein. While the wearisome mutual recriminations of Newton and Flamsteed

420

over a period of more than two decades are by no means an unprecedented example of science in the service of aggressive needs, Newton's vindictive pursuit of Flamsteed is perhaps more thoroughly documented than most. Unfortunately, as is usually the case, it is the victim who chronicles the story of his sufferings over and over again, finding a modicum of relief in the obsessive recapitulation of his persecution.

At the height of his power, Newton behaved toward Flamsteed, four years his junior, his younger brother in the Royal Society, as though he were a menial, and he made no effort to hide his condescension, if not his contempt. Newton looked upon Flamsteed as nothing more than a convenient source of data for his theories, a tool. And yet this was no schoolboy who was being maltreated, but a member of the Royal Society's Council, with an extensive correspondence among European scholars, the author of more than two-score papers in the *Philosophical Transactions,* a man who had devised novel methods of observation and was among the first to use an accurate timepiece and optical means for determining stellar coordinates. Flamsteed was as arrogant as Newton, and he dared to talk back to the president of the Royal Society, even to criticize the *Principia*—unpardonable sins.

Both Newton and Flamsteed were profoundly religious, and their works were dedicated to God as a worship. Both believed themselves to be of the elect, but they were also deeply concerned with what men thought about them, since they lived in a hostile world rendered even more nasty and brutish by their imaginings. The two troubled creatures—one the son of a tradesman, the other the son of a yeoman, now great officers of the Crown and rivals for world fame, each believing that he was divinely ordained—were almost fated to clash. The confrontation of several Christs in one asylum has been studied by clinicians. Newton and Flamsteed, though neither of them was psychotic, enacted a similar tragicomedy on the broader stage of the English scientific world.

Our most detailed consecutive account of the quarrel from 1704 to 1716, when it blazed in the open in the scientific and political world, is the "Original Preface" that was suppressed by the editors of Flamsteed's *Historia Coelestis* when the work appeared posthumously (1725). The preface, written by Flamsteed in February 1717, concentrated on Newton's unjust and unremitting harassment of the author; one did not cast such aspersions upon the character of the divine Newton with impunity, and censorship was invoked.[31]

The preface presented a lurid picture of Newton as a power-lusting, lying, conniving, treacherous monster, using his influence at Court and his intimacy with Lord Halifax to do Flamsteed out of his star catalogue, his money, his independent position as Royal Astronomer. Flamsteed depicted himself as a long-suffering martyr whose devotion to science and the revelation of God's works would not allow him to issue an imperfect star catalogue, a man who was the object of a conspiracy in which hypocritical Newton and atheistic Halley were the prime movers. They had vied for the favor of the Prince of Denmark, and through chicanery had forced Flamsteed to surrender his manuscripts, making arrangements with booksellers that robbed him of his due, for the Prince had donated £1200 for their publication. Flamsteed was the righteous man of God pursued by a political manipulator and a band of adulators constantly singing his praises. Since Flamsteed would not join them, he had to be crushed, and each move in the long, drawn-out story of official intrigue was, in Flamsteed's reconstruction of events, consciously planned by the arch-villain.

Despite Flamsteed's obvious exaggerations, the account carries some conviction and cannot be dismissed as nothing more than paranoid confabulation. Newton would brook no opposition and was quite capable of destroying a man who crossed him. Flamsteed's version of 1717 is, in much of its detail, corroborated by letters that he wrote to friends at the time the events were taking place, so that if he fantasied, he at least clung more or less closely to the frame of his original imaginings. Nothing in Newton's correspondence contradicts the facts presented, and extant manuscript drafts of agreements and royal orders, in Newton's hand, bolster Flamsteed's central contention that it was always Newton who was pulling the strings. In modern bureaucracies, scientists have often been adept in the art of the cabal, which they quickly learned from their political colleagues when the skill did not come naturally.

Newton's mechanics were astute. He operated through a Committee of Referees who, though members of the Society, were appointed not by it, but by the Prince of Denmark on Newton's recommendation. He lied, used guile, and intimidated his victim with threats that he was guilty of *lèse-majesté* when he refused to surrender his observations. In a bewildering scene in Crane Court after the Society was installed in its new building, Newton—supported by Sloane and Mead—excoriated the victim and called him names—puppy was the least of them, according to Flamsteed.[32] In the end, Newton won—the first British star catalogue was published in 1712 without Flamsteed's consent and under the editorial direction of Edmond Halley whom he loathed. Flamsteed had been persuaded or forced to surrender to the Committee of Referees a record of his original observations and an incomplete set of star-places. Some of the papers had been put under seal in Newton's possession, and Flamsteed charged that he had broken the bond and released them. The printing proceeded haltingly until Prince George's death, when the Committee gave Halley—the cruelest cut of all—the task of publishing whatever was in their hands and then filling out the volume with his own observations. The 1712 edition that was pulled out of this chaos is a veritable hodgepodge, because there were numerous unresolved problems of identification when Halley assumed control. In addition, Halley's introduction to what was essentially Flamsteed's lifework made brutal reflections about the Royal Astronomer's capacities and accuracy.

Because of his relationship with the government, Newton had thus been able to force Flamsteed to surrender his observations and to have them printed not as the isolated astronomer would have had them appear, but as Newton the administrator dictated. Though he received a salary from the government, Flamsteed still thought of himself as the lone, autonomous servant of God and of his work as an offering. Newton, in the name of the superior interests of organized science and the kingdom, treated him like a rebellious clerk whose peculiarities would not be tolerated. The novelty of this act of intervention and command has been ignored by commentators, though it presaged a new form of scientific organization and control.

While dealing with Flamsteed as an internal threat to his authority, Newton managed at the same time to grapple with a foreign menace. In a published series of Latin documents—mostly translations of letters about the calculus to and from John Collins in the 1670's—known for short as the *Commercium Epistolicum* (1712), a committee of the Royal Society adjudicated a contest over priority in the invention of the calculus in favor of its own president, aged seventy, against one of its oldest foreign members, aged sixty-six.

In a joust over precedence in the new philosophy, the Knight from Woolsthorpe and the Freiherr from Leipzig had abided by no known set of chivalric rules. At the height of the contest, after repeated letters from Leibniz to Hans Sloane, Secretary of the Society, complaining that Dr. John Keill, a fellow member, had insulted him, Newton the president formally brought together his adherents under the guise of what he grandiloquently called "a large committee of distinguished persons of several nations expressly assembled by order of the Royal Society," to judge the merits of Leibniz' accusation. The nations represented on this much-touted impartial committee turned out to be English, Scotch, and Irish, with a Prussian ambassador and a Huguenot émigré later thrown in for continental flavor. The decision of the Committee insinuated plagiarism on the part of Leibniz, though its report was required only to exonerate Keill from the charge that he had injured Leibniz during a polemical exchange, or to confirm it.

Newton was so well protected that publicly the affair appeared to be a Keill-Leibniz controversy; he operated exclusively behind the scenes and with consummate skill. There is only one document in which he took specific personal responsibility for what was said—his reply to the Abate Conti in 1716; for the rest, he was the grand strategist who refused to be revealed. And when he deigned to answer Leibniz through Conti on that one occasion, it was by *force majeure;* for Conti, a Venetian aristocrat sojourning in England, and Princess Caroline of Anspach had playfully decided to act as intermediaries in a reconciliation attempt, and Newton had no choice but to go along with their efforts.

The exchange of letters between Leibniz and Newton through Conti in 1716 only brought into the open a war that had been waged clandestinely since the turn of the century. Two of the greatest geniuses of the European world—not only of their own time, but of its whole long history—had been privately belaboring each other with injurious epithets and encouraging their partisans to publish scurrilous innuendoes in learned journals. In the age of reason, they behaved like gladiators in a Roman circus. Here were two old bachelors—Leibniz not far from death, Newton with a decade more of life—each fighting for exclusive possession of his brainchild, the right to call the invention of the calculus his own and no one else's. The contest transcended the specific issue of priority of invention to embrace rival conceptions of the nature of matter, substance, the cosmos, God's providence, time, space, miracles. Their views of all things in the heavens and on earth became polarized as they stalwartly assumed opposite positions, exaggerating their differences, grossly caricaturing each other's

424

opinions like schoolboys in debate. Their common commitment to advancing the new philosophy was totally forgotten.

For many years, others had perpetrated the hostile acts for the principals, who sedulously avoided an open confrontation—though the manuscripts now betray the extent to which they supervised the verbal assaults of their hangers-on when they did not themselves compose them under the cover of anonymity. Newton had a more numerous troop. He was in London, president of the Royal Society, embattled defender of the English nation in a war where world scientific prestige was at stake. Though Leibniz, too, had been president of an academy, it was in backwoods Berlin, and his last years were spent as a lonely old man in Hannover writing dynastic history for the head of the House of Brunswick who had become King George I of England. Leibniz had his adherents among the great continental scientists—Johann Bernoulli, Christiaan Huygens—but they were leery of engaging with Newton and only reluctantly allowed themselves to be drawn into the fray.

Leibniz was no innocent, and when he attacked Newton for his revival of scholastic philosophy and his belief in occult qualities, he knew the barbs would sting.[33] Like an envious schoolmaster, Leibniz boasted, almost pathetically: "I am surprised that the partisans of Mr. Newton produce nothing to show that their master has communicated a sound method to them. I have been more fortunate in my disciples." He smugly assured Conti that Wren, Flamsteed, and Newton were all that remained of the scientific "*Siècle d'or d'Angleterre*" and that their day would soon be done.[34]

Of the scores of documents that Newton prepared on the Leibniz controversy, the review, or *Recensio*, of the *Commercium Epistolicum* which he himself wrote and published anonymously, "An Account of the Book entituled Commercium Epistolicum Collinii & aliorum, De Analysi promota; published by order of the Royal Society . . . ," reveals the lengths to which he resorted to annihilate a foe. All but three pages of the *Philosophical Transactions* for January and February 1715 are devoted to this jejune recapitulation of the quarrel, beginning with proof of Newton's first discoveries in the sixties. Its text, interspersed with Latin quotations and mathematical proofs, was hardly likely to have great popular appeal, but the sharp edge of the polemical passages and the bite of the attack could be understood by anyone who perused the volume. While the piece is unsigned and purports to be a rectification by an editorial "we" of imperfect summaries published abroad, at one point near the end where a solemn warning is issued to Leibniz, the author of the review lapses into the singular personal pronoun. His identity is unmistakable. "And in the meantime I take the Liberty to acquaint him, that by taxing the Royal Society with Injustice in giving Sentence against him without hearing both Parties, he has transgressed one of their Statutes which makes it Expulsion to defame them."[35]

Newton's subtle and eminently persuasive structuring of Leibniz' intentions, the uncovering of a monstrous plagiarist plot, tells us far more about Newton than it does about Leibniz, for papers have since revealed that Leibniz' method was actually inspired by reading some Pascal writings in Paris, as he had testified.[36] Newton hoarded a great part of whatever he wrote and always lived in a circumscribed geographic area, while Leibniz roamed from royal court to royal court—from Muscovy to Berlin, Vienna, Hannover, Paris—in quest of personal preferment and support of his grand projects for the unification of mankind and the promotion of knowledge. In his hour of need, he was caught without written proof, and at the very moment when he hoped to be invited to England as a royal historiographer by the head of the House of Brunswick-Hannover, George I, for whose glory he had labored day and night in the archives, he found himself accused of a flagrant falsification of scientific history.

Reading the indignant peroration of the *Recensio*'s charge to the jury, one almost forgets that Newton himself is delivering the verdict, that he appointed the Committee of the Royal Society, that he edited the documents of the *Commercium*, adding his own footnotes and sometimes selecting for publication extracts rather than the full texts, that he interjected numerous unsupported inferences, and that he would in 1722 republish the *Commercium* with further emendations that were not signaled in any preface or introduction.[37] On occasion, Newton's cold cruelty assumed unbelievable proportions. In his *Historical Memoirs of the Life of Dr. Samuel Clarke,* William Whiston reports in passing: "He [Mr. Jackson] heard Sir Isaac Newton also pleasantly tell the Doctor [Clarke] that 'He broke Leibniz's Heart with his Reply to him.' "[38]

The republic of science had become too small for both Newton and Leibniz, as the Royal Society had once been for Newton and Hooke. A quarrel which had its origins in a classical priority fight had been fanned into a great conflagration. Leibniz could sometimes look away and jest about the struggle, but he was nonetheless devoured by it. This, rather than the noxious potions he took for gout, may have killed him. During his lifetime, he stood a condemned plagiarist, for who would gainsay the verdict of the Royal Society of London in a judgment that Leibniz himself had demanded? He died alone, and nobody of consequence attended his funeral. Newton regurgitated the case repeatedly in Latin and in English, ungallantly pursuing Leibniz even beyond the grave—witness the five hundred-odd folios of manuscript devoted to self-vindication and attack in the University Library in Cambridge, in addition to the stray papers at the Mint, into which his great wrath poured itself. His obsession lasted for a quarter of a century, and nowhere are the destructive forces in his character more visibly on the rampage than in this vendetta.

By the early-eighteenth century, Newtonian science had acquired many faces, and it showed them all: For the young scholars, it was a scientific philosophy; for the bishops, it was a proof of the existence of God; for the merchants, it offered the prospect of reducing losses at sea; for the King, it was an embellishment of the throne; for aristocrats, it was an amusement. Thus, it could be assimilated in many different forms—not excluding "Newtonianism for the Ladies"[39]—a protean quality that is almost a prerequisite for universalist doctrines. In order to secure itself, the science of Isaac Newton used certain of the mechanisms of a conquering new religion or political ideology. It triumphed, a truth in its day, but it seems to have availed itself of the same apparatus as any other kind of movement. Followers were assembled and bound to an apotheosized leader with ties of great strength. An internal institutional structure was fortified. The word was propagated by chosen disciples. Since the doctrine was rooted in a national society, its relations with the government gave it special privileges and emoluments. It became the second spiritual establishment of the realm, and at least in its origins presented no threat to the primary religious establishment that it was destined to undermine and, perhaps, ultimately to replace. As in many militant doctrinal movements, the truth was not allowed to fend for itself, and on occasion the sacred lie and the pious fraud became means to a higher end.

The content of Newtonian science might have prevailed without the personal force that Newton exerted. But with his extraordinary genius and energy, he was able to impose on the Western world a personal scientific style and a movement that reflected

427

his character. There was perhaps something valid in Leibniz' prognostication of the imminent decline of English science, for Newton's grip on the establishment did, in fact, stifle inventiveness for a time: The immediate followers were mere epigoni. Newton's great power as both the creator of a closed scientific world view and the organizer of its institutional framework has had analogies in both earlier and later generations and in other fields of endeavor —with similar consequences.

REFERENCES

1. The Royal Mint Library, Newton MSS., Vol. 2, fol. 334, John Chamberlayne to Isaac Newton, November 25, 1713.

2. See John Ball Keill, *Introductio ad veram astronomiam* (2d ed.; London, 1721), p. vi; Cambridge, King's College Library, Keynes MS. 130, Autograph drafts of portions of John Conduitt's intended life of Newton; Edmond Halley in the introduction of the *Principia;* Bibliothèque publique et universitaire de Genève, MS. français 602, fol. 58, minute of a letter from Fatio de Duillier to Jean-Robert Choûet, November 21, 1689.

3. William Stukeley, *Memoirs of Sir Isaac Newton's Life,* ed. A. Hastings White (London, 1936), p. 81.

4. Sir David Brewster, *Memoirs of the life, writings, and discoveries of Sir Isaac Newton* (Edinburgh, 1855), Vol. 2, p. 246.

5. Cambridge, King's College Library, Keynes MS. 136, Stukeley to Conduitt, June 26, 1727.

6. See J. Edleston (ed.), *Correspondence of Sir Isaac Newton and Professor Cotes* (London, 1850), p. lxxvii.

7. Thomas Hearne, *Remarks and Collections,* Vol. 6 (Oxford, 1902), p. 231 (September 25, 1718); Vol. 9 (Oxford, 1914), p. 293 (April 4, 1727).

8. William Whiston, *Memoirs of the life and writings of Mr. William Whiston* (2d ed.; London, 1753), Vol. 1, pp. 249-50.

9. *Ibid.,* pp. 250-51.

10. David Gregory, *David Gregory, Isaac Newton and their circle; extracts from David Gregory's memoranda 1677-1708,* ed. W. G. Hiscock (Oxford, 1937), p. 14.

11. Ralph Thoresby, *Diary,* ed. J. Hunter (London, 1830), Vol. 2, pp. 111, 117.

12. Sir Henry Lyons, *The Royal Society 1660-1940* (Cambridge, 1944), p. 121.

13. Cambridge, University Library, Add. MS 400B, fol. 669, Desaguliers to Newton, April 29, 1725.

14. Cambridge, University Library, Add. MS. 4005, foll. 1-7.

15. Brewster, *Memoirs of the life, writings, and discoveries of Sir Isaac Newton*, Vol. 2, pp. 243-44.

16. Stukeley, *Memoirs of Sir Isaac Newton's Life*, pp. 78-81.

17. Brewster, *Memoirs of the life, writings, and discoveries of Sir Isaac Newton*, Vol. 2, pp. 245-46.

18. Charles Richard Weld, *A History of the Royal Society* (London, 1848), Vol. 1, pp. 391-93. Weld quotes an anonymous contemporary report of the meeting, *An Account of the late Proceedings in the Council of the Royal Society, in order to remove from Gresham-College into Crane Court, in Fleet-Street* (1710).

19. A foreign visitor to the Society, the Frankfort traveler Zacharias Conrad von Uffenbach, still noticed the portrait in 1710; see *London in 1710, from The Travels of Zacharias Conrad von Uffenbach*, tr. and ed. W. H. Quarrell and Margaret Mare (London, 1934), p. 102.

20. Quoted by Weld, *A History of the Royal Society*, Vol. 1, p. 419.

21. D. Seaborne Davies, "The Records of the Mines Royal and the Mineral and Battery Works," *Economic History Review*, Vol. 6 (1936), pp. 209-13.

22. Newton, *Correspondence*, ed. H. W. Turnbull (Cambridge, 1961), Vol. 3, pp. 357-66, Newton to Nathaniel Hawes, May 25, 1694.

23. Cambridge, University Library, Add. MS. 4005, foll. 14-15, "Of Educating Youth in the Universities," printed in Newton, *Unpublished scientific papers*, ed. A. Rupert Hall and Marie Boas-Hall (Cambridge, 1962), pp. 369-73.

24. Stukeley, *Memoirs of Sir Isaac Newton's Life*, p. 81.

25. Weld, *A History of the Royal Society*, Vol. 1, pp. 420-21.

26. Brewster, *Memoirs of the life, writings, and discoveries of Sir Isaac Newton*, Vol. 2, p. 257.

27. Great Britain, House of Commons, *Journals*, Vol. 17 (1711-1714; reprinted 1803), pp. 641-42 (May 25, 1714), pp. 677-78 (June 11, 1714), p. 716 (July 3, 1714), p. 721 (July 8, 1714). See also Brewster, *Memoirs of the life, writings, and discoveries of Sir Isaac Newton*, Vol. 2, pp. 258-62, 265-66; Louis T. More, *Isaac Newton. A Biography* (London, 1934), pp. 562-63; William Whiston, *Longitude Discovered* (London, 1738), Historical Preface, p. v.

28. David Gregory, *David Gregory, Isaac Newton and their circle; extracts from David Gregory's memoranda 1677-1708*, p. 25.

29. Charles Hutton, *A Mathematical and Philosophical Dictionary* (2d ed.; London, 1815), Vol. 1, p. 557.

30. John Evelyn, *Diary*, ed. E. S. de Beer (Oxford, 1955), Vol. 4, p. 98 (September 10, 1676).

31. The preface was printed in Francis Baily, *An Account of the Revd. John Flamsteed, the first Astronomer-Royal* (London, 1835), pp. 71-105.

32. *Ibid.*, pp. 228-29.

33. Leibniz, *Die philosophischen Schriften*, ed. C. J. Gerhardt (Hildesheim, 1960-1961; reprint of 1875-1890 edition), Vol. 3, pp. 328-29 (Leibniz to Thomas Burnet, August 23, 1713).

34. Pierre Des Maizeaux, *Recueil de diverses pièces sur la philosophie . . .* (Amsterdam, 1720), Vol. 2, pp. 70-71 (Leibniz to Conti, April 9, 1716, *apostille*).

35. *Philosophical Transactions of the Royal Society*, Vol. 29 (1715), No. 342, p. 221.

36. J. E. Hofmann, *Die Entwicklungsgeschichte der Leibnizschen Mathematik während des Aufenthaltes in Paris, 1672-1676* (Munich, 1949), pp. 194-205.

37. John Collins, *Commercium epistolicum . . . ou Correspondance de J. Collins et d'autres savants célèbres du xvii* siècle, relative à l'analyse supérieure...*, ed. J. B. Biot and F. Lefort (Paris, 1856). Biot and Lefort collated the texts of the 1712 and 1722 editions, indicating additions, suppressions, alterations, and interpolations in what purported to be merely a new edition of the old *Commercium*.

38. William Whiston, *Historical Memoirs of the Life of Dr. Samuel Clarke* (London, 1730), p. 132.

39. Francesco Algarotti, *Sir Isaac Newton's philosophy explain'd for the use of the ladies*, tr. Elizabeth Carter (2 vols.; London, 1739). The original Italian version was published in 1737.

BARRY D. KARL

The Power of Intellect and the Politics of Ideas

I

A CONSCIOUSNESS of professionalism as a special shaping of a life-time career came late to popular American thought. The processes of specialized training, the articulation of standards, and the in-stitutionalization nationally of recognized methods of professional communication were established long before the breakdown of the national myth which decreed that unlimited opportunity shined equally on all by virtue of their citizenship in a democratic society and favored only those whose native intuitions and insights set them apart. The development of schools of business administration may have marked the beginning of the end, since of all the pro-fessions business was the most American and the most subject to interpretation by the chief canon of infinite mobility: that hard work and shrewd judgment would bring one to the top regardless of how far down one started. The sharpening distinction between skilled and unskilled followed the pace of industrialization seem-ingly without regard to myths of opportunity; and leaders like Andrew Carnegie puzzled in their declining years for ways to approximate for a society now aware of the costly necessity of education the freedom they seemed to recall as the legacy of their formative years.

The difficulties faced by successive generations in their efforts to understand the impact of education on the establishment of a career in an industrial age were a recurring source of instability in nineteenth-century American families as fathers sought for their

Much of this essay was written during my year as a Fellow at the Charles Warren Center for Studies in American History at Harvard University. A grant from the American Philosophical Society and the generosity of Washington University have aided my research.

431

sons careers which no longer existed as they had in father's day, or which failed to reflect the frontiers of ambition for a new generation. Fathers raised with the traditional professional trinity—the ministry, medicine, and the law—often saw engineering as a form of menial labor, politics as a slightly concealed version of thievery, and teaching as the refuge of the social and economic failure. Yet by the turn of the century, all three had become professions of an advanced order, as engineering drew upon and increased the resources of natural science, politics sought the specialized knowledge of economists, political scientists, and sociologists, and universities concerned themselves with the training of men for all of the new technical specialities.

Modern universities like Chicago and Stanford were built with the money of industrial leaders whose own educations had been a far cry from those they were providing for a new generation. Motivated more by their revolutionary industrial experience, than by alumnal recollections of good old college days, they succeeded in impressing at least the shape of their entrepreneurial skills on the talented academic leaders who assembled buildings and faculties with what seemed, at times, the same structural genius and whose fundamental sympathies were never too far from those of their benefactors. That they both often bought more than they bargained for, as recurring disputes over faculty radicalism indicate, should not obscure their own very real sense of innovation. The conflict in generation was not always between sharpened views of old and new, but rather conflicting views of the new. When one looks beyond struggles familiar enough in the history of the movement to secure workable canons of academic freedom, one notices the extraordinary level of agreement on a wide range of fundamentals between those industrial leaders who used their vast personal resources to build a modern system of higher education in America and the trained academics who assisted them and were assisted by them.

Chief among such agreements might well be the assumption that for those who would be trained to lead in the twentieth century, as contrasted with the leaders of nineteenth-century America, the route from rags to riches was no longer built on simple tailoring which any man handy with his hands could learn. Specialized training and a national professional structure in all modern fields had created a system that shaped and guided ambition, determined the course and consequences of the decisions which men were called upon to make at crucial stages in their careers, and provided the basic canons of method which those who would rise to leadership would be required to manipulate in order to be recognized as justifiably prominent men. So it had become in business, banking, and industry. So would it be in all the professions, including those of university life—their work with men like David Starr Jordan and William Rainey Harper could only have proved the point.[1]

That professionalism within the universities could share common ground with all other forms of professionalism tampers with the traditional view of the university as a place of refuge; that any kind of professionalism involves politics threatens equally sacred views, both in and out of the university, which hold skills and the training in them to be objectively beyond manipulation and subject only to community judgment. The politics which all forms of professionalism could be said to entail is not an easy subject for discussion, even in politics itself where terms like "wheeler-dealer" serve today, as "pol" once served, to express a distaste built upon an acceptance of the assumption that the search for power is necessarily conducted apart from—and conflicts with—a commitment to content and a pure sense of method. Yet professionalism in all fields has created platforms which one must mount before one can be heard; and access to those platforms is lined with guide ropes fashioned in the professions. Even the nation's poets, once the romantic ideal of the free soul, have become permanent inhabitants of academia, inhibited from time to time by its restrictions, but dependent nonetheless on its basic resources and willing, therefore, to chant their lays as they mount the ladder rung by rung.

Although the academic community is renowned for its concentration upon ideas, for its particular establishment of intellect as the basic substance of professional life, even for its increasing claim to status as a national community, it shares with all modern professions an awareness of the accepted routes to success and the leadership which that success may entail. Its academic robes and hoods are worn, more frequently than not, over conservative business suits. Its degrees and the institutions which award them, its national meetings, journals, and generally understood hierarchy of publishing houses are the nuts and bolts of the political machinery whose manipulation serves the establishment and distribution of ideas.

This is not at all to denigrate the central importance of ideas themselves, although it may easily be taken for that. Ideas are to the mechanisms of academic life what invention is to the mechanisms of industrial life. As invention waits upon recognition from an established community, financing from suitable resources, efficient production, and acceptance in a larger, more generalized community to assure continuity, so ideas and their promoters move through the stages of appropriate publication, significant professional reviews, promotion and tenure, activity within the profession through teaching, and, perhaps, broader public reception through the wider circles of professional publicity. While the stages are by no means intended to be correlative, the similarity of direction is interesting and possibly important.

Leadership in either case may well begin with a flash of insight; but the sparks need dry tinder, careful tending, and substantial supplies of fuel. To the extent, then, that such leadership requires a skill in the manipulation of the mechanisms and resources of the intellectual community, one can speak of a politics of ideas as the activity that takes place when men committed to the development of certain ideological positions which they seek to establish within the intellectual community achieve sufficient influence over the professional mechanisms of that community to assure their own continued research and production, the growth of a community engaged in the development of related interests, and the dissemination of the results of that work to the largest potentially interested public.

Professionally speaking, then, the power of intellect and the politics of ideas are, taken together, the basis of the establishment of what could be called a genuinely valid intellectual leadership. Intellect alone may provide sparks which illuminate worlds which others will govern, and that, obviously, may mark a man of brilliance in a generation. The capacity to act politically may give energy and direction to men whose ideas lack depth or continuity; and though that capacity may constitute power and authority for a period of time, it is not, in the sense to be emphasized here, intellectual leadership. Such leadership as the ability to generate ideas and give them effect in a modern world of professional intellectualism is leadership of the most traditional order and the subject of this essay.

Any examples one selects from more recent American history must be seen against the background of the development of the

American university in the period following the Civil War, for it is in the context of that somewhat peculiar confluence of interests that the politics of academic life received its shape. The concern of government, both state and federal, for more effective technical education at higher levels was expressed in the Morrill Act of 1862 which granted to each loyal state thirty thousand acres of land for each senator and representative then in Congress. The purpose of the land grants was the endowment of at least one agricultural college in the state. Twenty-five years later, the Hatch Act—with its establishment of state stations for agricultural experiment—widened even further the involvement of the federal government in educational development through its support of state institutions.[2] Such grants fed the beginnings of a national system through a shrewd exploitation of the interests of the states. In states like Wisconsin and Iowa, the pressure of the state university on the local academies with their often antiquated curricula and intense denominational interests served to improve the quality of academy education both by the example provided and by the interchanges of personnel.

Where private education was concerned, from the 1870's on the combination of reform ambition and personal self-memorialization led industrial leaders to confer large private resources on new collegiate enterprises. Both the public and private interests were guided by a newly emerging group of energetic academic entrepreneurs whose European educations spurred a sense of the need for revolutionary educational reform and whose persuasive skills gave state legislatures and philanthropists alike the assurance that ambitious efforts at modernization would be efficient and dignified. By the turn of the century, men like Chicago's William Rainey Harper, Wisconsin's Theodore Van Hise, Columbia's Nicholas Murray Butler, and Harvard's Charles W. Eliot provided a range of models that demonstrated amply both the dynamic successes and the inherent threats posed by a generation of giants.

Even as that generation's authority was reaching its zenith, however, it was being undermined by men who had the skill to develop plans and the wit to avoid the challenges posed by open confrontation in what was rapidly becoming a competition for resources among the universities as institutions and the institutionalization nationally of the various disciplines themselves. The development of national associations in various academic fields served not only to facilitate intellectual communication in the disciplines, but

435

also to provide resources for publication and to move individuals into national professional prominence, visible above the spires and turrets of their particular institutions.

By 1920 such individuals had been able to move more directly and on their own into entrepreneurial planning. That move coincided with more than a decade of the reorganization of philanthropy into the modern foundation as an institution governed by professionals; and as the giants stepped into the background, mounting the pedestals they had built for themselves, their places were taken by the developers of national groupings of academic associations and by professional foundation staffs within philanthropy. Such organizations as the American Council of Learned Societies and the Social Science Research Council, then, took over the modernization of the financing and planning of intellectual communication. This takeover by the academics of the management of their own resources was the heart of the intellectual revolution which took place in the 1920's; but it had, in its fashion, been carefully prepared.

The young turks who formed the American Economic Association in 1885 and who became justly renowned for their energetic espousal of social responsibility are an obvious example of the beginnings of change; but the more sedate historians from whom they broke are no less an example. That group, which included among its leaders Herbert Baxter Adams, had pushed historians to the national scene and had, by 1890, succeeded in getting a federal charter which entitled them to the publication and distribution of their proceedings by the Government Printing Office. Adams, prominent in the building of the social sciences at The Johns Hopkins, used his rapidly developing professional influence to press the careers of his students. When the historians met at Chicago in July 1893 (rather than at Christmas time, as was customary) to take advantage of the notoriety attendant upon the World's Fair celebrations there, Frederick Jackson Turner's paper, "The Significance of the Frontier in American History," although only one of some twenty-three papers delivered (and by no means the featured one) was given a remarkably central and even fulsome display in the report of the event which Adams wrote for the published proceedings of the association.[3]

Turner's paper was a tasteful and elegant exploitation of the Fair's major themes: westward expansion and the translation of the spirit of Columbian international exploration into national self-development (the separate state exhibits, including that of Turner's Wisconsin, supported that theme amply); census data and other technical innovations as newly developed resources for research (a well-attended Fair exhibit featured a group of "lady experts" demonstrating "a set of curious machines, electrical and mechanical, which were first used during the taking of the last census for tabulating returns"). The central occasion itself—the meeting of the World's Historical Congress in the sumptuous new building of the Art Institute on Michigan Boulevard—emphasized the national development of America's regional attractions toward the new internationalism which was to form one central thrust of the Progressive movement.[4]

Turner's subsequent career can serve as an example of the manner in which academic influence was exercised in the period prior to 1920. His performance at Chicago helped to establish the identification of his name with the "frontier" thesis which was already emerging as the general intellectual interest of his day, even though some of his contemporaries would prefer to associate their own initial interest in the subject with Theodore Roosevelt's *The Winning of the West,* which had begun to appear in 1889 and would conclude its six volumes in 1896. Turner's paper was given professional circulation in several other forms in the years which followed its delivery; and Turner's talents as teacher, as graduate counselor, and, apparently, as administrative entrepreneur in the building of a school of the social sciences at Wisconsin sufficient to attract such contemporary luminaries as Richard T. Ely—all helped in the development of his general reputation and influence. Although the *Wisconsin Bulletin* served for a number of years to distribute the writings of his students, as well as those of his colleagues, his well-known reluctance to publish the results of his own voluminous and continuous researches earned him, on at least one occasion, a gentle—but professionally very public—rebuke from one of his equally influential contemporaries, William A. Dunning, at the historians' meetings in 1917.[5]

The focus of Turner's power, then, was on the development of and distribution of ideas—not chiefly his own, in an absolutely literal sense, but the ideas of others influenced by his particular sense of originality. The focus of that process was primarily the institutions in which he worked, first Wisconsin, then Harvard. His forays on the national scene were confined to the meetings of the professional association. Although he was interested in government and describes having been raised in a family in which governmental involvement was, as it was for many families of his generation and locale, an acceptable avocation of a responsible man, he did not apparently take part in the national, or even local, political movements of his day. That extension of activity would wait upon a later generation.[6]

Turner, like his contemporaries Dunning and John W. Burgess, who built Columbia's faculty in political science and history, was extraordinarily effective within the framework of influence he set for himself. (It could be argued that the latter two had broader, if not greater, effect, even though they are relatively unknown to contemporary audiences.) Neither Dunning nor Burgess ever chanced to associate his name with a successful or popular thesis. Dunning was far too catholic in his own work and teaching, while Burgess sought to establish racial-political hypotheses popular among the Anglo-Saxon-ites of the ninety's, but so repugnant to later social scientists, particularly during the years which separated World War I from World War II. Burgess' continued espousal of them associated him irrevocably with evil. Turner's claim to originality has been challenged, and will undoubtedly continue to be, but with a justice with which he himself might have agreed. His claim to the validity of his thesis has been challenged as well; and there, too, it seems unlikely that a man so committed to the research and reorganization of evidence and hypothesis and so willing to acknowledge the insufficiency of research in his day would object to a solidly based critique.[7]

Nonetheless, one can come to bury Turner or resurrect Dunning and Burgess without ever revealing the very real power they shared in their generation: respect and authority within the intellectual community. That authority gave all three of them control over the resources of publication and research in their fields. By 1920, as their generation closed, it had brought them innumerable students to teach, students who seeded all levels of the profession—and in all of the proliferating social sciences—for another full generation, and more. It had made them friends outside their immediate professional communities to influence; and it had made them enemies and partisans to attack and defend their reputations in disputes which often extended well beyond the politics of their generation into the search for what must, somewhat blushingly, be called immortality.[8]

Our modern sophistication seems to resent that each generation creates its leaders in the available imagery of leadership, out of a selected group of the qualified, to be sure, but on bases which may not survive the generation intact. The problem makes the sustenance of reputation difficult, and earlier leaders may appear to have fallen not through any fault of their own, but through the processes of erosion which remove the ground on which they once stood. In modern life, the process moves with seemingly increased speed as the community of the competently educated expands. In intellectual life, as in political life, a man can consider himself rarely blessed if he and his laurels can be buried in the same grave.

The generation which had built America's institutions of higher learning had, by World War I, succeeded in most of its aims; but to the younger men approaching leadership, even those aims had become antequated in what they now conceived as professional ambition. Frederick J. E. Woodbridge, like Burgess, could boast of Columbia as "the Athens of the New World," but to a group who had come to find that brand of localism a restriction on the needs of its generation, the city-state—as a self-contained community related to other such communities by a loose national alliance—no longer seemed effective. The older generation had come to its profession accepting the assumption that teaching the young was what they were hired to do—and that included at least an acquiescence in the other administrative tasks involved in the general view of "education." Their research they financed themselves, at least until they had achieved sufficient reputation to attract funds from private benefactors on their own. That their publication might be financed institutionally by their institutions, or even by associations in the profession, had been part of their revolution. The new generation wanted more. They were emboldened by their experience in the Progressive movement from which many in the older group, experienced in the politics of university presidents and trustees, had kept a respectful, even if admiring, distance. Fired by government experience in World War I, the new generation had new plans. Returning from the war, they found the older attitudes timid and unimaginative and, above all, unrealistically committed to experiences and restrictions which the new demands of government, industry, and the foundations willing to continue the work of reform could not tolerate. The younger men took over the machinery, respectfully retired their teachers, and began the work. They could not know at the time that their own students would do much the same to them after the experience of World War II.

II

The 1920's, but specifically the war which so dramatically ended the previous decade, brought a new dimension to intellectual leadership in American academic life. Progressive techniques of influencing public opinion had undergone an essential transformation through such war groups as the Committee on Public Information and the Food Administration which utilized an incredibly broad range of talent from communities as seemingly disparate as newspapers, popular magazines, movies, and universities. The War Industries Board employed economists and statisticians, as well as the new enthusiasts for psychological testing and the Taylor management technicians. The Inquiry assembled historians and political scientists to advise Wilson at Versailles. The National Research Council worked to place natural scientists from universities in communication with their counterparts in clumsily, but urgently developing attempts at industrial research. Flooded with a level of academic talent it had used with sporadic and particular interest during the previous decade—the utility of technical information objectively researched had been noted by Theodore Roosevelt in his concern with labor-management relations and by William Howard Taft in his interest in a rational tariff structure—the federal government, even before the end of the Wilson Administration, paused in its involvement, just as it did in many areas of wartime government concern, leaving the academic community alone once again to develop its own directions, now irrevocably influenced by its tantalizing taste of federal power.[9]

Involvement with government had by no means been a new experience for many academics of the Progressive period; but that experience, however profound and enthusiastic, had been primarily local or state in character. Harding's inaugural address promised to continue the much vaunted use of "experts," even in the context of "normalcy"; but, as those academics who had worked in government during the war could well have testified, the federal government's failure to keep pace with many states in the ability to assemble and analyze social and economic data—let alone that of the cities which had pioneered in two decades of what they proudly termed "municipal research"—meant that an energy which would have challenged the political sagacities of men far shrewder than Harding and Coolidge would be required to press upon a conservative Congress of either party the necessity of expanding and improving federal resources. Even Franklin Roosevelt's considerable achievements in this area were bought from a reluctant and embattled Congress at great cost. Herbert Hoover vastly expanded the Department of Commerce to provide the nation's business and industry with technically competent guidance; and he envisaged even more such activity in his dreams of the Presidency. Through his eight very significant years as Secretary of Commerce, Hoover sought to build new relationships among government, business, industry, and the sciences, natural as well as social.[10]

As leading figures behind the founding of the Social Science Research Council in 1923, Charles E. Merriam and Wesley C. Mitchell represent rather well the new academic leadership that men like Hoover would consult, although in different fashion. Both had been involved in wartime agencies—Merriam in the Committee on Public Information, Mitchell in the Price Section of the Division of Planning and Statistics of the War Industries Board. The two had been colleagues on the very junior faculty levels of the University of Chicago in 1900—Merriam in political science; Mitchell in political economy. Both Veblen and Dewey were teaching there that year; Arthur Bentley, who had been an instructor in sociology in 1895-96, was working on a Chicago newspaper; Albion Small dominated sociology, J. Lawrence Laughlin, political economy. Laughlin and Veblen formed the extremes between which Mitchell moved—one a classicist with a willingness to entertain other positions, the other an iconoclast for whom sympathy served only to spur rebellion. Harper was at the peak of his powers and ruled his kingdom through the baronage of "head professors" whose lifetime tenure as department chairmen insured continuity, if nothing else. The university and the city were still touched by the magic of the exposition of 1893 and the spirit of a renaissance which inspired all but a younger generation of cynics who would remain to provide the base for a continuing rebellion.

Mitchell learned from Veblen the way Veblen learned from the world: by denying the example offered, but treating it with a fundamentally profound respect. By contemporary standards, Mitchell's career looks quite stable and conservative until one notes the institutional migrations and the quiet and repeated insistence that academic institutions are shaped not by the new traditions im-

441

posed by trustees and administrators, but by the faculties who teach in them. Harper had built publication and publicity for his faculty into his founding of the university by his establishment of the University of Chicago Press as, in its initial form, exclusive publisher to the Chicago faculty. It was a wise, but costly move and had to be modified later; nevertheless, it was certainly a recognition of a technique of the development of national stature which Harper's generation would initiate, and Mitchell's absorb. Like his contemporary and sometime colleague, Edwin F. Gay, Mitchell worked with the three essentials of academic leadership: the organization and direction of research, the publication and distribution of ideas, and the tapping of philanthropic resources for research and publication. Nonetheless, at least one important point would distinguish Mitchell's generation from that of Harper and Turner: They had sought to embed their aims in the building of their own institutions, drawing into their own universities the riches of opportunity for further research and development which resulted from their efforts. Mitchell and his generation would use the national professional organizations as a vehicle for the development of extra-university organizations that would accumulate resources and distribute them—but under the ultimate direction of nationally oriented professional groups.[11]

Merriam's early career, too, had an orthodoxy that is deceptive. He held appropriately spaced academic positions on the University of Chicago faculty between 1900 and 1920, from "docent" through standard professorial ranks, publishing books on political thought—his thesis in 1900 in the Columbia University series that served to single out the elite of that institution's higher training; and *American Political Theories* in 1903 which was a classic text for many years. He was also among the group who sought an active role in contemporary political life as a useful—and necessary—adjunct to scholarly research in politics. He brought his own research to the support of Chicago reform groups and moved directly into political life himself, so much so that until 1919 his future was clearly that of the scholar-politician nationally exemplified by Woodrow Wilson and Henry Cabot Lodge. To readers of Robert La Follette's *Progressive,* he was "the Woodrow Wilson of the West," although his scholarship at that point was probably somewhat less nationally known and accepted than Wilson's was by the age of forty-five. Merriam's teaching during those years had been interrupted at fairly regular two-year intervals by arduous campaigns for city councilman and mayor, each preceded by the then requisite party primary campaigns. His publications were increasingly associated with his political activities (*Primary Elections* in 1908, for example), and his production of students tended more to enrich the ranks of Progressive public officialdom than the publishing academy.

Thus, when he took the platform of the American Political Science Association at its meeting in December 1920 to call for new definitions of scientific research in politics, he was re-establishing for himself a career in political research, beginning with ideas which others in that postwar meeting had been arguing for some years, but dramatizing them far beyond the talents of any of those who had preceded him. With almost twenty years experience in organizing the philanthropic resources of Chicago to support research interests that the University administration was not willing to back, Merriam moved those skills, too, to the national scene, underplaying now the role of political reform as the vehicle of support, but not so much as to lose the essential attraction such implications had for local reformers. His capacity to compromise with traditional views without threatening progress, to outline the possibility and feasibility of organizational and financial support even before he knew clearly what either one would be, gave him a position of leadership provided to no one else by the ideas alone.

By 1925, when *New Aspects of Politics* appeared, his readers recognized it as a documentation of five years of active and intense engagement in an enterprise that had culminated in the founding of the Social Science Research Council in 1923. As time went on and the recollection of the initial professional exhortations faded, they would remember the experiences and the book as the collection of sparks, the record of the "happenings"—to use a later generation's term—that set them on their way toward the study of political behavior. Merriam would come to be known as the father of behaviorism in political science, although one can search his titles in vain for a use of the term, and it plays relatively little role as significant language in anything he wrote.[12]

When Merriam published *Political Power* in 1934, he was sixty years old, an established figure in his field and one of the influential social scientists of his generation. As a leading exponent of the empirical study of political behavior, Merriam could achieve a certain dramatic presence simply by the publication of a book that promised a new level of generalization. Later readers, even devoted ones, might find that drama difficult to recapture just from the text, until they recalled the circumstances under which they had first read or heard *Political Power*.

For those at Chicago who sat listening in the lecture room of the Social Science Research Building, the experience was filled with the sense of the richly suggestive mind with which they were, in varying degrees and at varying distances, familiar. Merriam in Chicago politics, Merriam and the management of what had come to be one of the country's most influential departments of political science, Merriam and the broad and imaginative distribution of social research funds through not only the Social Science Research Council, but also the Public Administration Clearing House, the Rockefeller Foundation's Spelman Fund, and his position on the National Resources Planning Board, the federal government in its pursuit of knowledge and data for social reform—Merriam stood before them in recollection, tall and white haired, recounting, in a voice still redolent of the Iowa countryside, an organization of the principles of politics for which they each could have supplied the particulars.

There was no discussion of Chicago politics, but thirty years of experience in governmental reform documented for Merriam and his audience a common set of sympathies and interests that underlay generalizations about political outlaws and community authority. Nor would anyone fail to catch the significance of the tale told about the first draft—that it had been written in a Berlin hotel room near the Reichstag in 1932 during the century's most crucial struggle for power. It was a fact he would acknowledge in his published preface, coolly concealing the intense concern and the fervent haste that had pressed the words to paper. An old-line Progressive academic who had twice seen his teachers' Germany fall before what he could only interpret as a failure of government and the public to bring resources of scientific theory to practical application, Merriam had become a master of the generalization of his own experience. He could assume that he spoke for his generation; and in many respects he did—although possibly in ways different from those he intended. "Merriam looked like a Roman Senator," Harold Lasswell recalled in 1962 when he prepared a preface for a re-issue of the book, "and spoke with unhurried authority." Professionally speaking, the age of hurry was over by 1934. Merriam had reached a point where he could quite clearly be considered a leader among the small group of American academics whose access to the newly reorganized generosity of

American philanthropists controlled the distribution of millions of dollars supporting social research. His bibliography was long and significantly influential. He commanded authority as well as respect.

The mechanisms of that authority had expanded well beyond those available to Turner's generation. The local and individual resources that based the previous generation's activities had, in the process of nationalizing their own ambitions, come to look to the federal government as an object of philanthropy. The administrations of Herbert Hoover and Franklin D. Roosevelt had both sought to utilize that rapidly growing and complexly interconnected network of small and large foundations, governmental and industrial research agencies, and academic associations which constituted the empire manipulated by men like Merriam and Mitchell. It was an empire in which command rested on prestige, prestige on ideas, and ideas on the essential power of an intellect to conceive, to persuade, and to achieve a position of influence on other intellects; and in that respect it was continuous with Turner's generation. But that generation considered it a triumph to have the federal government charter its association and provide publications for its yearly reports, ambitions sufficiently grand in their day, but scarcely even modest by comparison with those which World War I and its aftermath had spawned.

Merriam saw the science of politics as based upon the development of methods in all of the disciplines that could conceivably be relevant to politics; and the major achievements of his career, both in his writing and in his professional involvements, were built on the establishment of connections among the disciplines—not only their ideas, but their resources of intellect, method, and money for further research. At times, it seems as though the science of politics became for him the politics of social science, in all the variety, breadth, and inherent conflict which can reside in disciplinary points of view. Mitchell, on the other hand, was an economist, first and finally. Broadly humane, as Merriam was, and as deeply committed to the improvement of the social condition, Mitchell's essential science was economics, his research was economic, and he returned to the confines of his discipline for encouragement, intellectual rejuvenation, and that kind of basic relaxation which great scholars seem to find in their exhausting struggles with the intransigent fundamentals of their discipline. Merriam enriched political science by broadening it. Mitchell enriched economics by

445

deepening it. Their individual contributions cannot be measured by each other; but their joint contribution in the early days of the SSRC and in the planning boards of the New Deal is amply clear in the developments in the social sciences during the twenties and thirties.

Merriam's organizational talents lay in his quick, at times almost intuitive, recognition of the importance of new ideas and in the great efficiency with which he created and reorganized institutional structures for dealing with those ideas—giving them publicity and distribution as well as finding the financial means to further their development. However odious the comparison might have been to the Progressive core of his personal politics, he shared with banking entrepreneurs like Andrew Mellon an affinity for the new invest-ment. His imagination, like theirs, was capable of extension beyond his own experience and training, and his sense of urgency for implementation, like theirs, committed him to building under those ideas the substructure of institutional support that could increase their development and give continuing impulse to their effect. The method was not an easy one to observe. It had evolved over a period of more than twenty years when it reached its peak in the mid-twenties. A compound of the access which his political career had given him to the reformer-philanthropists of the Progressive period and the university and governmental involvement which his academic career had generated, the method was his personal refine-ment of practices he observed in a good many of his contemporaries, most notably and importantly, his brother John.

As a paleontologist and geologist at the University of California at the turn of the century, John Campbell Merriam had quite early in his career learned to utilize the well-supported hobbies of local amateur explorers as a source of research funds for his departmental interests. Summer travel in the Sierras could be interesting not only to students and colleagues, but to business people who could combine a fascination with rocks and crustacea with an awareness of other values of mineral discovery. The search for gold which had spurred the adventures of an earlier generation had gone through a vast sequence of scientific refinements as new resources attracted new attention. The relation between fossil re-mains and oil deposits, for example, was of more than geological and historical interest. Politically speaking, the concern could be transferred easily enough into the conservation movement, the planning of the rapidly growing cities and towns of northern

California, and the administration and development of the University.

John Merriam left the deanship of the University of California in World War I to work on the National Research Council in Washington, to help coordinate relationships between industry, academic scientific research, and government in pursuit of the nation's war aims. The active interest of Herbert Hoover during his brief period as president of the American Engineering Council helped sustain the NRC after the war. Hoover's continued interest during his period as Secretary of Commerce was one of several important factors that expanded the research activities of the NRC, attracted to it more private and public funds for research distribution, and contributed to its broadened involvement in social science and government. John Merriam remained with the NRC in numerous administrative and committee posts after he took over the presidency of the Carnegie Institution in Washington. As a sometime adviser to President Hoover, he was instrumental in bringing his brother's concern with his fledgling SSRC into governmental activity considerably sooner than might otherwise have been the case.

Through the twenties and into the thirties, the combined roles of the Merriam brothers as advisers in the distribution of research funds from foundations, as well as the selection of college presidents, government administrators, and key faculty members around the country, provided a remarkable center of influence and power, as the correspondence between them only begins to indicate. The NRC, like the SSRC, served as a clearinghouse and advisory service for interested donors and as a broker for setting up working operations in the relationship between interested research personnel, sources of finance for research, and various governmental, public, and private agencies interested in benefiting from the research.[18]

What an earlier generation would surely have designated as an academic research "trust" was formed under the direction of the councils. Unlike the entrepreneurs whose trusts had produced the funds they were manipulating, the academic entrepreneurs were committed to operation within a community whose devotion to ideas subjected them to rather different standards of truth, scientific validity, and ultimate social value, even while they found themselves unavoidably—and surely unadmittedly—borrowing heavily from the economic and political tradition that had produced them. While they also borrowed as much skill and method from their observations of men like Harper as Carnegie and Rockefeller, their own innovations were equally important. The emphasis upon the support of the research of younger men was a frank recognition of rebellion against the practice of educational institutions which placed heavy work loads on new, unpublished scholars during precisely those years when they could be making significant contributions to research. The focus on research groups and national communities of interest was in sharp contrast with the "great" man views established by Harper, as well as with the local approach that institution building was bound to give to the work of the previous generation. But it was not only the academic and industrial tradition which men like Merriam and Mitchell could draw on in their evolution of the methods of their generation.

Men like the Merriam brothers, or Harold Ickes, or Herbert Hoover all moved to the urban national and international scene from similar backgrounds in American rural life. Rural government, as such, was considerably more distant from the daily life of the citizen than urban politics had come to be for those bred in cities; and the different sense of government expressed by those raised in the rural townships of the old Northwest—as Turner had been—from those raised in the much more judicially-oriented counties—as the Merriams were—made for rather interesting variations in point of view.[14]

Government in its contemporary sense, and in the sense in which they were to see it in adult, urban life was probably more apparent in the churches of their small communities and in the little academies and elementary schools whose finances they tended and whose operation and "policy" they superintended, than it was in "local" government, whatever that happened to be. Part of their reaction to urban politics when they came upon it resulted not only because it was often highly corrupt, by their standards, but also because their standards were of a strikingly different order than those familiar to the urban merchants who worked to reform city politics (or to gain their own advantage from it) and whose methods were nonetheless compatible with those which the new group was going to develop.

The adoption of a complex of political manners by leaders of the academic community was influenced not only by the fact that such men continued to involve themselves throughout the Progressive period and into the New Deal in local and national political life, but also by the nature of the academic community itself. The relationships among American universities which moved into positions of prominence after the 1880's share interesting similarities with the relations existing among the states and governments within the states. Often regionally unique in their traditions, resources, points and manners of origin, relative qualities at various points in time, they nonetheless form a loose federation through their exchanges of faculty members and programs of education along routes of national professional communication as legally informal, so to speak, but as deeply embedded in the process of intellectual life as the American party system is in the process of political life. Like the systems of party politics and their relation to federal, state, and local political institutions, American academic life can be looked at from two distinct points of view where questions of politics are concerned. The politics of professionalism within any given educational institution or group of institutions can be made relatively clear, as can the political organization of the national associations in the disciplines. What is always unclear is the relation between the national organization and the relationships it determines among the various institutions whose faculties share a kind of dual citizenship as they work within their own departments and institutions and as they relate to the colleagues they join yearly in the national association. Membership in the association may be determined, in effect, by statute, as in the case of medicine or law, or simply by subscribing to a journal. Like the system of American party organization, however, with its quadrennial conventions, the emergence of national leaders and their relation to the local political institutions in which, generally speaking, they must at some point have originated is not so easy to describe.

Similarly within the academic community a system of politics has emerged that depends as much upon the development of cadres of present and future personnel and upon the distribution of resources, jobs, prestige, and the like as does the national political system. "Patronage" exists, is whispered about from time to time as a kind of corruption, and serves to organize loose parties whose debates are conducted largely at national meetings and in the review sections of journals. That such politics and the leadership which moves along its channels into national prominence should adopt parallels to American politics is no accident, nor is it simply a product of several generations of experience. Much of American life operates through similar federalisms. The practice partakes of a kind of necessity in a highly dispersed, but democratically committed

449

society as a means of dealing with fundamental differences without doing permanent damage to the illusions of consensus inherent in supporting the will of some kind of organized public. That the operation of politics in the academic community tends to be looked upon with distaste and played down as much as possible may be related as much to manners as to the marked resemblance such an attitude bears to the traditional American conception of politics as a professional pursuit. Politics is a dirty game. Professors and intellectuals—like Presidents, oddly enough—are supposed to be above such things. Yet, like aspiring Presidents, academics who seek to give their ideas useful public and professional support and who desire some measure of effect cannot achieve their aims by the simple announcement of their virtues.

Academics then, who wish to see their research interests and their ideas supported by government move through successive levels of politics, taking with them the politics of the profession in which they have been engaged, which is in turn derived from the experience of community politics. The influence and the relationships—to judge by a figure like Charles Merriam—are as pervasive as they are confusing. By 1933, when Merriam was seeking to move the national social research community which he had helped build to the service of the federal government, he was at the peak of his own power in that community. Yet despite his deep commitment to the scientific bases of the ideas that that community represented and the inherent and essential rationality of their methods, his power rested upon unresolved conflicts in point of view as capable of generating intense disputes and as much in need of compromise as those being manipulated by the President he advised. The story of the National Resources Planning Board is as much the story of the politics of science as of the science of politics. It helped teach the students of Merriam and his colleagues the methods with which, in their time, they would replace his leadership with their own.

The decline of the power of the Progressive generation came during World War II, a product of the experience of the New Deal and the war and, of course, the graceless erosion of age. The relation between theory and practice so frequently enunciated by Merriam and Mitchell began, at least in Merriam's case, to appear to be a mystique unsupported by the research he had generated and the practical experiences he had made possible. To returning veterans, many of the remaining voices of the Chicago School

450

seemed at times elegantly formal, a bit old-fashioned. Yet the organization the new generation was about to take over was one which had taken some thirty years for the generation which had taught them to build, and thirty years of work before that. It was a complex national system, a wealthy one, a powerful one, and—with a postwar educational revolution under way financed by federal funds (the G.I. Bill and then direct governmental research projects)—a political factor of a new order. The new generation would assume as given what the previous generation had celebrated as victory and proceed to new battles.

III

A narration such as this which halts so visibly on the rim of the present assumes sufficient risk without attempting anything so absurd as a conclusion. Anyone familiar with the present-day disputes in the fields once dominated by Turner, Dunning, Burgess, Merriam, and Mitchell is no likelier to be soothed by being told that the past is prologue than he is encouraged, say, by the suggestion that the present is epilogue. The future has a way of violating enchantments with prose—which is only to say that historians live no more happily ever after than do political scientists or economists.

One reason, perhaps, for calling attention to what has been called "the politics of ideas" is to indicate, at least, a methodology of continuity that can serve to clarify the transmission of ideas and their development and that might avoid—or less ambitiously "modify"—the tendency to render past intellectual achievements obsolete and to lose thereby such assurance as tradition can give to our sense of purposive, intelligent direction. The trouble with the view of intellectual politics presented thus far is that it may seem too recognizable and too real to be consistent with acceptable traditions, and may indeed be used against those traditions as some kind of demonstration of an inherent falseness in powerful minds.

The view that a politics of ideas is anti-intellectual, therefore, is a contradiction, but an important one, even if it misses the point. A destructive critique of past intellects serves the present more than it aids in a reconstruction of the past if the objective relevance of brilliant ideas is to be diminished by revelations of the essential humanity of the generations of men who move ideas and provide them with the continuing base of their transmission. One might better question the intransigent romanticism that presses us to create unrealistic models of ideal behavior which fail to stand the test of closer historical analysis.

The politics of ideas is the method by which ideas are brought into working relationships with the resources of their time, among them the processes by which new generations are to be educated to advance knowledge and to sustain the pace of its transmission. An approach so generational in its focus is bound to raise questions of "greatness," if not of anti-intellectualism, since the view that important ideas are more the products of a generation's concerns than of individual genius leads ultimately to the conclusion that greatness at any moment is the product of an individual's manipulative or political skills rather than of a peculiarly productive mind. Again, that is not a necessary conclusion except for the persistence of two related beliefs: first, that charisma, if that term is allowable at this point, is the product of magic rather than a skill in creating magical illusions; and, secondly, that Rhetoric, which in classical belief was a highly skilled art, is somehow false, a form of verbal trickery which is contrasted with simple truth.

This study has attempted to suggest that similar processes operate at all levels in the communication of ideas, and that greatness in a generation may rest as much on skill as on romantically isolated visions of peculiar wisdom. This is not to deny the importance of insight, but rather to argue that insight takes place in a context in which the acceptance of ideas by a community concerned with criticism and continuity plays an important role in the rise and fall of leadership. That context changes historically as the ideas affect the community, causing it to re-examine its views, testing insight against experience, and seeking new leaders to replace the old.

The relation between social theory and practical politics looked a good deal simpler to the Progressive generation than it has looked since, although one might argue that their relatively brief period of hearty enthusiasm produced the basic opportunities for genuine involvement which the present generation enjoys—if that is the right word. Turner and Ely at Wisconsin, Burgess at Columbia, and the later generation—Merriam at Chicago, Gay at Harvard and the New School, and Mitchell at Columbia and the New School—built institutional arrangements that could generate continuous training in governmental research. Charles A. Beard, even at the peak of his disgust with academic institutions, aided in developing the New York Bureau of Municipal Research and its Training School for Public Service into an effective instrument for reforming government. All, in one way or another, accepted social activism as a responsibility that could utilize their best thinking without necessarily damaging the logic of their ideas.

Chicago businessmen who found George Herbert Mead's paradigm of action unintelligible in his writings apparently found him persuasive when he appeared at their City Club to discuss educational problems in Chicago.[15] Dewey's Chicago career was steeped in political conflict which bled into his later writings, although the gentling of the pulse and the orderly flow of thought to thought conceal all of the scars and most of the sounds of the battle. During the more formalistic period of Progressive reform, when new charters and new electoral methods were looked upon as the real center of useful change, men like Merriam and Beard learned to move with the political tides that beached some plans and flooded others, but supported enough change to keep the sense of improvement in political life moving forward. Despite the repeated assertion that politics could be made more scientific, reform fervor demanded a kind of flexibility that might wreak havoc with the sense of system on which a scientific point of view would have to rest.[16]

Merriam's students often respectfully followed his injunctions that they expand the scientific nature of their research at the same time that they admired his sure instinct for the practical methods of politics. None of those who puzzled about the relation of the two ever resolved his own sense of suspicion that there might be a fundamental conflict. He knew Chicago the way few men of even his self-consciously urban generation knew any American city. He guided numerous studies of the city's politics and government, studies which were to become classics in the emerging field of urban politics; yet he continued to participate as directly as local party disputes allowed—and it was never enough to suit his interest —in the hearty brawls which characterized Chicago politics in the 20's and 30's. By the time he retired in 1940, there were no longer students who identified him as a Progressive. The science of politics and the practice of politics met in his personality without anachronism, but with an increasing individualism that would set him apart from the newer groups whose sense of science he had helped create. The questions that their observations of him might have produced were at the base of the problem of relating scientific social research to government and the almost metaphysical problems of the essential relations among systematic ideas and the men who use such ideas to assert their leadership.

Although Merriam undoubtedly dreamed of himself as a builder of systems, the reality of his career proved otherwise. His last major work was entitled *Systematic Politics,* but when it appeared in 1944, it was received with a respectful nostalgia that concealed the strong belief among the younger, postwar generation of political scientists that it was neither systematic nor political in its basic restatement of ideas with which they were familiar and about which they now had many doubts. New studies of politics, many of them by Merriam students, showed a methodological elegance that he had never achieved, partly because he had rejected the separation of method and structure from the ongoing process of politics itself.

Within a decade of the publication of *Systematic Politics,* writers like Daniel Boorstin, Louis Hartz, and Richard Hofstadter were enunciating important variations on what had become a major postwar theme: a questioning of the plausibility of describing a consciously practiced system of American political ideas. Americans, according to them, had either refused to create systematic political ideas, or had been unable to recognize those that they were in fact using, or had misused the ones they did attach to their political behavior. In an important respect, they were all describing accurately, if unintentionally, the revolution against the heart of the Progressive commitment to the mastery of political ideas as the basis of political action. It was a revolution, as well, against the bases of intellectual leadership that Merriam represented.

Intellectually speaking, Merriam's leadership rested on beliefs that would, in time, appear paradoxical. First, he inherited a nineteenth-century conviction that academic production should, at its best, involve the creation of comprehensive systems of philosophic thought, regardless of the field of study. Secondly, he accepted his own generation's concern with specialization in technical research, the need for more accumulation of organized data, and the necessary refinements of method in social science. Finally, he came to believe, more and more, that social research, however technical or specialized its base, ultimately had to be brought to the service of the whole of society by the whole of society; that it was not of, or for, or imposed by any special group. Inherent in the relationship among the three points were conflicts that could appear insoluble to men less convinced of the fundamental soundness of all three positions.

With respect to the creation of a comprehensive system of thought, Merriam, like John Dewey, sought to pursue every avenue of interest his disciplinary involvements suggested, interweaving insightful hints with judgments about research in such a way as to attract interest and provoke work by others. Dewey's enthusiastic invasions of each and every field of philosophy were not equally successful, as students of his work were once willing enough to admit, and the successful ones were not always on a sustained level of quality. Yet Dewey survives, his stature grows as an intellectual corpus evolves in a form greater than, and justifiably so, any of its parts. Similarly for Merriam, one can develop a model of his intellect that is considerably more imposing than the written relics which survive, once one relates the texts to the context of their times to observe a mind in action, the soul of intellectual leadership. He wove his own sense of system in and through the work of others; and his political manipulation of the intellectual life of his times is as much a part of his system as his published writings.

Since the 1880's, as this essay has tried to suggest, American intellectual leadership has depended upon the ability to create and to lead an ever more complex series of communities—local, institutional, regional, and national. Such communities may bring together systems of thought so deeply in conflict with one another that their continued association may depend on an avoidance of the fundamental confrontation of ideas through the operation of a politics built not on the subtleties of ideas, but on the realities of power. That power resides in the institutions and associations through which ideas are communicated; and it is manipulated by men who manage sufficient identification with ideas to justify their right to control the power. The conflicts they adjudicate may involve basic differences resulting from the effects on a discipline of specialization, the particularism of method and subject matter which the research promoted by men like Merriam seems inevitably to bring about. Merriam's search for systematic generalization would seem at times to run counter to his pressure for more specialized research were it not for the commitment to interdisciplinary communication that led him to see himself as a functional, rather than substantive, modern Aristotle, interrelating the sciences by forcing them to focus upon one another's problems. The resulting association made the establishment of useful relationships possible with-

455

out demanding strict adherence to any logical sequence of subject matter, or first principles or method. The ultimate social utility of all knowledge was the guiding assumption and the one generalization worthy of continuous repetition.

A basic pragmatism built upon an adherence to morally and politically simple ideas was the method whereby Merriam's generation effected a compromise between the tradition of system building in which they were educated and the rapidly and complexly diversifying society which they were called upon to manage. Trained to view the history of Western thought as a sequence of unifying systems, they sought to establish a place for themselves in what they accepted as an honorable continuity. The effects of technological diversity were sufficient to force reconsideration which could result either in Mitchell's immersion in specialization, broken by periodic resurfacings generated by social and professional responsibility, or in Merriam's commitment of himself to a whole community—social, political, and intellectual—which constituted at least a sense of system, the parts of which would have to be analyzed in depth by others. It is worth noting, perhaps, that Mitchell represented social science to Herbert Hoover, and Mitchell left the New Deal when he could no longer accept national planning as a part-time, semi-professional, semi-political endeavor. Merriam represented social science to Franklin Roosevelt, whose broad brush painted politics over even the most systematic structures and gave them a reason for working that overcame, at least for a time, the obvious lack of precision.

Whether or not one such man can both organize modern intellectual communities and take advantage of the opportunities for new insight and research which the existence of such communities makes possible is the question which points to at least two quite different functions of intellectual leadership. The first—the administration and politics of ideas—shares with all forms of politics an emphasis upon the possible, on resources available, and on personal and professional judgments about the talents of others. The second —the formulation and communication of ideas—shares with the arts and sciences, in general, an emphasis upon logic, the systematic structuring of ideas, and abstractions of formal analysis.

Men like Merriam and Turner and Beard sought combinations of the two approaches to leadership. Even in the loosely arranged federation of the American intellectual world, a significant demonstration of both is a prerequisite of leadership. All three men were viewed in their respective generations as leaders, even though their writings, unlike those, say, of Veblen or Dewey, have moved in and out of "classical" status with a remarkable kind of critical abandon.

A work that achieves status as a classic must be capable of being lifted from its historical environment, like Turner's paper, for example, without violating a sense of meaning, regardless of the author's intentions. Like the Turner essay, its relation to its original environment may continue to serve as a source of debate. The spiritual, Hegelian Turner, for example, was more immediately extractable and persisted, at least generally speaking, as the basic Turner until the recent rediscovery of the economic, geopolitical Turner. The same is true of some of Merriam's writings, which are just now being reactivated, and certainly of Arthur Bentley's presumably forgotten masterpiece. The ingredients of environment are interesting to point out, as in the case of Merriam's *The Making of Citizens*, which appeared in 1931 as the capstone and philosophical summary of a series of books on civic education in various countries of the world and which has recently been referred to, quite correctly, as a singularly important series with no predecessors and no successors.[17]

As this discussion has tried to suggest, intellectual leadership in any generation is considerably more complex a matter than a listing of "Great Books" or a recounting of thirty years of cumulative judgment might suggest. In the long run, a man's writings may become classics without his being an intellectual leader, in the sense described here, either to the generation that first read those books and may or may not have recognized their classical potential, or to the later generation that comes upon his work out of its original context and recognizes in it the more general virtues which give it universal interest. Indeed, such belated recognition may deceive a later generation into positing a dynamic leadership that did not exist at the time, just as the later discovery that a man's writings have not achieved such status may lead to the after-the-fact denial of a leadership that really did exist.

Turner's leadership in American historical writings between 1893 and 1933 is not changed by newly emerging criticisms of his methods and approaches. Charles Beard's waspish attacks on the academic community, his insistence after World War I that he remain on the fringes of that community (albeit well-displayed), and that community's rejection of him as World War II approached cannot deny the real leadership he exercised throughout his professional life. The discovery of the great importance which his own generation failed to see in the writings of Arthur F. Bentley does not make him, retroactively, an intellectual leader in his time, although the curious fate of political philosophy in both politics and philosophy between his generation and ours must also be taken into account. The relation between a presentness of effect—a kind of charisma, if you will—and the grinding processes of critical judgment over time is compounded of complexities that include ideas and systems of ideas, but a great deal else as well.

What this essay has been trying to suggest, then, is a way of relating intellectual leadership and historical experience in a fashion that will neither insist upon ideas as the ultimate driving force nor relegate them to some behavioral limbo in which they are subjected to and mastered by the mechanisms of a malevolently secret politics of manipulation.

Ideas are the materials of intellectual leadership, but they are not the only materials. They share status in their historical time with such powerful and often fearful forces as rhetorical skill, money, and political position in a professional community. Regardless of the tendency of later generations to fix ideas on a printed page and to identify them by title and author, they are born in a historical community, circulate through established channels, and are declaimed from clearly identifiable platforms. The ultimate survival of the printed page does not give it greater claim to reality in a truly historical sense. If it is true that in the long run ideas tend to survive other elements more immediately associated with historical milieu, it is all the more important to understand the mechanisms of intellectual leadership. The difference between "influence" and "leadership" might well come to rest on some closer definition of the relations among ideas, considered in and of themselves, and the technical talents and active careers of the men who give ideas their contemporary currency.

Although the suggestion of models is a dangerous method for a somewhat old-fashioned historian to begin using, examination of the careers of a few of the intellectual leaders in America over the past half century or so does seem to indicate the elements of a fairly recurrent pattern. A man may begin his career as an academic influential by enunciating a point of view in a fashion that is in some way sufficiently striking or attractive to identify that point of view with his particular statement of it, rather than with the statements of others in his generation who may be saying the same or similar things. This may, of course, involve a monumental scholarly achievement, to use that worn but irreplaceable phrase; or the attraction may rest on style of presentation, on the selection of an occasion uniquely appropriate to the profession, on the choice of one medium rather than another—indeed, on a host of factors which could be called "publicist" were that old term not already freighted with so many pejorative meanings in the intellectual community.

The politics of influence may follow the initial impact if the individual involved indicates in any way a willingness to take advantage of the opportunities open to him: by establishing himself in an institution that will give him a prominent position in the community or by using his own growing reputation as a device for giving the institution with which he is already established an influence associated more directly with him; by careful consideration of the recommendations he makes to sources of scholarship and research funds on the distribution of their resources, as well as by the attraction of such resources himself for his own work and work which goes on under his direction; by the selection of colleagues whose reputations will reinforce his own and by the training of students whose work will reflect his interests; by the sustained management of a reputation within the profession through the various purely professional routes—appearances on programs at the meetings and influence in the structure of those programs, involvement in the management of journals and their book reviews, influence in the writing of textbooks and the selection for publication of books in his field.

The last stage of influence may rest on the most complex shift of all—from national reputation in the relative privacy of his professional field to national public reputation and the consequent influence in areas that may reach well beyond his purely professional occupation. At this point, he may actually move into government— as an adviser, an administrator, a statesman, or a politician. The extent to which his public reputation rests upon his professional reputation may depend solely upon the nature of the public job and how much the tasks he is now called upon to perform are, in fact, related to his specialized training. The undercurrent of professional criticism of him which seems inevitably to attend his exercise of a public career indicates an additional problem in the tracing of stages: that from a professional point of view each stage critically threatens the previous one.

Academic power of the second stage may occasion questions about the continuing quality of the publication that initiated the reputation in the first place. Performance in a public career may give rise to questions about continuing professional competence. The price of upward mobility—if that is the proper designation of the direction—may well be the previous basis of influence; and the man who ascends the ladder may find his critics carefully removing the rungs as he passes them. While descent is by no means impossible, it depends on the extent to which real attachment is maintained to the ideas, the research, the scholarship—whatever it happens to be—on which the initial influence was predicated. If that sounds like a simple matter for any man of good conscience and mature responsibility, it might be well to recall Antony's concern over Caesar's reputation. Funeral orations are useful and, as the still present practice of the *Festschrift* testifies, it is possible to have friendly and affectionate recollections of the great and once-powerful. Most of them, however, are neither written nor delivered in the sight of the bloody corpse.

The politics of influence is no game. Its purpose may always be to facilitate the development and the utility of ideas; but it *is* politics. Battles are fought; there are winners and losers; and there are painful wounds and scars which prickle when the weather changes.

The increasing professionalism of the past half century has made the process of becoming intellectually influential much more complex than it used to be. The professionalization of the intellectual has sharpened the lines between thoughtful and informed writing, on the one hand, and the trained products of professional research, on the other. No one today would find it easy to take William A. Dunning's professional evaluation of Theodore Roosevelt as one of the more important American historians of his generation as seriously as he did. We tend not to think of Henry Cabot Lodge as a great scholar, and we reckon Woodrow Wilson's scholarship by standards considerably more complex than those current during the active phase of his academic career.

As the manipulation of ideas ceases being simply the province of all humanely educated men and becomes more involved in the vast array of rapidly proliferating specializations, the line between the politics of ideas and the power of ideas becomes sharper and more confusing. The politics of ideas appears more and more a specialization in and of itself, a kind of parasite living on thought.

Such a view may, however, be an illusion of our own creation which conceals one fact with which nature is already familiar: that it is man that views the parasite as evil, not nature. Some parasites, like orchids, for example, may be even more attractive than the hosts on which they live, and infinitely more valuable. In the world of ideas, they may function to create an order which would not exist without them, to generate a sense of purpose, to kindle ambition in others, to promise fulfillments which no one may ever know, but which all require as the essential source of initiating energy.

The world we inhabit may make parasites of us all in the sense that we feed on a common body of ideas; a significant portion of any intellect we develop is forever dependent upon those from whom we have learned, those of our contemporaries with whom we debate, and those whom we teach. The survival of the printed page with its final determination of the sources of mastery may be the one gracious illusion that history allows us; but it may conceal the political process by which ideas are passed from generation to generation and by which the men who lead in the intellectual world come ultimately to represent the ideas with which they lead.

REFERENCES

1. There are innumerable histories of American universities, most of which tend to be "house" histories devoted to internal memorialization and thus are inclined to an approach which avoids anything which might be interpreted as criticism. A remarkably notable exception must surely be the two-volume *The University of Wisconsin* by Merle Curti and Vernon Carstensen (Madison, Wisconsin, 1949). Recent studies which are useful are Richard J. Storr, *Harper's University* (Chicago, 1966); and Laurence R. Veysey, *The Emergence of the American University* (Chicago, 1965), although the review of the latter by Daniel Boorstin in *Perspectives in American History* (Vol. 1; Cambridge, 1967) makes some important points about the weaknesses in the writing of university history.

2. For a full account of such developments, particularly with respect to the sciences, see A. Hunter Dupree, *Science in the Federal Government* (Cambridge, 1957), as well as the essays in *Science and Society in the U. S.*, eds. David D. Van Tassel and Michael G. Hall (Homewood, Ill., 1966).

3. *Report of the American Historical Association, 1893* (Washington, D. C., 1893). The featured paper, probably, was Mrs. Ellen Hardin Walworth's "The Value of National Archives to a Nation's Life and Progress."

An equally official summary by William F. Poole of the Newberry Library and chairman of the Chicago Committee appeared in *The Independent*, July 20, 1893, p. 13, and does not mention Turner's paper. A total of thirty-three papers were included in the volume. Twenty-three of them were read during the course of the meetings.

4. These details combine material in Poole's summary with description in *The Cosmopolitan*, Vol. 15, No. 5, devoted to the Fair.

5. The descriptions of Turner and his influence are too numerous to note; the bibliography exceeds Turner's. The essays in O. Lawrence Burnette, Jr., *Wisconsin Witness to Frederick Jackson Turner* (Madison, 1961), are very useful, as is the essay in *Turner, Bolton and Webb*, Wilbur Jacobs, *et. al.* (Seattle, 1965). An important account of Turner's organizational skills is in Merle Curti and Vernon Carstensen, *The University of Wisconsin*, Vol. 1 (Madison, 1949), but see also the account in Richard T. Ely's autobiography, *Ground Under Our Feet* (New York, 1938). Dunning's sad reference to Turner's dilemma can be found in "A Generation of American Historiography," *Report of the American Historical Association, 1917.* "For the perpetuation of the spirit and method of these writers in the twentieth century, it is unnecessary to mention to this audience how potent has been the influence, and how disproportionately scanty, alas! the historiographic output, of our Turner."

6. Joseph Schafer, "Turner's Autobiographical Letter to Constance Lindsay Skinner," in Burnette, *Wisconsin Witness. . .*

7. Lee Benson, *Turner and Beard, American Historical Writing Reconsidered* (New York, 1960), gives important historical background on the thesis; comprehensive critiques of the theory itself can be found in George Wilson Pierson, "The Frontier and American Institutions," *The New England Quarterly*, Vol. 15, p. 224; a defense in Stanley Elkin's and Eric McKitrick, "A Meaning for Turner's Frontier," *Political Science Quarterly*, Vol. 64, p. 323.

8. In addition to the various *Festschriften* in their honor (Dunning alone has two, one put together by historians and political scientists, the other by a broader range of social scientists he trained), see Howard W. Odum (ed.), *American Masters of Social Science* (New York, 1927), for such things as Charles Merriam's appreciation of Dunning, and Carl Becker's of Turner.

9. Herbert Heaton provides a fascinating account of professional economics and the War Industries Board in *A Scholar in Action; the Life of Edwin F. Gay* (Cambridge, 1952). Lawrence E. Gelfand, *The Inquiry* (New Haven, 1963), is a useful and important account of that effort. J. R. Mock and Cedric Larson's *Words That Won the War* (Princeton, 1939) is about the only recent study of the Creel Committee, and it badly needs redoing. Despite its very real importance in evaluating the relation between the war and the New Deal, little has been done on the War In-

dustries Board; but see William E. Leuchtenberg, "The New Deal and the Analogue of War," in *Change and Continuity in Twentieth-Century America*, eds. Braeman *et al.* (Columbus, Ohio, 1964).

10. Typical of Hoover's appeals for "pure" research and its utility to industry is his speech before the American Society of Mechanical Engineers, New York, Dec. 1, 1925, "The Vital Need for Greater Financial Support of Pure Science Research." *Reprint and Circular Series of the National Research Council*, No. 65.

11. Lucy Sprague Mitchell's biography of her husband and herself, *Two Lives* (New York, 1953), will someday take its well-deserved place among the classics of such literature in America. It is rich in many things, among them the history of this period. Roger W. Shugg's essay *The University of Chicago Press, 1891-1965* (Chicago, 1966) gives a good bit of information on Harper's initial intentions and their evolution. And, of course, Joseph Dorfman's *Thorstein Veblen and His America* (New York, 1934) is extremely useful in documenting some of the problems of generational transition.

12. Within a decade of his death in 1953 the evaluation of Merriam's role had begun. The first effort was a critical attack: *The American Science of Politics* (London, 1959) by Bernard Crick. But see V. O. Key, Jr., "Issues and Problems of Political Science Research," *The Status and Prospects of Political Science as a Discipline* (Ann Arbor, 1960). In an interesting retrospective article published in 1964, Lindsay Rogers discusses rather critically Merriam's career and its relation to Columbia University's department of political science ("Notes on Political Science," *Political Science Quarterly*, January 1964). "Fact and Value in Charles E. Merriam" by Tang Tsou (*Southwestern Social Science Quarterly*, June 1955) makes some important comments concerning the later stages of Merriam's political thought. See also Evron M. Kirkpatrick, "The Impact of the Behavioral Approach on Traditional Political Science," *Essays on the Behavioral Study of Politics*, ed. Austin Ranney (Urbana, Ill., 1962); *The Limits of Behavioralism in Political Science*, ed. James C. Charlesworth: particularly the contributions by Heinz Eulau and David Easton. In 1963 Gabriel A. Almond and Sidney Verba prefaced their study, *The Civic Culture*, with a tribute to Merriam, stated again in different terms by Almond in his presidential address to the American Political Science Association in 1965. A recent attempt at a history of the profession, *The Development of Political Science*, by Albert Somit and Joseph Tanenhaus (Boston, 1967) casts some light on Merriam's relation to the discipline. A biographical essay on Merriam by the author will appear in the *New Encyclopedia of the Social Sciences*. A fuller biographical study, also by the author, may someday be completed.

13. Detailed documentation of these points will have to await the publication of the Merriam biography. Although foundation reports of the period provide ample evidence for the amounts of money going into research and the types of research being financed, the gradual emergence of academic organizations as distributors, plus the methods being used by

foundations in their own corporate reorganizations, make detailed trac-
ings difficult. The papers of Charles Merriam at the University of Chicago and those of his brother John, divided between the Bancroft Library at the University of California (up to 1920) and the Library of
Congress, give as much real detail as one needs to map the course of
academic influence which they controlled.

14. Turner's recollections of his father's activities at town meeting is described in his letter to Constance Skinner (see note 6 above). Merriam
recalled state legislatures and, most of all, church board meetings when
he thought of his childhood recollections of government. Louis Brownlow, one of Merriam's closest associates in his later years describes the
traveling county judges in Missouri. For all of them, the federal government, outside presidential years, was represented persistently only by
the post office. (Louis Brownlow, *A Passion for Politics* [Chicago, 1955],
particularly Chapter 2.)

15. The *Bulletins* of the City Club of Chicago, which for many years published full accounts of discussions at their regular luncheon meetings,
give an important indication of just how catholic such discussions were:
University professors, local ward bosses, businessmen reformers, social
workers, not only from Chicago, but from other cities as well met to
debate educational reforms, local and national elections, and to indulge
in significant comparisons of problems.

16. While the political side of Merriam's career is evident from time to time
in his writing (*Chicago, A More Intimate View of Urban Politics* [New
York, 1929], for example), Beard's has been too much obscured by his
historical writings, which would, in turn, be illuminated by more interest
in his activities as a political and administrative reformer. See H. K.
Beale (ed.), *Charles Beard: An Appraisal* (Lexington, Ky., 1954).

17. In his paper "American Election Analysis" (delivered to the American
Political Science Association, September, 1967), Richard Jensen calls attention to Turner as a social scientist and credits him quite properly
with pioneering which went well beyond a view of the frontier as a
source of democratic ideas. Peter H. Odegard's introduction to the John
Harvard Library edition of Arthur F. Bentley's *The Process of Government* (Cambridge, 1967) suggests that it was Bentley's incredibly in-
sulting treatment of his contemporaries which may have helped him into
relative obscurity after the 1908 publication of his book, not that important people failed to read or to review his efforts. It is also true that the
level of generalization and analysis at which he chose to work was not in
vogue in political science or history in his day, although it was in philosophy where he remained a known and relatively important figure. Odegard's introduction, too, if read for its contemporary political tone, could
raise some interesting speculations on the relation between the decline
of Merriam's reputation and the rise of Bentley's among some of today's
political scientists. One reference to Merriam's *Civic Education* studies is
in Almond and Verba's *The Civic Culture* (Princeton, 1963); but it has
also been commented upon elsewhere.

BRUCE MAZLISH

James Mill and the Utilitarians

MOST STUDIES of leadership tend to center on dramatic and revolutionary figures, guiding powerful mass movements. A Lenin or a Hitler, a Communist or a Nazi Party are attractive to scholars by the inherent spectacular nature of their force and influence. Moreover, while there are intellectual dimensions to such movements, they rapidly become subordinated to the political aspects of leadership, and the scholar can concentrate happily on the twists and turns of power and party relations, dealing with intellectual questions only in the guise of ideology.

Yet, most political leadership is not exercised in this fashion. On the one hand, ordinary politicians and statesmen do not have charisma, or at least not mass charisma. On the other, the sort of intellectual leadership—say, of a Voltaire—that strongly influences public opinion and in that way shapes political developments is not directly linked to the world of politics. Thus, the union of thought and action extolled, for example, by the Marxists has been a fairly rare specimen, at least until modern times.[1]

If, however, we look for an instance of combined intellectual (where the intellectual aspect is serious) and political leadership, though exercised and executed in a low key, we might find of great interest the historical phenomenon known, variously, as Utilitarianism, Radicalism, or Philosophical Radicalism (generally, we shall refer to it as Utilitarianism). That Utilitarianism was important needs little demonstration. As a doctrine, it dominated English intellectual life in the early-nineteenth century. As a movement, it may be said to have been the most vital force in bringing about, for example, the Reform Bill of 1832.

The Utilitarian creed, as summarized by John Stuart Mill, meant:

In politics, an almost unbounded confidence in the efficacy of two things: representative government and complete freedom of discussion. . . . In psychology . . . the formation of all human character by cir-

465

cumstances, through the universal Principle of Association, and the consequent unlimited possibility of improving the moral and intellectual condition of mankind by education.[2]

To this, one ought really to add an economic doctrine—a belief in free trade and industry, based especially on the theories of Thomas Malthus and David Ricardo, aided by Jeremy Bentham and James Mill—and a desire for legal reform, based on the work of Bentham.

As a movement, we may view the Utilitarian pressure for representative government, culminating in 1832, as a "peaceful revolution." It avoided the excesses and drawbacks of the French Revolution of 1789 and brought to England the gains originally sought across the Channel by the *philosophes* and physiocrats. It marked the official supremacy of the English middle classes and was consciously directed against "aristocracy." To use the terms of today, it insured that the modernization process—political, economic, and intellectual—in England would be carried out for, if not by, a bourgeois elite, impeded but not frustrated by a traditionalist, and sometimes reactionary, upper class.

Who was the "leader" or "leaders" in charge of this quiet revolution? Only two candidates present themselves: Jeremy Bentham and James Mill. As in so many other leadership situations, we have a dualism here. A study of their intimate personal relations shows us that the characters involved shifted roles, with each in due season and situation being the leader and the led. Let us look first and briefly at Bentham's claims.

Born in 1748, his father well-to-do and a political Jacobite, Bentham received an education befitting a child prodigy. Intended for the practice of the law, he became instead a reformer of the law. Starting as a Tory, he ended his life as a radical, his death in 1832 coming two days after the third reading of the Reform Bill. A hermit of sorts, unmarried, he lived most of his life in his books, pouring out unreadable and badly organized works on the civil and penal law, education, ethics, religion, and political economy. Without the assistance of disciples, such as the Frenchman Dumont, much of Bentham's work would never have seen print. Happily, however, by attraction of character and intellect, Bentham gathered around him a group of men prepared to receive his doctrine and to publish it abroad.

One of these men was James Mill. And it was the fortunate confluence of their meeting that made for the Utilitarian movement. When the two men first met in 1808, Bentham was sixty years old, yet still scarcely known to the English public; Mill was thirty-five, struggling to support a growing family, and with only some small reputation as a writer and journalist, his major work on the history of India still ahead of him. Bentham needed an intelligent disciple and a forceful man to make a political philosophy and party out of his Utilitarian doctrines; Mill needed—psychologically and economically—a patron and a philosophical mentor under whom he could serve with security. As Elie Halévy says of Bentham: "It seems as though the intrusion into his life of James Mill was needed to make him a democrat. . . . It was to James Mill that this hermit, this maniac owed the fact that he became the popular chief of a party that was half philosophical and half political."[3] As Bentham himself saw the relation, writing about Mill in 1828 to a friend: "For these three or four-and-twenty years he has numbered himself among my disciples; for upwards of twenty years he has been receiving my instructions; for about the half of each of five years, he and his family have been my guests."[4] And Mill phrased it in a letter to Bentham of 1814, talking of "the cause [Utilitarianism] which has been the great bond of connection between us . . . that system of important truths of which you have the immortal honour to be the author, but of which I am a most faithful and fervent disciple . . . nobody at all so likely to be your real successor as myself. . . . I am pretty sure you cannot think of any other person whose whole life will be devoted to the propagation of the system."[5]

As a self-proclaimed disciple of Bentham, James Mill became a leader, intellectual and political, in his own right. Nor ought we to be surprised at this pattern of leadership (though in this case it may have some unique features): After all, Lenin "followed" Marx, and Stalin "followed" Lenin. In the first place, Mill was a powerful thinker, able to add significantly to the received doctrine. "It was James Mill," as Halévy informs us, "who, having become a Benthamite, perceived the logical link which connected the ideas of Bentham and Malthus, became a Malthusian and made use of Ricardo to incorporate the ideas of Malthus with the tradition of Adam Smith."[6] Next, there are many testimonials to Mill's force of character, to his almost charismatic qualities, exercised as they were, however, only in small and select circles, and it was these qualities that allowed him to shape a political "school." Beyond this, he was a master propagandist and polemicist, spreading the Utilitarian doctrines and desires to a middle-class audience by such means as the new periodical press.

Ultimately James Mill, like almost every other leader, provided not only a doctrine and a method by which to propagate it, but also a prototype of the personality and character of the men who were to live by and for it. To quote Halévy again:

A new type of humanity, with its virtues and its failings, began to be sketched out around Bentham, thanks not to Bentham but to James Mill. . . . He was nothing more than the man of abstract convictions, a living example of the Utilitarian morality and of the absolute identification of private interest with the good of humanity . . . without eyes or ears for the beauties of nature and art, having systematically destroyed in himself the spontaneous impulses of feeling.[7]

At this point, to use Eriksonian terms, we see that Identity has become intrinsic to Ideology. Our task, now, is to see how James Mill's development of his own identity allowed him to offer a certain type of leadership to a significant number of his contemporaries searching for an ideology and an identity of their own.

There is little evidence about James Mill's early life, and this for two reasons. First, he was not a "hero" nor a "great" man, such as a Napoleon or even a Robespierre, and his contemporaries did not, therefore, treasure up mementos of his youth and family background. The second reason is more important and revealing. As we shall see, James Mill rejected his own past and, as a "self-made man," looked almost entirely to the future. This was true to such an extent that his own son, John Stuart Mill, with whom he spent an incredible amount of time, knew almost nothing of his father's Scottish background. Thus, James Mill's biographer, Alexander Bain, had to obtain what information he could from parish registers, conversations with surviving friends and neighbors, and extant collections of letters; luckily, Bain did his work well, and the biography is invaluable.

Fortunately there is also enough material for us to discern a number of psychological patterns operating in James Mill's life, and it is on these, rather than on a substantial chronological account of his development, that we shall focus. The psychological patterns chosen are those that correspond meaningfully to aspects of Utilitarianism.

The first psychological trait to be noted is Mill's quality as a self-made man, without a past. The facts are, briefly, that he was born in 1773 in Logie Pert, a Scottish parish of about seven hundred inhabitants. His father, James, was a shoemaker. His mother, Isabel Fenton, had been a servant girl in Edinburgh. Then, at age seven-

468

teen, she had married James Milne. Isabel was the daughter of a farmer, and with the legend of better times in her background, she was proud and even haughty. Changing the undistinguished family name of Milne to the less common Mill, she sought to realize her ambitions in her first-born son, James. To him was allotted one of the three rooms in the house for a study, and here he was commanded to study. A younger brother, Will, was set to the shoemaking trade, and a sister, May, was made to take care of the cow.

James Mill was gifted by nature. Pushed on by his mother, he soon came to the attention of the parish minister. From the parish school, he went on to Montrose Academy, where he boarded, until, at the age of eighteen, he came to the notice of Sir John and Lady Jane Stuart. It was they who sponsored him at the University of Edinburgh. At the university, Mill took special training in divinity (Lady Jane's special desire), while reading widely on his own in the secular authors of the Enlightenment (and we must recall that, entering in 1790, Mill was living through the stirring events of the French Revolution and its aftermath). In 1798, licensed as a preacher, Mill gave itinerant sermons and waited for a permanent post, without success. Finally, in 1802, approaching thirty and without a living, Mill decided to seek his fortune outside barren Scotland. Sir John Stuart, off to attend to his duties in Parliament, gave his protégé a seat to London in his carriage.

Once in London, Mill never really looked back. Like other thrusting young men of the time, he was delighted with his new possibilities. Quickly, he secured a job as a hack writer, then within a year persuaded a publisher to set him up as editor of a new periodical, and two years later was also editing a newspaper. As he wrote to a friend back in Scotland:

I am extremely ambitious to remain here, which I feel to be much the best scene for a man of letters. . . . You get an ardour and a spirit of adventurousness, which you can never get an idea of among our over-cautious countrymen at home. Here everybody applauds the most romantic scheme you can form. In Scotland, everybody represses you, if you but propose to step out of the beaten track.[8]

Moreover, there was nothing any longer to hold him to Scotland. His mother, worn out by cares, had died of consumption (as had his brother Will). In any case, she had trained James Mill to go on without her; this was her ambition, as much as his, at work. His father had become paralyzed as well as bankrupt, and Mill's only future filial act was painstakingly and scrupulously to pay off the family debts. His sister May had never meant much to him in any case, and her subsequent marriage to a journeyman shoemaker retained her in a way of life that was no longer Mill's. Small wonder that Mill turned his back so completely on his origins.

Mill's personal rejection of the past and its conditions coincided with two factors. The first was political. The late-eighteenth- and early-nineteenth-century society was in a mood to reject existing authority. Government based on traditions, privileges, and prescription—to use Burke's term—was under attack. The appeal to natural, and hence timeless, rights was the battering ram in France. In England, the French Revolution and its excesses, coupled with the ensuing war between England and France, discredited this particular ideological possibility. It was Bentham's genius to offer at this moment the creed of Utilitarianism, with its appeal to a scientific "felicific calculus" as the guide to legislation, in place of the natural rights theory. Thus, the attack on "antiquities" as the basis of legitimate government could go on even more vigorously than before. In this attack on the past, Mill was able to combine his personal experience and his philosophical convictions in a powerful, if unconscious, identity.

The second factor was economic. The Industrial Revolution opened the way to large numbers of new men, of humble origin, to rise by their own efforts. Psychologically, as well as socially, they seemed to have to stress their independence, their "newness," and their self-made quality. We see these traits in caricature in Dickens' Mr. Bounderby of *Hard Times*. Dickens describes him as "a man who could never sufficiently vaunt himself a self-made man. A man who was always proclaiming . . . his old ignorance and his old poverty." Successful in business, Bounderby spreads the myth that he had been deserted by his parents, left in the gutter, and had thus risen all on his own. There is a delicious denouement to the book when Bounderby's mother, whom *he* had deserted, accidentally appears. James Mill, himself, never went to such lengths. But his own repression of the past fitted in with the psychological needs of many in the middle classes for whom he wrote, and his stress on self-origin and independence (about which we shall say more later) tied in nicely with the notions of economic *laissez-faire*. It is as if James Mill were talking of himself and many of his followers when he eulogized his friend, David Ricardo, on the latter's death. "Mr. Ricardo had everything to do for himself, and he did everything.

. . . He had his fortune to make, he had his mind to form, he had even his education to commence and to conduct."[9]

At this point, a number of other elements cohere about the notion of the self-made man. The first is education. Throughout his life, James Mill was deeply interested in the problems of teaching and learning. His personal training of his son John Stuart is one of the famous pedagogical sagas of all time. He was deeply involved in the important Bell-Lancaster controversy and worked with Bentham to set up a Chrestomathic School in 1814. Later, in 1824, he was one of the founders of London University.

The basis of Mill's educational beliefs was in psychology. Without engaging ourselves in the difficult and lengthy subject of associationalist psychology, we can note for our purposes its stress on character being formed by sensations and thus by experience. Through the right experience—that is, education—man could be shaped according to the calculus of pleasure and pain to almost any desired form. Psychologically implicit, though not logically so, is also the view that a man could shape himself by exposing himself to the right environment. In any case, the rejection of an innate, hereditary character, in favor of one that could be shaped afresh, chimed in with the general rejection of "antiquities" and hereditary privileges. Man—and society—could be educated on a new basis.

The ethic of hard work, of the need to labor, also fitted into the general scheme. "He who works more than all others," Mill admonished his son, "will in the end excel all others."[10] And Mill suited his actions to his words, putting in prodigious hours at his writing and editing. Like so many others in nineteenth-century England and Scotland, having rejected the Calvinist dogmas, Mill retained the Calvinist ethos in a secularized form. Needless to say, one educated and shaped oneself and others through hard work: Character was "produced" just as was any other commodity.

Those who did not work were unworthy in two ways. They were parasites, and they were likely to be stupid. In his *Essay on Government,* Mill put the matter succinctly:

There may be a strong presumption that any aristocracy monopolizing the powers of government would not possess intellectual powers in any very high perfection. Intellectual powers are the offspring of labor. But a hereditary aristocracy are deprived of the strongest motives to labor. The greater part of them will, therefore, be defective in those mental powers.[11]

Contemporary with Mill, of course, the Saint-Simonians were making the same point about productive and unproductive classes (indeed, Sièyes had already laid the powder trail of this line of thinking, calculated to blow up the bastions of privilege, in his "What Is the Third Estate" pamphlet of 1789). On this basis, the Saint-Simonians then extolled the "industrialists" and their right to political as well as economic leadership. What Mill contributed was a synthesis of his various ideas on education, labor, and the rejection of the past with the charge against a privileged and stupid aristocracy.

Into the place of the latter stepped men like Mill himself: self-made, hard-working individuals of the "middle rank." Mill announced their claim to rule in no uncertain terms:

> There can be no doubt that the middle rank, which gives to science, to art, and to legislation itself their most distinguished ornaments, and is the chief source of all that has exalted and refined human nature, is that portion of the community of which, if the basis of representation were ever so far extended, the opinion would ultimately decide.[12]

In back of this view lay Mill and the Utilitarians' general conception of government. The purpose of government is to attain the "greatest possible happiness of the greatest possible number." The way to this end is to protect men in the fruits of their labor: Government has no other function. Only a representative government, whose interests are identical with the community at large, can be expected to protect and not prey on the generality of citizens. How happy a conclusion for Mill and the Utilitarians that the one group whose interests are identical with all is the middle class (whose "wisdom" the lower classes will always allow to guide them)!

Another pattern in Mill's life seems to have been his strong fear of dependency and dependent relations. Such a personal pattern, too, fitted consistently with the Utilitarian stress on individualism. Yet, in fact, Mill was extremely ambivalent in his feelings and behavior and constantly put himself, or allowed himself to be put, in the position of a protégé or disciple. Would we be wrong if we also claimed that the vaunted economic independence asserted by the commercial and industrial proponents of *laissez-faire* was, in fact, based on the covert, if not overt, protection, patronage, and support by the state? Alas, such an affirmation can only be stated, not supported, here.[13]

For Mill, however, the ambivalence about dependency can be demonstrated. His proud independence, fostered by his mother, may be illustrated by the story that James Mill gave up his hopes for advancement in Scotland and resolved to go to London because of an incident in a nobleman's family (not the Stuarts) when he was motioned to leave the dinner table with the ladies. According to the story, Mill "gave up his situation [as tutor], and determined to trust to his pen and his own exertions." The theme is the same at the end of his life. Brougham, writing a memorial of James Mill, commented that he "afforded a rare example of one born in humble circumstances, and struggling . . . with the inconveniences of restricted means, nobly maintaining an independence as absolute in all respects as that of the first subject in the land."[14]

As we have seen, however, there was another side to this proud independence. James Mill the self-made man was always being helped, *being patronized* by others. First, he received very special attention from his mother. Next, the Stuarts were, in fact, his patrons. Once in London, Mill married a girl above his own station, who brought him a dowry and whose mother bought him a house (in return for a very low rent). Later, he became the acknowledged disciple of Jeremy Bentham and lived advantageously with his "master" for a number of summers. Francis Place, the master tailor, lent him money.

James Mill felt the threat to his independence in these relations. Scrupulously, he paid off his debt to Place. When his own father, Mill senior, went bankrupt, he paid off these debts as well. In 1814, when Bentham took umbrage at one of Mill's actions, Mill wrote him that "it has been one of the great purposes of my life to avoid pecuniary obligations, even in the solicitation or acceptance of ordinary advantages—hence the penury in which I live." Then Mill added rather cryptically: "To receive obligations of any sort from you was not a matter of humiliation to me, but of pride. And I only dreaded it from the danger to which I saw that it exposed our friendship."[15]

Dependence and independence—these were the poles of Mill's relation to Bentham and all other figures of authority. "The voluntary servant of Bentham," Halévy comments, "he became a tyrant everywhere else than with Bentham—a domestic tyrant when he was concerned with the upbringing of his children; a social tyrant when he was concerned to develop, to organize and to create the Benthamite group."[16] Yet, as we have already noted, Mill would never have become a leader unless he had first been able to become the disciple of Bentham.

In his *Group Psychology and the Analysis of the Ego*, Freud describes the ideal leader, the "father of his people" (that is, of the primal horde). Asserting that the will of the leader needed no reinforcement from others, Freud declares that "his ego had few libidinal ties; he loved no one but himself, or other people only insofar as they served his needs. To objects his ego gave away no more than was barely necessary." Freud's conclusion is most interesting: "He, at the very beginning of the history of mankind, was the 'superman' whom Nietzsche only expected from the future."[17]

How does Mill measure up to this picture of the "superman"? "He loved no one but himself." Certainly, Mill had no overt love for his original family, except perhaps for his mother; and this last was hardly demonstrative.[18] His wife, after the first year or so, he treated with disdain. His firstborn, John Stuart, lamented the absence of loving parents and admitted, in turn, that he respected, but did not love his father.[19] Of all James Mill's friends, only Ricardo seemed to have awakened strong and tender feelings; and it was his death that Mill lamented openly. Otherwise, Mill's reputation and much of his power were seen to lie in his absence of feelings—in short, of libidinal ties. Even Mill's friendly biographer, Bain, admitted as much:

It is a consequence of the determined pursuit of one or two all-comprehending ends, that a man has to put aside many claims of mere affection, feeling, or sentiment. Not that he is necessarily devoid of the warm, social emotions: he may have them, in fair measure; not, however, in an overpowering degree. It is that they stand in his way to other things; and so are, on certain occasions, sacrificed; leading thereby to the reproach of being of a nature hard and unfeeling. Such was Pitt, and such was Mill.[20]

Feeling and passion were exactly what Mill repressed in himself. Indeed, this is what his son, John Stuart, so bitterly deplored and so openly testified to: "For passionate emotions of all sorts," he tells us in the *Autobiography*, "and for everything which has been said or written in exaltation of them, he professed the greatest contempt. He regarded them as a form of madness."[21]

To defend against such "madness," James resorted to intense self-control. Only at home did he give way to his aggressive and thwarted feelings. As Bain tells us: "He could exercise perfect self-control in his intercourse with the world . . . but at home he did not care to restrain the irritability of his temperament. . . . The

474

thing that has left the most painful memories was the way that he allowed himself to speak and behave to his wife and children before visitors."[22] In the public arena, however, as an intellectual and political leader, Mill exhibited rigid control of his emotions—and this we have already suggested was a major part of his success.

The power and the control found some of its dominion necessarily exercised in relation to sex. For example, Mill warmly congratulated a friend on being "past the hey-day of the blood when the solid qualities are apt to be overlooked for the superficial"; he opposed dances "such as slide into lasciviousness"; and he, who had nine children of his own, extended his personal and psychological needs to public ones and became one of the first exponents of birth control. Here, the connection of bourgeois economics and sexuality, so handily linked in Malthus, becomes obvious, and the mechanism of sublimation is brought evidently into play. As Peter Cominos has shown for a later period, the abstraction of *Homo Economicus* required a tandem mate in an abstraction of *Homo Sensualis;* and part of Mill's "moral superiority" over his contemporaries was the strength of his control in both areas: work and sex.[23]

At what point, or points, does James Mill, having rejected his past identity, take on another in which all of the elements that we have discussed fuse into the public figure of an intellectual and political leader? When does he go through what might be called his "crisis of identity"?[24]

The first point, in what must be conceived of as a cumulative development, would seem to have occurred in 1802. At that moment, Mill took two decisive steps. He left Scotland, psychologically and physically. And he gave up the ministerial calling for which he had been intended by both his mother and his first patrons, the Stuarts. The first of these steps supported Mill's sense of being a self-made man and gave him a new identity as an Englishman; fortunately, there was no "nationality crisis" connected with this step, for nineteenth-century England—unlike, say, Germany—was set in its self-definition. The second of these steps led to a shift from a religious to a secular career. In this it was prototypic of a whole wave of opinion and social change engulfing the late-eighteenth and early-nineteenth centuries.[25]

Mill now became a "man of letters." As such, to use other terms, he may be called a member of the "intelligentsia." Unlike Russia, however, England was graced with a large and growing middle class, interested in supporting such a man as Mill within the Establishment, rather than forcing him outside into revolutionary activity. In fact, the middle class needed men like Mill, steeled to lead the middle class itself *into* the Establishment. The relation was reciprocal. Within a year of coming to London, Mill was able to earn a decent living by his pen.

Mill's position was, nevertheless, precarious, dependent on the day to day success of his writings. To remedy this, shortly after the birth of his first son, he began his *History of British India,* in an attempt to establish an independent and secure reputation. Alas, instead of the planned three years, it took Mill twelve years of anguished effort to complete the work. In the meantime, the second apparent point in his crisis of identity seems to have come in 1808.

In that year he met Bentham and became his disciple, and at the same time he began firmly and even publicly to renounce his previous religious views. Although he had given up the ministerial career in 1802, Mill had at first held on to the religion. Indeed, he still went to church, and he had all his children baptized. But under the influence, and support, of Bentham he now began to attack the clerical establishment (but not Christianity itself) fiercely and stridently (though modulated in print for reasons of prudence).[26] Thus, by the age of thirty-five he had finally revolted completely against at least the form and specific content, though not the psychological direction, of his ambitious mother's training.

The third nodule in his crisis of identity seems to have been the publication in 1817 of the *History of British India,* establishing Mill's reputation firmly. On the strength of the book, Mill was appointed to the post of examiner in the East India Company. Now, Mill was financially secure, and he had made the move from a pure "man of letters" to a high-level civil servant. (At the end of his life, in fact, he rose to the top of his office.) Still, he remained true to his radical beliefs, and on this basis he gave leadership to the Utilitarian movement, culminating as it did in the Reform Bill of 1832. Bain has caught the flavor of his leadership: "Mill, I take it, while so daring as to be accounted revolutionary, was really the safest politician of his age. In the first French Revolution, no such man was to be found."[27] In sum, Mill had achieved his full identity: He was a revolutionary leader, whose energies and ambitions were safely channeled in the ways of reform. Character and circumstance, personality and party, individual and class—all combined in Mill and the Utilitarians in a special and mutually advantageous symbiosis.

Until now, we have centered our attention on the formation of Mill's character. We have tried to indicate the coherence between his traits—self-making, rejecting the past, fearing dependency and yet ambivalent thereto, and emphasizing self-control, education, and hard work—and some of the doctrines of Utilitarianism (and our assertion of coherence must not be mistaken for an assertion of causation, which is out of place in an analysis such as this). At this point, we need to shift our focus and to ask such questions as: What was the social and political structure of England in which leadership could be exercised? Who, in fact, were the members of the Utilitarian movement? Why did James Mill, and not some-one else, become the leader of the movement? What particular methods did he use to implement his leadership? In short, we need to bring the party into correspondence with the personality.

Let us take the question of political and social structure first. A cliché of political philosophy at the time was that public opinion ruled political life, if not at first, then ultimately.[28] Hence, whoever shaped public opinion at large might be thought to shape the politics of England. In a gross sense, one might claim that a John Wesley, a William Cobbett—men whom one might label dema-gogues (with the Greek meaning of the word in mind)—appealed to the country at large. James Mill was certainly not this sort of leader, nor were the Utilitarians interested in appealing to this sort of audience.

In fact, of course, in nineteenth-century England there was no such thing as an undifferentiated public. Wesley, for example, ap-pealed mainly to lower-middle-class and laboring groups left un-touched by the Church of England, and Cobbett to dispossessed agricultural workers and others of the lower classes who were uprooted by the growing industrialization of the country. To all intents and purposes, aside from mob actions, the working classes of early-nineteenth-century England might be dismissed from con-sideration as serious participants in the political process.[29] That process went on mainly in Parliament, dominated as it was before the Reform Bill by the "landed interest"; in the law courts, re-flecting largely the interests and desires of those already in power; and in the local government of the counties, administered by and for this same group.

To the "landed interest" we must add the beneficed clergy of the Church of England, often appointed to their well-endowed posts by the "landed interest"; the members of the professions: army,

477

navy, and bar; and the class of very rich men who hoped to become part of the landed aristocracy, either for themselves or their children. Generally known as Tories, these constituted the factions or groups that controlled Parliament, hence the sources of legislation, and whom Mill's son John Stuart called the Privileged Classes.[30] Clearly, this was not the audience for Utilitarian ideas and persuasions.

Against the aristocracy and their privileges stood the middle class, but generally with only a partial vote and therefore only a partial possibility of making their voices heard in Parliament; certain individuals from the aristocratic class "whom some circumstance of a personal nature has alienated from their class" (to quote John Stuart Mill again); and, in the background, the working classes.

Parliament, of course, met in London. Of outstanding importance in the political history of the time was the county of Westminster (thus matching the county of Middlesex, scene of Wilkes' activities in the 1770's). Until 1807, its seventeen thousand electors had dutifully elected one Whig and one Tory, the two faces of aristocratic parliamentary control. Then, sensationally, it elected Sir Francis Burdett as a popular and independent candidate (another Radical, Lord Cochrane, was elected with him), supported by such "democrats" as William Cobbett and Francis Place. This accidental spark was flamed into a permanent political conflagration by the fortunate meeting of Bentham and Mill the next year and the gradual formation around them of a Utilitarian, or Radical, party. Basing themselves pragmatically on the shopkeepers and tradesmen of Westminster, the Utilitarians used Westminster as the pivot for their lever on Parliament and as the model for their arguments in favor of parliamentary reform.

In this hasty perusal, we have our answer as to the target population at whom the Utilitarians aimed their appeal: the electors of Westminster, as "representatives" of the ten-pound middle-class electors of the towns of England, and, above them in station and intellect, the men of the aristocratic and professional classes "whom some circumstance of a personal nature has alienated from their class." Let us look at this last group closely, for they, of necessity (with some additions, of course), had to constitute the politically active "leadership cadres" of the Utilitarian movement as well as its primary "audience."

Initially, it must be noted that the Utilitarians were not a highly structured, well-knit group. Mill deplored this state of affairs constantly. Sir Francis Burdett, for example, scion of an aristocratic family, married to the daughter of a banker, became a radical of sorts after 1807, only to end his political life as a Tory. At the other end of the social scale, William Cobbett started out as an anti-Jacobin journalist and demagogue, only to switch around in 1807, by supporting Burdett and then, though in undependable fashion, the Radicals thereafter.

So amorphous and shifting a group as the Radicals is hard to bring into focus. For convenience, however, we can fix the political kaleidoscope at one or two patterns. A group of identifiable "members" can be made out from, say, 1808 to 1824, led and influenced primarily by James Mill. In the latter year, new young men are recruited to the movement, circling around James Mill's son John Stuart, who serves, however, mainly as his father's alter ego. A final formation can be discerned in the first reformed Parliament, only to fall apart disastrously after 1835.

In our first group portrait, we would have, of course, Bentham and Mill. With them is the exemplary and unique Francis Place, a self-made working man (he rose to be a master tailor, head of a thriving business), with unusual connections and organizational skills and, moreover, the only real contact with the artisan population of London. As Radical M.P.'s, we can cite Mill's dearest friend, David Ricardo, Joseph Hume (whose 1813 meeting with Place brought him into the fold), Henry Brougham (a boyhood friend of Mill's and mostly a Whig rather than a Radical), Sir Francis Burdett, and John Cam Hobhouse (Lord Broughton). As journalists and editors, Albany Fonblanque (who took over the editorship of the *Examiner* in 1830), Dr. Southwood Smith (contributor to the *Westminster Review*), Colonel Perronet Thompson (a long-time Radical, who kept the ailing *Westminster Review* going for five years, from 1830 on), and, of course, William Cobbett. As intellectuals and theorists, George Grote, the historian (introduced to Mill by Ricardo in 1818), J. R. M'Culloch, the economist, and John Austin, the legal philosopher. Hovering just outside this group seems to have been the eminent legalist, Sir Samuel Romilly (actually a Whig), and transcending it, though part of it, the old reforming war horse, Major John Cartwright.

In our second picture, we must add as new faces surrounding John Stuart Mill: the M.P., John Arthur Roebuck, the Unitarian minister and editor of the *Morning Register*, William J. Fox, Charles Austin (brother of John), Edward Strutt (Lord Belper), Hyde and

Charles Villiers, John Romilly (son of Sir Samuel), George John Graham, and Charles Buller.

These form more or less the hard core of the Utilitarian movement. After the Reform Bill, Tory alarmists claimed that Radicals in the Parliament of 1835 numbered about 190. But this included, in addition to about twenty-one of the foremost Radicals, the leaders of the Political Unions of 1831-32, a number of mere time-serving Whig-Radicals, and about a hundred Irish members, functioning as what is called O'Connell's "tail."[31] Such a diverse gathering had no common creed nor political platform and was a "Radical group" only for expediency. By the time of Mill's death, in 1836, the coalition was already in the process of falling apart.

Why was it James Mill who led the Utilitarians? His contemporaries amply attest to the fact that he was the leader and hint at the reasons why. As his son tells us:

By his writings and his personal influence he was a great centre of light to his generation. During his later years he was quite as much the head and leader of the intellectual radicals in England, as Voltaire was of the *philosophes* in France. . . . In the power of influencing by mere force of mind and character, the conviction and purposes of others, and in the strenuous exertion of that power to promote freedom and progress, he left, as far as my knowledge extends, no equal among men.[32]

Is this a hyperbolic view offered out of filial devotion? It would seem not. Typical of many other such comments are those by the journalist John Black:

Mr. Mill was eloquent and impressive in conversation. He had a great command of language, which bore the stamp of his earnest and energetic character. Young men were particularly fond of his society, and it was always to him a source of great delight to have an opportunity of contributing to form their minds and exalt their characters. No man could enjoy his society without catching a portion of his elevated enthusiasm. Many of the men in whom the country now places its warmest hopes benefited largely by the enlightened society of Mr. Mill.

By Albany Fonblanque:

One of our master-minds . . . one that has given the most powerful impulse, and the most correct direction to thought. . . . His conversation was so energetic and complete in thought, so succinct, and exact *ad unguem* in expression, that, if reported as uttered, his colloquial observations or arguments would have been perfect compositions. . . . It was hardly possible for an intelligent man to know James Mill without feeling an obligation for the profit derived from his mind.

And by George Grote, who notes Mill's "strenuous character, earnest convictions, and single-minded devotion to truth, with an utter disdain of mere paradox" and concludes:

It may be conceived that such a man exercised powerful intellectual ascendancy over younger minds. Several of those who enjoyed his society —men now at or past the maturity of life, and some of them in distinguished positions—remember and attest with gratitude such ascendancy in their own cases: among them the writer of the present article, who owes to the historian of British India an amount of intellectual stimulus and guidance such as he can never forget.

Bain adds that Grote frequently remarked that "Mill's personal ascendancy with men of wealth among the dissenters and among liberal politicians generally, and the trust that they placed in his judgment, had a great deal to do with the obtaining of the requisite funds."[33]

Confirmation of Mill's powers comes inadvertently even from an unfriendly critic. Thus, Bowring, one of Bentham's later disciples and envious of Mill, states, rightly or wrongly, that Bentham complained of Mill:

He will never willingly enter into discourse with me. When he differs he is silent. He is a character. He expects to subdue everybody by his domineering tone—to convince everybody by his positiveness. His manner of speaking is oppressive and overbearing. He comes to me as if he wore a mask upon his face.[34]

As we can see, from an adverse side, here is the same testimony to Mill's strength of character and conversation. In personal confrontation, Mill obviously had what Thomas Mann (in *The Holy Sinner*) might have referred to as "moral superiority," and Max Weber designated in part as charisma. As Bain sums it up:

In spite of all that is said of his arrogant manner, he made his way in society, and gained over people his superiors in rank. . . . Whether, as John Mill said, he was pre-eminently adapted for a prime minister, he was at all events a born leader—a king of men.[35]

Did Mill gain over people "his superiors in rank"—and a look at the 1808 or 1824 list of Utilitarians reveals how many of them were upper class—because he "represented" them in some way, or because he was "marginal" to them? The case looks suspiciously like Edmund Burke's ascendancy earlier over the Whig aristocrats whom he, as the "outsider," admired so extravagantly and whose unarticulated views he formulated so persuasively. For example,

481

Burke was Irish and Mill, Scottish; thus both were marginal to English politics. Both had their fame and fortune to make, and both made it into the company if not into the ranks of the upper class. And so forth.

But there the analogy stops. Burke eulogized the aristocracy and abandoned his possible leadership of the middle class. Mill fiercely attacked the aristocracy and never pretended, as Burke did, to their way of life; instead, he was middle class to his marrow and representative of that class in its most intimate traits of sobriety, hard work, and moral commitment. True, Bentham putatively impugned Mill's motives in attacking the aristocracy: "His creed of politics results less from love for the many than from hatred of the few. It is too much under the influence of social and dissocial affection"; and we catch an echo of this criticism in Grote's first impression of Mill:

His mind has, indeed, all that cynicism and asperity which belongs to the Benthamian school, and what I chiefly dislike in him is, the readiness and seeming preference with which he dwells on the *faults and defects* of others—even of the greatest men!

Nevertheless, for whatever reasons and in whatever modes, Mill's dislike of the aristocracy was representative of himself and his middle-class identity. It allowed him, as Bain remarks, to get "hold of the more intelligent minds of the growing middle class in our great centres of industry."[36]

As for the aristocrats in the Utilitarian movement, those "whom some circumstance of a personal nature has alienated from their class"—the Sir Francis Burdett's of the time—with them Mill's position was obviously "marginal." Yet, as Grote has told us, he won them over, in a sweeping and profound way. Surely, this was because, out of strength of mind and character, Mill voiced better than they could their own highest aspirations for society and the good of man. He offered them a total ideology—a psychology that gave certainty to their hopes and views on education and knowledge, a morality that could be calculated scientifically, an economic theory that left no doubts as to its rightness, and a political philosophy that justified their most earnest efforts at reform—and exemplified that ideology for them in his person.

No one else could have done it, or so we are told by Bain: "Had Mill not appeared on the stage at the opportune moment, the whole cast of political thinking at the time of the Reform settlement must have been very inferior in point of sobriety and ballast to what it was. His place could not have been taken by any other man that we can fix upon."[37] In the words of Packe: "James Mill, by reason of his long influence on the works of Bentham, as well as of his own steady service for the cause during the last twenty years, stood at the conflux of many tributaries and currents, contrary and unruly though they often were, as they flowed towards the great sea of democratic progress."[38] It is exactly because he was both representative and marginal, leader and disciple, that Mill was able to stand at the "conflux" of the many currents that brought reform, and not revolution, to England in 1832.

In analyzing the elements of Mill's leadership we wish to look also at the methods he employed. We have seen that his personal ascendancy within the Utilitarian elite depended on his force of character and intellect, manifested in dialogue. Those who heard him, especially the young, eagerly became his followers, like converts to a new religion.

As a writer to the "general public" (that is, middle-class readers), Mill's appeal, at least at first glance, seems a little less compelling. Bain suggests that "although he took great pains to get rid of Scotticisms, he did not attain a mastery of good English idiom."[39] This seems superficial and, perhaps, prejudiced. Mill's strength was in combining forceful logic with total lucidity, crushing sarcasm with penetrating invective. As a polemicist, he was superb; as a teacher and expositor of a "message," incomparable. His very faults—lack of depth (sometimes of penetration) and of subtlety, absence of feelings—were his strengths in appealing to his potential Utilitarian audience. They wanted a clear and uncomplicated doctrine, and Mill gave it to them with an air of total certainty. Indeed, his style superbly matched his content.

Mill, in fact, was primarily a journalist, a man of letters, and an intellectual. He took full advantage of the new "technological" possibility: the periodical (whose influence was shortly to be powerfully extended by the coming of the railroads, which would convey almost immediately the London journals to the provinces).[40] From the first, he edited and established, or helped edit and establish, the vehicles for much of his own writings: *The Literary Journal* (1802-06), *St. James Chronicle* (1805-08), *The Philanthropist* (1811-17), and the famous *Westminster Review* (1824, merged in 1834 with the *London Review*). During this period, he also wrote extensively for other journals: *Edinburgh Review* (until he broke with it in 1813), *Morning Chronicle,* and the Supplement to the *Encyclopedia Britannica.* It can be said with certainty that Mill's leadership over the middle class coincided with his genius at using the periodical press.

Why did he not seek to lead the Utilitarians also from within Parliament? We know that, on his first arrival in London, he listened with fascination to Pitt and Fox in the House of Commons. We are told that he had a full, strong, clear voice. Yet he never chose to lead by oratorical means, either in Parliament or on the hustings. We can only guess, and guess badly, as to the reasons. We know that, as an itinerant preacher before 1802, Mill was no great success. His humble peasant congregation could not understand a word he said. "I've heard him preach," one of them is claimed to have said, "and no great han' he made o't."[41] We can also conjecture that, burdened with family cares, insecure financially, his time obligated to his writing and to teaching his son, Mill could not imagine chancing his life in the corrupt and fickle atmosphere of parliamentary politics. Someone would have had to "patronize" him and in such a public fashion that Mill would probably have shied from this threat to his independence. Whatever the reasons, Mill never ran for Parliament. Consequently, the Utilitarians never had an effective and powerful leader where, at least in the short run, perhaps it counted for most.

If Mill did not lead directly in Parliament, he persuaded others, like Ricardo, to enter it. Mill's power was always behind the scenes, exercised directly only over those who formed the circle of his acquaintances. His was a force that could spur others, with his help, to start journals, launch educational experiments, publish their own work (he had this effect on both Bentham and Ricardo), and strive to put together a political coalition. It was a leadership exercised more by character and intellect than by organizational or oratorical abilities; these latter were in Mill's possession, but he seems not to have used them to the fullest extent. In all of this, he was true to the deepest elements of his personality, if not always to the immediate needs of his political party.

We must now ask whether the mark of a great leader is his ability to radiate influence even after his death, to inspire others by the long-range effect of his ideas, and to persist as a living force through the institutions that he has set up to perpetuate his doctrines. Mill left behind him no formal party structure; his periodicals had a relatively ephemeral existence; and only London University, more Bentham's creation than his, persisted.

In only one area—India—did his ideas seem to have a persistent, long-lasting effect. His influence here was based on *The History of British India*, which laid down the correct principles, and his post as examiner in the East India House, which allowed him strongly to shape policy. The result of Mill's work and that of his disciples, as Eric Stokes sums it up in a masterly book, *The English Utilitarians and India*, was that "in the sixties and seventies of the nineteenth century there eventually emerged a structure which substantially realized James Mill's ideals of Indian government."[42]

Elsewhere, however, most of Mill's ideas soon became dated. True, the Reform Bill was only partial in that further extensions of the parliamentary suffrage were required in the years that followed after 1832, but this was more a question of time than of principle, and the principle itself had little new life to it. So, too, by the mid-nineteenth century, Mill's ideas on psychology, and even education, began to appear naïve and even simple-minded. His "little England" ideas on international relations dropped out of fashion: such a statement as "The business of a nation is with its own affairs. That is not only the general rule, but one to which it is not easy to conceive a case of exception" was hardly calculated to appeal to either the coming internationalists or imperialists.[43] Most importantly, however, his ideas on economic and class relations, and the tone in which he expressed them, became the most dated of all his doctrines. We catch the flavor of his antipathy to "socialism" in the following:

These opinions [i.e., Hodgkin's], if they were to spread, would be the subversion of civilised society; worse than the overwhelming deluge of Huns and Tartars. . . . If a man preaches this doctrine without seeing what it is, he is below being treated with argument; if he preaches it, knowing what it is, hanging, a thousand times repeated, would be too small a punishment for him.

There are condescension and overconfidence in Mill's remark:

I should have little fear of the propagation among the common people of any doctrines hostile to property, because I have seldom met with a labouring man (and I have tried the experiment upon many of them) whom I could not make to see that the existence of property was not only good for the labouring man, but of infinitely more importance to the labourers as a class, than to any other.[44]

In short, Mill was the spokesman for the middle class at the

485

beginning of the nineteenth century; for the growing numbers and movement of the "labouring men" he had absolutely no message, or hint of one, to bequeath. Moreover, when the threat of the labor movement grew great, Mill's inability earlier to have taken it seriously meant also that his ideology provided little for his middle-class followers in the way of an effective defense.

Mill's leadership, then, would appear to have been mainly for the moment. The prime source of his leadership, his character, died with him. Or worse, it lingered on as a caricature. In books such as Dickens' *Hard Times*, Mill became a figure of fun, as in the "character" of Gradgrind. Mill thus became an abstraction—the Utilitarian—rather than surviving as a set of meaningful doctrines. Yet, the caricature, in stressing Mill's personality, caught an important glimpse of the truth about him.

There is, however, one final point to make. Another quality of a great leader, all too often overlooked, is his ability to provide for a successor: what might be called, with the Soviet experience in mind, the "Successor Problem."[45] In this, Mill was eminently successful. He had trained his own son, John Stuart Mill, to carry on after him. And John Stuart followed his father in the best sense of the term—by holding on to the logical and analytic method that James Mill had taught him so carefully, but applying it to the acquisition of new, and broader, opinions. Thus, John Stuart Mill was able to offer the same intellectual and, to some extent, political leadership that his father had offered earlier, but now to a new generation and on a wider front. In this way, then, in the true sense of "generational" creativity, leaving his character (with suitable modifications) worked into his son, James Mill transcended his death and the limitations of his doctrine.

As can be seen from our case study of James Mill, leadership is a subtle thing and can take many forms. This suggests that the critical task of a theory of leadership is to allow conceptually for a variety of ways in which a human, and humane, person can provide inspiration and guidance for his followers and—to borrow a good liberal, Utilitarian notion—for his fellow men.

REFERENCES

1. Matters change in the contemporary world, for good reasons into which we shall not enter here.

2. This is the summary offered by John Stuart Mill, *Autobiography*, Chapter 4. In the Liberal Arts Press edition (New York, 1957), it is pp. 68 and 70.

3. Elie Halévy, *The Growth of Philosophical Radicalism*, trans. by Mary Morris (Boston, 1955), pp. 255, 306.

4. Alexander Bain, *James Mill. A Biography* (1882) (New York, 1967), p. 326.

5. *Ibid.*, p. 137.

6. Halévy, *The Growth of Philosophical Radicalism*, p. 307.

7. *Ibid.*, p. 309.

8. Bain, *James Mill. A Biography*, p. 37.

9. *Ibid.*, p. 212.

10. *Ibid.*, p. 397.

11. James Mill, *An Essay on Government*, ed. Currin V. Shields (Indianapolis-New York, 1955), p. 53.

12. *Ibid.*, p. 90.

13. For support, see Lionel Robbins, *Theory of Economic Policy in English Classical Political Economy* (London, 1952); William Letwin, *A Documentary History of American Economic Policy Since 1789* (Garden City, 1961).

14. Bain, *James Mill. A Biography*, pp. 29, 461.

15. *Ibid.*, p. 139. Needless to say, patronage was a commonplace in Mill's time, though beginning to disappear. Nevertheless, the psychological effect on Mill had its own uniqueness.

16. Halévy, *The Growth of Philosophical Radicalism*, p. 308.

17. Sigmund Freud, *Group Psychology and the Analysis of the Ego*, trans. James Strachey (New York, 1960), p. 71. Freud adds that "the great majority of people have a strong need for authority, which they can admire, to which they can submit and which dominates and sometimes even ill-treats them."

18. A psychoanalytic explanation might proceed as follows: Mill's mother lavished attention and effort on the young James, all calculated to appeal to his narcissistic feelings. Her successful efforts to push and to harden him for struggle by rigid discipline undoubtedly made him feel special—but not necessarily loved. We can conjecture that, unconsciously, Mill resented his stern, cold, and unloving mother, without ever being able openly to express such feelings. Such an assumption allows us better to understand Mill's harsh treatment of his wife—was he getting his "own" back again?—and his stern disciplining of his own children (especially John Stuart, his firstborn), who, in any case, perceived *him* as unloving.

Had James Mill "identified with the aggressor," so to speak? (See, for example, Anna Freud, *The Ego and the Mechanism of Defense.*) As for the self-made aspect of Mill, this begs for an explanation in oedipal terms. In the basic Oedipus fantasy, catered to in this case by the excessive attention and hopes centered on Mill by his mother, the child wishes to become his father in relation to his mother—or to become his *own* father, hence, self-created. Often, this last expresses itself in fantasies of saving the father: The child gives "back" life to the father, thus denying the wish to kill him—and as a result purchases his own life afresh; one thinks of Mill's paying off his father's bankruptcy debts. The Oedipus complex may also express itself in fantasies of what Freud called a "family romance": For example, my real parents are the Stuarts, not the obscure and humble shoemaker named James Milne; and one notes that Mill named his firstborn John Stuart after his patron, rather than after his real father. (Though this was a common custom at the time on the social level, we can conjecture that the name had deeper meaning for Mill on the personal level.) Such an analysis in depth as the above is not required foɪ our work here, but it is along some such lines that further inquiry might proceed.

19. Psychologically, of course, John Stuart Mill's admission is an oversimplification. We must also note Mill's statement that his father softened later in life and was therefore loved by his other children.

20. Bain, *James Mill. A Biography,* p. 422.

21. John Stuart Mill, *Autobiography,* p. 33.

22. Bain, *James Mill. A Biography,* p. 334.

23. See Peter T. Cominos, "Late-Victorian Sexual Respectability and the Social System," *International Review of Social History,* Vol. 8 (1963), Parts 1 and 2, for a most interesting and suggestive treatment.

24. The term "crisis of identity" is inspired, of course, by Erik Erikson's work. Nevertheless, I have refrained from using his term "identity crisis," because I am not referring to that crisis which arises at a particular stage, generally in adolescence, when the somatic, ego, and social developments come together and provide the material for a specific "identity crisis." Indeed, for James Mill, it would be difficult to deal with this developmental stage adequately, because of a shortage of material. The notion of a continuing and cumulative "crisis of identity" is, however, intrinsic to Erikson's theory of the developmental stages of man. See further, Erikson's *Childhood and Society* (New York, 1963).

25. In Erik Erikson's classic work, *Young Man Luther* (New York, 1958), Luther's crisis differs in that it involves the reaffirmation of a religious identity and coincides with, if not inspires, the working out of a new territorial, and perhaps "national," identity.

26. Halévy, *The Growth of Philosophical Radicalism,* p. 291, suggests that "Mill was apparently converted to irreligion not by Bentham, but by

Miranda, a former general of the French Revolution, and a revolutionary general in South America."

27. Bain, *James Mill. A Biography*, pp. 421-22.

28. See, for example, various of David Hume's political essays.

29. E. P. Thompson, *The Making of the English Working Class* (New York, 1966)—which is rapidly becoming a classic, in part because it combines a political with an economic treatment of the working class, two aspects of the subject hitherto rather strangely kept apart—takes a slightly different view of the subject.

30. John Stuart Mill, "Reorganization of the Reform Party," *Essays on Politics and Culture*, ed. Gertrude Himmelfarb (Garden City, 1963). This article is a splendid analysis of the situation by one who was in a position to know. In addition to the Tories, of course, there were also the Whigs—the other face of the Privileged Classes—generally from the same social background. As Francis Place remarked about the Whigs in 1807, they were "Tories out of place." See Graham Wallis, *The Life of Francis Place* (London, 1951), p. 40.

31. See *The English Radical Tradition, 1763-1914*, ed. S. MacCoby (New York, 1957), pp. 7-8; and Michael St. John Packe, *The Life of John Stuart Mill* (London, 1954), p. 192. In my depiction here of the Utilitarian group, I make no claim to completeness.

32. Mill, *Autobiography*, p. 132.

33. All the preceding quotations are from Bain, *James Mill. A Biography*, pp. 457, 458, 459, 263.

34. See Bain's evaluation of this statement, *ibid.*, p. 463.

35. *Ibid.*, p. 425. The problem of what is "charisma" is a perplexing one, as so ably attested to by Robert Tucker's article and by various other contributions to the Conference on Leadership. I, myself, find Tucker's general treatment persuasive and helpful. I would like to add to what he says, however, an additional emphasis on one aspect of the problem: the fact that "charisma" must be viewed in terms of the shift in the last one hundred and fifty or two hundred years from a basically religious to a basically secular orientation in life (indeed, a shift, as Tucker points out, mirrored in Weber's borrowing the religious term for political usage). Thus, while ideologies have strong religious elements, they do, in fact, differ significantly from the great religions. "Superhuman" becomes "Superman," and power is not derived from contact with the Gods, but from the People, the Race, the Class, or History; or just Character. This shift, I believe, makes it necessary, as Tucker indicates, to rethink our usage of the term "charisma." We need to think more in psychological than in religious categories. Freud's ego with "few libidinal ties" perhaps shows us one path. Mill's leadership "by mere force of mind and character" suggests another. For example, President Johnson, or so we are told, seems to exert an almost uncanny power over others in direct conversation,

though he appears to lack this power over large crowds. Lenin, it would appear, had the same power in both situations. (As Tucker says of a leader: "He can even manifest some of his charisma in the inspired way in which he conquers dissent by the sheer power of his political discourse.") Do we attain conceptual clarity by restricting the term "charisma" to the sort of hypnotic power that is exercised only over large groups, or by insisting that it is out of some supernatural religious or messianic quality rather than out of some strange strength of character (still to be more precisely defined, probably in terms of interpersonal relations)? My own belief is that the "characterological" as well as the "religious" side of charisma (though the two ought never to be totally separated) needs more to be emphasized.

36. *Ibid.*, pp. 461, 180-181. Is it in this attention to the faults and defects of others that we find the occasional break in Mill's self-control in public and the link to his private tyranny in his home?

37. *Ibid.*, p. 447.

38. Packe, *The Life of John Stuart Mill*, p. 102.

39. Bain, *James Mill. A Biography*, p. 425.

40. See, for example, D. W. Brogan, "The Intellectual Review," *Encounter* (November, 1963).

41. Packe, *The Life of John Stuart Mill*, p. 7.

42. Eric Stokes, *The English Utilitarians and India* (Oxford, 1959), p. 80. The question of James Mill's influence on India, and on British ideas of empire, is interestingly pursued in Francis G. Hutchins, *The Illusion of Permanence. British Imperialism in India* (Princeton, 1967).

43. Bain, *James Mill. A Biography*, p. 366.

44. *Ibid.*, pp. 364-465. Mill was voicing these sentiments in 1832.

45. For comments on the "Successor Problem," as evinced, for example, in the Soviet Union, see the recent issues of the *Problems of Communism*.

CUSHING STROUT

William James and the Twice-Born Sick Soul

> *I became a doctor through being compelled to devi-*
> *ate from my original purpose; and the triumph of*
> *my life lies in my having, after a long and round-*
> *about journey, found my way back to my earliest*
> *path.* —SIGMUND FREUD

HISTORICAL DETERMINISM was much in fashion in 1880 when William James published his essay on "Great Men and Their Environment." He had to attack the superstition, derived from Herbert
Spencer, that great men were mere resultants of that "aggregate of
conditions" out of which both they and their society had arisen.
Spencer's method, as James pointed out, was like that of "one who
would invoke the zodiac to account for the fall of the sparrow."[1]
To offer the whole past as an explanation of something specific in
the present was no better than explaining every event by saying
"God is great." James acknowledged that society, in Darwinian
terms, could preserve or reject the great man, but it did not make
him before he remade it. Physiological forces, with which social
conditions had no discernible connection, genetically produced the
hero. Even at the level of intellectual history, the same Darwinian
point applied: Society confirmed or refuted the spontaneous variations of ideas produced in great thinkers by the "functional activity
of the excessively instable human brain."[2]

Certainly the movement of pragmatism cannot be explained
apart from William James who became, as Ralph Barton Perry has
said, "the Ambassador of American Thought to Western Europe."
It is consistent with James's theory of the great man to note that
social circumstances played their part in favoring the development
of pragmatism into a force which influenced American philosophy,
psychology, religion, political theory, education, and historiog-

raphy. Voluntaristic, democratic, "tough-minded," and optimistic, pragmatism had qualities well suited to American culture at a time when science had great prestige and humanistic values needed new underpinnings because of the erosion of older theological supports. But it was James's own wide-ranging intellectual curiosity, his familiarity with Europe and its languages, and above all his fervent conviction that pragmatism was "something quite like the protestant reformation" and destined for "definitive triumph" that made him "the revivifying force in European thought in the decade and a half preceding the outbreak of the First World War."[3] Intellectually gregarious, gifted with a talent for popular lecturing, passionately attached to American life by affection and critical commitment rather than by habitat, he was (like Franklin and Jefferson) a cosmopolitan American who could speak to the world in a voice that resonated with a specific identity.

Yet James's own struggle for forming a personal identity and finding his proper vocation was acute. His growth to greatness was precarious and painful, vulnerable to chronic debility, depression, and distress. James's theory of the great man has one conspicuous weakness: It does not cover himself. There is more to the great man than favorable social conditions, the spontaneous variations of genetics, or what James called the "seething caldron of ideas" in the "highest order of minds." He believed that the "genesis [of ideas] is sudden and, as it were, spontaneous,"[4] but the history of his own development is a refutation of any such sudden spontaneity. Spontaneity was in his case a hard-won achievement of a personality threatened by imminent disorganization. What James needed to round out his theory of the great man was an ordered way of talking about the inner history of the great man's relation to himself and to the significant others in his family.

In this sense, the great man is made, in part, by that intimate society, filled with resounding echoes of the world in the significant speech, gesture, and silence of parents and siblings, which he in turn remakes by his appearance in it. If he is truly great, he conspires with circumstance to turn his private conflicts into public issues with relevance for others. He learns to speak not only to his family and his society but, in principle, to all men. Paradoxically, he might even learn to speak to all men just because on certain matters he cannot speak openly to his family. The sign of that inability would be a kind of sickness, a bafflement of development, referring to the unspeakable. For such individuals, as Erik H. Erikson has taught us in *Young Man Luther*, the identity crisis of early manhood may be a period in which endangered youths, "although suffering and deviating dangerously through what appears to be a prolonged adolescence, eventually come to contribute an original bit to an emerging style of life: the very danger which they have sensed has forced them to mobilize capacities to see and say, to dream and plan, to design and construct, in new ways."[5] Erikson suggests that "born leaders seem to fear only more consciously what in some form everybody fears in the depths of his inner life; and they convincingly claim to have an answer."[6] The conscious fear that James grappled with was the apprehension that scientific determinism, what he called "medical materialism," would leave no meaningful space for the human will. That fear was closely connected with his fears as a member of the James family. I propose to analyze that linkage in narrative form, trying to do justice to the relevant claims of psychoanalysis, history, and philosophy.

The historian is justified in asking the James family to sit for a portrait of upper-class Victorian life. The bearded, revered, religious father, the domestically devoted mother, the effusive language of family endearment, the endless trips to Europe for convalescence—all these familiar features we recognize with the usual smile. The intellectual issues of James's life—the conflict between science and religion, the revolt against rationalism, and the moral cult of "the strenuous life"—are part of the texture of that period, which writers like Walter E. Houghton have brought to vivid life.[7] James's own depressed invalidism also had many counterparts in the lives of other eminent Victorians, like Mill, Darwin, and Jane Addams. A pre-Freudian, James was inevitably a mystery to himself, but he welcomed the work of Freud and his pupils on the ground that it might shed light on "the twilight region that surrounds the clearly lighted centre of experience." He looked forward to biographical studies that would show "the various ways of unlocking the reserves of power" exemplified in individual lives.[8] Let us begin, therefore, with a striking peculiarity of James's career—the long deferment of a youthful philosophical ambition, which he did not fully commit himself to as a vocation until he was nearly sixty.

William James first decided to become a painter. As a boy he had shown a spontaneous interest in drawing, and with his first real youthful friend shared a hope of becoming an artist. Unfortunately, in 1859 his father whisked young William off to Europe, away from

his friend and from William Morris Hunt's studio at Newport. The
father explained to a friend:.

> Newport did not give the boys what they required exactly, and we didn't
> relish their separation from us. Willy especially felt, we thought, a little
> too much attraction to painting—as I suppose from the contiguity to Mr.
> Hunt; let us break that up, we said, at all events. I hoped that his career
> would be a scientific one . . . and to give up this hope without a struggle,
> and allow him to tumble down into a mere painter, was impossible.[9]

In the end, the elder James relented because his son pleaded, very
respectfully and humbly, that his life "would be embittered" if he
were not allowed to try painting. The father need not have worried;
the son himself echoed his father's judgment by declaring before
entering Hunt's studio: "There is nothing on earth more deplorable
than a bad artist." For a conscientious boy who much admired his
father, this venture in vocation must have engendered a bad conscience. Within the year he had abandoned art school, though he
kept up his drawing for several years. In 1872, he was to confess
that he "regretted extremely" letting it die out.[10] Meanwhile, the
Civil War was a call to action, and in 1861 both William and Henry
sought to enlist in the Union Army. Once again their father had
other plans: "I have had a firm grasp upon the coat tails of my
Willy and Harry, who both vituperate me beyond measure because
I won't let them go."[11] Both boys soon developed illnesses that in-
capacitated them for service anyway, and it was the younger
brothers, Wilkinson and Robinson, the forgotten Jameses, who with
father's blessing joined the army.

In 1861, William dutifully gave his father a plan of his future
life: to study chemistry, anatomy, and medicine as preparation for
spending several years with Louis Agassiz in natural history. The
plan was shaped to his father's hopes for him. That fall William entered the Lawrence Scientific School in Cambridge as a student of
chemistry. "Relentless Chemistry claims its hapless victim," he
wryly wrote to a friend. As his teacher later recalled, nervous illness
began to interfere with his work at this point.[12] In 1863, he entered
medical school where Jeffries Wyman taught, a man for whom
James had "a filial feeling," perhaps because Wyman was also an
excellent draftsman. The next year, under the spell of the "god-
like" charm of Louis Agassiz, William went to Brazil as part of an
exploring and collecting expedition. There he caught varioloid, a
mild form of smallpox, and spent over two despondent weeks in the

hospital, resting his eyes and rethinking his future. His experience convinced him that he hated collecting and was "cut out for a speculative rather than an active life." Having recovered the use of his eyes and having lost his respect for Agassiz's pretensions to omniscience, he joyfully returned home with a new resolution: "When I get home I'm going to study philosophy all my days."[13]

Privately James read philosophy voraciously, but publicly he resumed his medical studies and undertook a brief internship at the Massachusetts General Hospital. His comments on the medical profession, excepting surgery, were always contemptuous, convicting it of "much humbug." Nevertheless, his disenchantment with Agassiz and natural history forced him to consider medicine as a possible career unless he were to abandon the scientific bent of his education. In retrospect, the Brazil expedition gave him a "feeling of loneliness and intellectual and moral deadness." In the fall and winter of 1866, he complained of digestive disorders, eye troubles, acute depression, and weakness of the back. His symptoms are characteristic of hypochondriasis, and in psychosomatic illness unconscious imitation often plays a part in the selection of discomforts. He revived those symptoms which he had felt in Brazil, and he now also spoke, in revealing language, of a "delightful disease" in the back "which has so long made Harry so interesting."[14] Henry had developed this symptom from a trivial accident incurred while he was trying to put out a fire in 1861. When his father was thirteen, he had sustained under similar circumstances an injury that led to a leg amputation and two years in bed. William's back and eye trouble provided him with an excuse for not practicing medicine. Shortly before taking his exams for the medical degree in 1869, he wrote his brother: "I am perfectly contented that the power which gave me these faculties should recall them partially or totally when and in what order it sees fit. I don't think I should give a single damn now if I were struck blind."[15] In the winter of 1866, he felt himself on the "continual verge of suicide" and sometime during these years he was paralyzed in panic fear by the image of a greenish, withdrawn epileptic idiot whom he had seen in an asylum. *"That shape am I,* I felt, potentially," he confessed, and for months he dreaded being alone in the dark.[16]

What did this paralyzing recollection mean? As a medical student he might easily have read the well-known work by the English doctor William Acton, *The Functions and Disorders of the Reproductive Organs.* Steven Marcus has pointed out in *The Other Vic-*

torians that Acton's book is a classic statement of Victorian attitudes toward sex; indeed, one of Acton's themes is the moral need to break willfully the habit of introspection in order to ward off the temptation of masturbation, luridly imagined as a threat to sanity. Acton points up his moral by a description of inmates of an insane asylum: "The pale complexion, the emaciated form, the slouching gait, the clammy palm, the glassy or leaden eye, and the averted gaze, indicate the lunatic victim to this vice." This image resembles James's memory of the epileptic patient, and in the late 1860's he was unsuccessfully courting Fanny Dixwell, whom his friend Oliver Wendell Holmes, Jr., married in 1872. James was thirty-six when he married, and no doubt sexual frustration had plagued him, but his vocational problem persisted after 1878. That hideous figure, we may speculate, objectified not only the self-punishing guilt in his own symptoms, but also his fear of being trapped in a medical career which seemed to be his only option after his disillusionment with natural history. Neither Wyman nor Agassiz had shaken his belief that his father was, as James had written in Brazil, "the *wisest* of all men" he had ever known.[17] And his father was a metaphysician—not a physician.

James defined his dilemma to a despondent friend: "I am about as little fitted by nature to be a worker in science of any sort as anyone can be, and yet . . . my only ideal of life is a scientific life."[18] His whole program, outlined to his father in 1861, had collapsed along with his health and spirits. In submitting his prospectus, he had prophesied wryly that the last stage would be "death, death, death with inflation and plethora of knowledge."[19] That jest had come symbolically true, as if he had unconsciously feared the worst in the pursuit of his scientific career. In 1867 he sailed for Europe, which served him as a psychic moratorium from commitment. Subjecting himself to the tortures of the baths and galvanic remedies, he felt ashamed not to be earning money like his brothers. He found solace in the theater, art galleries, music, novels, and glimpses of pretty *frauleins,* while he read philosophy and dutifully attended university lectures on physiology. After passing his medical exams for the degree in 1869, he wrote a sketch of his philosophical gropings which put his own pain at the center of things: "Three quantities to determine. (1) how much pain I'll stand; (2) how much other's pain I'll inflict (by existing); (3) how much other's pain I'll 'accept,' without ceasing to take pleasure in their existence."[20] To a friend he confessed: "I am poisoned with Utilitarian venom, and sometimes when

I despair of ever doing anything, say: 'Why not step out into the green darkness?' "[21] Similarly greenish in hue was his image of the idiotic, epileptic patient, huddled in the corner of his cell. To stick to his chosen path would be, in short, a kind of suicide. He could not find himself in medicine nor the acting self in medical materialism's picture of the world.

By 1872 James had discovered a desperately needed sense of initiative in the French philosopher Renouvier's arguments for free will. He also passed up an opportunity "to strike at Harvard College" for a subprofessorship of philosophy, accepting instead an appointment there to teach physiology. "Philosophy I will nevertheless regard as my vocation and never let slip a chance to do a stroke at it," he confided to his diary.[22] Reluctant to accept a reappointment in physiology because he had such "arrears of lost time" in "the line of mental science," he nevertheless acquiesced on psychological grounds: "Philosophy as a *business* is not normal for most men, and not for me." Philosophic doubt was too unnerving because he was not yet prepared to make that much of a bid for autonomy: "My strongest moral and intellectual craving," he confessed, "is for some stable reality to lean upon."[23] In 1874, thirteen years after the onset of his psychosomatic troubles, his mother complained: "Whenever he speaks of himself he says he is no better. This I cannot believe to be the true state of the case, but his temperament is a morbidly hopeless one, and with this he has to contend all the time, as well as with his physical disability."[24]

In the year of his marriage in 1878 he signed a contract to write the *Principles of Psychology*. He spent twelve years on the book, delivering it at last like a man relieved of a kidney stone. "Seriously," he wrote an admiring reader, "your determination to read that fatal book is the one flaw in an otherwise noble nature. I wish that I had never written it."[25] As Perry notes, "he never afterwards produced any considerable article or book on the standard problems of psychology."[26] Not until the late-1890's, however, did he cut himself free of the laboratory work which he had always disliked; he advised a fellow-sufferer to study philosophy with a good conscience because the best thing a man can work at "is usually the thing he does most spontaneously." Not until 1899 could he write:

I have surrendered all psychological teaching to Munsterberg and his assistant and the thought of psycho-physical experimentation and altogether of brass-instrument and algebraic formula psychology fills me with horror. All my future activity will probably be metaphysical—that is,

497

if I have any future activity, which I sometimes doubt. The Gifford Lectures . . . are a fine opportunity were I only able to meet it.[27]

At the age of fifty-seven James was at last prepared, with some trepidation, to give his full attention to those philosophical issues which had defined his ambition at the age of twenty-three. Suffering from a valvular lesion of the heart, he then spent six years trying to resign from Harvard. Four years after his resignation he died, convinced that his philosophy was "too much like an arch built only on one side."[28] Nearly all his major philosophical work, as Perry points out, began when he thought his professional career was finished.

The basic clue to understanding James's search for a vocation is provided by Erikson's remark in *Young Man Luther* that it is usually a parent, who has "selected this one child, because of an inner affinity paired with an insurmountable outer distance, as the particular child who must *justify the parent*," that by an "all-pervasive presence and brutal decisiveness of judgment" precipitates the child into "a fatal struggle for his own identity."[29] If in contemporary America that parent would usually be the mother, in Victorian America it would have been the father. It is significant that James's vivid memory of the shape in the asylum closely resembles a similar experience his father suffered in 1844 when he felt "an insane and abject terror" before "some damned shape squatting invisible" to him within his room "and raying out from his fetid personality influences fatal to life."[30] Henry James, senior, had written Emerson one or two years earlier to seek help:

What shall I do? Shall I get me a little nook in the country and communicate with my *living* kind, not my talking kind—by life only—a word, may be, of *that* communication, a fit word, once a year? Or shall I follow some commoner method, learn science and bring myself first into men's respect, that thus I may the better speak to them? I confess this last theory seems rank with earthliness—to belong to days forever past.[31]

Son of a rich Calvinist merchant, William's father had been cut off without a legacy because of his worldly tastes and heretical opinions. He had temporarily fled college to work as a proofreader, made an abortive attempt to please his father by studying law, and revolted against the Presbyterian orthodoxy of Princeton Theological Seminary to become an original, if obscure and eccentric, theologian. Having broken his father's will, he was able by his inheritance to devote himself entirely to his writings and to his remarkable family, whom he shuttled constantly about in America and Europe. In 1846 he was rescued from the "endless task of conciliating a stony-hearted Deity"—*his* father's Calvinist God—by a conversion to Swedenborg, as William would be rescued from propitiating the deterministic god of medical materialism by conversion to the philosophy of Renouvier and the idea of free will.

"The children were constantly with their parents and with each other," as William's son later described his father's childhood, "and they continued all their lives to be united by much stronger attachments than usually exist between members of one family."[32] The elder James refused to send his sons to college out of contempt for a gentleman's conventional education. Depositing them briefly with a succession of instructors, he involved his sons mainly with his own spirited intellectual and moral reactions to the world. In his eldest son he must have seen an opportunity to realize his own forsaken alternative of trying to "learn science" and bring himself "into men's respect." A visionary advocate of freedom and spontaneous love, he was also a fierce polemicist. In the family circle as with strangers, the elder James spoke his mind with trenchant, witty, and brusque decisiveness. "What a passion your father has in writing and talking his religion!" exclaimed Oliver Wendell Holmes, Jr., a tough-minded skeptic. "Almost he persuadeth me to be a Swedenborgian."[33] For William, his father was a vivid, perpetual presence. After his father's death in 1882, the forty-year-old son made a significant confession:

It is singular how I'm learning every day now how the thought of his comment on my experience has hitherto formed an integral part of my daily consciousness, without my having realized it at all. I interrupt myself incessantly now in the old habit of imagining what he will say when I tell him this or that thing I have seen or heard.[34]

His father was still an inner court of tribunal for him long after that is normally the case.

In this family it was easy for William to resolve his feelings and thoughts about his father because his mother had a soft spot for Henry, who was known in the family as "the Angel." Father himself, after his wife's death in 1881, felt that he had "fallen heir to all dear mother's fondness" for Henry, who had "cost us the least trouble, and given us always the most delight."[35] William, the oldest brother, had reason to be envious of Henry, who first achieved literary fame and financial independence. William's "hypochondriacal condition"—as his family called it—involved a set of highly charged elements: his career choice, his attraction to philosophy, but fear of embracing it; his dislike of practical scientific work, whether as collector, medical student, or laboratory psychologist; and his need to become financially independent. His father was closely linked to all these issues, and because Henry was obviously the mother's favorite, it was especially important for William to feel that he was in good standing with his father.

The sickness in this family gives deeper meaning to Perry's innocent remark about the James household that "the region of family life was not empty, but was charged with palpable and active forces." There is a strong hint of suppressed hostility in Alice James's confession that in her hysteria she sometimes felt "a violent inclination" to throw herself out of the window or "knock . . . off the head of the benignant Pater, as he sat, with his silver locks, writing at the table." The same point could be made of the benign father's remark to Emerson that he "wished sometimes the lightning would strike his wife and children out of existence, and he should suffer no more from loving them."[36] As the head of a religion with only one member, the father's life had something of the smell of futility about it, and his son felt uneasy about the prophet's role. "Certainly there is something disheartening in the position of an esoteric philosopher," he wrote in a letter he did not want shown to his father.[37] Although he followed his father's wish for a scientific career, the son could not but be aware that his father believed that science was ultimately inferior to metaphysics and religion. During his depressed years in Europe, he received from his father a nineteen-page letter of ontological speculation which boasted: "I am sure I have something better to tell you than you will be able to learn from all Germany—at least all scientific Germany. So urge me hard to your own profit."[38] Ambivalently attracted and repelled by both science and philosophy—an ambivalence connected with his feelings about his father's wishes, attitudes, and example—the son found his path hard to see clearly. He could not follow both his father's example and his advice—yet he tried to do both. The "sicker" he became, the more guilt he felt for prolonging his financial dependence. In his worst years, he made himself a pathetic parody of his father—a crippled philosopher without a job. "The crisis in such a young man's life," as Erikson has noted, "may be reached exactly when he half-realizes that he is fatally overcommitted to what he is not."[39] James made that discovery in medical school.

These emotional issues were linked to intellectual conflicts, for young men need ideological convictions to support their growing identity. During his period of invalidism, William wrote his brother Henry that their father was "a religious genius," but unfortunately his "absence of *intellectual* sympathies of any sort" made it hard to respond to "the positive side of him."[40] William James found himself in late adolescence "tending strongly to an empiristic view of life." Unlike his father, he was willing to believe that "God is dead or at least irrelevant, ditto everything pertaining to the 'Beyond,' " but the consequences left him full of doubt. The problem was "to get at something absolute without going out of your own skin!"[41] During his depression years, he was "going slowly" through his father's books; though he was impressed with their "definite residuum" of "great and original ideas," he could not find in them an explanation of his own torments. "For what purpose we are thus tormented I know not," he wrote his suffering brother in 1869. "I don't see that Father's philosophy explains it any more than anyone else's." He could not bring himself into so much sympathy "with the total process of the universe as heartily to assent to the evil that seems inherent in its details." He refused to "blink the evil out of sight, and gloss it over. It's as real as the good, and if it is denied, good must be denied too. It must be accepted and hated, and resisted while there's breath in our bodies." Like his father's peculiar blend of Swedenborg and Calvin, scientific determinism seemed to make these evils inevitable too—on physiological grounds. In April 1870, he finished reading Renouvier's essay on freedom and made his first act of positive belief: "My first act of free will shall be to believe in free will."[42]

James found a solution to the problem of determinism by sustaining a thought *"because I choose to* when I might have other thoughts." If he could not yet choose his vocation, he could validate choice in principle, and that freedom was enough to defend the moral power to fight evil. Erikson has relevantly observed that an aggravated identity crisis tends to generate a state of mind in which actual commitment is minimized, while an inner feeling of retaining the power of decision is maximized; at such a time, a person attempts to rebuild the shaky identifications of childhood, as if he wanted to be born again.[43] The general problem of determinism for William gained personal force from its association with his medical-scientific training and his need to find autonomy as a person. This issue was also intimately related to his involvement with his father.

In his diary for 1868 the son noted: "My old trouble and the root of antinomianism in general seems to be a dissatisfaction with anything less than grace." He acknowledged that his antinomian tendency was partly derived from the example of his father, who always made "moralism the target of his hottest attack, and pitted religion and it against each other as enemies of whom one must die utterly, if the other is to live in genuine form."[44] The elder James routinely condemned moralists as prigs who believed that their good works entitled them to salvation. His "amiable ferocity was," as Perry well puts it, "an exercise in contempt for selfhood, on his own part and in behalf of others."[45] This contempt was an unrecognized threat to a conscientious boy struggling to find his own sense of self and to be responsive to his father's attitudes. The elder James believed that men fell from grace individually, but could be saved collectively in a redeemed socialized society. His son, however, needed an individual salvation not only through faith, but also in works. To translate this theological idiom, he needed to believe that there was point and purpose to some particular work of his own with social meaning. He would finally save himself through his writing, finding courage in Carlyle's gospel of work, forgetting complaint and rapture alike in "the vision of certain works to be done . . . for the leaving of them undone is perdition."[46] To his father's antinomianism, he would oppose an Arminian emphasis on work, a moral equivalent for "the strenuous life" idealized in his period by Roosevelt, Holmes, and the naturalistic novelists London, Norris, and Dreiser.

The connection between the intellectual and emotional development of William James can be followed in the growth of his work and the betterment of his health, as he successfully, but slowly came to terms with his father's teachings and example. Four days before his father died in 1882, the son wrote him from Europe: "All my intellectual life I derive from you. . . . What my debt to you is goes beyond all my power of estimating—so early, so penetrating and so constant has been the influence." And he concluded this great and touching letter with a final benediction: "Good-night, my sacred old Father! If I don't see you again—Farewell! a blessed farewell!"[47] At the age of forty, the son would also very slowly bid farewell to his scientific career and gradually move from psychology toward those deep interests he shared with his father in religion and metaphysics. As he abandoned his image of himself as a scientist, he learned to yield to his spontaneous interest in philosophy, which had been born in his crisis of health and career in Brazil. He would increasingly see himself as well enough in body and strong enough in ego to become a philosopher by vocation, assimilating and rejecting aspects of his father's personality in a new configuration.

The father died a year after the mother. James was now the eldest in the family. He was alone in Europe, seeking respite from the burdens of his own family and having trouble getting his book under way. He was also in correspondence with Renouvier, whose philosophy had "saved" him in 1870. In the French philosopher, James found much-needed intellectual sympathy and encouragement for his own philosophical talents. "Your thinking," the Frenchman told him, "springs from a source that is original and profound, and bears the stamp of what you yourself feel—of something that comes, indeed, from your very self." The American was, he felt, much too modest about his philosophical efforts. "It seems to me when I read you," he wrote him, "that you are called to found an *American philosophy*."[48] The power of Renouvier's productive energies in his old age would later prompt James in his last years to form the intention of writing "a somewhat systematic book on philosophy—my humble view of the world—pluralistic, tychistic, empiricist, pragmatic, and ultra-gothic, *i.e.*, non-classic in form."[49] By then, Renouvier himself would seem "too classic in the general rationalism of his procedure," and James would be too near the end of his life. In 1883, however, he was undergoing a new sense of health and direction. Suffering from eye trouble, he had written but six pages of the *Psychology*. Two weeks after hearing of his father's death, he wrote his brother Henry that he felt "a different man" and was resolved to return home to his wife and children, amazed that a "change of weather could effect such a revolution."

In the winter following his father's death James wrote "The Dilemma of Determinism"—a blow for freedom against both scientific and religious monistic views of the world and the first of the characteristically Jamesian essays on the open universe which he had struggled to glimpse out of the pain of his own constricted conflicts. That same year, in filial tribute, he edited his father's *Literary Remains*, as he had promised, and in the following year he noted a definite improvement in his eyesight: "It has continued gradually, so that practically I can use them all I will. It saves my life. *Why* it should come now when, bully them as I would, it wouldn't come in in the past few years, is one of the secrets of the nervous system which the last trump . . . may reveal."[50] James now found in Josiah

Royce a worthy beloved opponent, provoking James's "highest flight of ambitious ideality," as he affectionately told him, to become his conqueror and "go down into history as such . . . rolled in one another's arms and silent (or rather loquacious still) in one last death-grapple of an embrace."[51] It was as if he had transferred some of his emotions about his father to the monistic religious idealist he had brought to Harvard in the year of his father's death.

The accounts, however, were not yet settled with his scientific career. Not until the late-1890's had he worked himself free of laboratory work. Philosophy was still a source of morbid feelings. In 1895, he confessed to a fellow philosopher:

I am a victim of neurasthenia, and of the sense of hollowness and unreality that goes with it. And philosophic literature *will* often seem to me the hollowest thing. . . . —When it will end with me I do not know. I wish I could give it all up. But perhaps it is a grand climacteric and will pass away. At present I am philosophizing as little as possible in order to do it the better next year, if I can do it at all.[52]

That summer he delivered his famous lecture on "The Will to Believe"—the justification of believing, under certain circumstances, beyond the evidence, the argument of a man who, as Perry notably remarked, had always "suffered from incredulity." At the turn of the century, a heart lesion forced him to postpone the Gifford Lectures, finally published in 1902 as *The Varieties of Religious Experience.* This book was his grand effort to incorporate "Father's cry" that "religion is real," a cry the son had earlier resolved some day to voice.[53] Now he did so on his own terms. He, like his father, was a "twice-born sick soul," the type he placed at the center of religious insight, and like his father, James was now convinced that religion was closer than physical science to ultimate reality: "Assuredly the real world is of a different temperament—more intricately built than physical science allows." Religion, because of its concern for the private destiny of the individual, grasped the personal nature of reality, which science lost hold of in its search for symbolic generalizations. Like the psychiatrist, the artist, and the existentialist philosopher, James felt that the self was the locus of fundamental reality: "The axis of reality runs solely through the egotistic places —they are strung upon it like so many beads."[54] Yet James remained honestly agnostic, making no personal "over-beliefs" in God or immortality and steadfastly refusing to give any cosmic apology for evil. While his sympathies went out to the "sick souls," who had a more profound sense of existence than the "healthy-minded," he was also drawn to the healthy-minded pluralists who resolutely gave no quarter in their struggle with evil. This divided sympathy reflected his personal history. He had been a sick soul who became healthy minded through intellectual resistance to scientific and theological monism. While he always felt that his episode of panic fear had a religious bearing because he had afterwards clung in desperation to scriptural texts, it was rather through his own "twice-born" pluralism that he made an original contribution to the varieties of religious experience.

Having settled his intellectual accounts with his father, he was now prepared to devote himself to philosophy, writing freely "without feeling in the least degree fatigued." But he had only a few years left. "I live in apprehension lest the Avenger should cut me off," he wrote in 1906, "before I get my message out. It is an aesthetic tragedy to have a bridge begun and stopped in the middle of an arch."[55] James died with his "somewhat systematic" book unfinished. He had been able to assure Royce in 1877 that "a young man might rightfully devote himself to philosophy if he chose," an assurance James found so very difficult to achieve for himself.[56] From a psychoanalytic point of view, the resolution of critical emotional issues in infancy "will determine whether an individual is apt to be dominated by a sense of autonomy, or by a sense of shame and doubt," and the way in which adults meet the child's shame and doubt "determines much of a man's future ability to combine an unimpaired will with ready self-discipline, rebellion with responsibility." Significantly, the father's crisis happened when the son was two years old, struggling to form his first sense of will. His later development illustrates the psychoanalytic point that "the neurotic ego has, by definition, fallen prey to overidentification and to faulty identifications with disturbed parents."[57] The historian must add that while the elder Henry James had made the son's struggle for identity particularly difficult, he had also made the resolution of that struggle particularly fruitful. His influence largely determined the kinds of problems that would be central for his son's intellectual development. That influence delayed the son's maturity, but it also enriched it by giving him that double focus on science and religion and that note of authenticity in dealing with the issues of freedom and determinism which stamped his work as vividly original. The father must also have engendered the son's charming tolerance of cranks and vigorous scorn for prigs of all kinds. William James had selectively assimilated and rejected what his father meant to him in a struggle of fifty years' duration.

The creative man, as Erikson has observed, has to face the risks of neurotic suffering:

Once the issue is joined, his task proves to be at the same time intimately related to his most personal conflicts, to his superior selective perception, and to the stubbornness of his one-way will: he must court sickness, failure, or insanity, in order to test the alternative whether the established world will crush him, or whether he will disestablish a sector of this world's outworn fundaments and make a place for a new one.[58]

James would have understood this point better than most philosophers. "In any minute of moral action where the path is difficult," he wrote George Santayana, "I believe a man has deeper dealings with life than he could have in libraries of philosophizing."[59] His own life was a painful, eloquent witness to this truth.

Most people, faced with such a parent as James had, learn how to evade or compromise in order finally to get their way. William's own son, "Billy," tried medical school for a melancholy year and then happily took up painting—the reverse of his father's sequence. Others make nothing distinctively great out of similar troubles. William's Swiss friend Théodore Flournoy was also depressed by his laboratory work in psychology, but could never marshal the strength to follow James's advice to give it up for philosophy. Sometimes, as Erikson has remarked, an individual feels "called upon" instead to "try to solve for all what he could not solve for himself alone."[60] By whom and by what he is called, the psychoanalyst adds, are mysteries which only theologians and bad psychologists dare to explain. James himself believed that individuality is founded in "the recessess of feeling, the darker, blinder strata of character."[61] In *The Varieties of Religious Experience,* he modified his earlier theory of the great man and offered a radical explanation for the mystery of his appearance: "Thus, when a superior intellect and a psychopathic temperament coalesce . . . in the same individual, we have the best possible condition for the kind of effective genius that gets into the biographical dictionaries."[62] Such men are possessed by their ideas, he added, and inflict them, for better or worse, upon their contemporaries. It is part of the ethical meaning of James's greatness that in this case the suffering was his, the enlightenment ours.

Looking backward, it seems an extraordinarily symbolic moment in time when James met Freud at Clark University in 1909. A decade earlier James had praised Freud's work on "the buried life of human beings"—that "unuttered inner atmosphere" in which the nervous patient "dwells alone with the secrets of its prison-house," full of "old regrets, ambitions checked by shames and aspirations obstructed by timidities," breeding "a general self-mistrust."[63] James spoke from experience, but unlike Freud, he was never able to systematize his troubles into a revolutionary new theory of the mind. Rather, his genius was for sketching a world in which truth was profoundly human and, like action itself, a genuine addition to a reality still in the making. "Admit plurality, and time may be its form," he wrote in "The Dilemma of Determinism," a remark which points toward a profoundly historical view of the world. Pluralism characterized his life as well as his thought. Perhaps the incompleteness of his philosophy is a mark of his failure to achieve that masterful and compelling power which the greatest thinkers have, exerting their force on followers and critics alike for generations to come, as Freud certainly did. But in an age when all systems are undergoing revision, and many have collapsed beyond repair, there is still something fertile in James's critique of "the block universe" and the synoptic vision which would claim to encompass it.

Psychology itself now reflects a more existential and historically oriented mode of analysis, of which Erikson's work is a primary example. Surely the author of *The Varieties of Religious Experience: A Study in Human Nature* would have found *Young Man Luther* a deeply congenial book. It is aesthetically satisfying that the kind of study which Erikson's book illustrated and spurred a decade ago should be luminously relevant to explaining William James's troubled history. James would not have been surprised, for he knew that the discovery of the "subliminal self"—as he called it—was the door through which entered the experiences that have had emphatic influence in shaping religious history, including (we must add) his own.

For James, however, the subconscious was not always the same concept that it was for Freud. Sometimes James spoke in Freudian terms of "whole systems of underground life, in the shape of memories of a painful sort which lead a parasitic existence, buried outside the primary fields of consciousness, and making irruptions thereinto with hallucinations, pains, convulsions, paralyses of feeling and of motion, and the whole procession of symptoms of hysteric disease of body and of mind."[64] He could also say that "on our hypothesis it is primarily the higher faculties of our own hidden mind which are controlling," a position reminiscent of the transcendentalists.[65] This dual emphasis partly reflected his distinction between the *"farther* side" and the *"hither* side" of the subconscious self; he focused on the nearer side in order to examine religious experience. Certainly he had something of the healer in him—a residue of his medical training, as well as something of the Swedenborgian mystic, like his father. Unfortunately, James's interest in the cults of "mind-cure" and Christian Science made him vulnerable to being classified as a facile "positive thinker." We too often forget that in his mature work, the *Pragmatism* of 1907, he cried out with a tragic sense that John Dewey never had:

Is the last word sweet? Is all "yes, yes" in the universe? Doesn't the fact of "no" stand at the very core of life? Doesn't the very "seriousness" that we attribute to life mean that ineluctable noes and losses form a part of it, that there are genuine sacrifices somewhere, and that something permanently drastic and bitter always remains at the bottom of its cup?[66]

And he associated this theme with his willingness to treat pluralism as a serious hypothesis.

James presented pragmatism as a reasonable synthesis of the two temperaments he called "the tough-minded" and "the tender-minded," but he personally believed that "the prodigal-son attitude . . . is not the right and final attitude towards the whole of life."[67] In the end, he remained a sympathetic agnostic, flirting with the idea of a finite God who needed men. In his more "tough-minded" moments, as Donald Meyer has acutely noted in *The Positive Thinkers,* James was (in retrospect) an important figure in the history of the movement which—from Anna Freud through Heinz Hartmann, Ernst Kris, and David Rapaport, to Erik Erikson—has developed an existentially oriented ego-psychology.[68] For all of them, the life of the self is portrayed not as a bland voyage on a smooth sea, but as a rugged willingness to encounter conflict and evil and so to transform oneself. A thinker sometimes comes into perspective as a leader only after those who come later can identify him as a forerunner of their own leadership. William James was such a man, and those who can revise our conception of ourselves are surely, at last, as influential as any leaders that history knows.

This paper is deeply indebted to close collaboration in research with Dr. Howard M. Feinstein, a friend and practicing psychiatrist in Ithaca, New York.

REFERENCES

1. William James, *Selected Papers on Philosophy* (Everyman Edition), p. 180.

2. *Ibid.*, p. 181.

3. Letter to Henry James, May 4, 1907, *Letters of William James*, ed. Henry James (2d ed.; 2 vols; Boston, 1926), Vol. 2, p. 279; H. Stuart Hughes, *Consciousness and Society: The Reorientation of European Social Thought 1890-1930* (New York, 1958), p. 397.

4. William James, "Great Men and Their Environment," *Selected Papers*, p. 192.

5. Erik H. Erikson, *Young Man Luther: A Study in Psychoanalysis and History* (New York, 1958), pp. 14-15. Erikson's concept of the identity crisis has proved to be of great value in understanding James.

6. *Ibid.*, p. 110.

7. Walter E. Houghton, *The Victorian Frame of Mind 1830-1870* (New Haven, 1957), especially pp. 58-109.

8. Ralph Barton Perry (ed.), *The Thought and Character of William James* (Boston, 1935), Vol. 2, p. 122. Perry explains James's troubles only by reference to "morbid traits," as if they had no history.

9. *Ibid.*, Vol. 1, p. 192. (Hereafter cited as *TCWJ*.)

10. Letter to Charles Ritter, July 31, 1860. *Ibid.*, Vol. 1, p. 193; letter to Henry James, Jr., October 10, 1872. *Ibid.*, Vol. 1, p. 330.

11. Quoted by Leon Edel, *Henry James: The Untried Years, 1843-1870* (Philadelphia, 1953), pp. 174-75.

12. Letter to Katherine Temple, September, 1861. *Letters of William James*, Vol. 1, p. 40; *ibid.*, Vol. 1, p. 32. (Hereafter cited as *LWJ*.)

13. *TCWJ*, Vol. 1, p. 220. Letter to his family, May 3-10, 1865, *ibid.*, Vol. 1, p. 219.

14. Letters to Tom Ward, May 24, 1868. James Papers, Houghton Library, Harvard University; September 12, 1867, *TCWJ*, Vol. 1, p. 244.

15. Letter to Henry James, Jr., June 12, 1869, *TCWJ*, Vol. 1, p. 300.

16. Letter to Tom Ward, January, 1868, *LWJ*, Vol. 1, p. 129; *TCWJ*, Vol. 2, p. 675.

17. *TCWJ*, Vol. 1, p. 142.

18. Letter to Tom Ward, October 9, 1868, *ibid.*, Vol. 1, p. 287.

19. Letter to his father, November, 1861, *ibid.*, Vol. 1, p. 211.

20. *Ibid.*, Vol. 1, p. 302.

21. Letter to Tom Ward, October 9 (1868), *ibid.* Vol. 1, p. 287.

22. February 10, 1873, *ibid.*, Vol. 1, p. 335.

23. Letter to Henry James, Jr., October 10, 1872; *ibid.*, Vol. 1, p. 341; Diary, April 10, 1873, Vol. 1, p. 343.

24. *Ibid.*, Vol. 2, p. 673.

25. Letter to Mrs. Whitman, October 15, 1890, *LWJ*, Vol. 1, p. 304.

26. *TCWJ*, Vol. 2, p. 125.

27. Letter to Theodore Flournoy, September 19, 1892, *LWJ*, Vol. 1, p. 325; to Carl Stumpf, September 10, 1899, *TCWJ*, Vol. 2, p. 195.

28. William James, *Some Problems in Philosophy* (New York, 1911), p. viii. See my "The Unfinished Arch: William James and the Idea of History," *American Quarterly*, Vol. 13 (Winter, 1961), pp. 505-15.

29. Erikson, *Young Man Luther*, p. 65.

30. Quoted by Austin Warren, *The Elder Henry James* (New York, 1934), pp. 56-57; *TCWJ*, Vol. 1, p. 21.

31. Letter to Emerson (1842?), *TCWJ*, Vol. 1, p. 43.

32. *LWJ*, Vol. 1, p. 19.

33. Letter to W. J., December 15, 1867, *TCWJ*, Vol. 1, p. 507.

34. *Ibid.*, Vol. 1, p. 142.

35. Letter to Henry James, Jr., May 9 (1882?), *TCWJ*, Vol. 1, p. 112.

36. *Ibid.*, Vol. 1, p. 171; F. O. Matthiessen, *The James Family* (New York, 1961), p. 276; *TCWJ*, Vol. 1, p. 3.

37. Letter to O. W. Holmes, Jr., May 15, 1868, *TCWJ*, Vol. 1, p. 517.

38. Letter to W. J., September 27, 1867, *ibid.*, Vol. 2, pp. 711.

39. Erikson, *Young Man Luther*, p. 43.

40. *TCWJ*, Vol. 1, p. 151.

41. Letters to O. W. Holmes, Jr., May 18, 1868, *ibid.*, Vol. 1, pp. 516-17; to Tom Ward, October 9, 1868, *ibid.*, Vol. 1, p. 287.

42. Letters to Henry James, Jr., October 2, 1869, *ibid.*, Vol. 1, pp. 306-8; May 7, 1870, *LWJ*, Vol. 1, p. 158; Diary, February 1, 1870, and April 30, 1870, *TCWJ*, pp. 322-23.

43. Erik H. Erikson, "The Problem of Ego Identity," *Psychological Issues*, Vol. 1 (1959), pp. 123-24, 129.

44. Diary, April 21, 1868, James Papers, Houghton Library, Harvard University; *TCWJ*, Vol. 1, p. 164, quoted from introduction, *The Literary Remains of the Late Henry James.*

45. *TCWJ*, Vol. 1, p. 133.

46. "The Dilemma of Determinism," *Essays in Faith and Morals*, ed. R. B. Perry (New York, 1947), p. 174.

47. Letter to father, December 14, 1882, *LWJ*, Vol. 1, pp. 218-20.

48. Letters to W. J., May 28 and September 5, 1882, *TCWJ*, Vol. 1, pp. 678-79.

49. *Ibid.*, Vol. 1, p. 710.

50. Letters to Henry James, Jr., January 23, 1883, *ibid.*, Vol. 1, p. 389; April, 1885, *LWJ*, Vol. 1, pp. 242-43. He did complain again about his eyes in 1887, but not severely, and presbyopic spectacles seem to have solved the problem. *LWJ*, Vol. 1, p. 262. In his pictures he does not wear spectacles.

51. Letter to Josiah Royce, September 26, 1900, *TCWJ*, Vol. 1, p. 817.

52. Letter to G. W. Howison, July 17, 1895, *ibid.*, Vol. 2, pp. 207-8.

53. *Ibid.*, Vol. 1, p. 165.

54. William James, *The Varieties of Religious Experience: A Study in Human Nature* (New York, 1928), pp. 519, 499.

55. Letter to Theodore Flournoy, February 8, 1905, Robert C. LeClair (ed.), *The Letters of William James and Theodore Flournoy* (Madison, 1966), p. 163; to Henry James, Jr., September 10, 1906, *LWJ*, Vol. 2, p. 259.

56. *TCWJ*, Vol. 1, p. 779.

57. Erikson, *Young Man Luther*, p. 255; Erikson, "Identity and the Life Cycle," *Psychological Issues*, Vol. 1 (1959), p. 90.

58. Erikson, *Young Man Luther*, p. 46.

59. Letter to George Santayana, January 2, 1888, *TCWJ*, Vol. 1, p. 403.

60. Erikson, *Young Man Luther*, p. 67.

61. James, *Varieties of Religious Experience*, pp. 501-2.

62. *Ibid.*, pp. 23-24.

63. William James, *Talks to Teachers of Psychology* (New York, 1916), p. 203.

64. James, *Varieties of Religious Experience*, pp. 234-35.

65. *Ibid.*, p. 513.

66. William James, *Pragmatism: A New Way for Some Old Ways of Thinking* (New York, 1919), p. 295.

67. *Ibid.*, p. 296.

68. Donald Meyer, *The Positive Thinkers* (New York, 1965), p. 284.

Notes on Contributors

DAVID E. APTER, born in 1924, is professor of political science and director of the Institute of International Studies at the University of California, Berkeley. During the academic year 1967-68, Mr. Apter was visiting Guggenheim Fellow at All Souls College, Oxford. Mr. Apter is the author of *Ghana in Transition* (rev. ed., 1963), *The Politics of Modernization* (1965), *The Political Kingdom in Ghana* (1968), and *A Structural Theory of Politics* (forthcoming).

JAMES D. BARBER, born in 1930, is professor of political science and director of the Office for Advanced Political Studies at Yale University. Mr. Barber is the author of *The Lawmakers: Recruitment and Adaptation to Legislative Life* (1965) and *Power in Committees* (1966); he has also edited *Political Leadership in American Government* (1964). During 1968-69, Mr. Barber will be a fellow of the Center for Advanced Studies in the Behavioral Sciences, while he completes research on presidential leadership styles.

ERIK H. ERIKSON, born in 1902, is professor of human development and lecturer in psychiatry at Harvard University. Mr. Erikson's publications include *Young Man Luther* (1958), *Childhood and Society* (2d ed., 1963), *Insight and Responsibility* (1964), and *Identity: Youth and Crisis* (1968). Mr. Erikson is currently at work on a psychoanalytic study of the origins of militant nonviolence in Gandhi's life and in Indian history.

ALBERT O. HIRSCHMAN, born in 1915, is Lucius N. Littauer Professor of Political Economy at Harvard University. He is the author of *National Power and the Structure of Foreign Trade* (1945), *The Strategy of Economic Development* (1958), *Journeys Toward Progress: Studies of Economic Policy-making in Latin America* (1963), and *Development Projects Observed* (1967). Mr. Hirschman is also the editor of *Latin American Issues* (1961).

INGE SCHNEIER HOFFMANN is the co-author of *Coercive Persuasion* (1961). Mrs. Hoffmann has studied international affairs and social psychology at Harvard University and for several years was a research associate at the Center for International Studies at the Massachusetts Institute of Technology. She has been interested in the relationship of personality to intellectual and political history since her family emigrated from Vienna. Mrs. Hoffmann is spending this year at the Radcliffe Institute.

STANLEY HOFFMANN, born in 1928, is professor of government at Harvard University. Mr. Hoffmann is co-author of *In Search of France* (1963) and author of *The State of War* (1965) and *Gulliver's Troubles, or the Setting of American Foreign Policy* (1968).

JOHN F. HOWES, born in 1924, is associate professor of history and Asian studies at the University of British Columbia. He is the translator and adaptor of *Japanese Religion in the Meiji Era* (Tokyo, 1956; second edition, Tokyo, 1969).

BARRY D. KARL, born in 1927, is professor of history at Washington University in St. Louis. Mr. Karl is the author of *Executive Reorganization and Reform in the New Deal* (1963).

NIKKI R. KEDDIE is associate professor of history at the University of California at Los Angeles. She is the author of *Religion and Rebellion in Iran: The Tobacco Protest of 1891–92* (London, 1966) and *An Islamic Response to Imperialism: Political and Religious Writings of Sayyid Jamal ad-Din al-Afghani* (Berkeley and Los Angeles, 1968), as well as of numerous articles on the social and intellectual history of the modern Middle East.

HENRY A. KISSINGER, born in 1923, is professor of government and member of the executive committee of the Center for International Affairs at Harvard University. Mr. Kissinger is on leave from the university while serving as presidential assistant for national security affairs. He is the author of *A World Restored* (1957), Nuclear Weapons and *Foreign Policy* (1957), *The Necessity for Choice: Prospects of American Foreign Policy* (1961), and *The Troubled Partnership: A Reappraisal of the Atlantic Alliance* (1965).

FRANK E. MANUEL, born in 1910, is professor of history at New York University. Mr. Manuel is the author of *The New World of Henri Saint-Simon* (1956), *The Eighteenth Century Confronts the Gods* (1959), *The Prophets of Paris* (1962), *Isaac Newton, Historian* (1963), and *Shapes of Philosophical History* (1965). Mr. Manuel is also the editor of the *Dædalus* Library volume *Utopias and Utopian Thought* (1966). His *Portrait of Isaac Newton* is scheduled for publication in the fall of this year by the Harvard University Press.

BRUCE MAZLISH, born in 1923, is professor of history at the Massachusetts Institute of Technology. Mr. Mazlish is the author of *The Riddle of History: From Vico to Freud* (1966), the co-author of *The Western Intellectual Tradition: From Leonardo to Hegel* (1960), and the editor of *Psychoanalysis and History* (1963). Mr. Mazlish is currently engaged on a study entitled "The Case of James and John Stuart Mill: A Father-Son Relation."

DANKWART A. RUSTOW, born in 1924, is professor of international social forces at Columbia University. Mr. Rustow is author of *A World of Nations: Problems of Political Modernization* (1967); co-author and editor of *Political Modernization in Japan and Turkey* (1964), and co-author of *The Politics of the Developing Areas* (1960) and *The*

Politics of Compromise: A Study of Parties and Cabinet Government in Sweden (1955).

CUSHING STROUT, born in 1923, is professor of English literature at Cornell University. Mr. Strout is the author of *The Pragmatic Revolt in American History: Carl Becker and Charles Beard* (1958) and *The American Image of the Old World* (1963). Mr. Strout is also the editor of the two-volume study *Intellectual History in America* (1968).

ROBERT C. TUCKER, born in 1918, is professor of politics and director of the Program in Russian Studies at Princeton University. Mr. Tucker is the author of *Philosophy and Myth in Karl Marx* (1961) and *The Soviet Political Mind* (1963). He is also the co-author of *The Great Purge Trial* (1965). Mr. Tucker is presently at work on a case study in political leadership and personality to be entitled *Stalin and Russian Communism*.

ADAM B. ULAM, born in 1922, is professor of government at Harvard University. He is the author of *Unfinished Revolution* (New York, 1960), *Bolsheviks* (New York, 1965), and *Expansion and Coexistence* (New York, 1968).

INDEX

Abdülhamid, Sultan, 149, 153, 155, 156, 167, 219, 234–237
Academic community: government and, 440–441, 445, 452–453; government careers, 459–460; intellectual leadership, 431–464; politics in, 448–450, 459–460; professionalism, 431–433; publications, 439, 442; research and development, 442, 448–450, 452–453; respect and authority, 438; support of foundations, 436, 445
Acton, William, 495
Adams, Herbert Baxter, 436
Addo, E. A. Akufo, 116
Afghanistan, 151, 156, 158, 160
Africa: art, 130; new states, 19, 112–147
Afrifa, A.A., 141
Agassiz, Louis, 494–495
Agitators, political, 9–10, 173–175
Agrarian reform, 356–357
Ahmedabad textile strike, 36–41, 51–52, 56–60
Algerian war, 19, 289, 300, 304
Ali Jinnah, Muhammad, 150
Ali Paşa, Grand Vizier, 151, 154
Ambivalence, 36, 43, 46–47
American Council of Learned Societies, 436
American Economic Association, 436
American Political Science Association, 443
Amherst College, 186, 188, 193
Amponsah, R.R., 116
Anatolia, 215, 217–218, 221, 223–225
Ankrah, J.A., 115–116
Anti-intellectualism, 452
Apaloo, M.K., 116
Apter, David E., 14, 17, 72, 512; "Nkrumah, Charisma, and the Coup," 112–147

Arbuthnot, John, 405, 418
Arden-Clarke, Charles Noble, 131
Aron, Raymond, 291
Ashton, Francis, 404
Atatürk, see Kemal Atatürk
Atta, William Ofori, 128
Austin, Dennis, 127
Austria: in German Confederation, 329–331; relations with Prussia, 329–331, 334–341, 348–349
Austro-Prussian War (1866), 334, 348–349
Authority, charismatic, 14–23, 71, 118
A'zam Khan, Amir, 163

Baako, Kofi, 126, 129, 133
Balance of power, 328
Bancroft, George, 375
Barber, James D., 8, 12, 13, 28, 512; "Adult Identity and Presidential Style," 367–397
Barrès, Auguste Maurice, 262, 285
Barrow, Isaac, 409
Beard, Charles A., 452–453, 456, 457
Bell, David C., 189, 198
Ben Bella, Ahmed, 115
Bentham, Jeremy, 3, 466–473, 476
Bentley, Arthur F., 441, 457–458
Bergson, Henri, 262
Bernoulli, Johann, 425
Bernoulli, Nicolas, 409
Bernstein, Eduard, 96, 100, 107
Bible, teachings of Uchimura Kanzō, 196–205
Biographies, 4, 28; comparative treatment, 10; psycho-historical analysis, 5–6, 29, 33–68; See also Leadership
Bismarck, Otto von, 1, 9, 11, 23–24, 28, 317–353; art of the possible, 335–338; attack on Metternich system, 329, 331–340, 348–349;

Philosophers and Kings:
Studies in Leadership

Edited by Dankwart A. Rustow